Catholicism

ALSO BY John T. McGreevy

Parish Boundaries: The Catholic Encounter with
Race in the Twentieth-Century Urban North

Catholicism and American Freedom: A History

American Jesuits and the World: How an Embattled
Religious Order Made Modern Catholicism Global

Catholicism

A Global History

from the

French Revolution to Pope Francis

John T. McGreevy

W. W. NORTON & COMPANY

Independent Publishers Since 1923

For information about permission to reproduce selections from this book, write to
Permissions, W. W. Norton & Company, Inc., 500 Fifth Avenue, New York, NY 10110

For information about special discounts for bulk purchases, please contact
W. W. Norton Special Sales at specialsales@wwnorton.com or 800-233-4830

Manufacturing by Lakeside Book Company
Book design by Marysarah Quinn
Production manager: Lauren Abbate

ISBN: 978-1-324-00388-5

W. W. Norton & Company, Inc., 500 Fifth Avenue, New York, N.Y. 10110
www.wwnorton.com

W. W. Norton & Company Ltd., 15 Carlisle Street, London W1D 3BS

1 2 3 4 5 6 7 8 9 0

Contents

PART III

Vatican II and Its Aftermath, 1962–2021

Introduction

THIS BOOK TELLS THE STORY of Catholicism since the French Revolution. I wrote it for two reasons.

The first is to make an argument: a better understanding of Catholicism enhances our grasp of the modern world. No institution is as multicultural or multilingual, few touch as many people. The Chinese Communist Party, the European Union, the Central Intelligence Agency, and the International Monetary Fund possess global influence. But only the Catholic church includes extended networks of people and institutions in Warsaw, Nairobi, and Mexico City, as well as the most remote sections of the Amazon. Only Catholicism counts 1.2 billion baptized members, a majority of whom are people of color living in the Global South. Only a pope, as Francis did when visiting Manila in 2015, can attract six million people, perhaps the largest crowd in human history, to attend Mass in a driving rainstorm.

Historians increasingly recognize this. And the recent burst of superb scholarship on modern Catholicism makes this book possible.[1] Placing these books and articles in conversation makes visible patterns blurred when studying a single person, town, parish, diocese, or country. The biggest change in history writing in my lifetime has been the loosening of the clamps of the nation-state. Nation-states matter for the history of modern Catholicism, as this book demonstrates, but doctrines, people, and devotional objects also crossed borders with ease.

In previous studies, I have tried to understand Catholicism in one nation-state and through its missionaries.[2] This project is more capacious, beginning in the late eighteenth century and coming up to the present. It is not comprehensive. One analyst of recent global histories worries that their scope renders them incapable of assessing causation or sustaining a reader's interest.[3] Chastened, I've made this study as much a story as my narrative skills allow, sacrificing coverage for individuals and themes. Specialists will regret what is missing and rightly so.

Just as the first Christians in Corinth differed from the first Christians in Ephesus, no two contemporary Catholic communities are identical. Still, the patterns of Catholic globalism in the modern era, woven by migrants, missionaries, intellectuals, and diplomats, are unusually dense. One example: a generation after an impoverished fourteen-year-old girl, Bernadette Soubirous, reported that the Virgin Mary appeared to her in 1858 in the Pyrenees village of Lourdes, an astonishing 250,000 pilgrims descended upon the village each year. The same pilgrims carried small bottles of the healing waters of Lourdes back to their home countries for distribution and sale. Nurses placed Lourdes medals under the pillows of their patients. A journalist and Bengali convert to Catholicism told his readers that miraculous healings at Lourdes constituted "infallible proof" of God. Lourdes grottoes appeared in almost every major city in Europe, North America, and Latin America, and Pope Pius IX had one constructed in the Vatican gardens. In Paris, priests installed the city's first Our Lady of Lourdes shrine soon after the apparition, even as clergy from Paris working in Shanghai constructed a Lourdes grotto in China.[4] Brazilian bishops purchased accounts of the Lourdes apparitions while visiting Portugal and built Lourdes grottoes upon their return.[5] Vietnamese Catholics brought to serve as soldiers in France during World War I toured Lourdes soon after their arrival.[6] A popular Lourdes grotto lies a five-minute walk from the office where I type these words.

In contrast to Protestantism or Islam, Catholicism in the modern era included not just transient networks of individuals but an increasingly powerful center. A Vatican stamp of approval, after all, proved crucial for the spread of devotion to Lourdes. Over the course of the nineteenth and twentieth centuries, the organizational and symbolic reach of the papacy expanded. Papal bureaucrats built vigorous offices for doctrine, canon law, and missionary work, and a diplomatic corps staffed by ambassadors, or nuncios, fanned out across the globe. As recently as the eighteenth century, bishops rarely (if ever) visited Rome. Ordinary Catholics might not know the pope's name. A pope would have never convened an ecumenical council of bishops from around the world without the approval of monarchs and nobles. And yet at the First Vatican Council in Rome in 1869, Pius IX did just that. Fifty years later a new code of canon law assigned to the pope "the most complete and supreme jurisdiction over the universal Church."[7]

The second reason for this book is personal. Most of my life has been spent studying in, teaching at, writing about, and administering Catholic institutions. Almost daily I get asked (and wonder): how did we get here?

The long sweep of the nineteenth-century Catholic revival, the building of a vast, protective milieu of parishes, schools, and associations, the political crisis of the 1930s, World War II, decolonization, and the end of the Cold War have resulted in a church marked by unprecedented vibrancy (in sub-Saharan Africa and South Asia), concern for social justice (everywhere), and global connections. At Sacred Heart Cathedral in Guangzhou, China, a neo-Gothic church erected by French missionaries (and Chinese laborers) in the 1880s, roughly two thousand migrants from Nigeria worship each week at the Sunday afternoon Mass and socialize afterward.[8] A few years ago, when attending Mass with my family while on vacation in rural Minnesota, I learned that the celebrant was a priest from southern India. He handed out a typed copy of his homily so that his congregation, the descendants of German and Irish Catholic farmers who migrated to the region in the nineteenth century, could decipher his accented English.

Meanwhile, in much of the world, the number of observant Catholics is shrinking, even hemorrhaging. The structures built in the nineteenth and twentieth centuries barely stand. In 2020, in Ireland, once the source of missionary clergy and nuns for much of the Anglophone world, more bishops (two) were ordained than priests (one). The sexual abuse crisis has taken an incalculable toll, on survivors above all, but also on the credibility of Catholic institutions and the people who run them. The confidence of an earlier era—the West German magazine *Der Spiegel* explained to its readers in 1962 that the church had "achieved a unity and consistency in teaching and structure never before seen"—is a distant memory.[9]

The hinge point in how Catholics got from the French Revolution to the current moment is the Second Vatican Council (1962–1965), one of the most important events of the twentieth century. All Catholics live in its shadow. But that shadow is receding. Sixty years have passed since the warm, Roman afternoon of October 11, 1962, when Pope John XXIII, weeks after being secretly diagnosed with the cancer that would end his life nine months later, delivered the council's opening address. Arrayed in front of him in St. Peter's Basilica were 2,500 Latin rite Catholic bishops, patriarchs representing Eastern Rite Catholic churches, Protestant observers, theological experts, and reporters, even as millions of viewers watched on television. Speaking in Latin for sixty-four minutes, John XXIII asked his listeners to ignore "prophets of doom" who saw in "modern times nothing but prevarication and ruin." The church needed an "aggiornamento," or updating. It should "meet the needs of the present day by demonstrating the validity of her teaching rather than by condemnations."[10]

The last person alive who played a major role at the Second Vatican Council is another elderly man wearing white robes. He is the ninety-five-year-old Pope Emeritus Benedict XVI, formerly theologian Fr. Joseph Ratzinger. The day before John XXIII's opening homily, Ratzinger, only thirty-four, addressed the German-speaking bishops. He worried that "a Council of today, which the whole world, including non-Christians, will be watching" could not lock itself "in the cage of a medieval view of history, within which it cultivates a kind of ecclesiastical provincialism."[11] Just after the council, a relieved Ratzinger admitted that his fears had not been realized. He termed the final conciliar documents a "counter-syllabus" in reference to Pius IX's denunciation of the modern world in the 1864 Syllabus of Errors. The church had rebalanced itself, Ratzinger thought, after "the one-sidedness of the position adopted under Pius IX and Pius X in response to the situation created by the new phase of history inaugurated by the French revolution."[12]

Ratzinger returned to the historical fray in 2005, eight months after his election as pope. He now saw things differently. In an address to the Roman Curia, he regretted that the "mass media" and "one trend of modern theology" emphasized the council as an event of "discontinuity and rupture." Instead, he stressed the continuity of the council with the sweep of church history. Certainly, John XXIII desired reforms. But more emphasis should be placed on the determination of the bishops at the council—and even John XXIII in his opening address—to transmit Catholic doctrine in its wholeness and to counter "human dangers and errors."[13]

It is a subtle text and its plausibility need not detain us. What Benedict XVI recognized is that historical claims matter. That history happened to Catholics, too, was a revelation of the council, at once disorienting and exhilarating to believers conditioned to understand theirs as an unchanging church. The Canadian Jesuit Bernard Lonergan, writing just after the council concluded, described Catholicism as moving from a classicist worldview to one possessed by "historical consciousness." The classicist worldview understood human nature as "always the same" and applied universal principles to "concrete singularity." By contrast, Lonergan encouraged Catholics to begin with the human subject, not an abstract human nature, and use history to scrutinize "how the patterns of living, the institutions, the common meanings of one place and time differ from those of another."[14]

Benedict XVI is now frail and faltering. He resides in an apartment on the grounds of the Vatican, alone with a small staff, his books, and his piano. He occupies his days with reading, prayer, and visits from friends. His funeral will sever the living memory of the council from its history. It will begin the post post-Vatican II era.

Catholicism in the twenty-first century will be reinvented, as it was in the nineteenth. We just don't know how. If this book provides a savvy baseline as the process unfolds, it will have served its purpose.

Let's begin.

It is ten o'clock in the morning on January 21, 1793, in Paris's newly named Place de la Révolution. One hundred thousand onlookers swarm the plaza. They await the former king Louis XVI—citizen Louis Capet in revolutionary nomenclature—who arrives after a two-hour carriage ride through the narrow, foggy streets, surrounded by twelve hundred soldiers and accompanied by an Irish-born priest, Abbé Edgeworth, who this morning had given him communion in his prison cell. When his carriage arrives at the scaffold, Louis XVI at first resists, but then submits to having his hands tied. Leaning on Edgeworth, the former king mounts the stairs toward the guillotine. . . .

PART I

Revolution
and Revival

1789–1870

ONE

Revolution

In France and around the World

I

EVERYTHING ABOUT JANUARY 21, 1793, remained etched in Abbé
Henry Edgeworth's memory. The church bells ringing across Paris, rousing them at dawn. The carriage ride to the Place de la Révolution, crowds

Abbé Edgeworth blessing King Louis XVI before the king's
execution in Paris, January 21, 1793. *(Leemage/Corbis via Getty Images)*

pressing in on the street. As a conduit for messages from hapless counter-revolutionary plotters, Edgeworth had hoped for an attack on the king's captors. "A great number of people devoted to the King had resolved on tearing him from the hands of the guards," he wistfully recalled. For that reason, "I still did not despair of rescue at the foot of the scaffold."[1]

Edgeworth and Louis XVI did not know each other well. An Irishman educated in Toulouse and Paris, Edgeworth had been drawn into the royal court by service as confessor to the king's aunt. After Louis XVI's failed flight from Paris in 1791, the king requested Edgeworth's counsel. When the National Convention sentenced him to death, the king asked to meet one final time with his wife, Marie Antoinette, and their children. Edgeworth listened from the next room as the family said their goodbyes, the sobbing children clutching onto their father.

No serious rescue effort materialized. When the king reached the top of the scaffold stairs, Edgeworth announced, "son of St. Louis, go to heaven." The king prayed out loud "to God that the blood you are going to shed may never be visited on France." Edgeworth knelt at the base. Then the guillotine fell, and the crowd roared. Edgeworth recalled the executioner "showing the bleeding head to the mob, and sprinkling me with the blood that streamed from it." Not permitted to wear his clerical robes, Edgeworth then managed, to his own amazement, to blend into the vast crowd. He journeyed to the country home of Malesherbes, the king's lawyer and an early proponent of the revolution. Malesherbes and his family would die by guillotine a year after the king. He begged Edgeworth to "Fly, fly, my dear Sir, from this land of horror and from the tigers that are now let loose in it."[2]

Edgeworth flew to England. His own opposition to the revolution was longstanding. Even in 1789, during the revolution's first months, he had complained that "no nation in the world has ever undergone so complete a change of principles in so short a time. Modern philosophy has broke all religious, all social ties."[3] His anxiety deepened as revolutionaries placed church property, in Edgeworth's words, "at the free disposal of the nation." That clergy were required to take an oath of loyalty to the new regime as part of the 1790 Civil Constitution of the Clergy appalled him. Soon, Edgeworth predicted to an Irish friend, "we must practice our religion in corners and holes, as you formerly did in Ireland."[4]

In exile, Edgeworth became friendly with the greatest critic of the revolution, Irish statesman and member of the House of Commons Edmund Burke. Burke (an Anglican born to a Catholic mother) organized a fund for "Relief of the Suffering Clergy of France" and insisted "that a difference in religious persuasion will not shut the hearts of the English public against their suffering brethren, the Christians of France."[5] Edgeworth connected Burke with the Catholic bishop of Cork, Richard Moylan. Moylan worried about the "spirit of the French infernal Revolution" spreading to Ireland and urged "all friends of order" to rally around the British throne.[6]

Edgeworth eventually followed Louis XVIII, brother of the executed king and claimant to the throne, to a palace in Mitau, then part of the Russian Empire and now part of Latvia. Tsar Paul I funded Louis XVIII's exile, including a household of courtiers who replicated the rhythms of Versailles. Edgeworth stood at the king's right during the daily promenade and otherwise upheld the fiction of a continued unity between throne and altar. The distance from Paris, where Napoleon consolidated his authority, to Mitau permitted the fantasy of a popular movement to restore the monarchy. Napoleon's spies mockingly called Louis XVIII the "King of Mitau."[7] As late as 1800, Edgeworth speculated in a letter to his sister that "the French will sooner or later return to their former masters, though it be impossible at present to say by what means, or when."[8]

When Napoleon's armies sliced through northern Europe, Edgeworth aided wounded Prussian soldiers brought to the estate. Edgeworth's health deteriorated after he contracted a fever from an ill soldier. In 1807 he died at Mitau, far from his native Ireland and the France he had called home. Louis XVIII mourned "a friend and comforter, a benefactor." Clergy at an Irish seminary stored a set of Edgeworth's vestments. Once a year a priest donned them and said Mass in honor of Edgeworth and all victims of the revolution.[9]

II

Abbé Edgeworth's melancholy career is a footnote to the French Revolution. But a revealing footnote. Until the Second Vatican Council in the 1960s, no single event in the history of modern Catholicism was as momentous, none as disruptive, as the French Revolution and the subsequent Napoleonic Wars. One of the first Catholic analysts of the revolution, the diplomat Joseph de Maistre, predicted that its reverberations would be "felt far beyond the time of its explosion and the limits of its birthplace."[10]

He was right. The revolution became the default for how Catholics explained the corruption of the modern world. When another set of revolutions broke out in 1848, the leader of the Jesuits in Rome assumed that leaders of the revolts aimed to replicate the "grand revolution in France."[11] In 1932, Dublin's archbishop informed a presumably befuddled audience in County Cavan that the "[revolution had] inspired the whole modern attack on Our Divine Lord Jesus Christ and his Church."[12] A few bishops assembled in Rome for the Second Vatican Council remained fixated on the "phantom" of the revolution.[13]

This rupture was not inevitable. The importance assigned in Catholic memory to the destructive effects of the French Revolution blotted out the more ambiguous relationship between Catholics and revolutionary ideas. Many Catholics played leading roles in the first phase of the French Revolution, and many more would participate in subsequent democratic revolutions in Europe and North and South America.

Sketching the life of another French priest, Abbé Henri Grégoire, the man who chaired the National Convention that voted to execute Louis XVI, permits a different narrative. Grégoire described the same 1790 Civil Constitution of the Clergy that horrified Edgeworth as "based on the Gospels."[14] He was elected Bishop of Blois in the new Constitutional Church created during the revolution. He emphasized national unity to the extent of insisting that government officials standardize the French language and discourage the use of regional dialects. He advocated for toleration of Protestants and Jews, although he viewed traditional Jewish devotional practices with the same disdain that he expressed for traditional Catholic devotions. Jews, like Catholics, could become citizens only by discarding outdated and superstitious habits.[15]

Grégoire also became one of the first European abolitionists, urging the emancipation of enslaved people as a corollary of the revolutionary rights of man. He later chastised Thomas Jefferson for denigrating the intellectual capacity of people of African descent. "The more imposing and respectable the authority of Jefferson," Grégoire explained, "the more essential it is to combat his judgment."[16]

As a cure-citoyen, or priest-citizen, Grégoire introduced the American radical Thomas Paine to French revolutionaries. Paine had once explained to his readers that "monarchy in every instance is the Popery of government."[17] "Let us instruct, build and continually make people realize," Grégoire wrote, "that Christianity is the friend of the Republic [and] the friend of liberty, equality and fraternity."[18] He supported the decision to remove Louis XVI from his throne because "we must destroy this talisman whose magic power may still stupify many more people."[19]

III

BOTH MEN WERE PRIESTS, both lived much of their lives in Paris, and both were active during the revolution. Why did Abbé Grégoire and Abbé Edgeworth assess it so differently? And why did Abbé Edgeworth's understanding triumph within Catholicism?

To answer these questions is to enter a debate about the relationship of Catholicism to the modern world that began in the early eighteenth century. The debate arrayed Catholics on two sides: on the one side, those who focused on the papacy as the primary source of Catholic authority, termed "ultramontanists," or "over the mountains" to Rome. On the other side were advocates of Reform Catholicism, a catchall term lumping together overlapping traditions variously identified as Enlightenment Catholicism, Richerism, Gallicanism, Conciliarism, and Jansenism.[20]

For most of the eighteenth century, Reform Catholicism seemed in the ascent. The movement only lightly touched the rural masses, a disabling weakness that would become more apparent in the nineteenth century. It appealed, though, to some eighteenth-century popes, many bishops and clergy, and an assortment of Catholic kings, nobles, and lay leaders. Reform Catholicism exerted the deepest influence in France, where its advocates inherited a tradition of episcopal independence from the papacy dating back to the seventeenth century. But Reform Catholicism also held sway in the Austro-Hungarian Empire, parts of the Netherlands and Germany, northern Italy, and among elites in Spain, the Polish-Lithuanian Commonwealth, and Portugal. Outside Europe, Reform Catholicism exerted significant influence in colonial Brazil and much of Spanish-speaking Latin America. Groups of Reform Catholics lived in England, Scotland, and British North America.

The nuances of Reform Catholicism defy brisk summary, but its adherents essentially desired two things: a Catholicism more consistent with Enlightenment ideals of science and investigation and a church with more deference toward episcopal and even lay authority at the expense of the papacy.

The blend of Catholic and Enlightenment ideas became increasingly visible during the eighteenth century. The first European university to offer a course in experimental physics was run by Benedictine monks in Salzburg.[21] Bishops funded scientists studying astronomy and medicine, with a Bolognese bishop facilitating the use of corpses for medical research. Pope Benedict XIV, himself, promoted the career of Laura Bassi, the first woman to hold a position at the University of Bologna and one of the era's most distinguished scientists. He thought scholarly work a "way for women to inhabit the Palace of the Pope."[22] In colonial Venezuela, priest-scientists mapped the Orinoco River, and in colonial Mexico they traced the origins of syphilis to Europe, not the supposedly primitive New World.[23] A German Catholic pastor wrote of his search "for all that is true and good, wherever it may come from." Without this independence, a Catholic intellectual risked becoming a "slave to the establishment."[24]

The same Reform Catholics favored a subdued, less baroque piety modeled after that of the early church: they downplayed the exuberant devotions associated with Catholicism after the sixteenth century Council of Trent. The Spanish monk Benito Feijóo y Montenegro cultivated interest in the scientific method, even as he dismissed tales of witches and exposed fictitious (but popular) saints and miracles. The Italian priest Ludovico Muratori was even more influential, and he proposed that Catholics stress aid to the poor instead of endowments for chapels or Masses for the dead. Both men published scientific treatises: Muratori on electricity and inoculations against smallpox and Feijóo on botany.

Muratori also warned against an overreliance on devotions to the Virgin Mary and such "pagan" superstitions as ringing church bells to ward off storms. Not celebrating a saint's feast day, he informed his readers, did not mean that "cattle would perish [and houses] would be in danger of being burned."[25] Translations of Muratori's works appeared in the major European languages and became standard seminary textbooks. Austrian priests influenced by Muratori urged an abandonment of "useless theological-scholastic controversies."[26] In Kraków, the archdiocese in 1781 forbade the following rituals: celebratory gunfire at Easter and on the feast of Corpus Christi, throwing oats at the priest on St. Stephen's day (to mark the stoning of St. Stephen), parading a man dressed as Jesus on a donkey on Palm Sunday, and reenacting the funeral of the Virgin Mary.[27]

Benedict Maria von Werkmeister, a priest based in Stuttgart, placed himself on Reform Catholicism's cutting edge. He favored a German-language liturgy (and illicitly celebrated a Mass in German using his own translation), proposed strict limits on papal authority, suggested closing monasteries because they evoked a bygone medieval past, and urged toleration for believers from other faith traditions. "Religion," he wrote, "is . . . the essential or that which makes humans wiser, better, and happier: the church is only something accidental and exterior."[28]

This same focus on a more reasonable religion may have diminished missionary zeal. The Catholic evangelization effort beginning in the sixteenth century in South America, the Philippines, French North America, China, and the Caribbean depended on the mixture of empathy and exploitation that marked all missionary programs. Its successes meant that Catholicism in the seventeenth century could plausibly claim to be the most global religion in human history. Already by 1650, Jesuits had established parishes and schools in Havana, Goa, Lima, Beijing, Manila, East Africa, and Quebec.[29]

The ebbing of the missionary effort in the eighteenth century occurred in part because Reform Catholics defined orthodoxy more narrowly, discouraging inculturation into non-European societies. The "stupid superstitions" that Gaspar Melchor de Jovellanos battled in Spain were not identical to those held by Hindus in India, Buddhists in China, or Indigenous people in Baja California or East Africa.[30] But absorbing pagan beliefs seemed dangerous. The most famous dispute took place regarding China. A series of popes, culminating with Pope Benedict XIV in the mid-eighteenth century, criticized Jesuit missionaries for distorting the Christian message by wearing native silk robes, permitting use of the Chinese term "Lord emperor" for God, and allowing Catholic converts to practise some Confucian rituals. The Chinese, Roman authorities insisted, must abandon the "superstition of their parents."[31] In part as a response, the Chinese emperor began persecuting Christian subjects. By the end of the eighteenth century, fewer than eighty priests, mostly native-born Chinese, labored in the vast empire.[32]

The single most important development in Catholicism in the decades before the French Revolution was the suppression of the Jesuits. Virtually everything about the Jesuits worried Reform Catholics. The special vow of obedience Jesuits took to the pope seemed an open invitation to destabilize both the local state and the local church. Every Jesuit, complained one Mexican bishop, "is the enemy of the Sovereign Power, depending on a despotic government [that is, the papacy] resident in a foreign country."[33]

Many Jesuits made significant contributions to natural science, but even more were vocal defenders of Aristotle and the traditional canon along with papal institutions such as the Inquisition.[34] Given their ultramontane leanings, the Jesuit role as the primary educators of Europe's Catholic nobility seemed positively dangerous to Reform Catholics. One German bemoaned the opportunities possessed by Jesuits to "beat or coax infantile prejudices and dogma into the heads of young people."[35]

Jesuit piety was also suspect for its focus on popular devotions in Europe, many of which Reform Catholics assessed as "ignorant," "superstitious," and "mechanical."[36] Despite their professed devotion to reason and science, Reform Catholics dabbled in their own conspiracy theories. Did the Jesuits, they wondered, condone the assassination of unfriendly monarchs? Or turn wives against their husbands by manipulating them in the confessional?[37] Some Reform Catholics composed (or forged) texts demonstrating that the Jesuits sought to subvert secular and religious authorities.[38]

Supporters of Reform Catholicism orchestrated the suppression of the Jesuits in stages, beginning in the 1750s in Portugal. The powerful

Portuguese minister Sebastião José de Carvalho e Melo, known as the Marquis of Pombal, disliked the fact that Jesuit missionaries governed dozens of villages in colonial Brazil and Paraguay, beyond the reach of Portuguese authorities. Pombal expelled the Jesuits from Portugal's empire, not only in South America but also in Goa and Macao. He imprisoned some two hundred Jesuits in Portugal itself, half of whom died before their release.[39]

Pombal's machinations existed alongside parallel efforts in France and the French Empire and in Spain and the Spanish Empire. Everywhere Catholic monarchs and statesmen judged the Jesuits as overly independent of royal authority. The same monarchs and statesmen helped arrange a general papal suppression of the Jesuits in 1773—with the exception of the Russian Empire, where Catherine the Great ignored papal edicts. The cumulative effect of these suppressions was one of the largest seizures of property, including schools, churches, libraries, communal homes, and tracts of land, in modern history. In France, 103 Jesuit colleges closed. In Belgium, auctioneers sold plates, silver, chalices, and paintings. (State officials hoarded for themselves valuable paintings commissioned by the Jesuits from Peter Paul Rubens.)[40] From small communities of Jesuits in Goa, French Guiana, and colonial Louisiana, to massive Jesuit establishments in Rome, Mexico City, and Vienna, the society's twenty-three thousand men abandoned the priesthood, joined other religious orders, or became diocesan clergy. In Rome, an English Jesuit recorded the reaction when, after the doorbell rang at suppertime, a delegate from the Curia entered with a team of soldiers to read the papal brief of suppression out loud: "We all stood stupefied and only now and then looked at one another. It was well that no one fainted."[41]

The Marquis of Pombal expressed particular enthusiasm for a Reform Catholic text written by an auxiliary bishop of Trier in the Rhineland under the pseudonym Febronius. Febronius naturally disparaged the Jesuits, but his primary focus was on episcopal authority within the church and the importance of synods or gatherings of bishops and priests as checks on papal authority. He insisted that bishops received their authority directly from the apostles, not the pope.[42]

Concrete expressions of these Reform Catholic sentiments—with copious references to Febronius—occurred at the Provincial Council of Utrecht in the Netherlands in 1763 and the Congress of Ems in the Rhine valley in 1786. Smaller synods occurred in South America in Lima and Caracas and in North America in Baltimore and Mexico City. The delegates at Ems identified the pope as merely the "principal over-seer" of the bishops.[43]

The Synod of Pistoia, led by Bishop Scipione de' Ricci and held in 1786 under the auspices of Tuscany's Grand Duke Peter Leopold, the brother of the Habsburg emperor Joseph II, drew the most atten-tion. Despite heading a minor diocese, Ricci was a major intellectual, a Reform Catholic busily corresponding with peers across Europe, including Henri Grégoire.

The eighty-five published decrees of the synod—ranging from sup-port for liturgy in the vernacular to limitations on festivals—circulated through Reform Catholic networks. They appeared in translation in Vienna and Salzburg, and copies made their way to Spain to be scru-tinized by clerics and allied state ministers, some of whom also began a correspondence with Grégoire. Catholics in Beirut pondered their implementation.[44] In Mexico City, Reform Catholics sympathetic to the Synod of Pistoia urged Catholics to obey the "Apostolic Canon" and not be distracted by the "novelty, opulence, and sensuality" of pop-ular devotions.[45] One Scottish priest thought that "the good bishop of Pistoia . . . has set the example, even in Italy."[46]

IV

THE POLITICAL IMPLICATIONS of Reform Catholicism also became evident. The monarchs and rulers favoring Reform Catholicism—Joseph II in Austria-Hungary, Charles III in Spain, Peter Leopold in Tuscany, Stanisław August in Poland, and Joseph I in Portugal—did not consider themselves democrats, then a term of abuse more than a com-pliment. The textbook phrase "enlightened absolutism" describes their autocratic approach to reform.

Still, opposition to ecclesiastical authoritarianism—at least in the papal court—pushed many Reform Catholics to reflect on political rep-resentation. The primary goal of a string of patriotic revolts in the 1770s and 1780s—in North America, Asia, and Europe—was to change systems of political authority based on aristocratic status to some version of popular sovereignty. Even in the fifteenth century, questions about representation in the church had ricocheted into questions of representation within the polity, and by the 1780s, reformers repeatedly made unfavorable comparisons between the less hierarchical structures of the ancient church and the tendency of popes to consolidate their power. Similarly, they noted that ancient constitutions had once limited royal authority. Complaints about a "despotic" papacy segued into questions about political representation within an absolute monarchy.[47]

Reform Catholics also supported religious toleration. In an era when minority religious faiths everywhere existed on sufferance, Joseph II and other Reform Catholics proved much more likely to recognize interreligious marriages than their ultramontane rivals. Joseph II's 1781 Edict of Toleration granted Protestants property and civil rights and permitted freedom of worship, even if he still restricted the construction of Protestant churches and synagogues to side streets so as to "not look like a [Catholic] church."[48] Poland's King Stanislaw August denounced the Roman institution of the "Inquisition, terrible in its very name." French priests associated with Reform Catholicism encouraged Louis XVI to sign an Edict of Toleration that gave modest legal rights to Calvinists.[49]

Protestant rulers also demonstrated a growing appreciation of religious toleration. Dutch authorities in Holland and in colonies such as Sri Lanka edged away from efforts to punish or convert Catholics and allowed them, in the words of a Catholic petition, "the same freedom and liberty as the Heathens, the Mohammedans and the Buddhists."[50]

Movement toward toleration within the British Empire was equally uneven, but equally noticeable. In most of the empire, including England itself, Catholics enjoyed freedom of religious practice as a practical matter but with little legal protection. They often could not vote and faced restrictions on owning property, appointing bishops, and publicly displaying their faith. Almost everywhere potential Catholic officeholders were deterred by having to take test oaths denying the doctrine of transubstantiation. When the French colony of Quebec (most famously) and Caribbean islands such as Grenada passed into British hands in 1763, the question of what to do with significant Catholic populations became more pressing. In Quebec, the British governor general received explicit instructions to persuade Catholics to "embrace the Protestant religion, and to raise their children in it."[51]

Yet less than a decade later the British imperial strategy had shifted. In Grenada, the colonial authorities overcame complaints about "popery" and allowed Catholics—a majority of the free male population—to hold office and vote in 1768.[52] Members of Parliament in London, cognizant of the resentments brewing in their North American colonies, passed the Quebec Act in 1774, providing for full religious freedom and exempting Catholics from the test oath. By this they hoped to head off any rebellion in French Canada. A young firebrand in the colony of New York, Alexander Hamilton, expressed outrage: "They may as well establish popery in New York and the other colonies as they did in Canada."[53]

The same English Parliament proposed Catholic Relief, or the elimination of test oaths, in England itself. The proposal reflected a growing appreciation of religious tolerance as a Protestant virtue, as well as a more pragmatic goal: recruiting more Irish Catholic soldiers into the British army. A "Catholic Committee" of leading English Catholics discreetly lobbied for the bill's passage, even though Catholics could not legally appear in the king's presence, even for a moment.[54]

Just as the British army needed Catholic soldiers, the American revolutionaries after the Declaration of Independence in 1776 needed allies, and found them in Catholic France. The Franco-American alliance—in a war against Protestant Britain—diminished anti-Catholicism in the United States. The first Catholic bishop in the United States, John Carroll, enjoyed pointing out that a Protestant empire, Britain, had nearly crushed the United States "in its birth."[55] A mellowed Alexander Hamilton now urged the New York State Assembly to allow Catholics full voting rights due to the "little influence possessed by the Pope in Europe." No need, Hamilton assured his colleagues, "to extinguish fires which had many days subsided."[56]

The Catholic Relief bill that passed in England never became law in Scotland, as "Protestants and loyal subjects" rallied against its passage. Riots against the bill in Glasgow and Edinburgh demonstrated the tenacity of popular anti-Catholicism.[57] Similarly, some of the bloodiest riots in London's history occurred in 1780, with hundreds reported dead from fires set by anti-Catholic mobs.[58] But in England, as in its rebellious colonies, political leaders now deemed violent anti–Catholic agitation unacceptable. George Washington prohibited his soldiers from celebrating Guy Fawkes Day, or that "ridiculous and childish Custom of burning the Effigy of the Pope." King George III called the riots in London offensive "to all truly pious and good protestants."[59] English Catholics, in turn, expressed loyalty to the British Crown while distancing themselves from the papacy. "I am no Papist nor is my religion Popery," explained one English Catholic bishop in 1781. These are only to be found "in the kingdoms of Italy, Spain and Portugal."[60]

Sympathy for democratic reforms in the political realm and Reform Catholicism in the religious realm also became evident on the other side of the world. Goa remained under Portuguese control, and just as Pombal had favored Reform Catholic ideas in Portugal, he did so in the colonies. He pressed for greater toleration of the Hindu minority, permitted the building of Hindu temples and encouraged the public celebration of Hindu weddings.[61]

Yet Pombal and Portuguese rulers generated some of the same resentment among their colonial subjects that King George III did in British North America. A group of native–born priests led a revolt in 1787. Fully aware of the example set by the American Revolution, they worked at "implanting a new republic" led by native Goans. The revolt's leaders were betrayed in its first days, and fourteen priests eventually spent the better part of two decades in jail as a result, but the rebellion suggests the widespread availability of new political ideas.[62]

From Baltimore to London to Goa, then, and soon in Warsaw, Madrid, and Mexico City, a Reform Catholic sensibility prompted discussion of limits on papal authority as well as sovereignty and constitutions. By the 1780s, new forms of representation within both church and state seemed a logical next step.

V

THE RECIPROCAL RELATIONSHIP between Reform Catholicism and new forms of political representation proved most consequential, and tragic, in France. Popular dissatisfaction with the monarchy fueled by its incapacity to manage the nation's finances had swelled in the 1770s and

1780s. Precisely because church and state in France were so intertwined, resentment grew against the web of taxes, tithes, and fees supporting bishops, abbots, and other clerics who lived in luxury. Clergy owned (and often farmed) some 10 percent of French property. Clerical positions and places in convents attracted parents eager to place unemployed younger sons or unmarriageable daughters in stable positions, but piety was often not required. When Emmanuel Sieyès, later one of the leaders of the revolution, entered the seminary, he did so because as the son of a tax collector he saw no other way to obtain a steady income. Sexual and financial scandals, from episcopal mistresses to frivolous spending, took a reputational toll. Two hundred priests and bishops were deemed necessary to serve the royal court at Versailles.[63]

Up until the revolution, dissatisfaction with clerical corruption could still be understood as part of a normal ebb and flow. Just as efforts to reform the monarchy seemed to bear promise in the 1780s, so, too, did that rarity, a genuinely pious king, Louis XVI, attempt to raise the ecclesiastical tone. He refused to appoint the openly skeptical Cardinal of Toulouse to the more prestigious see of Paris on the grounds that the holder of such a post "must at least believe in God."[64]

The corruption and cynicism associated with the church by its detractors did not eliminate a reservoir of popular piety. The irreligion of Voltaire, Diderot, and the philosophes was the leading edge of a skeptical current that would strengthen in the nineteenth century, but such views rarely disrupted the day-to-day flow of parish life and the sacraments. In the years before the revolution, living in the heart of Paris, Abbé Edgeworth wrote to a friend about his ministry to Irish immigrants and predicted that it would be unchanged "thirty years hence."[65]

When queried in the first weeks of the French Revolution in 1789, members of the three Estates General called by the king—one for clergy, one for nobles, and one for common people—evinced little hostility to religion. Fifty-two bishops were elected to the First Estate (for clergy), although they were outnumbered by over two hundred ordinary priests. These clergy expressed their desire to help the poor—whose situation they knew better than any other educated group in French society—but they also took this unusual opportunity to voice ecclesiastical grievances. For example: why were so many priests poor and why could only nobles become bishops? More radical priests pleaded for the election of bishops. "If election was restored [as in the early Church]," the clergy of the small city of Toul explained, "the face of the Church would be transformed; the voice of the people always decides more surely than the intrigues of a Court."[66]

The Estates General were succeeded by a National Assembly that rapidly became more antagonistic to traditional Catholicism. The National Assembly confiscated the landholdings of wealthy clergy and bishops and passed the Civil Constitution of the Clergy in the summer of 1790. The Civil Constitution required that citizens, not popes or kings, select bishops and even priests, that dioceses conform to administrative lines established by the revolutionary government, and that clergy take an oath of fidelity to the nation, the king, and the new constitution. Monasteries were suppressed.

Some Reform Catholic clergy and their allies expressed their opposition to these policies as "a frontal assault on our liberties."[67] A slightly smaller number welcomed them. They assessed the reforms as making Catholicism more authentic, not less, restoring "principles of the primitive church" lost in the haze created by Latin liturgies, baroque devotions, and obeisance to Rome. Far from doing any damage, Grégoire explained, the Civil Constitution of the Clergy will restore the Church to its "pristine discipline." He took the oath of loyalty on the first possible day, along with sixty-two like-minded priests.[68]

These changes in the first phase of the French Revolution could be understood for a last fleeting moment as the French version of a wider Reform Catholic project. After all, Joseph II's policies in the Austro-Hungarian Empire resembled those enacted in the first phase of the French Revolution. He had suppressed over half of the monasteries in Austria during the 1780s and considered contemplative houses dedicated to prayer "useless" and "sources of superstition." He focused governmental attention on the training of secular (or diocesan) clergy.[69] His toleration of Jews had encouraged some Reform Catholics, such as Henri Grégoire, to extend such toleration in France.

In Poland, too, statesmen in the early 1790s pondered declaring church lands part of the national patrimony and selling them to fund new government ventures. A Reform Catholic clergyman, Hugo Kołłątaj, saw the initial phase of the French Revolution as a giant step forward for liberty, and he had also spent time in Vienna, where he came to admire Joseph II's reforms. Typically, he criticized the Jesuits, urged a national episcopal synod, and stressed the independence of Polish Catholicism from direct oversight by the pope.[70] In Germany, monks sympathetic to Reform Catholicism applauded the revolution and saw the Civil Constitution of the Clergy as a way to purge "papal despotism."[71]

This precarious balancing act did not endure. No event in the French Revolution was more decisive than the Civil Constitution of the Clergy. When one dismayed French bishop noted that the Civil Constitution of the Clergy meant that unbelievers had as much say as "a single priest or bishop" in the episcopal selection process, revolutionary leader Maximilien Robespierre retorted that "the nomination of bishops is an exercise of political power." He saw no reason to "privilege the clergy over other citizens in this process."[72] A secular anticlerical revolutionary leadership now anchored one pole of the French discussion, forcing Reform Catholics to choose sides. Either they could declare loyalty to a church under siege or to a state increasingly antagonistic to Christian expression.

In the United States, at this exact moment, Maryland planter Charles Carroll, whose ideas about church and state had been shaped by Reform Catholicism, helped draft Article VI of the United States Constitution, which banned oaths of religious allegiance for public office, so aggravating for English Catholics. His cousin, soon to be Bishop John Carroll, had requested an English acquaintance to send him writing on the limits of papal authority and the desirability of the liturgy in the vernacular. For a time, John Carroll favored priests electing their bishops as recommended at the Synod of Pistoia.[73] Charles Carroll also served on the committee that drafted the first amendment to the United States Constitution forbidding a religious establishment and supporting free exercise.[74]

Distinctions between church and state drawn in the United States never seemed plausible in France, where church and state had so long been interwoven. Pius VI's verdict on the first phase of the French Revolution was uncertain, and he waited a full seven months before making a public statement. Abbé Edgeworth nervously predicted that the pope "will be firm."[75]

The Civil Constitution of the Clergy proved the tipping point. When Pius VI consulted his curial cardinals, the more pessimistic saw the Civil Constitution as a "schismatic system tending toward the total extermination of religion." The pope agreed and excommunicated priests and bishops willing to take the loyalty oath. His objections, articulated in a long letter addressed to the French bishops seated in the National Assembly, were in the first place ecclesiastical: the Civil Constitution "cuts down and subverts the Catholic religion."[76]

But his objections were also political. Pius VI's reaction to the Civil Constitution of the Clergy should be understood as the first strike in a counterrevolutionary Catholic movement that would solidify in the mid-nineteenth century and last well into the twentieth. He assessed "unrestrained freedom" as resulting in chaos and mobilized Catholics to resist a whirlwind that threatened to destroy both church and society.[77]

In the aftermath of the papal condemnation, the gap between Catholicism and the revolution widened with dizzying speed. Already almost all of the French bishops and slightly under half of the French clergy had refused to take the loyalty oath on a succession of wintry Sunday mornings. (They were termed nonjuring clergy.) Another group of clergy recanted their oath when learning of papal opposition. Formally prohibited from saying Mass or leading religious ceremonies in France, thirty thousand nonjuring priests fled to Belgium, Rome, England, Italy, Spain, and the United States, clutching their chalices and vestments. Meanwhile, the National Assembly banned any kind of religious apparel for priests or nuns. They should not, explained one legislator, be allowed to distinguish "themselves from the national mass by wearing a total or partial costume not established by the nation."[78] In the fall of 1792, terrified by approaching Prussian armies, Parisian revolutionaries began slaughtering perceived opponents (or suspected traitors), among them 223 nonjuring priests in one bloody September week.

Soon after the execution of Louis XVI, revolutionary armies confronted a full-fledged rebellion in the Vendée, an especially devout region in western France. The rallying cry of the Catholic masses became a primal scream of resentment against civic elites for persecuting clergy, disrupting parish life, and trying to eliminate processions and pilgrimages. A fish vendor and a wig maker helped lead the revolt.

By one estimate 200,000 men, women, and children died in the Vendée in less than two years of guerrilla warfare. Savagery marked the fighting on both sides, and the Catholic and royalist force eventually succumbed to the numerical and organizational superiority of the revolutionary armies.

Recognizing that Catholics were now disproportionately numbered among the revolution's opponents, revolutionaries shifted in 1793 and 1794 from reforming Catholicism to dechristianization. Civic authorities forbade public worship, replaced the seven days of the Christian calendar with a ten-day week (eliminating the Sabbath), and renamed churches, streets, and squares in an effort to eradicate France's religious heritage. In Strasbourg, revolutionaries seriously proposed (but could not manage) toppling the spire on the city's medieval cathedral in order to challenge the "people's superstition." They did manage to remove hundreds of statues from the exterior of the cathedral's nave. Militants lopped off the heads of the long rows of saints on the exterior of the onetime cathedral of Notre Dame in Paris (renamed a Temple of Reason) and carved "To Philosophy" over the cathedral doors. At the Parisian parish of Saint-Sulpice, the commune in control of the city stopped all Masses, and militants carried away chalices to be melted down for cash. A local philosopher, according to the pastor's account, "also gave a speech announcing that there was no more God and everything was a question of Nature." "This," wrote the pastor, "is the new religion or rather cult, established now in all the churches of Paris."[79] After a group of Carmelite nuns died at the guillotine for refusing to adhere to the Constitutional Church, friends found devotional pictures of Louis XVI hidden in their abandoned rooms.

In 1789, with its high standards of erudition, magnificent music, great cathedrals, charitable works for the poor, and churches in every village, Catholicism remained an inescapable part of French life. Five years later the French church stood bereft. The Mass had become illegal. Clergy and nuns had scattered. Traditional Catholic ministries in education and aid to the poor had been dissolved. The country's grand monasteries, catherals, and convents—some dating from the Middle Ages—had been emptied and their material treasures looted. Thousands of vacant church buildings dotted small towns and the countryside, with groups of furtive communicants sustaining links to a tradition once thought immemorial.

VI

JUST AS THE DEBATE over the Civil Constitution of the Clergy erupted in France, a group of plantation owners in Haiti burned Henri Grégoire in effigy. Grégoire had corresponded frequently with Toussaint Louverture, the Haitian-born leader of the rebellion of five hundred thousand enslaved people and free people of color that began in 1791 and eventually led to Haitian independence.

Grégoire supported the Haitian revolutionaries and eventually played a role in persuading the revolutionary leadership in France to support slave emancipation. Most Catholic clergy in Haiti, almost all French-born and many with a Reform Catholic sensibility, supported both revolution and emancipation.[80] "What pierced the heart with pain," complained one aggrieved planter, "was the thought that most of the parish priests had only remained among them [the rebels]."[81] Louverture requested from Grégoire recommendations for priests not only of "exemplary conduct" but also "religious and republican." He invited Grégoire to move to Haiti—an invitation Grégoire declined—and run the island's ecclesiastical affairs.[82]

Enthusiasm for the French Revolution and then a rebellion against a colonial power also characterized Ireland, if on a less grand scale. Protestants such as Theobald Wolfe Tone took the lead, arguing that if Catholics in France could support freedom and republicanism, so, too, should the Irish Protestant minority and the Irish Catholic majority demand freedom from England.[83]

Governor-General Toussaint Louverture. *(Photo by Stock Montage/Getty Images)*

More vehemently than Grégoire and Reform Catholics in France, Tone dismissed the importance of links to Rome. "Look at France," he exclaimed, "where is the intolerance of popish bigotry now?" Why worry about the "rusty and extinguished thunderbolts of the Vatican?"[84]

In 1798, twenty thousand people died during an explosion of violence that metastasized into a sectarian war of Catholic versus Protestant, despite the ecumenical ambitions of the movement's leaders. Those who joined the rebellion found themselves allied, unpredictably, with French revolutionaries against Ireland's British imperial masters. Irish bishops chose the other side, fearing that revolution would lead to anti-Catholic chaos. Encouraged by Vatican officials, bishop after bishop in Ireland denounced the "French disease" of revolution.

Abbé Edgeworth's close friend, Cork bishop Richard Moylan, proved especially vocal in his attack on "atheistical incendiaries."[85] In nearby Scotland, bishops dismissed "emissaries of impiety and rebellion." In faraway Newfoundland, where 80 percent of the population was Irish-born, the Apostolic Vicar made clear that only British rule had made residents "the happiest people in either the old or the new world."[86]

VII

ON THE CONTINENT, the story was different. Here a populist reaction against Reform Catholicism and French anticlerical armies strengthened ultramontanism. A crucial episode occurred before the French Revolution, in 1787, in Prato, near Pistoia, when rioting broke out after rumors spread that the Reform Catholic Bishop Ricci planned to destroy a relic, the Virgin Mary's cintola, or girdle. Protesters dragged the bishop's ceremonial chair out of the cathedral into the piazza and burned it. After several chaotic days, Ricci's patron, Duke Leopold, sent in troops to calm the crowds, but Ricci eventually abandoned the diocese, never to return.[87]

Once the French Revolution took an anti-religious turn, revolutionary armies did the work of alienation more efficiently. The occupation of both Belgium and the Rhine valley during the first wars of the revolution in 1793–1794 and the simultaneous war with Spain created multiple small Vendées. Everywhere patriotic reaction against French imperial ambitions merged with a rejection of French anticlericalism. In Aachen, delegates to the local assembly refused to swear the oath to liberty and equality instituted by the French and instead adopted the following statement: "We swear to maintain the Roman Apostolic religion in all its purity and to support with all our power the sovereignty, freedom and welfare of the people of Aachen, So help us God and his dear saints."[88]

In the lands that later became Belgium, revolutionary armies implemented one of the fiercest repressions of religion since the Reformation. All exterior signs indicating a church were banned, as was the ringing of church bells. The occupation government suppressed all religious orders and began deportations of priests unwilling to swear an oath of loyalty to the revolutionary government. Some were deported to neighboring Prussia, others to a penal colony in French Guiana. A populist uprising against these measures turned into a civil war. Priests celebrated Mass in disguise and parishioners took pride in hiding the church bells—a game they called Klöppel Krieg—from exhausted French commissioners. One priest changed his clothes four times a day to evade capture and proudly wrote in the parish register in the tiny town of Sichem: "In spite of the terror I baptized all the children between 1797–1802."[89]

In Spain, censorship of the press limited popular knowledge of the French Revolution, but the roughly six thousand French émigré priests entering the country at the height of the anti-religious persecution filled in the gruesome details. Spanish priests and monks mobilized the faithful with exhortations against "irreligious men" determined to shatter Spain's unity of "faith and country."[90]

Napoleon's ascendancy within the French army accelerated this pattern. Napoleon's basic sympathy for the revolution made him an ally of Reform Catholics, and he and his deputies saw part of their task as weaning Catholic peasants (and some clergy) from "the sort of superstition that often abuses natural occurrences." They proposed mandatory courses for clergy in math and science.[91] While Napoleon's armies established republics across northern Italy—for a *triennio*, or three-year period—his generals enlisted Reform Catholics to draft constitutions. In the Genoese Republic, a Bishop Ricci protégé authored a "political catechism" that attempted to persuade local peasants of the need for political and religious reform. Only the abolition of "superstitious" practices could lay the groundwork for a republic of self-governing citizens.[92]

These modest triumphs for Reform Catholics, however, could not counteract continuing unrest. Parish priests in Imola, having witnessed the looting endemic to Napoleon's armies, became unenthusiastic about democracies installed by bayonets. "They have suppressed St. Charles, and all the brotherhoods, abolished bequests, [and] imprisoned eleven of the cathedral canons in the castle," one diarist sardonically explained, "So democracy, that Liberty and Equality of the Republicans and the French, robbed our Italy." In southern Italy, one cardinal based in Naples led a guerrilla army of some seventeen thousand men against the occupying French armies. One of his victims—shot dead in his bed— was a bishop stationed in Calabria and allied with Bishop Ricci. The bishop's dying words were reportedly "Long live Jesus Christ, long live the republic."[93]

VIII

HENRI GRÉGOIRE bravely defended his Catholicism and the new Constitutional Church at the height of the Terror in Paris, even refusing to abandon his clerical clothing. When the Terror ceased, he again insisted that Catholicism was "in perfect harmony with liberal principles."[94] As always, Grégoire and other constitutional clergy demanded a church "as pure as it left the hands of Jesus Christ, as it was in the first centuries." Again, councils were held (in 1797 and 1801) to discuss the liturgy in the vernacular and other reforms. "Sensible men," Grégoire wrote, "will never confuse the Revolution with the crimes and disasters that accompanied it."[95] His influence extended to Spain, where the country's most prominent minister, Gaspar Melchio de Jovellanos, had long proposed, like French revolutionaries, to sell church lands as a mechanism for renewing the "pure and ancient discipline of the church."[96] Even as he advocated restraints on the papacy by invoking early church councils, Jovellanos wondered if some form of constitutional monarchy might serve as a check on royal absolutism.[97]

Anyone predicting the future of Catholicism in 1789 might have forecast a group of national Catholic churches, loosely linked to the papacy but fundamentally tied to local monarchs and even republican governments. This Reform Catholic ethos did not disappear after the French Revolution: Henri Grégoire's influence, for example, endured through his disciples in Mexico, Italy, and Haiti well into the 1830s.

But Abbé Edgeworth's account of Louis XVI's death was one small part of what became a more influential project. It distinguished Catholicism not only from the French Revolution but from the modern world it brought about. If for its proponents the French Revolution ushered in republican government and allied civil liberties, at least for a time, ultramontane Catholics described it as a "seditious and murderous" conspiracy led by anti-Catholic philosophes.[98]

A cluster of theologians, mostly based in Rome, had already begun to defend papal authority. They described the pope as the monarch of the church, much more than the first bishop among equals. The papacy preceded church councils, instead of deriving authority from them. Only the pope—not princes and government officials—should appoint bishops. The pope himself, acting on certain matters, might be understood as infallible.[99]

Ex-Jesuits, appalled by their treatment at the hands of Reform Catholics who had orchestrated the suppression of the Society of Jesus, took a leading role. One ex-Jesuit, François-Xavier de Feller, set up a print shop in Liège and rallied ultramontane opponents of Reform Catholicism and the French Revolution. He inveighed against Voltaire as the symbol of a secular Enlightenment but also against Reform Catholic figures such as Joseph II.[100]

Ultramontane polemicists such as Feller applauded Edmund Burke's 1790 *Reflections on the Revolution in France.* Burke's dismay at the course of the French Revolution rested upon what he saw as its abandonment of an established church and inherited political institutions. He pointed to the widespread confiscation of church property as an "unheard of despotism" of state over church.[101] A French bishop used Burke to pour scorn on the "metaphysical legislators" drafting the Declaration of the Rights of Man and the Citizen and in so doing "placing the germ of atheism in the preamble of their constitution."[102] In Poland, a papal nuncio denounced priests perceived as sympathetic to the French Civil Constitution of the Clergy. Such men were "infected with the dangerous maxims and pernicious systems of the Assembly of France."[103] As far away as Pondichéry, in India, missionary clergy refused to swear an oath of loyalty to the new French government, offered a requiem Mass for Louis XVI, and complained about local priests who "breathed only the air of democracy."[104]

Even as they issued a stream of documents condemning the revolution, Pius VI and his advisers turned their attention back to the Synod of Pistoia. The Vatican condemned the decrees of the synod in 1794, eight years after their promulgation, and directly linked the synod to the "revolutionary upheaval" shattering Europe.[105] Ricci complained to Henri Grégoire that their enemies desired to persecute all "good Christians who hope to reform abuses in Church or State."[106]

IX

PIUS VI DIED IN 1799, in Valence, France, as a captive of Napoleon. Many thought he would be the last pope. The entire Roman apparatus of curial cardinals, nuncios, and even Swiss guards lay in disarray. Napoleon's troops occupied Rome, and a republic had been declared. Most Catholic universities had closed, and missionary efforts had ground to a halt. The number of monasteries and convents had declined precipitously.

Forced to hold their conclave in Venice, not occupied Rome, the beleaguered cardinals managed to elect a new pope, Cardinal Barnaba Chiaramonti, or Pius VII. A pragmatist, Chiaramonti had attracted attention for a Christmas homily of 1797 in which had endorsed a "form of democratic government." "Do not believe," he stressed, "that the Catholic religion is against democracy."[107] He embarked on negotiations with Napoleon, who had just assumed dictatorial control of France, and the two men signed a concordat in 1801. Pius VII hoped to save the church; Napoleon hoped to fend off continuing Catholic resistance to his plans to remake Europe. State involvement in religion remained significant: the treaty limited the number of French clergy, affirmed the legality of the seizure of church lands during the revolution, and

arranged for clerical salaries to be paid by the state. The treaty guaranteed freedom of religion, but also declared Catholicism "the religion of
the majority of the French people." A bemused Napoleon reportedly
explained his tactics this way:

> It was by making myself a Catholic that I won the war of
> the Vendée, by making myself a Muslim that I established
> myself in Egypt, by making myself Ultramontane that I
> won men's hearts in Italy.[108]

In a few regions of Europe, the Reform Catholic impulse continued to crest. In Bavaria, the government now treated priests as state
employees and introduced religious toleration. Bavaria's foreign minister denounced monasteries (and confiscated their land) for rejecting "the
spread of enlightened principles."[109]

The primary optic remained that of a church besieged. Napoleon
forced Pius VII to journey to Paris and witness his crowning as emperor
in 1804 in the Cathedral of Notre Dame. (Characteristically, Napoleon
placed the crown on his own head.) Soon Napoleon would pressure
Roman cardinals into concocting from whole cloth an early Christian
martyr named Neopolis. The martyr was dubbed Saint Napoleon, and
his feast day was scheduled on August 15, the traditional feast day of the
Assumption of Mary, but more importantly Napoleon's birthday.[110]

These humiliations obscured a different story. In attempting to control the French church, Napoleon had partially liberated it. Even though
the French government still paid clerical salaries, the pope gained the
right in one swoop to remove all of the bishops of France and appoint
their successors. By ignoring bishops of the Constitutional Church, such
as Henri Grégoire, who lost his job in the episcopal shuffle, Napoleon
inadvertently strengthened the papacy.

On both the journey to Paris for Napoleon's coronation and the
return to Rome, Pius VII marveled at the crowds clustered on the side
of the road, drawn to catch a glimpse of the pope. (Former bishop Ricci
scrambled to get a papal audience when the Pope arrived in Florence,
noting to Abbé Grégoire that the pope's aides doubted his "orthodoxy.")[111] Sometimes priests rang bells or arranged for the organist to

play while they muttered the mandatory prayer for the emperor, Napoleon, under their breath. Pius VII had once found Napoleon captivating and was grateful that his attacks on the church had ceased. But in 1809 he finally broke with Napoleon, excommunicating him for annexing the Papal States to the French Empire. When confronted by French troops who demanded that he acquiesce to Napoleon's demands, Pius VII responded, "we must not, we cannot, we will not."[112]

Napoleon removed the pope from Rome—to a bishop's palace in Savona, in northern Italy, where he remained under house arrest for five years. But Pius VII's resistance to Napoleon's demands inspired his flock. As one contemporary later commented, "the detention of the Pope and the annexation of the States of the Church to France were the caprices of tyranny by which [Napoleon] lost the advantage of passing for the restorer of religion."[113]

Pius VII's release in 1814 and Napoleon's final defeat a year later meant a new beginning. Word of the pope's release spread around the world, reaching even Shanxi Province, where Jacobus Wang, one of the few remaining Chinese priests, wrote to congratulate the pope on his freedom.[114] By then, the pieces of the ultramontane Catholic worldview were locked in. Its proponents heralded feast days, processions, saints, and miracles. They disparaged any idea of revolution, and their focus on hierarchy and authority made ideas of representation and popular sovereignty unacceptable in the church and less welcome in the state. They thought state endorsement of the church a worthy ideal, but only with ecclesiastical independence from state authority. They exalted the status of priests, bishops, and especially the pope. They understood themselves to be battling Protestant, Jewish, and secular foes.

Pius VII could not revive the shattered church of the old regime, so dependent on Catholic monarchs and divided by nationalist rivalries. He did not try. Instead, he immediately restored the Jesuits, reversing one of Reform Catholicism's signature achievements. Some of these Jesuits began explaining how "crimes of philosophy" and the wrong direction taken by the modern world had inexorably led to the persecution of the church in France.[115] And so the pope and his allies set about fashioning an ultramontane church in a postrevolutionary age.

TWO

Revival

Devotions, Miracles, and the Papacy

I

BORN IN DUBLIN IN 1778, Catherine McAuley was orphaned at a young age. She first lived with a Catholic uncle, then distant Protestant relatives, and finally an affluent Protestant couple, Catherine and William Callaghan. After the deaths of the Callaghans, McAuley inherited their estate. She persuaded a small group of women to join her in a new venture funded by her inheritance. Together they built and staffed a House of Mercy on Baggot Street, in Dublin, which opened in 1827 with Catherine and her friends in residence. They enrolled five hundred poor girls in a school and provided a home for young women attempting to find employment as maids and in laundries.

The neighbors on the prosperous thoroughfare protested. But a priest advising McAuley stressed that "if you would have a public institution be of service to the poor, place it in the neighborhood of the rich."[1] Dublin's archbishop, Daniel Murray, signed a petition that the women circulated door-to-door, conveying his endorsement of the school as preparing "poor girls" for the "duties of the humble state in life to which it has pleased God to call them."[2]

Jealousy from other Dublin-based women's religious orders could be shrugged off. Doubts expressed by Archbishop Murray about the informality of the arrangements on Baggot Street could not. McAuley should not be "designated *Sister*," Murray told Cardinal Mauro Cappellari, soon to be elected Pope Gregory XVI, since the women did not take vows or belong to a "legitimately established congregation."[3]

Against her inclination to simply gather like-minded women, McAuley petitioned Rome for approval. Along with two colleagues, she took vows of poverty, chastity, and obedience "until the end of my life." Once canonically recognized, she dedicated the Sisters of Mercy to the "visitation of the sick poor" and "protection and instruction of poor females."[4] Roman officials insisted that she add the phrase "the Parish priest shall always be consulted" when young women applied to join the order.[5]

McAuley's decision to begin a new women's religious order was not unusual. The number of nuns or women religious had declined over the course of the eighteenth century, a decline accelerated by revolutionaries who forced between thirty and fifty thousand women to leave their convents in the aftermath of the French Revolution.[6] But women like McAuley and bishops or priests inspired by such women founded a staggering 571 women's religious congregations in the nineteenth century. In France, the number of women religious increased from 12,300 in 1808 to 135,000 in 1878, and women religious by that time significantly outnumbered clergy (the opposite of the situation in 1789).[7] In Germany, women were four times as likely to enter a convent in 1908 as in 1866.[8] The number of nuns within Ireland grew from 122 in 1800 to 8,031 in 1901, a number that does not include a large number of Irish nuns working outside of Ireland.[9]

Importantly, women in these new religious orders balanced prayer and contemplation with active service in the world, instead of devoting their lives to prayer and contemplation alone, as would have been typical in the eighteenth century. Attracted to lives of service, perhaps wary of the day-to-day demands of family life in a world where the authority of husbands and fathers remained difficult to question, women religious formed the institutional backbone of modern Catholicism. They staffed schools, founded hospitals, and raised orphaned children. Where gaps existed between lofty ideals and weak governments, women religious stepped in. They focused especially on the tribulations endured by young women migrating from the countryside to urban areas, searching for work as maids and at risk of turning to prostitution. What McAuley did in Dublin, other women did elsewhere. Barbara Maix, founder of the Sisters of the Immaculate Heart of Mary, did similar work in Vienna and later in Rio de Janeiro.[10]

Leadership roles for women religious within the church frequently exceeded possibilities for women outside it. "You do not know," explained an envious Florence Nightingale, having observed Sisters of Mercy working as nurses in the British army during the Crimean War, "what a home the Catholic Church is. . . . There is nothing like the training (in these days) which the Sacred Heart or the Order of St. Vincent gives to women."[11] Bishops and priests competed to lure women's religious orders to their dioceses with promises of financial support. When a priest in Dundee, Scotland, asked the Sisters of Mercy to open a school, he admitted that they would be moving to a "dark and bigoted Protestant town." In recompense he offered "the prettiest and best Irish cow that could be found in Scotland."[12]

McAuley and her contemporaries absorbed and transmitted the piety of the ultramontane revival. They meditated on their own sins. "Since one sin alone required this expiation [of Christ's death]," McAuley instructed novices, "see how many strokes your sins added to the number."[13]

They also championed self-denial. McAuley thought the "most acceptable offering we can make to Him is the sacrifice of our self will."[14] Routinely, Sisters of Mercy—and other men and women in religious orders—gathered to listen as each individual member apologized for faults and errors within community life and endured public corrections from the mother superior or rector. Women religious often chose new names upon their admission to a community, sometimes the names of male saints, as symbolic breaks with their biological family. Occasionally their names were chosen for them. Some nuns challenged themselves to wear hair shirts or iron bands around their legs as a reminder of Christ's suffering. Women religious wore distinctive habits at all times, even during the heat of summer, identifying themselves as a separate caste. Friends and relatives, even parents, received only occasional visiting opportunities.

The rhetoric associated with the ultramontane revival meant that relations with other Christians became more strained. Dublin's Archbishop Murray avoided the term "heretic" when referring to Protestants and preferred "separated brethren" or even "beloved fellow-Christians." His ultramontane successors thought this vocabulary overly sensitive. The greater risk was to "delude Protestants and scandalize Catholics regarding salvation."[15]

McAuley, too, became more combative. She had spent her childhood surrounded by Protestant relatives, which testified to at least casual exchange between Protestants and Catholics in early-nineteenth-century Dublin. When she founded the first Houses of Mercy, she appreciated Protestants' willing to contribute to charitable bazaars and sign petitions in her support.

By the 1830s, though, McAuley understood herself to be competing against Protestants "employing wealth and influence to allure Catholics from their faith." Prior to the foundation of the House of Mercy, she explained, young girls would have fallen victim to the "Protestant influence in this neighborhood."[16] She and her colleagues worried that even "amiable" Protestant or unchurched acquaintances might be doomed to eternal torment "for want of a knowledge of the faith."[17]

McAuley died in 1841, inspiring genuine grief. The phrase "God's holy will be done," noted one bereft Sister of Mercy, seemed "difficult to say . . . sincerely."[18] She had requested a simple coffin laid in the earth like the poor. Her legacy was less simple. She helped construct the institutions of modern Catholicism. A century later, her successors worried about being trapped within them.

Mother Mary Catherine McAuley.
(Archives of the Sisters of Mercy)

II

WHAT HISTORIANS NOW TERM the ultramontane revival shaped every dimension of Catholic life from the early nineteenth century through the 1960s. It was a revival because a church near collapse emerged as a more potent source of meaning for tens of millions of people. It was ultramontane because it nurtured a particular set of theological and institutional forms. Its origins lay in parish missions, a better trained (and monitored) clergy, and activist nuns. Particular ideas about suffering and sin developed during the Reformation provided a foundation, but only the disarray caused by the French Revolution allowed ultramontanism to become the dominant form of Catholic Christianity.

If a single text sparked the revival it was *The Genius of Christianity*, written in exile in London and published in 1802 by François-René de Chateaubriand, a French nobleman and former military officer. In his youth, Chateaubriand had lamented priests serving as "vampires who suck your money, your blood, your very thought," but he had experienced an instant, emotional conversion upon learning of his mother's death. As he later reported, "my conviction came from the heart; I wept and I believed."[19]

Chateaubriand looked forward by looking back. He accepted Napoleon's concordat with the pope and prudently dedicated *The Genius of Christianity* to the French emperor. But in a Europe divided between secular and religious, revolutionary and counterrevolutionary, he yearned for a unity he associated with the Middle Ages. Across Europe and North America, Catholics devoured Chateaubriand's writings and found in them inspiration for a religious ideal standing against the revolution, certainly, but also broader than a nation-state.[20] That same year, Friedrich Schlegel, a German poet living in Paris, founded the journal *Europa*. He, too, thought "the great question" was whether a Europe marred by war and revolution could rebuild itself "as in the Middle Ages."[21] Along with his wife, Dorothea, Schlegel converted to Catholicism in 1808, and the couple lived with a like-minded circle of friends first in Munich and then in Vienna. They aimed to develop a Catholic "system of science" in opposition to the "revolutionary spirit of the age."[22]

Thirty years later, the famed English historian Thomas Macaulay glumly described the "progress of the Catholic revival." "We often hear it said," he explained, "that the world is becoming more and more enlightened, and that this enlightening must be favourable to Protestantism and unfavourable to Catholicism. We wish that we could think so." Quite the opposite:

> No person who calmly reflects on what, within the last
> few years, has passed in Spain, in Italy, in South America,
> in Ireland, in the Netherlands, in Prussia, even in France,
> can doubt that the power of this Church over the hearts
> and minds of men is now greater far than it was when the
> Encyclopaedia . . . appeared [in the 1760s].[23]

The geographical sequence is significant. The earliest centers of the revival were France, Germany, Belgium, and the Netherlands. It swept through North America soon after its origins in Europe, carried by migrants and missionaries. The fragility of institutional church structures in Mexico and South America and the region's more enduring Reform Catholic tradition meant that the revival only arrived there later in the nineteenth century.

The revival began with hearts, not minds. Chateaubriand championed popular devotions and thought ordinary believers "wiser than philosphers." Catechisms were simple. One 1840 manual encouraged nuns and priests to stick "simply to the text, without adding any explanations of complex questions, repressing the curiosity of the mind, so as to accustom them to treat matters divine with respect, and to make them more humble and more submissive to the simple beliefs of our faith."[24]

At the revival's core was a deepening attachment to the institution of the church. As one Polish priest explained:

> It is not enough to believe in Jesus Christ, to be a sim-
> ple Christian like the heretics [Protestants]; in addition
> it is necessary to be faithful, that is, to believe strongly
> and proclaim everything that the Church teaches; to be
> united with the bond of the Holy Sacraments and remain,

through one's pastor and bishop, unified with and obedient to the highest leader, the Pope.[25]

The first mechanism to spread an ultramontane Catholicism was the
parish mission. Typically, a week-long series of exhortations, opportunities for confession, and Mass, concluding with the erection of a
huge cross, missions were pioneered by Jesuit, Redemptorist, and Pas-
sionist priests beginning in the mid-eighteenth century. In France,
clergy organized a stunning fifteen hundred missions between 1815 and
1830.[26] In the Netherlands, the Protestant King William I attempted to
ban missions but found enforcement of this edict impossible given the
groundswell of enthusiasm among his Catholic subjects. The Protestant
governments of Baden and Prussia also banned missions, but eager participants simply crossed into Alsace and Belgium.[27]

Mission psychology pivoted between two poles: a doctrinal severity
centered on the horror of sin and everlasting damnation and a practical
piety aimed at persuading Catholics to view the sacraments (especially
confession) and the institutional church as their best shield in a bewildering, often hostile world. The severity is evident in the correspondence
of one Jesuit missionary trained in Switzerland and sent to Maine, in the
United States. He viewed missions as "spiritual weapons" for "reclaiming a very large number of bad Catholics" and converting the occasional
"Protestant or heretic." "Hardened sinners" must understand that eternal life depended on reconciliation with the church. He was appalled by
local Protestants of a more liberal bent who speculated that "there is no
hell, or if there is, it is not for men, as Christ ransomed us all."

At the same time, this missionary reassured his listeners, "who seemed
lost without hope," that their sins could be forgiven in the confessional.
Damnation could be evaded.[28] As a leading ultramontane theologian
in Rome explained, men and women not in a "culpable state of heresy,
schism or unbelief" would not "suffer the eternal torments of hell." The
"goodness and mercy of God" were too great.[29]

Reform Catholics had a different view. At the 1786 Synod of Pistoia,
the assembled clergy attacked the "irregular noise of these new practices
called 'exercises' or 'missions.'" Such events rarely succeeded in "producing a real conversion."[30]

This suspicion of parish missions demonstrates how Reform Catholics never strayed far from their elite roots. Their more restrained, contemplative Catholicism, disdainful of processions and pilgrimages, did not penetrate beyond a stratum of educated clergy and laypeople. The leaders of the ultramontane revival, by contrast, possessed a genius for tapping into the spiritual longings and fears of ordinary men and women. They recognized the comfort that came from a renewed attachment to the institutional church through its sacraments, the peace of mind derived from a conviction that even the most habitual sinners would be saved. Mass attendance increased markedly, even in countries such as France and Spain, where anticlericalism possessed deep roots. The same clergy stressed the importance of "regularizing" marriages (and forbidding informal cohabitation). They urged the anointing of the sick before death, proclaiming the sacrament crucial to eternal life. Stories circulated of priests on horseback riding for miles to anoint a dying parishioner.

A second change brought about by the revival was a set of reinvigorated devotions, including the rosary, nine-day novenas to Mary, and forty-hour-long sequences of prayers to the Blessed Sacrament. Most of these dated from the sixteenth and seventeenth centuries (or even earlier) but were never more popular than during the nineteenth century. The most important such devotion was to the Sacred Heart. The central image—Jesus gazing directly at the viewer, with his pulsing red heart exposed and pierced by a lance—became one of the most widely distributed of the era, stamped, carved, or engraved onto countless holy cards, stained glass windows, statues, tracts, and pamphlets. Here Jesus came neither as a conquering savior nor as a wise teacher. Instead, he suffered with the devout.

Reform Catholic clergy found the devotion to the Sacred Heart distasteful. At the Synod of Pistoia, Bishop Ricci criticized it as "fantastical, womanish and ridiculous." (He allegedly kept in his dining room a portrait of Joseph II tearing up a picture of the Sacred Heart.)[31] Ultramontanes naturally took offense. When he condemned the Synod of Pistoia, Pius VI described criticism of the Sacred Heart as "false, rash and injurious."[32]

A Lyon Jesuit took a small French devotional group and transformed

The Sacred Heart of Jesus, statue from c. 1920 *(photo courtesy of David Morgan)*

it into an international movement devoted to the Sacred Heart, a group that numbered four million dues-paying adherents by 1900. He also founded *Le Messager du Coeur de Jésus* (The Message of the Heart of Jesus), the most influential Catholic devotional periodical of the nineteenth century. By 1926, Catholics in sixty-nine countries published versions of *Le Messager* in forty-five languages.[33]

This empathy with ordinary believers was also displayed in a distinctive focus on the miraculous. Most Protestant intellectuals believed that miracles had ceased with the deaths of the apostles, and miracles occupied an uncertain space in many Protestant churches. Miraculous healings, certainly, were discredited by association with Catholicism and in the nineteenth century were understood by educated elites as incompatible with a belief in modern science.

Catholics believed otherwise. A cluster of alleged miraculous events in the 1840s—the exhibition of Christ's Holy Robe at Trier in Germany in 1844; the appearance of the Virgin to three children at La Salette in France in 1846; the winking Madonna at Rimini on the Adriatic coast in 1848—signaled a renewed fascination with bridges between the human and the divine.

The events at Trier, a city in the Rhine valley, were the most startling. In the late eighteenth century, Reform Catholic bishops uneasy with the legend that a robe worn by Christ had made its way in perfect condition to Trier, had discouraged pilgrimages and even the robe's public display. Those pilgrims allowed to see the garment were instructed to desist from "bellowing" and to "abstain in future from all clapping of the hands, waving of the finger, and kissing."

What embarrassed Reform Catholics inspired ultramontanists. In the 1840s, at the urging of a new bishop, the Trier coat was again displayed, this time with an emphasis on the seamlessness of the garment reflecting the unity of German Catholics, "be they rich or poor, polite or humble, governors or the governed." Five hundred thousand pilgrims—the largest gathering in German history until that point— trooped through the cathedral to see the robe in seven weeks, at the rate of ten thousand visitors a day, overwhelming (and enriching) local merchants. Observers noted the pilgrimage's popularity with women and its disciplined, orderly character, with ten bishops and close to three hundred priests leading parish and diocesan groups. To the most promi- nent German Catholic writer of the era, Joseph Görres, the pilgrimage signaled "the unity of the Church."[34]

Protestant ministers and editors mocked adoration of the robe at Trier. So did some Catholics. Uneasy with the emerging alliance between lower-class Catholics and ultramontane clergy, Fr. Johannes Ronge left the Roman Catholic Church and founded the *Deutsche Katholiken,* or German Catholic Church, in one of the first schisms of the nineteenth century, all of which were reactions in some way against ultramontanism. (They included another schism in Germany in the 1870s, one among Polish-speaking immigrants in the United States, and one in the Philippines.) He disparaged pilgrims from "the lower classes, very poor in any event, oppressed, ignorant, dull-witted, super- stitious and, some of them degenerate."[35] Ronge's influence extended across the Atlantic. Eager to welcome "Rongianers," the Boston min- ister Theodore Parker hoped that "science" would end such charades as the Holy Robe at Trier.[36]

III

ULTRAMONTANE THEOLOGIANS saw only disaster coming out of the French Revolution, especially the ongoing efforts of revolutionaries— often aided by or inspired by Reform Catholics—to assert civic controls over religious institutions. One of the young theologians associated with the ultramontane school, Mauro Cappellari, concluded his seminary training with a thesis defending papal infallibility as well as a treatise attacking the Synod of Pistoia. In 1799, he published a five-hundred- page study with the revealing title *The Triumph of the Holy See and the Church against the Attacks of Innovators.* Its publication was considered a daring gesture given Cappellari's hostility to revolutionary activity and the presence of French troops in Rome. It attracted few readers. Thirty-two years later, it would be translated into four languages and reprinted in multiple editions after its author was elected as Pope Gregory XVI.

More than ever, Rome became a training ground for a clerical elite. Bishops sent talented seminarians there to prepare them to take up important positions upon their return home. As early as 1820, one astonished Montreal visitor to the Roman dicastery in charge of missions, the Propaganda Fide, observed seminarians reciting texts in fifteen languages, from Irish to Flemish to Coptic.[37] The rector of Rome's Irish College described its mission as "introducing Roman maxims into Ireland and uniting that church more closely with the Holy See."[38]

The shift toward Rome was also intellectual. Joseph de Maistre spent two decades pondering the legacy of the French Revolution from a consular post in St. Petersburg. He acknowledged corruption within the monarchy and the clergy, but he regretted democracy within the state and within the church even more. De Maistre's 1819 *Du Pape* argued for papal primacy at the expense of authority held by bishops or church councils. "There can be no European religion without Christianity," he explained in a syllogism that would have startled eighteenth-century Catholics, "there can be no Catholicism without the pope; there can be no pope without the sovereignty that belongs to him."[39]

De Maistre's death in 1821 and his layman's status limited his initial influence. But his visibility from an out-of-the-way perch in St. Petersburg reflects the disordered state of Catholic intellectual life. The closure of most European Catholic universities during the revolution and the Napoleonic Wars swept away a once vibrant ecosystem of publishers, learned societies, and scholars. Catholics also battled a post-revolutionary conventional wisdom that associated Protestantism with political liberty, prosperity, and toleration. James Mill, the economist and father of the English philosopher, encouraged Catholics to abandon a faith so "unfavourable to their progress in reason and virtue."[40] One young French ultramontane, Frédéric Ozanam, tried to rally Catholic students at the Sorbonne to challenge every "rationalist professor." No one should be allowed to profess that the "institution of the papacy was passing" or that the clergy "consistently favored despotism."[41]

In Germany, small groups of Catholic scholars worked on the intellectual margins of Protestant universities. Some of these scholars taught at the University of Bonn, where their leader, Georg Hermes, explicitly drew upon Immanuel Kant to demonstrate the rationality of Christian faith. His association with Enlightenment ideas and Reform Catholicism made Hermes suspect to ultramontanists now gathered in Cologne and Rome, as did his refusal to lecture in Latin. That ultramontanes now controlled the levers of power became clear when Gregory XVI issued an unexpected condemnation of Hermes's work as "false" and "rash" in 1835. The ultramontane archbishop of Cologne compelled priests on theological faculties to reject theses associated with Hermes. His successor reassigned priests tainted by association with Hermes to "the darkness of a lonesome little village."[42]

The Italian Jesuit Giovanni Perrone, one of the consultors who recommended the placement of Hermes's work on the Index of Forbidden Books, was not a neutral arbiter. Based in Rome, he taught at the Collegio Romano, handed over in 1824 by the pope to the newly restored Jesuits. Perrone favored a different theological school, termed scholastic or neo-Thomist. As the name suggests, the Jesuits and Dominicans who led this enterprise saw themselves as recovering the wisdom of Thomas Aquinas and the scholastic theologians of the Middle Ages.

Even within the church, the neo-Thomist task was formidable. Four decades had passed between the Jesuit suppression in 1773 and their restoration in 1814, and the French Dominicans had been exiled during the French Revolution. One Irish Jesuit scanned the room at a gathering of the world's Jesuits in 1829 and admitted that "the Society can no longer boast of so many brilliant men as she had in the age when Scholasticism flourished."[43]

The work of these neo-Thomist scholars rested upon a particular reading of history: Protestant and Enlightenment intellectuals might prattle on about a "solitary subject" but such a notion was untrue to the dense familial and social worlds humans inhabited. The mistaken individualism taken in philosophical matters had religious implications, producing, in the words of Perrone, men and women "who reject the Catholic Church and follow the fantasies of their private spirit."[44]

All of this would later be spelled out in fine-grained detail. In these early years of the 1830s and 1840s, scholastic or neo-Thomist theologians and philosophers struggled to sort out their presuppositions. The theologian John Henry Newman's conversion from Anglicanism to Catholicism was one of the great ecclesiastical events of England's nineteenth century, and Newman's writings on doctrinal development and conscience would later exert enormous influence within Catholicism. In 1846, just after his conversion, Newman made his first visit to Rome. He became disillusioned. He feared that the Roman Jesuits displayed a "deep suspicion of change with a perfect incapacity to create anything *positive* for the wants of the times."[45] Still, in the 1840s, Newman could at least discuss doctrinal development with Roman interlocutors. Giovanni Perrone admiringly quoted Newman at length.[46]

These cordial exchanges would not endure. In the 1850s and 1860s, Neapolitan and Roman Jesuits would join with like-minded Dominicans and triumph over Catholic rivals. Their scholarship became deeply ahistorical, abandoning ideas of doctrinal development and using Aquinas and his sixteenth- and seventeenth-century interpreters as the basis for answering contemporary questions. This neo-Thomist project would provide the scaffolding for the ultramontane milieu, the core of seminary and university education and a counterpoint to more secular philosophical traditions. Two brothers trained as neo-Thomists in the 1830s in Italy would become especially influential. The older brother, Giuseppe Pecci, grew up to become a leading Jesuit theologian and seminary rector. The younger brother, Vincenzo, became a diocesan priest, papal nuncio to Belgium, bishop, and cardinal archbishop of Perugia. In 1878 he would be elected Pope Leo XIII. He then made his older brother a Roman cardinal.

IV

OVER TIME, bishops and priests, along with women religious such as the Sisters of Mercy, became formed in an ultramontane image. One shift was social location. In the eighteenth century, many bishops, certainly, but often leading clergy and women religious, too, had been raised in aristocratic families. To serve as bishop or abbot or mother superior meant a guaranteed income and high status. In German-speaking Europe and in Latin America, aspiring clergy often studied at universities, not seminaries.[47]

Many of these bonds between the priesthood and the aristocracy were severed during the nineteenth century. Certainly, the assumption that taking on an episcopal role guaranteed great wealth no longer held. The willingness of states to confiscate church lands as a source of revenue did not cease at the end of the French Revolution. In Spain, to take the most extreme example, 83 percent of the property belonging to religious orders was seized by the 1840s.[48] In Mexico, clergy associated with Reform Catholicism proposed confiscating available church land as part of the "rights of nations and governments."[49] Even in countries where Catholics owned no vast tracts of land, such as the United States, former president James Madison cautioned "against the wealth of ecclesiastical corporations" and lauded reformers in Europe and Latin America for rectifying "that disordered state of things."[50]

Recruitment for the clergy shifted to bright young men from the peasantry. After all, as one German theologian put it, "few members of the aristocracy have any desire to serve [the Church]."[51] Cologne's cardinal archbishop, Johann Geissel, was the son of a poor winegrower. A newly appointed French bishop, older local clergy worried, would surround himself with "relatives from the working class and without education."[52] In India, ultramontane missionaries proved more willing than their Reform Catholic predecessors to ignore the boundaries of caste.[53]

Religious orders expanded at an impressive rate. Along with the even greater number of women's religious orders, dozens of male religious orders were founded in the early nineteenth century, including the Marianists (1817), Oblates of Mary Immaculate (1826), Resurrectionists (1836), and Congregation of Holy Cross (1837), all marinated in the devotional piety of the revival and often begun by men with personal experience of persecution during the French Revolution. Older religious orders such as the Dominicans, the Franciscans, and the Redemptorists reinvigorated themselves. The six hundred aged Jesuits alive at the order's refounding in 1814 grew to seventeen thousand men by 1914.

French revolutionaries had raised doubts about celibacy along with so much else, and many intellectuals scorned it as "unnatural." A salacious popular literature mocked priests as sexually avaricious.[54] Delegates to the National Assembly passed laws permitting priests to marry, and several thousand priests did. As the revolution descended into the Terror, celibacy became described as a "social crime," since married priests were presumed more likely to become good republican citizens. One Robespierre protégé denounced men vowed to celibacy "who wish to isolate themselves further from their fellow man and to violate natural and social law." Revolutionaries funded clerical weddings.[55]

Napoleon and Pope Pius VII agreed to forbid clerical marriages in the Concordat of 1801, although it took longer to sort through the several thousand existing unions. Roman officials chose not to highlight clerical marriages and quietly informed local bishops that they were willing to legitimize these marriages and make the clergy (and their wives) laypeople in good standing instead of excommunicating them. Vows of chastity—taken as priests—could be abrogated given the "frightening . . . circumstances of the Revolution."[56]

Still, questions persisted. In French Catholic New Orleans, a newly installed ultramontane bishop banned a priest from celebrating Mass because he was living with his housekeeper and their children, who called him "Papa." Led by the mayor, the city erupted in protest with many petitions signed in support of the beloved, if decidedly not celibate, clergyman.[57] In Mexico, a crusading journalist blasted celibacy in a celebrated 1825 pamphlet as an addition "that you [theologians] have made to the Gospel written by the Apostles."[58] A group of Catholics in the Grand Duchy of Baden called for an end to mandatory celibacy in 1828 and addressed their plea, significantly, not only to the local archbishop but the local archduke and legislative assembly.[59] They understood vows of celibacy for clergy as proof that it was "more than ever necessary . . . to separate the Catholic church from the Roman curia."[60]

The gap between celibacy as an ideal and celibacy as a lived reality could be wide. In regions of the world with few priests, clerical families were widespread. Half of all clergy in the Brazilian diocese of Salvador are estimated to have lived in common-law relationships with wives and children, a practice that while accepted at the village level made priests vulnerable to blackmail if they wished to advance their careers.[61] Brazilian clergy and statesmen associated with Reform Catholicism frequently denounced celibacy as a relic of an unenlightened age.

Legislators proposed that bishops be allowed to ordain married men as priests, "as occurred in the primitive Church, as occurs today in the Greek church and among the Reformed Christians."[62]

Under pressure, ultramontane theologians forged a response, first by attributing weaknesses in sexual discipline to the loose standards set during the eighteenth century. Married clergy preoccupied with their families, they also asserted, would be drawn away from ecclesiastical institutions. A celibate priesthood promoted loyalty. Why is it, one defender of celibacy asked, "that enemies of celibacy always seem to be hostile to the Pope while its defenders are on his side?"[63]

This emphasis on the priesthood as a separate caste even became evident in dress. In the eighteenth and much of the nineteenth century, a more aristocratic clergy had dressed in ways appropriate for their social class. One German Reform Catholic bishop favored a military uniform decorated with medals. Some Irish priests sent to India wore trousers and cutaway coats in the manner of Protstant ministers because it afforded them "access to society." But by the 1840s, ultramontane bishops had begun to require the Roman collar or robes for all clergy.[64]

Over the course of the nineteenth century, clerical careers became more regimented, structured by orderly training and intensive monitoring. Scandals, endemic to a system where clergy could have remarkable day-to-day autonomy despite a formal chain of command, became less frequent. These better socialized priests displayed a greater esprit de corps, an enhanced sense that the clergy as a group had a distinctive and vital role to play as "soldiers of God." Or as one priest in Le Mans, France, explained to his parishioners in the 1830s: "The Gospel gave the Church [that is, the clergy] the right to command; it imposes on you the duty to obey."[65] The sheer number of clergy indicated renewed vibrancy. In 1800, there was one priest for every 2,676 Catholics in Ireland and in 1901 one priest for every 1,126. The ratio also became considerably more favorable in France and Germany.[66]

V

MISSIONARY EFFORTS after the French Revolution collapsed. Napoleon closed the Propaganda Fide and carted its archives to Paris while orders of priests and nuns dedicated to missionary work teetered on the edge of extinction. In Vietnam, a mournful letter from a French missionary in 1805 tallied the numbers: a few isolated "European priests" and "recently ordained Cochinchinense" ministering to over ten thousand Catholics. "Judge for yourself," he concluded, "what a dearth this poor mission suffers."[67] In Africa, modest Catholic communities in the kingdom of the Kongo, Angola, and Senegal fell into disarray.[68] In once major sites of missionary activity such as China, persecution increased— one French priest was beheaded in Chengdu in 1815—as rulers hostile to Christianity detected a vacuum. Only determined efforts by native Chinese ensured the persistence of Catholic communities.[69]

During the nineteenth century, an expanded missionary program would lessen the isolation of Catholics in all of these places, creating a more integrated, more Roman church. Priests, nuns, and brothers came from the regions of Europe touched by the ultramontane revival. Tiny Luxembourg sent missionaries to Africa, South Asia, China, North America, and South America.[70]

French missionaries were the key, even if French people never migrated in significant numbers. The revolution left permanent scars, and Catholicism in certain regions of France never recovered its previous vitality. But in other regions the Catholic culture deepened, and French Catholics took on responsibility for the global church. By one estimate, French priests, nuns, and brothers numbered two-thirds of the Catholic missionary total in 1900.

French benefactors also did the underwriting. A laywoman, Pauline-Marie Jaricot, founded the most important funding organization for Catholic missions, the Oeuvre de la Propagation de la Foi, in Lyon in 1822. It encouraged regular donations from ordinary Catholics in France—five centimes a week—to support mission work. Within a generation, the organization enrolled tens of thousands of members, and the organization's journal quickly became one of the most important print publications of the era, with a circulation of 178,000 by 1846 and translations into English, Polish, Italian, German, Spanish, Dutch, and Portuguese. A single issue included letters from missionaries in the Seychelles, Scandinavia, China, Japan, Korea, India, Libya, the United States, Canada, and Oceania.[71] Fundraising was global (and effective) too, with contributions from many countries. Successful benefaction campaigns resulted in a budget over ten times that of the Propaganda Fide in Rome, where officials maneuvered (without success) to gain control of the Propagation de la Foi funds.[72]

Another French missionary society, the Holy Childhood Society, founded in 1843, reflected the importance placed by ultramontane Catholics on the sacraments. Its goals were simple: "the administration of baptism to children in danger of death and the purchase and adoption of a great number of others." Children burdened by original sin, Catholics concluded, must be absolved by baptism even if their parents had no desire for the sacrament. Within France, the practice of infant abandonment was rife, but orphanages took up the sacramental and institutional slack. Outside of France, members of the society focused on China, where infant abandonment was even more prevalent. They organized European and North American Catholic children to bear the psychic weight of praying for the souls of "pagan" Chinese infants and enumerated with startling precision the exact number of souls saved. Again, weekly donations were requested, and again, considerable sums were raised. Soon the journal for the association appeared in fourteen languages and funded programs in Indochina, India, and Africa.[73]

German missionary societies also formed on the model of the Propagation de la Foi. The Leopoldine Society (1829) in Vienna and the Ludwigs-Mission Verein (1838) in Munich mobilized German-speaking Catholics to fund missionaries, primarily in the United States. As in France, small weekly contributions came from parishioners, but unlike France, significant direct support also came from Catholic royalty, including the Habsburgs in Vienna and the Wittelsbach royal family in Munich.

Competition spurred the missionary effort, since everywhere Catholic missionaries ventured they encountered Protestants who had gotten there first. (The reverse had been true in the sixteenth and seventeenth centuries.) In southern India, the first missionary priests to visit the area in a generation worried that Methodists would "pollute" the region.[74]

Competition was especially keen in North America. Prominent Protestant ministers, such as Ohio's Lyman Beecher, authored widely distributed tracts warning of Catholic infiltration into the vast region west of the Appalachian Mountains. In turn, the Father General of the Jesuits requested (and received) volunteers to combat "ministers of error" (that is, Protestant clergy.)[75] In a remote village in the Canadian Great Lakes region, a Catholic missionary bumped into a Protestant counterpart, who immediately explained how a backward Catholicism was impeding the "progress of civilization."[76]

In much of Asia, Catholic communities had over the course of the late eighteenth and early nineteenth century become isolated from Rome. Their joy when reconnected to missionaries was palpable. In Japan, villagers in the area around Nagasaki approached the first French Catholic missionaries to appear in the region in over one hundred years. They recited the Hail Mary, the Our Father, and asked about Lent. "The hearts of all of us here," they explained, "do not differ from yours."[77] In Vietnam, a French apostolic vicar traveled through the Mekong Delta in 1828, regularly passing through small Catholic communities that had not seen a priest—native or foreign—in decades. Some communities had not been visited by a bishop for over one hundred years.[78]

The same clergy noted, with varying degrees of empathy, that local practice after the French Revolution and the disruption of missionary programs had veered from orthodoxy. In India, missionaries complained that locals had "reverted" to their "paganism." "Errors" and "depravity" needed correction.[79] In China, missionaries tried to ban a local custom of setting off fireworks at the moment the host was elevated during the Mass.[80]

In locations as diverse as China and the North American frontier, the absence of clergy meant that Indigenous laywomen took on new roles as catechists and parish leaders. In the view of one skeptical missionary to China, women had "usurped the functions of [an] administrator" because they "led the changing of prayers at the church, gave pious readings, [and] admonished delinquents."[81]

VI

ULTRAMONTANISM ALSO TOOK material form. Sales figures are elusive, but the number of religious book titles increased dramatically in the mid-nineteenth century as the Catholic component of the publishing revolution. French titles were probably the most widely distributed, then English language texts. Prayer books and catechisms were also distributed through an extensive German-language Catholic publishing network.[82]

Stained glass, crosses, statues, rosaries, and paintings came from Munich and Paris, mass-produced by the many firms that sprang up to meet global demand. A Swiss firm with a New York City branch office, Benziger Brothers, became the largest distributor, with items ranging from inexpensive figurines and prints affordable to working-class Catholics to life-size statues of saints. Benziger also distributed readers for Irish Catholic schools in the United States, Australia, New Zealand, and other sites of Irish Catholic migration. Convent diaries in isolated towns in French Catholic Louisiana repeatedly mention the arrival of new religious goods, including Sacred Heart pendants, statues of the infant Jesus, holy medals, and scapulars.[83]

The material consequences of the ultramontane revival were also artistic and architectural. Small groups of Catholic painters rebelled against the longtime focus within the art establishment on classical subjects and shared in the yearning for the medieval period. Drawn to the philosophical and theological texts of the Catholic revival, their paintings emphasized the continuity of the sacraments through the mediating institution of the church. One group of German painters who moved to Rome—the Nazarenes—lived in a converted monastery, wore old German cloaks, and grew their hair long, severely parted in the middle, in an homage to Raphael, the artist they most admired. One of the leading figures read essays out loud from neo-Thomist periodicals to his family after dinner. Their critics, in turn, mocked these artists for their loyalty to the "crass dogmatism of dark and depleted centuries."[84]

The impact of ultramontanism on church architecture was even more profound. "One cannot enter a Gothic Cathedral," Chateaubriand wrote, "without feeling a kind of shiver of awe and a vague sentiment of the Divinity."[85] Thirty years later, Augustus Pugin, the most influential English architect of the nineteenth century and a Catholic convert, began designing what would become dozens of new Gothic churches. The opening sentence of a Pugin manifesto conveys his philosophy: "On comparing the Architectural Works of the last three centuries with those of the Middle Ages, the wonderful superiority of the latter must strike every attentive observer."[86] Pugin thought it crucial to saturate church buildings with statuary, stained glass, and "sacred representations." Fear that such objects would lead to a "superstitious reverence" was misplaced; instead, the right combination of structure and decoration could "improve and elevate the religious feelings of a nation."[87]

This neo-Gothic sensibility was new. Many Catholic churches built in the eighteenth and early nineteenth centuries—such as La Madeleine in Paris—displayed a classical facade, and Benedict XIV had acted as a patron for classical buildings in Rome.[88] When Bishop John Carroll of Baltimore commissioned the first Catholic cathedral built in the new United States in 1805, he hired Benjamin Latrobe, the architect of the United States Capitol Building. Asked to choose between Gothic and classical designs, Carroll chose classical, complete with Greek columns fronting the church.[89]

Pugin's influence meant that Greek columns became incongruous. By 1850, Gothic dominated. Cementing this view was a long controversy in Cologne, whose unfinished Gothic cathedral, including an antique medieval crane, towered over the city, and whose completion became an international Catholic cause. When Friedrich Schlegel sauntered across the Rhine valley just after 1800, he paid special attention to the "unparalleled" Gothic buildings in Cologne. "Were it [the cathedral] completed," Schlegel wistfully concluded, "Gothic art might boast having produced a giant work, worthy of rivaling the proudest edifices of ancient or modern Rome."[90]

Pugin visited Cologne and championed the cathedral's reconstruction. There he met with an admirer, August Reichensperger, the leader of the movement to finish the Cologne cathedral who worked also as a Catholic journalist and eventually a member of the German parliament. When Prussia's Protestant King Friedrich Wilhelm IV offered to conciliate his Catholic subjects with funds to complete the cathedral in 1840, Reichensperger seized the opportunity. He had long regretted that the "Middle Ages have only given us these fragments." The cathedral "breathed through and through the spirit of Catholicism" and formed a "most vital opposite to Protestantism."[91]

Not everyone found the neo-Gothic style appealing. When the Sisters of Mercy arrived in London in 1839, they occupied an unfinished Pugin convent. "I do not admire Mr. Pugin's taste," complained Catherine McAuley, "though so celebrated—it is quite the old heavy monastic style."[92] Still, through travel and correspondence, Pugin quickly built an international network of architects and artisans. (His architect son, Edward, sustained this network after his father's death in 1852.) These Irish, Canadian, French, and Australian protégés all brought enthusiasm for the neo-Gothic to their own countries. One Canadian bishop, dedicating St. Patrick's Church in Montreal, delighted in the fact that this new building "would compare with the old churches, now in ruins," that had marked medieval Ireland.[93] A German architect designed a massive neo-Gothic church for the remote South Indian village of Vadakkankulam.[94]

The baroque style was less common but even more ultramontane. Often associated with the Jesuits because of the archetypically baroque Gesù church in Rome, the frescoes, side altars, and statuary in baroque churches seemed to skeptical observers calculated to overwhelm visitors. The Swiss historian Jacob Burkhardt coined the phrase "Jesuit style" as an epithet. He complained, "The Jesuits were as insincere in

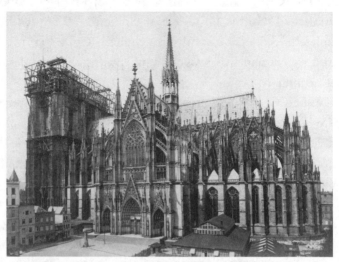

Cologne cathedral, under construction c. 1890. *(Archive Photos/ Getty Images)*

their architecture as they were in every other aspect of the spiritual life of the people; they wished only to dazzle them." He contrasted the "inner poverty" of baroque architecture with its "raw effects." In both Montreal and Philadelphia, Jesuits and their architects made "exact comparisons" between their new churches, also named Gesù, and the Roman namesake.[95]

The fascination with the medieval period reshaped the liturgy itself. In the early nineteenth century, liturgical rites varied widely across the Catholic world. A Roman rite existed, but in France, for example, a variety of older rites predominated, with priests in Paris using different prayers than priests in Lyon or Marseilles. As late as 1840, only eighteen out of over eighty French dioceses used the Roman missal.

As nationalists, Reform Catholics favored civic uniformity through a common language and common school texts, but as Reform Catholics they defended liturgical diversity. In some of the German-speaking principalities, Reform Catholic clergy experimented with saying the Mass in German. One of their ultramontane opponents wrote Gregory XVI to complain that in Baden "every lowly clergyman dares to tinker with the worship service, with the handling of the sacraments, to celebrate the Holy Mass in [the] German language, to present his very own catechism."[96]

By contrast, ultramontanists welcomed checks on nation-states, but favored centralization and uniformity within the church. France's Prosper Louis Pascal Guéranger, deeply influenced by Chateaubriand and de Maistre, argued that the Roman liturgy represented the apex of worship. Guéranger unsurprisingly proved an enthusiast for the neo-Gothic revival led by Pugin, as well as another medieval artistic form, Gregorian chant. He purchased one of France's many abandoned monasteries, studied medieval musical notation systems, and recruited aspiring monks. One protégé proclaimed the abbey's mission: "The music of the past better understood will be greeted as the true music of the future."[97]

Since Guéranger's goal was a uniform liturgy, he thought using vernacular languages instead of Latin was nothing more than an "anti-liturgical heres[y]." Should Mass be said in French, German, Italian, or Portuguese, he predicted, "the people will find that it is not worth their while to leave their work or entertainments to go to Church to hear the same language that is used on the streets."[98]

Guéranger launched a fierce campaign against bishops insufficiently enthusiastic about the Roman liturgy. "It is a matter only," asserted one protégé, "to pray as they do at Rome, in the same words, on the same days, with the same ceremonials, from one extremity of the world to the other."[99] In the United States, ultramontane bishops substituted the "Roman ritual" for traditional English practices. In Canada, another ultramontane bishop reported to Rome that "the faithful are wonderfully uplifted by the splendor of divine worship since it is conducted as much as possible according to Roman forms."[100]

VII

PRACTICAL ISSUES OF episcopal and parish appointments garnered much attention. Odd as it sounds to contemporary Catholics, the tradition of the pope appointing bishops around the world is a recent one. Ministers and monarchs appointed most of the world's bishops into the twentieth century, usually with the curia and pope holding only veto power. In 1829, the Holy See had appointed just 24 of the world's 646 bishops; 67 were elected by local clergy and 555 nominated by monarchs and presidents.[101]

Those parts of the world designated as "mission" territories, such as the United States, the Middle East, Africa, China, and South Asia, fell directly under the aegis of the Propaganda Fide, theoretically allowing Rome more control. Even in these regions, though, traditions of consultation endured. John Carroll's selection as the first bishop in the United States needed an assist from Benjamin Franklin, who lobbied for Carroll's appointment in correspondence with curial bureaucrats. Despite protestations of neutrality, Franklin enjoyed acting the part of an Old World prince.[102]

In much of the world, officials at the Propaganda Fide knew they had to maneuver episcopal appointments through the gauntlet established by Catholic imperial powers. The situation was especially tricky in India, China, and Latin America. In India, from the sixteenth century onward, the Portuguese government nominally controlled the right to make episcopal appointments. By the 1830s, the presence of priests from Ireland (ministering primarily to Irish Catholic soldiers in the British army) and missionaries from France, Germany, and Italy made this situation untenable. Following much bureaucratic jousting, Gregory XVI reorganized the missions in India and installed apostolic vicars (not bishops who possessed more autonomy) reporting directly to the Propaganda Fide. The men dispatched as missionary priests from Rome to Calcutta were assessed on their "attach[ment] to the Holy See." They wrote home of encounters with "ignorant Christians" and "schismatic priests" who thought the "Pope has no jurisdiction over them."[103]

In China, beginning in the 1840s, the Catholic missionary effort became integrated with the French Empire through a sequence of Sino-French treaties that permitted Catholic evangelization but only under French auspices. French bishops, not Roman officials, controlled and monitored missionary efforts. Missionaries from other countries working in China needed French passports to identify them as *notre compatriote*, or "our countrymen," if they wanted to venture beyond international ports into the Chinese interior.[104]

The issue of episcopal appointments was even more fraught in Latin America. Leaders of newly independent nations, such as Colombia, Mexico, Ecuador, and Peru, assumed that appointment rights once exercised by the Spanish Crown transferred to new national governments. Roman officials disagreed. They thought the move from monarchy to republic meant an opportunity for Rome to control appointments, especially given the intermittent anticlericalism evident among elected Latin American leaders. They refused to recognize the new Haitian republic in part because that republic's leaders demanded the right of appointment. Curial representatives predicted that if such episcopal appointment rights were granted to Haiti's rulers, other Latin American leaders "will not delay in demanding the same."[105]

The result was a standoff. As bishops appointed by Spanish monarchs died off, they were not replaced. In 1825, only one officially appointed bishop worked in the countries of Ecuador, Peru, Bolivia, Chile, and Argentina. By 1829, none worked in Mexico or Central America. Only bishops could ordain clergy and so the number of clergy fell precipitously. Over four thousand priests worked in Mexico in 1810; just over two thousand in 1834. In Argentina, the absence of bishops meant only thirty-five priests served the region around Buenos Aires in the early 1850s.[106] Eventually, Gregory XVI rebuilt this ecclesiastical infrastructure. More pragmatic than his predecessors, he hammered out concordats or treaties with almost every nation in Latin America and granted even many republican governments the right to nominate bishops.

Another type of conflict occurred at the parish level. In parts of Europe with strong Reform Catholic traditions, such as France, Poland, and the Rhine valley, lay leaders approved the appointment of pastors, and indeed such consultation had been a recommendation of Febronius, the eighteenth-century Reform Catholic writer and bishop.[107]

These traditions crossed the Indian and Atlantic Oceans. In Bombay, English, Irish, and Indian Catholic parishioners insisted on elections for parish clergy instead of viewing their parishes as "private property of the bishop." High-caste lay Indian Catholics especially resented assertions of episcopal authority.[108] In both Canada and the United States, a tug-of-war occurred between laypeople and priests sympathetic to Reform Catholicism and ultramontanists who disliked such divided authority. Typically viewed as ethnic battles between French and Irish (in Canada) or French, German, and Irish (in the United States), these episodes were often that, but they were also examples of Reform Catholics attempting to restrain an ascendant ultramontanism.

In Montreal, Louis-Joseph Papineau, the leading "patriote" of the era and a founding figure of Canadian nationalism, demanded representation of "notables" in parish councils so as to avoid a "taxation without representation" that occurred when clergy spent funds collected from parishioners without accountability. "In spite of your splendid robes," he told his bishop, "you are incapable of seeing or feeling, yet you claim a divine right to control everything. Can anything be more anti-national or anti-patriotic?"[109]

Parallel governance disputes existed in the United States. In Louisiana, lay committees of French-speaking Creoles paid parish bills and collected parish funds. The first bishop of New Orleans disliked this practice and worried that such parishioners sympathized with the French

Revolution. It seemed to him that "rebellion is in their hearts and their minds are imbued with the maxims of democracy."[110]

A few decades later, the trustees of St. Louis Cathedral in New Orleans ingeniously argued that the sovereignty of the Spanish and French monarchs had now passed to "the people" as the sovereign power in the democratic United States. And so the people—lay Catholic trustees—should approve any nomination for bishop or pastor. Ultramontane clergy and their supporters fought back via state legislatures, secular courts, and the pope. They arranged for Gregory XVI to issue a papal brief denouncing this "wound . . . inflicted on Episcopal authority." They also persuaded the Louisiana Supreme Court to thwart the lay trustees.[111]

VIII

WHEN THE ENGLISH WRITER Frances Trollope toured Belgium in the early 1830s, she termed its people "deeply and severely Catholic." To her amusement, she reported much talk of relics and miracles, and she included a disapproving description of churches jammed with decorations and statues of the Virgin "tricked out in tawdry finery."[112] What fascinated Trollope was not, as she imagined, a retrograde Catholicism yet to be liberated from the Middle Ages. The Belgium she documented was then in the throes of the ultramontane revival, and a brief sketch of the revival in one country allows more purchase on the whole.

The first mission preachers appeared in Belgium in the early nineteenth century. Their presence, signaling the rebuilding of the church after the long occupation by often anticlerical French troops during the revolution, brought native Catholics to tears. The number of male religious in the country tripled in just twenty-five years after 1829.[113]

The number of women religious increased at an even faster rate. By 1846, ten thousand women religious worked in Belgium. Before 1789, most of these women had lived lives of contemplation; fifty years later, fewer than 10 percent did, as they came to prefer lives focused on public service. Most women religious staffed hospitals and schools, while others ran "homes of preservation" and "refuge" for women trying to escape prostitution or make their way in an unfamiliar city. They began the first homes for the mentally ill. When Trollope encountered Sisters of Charity in a hospital ward, she found their spirit of self-sacrifice admirable. So effusive were her compliments, Trollope joked, that her friends might think she had "turned Catholic."[114]

The same missionary impulse propelled Belgians abroad, with the United States as the most important destination. (Later in the century missionaries from Belgium would journey to places as diverse as the Congo and Mongolia.) The most famous of these men, Jesuit Pierre De Smet, spent most of his career in the American West, and his tales of his encounters with Indigenous peoples became best sellers in Catholic Europe. De Smet and other missionaries organized mission campaigns, complete with monumental crosses erected in town squares, devotion to the Sacred Heart, and churches "well adorned with pictures and statues." He promoted the claim of a Flathead boy to have seen an apparition of Mary. De Smet's goal was a "Christian civilization" better than the "modern civilization" bequeathed to the world by the French Revolution.[115]

Brussels also came to Rome. After 1842, Belgian expatriates in Rome worshipped in a national church, Saint-Julien-des Belges. The Belgian bishops founded a college for seminary students to provide Roman seasoning. Belgian tourists also visited the city in growing numbers, expressing fascination with the catacombs (as a symbol of persecution) and the Colosseum (which invoked Christian martyrdom).[116] Belgian Catholics, like their ultramontane contemporaries around the world, favored Sacred Heart devotions, Roman liturgies, and neo-Gothic cathedrals. "Our heart needs to compose itself sometimes in the memory of all the great things of the Middle Ages," explained one devotée, "when people did not make railways but immense Gothic churches."[117]

This ultramontane revival—and the devotions, schools, associations, cathedrals, philosophical texts, and paintings it spawned—had analogues in other religious traditions. During this same period, Protestant evangelists crisscrossed not only Europe and North America, but also once-remote locales such as Australia and South Africa. Muslim scholars journeyed from Istanbul to Cairo to Calcutta to lay the groundwork for a more unified "Muslim world."[118]

Even so, the Catholic global community was distinctive. Its tentacles reached into the tiniest rural, Flemish-speaking parish, aristocratic homes in Brussels, and ecclesiastical offices in Rome. Its institutions constituted a milieu far more dense than anything that existed in the eighteenth century. As one Belgian Catholic explained:

> Catholicism is not only a doctrine, but an action. Catholicism is the people praying in our churches; it is the Sister of Charity sustaining the patient's head in our hospitals; it is the Christian brother using his life to instruct small children; it is the missionary evangelizing ignorant populations; it is the priest, from the parish vicar so loved by the poor and downtrodden to the pontiff sending his benediction *urbi et orbi*.[119]

THREE

Democracy

How Catholicism Fostered
and Inhibited Democratic Revolutions

I

NEAR DEATH, unable to work in either "mind or body," Fr. Servando Teresa de Mier invited friends and colleagues in Mexico City to a reception to observe him receiving last rites on the morning of November 15, 1827. Guests included the president of the Republic of Mexico, who had arranged for Mier to live in an apartment in the presidential palace as a token of gratitude for his service to the new nation.

The ceremony began with a procession including a military band. Mier's guests then gathered around his bedside as he received the last rites from Fr. Ramos Arizpe, a fellow priest serving as the Minister of Justice and Ecclesiastical Affairs. Mier had worked with Arizpe since 1810, when the two men attended the first democratically elected legislative assembly in modern Spanish history, the Cortes of Cádiz, and the two friends had each played a significant role in the fight for Mexican independence from Spain.[1]

This odd ritual—and Mier's death three weeks later—capped an eventful life. Born in 1765, Mier was educated in Mexico and ordained a Dominican priest. He achieved prominence by making the odd claim that Our Lady of Guadalupe had appeared to St. Thomas soon after the death of Christ and not to Juan Diego outside of Mexico City in

1531. Suspicious of Mier, the archbishop of Mexico City exiled him to Spain.[2]

Eventually, Mier made his way to France, where he became friendly with Fr. Henri Grégoire and other clergy of the Constitutional Church. He thought Grégoire nothing less than "the pillar of religion in France." Like Grégoire, Mier believed that the French Civil Constitution of the Clergy in 1790 did not contain "anything heretical." He admired the "wise" Bishop Ricci and the Synod of Pistoia and was dismayed by the pope's condemnation of its decrees.[3] After journeys to Portugal and Rome, Mier moved to London in 1811, where he helped edit the leading Spanish-language journal, *El Español*, and sustained contact with colonial revolutionaries.

For Mier, as for many Reform Catholics, little separated the political from the ecclesiastical. Like Grégoire, he believed in the affinity of Catholicism and republicanism, since "God gave his favorite people [the Israelites] a republican government." Mier and Grégoire both admired Thomas Paine and both wrote treatises on Bartolomé de las Casas, positioning the sixteenth-century Spanish defender of Indigenous peoples as a critic of nineteenth-century Spanish imperialism. Grégoire arranged for the reprinting and distribution of the 1797 homily of the future Pope Pius VII on the compatibility of democracy and Catholicism, and Mier's friends published editions in Spanish and English.[4]

After participation in a failed rebellion in Mexico followed by another imprisonment, Mier retreated in 1821 to Philadelphia, which had become a center for Reform Catholicism. He immediately fell into a community of Spanish-speaking Catholic exiles, some of whom also had participated in the Cortes of Cádiz. This group found common cause with Irish Catholic émigrés, many of whom had fled to the United States after the failed 1798 revolution in Ireland and joined the Democratic-Republican party led by Thomas Jefferson. For all of these men, the United States with its republican government and strong religious institutions seemed a better model than France, where, in Mier's words, the abandonment of religion during the revolution had led to the "demoralization of the people."[5]

Enthusiasm for republican or democratic government extended to the parish level. Together, Irish and Latin American Catholics led a fight for parishioner control of the finances and pastoral appointments at St. Mary's Church. Despite having just arrived in Philadelphia, Mier jumped in. Along with his allies, he defended the rights of lay parish trustees and a charismatic if erratic Irish pastor, William Hogan, against an Irish-born bishop, Henry Conwell, in what became the country's most significant trustee conflict.[6]

The rhetoric was heated. In the same breath Mier denounced Spanish bishops who "established crusades against [Mexican Catholic] patriots" and the recalcitrance of Bishop Conwell in Philadelphia. The key was "to distinguish the *church* from the *bishops*, and *religion* from its *abuses*."[7]

Mier's opponents termed him an "infidel Mexican priest . . . lately escaped from the prison of the Inquisition." Mier retorted that "citizens of the United States and every civilized country" should consider it "honourable" to be imprisoned by the Inquisition. The embattled Bishop Conwell, in a reference to the French Revolution, feared the "success of these Jacobins."[8]

In 1830, Roman officials charged another Irish-born bishop, Francis Kenrick, educated in Rome, with restoring order. Laypeople in Kenrick's view should be "obedient subjects of the ruler," and by ruler he meant pastor or bishop. Priests should exhibit "docility." He confronted trustees—dressed in full episcopal regalia—and to the delight of another Philadelphia pastor and soon-to-be bishop in New York City, John Hughes, "made them eat their words." When resistance from members of the congregation did not cease, he threatened excommunication and stated that "Catholic principles of church government" admitted no role for laypeople beyond "obedience and subjugation."[9]

Well before Kenrick's arrival in Philadelphia, Mier had returned to Mexico, where he became one of the leading figures in the successful movement to declare independence from Spain. On the legislative floor he recalled his time among the "constitutional clergy of France" and the need for the state to appoint bishops and the people to elect their pastors. When in France, he noted, "we had nothing to do with Rome except for the bishops sending the pope letters of communion as in the primitive church."[10]

Mier never abandoned his conviction that the state should endorse Catholicism as the official religion, even if he readily admitted the importance of practical tolerance. But when Pope Leo XII made a futile plea for the Latin American subjects of King Ferdinand VII to remain loyal to the Spanish Crown, Mier authored a scathing response. Addressing "señor Papa" in an insolent tone, he aligned himself with the "many Catholic authors" who saw in such requests a "new doctrine" of papal authority. The "court of Rome" must shed its "ambitious pretensions."[11]

Mier's travels from Mexico to Spain to France to Rome to Portugal to England to the United States to Cuba and finally back to Mexico reflected the flux of an era when successive revolutions convulsed the Atlantic world. His life exemplified the strength of the Reform Catholic tradition, diminished in northern Europe but still vital in central Europe, the Iberian Peninsula, and Latin America. Its advocates professed sympathy for national ecclesiastical traditions, a more restrained piety, and the authority of church councils as opposed to the papacy. They stressed a lay voice—an educated, property-owning, male lay voice—and the rights of not only monarchies but republican and constitutional governments to appoint bishops and even pastors.

Just before his death, Mier complained to a friend that France was now "covered" with Jesuits and that a resurgent ultramontanism had "swallowed everything." Newly appointed French bishops seemed to him "fanatics." He quoted with approval a letter from Henri Grégoire, urging Latin Americans to remain Catholic but "reject in force the pretensions of the Roman Court, so ominous to the freedom of nations."[12]

II

HOW CATHOLICS WOULD RESPOND to what historians sometimes term the Age of Democratic Revolutions was not obvious.[13] Between the American Revolution in the 1770s and various European revolutions in 1848, at least twenty democracies sprouted (and withered) on both sides of the Atlantic, with the Mexican Republic supported by Fr. Mier as one of the most notable of these experiments.

Because so many ultramontanists, beginning with Joseph de Maistre and continuing through authoritarian Catholic leaders in the 1930s, voiced skepticism about constitutions and republican government, historians have neglected a wider Catholic political repertoire. Just as an

"uncompromising Protestantism" could support democratic nationalism in early-nineteenth-century Britain, the Netherlands, Prussia, and
the United States, so, too, did Reform Catholics support constitutions
and representative governments from Spain and southern Italy to Mexico and much of Latin America.[14]

An early indication that Catholics in southern Europe and Latin
America were developing their own version of constitutional government became visible in Mexico. The first revolts against Spanish colonial rule began in 1810, with native-born priests leading an uprising
not only in the realm of ideas but on the battlefield. After Mass in the
village of Dolores, with the townspeople called into the main square
by the ringing of church bells, Fr. Miguel Hidalgo organized an army
eventually numbering thousands of men and dedicated to overthrowing
the Spanish colonial government.

Placing an image of Our Lady of Guadalupe on the banners held
by his troops, Hidalgo merged religion with a nascent Mexican
national identity. He and his allies professed their loyalty to the Spanish king, Ferdinand VII, and their opposition to the putatively godless French who controlled much of Spain until 1814. But Hidalgo
was also interested in Reform Catholicism. Educated by priests connected to Reform Catholic circles in Europe, Hidalgo came from an
elite family and questioned papal authority, the virginity of Mary,
and clerical celibacy. (He fathered several children with a succession
of common-law wives.) Venezuela's Simón Bolivar, another Latin
American leader eager to end Spanish colonial rule in the region,
thought Catholicism an "exclusive and intolerant religion." But he
envied how Hidalgo and "the leaders of the [Mexican] independence
movement have happily profited from fanaticism with the greatest
skill, proclaiming the famous Virgin of Guadalupe as queen of the
patriots."[15]

Most bishops in Mexico, almost all from Spain, opposed Hidalgo's
insurgent army, some by excommunicating rebels and predicting they
would go "infallibly to hell."[16] The influential Michoacán bishop, Manuel
Abad y Queipo, despaired of Hidalgo, a friend, leading the rebellion and
after his capture ordered his execution.

Still, only a year later, during the chaos created by Napoleon's armies, an election was held in Cádiz, Spain, for a Cortes, or assembly. The Cortes retained the monarchy—although King Ferdinand VII did not attend its sessions—but proclaimed national sovereignty, civic equality, and universal male suffrage. The constitution drafted at Cádiz became influential not only in Latin America but also in Greece and India.[17] Delegates claimed to transform Spain from a "Catholic monarchy," to a "nation of Catholics."[18]

Deliberations in Cádiz resembled those in Paris in 1789. Priests constituted one-third of the delegates, their presence at a democratic assembly a symbolic rejection of the alliance of throne and altar so central to Spanish history. Some religious orders were abolished, again as in France. In Seville and other Spanish cities, much as in France after the Civil Constitution of the Clergy, Spanish citizens swore oaths of loyalty to the constitution after Mass and the constitution itself was read during the service.[19] The Reform Catholic commitments of the assembly meant that delegates might discuss the relationship between the executive and the legislature on one day and ponder how to eliminate pilgrimages and prune overly exuberant devotions on the next.

Despite the enthusiasm that it generated, the Spanish constitutional regime of 1812 was short-lived. Napoleon's defeat and the evacuation of the French armies became King Ferdinand VII's opportunity, and he managed to restore the Spanish monarchy in 1814. Ferdinand VII reestablished the Inquisition and permitted the newly restored Jesuits back in the country. Mission campaigns began, and support for religious tolerance ebbed. One prominent Spanish ultramontane asked:

> Are we in Spain, or in Holland and North America? . . .
> Which tolerance are we talking about? That of another
> religion, or that of people who are unfortunate enough to
> profess it? If we are speaking of tolerance of another reli-
> gion, Catholicism is as intolerant as light is of darkness,
> and truth is of lies.[20]

Another ultramontane writer took the time to condemn not just the standard villains of Luther and Calvin, but the Habsburg emperor Joseph

II, Bishop Ricci, and other Reform Catholics for provoking the French Revolution and inspiring delegates at the Cortes of Cádiz.[21]

Still, Reform Catholic ideas continued to spread across the Spanish and Portuguese empires. The first European to call for the independence of Latin American nations, a Belgian bishop, warned his readers that Latin American Catholics with "republican" sympathies would not listen to either Spanish Catholics opposed to liberty or "Rome and her thunders."[22] Bishop Queipo, in Mexico, had opposed Miguel Hidalgo's populist revolt, but he also thought the 1812 Spanish Constitution "the most liberal, the most just and the most prudent" such document devised.[23] A Reform Catholic bishop became the first president of Ecuador under its new constitution.[24]

An unsuccessful republican revolt in Pernambuco, in northeast Brazil, in 1817 was often termed the "revolution of the priests" because of the participation of clergy trained at a seminary founded by a Reform Catholic bishop. The revolution's leading figure melded science and faith by working as a botanist and a theology professor.[25] Another leader of the Pernambuco revolt, Fr. Antônio Gonçalves da Cruz, met with the former United States president, John Adams. Adams had long scoffed at the idea of Catholics in South America supporting "free government." More likely, he thought, to establish "Democracies among the Beasts, Birds or Fishes." After meeting the congenial Gonçalves da Cruz, Adams wavered. Perhaps, he speculated, "the Age of Reason is not ended."[26] A Boston newspaper hailed Cruz as one of the "very patriotic" Catholic clergy, eager to "resist tyranny and establish liberty [just as] our clergy did in 1775."[27]

That the Spanish Constitution of 1812 declared Catholicism the state religion might seem puzzling. (It puzzled Thomas Jefferson, who admired the constitution but expressed disappointment at the "intolerance of all but the Catholic religion.")[28] After all, the same Cádiz assembly abolished the Inquisition in order to protect national sovereignty from Roman influence—this pleased Jefferson—and expelled the papal nuncio. And yet the constitution reads: "The religion of the Spanish nation is, and ever shall be, the Catholic Apostolic Religion and only true faith. The Nation shall, by wise and just laws, protect it and prevent the exercise of any other."

In Haiti (1804), Venezuela (1811), Spain (1812), Naples (1820), Spain again (1820), Portugal (1822), and Mexico (1824), constitutions drafted in a Reform Catholic key defined Catholicism as integral to national identity. In Naples, legislators added the term "public" to the subsection on Catholicism as the national religion, implying that private practice of other creeds would not constitute a crime. Even this modification proved controversial and was dropped before the final vote. The Chilean Constitution of 1822 tolerated individual dissent from Catholicism only as long as it did not lead to "calumnies, affronts or crime." Simón Bolivar judged religion an entirely private—indeed absurd—matter, but even Bolivar drafted a constitution for Colombia in 1828 declaring that "the government supports and protects the Roman Catholic Apostolic religion as the religion of Colombians."[29]

This melding of religion and the state occurred because Reform Catholic clergy and politicians assumed that religion needed to support the state, not be separated from it. In the eighteenth century, Reform Catholics had pledged their loyalty to royal authority as one means of unifying the state and checking the power of the papacy. In the nineteenth century, republican governments were substituted for monarchies in some countries, but the principle of integrating church with state remained. Bishops and clergy still sat in parliaments, swore in presidents, and dictated legislation on moral matters.

The desire to weave together Catholicism and the state rested in part on an absence of religious diversity. In southern Europe and Latin America, Catholics were the overwhelming majority of the population, often with over 90 percent of residents baptized. Contact with clergy might be episodic in rural regions but a Catholic culture was widespread. (The religions of enslaved people in Latin America were more diverse, but many enslaved people also identified as Catholic.) Even leaders of the Italian republics of the 1790s viewed endorsement of Catholicism as part of a "religious social contract."[30] A Benedictine monk elected to the Neapolitan parliament explained his preference for a state religion this way:

> Having just the one religion, we do not need to proclaim
> freedom of worship, as other countries, where there are

followers of different religions, have been obliged to do. Happy as we are to have this powerful bond, we will not live in fear of those bloody scenes between Catholics and Protestants witnessed even in recent years in France.[31]

Small groups of Jews and Protestants lived in even the most Catholic countries, and Reform Catholics proved more accepting than their ultramontane Catholic contemporaries of this pluralism. One Protestant observer complimented a Portuguese bishop in Rio de Janeiro—where the constitution declared Catholicism the state religion—for being "perfectly and sincerely tolerant of every sect, while he is warmly attached to his own."[32] Even so, Reform Catholic leaders only accepted the rights of groups to worship, not the rights of individuals to proselytize. The same Uruguayan constitution that made Catholicism the official state religion carved out rights of worship for specific groups, such as Anglicans, Swiss German evangelicals, and Waldensians, but not freedom of religion for individuals.[33]

Another liberal revolution occurred in Spain in 1820. Reform Catholics who had gone underground after 1814 resurfaced and began speaking again of constitutions and democracy. Fifty-four priests were elected to the reestablished Cortes, and priests explained the new constitution "to all their parishioners on Sundays and on festival days." It still seemed possible that democracy could be supported by "the pure faith, without obstacles, without superstition or fanaticism."[34]

This second Spanish revolution of 1820 gave Mexican patriots the opportunity to declare their own country's independence. After much turmoil, the republic established in 1824 exemplified Fr. Mier's vision in that the constitution declared Catholicism the "religion of the Mexican nation." All parishioners attending Mass in Mexico City on one October Sunday swore an oath to the constitution and listened as priests explained the document.[35]

In Spain, democracy was again short-lived. The wily Ferdinand VII reclaimed his throne in the early 1820s, abolished the Cortes, and began imprisoning or exiling his opponents. His officers executed fifty priests supportive of the revolutionary government and now deemed traitors to the nation. Ferdinand's allies accused Havana's Reform

Catholic bishop of supporting Bishop Ricci and the Synod of Pistoia.[36] In neighboring Portugal, ultramontane Catholics argued that the appalling ideals of the French Revolution must not be allowed to corrupt "the best institutions" with "perversity, disorder and general annihilation."[37]

By contrast, Latin America had become a global leader in republican government by 1830, with male suffrage more widespread than in any other region.[38] One of Fr. Mier's protégés, José Luis Mora, perhaps the most important Mexican intellectual of the era, admired the constitutional reforms passed by the Cortes of Cádiz. He criticized the needless expenses of pilgrimages and popular devotions and republished in Mexico Reform Catholic texts first published in Spain.[39] But Mora expressed grave doubts about the capacity of the church to adapt to the new world of constitutions and democracy. "Instead of inspiring youth with a spirit of inquiry and doubt," he feared, "[Catholic clergy] will . . . instill habits of dogmatism and disputation."[40]

III

WHILE REFORM CATHOLICS in Spain and Latin America launched democratic revolutions, the political implications of the ultramontane revival in northern Europe remained uncertain. Joseph de Maistre— skeptical of representation in both church and state—had no doubts. "To hear the defenders of democracy talk," de Maistre mockingly explained, "one would think that the people deliberate like a committee of wise men, whereas in truth judicial murders, foolhardy undertakings, wild choices, and above all foolish and disastrous wars are eminently the prerogatives of this form of government."[41]

The Holy Alliance created at the Congress of Vienna in 1815 strengthened monarchical governments with strong ties to the papacy. Some Reform Catholic suspicions persisted, especially in the Habsburg Empire, where the emperor refused to permit bishops to travel to Rome for their ordination, since they might "return to their dioceses as Roman converts . . . doing more harm than good to church and state." [42]

Other Catholics had begun a reassessment. The French Revolution and the Napoleonic Wars had demonstrated the dangers of revolution and the need to mobilize religious influence on behalf of newly vulnerable monarchies. The Austrian chancellor, Metternich, once sympathetic to Reform Catholicism, now saw an alliance with the papacy as crucial to stabilizing the Habsburg Empire and worked to diminish Reform Catholic tendencies at the royal court. Papal officials expressed delight that leaders such as Metternich "have realized that the best defense of their thrones . . . lies in the true religion, which makes subjects faithful to their sovereign."[43]

In Canada, Archbishop Plessis, of Quebec, instructed his clergy never to criticize the king or the parliament and warned against "the spirit of democracy [that] is wreaking havoc among us." As he privately explained to the British governor general in a tone echoing Catholic defenders of monarchy in Europe, "our altars protect the Throne as the Throne protects them."[44] In 1819, Plessis and a group of clergy journeyed to a "degraded and degenerate" France and met with one of their heroes, Joseph de Maistre.[45]

Catholics in the United States also responded to ultramontane signals. In the 1780s, Bishop John Carroll had expressed sympathy for Reform Catholicism, but he recoiled from the 1790 Civil Constitution of the Clergy as an effort to reduce religion by "a slavish obsequiousness to the civil power."[46] When contacted by Henri Grégoire in 1809, Carroll declined his request for cooperation out of distaste for "some of the principles avowed in the pamphlets and proceedings of what is called the Constitutional clergy." He thought that "late and present events" merited caution and judged it more important to sustain the "independent jurisdiction of the Holy See and episcopacy."[47]

The brightest prospect for a unity of democracy and ultramontanism came from Ireland in the person of Daniel O'Connell, the most important Irish politician of the nineteenth century. O'Connell had fled his Catholic boarding school in Belgium during the French Revolution. He was horrified to meet Irishmen who, after witnessing Louis XVI's execution, thought the deed justified "for the cause." At the time, he later recalled, he "thoroughly detested the revolutionists and the democratic principle."[48]

But O'Connell's views changed. Over the next three decades,

O'Connell became an inspiration to Catholic democrats around the world. In 1823, he formed a new Catholic association that focused on a variety of issues, including British prohibitions on Catholic chaplains visiting prisoners, the paucity of Catholic burial grounds, and bias against Catholics in the armed forces and the judiciary. A "Catholic rent" of one penny per month paid to O'Connell's movement mobilized the country's peasantry.

The Catholic emancipation campaign led by O'Connell—demanding the right of Catholics to sit in the British Parliament without swearing allegiance to the king or admitting, as then required, that veneration of Mary and the saints was "idolatrous"—

Daniel O'Connell. *(Courtesy of Rare Books and Special Collections, Hesburgh Library, University of Notre Dame)*

culminated with a victory in 1829. Parliament finally permitted Catholics to hold office not only in England, but also in Ireland, South Africa, and other parts of the British Empire. (Catholics in what is now Quebec and Ontario had long possessed this ability.)

Restrictions remained. Catholic students could enroll at Cambridge but were not allowed to take a degree; they could not even enroll at Oxford. Jesuits were banned from coming "into this realm" (although this provision was not enforced), and priests were not to wear habits "save within the usual Places of Worship of the Roman Catholic religion."[49] Still, the principle of Catholic participation in public life had been won. Reflecting on an electoral triumph in County Clare, O'Connell described election day as "in reality, a religious ceremony." Priests marched with parishioners carrying banners with such messages as "Vote for our Religion." Or as he concluded, "honest men met to support upon the altar of their countryman the religion in which they believed."[50]

IV

OBSERVING DANIEL O'CONNELL in the late 1820s were an extraordinary trio of French Catholics. All would play significant roles in modern Catholic history, and their sympathy for democratic reform would demonstrate the uncertain political trajectory of Catholicism in the age of democratic revolutions.

The three friends or "liberal ultramontanists" were Charles Montalembert, a lay nobleman; Henri Lacordaire, a priest who would reestablish the Dominican order in France; and Félicité de Lamennais, a Breton priest. Lamennais was the leader, and his essays on religious belief in the aftermath of the revolution circulated across Catholic Europe, North America, and South America. Like de Maistre, with whom he cheerfully corresponded early in his career and whose *Du Pape* he praised, Lamennais initially defended monarchical government. The corruption of Reform Catholicism had led to the French Revolution and explained how a "Christian monarchy" had "degenerated into a democracy."[51]

Lamennais—again like de Maistre—did not begin with politics. Instead he rejected a Catholicism in any way subservient to a state or claiming independence from the papacy. This view ran against the grain in 1820s France, where the state still paid clerical salaries. Lamennais wondered how French bishops distinguished governmental endorsement from governmental oppression. After all, he pointed out, the same nominally Catholic French government proved willing to ban the Jesuits in 1828 and funded a "Ministry of Religion which works ardently to corrupt all sources of teaching." The intertwining of church and state led to "pressure for a break with Rome and the establishment of a national church which would represent only folly."[52]

Lamennais knew that younger ultramontane clergy found government restrictions on parish missions patronizing. Who would evangelize a France drifting away from orthodoxy? Not timid bishops appointed by the state. "By binding the cause of religion inseparably to that of the Government which oppresses it," Lamennais regretted, "they are preparing a general apostasy."[53]

Ireland seemed a happier case. Lacordaire admiringly termed

O'Connell the "Pope of Ireland," and lauded the Irish Catholic willingness to "defend and demand" their freedom. "Of all the populations
of Europe," Lamennais explained, "the most indigent is that of Ireland,
and yet nowhere is religion more endowed."[54] O'Connell reciprocated
by expressing disdain—"as a Catholic"—for a French church still sub-
mitting episcopal nominations for approval by government officials.[55]

Lamennais also reconsidered what his ultramontane theology might
mean for politics. Daringly, he became convinced that Catholicism
needed open debate and freedom of religion to thrive and that the people needed the opportunity to vote for their political leaders. He rejected
the instinctive ultramontane desire to support authoritarian monarchs
against populist agitation, because it betrayed a piety and theology that
claimed to respect the aspirations and struggles of common people.

Lamennais's opportunity to voice such views came during the European revolutions of 1830, a series of loosely linked revolts beginning in
France but extending to Belgium, Poland, and northern Italy. As crowds
again took to Parisian streets, Catholics with memories of the Terror in
the 1790s trembled. (The archbishop of Paris hid in a convent.)

Lamennais thought the revolutions providential. The church must ally
itself with the desire of the people for democratic government and basic
liberties such as freedom of the press and freedom of religion. No longer
should Catholics assume that monarchs in Paris, Vienna, and Madrid
would shelter them from revolutionary storms. Better to welcome a
"popular reaction against absolutism" and the collapse of a "worn-out
order."[56] Watching from Ireland, O'Connell exulted in the idea that the
revolution had dismayed "the tyrants and oligarchs of the world."[57]

Montalembert, Lammenais, and Lacordaire chose this moment to
found *L'Avenir* (The Future), a newspaper emblazoned with the motto
"God and Liberty." In its eighteen-month existence, the journal circulated across Europe and North America with issues passed hand to hand.
The editors insisted that the proliferation of constitutional governments
around the world required "Catholics to give the world a model" of
how to blend religious and political commitments.[58]

The young ultramontanes paid special attention to Belgium and the
United States. The influence of Lamennais in Belgium was strong, and
Belgians elected a number of priests who admired Lamennais to the

country's first national assembly. The Belgian Constitution of 1830, drafted primarily by Catholics, granted freedom of religion to all citizens. "As in Belgium" became shorthand for the idea that Catholicism and republicanism could coexist.[59] Lacordaire pondered leaving France to work as a missionary in the United States, since only in such a "free, populous, young" country could the "Catholic revolution" move in sync with the "political revolution."[60]

They also looked east. Polish revolutionaries launched a revolt against the Russian tsar in 1830, a challenge that generated enthusiasm around the Catholic world. The tsar's crushing of the revolt meant a dispersion of Polish intellectuals, especially to Paris, where they quickly attached themselves to the liberal ultramontanes. Montalembert championed a "free and Catholic" Poland in the name of "Catholics of France."[61]

Crucially, these liberal ultramontanists saw no future for Reform Catholicism. At one time an alliance between the two impulses, both in their own way committed to a Catholic foundation for republican government, seemed possible. O'Connell welcomed the revolution that toppled Ferdinand VII in Spain in 1820 as an "auspicious circumstance."[62]

But different theological assumptions prevented a united front. Reform Catholics deplored an intrusive papacy, while liberal ultramontanes saw the papacy as protection against intrusive governments. O'Connell became disenchanted with the anti-papal contours of the revolution in Spain. In a speech that infuriated Spanish exiles in London, O'Connell denigrated "the attempts of the Cortes to ingratiate themselves with the English *Liberals* and their press." He compared them with French revolutionaries during the 1790s and wondered if they desired the "overthrow of the Catholic religion."[63]

Ultramontane scorn for Reform Catholicism also became visible in France. When Henri Grégoire lay dying in 1831, one of the few surviving members of the constitutional clergy and the symbol worldwide of the Reform Catholic tradition, the archbishop of Paris refused him the last sacraments unless he renounced his forty-year-old endorsement of the Civil Constitution of the Clergy. (Independent to the end, Grégoire refused. The first sentence of his will blasted "ecclesiastical [and] political despotism.")[64] Montalembert mocked Grégoire's supporters. "Earn the salary the government has thrown to you," he sneered, "kiss the rings of the government-appointed bishops." In Haiti, by contrast, where Grégoire had long been admired for his opposition to slavery and his Reform Catholicism, his death was marked by a national day of mourning.[65]

The prospects for an ultramontane version of democracy soon dimmed. Knowing that many French bishops despised *L'Avenir* for its attacks on the episcopacy, Montalembert, Lamennais, and Lacordaire traveled across the Alps in 1831 as "pilgrims of God and liberty" in order to persuade the pope of their orthodoxy.[66]

While they awaited an audience, the Polish community in Rome welcomed them, bestowing upon Lamennais a chalice in gratitude for his advocacy of their cause. Ominously, Gregory XVI chose this moment to condemn the Polish revolt against the tsar as an unlawful rebellion against a legitimate ruler. This papal edict shocked Polish Catholic rebels but also did not augur well for Lamennais, on record as calling the tsar a despot.[67]

Perhaps Lamennais should have expected as much. From the first days after his election in 1831, Gregory XVI had struggled to quell a revolt in the northern sections of the Papal States, the portion of the Italian Peninsula governed (ineptly) by the Holy See. He had initially welcomed some of Lamennais's ideas, and the shocked representative of the Habsburg Empire to the papal court reported hearing curial officials deem some revolutions "justified as Catholic causes."[68] Papal government must be saved "from itself," Metternich bluntly responded.[69] He knew that Lamennais had found a ready audience among some Catholics in Turin and other parts of northern Italy.[70]

What Gregory XVI could not countenance was revolutionary nationalism. Out of desperation, Gregory XVI permitted Metternich to send the Austrian army to quash the revolt in northern Italy. Metternich also complained about *L'Avenir* to Rome and used his spy network to swipe Lamennais's letters (where Lamennais bemoaned the intrigue surrounding the papal court) and send them to the pope with his own annotations. Representatives from the governments of Russia and Prussia also lobbied Gregory XVI, unhappy to see any Catholic journal countenance revolution and worried about restive Polish and German Catholic populations within their midst. The Irish priest Paul

Cullen, one of Gregory XVI's colleagues from their days of working together in the offices of the Propaganda Fide, characterized the revolutionaries this way: "irreligion in its broadest sphere, the vilest hatred against the Catholic religion and especially its supreme head the Pope, a desire to overturn all established authorities, and to destroy all order."[71]

Entreaties from the great powers made Gregory XVI less inclined to support Lamennais, but so, too, did the dossier compiled in the Holy Office. It included a defense by the foremost Italian disciple of Lamennais, Gioacchino Ventura, who described him as a writer of the "first rank." Lamennais in this reading had demonstrated to Catholics around the world that the church did not invariably stand for the "despotism of kings" at the expense of "political liberty."[72] Other consultants were less admiring. They deplored the "disastrous" doctrines of Lamennais, allegedly imbibed from Voltaire and Benjamin Franklin. Popular sovereignty might work for a "Protestant people" accustomed to a society where each person is his or her own arbiter of the law, but not for a "Catholic people" faithful to compacts with king and God.[73]

After struggling for months to gain an audience with the pope, only to be baffled on the occasion by desultory chitchat, Lamennais retreated from Rome to Munich. During a banquet in his honor, he was handed a fresh-off-the-press copy of Gregory's XVI's 1832 encyclical, *Mirari Vos.* Here Lamennais encountered ultramontanism shorn of democracy and civil liberties. Gregory XVI held that freedom of conscience was liable to "spread ruin." Freedom of the press seemed "monstrous" because of the propensity to equate truth and error.[74]

Lamennais and the other young ultramontanes initially thought they should submit to the encyclical and continue their work. Surely the pope's words did not possess a "dogmatic character."[75] The pope, Lamennais thought, "is a good monk. He knows nothing of the world. He has no idea what the Church is like."[76] One Belgian disciple agreed that the pope referred to Lamennais in "only a few passages," but he still worried about the "effect it would produce in France, in England, in Ireland, in Germany!"[77]

So Lamennais kept writing. In 1834, in another messianic best seller, he again celebrated "liberty" and mourned those who think "the people are incapable of understanding their own interests."[78] Gregory XVI reciprocated by denouncing Lamennais, this time by name. The bishop of Rennes forced Lamennais's brother, also a priest, to disavow him. In Quebec, onetime admirers of Lamennais took their papal cues and prohibited "anything [being] taught of the books, system or doctrine of that Author." Rectors snatched issues of *L'Avenir* out of seminary libraries.[79]

An embittered Lamennais now publicly denounced the "horrible system of [papal] tyranny which today burdens the people everywhere." He told a colleague that the church "was in a state of complete decadence." Friends pleaded with him to recant. "All agree that deplorable procedures have been used against you," one explained, "but all agree that you have lacked humility."[80] Lamennais did not agree. He abandoned Catholicism and confessed to Montalembert to having long held "very great doubts on many points of Catholicism, doubts which have become stronger since."[81]

One of Lamennais's correspondents during these fateful days was Giuseppe Mazzini, the world's foremost advocate of democratic nationalism. Mazzini founded the "Young Italy" movement just after the revolutions of 1830, and the term reflected his desire to replace the Old Europe of treaties between popes and kings with republican governments. "We will not attempt any alliances with the kings," he announced. "We will not delude ourselves that we can remain free by relying on international treaties and diplomatic tricks."[82]

Lamennais's influence on Mazzini was immense, and references to the Breton writer's "inspired pages" peppered Mazzini's prose.[83] Both men shared an antagonism toward Catholicism in its conservative, ultramontane form, and this clash between ultramontanism and liberal nationalism would soon become a fundamental organizing principle of the nineteenth century. Mazzini invoked the Reform Catholic hero, Bishop Ricci, as an intellectual ancestor who recognized the need to "establish the [principle of the] supremacy of the whole church over the pope in order to save . . . Christianity and religion from the ruin that threatens them."[84]

To Lamennais he was more direct. "The Rome of the Pope condemns you," he confided. Only "the Rome of the people will succeed."[85]

V

GREGORY XVI HAD denounced Lamennais, but the dream of an ultramontane democracy did not die. Henri Lacordaire, another of the French liberal ultramontanes, still championed "free governments" as confirmed "by the example of Belgium, Ireland, the United States and the republics of [South] America."[86] One of Daniel O'Connell's clerical supporters in Ireland, Bishop John MacHale, mischievously offered an after-dinner toast to "the people, the source of all legitimate power." (Word of the toast reached Rome, and a curial official rebuked an unrepentant MacHale for provoking imperial British authorities.)[87]

One problem faced by these Catholic democrats was increased confessional tension. Protestants watched the ultramontane revival with dismay, and just as Catholics touched by the revival became more intolerant of ecumenical dialogue, so, too, did Protestants. During the 1830s and 1840s, proponents of the "Second Reformation" emerged in England, Germany, the Netherlands, Switzerland, the United States, and Canada. They founded dozens of Protestant associations with such titles as the Evangelical Alliance, the Protestant Association, and the Protestant League and produced histories of the Reformation that painted Luther, Calvin, and other reformers in heroic colors.[88]

Allied with these Protestants were anticlerical nationalists, much like Mazzini, raised in Catholic countries such as Italy, France, and Mexico but wary of ultramontanism. They rolled their eyes at the religiosity of their Protestant allies—German radicals found it preposterous, for example, that Anglo-American Protestants lobbied for the Sunday closure of beer gardens—but found it easy to join forces against the Roman church, what one contemporary named as our "common enemy."[89]

Both Protestants and anticlerical nationalists stressed Catholicism's enervating effects. A member of Parliament from Glasgow explained: "In Ulster where Protestantism preponderates, there is wealth, comfort, peace, freedom, knowledge, enlightened and real loyalty. In Connaught, where Popery predominates, there is penury, misery, slavery."[90] Switzerland became another proof point. One minister crossing the border from Catholic Turin toward Protesant Geneva concluded that "the people who drink the stream of Romanism and live on that side, are lean, poor and ignorant."[91]

The notion that Catholicism diminished economic progress was reinforced by a conviction that Catholicism generated retrograde views on the family. The increase in the number of women choosing to enter religious orders—consciously rejecting marriage and the patriarchal family—seemed positively dangerous. Protestant and secular reformers across Europe and North America promoted tales of nuns allegedly imprisoned in convents or lured away from their families. In France, an English Protestant father sparked an international debate by alleging that his twenty-one-year-old daughter had been lured under false pretenses into a French convent.[92] Rumors of imprisoned Protestant girls in Boston led to the burning of an Ursuline convent in 1834. The next year Protestants bitterly complained about "a nunnery" with an attached school in Newfoundland and attempts to "ensnare the poor and ignorant into the trap laid for them."[93]

The most controversial issue in the 1830s was marriage. The problem was simple: how should the state regulate interfaith marriages? In Cologne an aristocratic archbishop, Count Ferdinand August von Spiegel, and the Prussian state negotiated an agreement that Catholic priests could passively "observe" Protestant-Catholic marriages conducted by a Protestant minister. Girls born to Protestant-Catholic marriages would be raised in the faith of the mother and boys in the faith of the father.

This marital détente collapsed in 1837 when a newly appointed ultramontane archbishop with the formidable name of Clemens August von Droste-Vischering angered Prussian officials by insisting that all children of mixed marriages be raised as Catholics. Hardliners in the Roman curia came to his support. Prussian authorities responded by imprisoning Archbishop Droste-Vischering for disturbing the region's religious peace, and this imprisonment made the ultramontane revival a political as well as a religious event. As one of Daniel O'Connell's friends explained, the Cologne crisis demonstrated that "if we consider the State of the Church in Switzerland, Russia, Prussia and elsewhere, we will find it suffering more now from persecution than it has for centuries past."[94]

Advocates on all sides furiously drafted pamphlets, the most famous by Munich's Joseph Görres. (Görres had arranged for the translation of Joseph de Maistre's *Du Pape* into German in the 1820s.) Görres stressed loyalty to the papacy. "I cannot and may not appeal to other than the pope," he pronounced, the "head of the whole Church." The idea that Protestant Prussian bureaucrats would dictate how Catholics understood sacramental marriage was intolerable.[95]

These tensions between Protestants and Catholics, or secular nationalists and Catholics, extended to South America and then back again to Europe. Lamennais's first Spanish translator, Francisco Bilbao, came to public attention for his attacks on the church and its hierarchy in Santiago, Chile. Bilbao assessed Catholicism as in direct opposition to the "human self" and the need for free trade, public education, and representative government.[96] In the early 1840s he made his way to Lima and then Paris, where he again found himself in a maelstrom of anti-Catholic agitation. Eugène Sue had just published a serialized novel, *Le Juif Errant*, that became one of the century's best sellers. Despite the title—"The Wandering Jew"—the plot revolved less around Jews than around crafty Jesuits maneuvering a vast fortune away from an honorable but needy French Protestant family. In Colombia, legislators referenced the novel in an ultimately successful campaign to expel the Jesuits. In Belgium, crowds inspired by the novel vandalized Jesuit residences and schools and chanted anti-Jesuit slogans in the streets.[97]

Bilbao chose this moment to enroll in a course on the Jesuits offered by the historians Jules Michelet and Edgar Quinet at the Collège de France. He learned there that Jesuitism and ultramontanism menaced new nation-states. Michelet and Quinet compiled their lectures into another anti-Catholic text, *The Jesuits*, with global circulation. The choice patriots faced was stark: either "Jesuitism must abolish the spirit of France," Michelet and Quinet explained, "or France must abolish the spirit of Jesuitism."[98] After reading Michelet and Quinet, a Colombian statesman wondered if a Jesuit's "patria" (or homeland) would always be the Society of Jesus, not Colombia, or any single nation-state.[99]

VI

ON HIS SPEAKING TOURS in the 1840s, Daniel O'Connell demanded the repeal of the union between England and Ireland. He continued to see the papacy as the "spiritual authority" and the "centre of unity, the safeguard of the Church."[100] In contrast to the 1820s, however, when bishops supported O'Connell's campaign for Catholic emancipation without hesitation, the episcopal response to O'Connell's repeal campaign was guarded. Some bishops welcomed O'Connell's efforts; others expressed doubts. The combination of democracy and ultramontanism, so alluring in the 1820s, had lost some of its luster. "It is the first time," wrote O'Connell, "that the people and any part of the Irish hierarchy were divided."[101] The English priest (and future cardinal) Nicholas Wiseman was dismayed by O'Connell's efforts. "I can see no Catholicity," he complained. "I fear it is thoroughly of this world. Repeal, universal suffrage, democracy etc. I have all along hated them and detested them and do so as yet."[102]

British government officials asked Gregory XVI to "discourage agitation" in Ireland. (The pope, who admired O'Connell, did nothing of the sort.)[103] The same British officials—working hand in glove with aristocratic English Catholics—weaned some Irish bishops away from O'Connell's movement by modifying laws forbidding bequests to the church. They arranged increased public funding for the Irish Catholic seminary at Maynooth, which provoked shrieks of protest from newly mobilized Protestant evangelicals in Parliament who accused the government of funding "a Popish Establishment."[104]

Gregory XVI's unexpected death in 1846 seemed an opportunity for O'Connell and other democratic reformers, since Gregory XVI's successor, Giovanni Maria Mastai-Ferreti, or Pius IX, offered a more conciliatory vision of the church's role. Pius IX began his papacy by authorizing the first legislative assembly for the Papal States and granting amnesty to political prisoners languishing in papal jails. Celebrations around the world, often led by non-Catholics, marked the apparent reconciliation between the papacy and new ideals of freedom. "The Pope's object," explained one Irish priest based in Rome to a colleague across the Atlantic, "is to gain the affections of his own subjects by useful reforms, and to re-establish that paternal form of government which is best adapted to the common Father of the faithful."[105] When Pius IX greeted Belgian visitors, he praised the country's combination of democracy and Catholicism. "Thanks to liberty, religion flowers in Belgium," he said, "and it will flower more and more." Belgian students reportedly decorated their rooms with portraits of the pope next to portraits of George Washington.[106]

Gravely ill, Daniel O'Connell decided to journey to Rome and meet this reform-minded pope. When he reached Paris, Charles Montalembert insisted on paying tribute to his shivering friend, wrapped in a blanket and barely able to leave his chair. "Wherever Catholics begin anew to practice civic virtues," Montalembert proclaimed, "and devote themselves to the conquest of their legislative rights under God, it is [O'Connell's] work." No one had done more "for the political education of Catholic people."[107]

O'Connell never reached Rome, but his heart did. He died in Genoa in 1847 after requesting that his heart be carried to Rome, where it was displayed in the chapel of the Irish College, and his body returned to Ireland. At a massive two-day ceremony in O'Connell's honor, encouraged by Pius IX and held at one of Rome's largest churches just a short walk from St. Peter's, Fr. Gioacchino Ventura electrified the audience by denying the need to unify "throne and altar." O'Connell's life conveyed a different message. He had proven that "religion could only be victorious by the aid of liberty."[108]

A new era seemed to have dawned.

FOUR

Triumph

1848, Vatican I and the Consolidation
of the Catholic Revival

I

THE ASSERTION THAT Alexis de Tocqueville and Charles Montalembert were two of the most important French intellectuals of the nineteenth century is uncontroversial. To view them in tandem is less common.[1] Yet their lives bear comparison. Born five years apart, both men grew up in aristocratic families scarred by the revolution. Tocqueville's father served in the royal constitutional guard, and his parents narrowly escaped the guillotine. Montalembert's father fled France in the desperate emigration of 1792 and returned only in 1814.

Neither man followed his father into a military career. Instead they achieved renown as writers and politicians. Montalembert became one of the closest associates of Félicité Lamennais and joined him in heralding a new union between Catholicism and democracy. Tocqueville shot to fame with the 1835 publication of his *Democracy in America*, where he identified Catholics as the "most republican and democratic class in the United States." He rejected the claim made by some radicals during the French Revolution that the "Catholic religion [was] the natural enemy of democracy."[2] When he visited Ireland and met with a group of bishops and clergy, he reported "extremely democratic" sentiments.[3]

When in Paris, the two men dined together. When not in Paris, they corresponded. Friendship did not ensure agreement. Montalembert wrote biographies of medieval saints, delved into arcane liturgical practices, and tramped through abandoned abbeys. He helped England's Augustus Pugin obtain French commissions for neo-Gothic church buildings and described the cathedral of Notre Dame as the centerpiece of French civilization. After visiting Rome, he dismissed the Forum and the Colosseum as making "no impression on my anti-classic soul."[4]

Tocqueville's sensibility was more austere. He dutifully practiced his Catholicism and occupied the family pew in his ancestral village, despite private doubts. He served on the board of the missionary Holy Childhood Society, dedicated to baptizing infants in China. But he mistrusted ultramontane exuberance. He wryly termed Montalembert, with his many enthusiasms, "the greatest enemy of Catholicism since Voltaire."[5]

II

THE 1848 REVOLUTIONS were the turning point. As monarchies collapsed, governments formed, and revolutionaries drafted constitutions, from Naples to Budapest to Copenhagen to Paris, new possibilities for Catholicism became visible. A priest from Vienna joined a Protestant minister and a rabbi in mourning the deaths of five students in a revolutionary skirmish. "The old and new testament marched together under freedom's banner," he later wrote. He expressed delight in seeing activists from across Europe working in "fraternal, magnificent concord."[6]

Many Catholics delighted in these new democratic governments. Montalembert's close friend, Dominican priest Henri Lacordaire, served as a delegate in the new constituent assembly of the Second French Republic, and Tocqueville noted the election of numerous priests to the assembly as part of the "quite unexpected return of a great part of the nation to a concern with religious matters."[7] "My knowledge of history," declared an excited liberal ultramontane, Frédéric Ozanam, "forces me to the conclusion that democracy is the natural final state of the development of political progress and that God leads the world thither."[8]

In Berlin, German Catholics played a significant role in the revolutionary Frankfurt Parliament. A handful of leading Catholics, not only Protestants, advocated banning the Jesuits from Prussia, and a few Cath-

olics urged the end of mandatory clerical celibacy. More radical Catholics urged the election of parish clergy, harkening back to the first years
of the French Revolution.[9]

These hopes soon withered. The 1848 revolutionaries had revived
the animating vision of the French Revolution: unified nation-states
with free male citizens possessing the right to vote along with civil
liberties such as freedom of speech and freedom of association.[10] The
same revolutionaries had not resolved, and would soon exacerbate,
tensions between these new nation-states and an international church
still claiming its own territory (in the Papal States) and its own schools
and associations.

The second phase of the revolutions beginning in the summer of 1848
marked a shift in tone. Revolutionaries became more violent, especially
as kings and ministers began to regain control in Vienna, Paris, and
Berlin. This reassertion of monarchical authority could allow for more
latitude for Catholics—Tocqueville later noted that Catholic friends in
Bonn delighted in a "real freedom" under a Prussian Protestant king—
but meant the abandonment of democracy as a political goal.[11]

The revolutions also became entangled with the fate of the papacy.
Beginning in the early 1840s, two scholarly priests, Fr. Antonio Rosmini
and Fr. Vincenzo Gioberti, had become leaders of the Risorgimento, or
movement for Italian independence. They desired consolidation of the
various Italian states into a single nation, constitutional government,
and the expulsion of foreign troops from Italy.

Rosmini studied Tocqueville's *Democracy in America*. Gioberti drew
from Reform Catholic sources and expressed admiration for Henri Grégoire, who in his eyes exhibited "love of humanity and country and a
truly evangelical spirit of charity."[12] Both Rosmini and Gioberti mistrusted the Jesuits because they seemed independent of nation-states, and
Gioberti defined the Jesuits as the "enemies of nationalities." In Spanish
translation, Gioberti's writings inspired anti-Jesuit oratory across Latin
America.[13]

Some of the Risorgimento's champions, such as Giuseppe Mazzini,
were anti-Catholic and desired an Italy freed from any taint of an archaic
papacy. Rosmini and Gioberti disagreed. Both men thought that Italian unity required the pope as the symbolic head of the nation. Only

the papacy could inspire the "fraternity" and "natural equality" necessary for a stable national government, and both men welcomed the election of Pius IX. But as reformers grew more radical over the course of 1848, Pius IX became more uneasy. When Mazzini published a letter to the pope demanding that he support a united Italy, Pius IX responded by denouncing "nationalist fanaticism" as inconsistent with a "universal church."[14]

Revolutionaries assassinated Pius IX's first prime minister for the Papal States on the steps of the new legislative assembly in November 1848, making the pope legitimately fearful for his life. Ten days later, traveling incognito in an unmarked carriage, he fled Rome for the seaside town of Gaeta. In his absence, Roman citizens declared a republic, wrote a constitution, and proclaimed full religious liberty. They seized church property and declared the Roman republic linked to the rest of Italy by "common nationality."[15]

Mazzini entered Rome in triumph. He predicted that Pius IX would be "the Louis XVI of Papal Rome."[16] Mazzini's friend and ally, the American feminist Margaret Fuller, reporting from Rome for the *New York Herald Tribune*, caught the mood. Where three years earlier she had praised Pius IX as a "thoughtful, noble-minded man," she now proclaimed that "not only Jesuitism must go but the Roman Catholic religion must go. . . . The influence of the clergy is too perverting, too foreign to every hope of advancement and health."[17]

Once again, foreign troops, this time from France, came to the pope's rescue and defeated the ragtag republican militia in 1849. Only when French troops had secured the city did Pius IX return to Rome, determined to protect his political authority in the Papal States and his religious authority within the church. He arranged for the writings of those Italian priests who had supported the Risorgimento—notably Gioberti and Rosmini—to be placed on the Index of Forbidden Books. As a symbol of his new disposition, Pius IX took to carrying a locket containing the eucharistic host, which had been worn by his predecessor, Pius VI, during his imprisonment after the French Revolution.[18]

The pope's recalcitrance infuriated Tocqueville, who briefly served as French foreign minister and negotiated with Vatican diplomats. France cannot support papal government, Tocqueville complained to a friend, with nothing to show for it but "having reestablished the cardinals and the abuses of the clerical administration in place of the Roman Republic. Our honor, the interests of France, and even the interests of the Church preclude this."[19] For a moment during the revolutions of 1848, Tocqueville later observed, the French clergy had "discovered that the motto of the Republic dated back to the gospels." Now liberal French Catholics had been "reduced to silence" while conservative clergy and laity treated "the Republic and liberty as mortal sins."[20]

III

THE TRAVAILS OF PIUS IX made him more visible to ordinary Catholics, not less. Catholic globalization in the nineteenth century rested on migrants and missionaries departing Europe, but it also depended on Catholics from other parts of the world turning their attention to Rome. To view this emphasis on Rome as nothing more than an assertion of papal authority would be mistaken. Just as often, ultramontane fervor sprang from the grassroots. Tocqueville knew that "the revival of the Catholic spirit across the world" demanded study. As he told one English friend:

> It was not a matter of the pope seizing power over the
> faithful, but of the faithful themselves calling on the pope
> to become absolute master of the church. And this ten-
> dency was, if not universal, then widespread throughout
> the Catholic world. The papal position we see today was
> not so much a *cause* as an *effect*.[21]

One dimension of this papal focus was ecclesiological. "The highest duty of bishops," wrote one prominent French ultramontane, "is obedience to the Pope."[22] Once a minority view, Joseph de Maistre's exaltation of the papacy as the cornerstone of ecclesiastical authority became conventional Catholic wisdom, and his writings were avidly read from Poland to Chile.[23] More liberal ultramontanes such as Frédéric Ozanam despaired of the vogue for de Maistre, whom Ozanam called a member of the "school of hatred."[24]

Exercising papal authority in unprecedented ways became routine. In 1854, Pius IX declared Mary's conception immaculate, or without sin, with minimal episcopal consultation. The idea had long been popular among ordinary Catholics and particular religious orders, such as the Franciscans. But it lacked a scriptural pedigree and widened the already yawning gap between Catholics and Protestants. In New Orleans, French Jesuits from Lyon delighted in naming their grand new church and college Immaculate Conception and offered a series of public lectures on the topic. One mischievously remarked that focusing on the dogma will "scare" the "rich American Protestants."[25] In Guatemala City, travelers marveled at the illumination of the city's main buildings in honor of the dogma, "the most beautiful [celebration] I have seen in all of America."[26]

Four years later, Pius IX sparked an international furor by condoning the forced conversion and kidnapping of Edgardo Mortara, a Jewish boy from Bologna, and raising him as a protégé in Rome. Mortara had been secretly baptized by a Catholic servant working for the family, and according to the letter of church law, when baptised he should be raised in the faith. Secret baptisms occurred across the Catholic world in the nineteenth century, from North Africa to the United States, because of the fear that unbaptized children could not reach heaven.[27]

The crucial difference in the Mortara case was the actual removal of Edgardo from his home by police from the Papal States. This abduction outraged public opinion, catalyzing Jewish solidarity across national lines. Many Catholics, too, were embarrassed by papal acquiescence in the kidnapping, but the ultramontane press framed the conflict as one of Catholics versus a corrupt and hostile world. "In the past," explained one Parisian editor, "Christians would have accepted the Papal decision: now the same people criticize his action. A revolution in values and beliefs has shaken modern society and pagan prejudices have taken precedence over eternal verities."[28]

In 1864, the pope issued the encyclical *Quanta Cura*, with its notorious appendix, The Syllabus of Errors. The chaotic preparation of this document meant that Pius IX may not have seen the final version before publication. But its final proposition famously rejected the idea that "the Roman Pontiff can, and ought to, reconcile himself, and come to terms with progress, liberalism and modern civilization."[29] In Poland, observers began to ask exactly how Catholics would oppose "modern civilization."[30]

Other markers of ultramontanism included an astonishing five million Catholics signing petitions in the pope's support in 1859, when Italian armies again threatened to conquer the Papal States. One priest from a tiny village in rural Ireland reported parishioners asking him, "How is the Holy Father? Will they banish him?"[31] Twelve thousand soldiers from across the Catholic world enlisted as Zouaves, or soldiers, in the papal army. An Australian bishop said of his country's Zouaves, "we talk our faith: they have wrought theirs."[32]

Contributions from ordinary Catholics also became central to papal finances. The mechanism was Peter's Pence, an appeal to Catholics around the world to assist a besieged pope. France, as the wealthiest Catholic country, contributed almost half the total before 1870, but donations came in significant amounts from North America, South America, India, and Africa. Pilgrims journeyed to Rome in growing numbers, gathering in St. Peter's Basilica, in the words of one Scottish visitor, to console "the pope who never leaves his palace but is there visited by crowds of good Christians."[33]

IV

IN 1858 AT LOURDES, a village in the Pyrenees, a poor fourteen-year-old girl named Bernadette Soubirous claimed to see Mary. Local officials—civic and ecclesiastical—at first doubted Bernadette's claims, but her sincerity and the alignment of her vision with an ultramontane sensibility meant that she and her local supporters found allies up the ecclesiastical chain. That Bernadette claimed Mary had uttered the phrase "I am the Immaculate Conception" just four years after the proclamation of the dogma signaled the increasingly tight link between Rome and even the most remote provinces. Pius IX provided a papal endorsement of the visions as early as 1870 and formally approved Lourdes as a pilgrimage site in 1876.

The attention lavished on Lourdes was unprecedented but only the most visible manifestation of a resurgent interest in the miraculous. Beneath the iceberg tip of the great European and Latin American pilgrimage sites lay a vast block of apparitions, miracles, and healings, most never approved by the church, a few approved but of local interest. Alleged apparitions in Knock, Ireland, and Marpingen, Germany, echoed Lourdes in many of their details and how participants understood events. At Knock, a parish priest had arranged for Lourdes statues to be placed in the local church; in Marpingen, the three young witnesses at the apparition had heard a local school teacher discuss Lourdes.

Pius IX also promoted the idea of national seminaries in Rome, and French, German, Latin American, North American, and Polish seminaries were established during his reign in order to ensure Roman training for a clerical elite. Priests trained in Rome accounted for eleven of the seventeen bishops appointed in Australia during Pius IX's reign. In the United States, officially missionary territory until 1908, Bishop Martin Spalding could boast to the equally ultramontane Cardinal Paul Cullen, of Ireland, his former teacher in Rome, "Thank God! We are Roman to the heart."[34]

Pius IX's decision to restore the Catholic hierarchy in England and the Netherlands also enhanced Roman influence and demonstrated a pugnacious streak. In 1850, he appointed the first cardinal archbishop of Westminster (London) since the Reformation, a decision that set off protests across England. Prime Minister Lord John Russell publicly regretted the "assumption of power" evidenced in the papal decision even if he felt confident that the "liberty of Protestantism" would repel any effort "to impose a foreign yoke upon our minds and consciences."[35] In both England and the Netherlands, Catholics fought off accusations that they were "internationalist in nature."[36]

A generation of ultramontane Catholic newspaper editors across Europe and North America played a vital role in this Romanization process. By the 1850s, the *Freeman's Journal* in New York, *L'Amico Cattolica* in Milan, the *Dublin Review* in London (oddly), *La Revista Católica* in Barcelona, and *L'Armonia* in Turin exchanged news items and created a shared sense of battling liberal foes.[37]

The most prominent such editor was Louis Veuillot, of *Univers* in Paris. In the newspaper's first years in the 1840s, Veuillot's political orientation was unclear, and Montalembert and other liberal ultramontanes served on editorial committees. The revolutions of 1848 made Veuillot far more combative and spurred his attacks on what he considered an anti–Catholic liberalism outside the church and a false liberalism within it. *Univers* never counted more than eight thousand subscribers, but this number does not reflect its influence. Articles from *Univers* circulated across the world in the Francophone press and were translated into English in New York's *Freeman's Journal* and into Spanish in Chile's *Revista Católica*. "I believed," Veuillot wrote toward the end of his life, "that I was at the same time a soldier and a judge and that I had no business in making myself likeable."[38]

In this he succeeded. Veuillot's primary targets were bishops resistant to the ultramontane movement. When he visited Lourdes just months after the apparition, he instinctively composed a populist framing: "It's a miracle the administration doesn't want, in defiance of the people, who do."[39] That he berated bishops who as an ultramontane he might be expected to obey did not trouble him. He served only "the truth, in humility and poverty."[40] The aggrieved archbishop of Paris complained that Veuillot's assaults "turn upside down the entire economy of ecclesiastical government." To no avail the archbishop reminded French Catholics not to determine doctrinal truths from newspapers.[41]

Pius IX took Veuillot's side in these disputes and joined the publishing game by pressuring initially reluctant Jesuits to found a Roman journal, *Civiltà Cattolica*. Published in Italian, not the otherworldly Latin ordinarily used for church documents, with articles personally reviewed by the pope, *Civiltà Cattolica* enrolled subscribers, often Jesuits, in all parts of the world. Many became contributors to the significant sections of the paper devoted to foreign news.

Irish migrants avidly read not only the *Freeman's Journal* in Dublin but the *Freeman's Journal* in New York City and the *Freeman's Journal* in Sydney, all "soundly Catholic."[42] Santiago's archbishop Rafael Valdivieso, born in 1804, did not leave his home country until 1869. But he absorbed the global Catholic discussion through subscriptions to *Univers*, his favorite, along with *Civiltà Cattolica* and the *Dublin Review*.[43] One missionary writing from Cairo pleaded with colleagues to send him copies, even used copies, of *Civiltà Cattolica* and Milan's *Unità Cattolica*, since "we only know a little of what is going on in the world."[44] Catholics in Bombay met in 1866 to bemoan the absence of a "Catholic press worthy of the name." No longer should India's Catholics rely primarily on books or journals imported from Britain, France, and the United States. Given that Protestant publications flooded the subcontinent, Catholics needed to respond on a "grand scale."[45]

V

THE IRISH PRIEST Paul Cullen spent the 1848–1849 Roman Revolution barricaded within the walls of the Propaganda Fide on the city's Piazza di Spagna. He occasionally ventured onto the city's streets in a peasant disguise. Such cautions were understandable. Cullen itemized "Republican Atrocities" during the revolution, including murders of priests and desecrations of churches. When Cullen emerged from hiding, and when he later became the archbishop of Armagh in 1850 and archbishop of Dublin in 1852, he set himself to preventing any Irish variation on the Roman revolution. The Young Ireland movement shared barely a name with Mazzini's Young Italy, but for Cullen even a whisper of anticlerical nationalism was enough. "The Young Irelanders," Cullen complained, "desire to destroy all the power of the priests—they seem to act just as the Mazzinians did in Italy."[46]

The process of forging a Catholic social vision began, as Cullen's experience suggested, with sharp lines drawn between Catholicism and revolution. That many Catholics had favored the revolutions of 1848, just as they had favored the original French Revolution in 1789 and the Spanish revolution of 1812, was ignored or forgotten. The Spanish nobleman Donoso Cortes, for example, saw the attacks on Pius IX as a point of no return. In a widely reprinted address delivered in the Spanish assembly in 1849, Cortes asserted that dictatorships should frighten Catholics and other citizens less than revolutions. In Rome, Cortes asserted, the throne of Pius IX had almost been abandoned to the "throne of demagogues."[47]

So, too, in Canada. The new bishop of Montreal, Ignace Bourget, began his tenure by working to create a "petit Rome" with the full panoply of devotions, religious orders, and neo-Gothic churches. He denounced the revolutions of 1848 and Canadian nationalism. A beleaguered friend of Félicité Lamennais regretted the bishop's tone. "This

revolution in Italy," he complained, "has provided a pretext for endless attacks on democratic principles." He wondered, "Do [such bish-
ops] believe [they] are strengthening Catholicism by showing that it is
incompatible with liberalism?"[48]

The foes identified by ultramontane Catholics were typically liberal nationalists, now dominant in educated circles on both sides of
the Atlantic. Among their most prominent voices was England's John
Stuart Mill, who saw unified nation-states and representative government as logically connected and the individual—as voter, as negotiator
of contracts, as voluntary (and equal) marriage partner, and as owner
of himself and his labor—as the starting point for a just social order.
In the United States, Ralph Waldo Emerson extolled "self-reliance"
and later complained of "Romish priests, who sympathize, of course,
with despotism."[49]

Ultramontane Catholics accepted little of this, and indeed, Vatican officials placed some of Mill's writings on the Index of Forbidden Books. Mill had learned from his father that the Reformation had
been the "great and decisive contest against priestly tyranny for liberty
of thought." But ultramontane Catholics viewed the Reformation as
tragic, not liberating.[50]

Three intellectuals—the Catalan priest Jaime Balmes, the Mainz
bishop Wilhelm von Ketteler, and the Italian Jesuit Luigi Taparelli—
developed a Catholic alternative to liberal nationalism. Balmes offered
a different historical narrative. In contrast to secular and Protestant historians who traced the evolution of liberty and progress back to the
ancient Greeks and forward through the Reformation and the Enlightenment, Balmes equated progess with Catholicism.

The key text was his *Protestantism and Catholicity Compared in their
Effects on the Civilization of Europe.* Do not permit the false claim, he
warned his readers, that "innovators of the sixteenth century proclaimed the freedom of thought." Instead, remember the founding of
Oxford and the University of Bologna in the Middle Ages, the freedom
given to the European serfs, and the medieval origins of constitutional
government. Indeed, the "progress which has been made since Protestantism, has been made not by it, but in spite of it."[51]

Balmes lived almost his entire life near his birthplace in Barcelona, but his influence was vast, especially after the 1848 revolutions, with dozens of reprintings of his *Protestantism and Catholicity Compared* in multiple languages. One American convert termed *Protestantism and Catholicity Compared* "*the* book for our times," and its influence was especially significant in Spain and Latin America. The Argentine Fèlix Frias repeatedly referred to Balmes as a guiding light in his rejection of liberalism and his conviction that Catholics possessed a "true social theory."[52]

Bishop Ketteler probed another dimension of liberal nationalism, free markets. Ketteler worked as a young priest near the first sites of Germany's industrial revolution in the Rhineland and watched with foreboding the transformation of the landscape and the desperate migration of families from villages to cities. Just as Balmes worried about "steam civilization" destroying the social fabric of Catalonia, Ketteler, in a series of well-publicized sermons given in 1848, stressed limits on the "right to possess and use property." He despaired of a "stubborn, narrow interpretation of the property right" at a moment when "the poverty of the masses grows daily."[53] Ketteler inspired Adolf Kolping, a friend and fellow priest who had once worked as a shoemaker, to form a workers' association, termed the Kolping Verein, that soon enrolled tens of thousands of members and provided literacy training, instruction in bookkeeping, and other practical skills for men displaced from artisanal jobs.[54]

In its favoring of communal goals over individual rights, the ultramontane Catholic social vision as articulated by Ketteler resembled nothing as much as the first socialists. Ketteler regretted that "no word is more misused than the word, 'freedom,'" and socialists, too, thought liberal notions of individual freedom misleading.[55] Ferdinand LaSalle, the leading German socialist of the mid-nineteenth century, trumpeted a friendly correspondence with Bishop Ketteler, and a surprising number of ultramontane Catholics admired the young Karl Marx's critical assessment of the new industrial economy.[56]

Shared critiques did not lead to a common front. Ketteler did not reject private property, just what he considered a naive vision of economic freedom. Many socialists and communists, in turn, possessed a didactic certainty about the oppressive capacity of religion. Religion only distracted workers from class conflicts. Karl Marx called the Catholic clergy "dogs" and ridiculed Ketteler.[57]

The same vision of an organic society that made ultramontane Catholics among the first to decry the effects of industrialization impeded their recognition of slavery's horrors. Here the difference between Reform Catholics and liberal ultramontanes, on the one hand, and more conservative ultramontanes on the other was significant. Most Latin American countries, with the important exceptions of Brazil and Cuba, abolished slavery early in the nineteenth century in part because of the influence of Reform Catholicism. Reform Catholics, such as Fr. Mier in Mexico, supported abolition, as did a young Cuban priest, Félix Varela. Varela urged the abolition of slavery in both Cuba and the United States. He viewed the terms "Constitution, liberty and equality" as "polar opposites to the words slavery and inequality of rights."[58] His Havana bishop agreed.[59] In Brazil, some of the most important early abolitionists, such as Padre Feijó, alternated between pleas for the abolition of slavery and demands to abolish the requirement of priestly celibacy. (Feijó lived with his common-law wife and five children.)[60]

Liberal ultramontanes such as Montalembert also opposed slavery. He mocked the "infallible wisdom and virtue" of Americans for publishing newspaper advertisements offering rewards for fugitive slaves.[61] Daniel O'Connell welcomed African American abolitionist Frederick Douglass to Ireland and risked his popularity in the Irish diaspora by condemning the unwillingness of Irish Americans to support the abolition of slavery. "Dare countenance the system of slavery," he warned, and "we will recognize you as Irishmen no more."[62] In response, Irish Catholics in Savannah, Georgia, worried that "[O'Connell] has learned his lessons on Southern institutions from Northern abolitionists, the dire enemies of real liberties, and the notorious enemies of Ireland's religion."[63]

Conservative ultramontane Catholics equivocated on the topic of slavery. Gregory XVI condemned the trade in enslaved people in 1839—to applause from abolitionists—but this carefully worded papal statement evaded the larger question of the institution's morality. When a French Catholic nun, Anne-Marie Javouhey, founded a colony for formerly enslaved people in French Guiana, the local apostolic prefect dismissed "the project of the abolitionists, of which she is the head, [as] obviously a deception and a chimera."[64] Baltimore's bishop Francis Kenrick, trained at the heart of the ultramontane revival in Rome, made the opposite argument of Montalembert. He disdained "vain theories of philanthropy to the prejudice of social order" and encouraged the return of fugitive slaves to their owners.[65] When a priest visited abolitionist John Brown in his jail cell after Brown's failed 1859 raid on the Harper's Ferry Armory, the priest urged Brown to "recall an epistle of St. Paul to Philemon, where we are informed that he sent back the fugitive slave Onesimus from Rome to his master."[66]

Some Catholics owned (and sold) enslaved people. Members of the Carroll family, the most prominent Catholic family in the first decades of the United States, were also some of the country's largest slave owners. The Jesuits in Maryland, after a caution from the Father General in Rome not to separate husbands and wives, or parents and children, sold 272 enslaved people to slave owners in Louisiana to pay off debts incurred by Jesuit-run Georgetown University. One Georgetown Jesuit had recently denounced abolitionists as "would-be philanthropists," and he insisted that enslaved people were better off as property in the South than as free people of color in the North.

The day of the sale was traumatic. One report described enslaved people carrying rosaries, holy medals, and crosses as they prepared to

In 1865, the Sisters of Charity of Nazareth in the United States owned thirty enslaved people. This photo, taken at Nazareth, Kentucky, in 1912, is of those formerly enslaved people and their descendants. *(Courtesy of Archives of the Sisters of Nazareth of Charity)*

leave Maryland. An enslaved woman requested a blessing from a Jesuit on the day of the sale. She then asked, "What will become of me? Why do I deserve this?"[67]

VI

THE ITALIAN JESUIT Luigi Taparelli did not defend slavery as it existed in the 1850s, but he made the standard conservative ultramontane argument that "certain philanthropic declarations against slavery in the general meaning" had led to a "false idea of an inalienable right to freedom."[68] Taparelli devoted far more energy to articulating a new relationship between Catholics and nation-states. Born in Turin in 1793 to a noble Piedmont family, Taparelli entered the Jesuits as soon as they were reinstated in 1814. He became one of the founding editors of *Civiltà Cattolica* and an early proponent of neo-Thomism. He professed his admiration for Louis Veuillot.[69]

Taparelli's brother, Massimo, was an important advocate for Italian unity under papal leadership in the 1840s, and Luigi initially seemed willing to join his brother in promoting the Italian nationalist cause. But the events of 1848 pushed a generation of ultramontane Catholics into a more confrontational posture toward the nation-state, a rupture that would not heal until World War I. When nationalism united a people and deepened attachment to a particular language and culture, as opposed to substituting for religious loyalties, ultramontanists acknowledged its benefits. Irish Catholics defending themselves from British overlords, Polish Catholics mistrustful of Russian tsars, Mexican Catholics loyal to Our Lady of Guadalupe, and Croatian Catholics struggling for distance from Habsburg rulers all saw Catholicism as interwoven with the destiny of a particular people. In Canada, French ultramontanes insisted that "here more than anywhere else, the national interest is inseparable from the religious interest, and if liberalism disassociates itself from either one, it automatically becomes the enemy of the other."[70]

But Taparelli worried about "exaggerated nationalism" substituting for more fundamental ties of church, family, and local community. In his theoretical essays he foregrounded international communities and international law, not individual nation-states. Premature efforts to forge national unity—characteristic, in Taparelli's view, of nationalists influenced by Protestantism—almost always required violent state coercion. The regions coerced—Silesia, Brittany, and Alsace—were among Europe's most Catholic. This "conquest" seemed to Taparelli a high price to pay for the "idol" of national unity.[71]

Jesuits such as Taparelli offered an especially jaundiced perspective on nationalist rhetoric, in part because of the willingness of so many liberal nationalists to expel members of religious orders and confiscate their property. The Jesuits were expelled from over a dozen countries in the decades after 1848. Taparelli himself witnessed the expulsion of the Jesuits from Sicily by a revolutionary government in 1848. "Where is the unity of the nation," Jesuit Father General Jan Roothaan sardonically asked after he had been expelled from Rome, "in Italy, in Germany?" Forging a nation out of diverse regions and linguistic communities "produced precisely the opposite, disunion."[72]

Ultramontane Catholics helped coin the term "Latin America" to promote a religious identity broader than the nation-state. The Chilean priest José Ignacio Víctor Eyzaguirre explained in 1859 that "half a century of bloody revolutions" had done Latin Americans little good. No longer should Catholics tolerate distance "from the Church that has granted her all the goods of Civilization. . . . America owes everything to the Church, to religion, to her faith."[73] Eyzaguirre obtained a private meeting with Pius IX, who encouraged him to establish ties with Catholics across Latin America. By traveling from Brazil to Mexico, he built an impressive network.[74]

The most interesting experiment in Catholic nationalism occurred in Ecuador. Much of South America in the 1840s and 1850s remained locked in a pattern of regalism, or state control over the church. In Brazil, government officials not only appointed bishops but regulated the use of candles in churches. In Argentina, government officials selected the colors of clerical vestments. When Jesuits returned to Argentina after a long absence in 1843, they were shocked to find portraits of Argentina's strongman president, Juan Manuel de Rosas, on church altars.[75]

Ecuador's Gabriel Garcia Moreno, developed an ultramontane alternative. During visits to Paris as a young man he learned to despise the liberal anticlericalism he detected behind the 1848 revolutions. He read de Maistre and Balmes. After his election as president, Moreno signed a concordat with the Holy See in 1862 that made Catholicism not only the state religion but ultimately a requirement for citizenship, a rule less controversial than one might think, since over 95 percent of Ecuadorans were baptized Catholics. He rejected the individualist and Protestant values he and other Catholics associated with conventional nation-building projects.

The same concordat insisted that education at all levels in Ecuador would "conform to the doctrine of the Catholic religion." To that end, Moreno invited German Jesuits and French Christian Brothers into the country to take leadership positions in schools and universities and encouraged several different women's religious orders from France to take the lead on women's education. (He dismissed—and infuriated—local clergy and bishops by describing them as lazy.) He dedicated the nation to the Sacred Heart. After Moreno's assassination by political rivals, Pius IX paid for a sculpture of him to be placed outside the Colegio Pio Latino in Rome, recently opened to train Latin American seminarians. An inscription chiseled into the statue praised Moreno for his "Supreme Devotion to the Chair of Saint Peter."[76]

VII

SIXTY MILLION EUROPEANS left the continent over the course of the nineteenth and early twentieth centuries in one of the great migrations of modern history. The Catholic portion of the migration—probably over half—was led by immigrants from Ireland and Germany in the mid-nineteenth century and from Polish-speaking Europe, Spain, and Italy after 1870.[77] Joseph R. Biden's great-grandfather left the west of Ireland in 1850 and arrived in the United States at the outset of the migration, and Pope Francis's grandparents left their home near Turin in the 1920s and arrived in Argentina at its conclusion.

The Irish diaspora set the template, and Ireland had the continent's highest emigration rate. One million people left Ireland between 1815 and 1845 and another two million, or almost a quarter of the island's population, in the famine decade of 1846–1855. (One million Irish perished from hunger and disease.) Until the 1830s, Irish Protestant migrants, mostly from Ulster, outnumbered Catholics, and in some regions, such as Ontario, in Canada, they outnumbered Catholics by a ratio of two to one. But in the famine era, an overwhelming majority of Irish migrants were Catholic. Some moved directly to the industrial centers of England and Scotland, creating new Irish Catholic enclaves in Glasgow, Liverpool, and London. Even more left for the United States, for New York City most of all, but also Boston, Philadelphia, and San Francisco. Smaller but still sizable numbers moved to Australia and Canada.[78]

These Irish migrants—wherever they landed—depended more on Catholicism and its structures than any other set of institutions, ensuring that Irish Catholics, not Irish Protestants, would remain identifiable as a distinct community well into the twentieth century. Irish clergy founded All Hallows College in Dublin—with the approval of Gregory XVI and a commitment by the Propaganda Fide to stock the library— to train seminarians for the foreign missions, "since the Catholic inhabitants of the British Colonies and dependencies, and of the United States of America, are in great part descended from Irish emigrants." Rectors dispatched priests from the first graduating classes to the United States, Canada, South Africa, Madras, Bombay, and Scotland.[79]

A single well-placed Vatican official such as the Irish priest (and eventually cardinal) Paul Cullen engineered the appointment of Irish-born bishops in the United States, Ireland, Canada, Australia, South Africa, India, and New Zealand. Cullen's facility in Italian and ties to Gregory XVI and Pius IX allowed him to manipulate the levers of Roman power. Long after he returned from Rome to Ireland, Cullen subscribed to not only *Civiltà Cattolica*, but also the ultramontane *Armonia* based in Turin. "I would be lonesome unless I had the paper," he told one of his Australian protégés.[80]

The same bishops cajoled Irish nuns to staff the schools and social welfare institutions of the diaspora. The first foundation for the Sisters of Mercy outside of Europe occurred in Canada (in Newfoundland) in 1842. The first of what would become several dozen foundations in the United States was established in Pittsburgh in 1843. By 1850, Sisters of Mercy also worked in Australia and New Zealand. Later they journeyed to South Africa, Rhodesia, and India. In one six-year period, twenty-two Sisters of Mercy born in Ireland left their home for the rural Australian diocese of Maitland.[81]

British settler colonies, such as Canada, Australia, New Zealand, and South Africa, grew rapidly in the nineteenth century, and Irish Catholic migrants and their clergy and women religious facilitated this growth. Imperial officials in London shared with Irish bishops such as Cullen the goal of cultivating loyalty to the British Empire (or at least quashing dissent). In Canada, South Africa, and Australia, British support for Catholicism included funds for clerical salaries.[82] When an English priest was sent to minister to African, Portuguese, and French Catholics in the colony of Trinidad, local officials congratulated the populace, "more particularly that great majority of it that belong to the Church of Rome," for having received the "high sanction" of Parliament and the British Crown.[83]

Many Irish migrants, and almost all of the Irish nuns and clergy who followed them, had been touched by the ultramontane revival, prompting conflicts with native-born Catholics. When Irish Catholics migrated in large numbers to Glasgow, Scottish priests contrasted their own long-standing devotional practices with ultramontane enthusiasm for rosaries, scapulars, and novenas.[84] In Louisiana, French-speaking Creoles in New Orleans resisted the reforming efforts of Bishop Antoine Blanc, the product of a Lyon seminary at the heart of the ultramontane revival in France. One Creole editor accused Blanc of taking the side of the "Ultra-Montanists, against the Gallican Church." But Irish migration meant that Blanc had new allies. As the same editor explained:

> The Irish Catholics are, almost to a man, papists. The French Catholics are generally anti-Papal. Hence, the French Creoles of this city are true Americans; the Papal Irish are not; and cannot be, until they abjure, as the French have abjured, the tyranny of the Jesuit and other orders of Papal Priests.[85]

No comparable famine ravaged Germany, but a similar potato blight and then episodes of grinding economic distress pushed 5.5 million migrants out of German-speaking Europe between 1814 and 1914, with the largest number moving in the 1850s. Most German Catholic migrants came from the Rhineland and Bavaria. Most moved to the United States, with a significant minority to Brazil. But other countries received German Catholics too. Thousands of German Catholics from near Odessa migrated to Saskatchewan, where they organized their farms and villages around parish churches.[86]

Just as Irish bishops recruited Irish-born nuns, German bishops recruited German-born nuns. Mother Theresa Gerhardinger founded a women's religious order in Bavaria, the School Sisters of Notre Dame. Like her Irish counterparts, she began with a house for young women, but she soon aspired to begin a religious congregation. She began sending women out from Bavaria soon after the order's founding, to the United States in 1847 and then to Poland, Austria, Italy, Romania, and Czech-speaking lands.

German Catholics generally shared an ultramontane sensibility with Irish Catholics, and they re-created in North America feast day processions and schools "as in Europe." Still, as in Germany, some middle-class, educated German Catholics resisted the new ultramontane style. These tensions appeared in Buffalo's St. Louis Parish, where an ultramontane bishop and Alsatian parishioners went to court over issues of lay trustee governance. New York State legislators observing this conflict used the occasion to denounce "foreigners, educated in the most absolute doctrines of Papal Supremacy, who have no faith in progress, who regard the doctrine of individual independence as heresy."[87]

Politicians and Protestant ministers, especially, wondered how Boston and New York, as well as Glasgow and Geneva, would absorb large immigrant Catholic populations. In Boston, the prominent liberal minister Theodore Parker issued an illiberal warning: "This increase of foreigners is prodigious: more than half the children in your public schools are children of foreigners; there are more Catholic than Protestant children born in Boston."[88]

Parker's uneasiness was not unusual. Controversy around schools exploded in the mid-nineteenth century as legislators and church leaders debated how to integrate religion into newly founded systems of mass education. Montalembert and Tocqueville participated in the French debate. In opposition to French liberals demanding a unified, state-controlled "monopoly" from the Sorbonne down to primary schools, Montalembert and his allies formed a short-lived political party. "We are the sons of the Crusaders," he concluded in a rousing speech, "and we will not yield to the sons of Voltaire."[89] Tocqueville despaired at Montalembert's histrionics. He thought Montalembert veered toward attacking "freedom of thought itself, the very principle of lay education in France." At the same time, Toqueville conceded, Montalembert's opponents risked attacking "religion itself."[90]

In Ceylon, missionaries founded Catholic schools because government schools (run by the British) specialized in a "pretended neutrality" that permitted a definition of Catholicism as "pure idolatry."[91] In Philadelphia, Dublin, and Toronto, ultramontanists replaced bishops sympathetic to nondenominational education. In all three cities, ultramontanists demanded public support for Catholic institutions and disparaged the possibility of religiously neutral public schools in a Protestant environment. This more confrontational approach infuriated liberals committed to one-size-fits-all publicly funded systems. Toronto's Edgerton Ryerson, the founder of Canadian public education, accurately complained that "not long ago" Catholics worked with Protestants to support common schools. Now the "infusion of a new foreign element into our country" posed a new threat.

As educators grappled with this new religious diversity on both sides of the Atlantic, controversies raged about the particulars of religion in publicly funded schools. A young Boston boy, Thomas Whall, sparked an 1859 dispute by refusing to read the King James (or Protestant) version of the Ten Commandments out loud. The local schoolmaster beat Whall as a result. Urged on by a local Jesuit expelled from Switzerland in 1847, Whall's classmates then ripped the Ten Commandments out of their King James Bibles. Soon the city was in an uproar (and a legal dispute) as the Swiss Jesuit glided from criticizing an intolerant public school to founding a Catholic school. One of Boston's leading Protestant ministers, the Rev. Arthur Fuller, the late Margaret Fuller's brother, meditated on links between Whall's recalcitrance and

Margaret Fuller's fight against Pius IX in Italy. He feared that "in our own land Romanism allies itself with every false and anti-republican institution."[92]

VIII

EVEN AS IRISH and German Catholic migrants left their homelands, so, too, did the aftershocks from the 1848 revolutions extend beyond Europe. Everywhere the revolutions unleashed a debate over the nature of freedom, and everywhere liberal nationalists targeted ultramontane Catholicism. In the immediate aftermath of 1848, many ultramontane Catholics favorably compared the relative freedom they possessed in the United States with the hostility they had encountered in Europe. One Italian Jesuit expelled from Rome conceded that Catholicism would "never become the religion of the State" in the United States. But he still thought "it will be the better for being free of those oppressions which governments usually put on a Church."[93]

A few years later Catholics were less sure. The 1850s witnessed the most vigorous anti-Catholic agitation in American history. An anti-Catholic political party, the American Party, elected governors, senators, and representatives. Maryland's Henry Davis, later a US senator, divided Catholics into "those worthy of their Republican fathers" and "ultra-montanists or papists." On the Senate floor, US senators debated the credibility of a rumor that the Revolutionary War hero, Lafayette, had warned on his deathbed that "if ever the liberties [of the United States] are destroyed it will be by Catholic priests."[94]

A wave of popular speakers traveled on what became a global anti-Catholic lecture circuit, drawing large crowds and often inspiring violent attacks on Catholics and their churches. A strange man named John Orr took to dressing as the archangel Gabriel and offering harangues against Catholic influence, beginning in Scotland, where his lectures precipitated riots, extending to New York City and New England at the height of the anti-Catholic agitation of the 1850s, and ending his career in British Guiana.[95]

Somewhat more sober-minded veterans of the 1848 revolutions also circulated on the lecture circuit. An Italian ex-priest, Alessandro

Gavazzi, exiled from Italy after supporting the ill-fated Roman republic, toured England, Scotland, Ireland, Australia, the United States, and Canada to huge audiences, warning against Catholic influence. "Twenty years ago," he told his audiences, "the Papists in your country were . . . only native Americans. But, now, after so many hundred Jesuits have come to America from Europe; now, after so many thousand Roman Catholics have emigrated to this country, to be silent on the Popish system is no longer a duty, indeed it is a crime."[96] The exiled Hungarian revolutionary, Lajos Kossuth, addressed the United States Congress and in St. Louis accused the Jesuits of "warmly advocating the cause of Despotism."[97]

Anti-Catholic agitation cooled in the United States in the late 1850s as the slavery question consumed political life. Abraham Lincoln steered the Republican Party away from its most aggressive anti-Catholic rhetoric, while welcoming the support of anti-Catholic voters. He lamented that the Know-Nothing version of the US Constitution might as well read "all men are created equal, except negroes, and foreigners, and Catholics."[98]

In Mexico, by contrast, debate over Catholicism's role took center stage. As late as 1853, the Mexican statesman Lucas Alaman urged his colleagues not to denigrate Catholicism "because we believe in it and because even if we did not hold it to be divine, we consider it to be the only common bond that links all Mexicans when all the others have been broken."[99]

A new generation of Mexican liberals disagreed. They feared that clergy overly loyal to Rome could never fully commit themselves to a liberal nation-state. In 1855, they abolished clerical immunity from civil law. In 1856, they ordered ecclesiastical real estate of all types to be sold at public auction. In 1857, they rewrote the constitution and banned religious orders. Taking "religious vows" meant an "irrevocable sacrifice of individual liberty."[100] In 1861, they orchestrated the secularization of Catholic schools, hospitals, and charitable institutions.

If liberal government ministers tossing elderly nuns out onto the street and selling their convents infuriated Catholics, liberals could not countenance Catholic support for the Austrian emperor Maximillian, installed by France as Mexico's ruler for an unhappy three-year reign from 1864 to 1867. Maximillian had traveled to Rome for a blessing from Pius IX before embarking for Mexico, and one of the most ultramontane Mexican bishops, Pelagio Antonio Labastida y Dávalos, returned from exile in Rome to support Maximillian. The entire episode prompted the Mexican ambassador to the United States to ponder the "striking similarity which exists between the Church party of Mexico and the Slavery party in the United States."[101]

By this point, the church in Mexico, long the preeminent example of Reform Catholicism, had begun to take on an ultramontane hue. Bishop Clemente de Jesús Munguía, like his ultramontane counterparts in Europe, read Balmes and de Maistre, whom he lauded for "criticism of the first order." The revolutions of 1848 horrified him, as did the confiscation of church property in Mexico, especially by liberals nominally committed to property rights. Freedom of religion made sense in a country where many people practiced different faiths, but in an overwhelmingly Catholic Mexico, the promotion of Catholicism should be "one of the primary obligations of the government." He resented the mocking tone of the local governor—a member of the "liberal dictatorship"—when the governor described the bishop as just "one of many citizens."[102]

In the 1820s Reform Catholic priests such as Fr. Servando Mier had hoped to integrate state and church. In the 1860s, ultramontanists such as Munguía demanded church autonomy. When the local governor seized his seminary buildings and his private library and melted down the gold and silver in the local cathedral, Munguía left for Europe and eventually settled in Rome. There he discouraged Pius IX from negotiating with what he understood as an irremediably hostile government. He died just before Pius IX opened the first ecumenical council since the sixteenth century.

IX

THE TRIUMPH OF ULTRAMONTANISM occurred at the First Vatican Council. Over seven hundred bishops assembled in St. Peter's on December 8, 1869, a date chosen because it marked fifteen years since the definition of the dogma of the Immaculate Conception and five years since the release of the Syllabus of Errors.

To signal church independence, Pius IX decided against inviting any monarchs or heads of state, a decision that for the first time eliminated lay participation in an ecumenical council. As a French cabinet minister complained, "the church, through its supreme pastor, says to the lay world, to lay society, and to lay authorities: It is apart from you that I want to exist, to take action, to make decisions, and to develop, affirm, and to understand myself."[103]

The core issues of the council became papal primacy (or supremacy over other Catholic bishops) and whether a pope could declare himself infallible in certain circumstances. The notion of infallibility dated back to the Middle Ages, but only in the 1840s did ultramontane Catholics come to believe the doctrine indispensable. A string of books, notably one by Italian Jesuit Giovanni Perrone, made the case for papal infallibility independent of the bishops, or even absent the "consensus of the church." (Perrone highlighted Pius VI's condemnation of that perennial ultramontane fixation, the 1786 Synod of Pistoia.)[104]

The bishops at the council fell into two camps: a majority believing a strengthened papacy would allow Catholics to resist the incursions of aggressive nation-states, and a minority opposed to infallibility or at least dubious. Almost all bishops from the United States favored infallibility, as did every bishop from Latin America. Bishops from missionary regions generally supported the ultramontane majority. Catholics must counter Hindus and Buddhists, a French missionary bishop from Ceylon argued, who also believed "true religion" and "infallible authority" to be inseparable.[105] Sixty-two Irish-born bishops—representing the United States, New Zealand, South Africa, India, Canada, and Australia, as well as Ireland itself—gathered at the Irish College in Rome in honor of their patron, Cardinal Paul Cullen. "We drank," one member of this episcopal diaspora reported, "to the Pope's health and infallibility most enthusiastically."[106]

The conviction that the church needed a more conciliatory approach to the modern world drove the minority. Their leader behind the scenes, England's Lord Acton, had long recognized that "we are the flying fish who can neither swim with the Protestants nor fly in peace with the Catholics."[107] Acton's own anxieties about modern nation-states sparked his famous dictum about absolute power corrupting absolutely, but he still thought Pius IX's obstinacy tragic. He moved his family into a Roman apartment for the duration of the council and coordinated the publication of reports by his friend Ignaz von Döllinger, Germany's most prominent Catholic scholar, on conciliar debates. Döllinger had begun his academic career sympathetic to ultramontanism, but a visit to Rome with Acton in 1857—where he was forced to kneel three times before meeting the pope and then kiss his extended foot—proved disillusioning. He incurred Pius IX's wrath by asserting the value of historical scholarship as opposed to neo-Thomist philosophy. In response, Roman theologians coined the term "ordinary magisterium" to mark the importance of obeying church teachings as enunciated by the pope. "You see," Acton told Döllinger, "exactly how you are feared [in Rome], and how far they dare go against you."[108]

Perhaps the most visible episcopal leader of the minority was Croatia's Josip Strossmayer, who worked closely with Acton and Döllinger. In his native country, Strossmayer blended a nationalist and a Catholic sensibility. He disliked, for example, the Roman liturgy and schemed to allow Catholics in Montenegro to retain the old Slavonic liturgy.[109] His stress on the "divine and inviolable rights of bishops" proved unwelcome to the ultramontanes, some of whom also shouted down his conciliatory words about Protestants. After one such incident a bishop from the United States told Lord Acton that "there is certainly one assembly in the world rougher than the American Congress."[110]

Among the most influential members of the pro-infallibility majority were the Jesuits at *Civiltà Cattolica*. The "restoration of the principle of authority" was for them the issue.[111] "The very concept of the liberal Catholic," wrote the editors, is "an entirely repugnant combination."[112] Louis Veuillot, still a favorite of Pius IX, also set up house in Rome, eager to battle infallibility's opponents. Montalembert had long bemoaned Veuillot's "daily denunciations of every [kind] of rational freedom, not only in France but throughout Europe and America."[113]

In 1863, Montalembert had given two major addresses at Malines, in Belgium, on the importance of "A Free Church in a Free State" and emphasized his desire to see "democracy become liberal and liberty once again become Christian." He denounced "religious absolutism." The addresses provoked a stern, if private, letter of reprimand from the Vatican.[114]

Six years later, gravely ill, Montalembert knew he did not enjoy papal favor. His allies in France and Belgium noted that Louis Veuillot's version of ultramontanism "rejected as suspect" Catholics once thought above reproach, including Montalembert and Tocqueville.[115] Montalembert publicly regretted Pius IX's condemnation of "all modern liberties" and endorsement of "theocratic autocracy."[116] Once "acclaimed by all the liberals," the pope now authored "doctrines outrageous to common sense."[117]

An aggrieved Pius IX reciprocated, describing Montalembert as a "victim of his pride." Montalembert died in March 1870. On the night before Montalembert's memorial Mass at the Roman church of Ara Coeli, Pius IX canceled the service. A gleeful Veuillot stood outside the church at the scheduled time to inform bewildered attendees that they must avoid any hint of an anti-papal "demonstration." Pius IX permitted, and attended, a much smaller service in Montalembert's honor a few days later. Not one of the bishops then deliberating the future of the church joined him.[118]

In the last weeks of debate, conducted in the stifling heat of a Roman summer, another group of bishops pleaded with the pope for a delay. An angry Pius IX retorted, "I, I am tradition; I am the Church."[119] Some bishops left Rome before the vote to avoid defying the pope, and the final definition of infallibility was more limited than its most fervent advocates desired. Still, *Pastor Aeternus*, the document approved by the council, declared that "historical facts" could never disprove a "divinely revealed truth."[120]

The British prime minister, William Gladstone, a friend of Acton and Döllinger, expressed his dismay with the council's outcome. Leading English Catholics in the eighteenth century had rejected papal infallibility, Gladstone correctly noted, but now English bishops and the pope proclaimed it as dogma. He would soon begin a public relations campaign against a "vast conspiracy" originating in the Vatican. No good Catholic, in Gladstone's view, could be a good citizen, and the loyalty of Irish Catholics to Britain and Polish-speaking Catholics to Germany was an open question. Catholics seemed "estranged" from national life.[121]

Roman officials hounded bishops who had not supported the definition of infallibility into formally declaring their submission. One opponent, St. Louis's archbishop, Peter Kenrick, finally reconciled himself "intellectually to submission by applying Father Newman's theory of development."[122] But English convert and theologian John Henry Newman had opposed papal infallibility. He feared what the future might bring. "We have come to a climax of tyranny," he wrote privately. "It is not good for a Pope to live 20 years . . . [he] has no one to contradict him."[123]

The council ended not because its work was concluded but because Italian armies breached Roman city walls. Pius IX condemned this "sacrilegious" assault but could do nothing other than retreat to St. Peter's as the government of the Papal States collapsed. Centuries of papal rule over much of central Italy came to an end. He suspended the council and declared himself a "prisoner" of the new Italian state.[124]

The pope detested his new isolation, but he correctly predicted that Rome would remain "the capital of Catholicism worldwide."[125] Or as one Jesuit in the United States wrote to his superior in Rome, "The afflictions of the Holy Father have made ultramontanes of all of us here."[126]

PART II

The Milieu and
Its Discontents

1870–1962

FIVE

Milieu

Why Nationalists Attacked Catholics
and How Catholics Responded

I

IN 1880, when workers finally completed the great Gothic Catholic cathedral of Cologne, begun in the thirteenth century and restarted in the 1840s, the Protestant Prussian emperor, Wilhelm I, attended a dedication ceremony marking the occasion. The city's Catholic archbishop did not. He was in exile, administering the enormous Cologne archdiocese from the Netherlands.

Nationalism, in Germany and around the world, had become the stuff of ultramontane nightmares. After Otto von Bismarck and the Prussian army crushed the French in the Franco-Prussian War of 1870, he united multiple principalities into a new German nation-state. Most German Catholics had supported the war, even if the opponent was Catholic France. (The largest bell in the Cologne cathedral was cast from cannons seized from the French.) "We Catholics," explained Mainz bishop Wilhelm von Ketteler, "want to be second to none in terms of love of the Fatherland."[1]

Despite this support, Bismarck pivoted after the armistice and began a Kulturkampf, or culture war, against a Catholicism he deemed the new nation's most serious threat. Speaking in the Reichstag, Bismarck denounced the "international character" of Catholicism as obstructing "the development of Germany for the sake of foreign nations."[2]

Between 1871 and 1875, Bismarck's government expelled from the country almost all members of men's religious orders and some members of women's orders, limited enrollment in Catholic schools, required priests to possess German citizenship and pass exams in German culture, and gave the state the right to veto the appointment of parish priests if they proved politically troublesome. State officials imprisoned bishops who resisted these measures, forced other bishops into exile, and purged many Catholics from civil service positions.

In response, Bishop von Ketteler regretted that German liberals denounced anyone who "does not accept their interpretation of culture and reason [as] a child of darkness, an ultramontane on whom the truly cultured person looks down with disdain and arrogant contempt." He chided liberals willing to "elevate the state to the dignity of the immanent God." Equally troubling was liberal subservience to the "money power."[3]

Ketteler knew that these liberal-Catholic tensions were not unique to Germany. As far away as China, Catholics compared attacks on the church with ongoing persecution in Germany and described both Chinese and Prussian officials as the "forces of Satan."[4] In next-door Switzerland, a liberal government in Geneva expelled an ultramontane bishop and insisted that congregations elect parish priests sworn in by state officials.[5] In Mexico, liberals decided to expel all "foreign-born" Jesuits.[6] In Argentina, anticlericals burned a Jesuit college to the ground.[7] When a young Woodrow Wilson enrolled in a government course at Princeton University in 1878, he took careful notes on the problem of papal authority. The subject was vital, his instructor explained, "not only in European but also in American politics." (Wilson also penned an admiring portrait of Bismarck, singling out his willingness to check an aggressive Catholicism.)[8]

Some of the most venomous disputes between Catholics and nationalists occurred in Italy. Pius IX remained within the walls of St. Peter's, never venturing one mile across Rome to the new Italian Parliament and never welcoming an Italian head of state. He watched with fury as Italian state officials confiscated monasteries, expelled Jesuits, and encouraged anticlerical rallies. A less than exhaustive list of the terms of endearment Pius IX used to describe these state officials included: wolves, liars, satellites of Satan in human flesh, and monsters of hell.[9]

Fueling these conflicts on the liberal side was one of the great organizing narratives of the nineteenth century: that Catholicism opposed modernity, while Protestantism and liberalism furthered it. The authors of this narrative claimed that Catholicism literally impoverished nations unlucky enough to wallow under its dominion. The primary source was the Belgian economist Émile de Laveleye's *Protestantism and Catholicism, in their Bearing upon the Liberty and Prosperity of Nations.* (Britain's prime minister William Gladstone provided an introduction to the English translation.) Using the "scientific impartiality of the physiologist and naturalist," de Laveleye concluded that Protestant churches remained loyal to the nation-state, while Catholic priests formed a "caste, having a special interest differing from that of the nation." A Catholicism fascinated by miracles and pilgrimages lay "outside the atmosphere of modern thought."[10] The Inquisition (much exaggerated in this nineteenth-century retelling) and the persecution of Galileo (much simplified) told knowledgeable observers exactly what they needed to know about the relationship between a "clericalist" Catholicism and progressive ideas.[11]

The German scholar Max Weber's celebrated 1903 claim of an intimate relationship between Protestantism and capitalism should be understood as a variant of this literature. Weber cited de Laveleye's arguments about Catholicism's backwardness, and his work, too, responded in part to a polarization between liberals and Catholics in his native Germany. Like many German liberals, Weber regretted the continued influence of Catholicism on German peasants and workers. He argued that constitutive features of modernity, not only capitalism but modern science and free political institutions, depended on the emergence of a Calvinist asceticism.[12]

As in the 1850s, but with greater vehemence, the most potent disagreements involved schools, the institution liberals understood as the training ground for citizens and Catholics understood as the training ground for believers. In France, Prime Minister Jules Ferry and other republicans began a concerted effort to limit Catholic influence. They prohibited nuns from serving on the boards of the Catholic hospitals they had founded, required priests to register for military service, and, most of all, tried to secularize public education entirely, banning Jesuits from running secondary schools and limiting the ability of nuns to teach young girls.

The prominent French philosopher Charles Renouvier exaggerated, but only slightly, when he claimed that there are "two Frances in France, that of the clericals and that of the liberals."[13] The influence of French liberals such as Renouvier extended into Latin America, and Argentine and Colombian liberals, in particular, fought in the 1870s and 1880s to eliminate subsidies for Catholic schools and to secularize publicly funded education.[14]

In the United States, the normally taciturn President Ulysses S. Grant, an anti-Catholic Know-Nothing supporter in the 1850s, warned in 1875 that the country risked division, not between North and South but between "patriotism and intelligence on one side, and superstition, ambition, and ignorance on the other." He urged taxation of "vast amounts of untaxed church property," a transparently anti-Catholic plea, since only Catholics owned large numbers of schools, hospitals, and orphanages. The US Congress debated (and rejected) an amendment to the Constitution banning governmental aid to religious schools, but many states placed such amendments into state constitutions. Another Republican (and future president), James Garfield, worried about a Catholic assault on "modern civilization" as well as the "papal assault on secular schools in France and Germany."[15]

A second contentious issue was whether church officials would condone Catholic membership in so-called "secret societies." The most prominent of these were the Freemasons, whose members included Jules Ferry in France and numerous other republican leaders. Some Freemasons, such as Ferry, were resolutely anti-Catholic. Other Freemasons, as in much of South America, were themselves Catholic and opposed to ultramontanism and Roman authority, not Catholicism generally.

The most revealing dispute of this type occurred in Brazil. Church affairs slotted into the imperial bureaucracy in Brazil as part of the Ministry of Justice and, later, the Ministry of Interior. Pedro II, Brazil's emperor from 1831 to 1889, appointed bishops. Disgruntled priests sardonically referred to state officials involved in the process with the term "Your eminence," as if addressing a cardinal.[16]

Pedro II resented that Brazil's bishops had begun to assert their independence in the 1870s. All of the Brazilian bishops, for example, supported papal infallibility, which Pedro II opposed. One bishop in particular, Dom Vital of Olinda, denounced the presence of Freemasons in lay brotherhoods affiliated with Catholic parishes. He prohibited Freemasons from attending Mass and ordered them to choose between their affiliation with the Freemasons and their Catholicism. An infuriated Pedro II demanded that Vital be jailed, and so he was, at the exact moment that Bismarck was imprisoning bishops in Germany.

A third controversial issue was civil marriage, which had roiled Prussia and other German states in the 1830s and 1840s and Mexico in the 1850s. For liberals, civil marriage meant a necessary secularization of a key social institution. For ultramontane Catholics, civil marriage suggested yet another unwelcome step toward individualism by making an indissoluble sacrament authorized by the church into a provisional contract ratified by the state. Here again, from the Catholic point of view, was an incursion into the proper domain of the church.

The debate over the nature of marriage resumed in Vienna in the late 1860s, where the national assembly passed laws authorizing civil marriage. With characteristic tact, Pius IX declared the laws "null and forever invalid." They were neither, but they were controversial. The most uncompromising Austrian bishop, Franz Joseph Rudigier, encouraged Catholics to practice civil disobedience and denounced the civil marriage laws as aimed at "alienating believers from Christian truth." Convicted of disturbing the peace (although Emperor Franz Joseph hastily commuted his prison sentence), the unrepentant Rudigier delighted in receiving letters of support from admirers across Europe. One German bishop noted that the "whole world acknowledges you for what Austria has done to you."[17]

Marriage laws also deepened the liberal nationalist–Catholic divide in South America. In Brazil and Argentina, secular leaders saw civil marriage as necessary to encourage Protestant (usually German) immigrants whose marriages under existing law had no standing. In both countries, liberals began to draw sharper lines between religious and civil ceremonies. Marriage "has to do with a contract," one Brazilian reformer explained, "and when one is dealing with a contract, the church has nothing to do with it."[18]

II

POPE LEO XIII sold the last vessel of the decrepit papal navy, named, of course, the *Immaculate Conception* and berthed at the French port of Toulon, because the Papal States no longer existed and the papacy possessed no independent port. His election, after Pius IX's death in 1878, following the longest papal reign in modern history, marked a partial reset. He disparaged liberalism in the manner of his predecessor, and he defined religious freedom as practiced in the United States, for example, as a "hypothesis" less attractive than the "thesis" of state endorsement and support of Catholicism. He identified with fellow monarchs, and after Russian radicals assassinated Tsar Alexander II in 1881, he sent a message to the tsar's son and successor, Alexander III, pledging Christian unity. When Italian Freemasons and anticlericals erected a statue of Giordano Bruno in the Campo di Fiori, a short walk from St. Peter's, emphasizing that Bruno had been burned at the stake by church officials in 1600 for heretical views, Leo XIII encouraged bishops around the world to join him in condemning the provocation.[19]

Compared with Pius IX, though, Leo XIII articulated a forward-looking program. He had trained as a diplomat, in contrast to his undiplomatic predecessor, and he revitalized the papal diplomatic corps, sending the first ambassadors, or nuncios, invariably Italian priests trained in Rome, to Argentina, Nicaragua, Guatemala, Canada, and the United States.[20] He inaugurated a modern press office and gave interviews to acquiescent journalists.

Part of Leo XIII's agenda was intellectual. He unexpectedly made England's John Henry Newman, much abused by ultramontanists, a cardinal. (Newman accepted the honor with gratitude: "All the stories which have gone about of my being a half Catholic, a liberal Catholic, under a cloud, not to be trusted, are now at an end.")[21] He opened the Vatican archives to historians. He encouraged archaeological investigations in Rome, founded the first Vatican observatory, and endorsed scholarly investigation of the Bible through the new Pontifical Biblical Commission. As a young bishop in Perugia, Leo XIII had required his seminarians to study Dante, and as pope he promoted Dante as a unifying Catholic figure of the Middle Ages.[22]

More than any previous pope, Leo XIII also endorsed a philosophical program, neo-Thomism, named after Thomas Aquinas, yet another Catholic medieval figure. In contrast to contemporary liberals, neo-Thomists valued community over individual rights and justice or social order over free expression and religious freedom. An early neo-Thomist, Italian Jesuit Luigi Taparelli, was perhaps the first writer in the modern era to use the term "social justice."[23] "The true liberty of every human society," Pope Leo XIII announced in an 1888 encyclical that summarized neo-Thomist thinking, "does not consist in every one doing what he pleases." Genuine liberty "supposes the necessity of obedience to some supreme and eternal law."[24]

Leo XIII turned to Italian Jesuits affiliated with *Civiltà Cattolica* and the German Jesuit Joseph Kleutgen and commanded them to draft an encyclical, *Aeterni Patris*, requesting Catholic bishops and priests to study the "Angelic Doctor [Thomas Aquinas]."[25] More practically, the pope made cardinals out of staunch neo-Thomists and placed them in curial positions. One American seminarian studying in Rome told Baltimore's archbishop in 1881, "As your Grace is aware, scholasticism's star is now in the ascendant throughout the eternal city. The majority of professors not bred up as Thomists have been forced to vacate their chairs in favor of the Neapolitan schools of philosophy and theology."[26] Neo-Thomist scholars began journals in Paris, Louvain, and Madrid and founded a Thomistic Academy in Rome. Dominican priests began editing and publishing a new edition (in Latin) of Aquinas's writings.

This neo-Thomist movement would become the world's most global philosophical enterprise. Leo XIII nostalgically invoked a medieval Europe where scholars in Paris, Salamanca, Alcalá, Douay, Toulouse, Louvain, Padua, Bologna, Naples, and Coimbra worked on the same texts with the same methods. He could not replicate this scholarly universe, but already by 1890 less than one-third of the students at one important Thomistic center, the Gregorian University in Rome, were Italian, with the others from almost every European, North American, and South American country.[27]

Neo-Thomists did not see their philosophical or natural law arguments as entirely dependent on faith but instead accessible to all men and women. As a practical matter, though, despite a core of prominent non-Catholic admirers, neo-Thomism had only slight influence on the mainstream philosophical world even as it gained enormous influence within the church. The Catholic presence in the world of postsecondary education was similarly modest, with little progress made since the destruction of Catholic universities during the Napeolonic era. One partial exception was the United States, where the absence of state regulations allowed the founding of dozens of small Catholic colleges, with the Jesuits alone administering twenty-five by 1900. More typical was the situation in Dublin, where the Catholic university enrolled exactly 106 students in its first four years. Bishops ignored the project and (the few) affluent Catholic parents demonstrated their skepticism by sending their sons elsewhere.[28]

Like many secular and Protestant counterparts, Catholic institutions typically offered a curriculum with classical languages at its core, but even more mandatory Latin. The goal was to form future clergy and lay leaders. As Germany's Ketteler explained, "I would be a betrayer of the Church if I agreed for young candidates for the priesthood to study at the unbelieving universities."[29] One prospectus for a (never realized) Catholic university in Bilbao promised a place "where sciences will be learnt with orthodox criteria and which young men will leave fully armed against all modern errors."[30]

Leo XIII hoped to lessen Catholic isolation from the world of scholarly research. He encouraged Belgian Catholics at Louvain to develop a new research emphasis—including an institute on Thomistic philosophy. Local clergy launched a handful of pontifical research universities with direct ties to the papacy, including the Catholic University in Santiago (1888), the Catholic University of America in Washington, DC (1889), the Catholic University of Tokyo (1914), the Catholic University of Lublin (1918), and the Catholic University of the Sacred Heart in Milan (1921).

III

THE TERM "MILIEU" refers to the infrastructure built in the late nineteenth and twentieth centuries and in no other era would the conviction that Catholics needed their own institutions be so widespread, in no other era the organizational accomplishments more significant. Viewing the nineteenth century in retrospect, one prominent English political theorist writing in 1907 tallied "the Catholic revival and the growth of nationalism" as the century's most important developments.[31]

The bonds of the Catholic subculture were strongest in countries such as Germany, where they were forged in opposition to Prussian authorities. In the region of Silesia, populated by both German-speaking and Polish-speaking Catholics, Bismarck's officials charged fully one-quarter of the clergy with violations of regulations during the Kulturkampf and limited the ability of bishops to build new churches or fill vacant pastoral positions. The persecution was fierce—Pius IX encouraged German Catholics with a letter expressing his admiration for their endurance—but the ensuing solidarity among Catholics was memorable.[32] By 1900, some 90 percent of Catholics in the region attended Mass and confession during the Easter season, only 2 to 3 percent of births were outside of marriage, and virtually all Catholics married within the church. "It was pure joy to be a priest," recalled one clergyman a generation later, "where the people stood unified against the enemy like an unconquerable phalanx."[33]

Even in areas with less overt hostility, the Catholic instinct to join and build organizations proceeded apace. In Sacred Heart Parish in Edinburgh in 1883, a daunting list of parish organizations included the St. Vincent de Paul Society, Sacred Heart Society, Living Rosary, Bona Mors, Children of Mary, St. Aloysius Guild Sodality of Blessed Virgin Mary, Christian Mothers, League of the Sacred Heart, Guild of the Sacred Heart, Apostleship of Prayer, and League of Prayer.[34] Catholics (and even non-Catholics) in North America advertised homes for purchase or apartments for rent by a parish name—Holy Cross, Sacred Heart, St. Matthew's—instead of by residential district.[35]

Catholic institutions often absorbed functions—caring for indigent children, arranging adoptions, providing health care—neglected by nascent state bureaucracies, creating a parallel social welfare system. Protestants and Jews had some of the same ambitions and institutions, but Catholics took the lead, benefiting from the essentially unpaid labor of women religious, especially, but also of priests and brothers. In some countries, notably Ireland and Australia, women religious used state funds to run workhouses for women, often single mothers struggling with abandonment or poverty. Highly controversial in retrospect, these institutions at the time seemed a logical form of cooperation between a church eager to expand its influence and state authorities, including police officers who recommended clients and legislators who nominally oversaw such institutions.

At times, Catholics encountered a cooperative spirit, such as when nuns founded the first hospitals in small towns on the American and Australian frontiers. In Ireland, the British authorities conceded that state schools (except at the university level) would be publicly funded with effective Catholic control.[36] In Medellín, Colombia, Catholic groups struck an agreement with the city to try to eliminate begging by feeding and clothing paupers.[37]

In other settings the Catholic social welfare state was contested. An Italian Jesuit stationed in Italy informed a colleague of his fears:

> The Republican party [in Italy] wishes centralized government which tends to absorb all in the God-State; power, wealth, science, religion. Such is the tendency of the party which triumphed . . . in Switzerland, of Bismark [sic] in Germany. This is the purpose seen in Italy: Despotism presents itself under the mask of liberty.[38]

Orphanages became a flash point. By 1875, Protestant agencies in New York City, officially designated as "nonsectarian," had shipped an estimated forty thousand children given up for adoption, most of them Catholic, to non-Catholic homes outside the city. The foremost expert of the era warned of the "chilling formalism of the ignorant Roman Catholic." In response, New York Catholic nuns built an orphanage network capable of housing twenty thousand children annually and arranged for public funds from supporters in the city's Tammany Hall political machine.[39] An identical debate played out in Germany, where public authorities often neglected formal requirements to "take the ward's [religious] confession into account." Catholics argued that the religious training of a child was "no less important than good health care" and built their own institutions.[40] So, too, in Australia, where a Tasmanian bishop insisted that Catholic orphans not be compelled to rely on the "cold charity of strangers."[41]

IV

BUILDERS OF THE Catholic milieu confronted (and frequently overcame) two challenges. The first was urbanization. Most Catholics, like most people, lived in villages and on farms at the turn of the twentieth century, often in overwhelmingly Catholic settings. Ninety-nine percent of residents in the Slovenian region of Ljubljana, for example, registered as Catholic in 1905.[42] In Belgium, the number was 95 percent in 1914; in Argentina, 92 percent in 1910.[43]

These Catholic worlds were less stable than these census data suggest. Everywhere cities exploded in size in the late nineteenth century, and everywhere Catholic leaders accustomed to the identification of a parish church with a tightly defined geographical territory struggled to provide pastoral services. In Vienna, Warsaw and Kraków, some parishes counted one hundred thousand nominal members.[44] The population of Buenos Aires quadrupled between 1885 and 1914; the number of parishes almost doubled, too, but this still left almost forty-eight thousand members in a typical parish.[45]

In Barcelona, Madrid, and Spain's largest industrial cities, priests conducting surveys judged only 5 percent of the population as practicing. Men laboring in factories, in particular, often embraced a popular anticlericalism. Yet in smaller cities populated by farmers and shopkeepers, church attendance remained a family affair with well over 50 percent of men and women attending Mass each week. German Catholics proved more faithful in church attendance than German Protestants, and scholars, especially anxious Protestant scholars, charted high Catholic rates of adherence in many cities. In a more mobile world, the mechanisms for belonging provided by Catholic institutions proved compelling.[47]

The second and related challenge was migration across national borders. The initial German and Irish Catholic migrations of the 1840s and 1850s carried ultramontanism around the world, and both Germans and Irish continued to migrate in significant numbers up until World War I. A more diverse set of migrants left Europe in the late nineteenth century and a more diverse set of countries received them. The United States received twenty-nine million migrants between 1870 and 1914, and Canada, Argentina, and Brazil all received three or four million migrants.[48]

The most important Catholic migrations came from Polish-speaking lands, Spain, and Italy. Poland became an independent nation only in 1918, and until then Polish speakers resided in the Austro-Hungarian, German, and Russian empires. Most Poles emigrated within Europe, often to Germany and industrial regions such as the Ruhr. An additional several million Polish-speaking Catholics left Europe, primarily for North America. They, too, clustered in industrial regions, around both the Canadian and American sides of the Great Lakes. Some Polish migrants, like German Catholics, fled their homeland because of tensions caused by Bismarck's Kulturkampf.

Even more than Ireland, Poland had absorbed the Catholic revival before the migration began, and Poles quickly built some of the largest and most successful parishes and Catholic organizations in Germany and the United States. Over five hundred Polish Catholic parishes existed in the United States in 1900. Pastors of these parishes built Catholic schools and recruited Polish-speaking Catholic nuns, such as the Felicians and the Sisters of the Holy Family, to staff them. Polish Catholic children were more likely than Catholics of any other ethnic group to be enrolled in Catholic schools.[49]

The relationship of these Polish Catholic parishes, schools, and fraternal organizations—termed "Polonia" as a collective—with Irish or German Catholic leaders was fraught. In both Germany and the

United States, Polish Catholic pastors and lay trustees fought for local control of pastoral appointments and church finances, with limited success.[50]

The Spanish and Italian migrations possessed a different dynamic. Almost five million Spaniards migrated to Argentina, Cuba, and other countries in Latin America in the late nineteenth century. Unlike the Irish and German Catholic migrations of the mid-nineteenth century, but very much like the simultaneous Italian migration, Spanish migrants were virtually all baptized Catholics but with varying levels of identification with the church. Still, those Spanish Catholic priests and nuns who migrated to South America tended to come from the most devout regions of Spain, usually the north, and strengthened among Spanish-speaking Catholics the rituals of the Catholic revival. Even cities as far north as San Francisco witnessed Mexican and Spanish Catholics uniting to form a parish because Catholicism is "the soul of Spanish honor."[51]

The Italian migration was the most significant. Over sixteen million Italians left the newly unified country between 1870 and 1921. More dispersed than the Spanish migrants, slightly less than half of the Italians ventured elsewhere in Europe, while a majority crossed the Atlantic, primarily to the United States and Brazil but also to Canada and Argentina.[52] Irish and German priests and bishops in the United States frequently described Italian Catholics as negligent because so many Italian men skipped Sunday Mass, even if they resolutely attended family baptisms or weddings. Clerical trade journals published articles on "the peculiar kind of spiritual condition" that favored street processions and festivals over the building of parochial grade schools.[53]

The migration of first German and then Italian and Spanish Catholics to Latin America spurred that region's version of the ultramontane revival. As the country with the largest European migration (as a proportion of population), Argentina's Catholicism became the most oriented toward Europe, but continental influences were everywhere. In Brazil, for example, migrants clustered in southern coastal cities, where they quickly built networks of Catholic schools and cooperatives. After the collapse of the Brazilian Empire and the birth of the republic in 1889, the floodgates opened. Between 1880 and 1930, men's religious orders from across Europe—twelve from Italy, ten from France, four each from Holland and Germany, and three from Spain—established beachheads and often seminaries in Brazil. Women religious established houses for another ninety-six women's religious orders, primarily from France and Italy.[54] In Peru, Spanish Franciscan priests, clutching their devotional books and copies of *Civiltà Cattolica*, led popular missions in and around the city of Arequipa, where the density of Catholic organizations and buildings prompted the nickname "little Rome."[55]

Often, priests and nuns forced out of Germany or Italy by state authorities made their way to South America. In the region surrounding Medellín, over two hundred Catholic hospitals and charitable associations were founded between 1870 and 1920, most by women religious originally from France, Italy, or Spain.[56] In Argentina, a German Redemptorist priest founded popular workers' associations on the German model with night courses, access to lectures and newspapers, and welfare services. A generation later, he counted almost thirty thousand members and thirty-eight independently owned meeting places.[57]

Over time, Latin American Catholic piety—at least in urban areas—became more like the piety found in Europe and North America, with its miracles, novenas, and mission campaigns. Such devotions unsettled native-born clergy accustomed to both political and religious leadership. One disgruntled native Brazilian clergyman commented that "Our Lord does not leave France to work miracles in Brazil."[58]

In 1899, the first Latin American plenary council met in Rome with a focus on establishing "shared guidelines for responding to liberal governments, freemasonry and regalism [government control of the church]." Another agenda item was nurturing a more disciplined and Roman clergy. Bishops were encouraged to increase their support of the Colegio Pio Latino Americano, also in Rome, where seminarians could study "in the capital of the Christian world and under the watchful eye of the Roman pontiffs." Clerical graduates of the Colegio started to fill influential positions in Mexico, Chile, and Bolivia, staffing local seminaries and organizing curricula along Roman models.[59]

The Catholic neo-Gothic also arrived in South America, fifty years after replacing classical facades as the dominant architectural form in

Europe and North America. A French architect modeled the cathedral at La Plata in Argentina on the cathedrals of Amiens and Cologne.[60] A more robust Catholic press developed in the region, too, even in countries such as Mexico, which saw little migration. Drawing in part on the model of French Catholic journals such as *Univers*, Mexican Catholics founded newspapers and journals, notably *La Voz de México*, to better articulate "the excesses and disasters which accompany liberalism."[61]

Another consequence of these late-nineteenth-century migrations was enhanced ethnic diversity within receiving countries, small and large. In the South American nation of Suriname in the 1890s, for example, the local bishop navigated among English, Dutch, Portuguese, and Chinese Catholics.[62] In the United States, the country with the most ethnically diverse Catholic population, Detroit Catholics on any given Sunday could listen to a homily in twenty-two languages.[63] This multilingual cacophony prompted an international group of Catholics, led by a Catholic member of the Reichstag, Peter Paul Cahensly, and Italian bishop John Baptist Scalabrini, to urge "national" parishes for particular linguistic groups. Cahensly spent eighty days in the United States lobbying for better treatment of German Catholic migrants, as well as stimulating "some interest also for the Italians."[64]

With the personal encouragement of Leo XIII, himself of course an Italian, Scalabrini urged priests and bishops in Brazil and the United States to welcome Italian migrants and protect them from Protestant evangelists, even as he pleaded with Italian priests and nuns to follow their compatriots. He detailed heartrending scenes of anxious migrants crammed into boats in Genoa and Naples and fielded requests from Italian Catholics in remote areas of Brazil to send a sympathetic priest, "otherwise our children will lose the faith."[65]

Scalabrini also promoted the work of Mother Frances Cabrini and her newly founded women's religious order, the Missionary Sisters of the Sacred Heart of Jesus. Leo XIII had encouraged Cabrini to focus on Italian Catholic migrants (as opposed to the conversion of the Chinese), and Cabrini established foundations not only in the United States, England, and France, but also in Nicaragua, Brazil, Panama, the Philippines, and Argentina. When she first landed in New York

City, she found the city's religious diversity—"so many Protestants, so many Hebrews, so many sectarians"—bewildering. She nonetheless set to work founding schools and orphanages. Cabrini's brother migrated to Buenos Aires, and she established a school there in part to educate his children.[66]

At issue on both sides of the Atlantic was the relationship of churches to the nation-state. More nationalist Catholics, such as Archbishop John Ireland in the United States, distorted the modest requests of Cahensly, Scalabrini, and others for linguistic parishes into an "unpardonable" conspiracy to "meddle . . . in the Catholic affairs of America."[67] The nationalist vison articulated by Ireland and others would become widespread after World War I, but the dominant impulse in the late nineteenth century moved in the opposite direction. Mother Cabrini eventually became an American citizen, but her travels and identification with the church made her Catholicism more salient than any particular national identity. The ethnically homogenous nation-state did not seem an inevitability, and the Italian Jesuit Matteo Liberatore defended multicultural republics such as Switzerland and multicultural empires such as Austria-Hungary. The "unity of a state with a nation can be a good thing or a bad thing," he explained, "depending on the circumstances."[68]

Polish Catholics living adjacent to German Catholics in Silesia, French Catholics in English-speaking Manitoba, Catalan speakers in Spain, Flemish Catholics in Belgium, and German Catholics scattered across the prairies of the American Midwest and Canada all kept their distance from ambitious nationalist leaders. These ultramontane Catholics frequently took the lead in arguing for bilingual education, yet another marker of their detachment from nationalist programs. One bishop founded a women's religious order to staff French-language parochial schools in English-speaking Manitoba, since "if our people lose their language" they might lose interest "in all the holy causes."[69] In Silesia, German Catholics supported the right of Polish Catholic coal miners to sing religious hymns in Polish as they descended into the mines.[70]

V

THE UPHEAVAL OF the 1880s and 1890s, including a sequence of mass migrations, populist farmer movements, depressions, and labor protests, reached into every corner of the industrializing world and cast doubt on conventional solutions to economic inequality. The array of reforms marking the era, from municipal ownership of streetcars to child labor laws to public housing to agricultural cooperatives, stemmed from a desire to shield vulnerable families and communities from the unpredictability of global markets.

When it came to these economic dangers, liberals and Catholics discovered common ground. An international group of Catholics met several times in Switzerland and forwarded its reports—one arguing that capitalism had "favored the accumulation of riches in the hands of a few and has brought about the impoverishment of the masses"—to Rome at the request of Leo XIII. Matteo Liberatore published a series of articles critical of Adam Smith and laissez-faire economics, and an English bishop, Edward Bagshawe, denounced the "overwhelming power of the rich man" in his *Mercy and Justice to the Poor: The True Political Economy.*[71]

Cumulatively, this work inspired Leo XIII's 1891 encyclical, *Rerum Novarum*, which became the founding document of modern Catholic social thought. The term "democracy" is absent from the text. And yet the tone of *Rerum Novarum*—issued by a papacy understood by liberals as a citadel of reaction—was remarkable. Leo XIII began with an attack on the "misery and wretchedness pressing so unjustly on the majority of the working class." He denounced socialism and defended private property but also asserted that a "workman's wages [should] be sufficient to enable him comfortably to support himself, his wife, and his children."[72]

The most important Catholic social theorist of the early twentieth century, German Jesuit Heinrich Pesch, saw *Rerum Novarum* as the roadmap for a third way between unrestrained capitalism and socialism. Pesch had studied with economists at the University of Berlin, then the center of secular efforts to develop more socially minded alternatives to laissez-faire. (Because of the expulsion of the Jesuits from Germany during the Kulturkampf, he also spent time in exile near Liverpool and was horrified by the conditions endured by English industrial workers.) "There is no such thing," Pesch declared in the opening chapter of his major work, "as absolute self-sufficiency." He dismissed as "plutocratic" the "individualistic, free enterprise economic structure" recommended in standard textbooks.[73]

Pesch was not alone. In Brazil, the country's most important reform-minded priest declared that Catholics must "subject the despotism of capital to the laws of equity; demand of capital not only charity but the justice which is the right of the worker."[74] In Mexico, Catholics formed night schools, recreation centers, and mutual aid societies; property-owning conservatives termed them "white socialists."[75]

The career of Catholic University professor Fr. John A. Ryan in the United States reflected this Catholic vision. Ryan worked from a standard neo-Thomist template, and even his studies of wages and consumption contained excursions into lesser known texts by Thomas Aquinas. He admired the work of Pesch as "the most comprehensive treatise ever put forth in the name of political economy" and a success-ful effort to define "solidarity" as a Catholic principle more compelling than "individualism and Socialism."[76]

Ryan's recommendations—that employers provide a "living wage" capable of supporting a male breadwinner and his family and that the state regulate the working hours of women and children—placed him on the moderate left wing of American social reform.[77] The terms "liv-ing wage" and "family wage" circulated around the Catholic world, from Berlin to Mexico City to Sydney. In Australia, leading Catholics denounced "kings of business and finance" and endorsed the Labour Party for its focus on workers and a "living wage."[78]

Like so many early-twentieth-century Catholic reformers, Ryan viewed economics and theology as inseparable. I am "pursuing a post-graduate course in moral theology," he told a friend, "together with courses in economics." In a combination of academic duties unlikely today, Ryan taught both moral theology and economics at Catholic University. He argued that "economic inquiry is . . . intended to serve solely as a basis for ethical conclusions."[79]

VI

JOHN RYAN never exhibited anti-Semitism, and he became an admired ally of Jewish reformers. But repeated Catholic attacks on "capitalism" and "liberalism" opened a door for anti-Semitism in a reform key. Editors for *Civiltà Cattolica*, even as they criticized the assumptions behind laissez-faire economics and dismissed the claims of Adam Smith, published essays describing Jews as a threatening "nation within a nation."[80]

The most virulent Catholic anti-Semitism developed in central Europe. Kraków's Stanisław Stojałowski, chastised by his own bishop for ferocious attacks on wealthy Polish elites, also urged Catholics to beware of Jewish influence on public life.[81] The Czech priest Rudolph Vrba proposed measures to exclude Jews from public institutions, and the Polish Jesuit Marian Morawski argued for "reducing" their influence.[82] In Vienna, the Christian Social Party, founded by Karl Lueger, depended on support within the Catholic milieu, and its leaders, including Lueger, whose own religious convictions were unclear, drew on the ideas of prominent Catholic intellectuals. As mayor from 1890 to 1907, Lueger combined social reforms such as municipal ownership of streetcars with fierce, often anti-Semitic attacks on "large capitalism."[83]

The most notorious example of Catholic anti-Semitism occurred in France in the 1890s, where Catholics played a significant role in the campaign falsely alleging that Alfred Dreyfus, a Jewish military officer, had committed treason. Respected figures, such as the industrialist Albert de Mun, a key advocate of *Rerum Novarum* in France and earlier in his career the founder of a network of Catholic worker societies aimed at reproducing the solidarity of medieval guilds, saw what is "true and just in Anti-Semitism [as] directly linked to the very principle of the struggle against the spirit of the [French] Revolution."[84] News of the Dreyfus affair, in turn, sparked riots against Jews led by Catholics in Hapsburg-controlled Galicia and demands that Catholics boycott Jewish-owned stores. "We have plenty of Catholic stores in nearly every village," wrote one editor after regretting anti-Semitic violence, "but despite that we run to the Jew."[85] The same focus on community that enabled Catholics to pinpoint the disruptive impacts of industrial capitalism allowed Catholics to blame this disruption on the Jews.

VII

ACROSS EUROPE and North and South America, the uneven but steady advent of male suffrage invariably meant liberals complaining about priests influencing their congregations. "I became mad with rage," wrote one French liberal as voters marched to the polling place with "lists from their parishes, the confessional, the church."[86] A generation later in Colombia, priests were accused of distributing specific voting instructions to parishioners.[87]

Before the 1880s, Catholic political organizing occurred for the most part outside political parties. Massive congresses, most famously the Katholikentag in Germany, but also equivalents across Europe and South America, brought together tens of thousands of Catholics to discuss contemporary issues.[88] Catholic trade unions formed in much of northern Europe and parts of Latin America and doubled as organizations where debates about wages, strikes, and the distinctions between workers and management nurtured a political consciousness.

In Belgium, the Netherlands, Germany, Hungary, Austria, Italy, Chile, and Uruguay, conflicts between Catholics and liberal nationalists over schools and marriage laws prompted Catholics to go one step further: they decided to form confessional parties. The marquee example, followed with pride around the Catholic world, was the German Center Party, or Zentrum. Formed as Bismarck and his allies began the Kulturkampf, the Zentrum became the political party of choice for Catholic voters across Germany, a loyalty that endured until the collapse of German democracy in 1933.[89] The sentiment attributed to its hugely popular leader, Ludwig Windthorst—"no salvation outside the Zentrum"—indicated the ferocity of attachment. When German American Catholics organized their own version of the Katholikentag, they met beneath portraits of Windthorst and George Washington. German Catholics named a town after Windthorst in the Texas Hill Country. German Catholics in Canada organized a Katholikentag, too, and named a town after Windthorst on the Saskatchewan prairie.[90]

Leo XIII and his aides viewed confessional political parties with uneasiness; enterprises led by laypeople inevitably proved difficult to control. (At times Leo XIII bypassed Windthorst to negotiate directly with Bismarck.) But Leo XIII knew that political participation led to better results than abandoning politics. Even in overwhelmingly Catholic countries such as Chile, Conservative Party members came to see themselves as representing a devout minority, since many baptized Catholics did not practice their faith.[91] By contrast, no Catholic political parties succeeded in Brazil, Spain, or France. One wing of French Catholicism, especially, spurned democratic politics and spied a return to a Catholic monarchy over every horizon. Leo XIII dismissed these archaic yearnings for a world ruled by altar and throne. He urged Catholics in Spain (1882), France (1892), and Brazil (1894) to reconcile themselves to republican governments, although he never recommended democracy as a political system.

The more Catholics participated in the political world, the more embedded they became within it. In Mexico, Catholics seized the opportunity presented by open and (relatively) uncorrupted elections. In the state of Jalisco, the legislature and the governor promoted church-sponsored labor unions, youth organizations, and mutual aid societies for farmers.[92] In Germany, by 1914, the Zentrum, once a pariah within a Protestant nation-state, held the balance of power in a governing coalition. In the United States, Irish and German Catholics became bulwarks of the northern wing of the Democratic Party. In Britain and Australia, Irish Catholics and their descendants became a core constituency of Labour parties, which Britain's Cardinal Bourne thought embodied Catholic social thought "without knowing it."[93] Even in Italy, where some aristocrats had urged Pius IX to flee the country after Italian unification in 1870, a tacit recognition of the Italian state developed beneath formal papal demands that Italian Catholics not legitimate the new nation.[94]

VIII

LEO XIII'S DEATH led to the election of Pius X in 1903. Himself of humble background—his brother remained a postal clerk while he served as pope, and three unmarried sisters lived together in near poverty outside Rome—Pius X furthered the devotional and liturgical dimensions of the Catholic revival by promoting Gregorian chant around the world and encouraging frequent communion, even for children as young as seven. He inspected the appointment file for each bishop personally and required more frequent visits by the world's bishops to Rome for meetings with (and lectures from) curial officials.

On doctrinal matters, Pius X proved less willing to meet the world halfway. He spent much of his papacy scrutinizing what opponents termed modernism, a theological approach committed to understanding doctrine in light of individual experience and historical change. An informal group of scholars pursued these topics through private correspondence, journal articles, and books. Some of their ideas drew on John Henry Newman's analysis of the development of doctrine or the American philosopher William James on religious experience. A few pushed beyond conventional Christian boundaries, but most would seem unthreatening now.[95]

One of the most famous, or notorious, Catholic modernists was England's George Tyrrell, a convert from Anglicanism and then a feisty Jesuit until the Society of Jesus expelled him. Tyrrell baited Roman heresy hunters by noting the "sterilizing uniformity" of contemporary Catholic intellectual life. He took a swipe at papal infallibility for allowing a "monopoly of ecclesiastical power."[96] Even Tyrrell's friends worried that a penchant for controversy meant he "put on Post Cards things that most of us would have only in registered letters."[97]

Pius X found none of this tolerable and unleashed a network of spies to root out inklings of modernism in Catholic seminaries and universities. Faculty lost positions, journals were discontinued, and embarrassing claims were made. Curial officials, for example, marshaled in-house loyalists to maintain that Moses personally authored the first five books of the Hebrew Bible, ignoring contrary evidence provided by less inhibited scholars.

The Office of the Inquisition issued a statement in 1907 that denounced no less than sixty-five alleged modernist claims. A Roman-based consultant to the Curia, who drafted an encyclical for Pius X condemning modernism, privately concluded that the modernists had abandoned "all that has been always held as the legitimate object of natural theology."[98] The Holy Office composed an anti-modernist oath to be sworn by all candidates for the priesthood. The language was uncompromising, even absurd: candidates must "flatly reject the heretical invention of the evolution of dogmas."[99]

When on his deathbed Tyrrell refused to recant modernist positions, he was denied a Catholic funeral. A local bishop temporarily suspended a priest friend who had deigned to say a few prayers over Tyrrell's coffin during a burial service in an Anglican churchyard. A French bishop confided to one of Tyrrell's acquaintances that Pius X had "crushed many souls whom a little goodness would have kept in the right way."[100] Only Pius X's death in 1914, and Benedict XV's election, would end the anti-modernist crusade. The new pope immediately ordered the dismantling of the papal spy network.

IX

A 1914 SUMMER VISITOR to Lourdes, the most potent symbol of the nineteenth-century ultramontane revival, observed men and women from many nations walking through the village, dipping their feet in the healing waters, and attending Mass together even in the first days after the assassination in Sarajevo. A month later, though, he noted, "pilgrims of Lourdes, having gone home, clashed against one another, under the shadow of their own flags. Those who yesterday greeted each other as brothers and sisters, now were fighting as enemies."[101]

Pilgrims at Lourdes, 1914. *(Getty images)*

Just as the war shattered socialist illusions about class unity, so, too, did it demonstrate the willingness of Catholics to slaughter coreligionists. To be sure, some Polish Catholics in the German Empire were resistant to conscription, as were some Irish Catholics in Australia and French-speaking Catholics in Canada. But more Polish-speaking Catholics served in the German army than fought for Polish independence, just as far more Irish Catholics volunteered to serve in the British army than participated in the 1916 Easter Rebellion in Dublin. One Irish-born, Auckland, New Zealand, Catholic bishop served as a chaplain on the Western Front and received a commendation from King George V.[102]

In a phrasing that would have seemed bizarre to ultramontane Catholics in the mid-nineteenth century, a French priest declared in 1915 that God desired "national homelands" for all people and that "a soldier who dies for his country accomplishes an eminently religious act."[103] German bishops defined the German army's invasion of Belgium as a "textbook example of a just war," and in Vienna's St. Stephen's Cathedral, an Austrian homilist arranged to bless not only the assembled soldiers but their weapons.[104] "There is no perfect Christian," Belgium's Cardinal Mercier insisted, "who is not a perfect patriot." "Patriotism," he added, "is a sacred thing."[105] A few Catholics, such as the Viennese priest-politician, Ignaz Seipel, still defended multicultural empires and challenged the idea that "belonging to a nation represented the highest good of humanity." But Seipel's empire, Austria-Hungary, was on the verge of collapse.[106]

In retrospect, hints of this Catholic nationalism had been evident before the war. In Buenos Aires, a leading cleric urged Catholics to adopt an "authentic patriotism" that protected "property, family, religion [and] patria."[107] In the United States, where in the 1870s and 1880s exiled European Jesuits refused to vote and conducted classes on the Fourth of July, and where the country's leading political scientist in turn described the Jesuits as "unnational," a new generation of American-born Jesuits founded a weekly journal in 1909. They named it, astonishingly, *America*.[108]

SIX

Empire

Missionaries, Converts, and Imperialism

I

AT THE 1888 GERMAN CATHOLIC CONGRESS (Katholikentag) in Freiburg, a teenage boy garnered unusual attention. Recently brought to Germany from Cameroon by missionaries for instruction at a Benedictine school near Munich, Mbange Akwa mingled with attendees. Mbange came from an elite Douala family—an uncle was a chief—and he was one of the first Africans educated in Germany. His presence was applauded by the German-speaking world's most celebrated Catholic, Ludwig Windthorst, leader of the Catholic Center Party, or Zentrum. As Windthorst explained:

> We can clearly see that [Black Africans] are capable
> of developing, and because they are our fellow men,
> because, like all of us, they have God-given souls, we
> must do everything we can to make them see the light of
> the Gospel.[1]

Windthorst was not alone in seeing missionary work as an opportunity. Compared with Britain and France, German colonialism was belated, and early in his career, Windthorst had opposed imperial projects proposed by Germany's (largely Protestant) leaders. By 1888 his opposition had weakened. Beyond converting young Africans, he thought the shared project of colonial missions might weaken divisions between Protestants and Catholics, so bitterly evident during the Kulturkampf of the 1870s. Even Roman newspapers approvingly noted how Germans would now "support priests abroad" if they promised to "evangelize barbarian peoples." Protestants and Catholics could agree that such work was "essentially patriotic and national."[2]

Mbange's successes at school and in the workplace (as an apprentice baker) were chronicled in the German Catholic press. They seemed to justify colonialism through "civilizing" Africans. When Mbange requested to be baptized as a Catholic, his sponsors made it an event. The papal nuncio to Bavaria performed the ceremony, Windthorst served as godfather, and the prominent Catholic writer Emilie Ringeis served as godmother. Mbange's German baptismal name was Andreas Ludwig (after Windthorst) Mbange.

Mbange returned to Cameroon after three years in Germany. The church there needed him. In the first thirteen years of the Cameroon mission, seven German priests, thirteen German brothers, and two German sisters died from tropical diseases.[3] These missionaries arrived in Cameroon without a word of language training and resented having to communicate at first in the "pidgin English" known by Cameroonians through contact with British traders. According to one account, Mbange did a "wonderful job translating [into the Indigenous language of Douala] the catechism and the Gospels."[4] He became the leader of the lay catechists, who did most of the work to establish Catholicism in the region. German clergy running the missions admired his work, even if one regretted that Mbange was "not able to replace a priest."[5]

II

IN 1910, Europe remained home for two-thirds of the world's 290 million Catholics, with only one million Catholics in sub-Saharan Africa and perhaps fifteen million Catholics in Asia (most of whom lived in the Philippines). These ratios would flip over the course of the twentieth century; by its end, most Catholics lived in the Global South.

This process began in the late nineteenth century with a renewed missionary effort. Pope Leo XIII placed great emphasis on missions and reorganized the Propaganda Fide in Rome to better financially support missionary schools and centers. Curial officials regulated—or attempted to regulate—marriage controversies and liturgical disputes and convened synods of missionaries and local clergy to develop common procedures. Synods, once vehicles to oppose Roman authority, as in the Synod of Pistoia in 1786, became mechanisms for Roman control.

Priests and nuns founded dozens of new missionary societies, including the first such societies in North America.[6] In 1868, sixty-eight foreign missionaries, almost all from France, worked in Vietnam, but by 1900, there were four hundred French missionaries and dozens more from Italy and Spain.[7] In China, the number of priest missionaries increased from two hundred in 1860 to nine hundred in 1899.[8]

Protestant missionaries still outnumbered Catholics, but the competition spurred Catholic efforts. One priest founded a seminary to train missionaries in Portugal. He wanted to ensure that the version of "European civilization" encountered by Indigenous people in Angola would be filtered through a Catholic lens, not through Protestants or secular colonial officials. Colonial officials horrified him by soliciting contributions for a new "statue of Voltaire."[9]

The ethos remained impeccably ultramontane. Lourdes grottoes proliferated, as did devotions to the Sacred Heart. In China's Shanxi Province, missionaries organized Corpus Christi processions in the 1880s up and down the paths of Catholic villages, with clergy in their robes, clouds of incense, and men and children in line. (If their feet were bound, Chinese women could not march in the procession, and Catholic clergy were among the first foreigners to try to abolish this practice.)[10] In Uganda, converts took to wearing miraculous medals and credited such medals with protecting them during civil wars, just as French Catholics wore such medals in times of peril. French missionaries described Ugandan Catholics dipping the medals into water and then drinking the water for its healing effect or using the medals to ward off lions and leopards on the way to church.[11]

Missionaries incessantly encouraged Catholics to form their own associations. While the term "Catholic milieu" typically refers to Europe and North America, it applies as well to Asia and Africa.

White Father missionary instructing students in German, probably in East Africa, c. 1900. *(Archiv Zentralkomitee der deutschen Katholiken)*

Everywhere Catholics built dense networks of organizations and nurtured self-segregation. They also became more likely to see their institutions as exclusively Catholic. Catholic schools in the United States had long welcomed Protestant students, and now in South Asia they welcomed Hindu students and in North Africa Muslim students. But Vatican officials began issuing cautions about admitting too many non-Catholics—"infidels" and "heretics" in the vocabulary of the time—even in societies where Catholics remained a tiny minority.[12] Italian missionaries in Shanxi Province became less willing than their predecessors to approve marriages between Catholics and non-Catholics or to permit Chinese Catholics to attend ancestor rituals or non-Catholic funerals.[13]

The most rapid Catholic growth in the early twentieth century occurred in Africa. Isolated missions had long existed on Africa's Indian and Atlantic Ocean coasts, along with Catholic communities dating from the sixteenth century in regions such as the Kongo. But only in the late nineteenth century did the opening of the sub-Saharan interior of the continent to Europeans produce, in the words of one missionary, a "true enthusiasm."[14]

The most important instigator was French bishop (and then cardinal) François Lavigerie. Lavigerie founded the Missionaries of Africa in 1868, commonly known as the White Fathers for their distinctive robes, and dedicated them to work in Africa. (A painting of Lavigerie now in Versailles shows him in his scarlet cardinal robes, pen in hand, his hat resting on a map of Africa.)[15] In reports urging Vatican officials to take greater interest in Africa, he warned against the maneuverings of "German and English Protestants" and "free thinking" French.[16] He judged social and political conditions in the interior of Africa with local tribes and princes "precisely in the state where Europe was in the Middle Ages" and hoped to establish an African Catholic civilization.[17]

Other men's religious orders—including Spiritans in East Africa and Holy Ghost clergy in West Africa—initiated major missionary programs. The work of Daniele Comboni, a priest (and then bishop) from Verona, is typical. Comboni made several voyages down the Nile into what is now Egypt and Sudan. He shopped his "plan for the regeneration of Africa" to Pius IX and various curial cardinals, urging coordination and focus in Catholic efforts. Cheerfully terming himself a "hustler and a mendicant," he made fundraising trips to Germany, where a committee to support missions in Africa had already formed, as well as to Austria, France, Belgium, and England.[18] He saw the fundamental problem for the continent as the "yoke of fetishism" and the continued "invasion of Islam." The haphazard Catholic response, with dozens of religious orders beginning work on the continent with little overall direction, dismayed him.[19]

The day-to-day workings of Lavigerie, Comboni, and other missionaries who descended on Africa remain little studied. In Africa, especially, but also in East and South Asia, missionary efforts began with priests or nuns struggling to learn Indigenous languages, and their work almost always depended on the training of native-born catechists such as Mbange Akwa, who in turn translated devotional practices and basic catechetical points. In the southeast of present-day Nigeria, Holy Ghost Fathers catalyzed the work of the missions, but only when Igbo men and women became catechists did a significant number of their friends and neighbors convert. In 1906, thirty-one missionary priests, brothers, and sisters worked in the region; in 1918, thirty. During the same period, the number of native-born catechists grew from 33 to 552.[20]

Here, too, the desire for a Catholic milieu became evident. Some missionaries built almost self-enclosed worlds, fueled by a grandiose sense of purpose. Belgian missionary (and bishop) Victor Roelens served in the northern Congo for over forty years. Given the fragility of the Belgian colonial state, he exerted tremendous control over the schools and municipal governments of the region. He once informed his superiors that he planned to "constitute a little republic, and I will be its president." He even printed his own currency.[21] In Uganda, the Christian God was treated as a king of kings, and when chiefs of various tribes converted to Catholicism, they spurred entire villages to follow them. Marian devotions and adoration of the Blessed Sacrament became especially popular, particularly as they were absorbed into Indigenous religious practices. The reverence shown to church workers—catechists as well as priests and nuns—made families eager to have a son or daughter enlist in church work. After five years of intensive evangelization in Buddu (near Lake Victoria), the number of annual adult baptisms rose from 147 in 1891 to 2,729 in 1896. By World War I, the pace of conversions was accelerating, more from African-to-African contact than from direct encounters with European missionaries.[22]

III

AT THE BEGINNING of their evangelization efforts, Lavigerie and other Catholic missionaries insisted on their independence from nation-states. As Lavigerie stressed, "We say 'Christians and Apostles,' not 'Frenchmen or Europeans.' It would make no sense to turn Africans into Frenchmen or Europeans, since such a metamorphosis would unfit them for the task they have to fulfill."[23] Other French missionaries, contemporaries of Lavigerie, focused on converting Muslims, but also conveyed respect for Africans as innately religious even if they had not yet accepted Catholicism as the true faith.[24]

Leo XIII made similar observations when he addressed the emperor of China, explaining that missionaries from "very diverse" Catholic countries would make no "distinction of country or race."[25] Writing to Catholics in India, the pope insisted that "indigenous clergy" must not be limited to "aiding [European] missionaries" but "replacing them."[26]

This cosmopolitan sensibility had waned by 1900. The great era of imperial expansion overlapped with and reinforced the great era of Catholic expansion, and lines between imperial and religious ventures often blurred. As early as the 1840s, in Tahiti, when a British Protestant missionary helped persuade the queen to expel two Catholic missionaries, a French admiral immediately arranged for more Catholic missionaries to take their place in order to forestall Protestant influence. French bishops successfully pleaded with Napoleon III to send ships and troops to the Vietnamese coast to protect missionaries.[27]

The identification of missionaries with colonial officials often had sociological dimensions. Belgian Catholics in the Congo, Portuguese Catholics in Mozambique and Angola, Dutch Catholics in Indonesia and the Caribbean, and Spanish and then American Catholics in the Philippines worked with colonial administrators, educating their children and sharing the travails of expatriate life. The most influential alliances were struck between colonial officials and Catholic missionaries working in the French Empire, which stretched from Lebanon to Madagascar to Senegal to China to Vietnam. Even former French colonies depended on the mother country. In Haiti, every bishop and archbishop in the late nineteenth century trained in a seminary dedicated to providing clergy for Haiti but located in the French region of Brittany.[28]

This French missionary empire rested on a paradox. As in so many countries, Catholics in late-nineteenth-century France battled hostile government officials eager to close Catholic schools and limit Catholic influence. As late as 1901, after conflicts between liberals and Catholics in most of Europe and North and South America had subsided, a deeply anticlerical government banned men's religious orders in France, with the intended result of closing ten thousand French Catholic schools and the unintended result of sending thirty thousand priests, brothers, and sisters out of France, deepening missionary networks around the world.[29] In 1905, the same government separated church and state. Only such a step, according to the French senator and future prime minister Georges Clemenceau, could save the country from becoming "the France of Rome" as opposed to "the France of the revolution."[30] Clemenceau became so identified with attacks on Catholicism that Catholic

groups disrupted his visit to Brazil, organizing protests against his pretensions to "teach Brazil the principles of democracy."[31]

Some of this hostility between government officials and Catholics
transferred to the empire. In Tahiti, administrators expelled Catholic
nuns from the local school in an effort to create "education outside the
missions."[32] In Rufisque, a Senegalese port town, a colonial mayor in
the summer of 1884 ordered a local priest to hang the tricolor French
flag on the church building on Bastille Day. The priest refused. The
mayor attached the flag himself. The priest tore it down and threw it in
the mud. The mayor took the occasion of Bastille Day to praise the education offered in the local school for breaking down "the old ramparts of
superstition and intolerance."

These tensions are not the dominant story. Even in Rufisque, nuns
and the occasional priest on state payrolls taught elementary school children, providing an inexpensive and irreplaceable labor pool for colonial administrators tasked with educating future citizens. When colonial
administrators pondered firing all of the Catholic nuns in Senegal, African Catholic parents devoted to the nuns would not permit it. "There is
not a single woman in the assimilated population of St. Louis [in Sen-
egal]," one administrator complained, "who did not attend this [Catho-
lic] school and does not ardently desire that her daughter do the same."[33]
The same France where one politician could declare in the Chamber of
Deputies that "ultramontanism or clericalism" was the "all-powerful"
enemy was also the France described by Catholics as the eldest "daughter
of the church."[34]

On balance, imperial competition between France and Britain and
Catholic enthusiasm for the French language commended missionaries and their work even to anticlerical officials. Jules Ferry, the French
prime minister, Freemason, and scourge of Catholic schools, made a
pilgrimage to the cathedral of Cardinal Lavigerie in Algiers to offer his
support for Lavigerie's work in Africa.[35] French Protestants, formally
granted equality with Catholic missionaries, repeatedly complained of
favoritism toward Catholics and, among colonial administrators, indifference to principles of religious freedom. Meanwhile, in Madagascar,
colonial prefects congratulated Catholic clergy for "the work of patriotism that you have pursued for long years."[36]

This reconciliation between Catholic and imperial interests was obvious across the world by the early twentieth century. Bitter divisions between Belgian liberals and Belgian Catholics in the 1870s over education policies, for example, dissolved in the early twentieth century as they joined forces to support colonial ventures in the Congo.[37] German Jesuit missionaries in Shanghai, banned from working in Germany itself, welcomed Prince Heinrich, brother of Kaiser Wilhelm II, on his tour of East Asia.[38] The German government, not the church, funded the first scholarly chair in Catholic mission studies at the university of Münster. When its first occupant published an account of German Catholic missions in Africa, he dedicated it to Kaiser Wilhelm II.[39]

In the United States, Catholics and Protestant allies rewrote biographies of seventeenth- and eighteenth-century missionaries, such as the Jesuit Jacques Marquette (in the Midwest) and the Franciscan Junipero Serra (in California), so as to place them alongside the Pilgrims and Puritans as the founders of Western civilization on the continent. Statues of Marquette (nominated by legislators from Wisconsin) and Serra (nominated by legislators from California) were placed in the US Capitol Building in Washington, DC.[40] American Catholic missionaries sent to the Philippines after the American military took control of the islands in 1898 found themselves dining with Governor General (and future president) William Howard Taft. The vice president (and another future president), Theodore Roosevelt, flattered these missionaries by encouraging them to make Filipinos "better Catholics and better citizens."[41]

Ironically, Vatican officials found it especially easy to establish unfettered lines of communication between Rome and Catholics in the Protestant British Empire. A significant percentage of the soldiers in the British army were Catholic, typically Irish Catholic, and required spiritual sustenance. As early as the 1820s in India, James Mill, an official with the East India Company, agreed to pay the salaries of Catholic priests, since, as he sardonically put it, "they have, at least, as strong a claim upon our bounty as the Hindoo and Mahomedan priesthood."[42]

Irish Catholics in settler colonies such as New Zealand, Australia, and South Africa developed close ties to British colonial authorities, with Leo XIII himself acknowledging that "it cannot be doubted that the well-being of Ireland is connected with the tranquility of the whole [British] Empire."[43] In turn, British Foreign Office officials hoped to persuade Vatican officials to tamp down nationalist Irish priests.[44] In British-controlled South Africa, Irish bishops supported the British in the war against the Afrikaner Boers, silencing a Dutch priest who voiced his opposition.[45]

IV

ALONG WITH bringing Catholicism, missionaries in the late nineteenth century began to stress that they brought "civilization," a user-friendly imperial concept. One dimension of civilization where Catholics played a leading role was the effort to eliminate slavery in Africa. This was surprising. Ultramontane Catholics in the mid-nineteenth century had been conspicuous for their reluctance to recommend the abolition of slavery, so opposed were they to the individualist (at times anti–Catholic) rhetoric they associated with liberal Protestant or secular abolitionists. Beginning in the 1850s and 1860s, though, French and Italian Catholic missionaries frequently encountered enslaved people in Africa, and they saw in these men and women not simply vulnerable human beings but potential Catholics. Unlike West Africa, where Portuguese Catholics had taken a leading role, the slave trade in eastern and northern Africa was dominated by Muslims, which made it easier for these Catholic missionaries to mount a critique.

On-the-ground distinctions between slavery and other forms of coerced labor were hard to parse, and Europeans often struggled to understand the status of the men and women they encountered.[46] But the advantages of claiming to rescue enslaved people from the clutches of Islamic slave traders were clear. Such ransoms meant allying Christianity with "civilization" while linking Islam to barbarism. Or as Daniele Comboni explained after describing markets for enslaved people in Khartoum and Cairo, "Only Catholicism will be able to restore full freedom to a large part of the human family which is still groaning under the shameful yoke of slavery."[47] He added later that Muslim rulers of cities such as Zanzibar would cheerfully agree on paper to abolish the trade in enslaved people to please English diplomats, but would actually do nothing, since for them "the Koran is the word of God and does not forbid but permits the trade in human flesh."[48]

In missions near Lake Victoria and Tanganyika, White Fathers detailed the activities of Islamic slave traders and ransomed enslaved women and children. In Zanzibar, priests carried bags of coins in order to purchase enslaved people at auction and grant them their freedom.[49] Cardinal Lavigerie (in North Africa) and Daniele Comboni (along the Nile River) even organized informal armies to try and protect Indigenous villages from raids by slave traders.

The same 1888 meeting of the Katholikentag attended by Mbange Akwa included a rousing endorsement of the efforts of Cardinal Lavigerie to eliminate African slavery. The next year, in Brussels, diplomats from almost every European nation invoked Lavigerie as they signed a treaty in support of slavery's abolition. Lavigerie sparked the formation of Catholic antislavery organizations in France, Belgium, and especially Italy and encouraged Leo XIII to address the topic.[50] The leading Brazilian abolitionist, Joaquim Nabuco, long dismayed by ultramontane hesitation on the issue, met with Leo XIII in 1888 and was delighted when the pope promised to say "a word" against slavery. (Leo XIII allegedly added: "when the Pope has spoken, all Catholics have to obey.")[51]

The pope directed his 1888 encyclical on the topic, *In Plurimus*, to Catholics in Brazil, which had just abolished slavery. In an act of creative amnesia, Leo XIII described the church as continually working toward slave emancipation. Using a resonant phrase that would echo down through Catholic social thought in the twentieth century, he declared slavery a violation of "human dignity."[52]

V

AFRICAN STUDENTS studying in Europe, such as Mbange Akwa, drew considerable attention, but formerly enslaved people offered the most powerful testimony of a multiracial religious community. Daniele Comboni brought twelve freed Sudanese girls to the Vatican to meet Pius IX himself in 1867. He arranged the girls in a row along a wall near the Vatican library, and Pius IX arrived at 5 p.m. Captivated by their presence, the pope strolled through the Vatican gardens with the girls. Cruelly, he made a reference to Africans as "ungrateful" and, in his experience—a single trip as a young priest to South America where he met some Africans—potentially "thieves and liars." Comboni immediately responded that Europeans would be thieves and liars, too, "if they found themselves in the sad condition of slavery." Pius IX agreed and then expressed delight as the girls spoke of their belief in the pope as the "representative of Jesus Christ" and of their determination to evangelize their homelands. He awarded them medals and thanked them.[53] Twenty years later, Cardinal Lavigerie brought another group of formerly enslaved people to Paris to rally Catholic antislavery activists, and to Rome to visit Leo XIII.[54]

Sister Josephine Bakhita became the most prominent of these men and women. Her own recounting of her story, a document she dictated at the wish of her mother superior in 1910, is a gripping narrative.[55] Other formerly enslaved Catholics from East Africa and elsewhere composed similar accounts, and these stories were used as fundraising tools and to raise awareness among Europeans about the plight of African Catholics.[56]

Bakhita was born in about 1869 in a village southwest of Khartoum. Her family were members of the Daju people. When Bakhita was about nine and playing in a field, two men armed with knives kidnapped her. "I was petrified," she remembered, and she shrieked for her mother and father as she was carried away. Her captors gave her a common Arabic name, Bakhita. She was sold at auction, managed to escape her first owner, but was captured and sold again to a Turkish general. She assisted the general's wife and mother, but the two women beat her mercilessly when she inadvertently touched their hair while dressing them. They ordered tattoos to be carved into her breasts and stomach to identify her as their property.

When the general decided to return to Turkey, a friendly Italian diplomat ransomed her, and two years later—just before the Mahdi (or Islamic) armies captured Khartoum in 1885 after a long siege—the diplomat took her back to Italy. He almost certainly knew Fr. Comboni and was influenced by the priest's efforts to free enslaved people. "I can still taste the joy I felt at the time," Bakhita recalled. After journeying with the diplomat and his family through the Suez Canal and across the Mediterranean, Bakhita found work as a nanny with an aristocratic family in the Veneto region of Italy. The family did not encourage Bakhita to learn about Catholicism. Still, when a local Catholic gave her a tiny silver crucifix, she hid it in her room. The family placed Bakhita in a home run by Canossian nuns while they returned to Sudan for business. Upon their return to Italy, the wife of the family decided to take Bakhita with her on yet another trip back to Sudan, to the port city of Suakin, and put her to work in a family-owned hotel. Bakhita refused to return to her homeland and asked to live in the house run by the Canossians, where she was preparing to convert to Catholicism. She could not be forced to leave, since, as she put it, in Italy "the slave trade is not allowed."[57]

Her furious employers appealed to local officials and even Venice's cardinal, all of whom sided with Bakhita. A month later she was baptized. She immediately decided to enter the Canossians, and four years later, in 1896, another Venetian cardinal, Giuseppe Sarto, attended the ceremonies as Bakhita took her final vows. Sarto would be elected as Pope Pius X in 1903 and would support efforts to mobilize Catholics against slavery in Africa, personally blessing each delegate at an antislavery conference held in St. Peter's in 1907. Bakhita settled into life as a Canossian religious woman assigned to a convent in the mountain town of Schio, mastering the local dialect and developing a regional reputation for holiness.

VI

BY THIS TIME, Catholic missionaries collaborating with imperial officials faced a problem: the closer the alliance between the church and imperial states became, the more likely they were to alienate Indigenous Catholics by propagating racist assumptions of superiority. This dynamic had existed from the beginning of the missionary effort. As early as 1865, Comboni regretted that a French Catholic bishop in Dahomey did not believe that native-born Africans could serve as "catechists, teachers, artists and least of all Priests."[58]

Catholics rejected the most appalling versions of scientific racism, such as polygenesis or the idea that separate races might be separate species. One Mississippi bishop urged local Jesuits to criticize the "abominable idea of the plurality of races," and the Holy Office in Rome rejected any notion of a curse on peoples of African descent. All people were members of the "great human family."[59] The very act of encouraging conversions presumed commonality, and the first German Catholic missionaries to Cameroon stressed that they did not see Africans as "objects of exploitation" but instead as "companions of humanity, a brother loved by God." The piety these missionaries found in converts in Cameroon was "incomparably greater" than among some "tired" and "civilized" Catholics in Europe.[60]

Still, missionary efforts to "civilize" people of color almost inevitably assumed a racial hierarchy. In New Orleans and in Capetown, South Africa, for example, Black and white Catholics worshipped together until the end of the nineteenth century. Catholic churches were much more likely to be integrated than their Protestant counterparts. But Catholics eventually conformed to segregationist patterns. In New Orleans they did so against the wishes of French-speaking Creole Catholics, some of whom were then challenging state laws mandating segregation in public institutions. In both South Africa and the United States, white bishops, priests, nuns, and laypeople acquiesced in—or furthered—what Baltimore's Cardinal Gibbons ruefully termed the "caste system."[61]

Racial hierarchies also became visible in the evangelization of Indigenous or aboriginal peoples. In the late nineteenth and early twentieth centuries, Catholic missionaries worked with Indigenous peoples in North and South America, Australia, New Zealand, and Polynesia. Maori people in New Zealand, Dakota people on the American Great Plains, Tahitian people on Pacific islands, and Bororo people in the Amazon all encountered the ultramontane revival.

The pattern in South America was typical. After a long hiatus, missionaries in the late nineteenth century reached Indigenous peoples in all corners of the continent. These missionaries used familiar strategies, holding parish missions, urging penitents who had not seen a priest in years to attend confession, and erecting crosses in villages. Just as missionaries built educational and social welfare institutions among German and Italian Catholic immigrants clustered in coastal cities of Brazil, so, too, did they take on similar roles with Indigenous peoples, some of whom had been Catholics since the sixteenth and seventeenth centuries.

Salesian priests from Italy and Claretian priests from Spain helped establish schools and missions among Indigenous peoples in Brazil, and government officials relied on missionary clergy to calm local rebellions. Dominican priests from Spain did similar work among Indigenous peoples in Colombia. When the Spanish lost control of the Philippines after the war with the United States in 1898, a group of Dominicans stationed there traveled back across the Pacific Ocean to begin work with Indigenous peoples in Peru.[62]

In Canada, Australia, and the United States, competition with Protestants for Indigenous converts was an added variable. Catholics in the United States resented governmental attempts to equate Protestant with American. They bristled when the US commissioner of Indian Affairs described Catholic requests for public funding for their Indian schools as "un-American, unpatriotic, and a menace to our liberties."[63] The founder of the secular and government-funded Carlisle Indian school in the United States complained about a priest "speaking against the Indians sending their children to Carlisle, or away to school."[64]

Over time, Catholics became charged with operating their own schools, often boarding schools, with the explicit goal of detaching Indigenous or aboriginal peoples from their traditional way of life. Priests and nuns running the schools separated children from their families, often with little notice. They trimmed hair on boys and mandated unfamiliar foods. They banned traditional dress. In Australia's isolated northwest coast, German priests and Irish nuns sent any son or daughter of an aboriginal woman and a Malaysian or Indonesian man away from the child's parents, so convinced were they that mixed-race children could not thrive in their home villages.[65]

The same missionaries often did defend the prerogatives of Indigenous peoples, and genuine Indigenous or aboriginal Catholic communities did form. Catholic missionaries were more likely than Protestant counterparts to permit the use of (and learn) Indigenous languages, although even Catholic missionaries occasionally punished students for "talking Indian."[66] Salesian priests in the Amazonian state of Mato Grosso saw themselves as protecting Bororo people from "persecution" by government officials even as they tried to "eradicate the numerous, erroneous, and immoral superstitions of their tribe."[67] In British Columbia, Oblates of Mary Immaculate missionaries fought to keep traditional fishing lands under the control of the Dakelh people.[68] In the United States, Joseph Pawnee-no-pah-she, a Catholic Osage tribal governor, traveled to Washington to make the point that tribes, too, possessed sovereignty and should be able to welcome Catholic missionaries and schools if they chose to do so. "Religion among the whites," the Osage delegates wrote, "is a matter of conscience and voluntary choice . . . why should it not be so among the Osages?"[69]

Underpinning the idea that Indigenous culture must be transformed was a profound sense of racial superiority. Present from the beginning, this racism had been submerged in the early nineteenth century beneath a romantic, if also condescending, understanding of Indigenous peoples as uncorrupted by modern mores. In 1850, a Swiss missionary in Maine spoke with awe of the "savage eloquence" of Penobscot people uncontaminated by "overwrought civilization." One French priest hoping to work with Indigenous peoples in the Rocky Mountains was disappointed to learn he had been assigned to a mission of lesser "prestige": French-speaking Catholic Louisiana.[70]

By 1900, hierarchies were more clear. An Italian missionary in the Pacific Northwest of the United States described the Blackfeet people as inhabiting an "uncivilization." Another missionary described the Coeur d'Alene people as debilitated by "degraded habits" and "foolish superstitions."[71]

Asian Catholics issued some of the first challenges to European and North American assumptions of racial superiority. In the majority Catholic Philippines, armed resistance to the American occupation of the islands after 1898 was crushed in a brutal military campaign, but both Spanish and American Catholics recognized that a growing number of Filipino Catholics desired political independence. Filipino antagonism toward Catholic leaders for their alliance with American occupying forces—one American priest in Manila thought independence for the Philippines plausible "only after the present generation is in the grave"—helped spur the formation of a popular schismatic church led by a former Catholic priest: the Iglesia Filipina Independiente, "established in the Philippines for Filipinos."[72]

In China, nationalists directed their animus at all Christians during the 1900 Boxer Rebellion, but Catholics with international ties and European-style churches came under especially savage assault. The just constructed French neo-Gothic Cathedral in Beijing endured a two-month siege as over three thousand European and Chinese Catholics, fearful for their lives, huddled inside the structure. Mobs murdered thousands of Catholics, perhaps tens of thousands, including three bishops and over thirty priests. The Jesuits saw their parishes decrease from 674 to 58 and their schools from 221 to 49. Numerous Franciscan missions were left in shambles. Even tiny Catholic villages were occupied, with captives tortured and demands made that villagers renounce Catholicism. After the European powers quashed the rebellion, they squeezed indemnities out of the enfeebled Chinese empress. By using the funds to rebuild and expand Catholic churches and facilities, local Catholic leaders heightened tensions between Chinese Catholics and their non-Catholic neighbors.[73]

Underwriting these tensions were a more self-conscious and aggressive Chinese nationalism, on the one hand, and Western assumptions of cultural superiority on the other. French missionaries in China, for example, explained to skeptical Vatican officials that, "The native priest, apart from some honorable exceptions, is not equal to the European in efficiency, intelligence, administrative ability, [and] reliability. Giving these mission churches too much independence too soon is not desirable in their own interest." When a German Catholic missionary met with the alleged seventy-sixth descendant of Confucius, Kong Lingyi, in 1902, he dismissed him as knowing "almost nothing of the situation and learning of Europe." The Chinese sage, he noted sadly, "lived a thoroughly Chinese existence."[74]

Shocked by the Boxer Rebellion, Léon Joly, a French priest immersed in the missionary literature, published a widely discussed assessment of Catholicism in China in 1907. Joly never visited East Asia, but even from his Parisian study he knew that some missionary priests refused to eat at the same table with their Chinese clerical colleagues and over time had become more cloistered within European compounds in China's cities. He asked missionaries to reflect on the fact that some converts seemed eager for baptism only to gain access to Church funds, while priests and nuns enrolled these "rice Christians" in order to inflate their convert totals. He deplored low numbers of Indigenous clergy and the complete absence of Indigenous bishops.

Joly acknowledged that most missionaries possessed good intentions. But he concluded that Chinese Catholics attached to a European Catholicism will always seem "renegades to the homeland, traitors allied with the foreigner."[75] Another missionary sympathetic to Joly was more blunt: "Our duty and honor is to work to render ourselves redundant." He went further: "The Chinese are in practice treated as inferiors, *by reason of race.*" European-led Catholicism in China risked becoming a "spiritual colony."[76]

A few other European Catholics—notably the Belgian Jesuit Arthur Vermeersch when writing on the Congo—irritated colonial authorities by wondering whether "civilization" could be brought by governments intent on exploiting local resources.[77] Bengali and Vietnamese Catholics took matters into their own hands. Working out of Calcutta, Brahmabhadhav Upadhyaya published a series of blistering editorials criticizing British rule, even as he urged European Catholic missionaries to adapt their evangelization strategies to local mores. Upadhyaya himself dressed as a Hindu monk and defended traditional caste distinctions. He described himself as at once Catholic and "emphatically Hindu."[78] In the Tonkin region of Vietnam, a French bishop writing from Hanoi worried that "indigenous priests and catechists" did not have "the deference nor the cordiality of the past." In 1907, three Vietnamese priests were sentenced to long prison terms

Three Vietnamese priests arrested for anti-French activities, 1909. *(Institut de recherche France-Asie/MEP)*

for rallying Vietnamese Catholics to "contribute by any means, labour or property, in the struggle against the French, so as to show patriotism and love of the Lord." A French missionary priest had turned them in.[79]

VII

MISSIONS AND IMPERIALISM structured the lives of Mbange Akwa and Josephine Bakhita. The work in Cameroon that Mbange helped jump-start had achieved significant success by 1914. Ninety-three missionaries staffed dozens of mission stations, and a much larger group of catechists ran schools for over twelve thousand pupils.[80]

During World War I, French and British troops expelled all German citizens from Cameroon, including the Pallottine priests and nuns overseeing Mbange's work. The departing priests handed the keys to mission churches to Mbange and other catechists, advising them to marry couples and give instructions in the faith.[81]

This wartime interlude of African leadership presaged the future. When Cameroon became governed through a League of Nations mandate in 1919, French Catholic missionaries maneuvered colonial officials into pressuring the Vatican to replace German missionaries with French missionaries. The cardinal in charge of the Propaganda Fide erupted in anger at the "misplaced patriotism" infecting French Catholics, but as a compromise he nominated as bishop in Cameroon a priest from Alsace fluent in both German and French.[82]

Over the next decade, the unwillingness of French colonial officials to consider democracy and self-determination in Cameroon provoked resistance to the colonial state.[83] At the same time Catholics in Cameroon and elsewhere began to press for native-born clergy. The number of such priests from missionary lands in Africa and Asia increased in the 1920s and 1930s from 2,670 to over 7,000.[84] Vatican officials also pressured bishops in the racially segregated southern United States to train African American men for the priesthood—encountering much resistance—and connections were occasionally drawn between evangelization in Africa and evangelization in communities of the African diaspora. Some European missionary orders, such as the Society of Divine Word, sent priests to work in Togo and in African American communities in Chicago. One French priest squabbling with his German colleagues over ecclesiastical boundaries in Africa suggested to curial officials, who disregarded him, that all Germans be sent to work for "the conversion of blacks in the United States."[85]

Native-born African catechists, such as Mbange, kept working. When Mbange died at the age of fifty-nine in 1932, his life was celebrated in German Catholic missionary publications as someone "who had no aberrations for which to repent and who served as a perfect example of true missionary service for forty years."[86] Mbange's son Benedict pledged to "continue the work begun by his father."[87]

Josephine Bakhita unexpectedly became a public figure at the same moment. For three decades she had worked as a cook, nurse's aide, and doorkeeper with the Canossian sisters. Her biography—a repackaging of the oral history she had dictated in 1910—was published in 1931 to acclaim and indicates how ties between Europe and Africa were deepening during this period. Benedict XV had recently beatified twenty-two Ugandan young men burned to death for their faith in 1885–1886. The ceremonies marking the event had drawn huge crowds, including two men spared execution by chance in Uganda almost forty years before.[88]

With reluctance, Josephine Bakhita obeyed the request of her religious superiors to make extended tours of Italy in order to raise funds for Catholic missions in Africa. Over a period of years, Bakhita journeyed from town to town and to every major city. Escorted by priests and nuns active in missionary work—her primary traveling companion was a Canossian nun recently returned to Italy from thirty-five years of work in Shanxi Province in China—she nonetheless became the campaign's primary attraction. Bishops and cardinals requested audiences. She also met—at their request—with both Benito Mussolini and his rival and occasional negotiating partner, Pius XI. Bakhita's was often the first African

Sr. Josephine Bakhita, n.d.
(Courtesy of Canossian Daughters of Charity)

face residents of villages and small cities had seen, and her presence in a religious habit guaranteed large crowds. At these public events, Bakhita would make a short speech and respond to questions about her enslavement and life in the Sudan. When she finished speaking, she reluctantly allowed people to touch her and to kiss a miraculous medal around her neck. Others in the audience thrust babies and sick relatives toward her for a blessing. Her uneasiness in these moments perhaps reflected her vulnerability as an African Catholic in a church long dominated by Europeans. Privately she complained that "everyone looks at me like a nice beast. I want to work, to pray for everybody, and not to look at people."[89]

SEVEN

Nation

A Catholic Nationalism?

I

MA XIANGBO WAS born in 1840 and raised in Jiangsu, a region north of Shanghai and on the Yellow Sea. Vincent Lebbe was born in 1873 and raised in Ghent, Belgium. The two men met after Lebbe began his missionary career in Shanghai in 1901.

A member of a family whose ancestors had converted to Catholicism in the seventeenth century, Ma attended the College of St. Ignace from grade school until his ordination as a Jesuit priest.[1] When Ma became director of his alma mater, other colleagues resisted his plan to reform the curriculum so as to allow the study of Chinese texts. Dismayed by this hesitation, eager for more contact with his family, and aggravated by perceived slights, such as superiors insisting that he teach astronomy, not Chinese literature, he left the Jesuits. "I have never been a French member of the Society," he told his superiors, emphasizing the adjective "French."[2] Not all the Jesuits in Shanghai were French—his beloved mentor was Italian—but Ma resented how treaties signed in the 1840s gave French Catholics and the French government the right to supervise Catholic activity in China.

Ma married and fathered two children. Working on behalf of the Chinese imperial government, he traveled throughout Europe and North America. He kept a discreet silence about his Catholicism

Vincent Lebbe in Tianjin in 1910.
(Archives Vincent Lebbe-ARCA.)

Ma Xiangbo, 1935. *(Ma Xiangbo 2"*
Whitworth University (2017). Album 13: Catholic
Action First National Congress in Shanghai, 1935.
https://digitalcommons.whitworth.edu/album13/90)

because of anti-foreign, often anti-Christian, sentiments permeating the royal court. A meeting with Pope Leo XIII in Rome in 1886 while on a diplomatic mission began Ma's reconciliation with the church.

With Chinese colleagues and the support of a few French Jesuits, Ma founded Zhendan University in 1902, whose Western name, Aurora, invoked not only the dawn but the collective hope of a generation of Chinese intellectuals to fuse Western and Eastern knowledge. The French Jesuits shied away from politics and over Ma's objections altered the curriculum to a more conventional focus on Western classics. Ma resigned and persuaded many of the school's students to enroll in a new university, Fudan, which he founded in 1905. He arranged for the reprinting of works by the seventeenth-century missionary, Matteo Ricci, contrasting Ricci's capacity for integration into Chinese culture with the rigidities of nineteenth-century ultramontanism. He later wrote Pius X urging him to send scholars with the sensibility of Ricci to China.[3]

An eleven-year-old Vincent Lebbe vowed to go to China after reading a biography of a French priest martyred there. Even before his arrival many years later he knew how missionaries should conduct themselves. "To be effective," he wrote, we must "stay in tune with our time, adapt to its customs, ideas and manners of expression."[4]

After only a few months in China, Lebbe identified completely with his adopted homeland. "I am Chinese," he wrote to a friend, "with all my heart, with all my soul, and with all my strength. China is my lot and my country, and the Chinese are my brothers." He signed the letter with his Chinese name, Lei Ming-yuan.[5] He read and endorsed the French priest Léon Joly's controversial work on the need for missionaries to adapt to Chinese culture and thought Joly had "held to the letter of the Gospel."[6] After Joly's death, one of Joly's friends gave Lebbe his chalice as a token of esteem.[7]

Like Ma and Joly, Lebbe was appalled by the behavior of many French missionaries. Some French priests, like French colonial administrators, rode in rickshaws. Lebbe rode a bicycle. Some of these same missionaries made only half-hearted efforts to learn Mandarin and rarely wore Chinese clothes. Lebbe spoke idiomatic Mandarin, braided his hair in a pigtail, and insisted on using chopsticks. French colonial officials discouraged papal envoys from visiting the country and thwarted requests from an enfeebled Chinese government to establish independent diplomatic relations with the Holy See. Lebbe described the neo-Gothic cathedral in Beijing, built in the 1890s and rising majestically over the city skyline only a short distance from the Forbidden City, as an "eyesore." Its style was "deliberately non-Chinese."[8]

Ma supported the Chinese Revolution of 1911, became a prominent lecturer on the new constitution, and was elected as the only Catholic in China's parliament. By then posted to Tianjin, Lebbe offered well-attended public lectures on Catholicism and on the need for Chinese independence from foreign control. Together with Chinese Catholic colleagues, he edited a newspaper that attracted one of China's biggest readerships. A dismayed French consul reported to the foreign minis-try in Paris that "the people, aroused by the prefect of police and also, I regret to say, by the Belgian missionary Lebbe, who is poorly controlled by his bishop, may at any moment be drawn into violent acts." The French consul and Lebbe's ecclesiastical superiors agreed to move Lebbe out of Tianjin, but Lebbe turned the patriotism displayed by French Catholics during World War I to his advantage.

> It has been the patriotism of the church in France dur-
> ing the years of war that more than anything else has
> returned the church there to the role it had lost. . . .
> What they do not forgive me is that I believe that, to save
> the Chinese, today especially, one must love not only
> the Chinese, but China, as one loves one's homeland, as
> a Frenchman loves France, to work to spread this love
> among priests, Christians, and pagans.[9]

French missionaries in China disagreed. "It seems," one bishop explained, "that the *European* Catholic episcopate will remain for a long time yet the only safeguard of the Catholic link with *Rome* and the sole upholder of practical belief in the infallible magisterium of the *church*."

A skeptical curial official wrote on the letter from the French bishop in blue pencil: "And why? And whose fault is that?"[10] His frustration reflected the gap between the Roman desire to cultivate local leader-ship and an insular French missionary culture. Benedict XV dispatched emissaries to investigate the condition of the church in China. Among their informants were Lebbe and Ma. "If true patriotism is praisewor-thy and praised in the churches of Europe," Lebbe had already insisted, "it is necessary to the Church of China, and one of the indispensable human conditions for Catholicism taking root in the people and draw-ing the masses to its bosom."[11] That a French flag hung in many Catho-lic churches was scandalous.[12]

In 1919, Benedict XV released an apostolic letter on the missions, *Maximum Illud*, that drew from Lebbe's writings. Evangelization without the goal of an Indigenous church was unacceptable. "The ideas . . . are 'our ideas,'" an excited friend reported to Lebbe.[13] Ma translated *Maximum Illud* into Chinese. French clergy in China were less enthralled. One privately called the apostolic letter "unjust" and "discouraging." Benedict XV, they said, was "badly informed."[14]

Lebbe spent much of the 1920s in Paris and Belgium working with Chinese and Vietnamese Catholic students. He urged the Chinese students to adopt two mottos: "China for the Chinese" and "the Church for Christ."[15] Ma helped the Vatican establish an apostolic delegation to China, headed by an Italian bishop, Celso Constantini. (Ma was chagrined not to be named ambassador to the Vatican in return.) Constantini labored over the next decade to fulfill the promise of *Maximum Illud* by convening clergy synods, discouraging Chinese Catholics from *koutou*, or kneeling, when meeting clergy, forbidding national flags in churches, sending seminarians to Rome for training, and encouraging experiments in Chinese-style church architecture (as opposed to neo-Gothic). As he explained, "the missions have remained foreign fiefs, without ever becoming local churches."[16]

Pius XI plotted an even more dramatic gesture. Lebbe had once written that "I would die happy if I could kiss the ring of the second [Chinese] bishop of China"—the first Chinese bishop had been ordained in 1685.[17] Pius XI fulfilled Lebbe's wish in 1926 when he plucked six

The first six Chinese bishops of the modern era, at St. Peter's in 1926. *(Archives Vincent Lebbe-ARCA.)*

Chinese clergy—three from a list supplied by Lebbe—to be ordained in Rome as the first native bishops in Southeast or East Asia. (An Indian Jesuit had been ordained bishop in 1923.) With much fanfare, the soon-to-be bishops traveled to Rome via Beijing, Tianjin, Shanghai, Hong Kong, Manila, Singapore, and Colombo.[18] Invited to the ordinations as a distinguished guest, Lebbe exuded vindication. "God is good," he wrote to a friend, as he anticipated a reception in Rome for the new Chinese bishops. "I am invited to give [in Rome] a lecture on indigenous clergy!" During the ceremonies surrounding these "historic hours, these unforgettable hours," he felt the "greatest joy possible for a missionary."[19] Afterward, he founded an order of Chinese brothers and an order of Chinese sisters. He mandated that these Little Brothers of Saint John the Baptist and Little Sisters of Saint Theresa use Chinese (not only Latin) in their daily prayers.[20]

II

THE SAGA OF Ma Xiangbo and Vincent Lebbe illuminates the challenge of building a global church in a nationalist age. After defending themselves against liberal nationalists in the 1870s, Catholics came out of World War I convinced they could be good patriots and good Catholics. The shared experience of the war had simultaneously lessened anticlericalism and reconciled many Catholics to the nation-state. Germany's Catholic political party, the Zentrum, placed the term *Volksgemeinschaft*, or "national community," on its banners and publicity materials. The French government honored Joan of Arc, long a symbol of the antiliberal Catholic right, with a national holiday in 1920, the same year that Benedict XV canonized her in Rome.[21]

The collapse of the Habsburg Empire also enhanced this Catholic nationalism. Bishops in the new state of Czechoslovakia vowed to "love, also in its new form, our Fatherland." Croatian, Slovakian, Slovenian, and Hungarian Catholics exhibited a newfound conviction in the need for unity between particular peoples and a particular state.[22] Poland's Roman Dmowski, one of the leading political figures in a Poland that had gained political independence only in 1918, published a pamphlet explaining his understanding of Polish nationalism:

> Catholicism is not an appendage to Polishness. . . . It is
> embedded in its essence, and in a large measure it *is* its
> essence. To attempt to dissociate Catholicism from Pol-
> ishness, and to separate the Polish nation from its religion
> and the church, means to destroy the very essence of
> that nation.[23]

The same pattern was evident beyond Europe. In Brazil, for example, the energetic archbishop of Rio de Janeiro, Sebastião Leme, authored a widely distributed 1916 manifesto urging Brazilian Catholics to take ownership of their society. "The Brazil that we see," he explained, "the Nation Brazil, is not ours. It is the minority's."[24] A Jesuit in British-controlled Ceylon urged local Catholics to avoid condemnations from the majority Buddhist population by becoming more patriotic.[25] In Senegal, missionaries preached "immortal glory to France" as they encouraged local men to volunteer for military service or looked the other way during forced recruitment drives. They boasted that French officials "have nothing to fear from the African Catholic."[26]

This Catholic nationalism informed Vatican diplomacy. The failed attempt of Benedict XV to negotiate an end to World War I in 1917 and the warm reception afforded Woodrow Wilson's Fourteen Points unnerved papal diplomats. One such diplomat, Eugenio Pacelli, the future Pius XII, assessed Wilson's goal as to "Americanize the whole world, making it Freemason so as to liberate it from its servitude to the Kaiser, the pope, and the priesthood."[27] Wilson, equally suspicious, told his cabinet that he thought Benedict XV planned to establish Roman Catholic nations in central Europe under "control of the papacy."[28]

Excluded from the League of Nations, a decision that embittered a generation of papal diplomats, Catholics forged their own alliances. With Benedict XV's encouragement, Pacelli and another future pope, Achille Ratti, elected Pius XI in 1922, began negotiating treaties or concordats with European and Latin American leaders. (Medieval Europe, Pius XI explained, had been a "true League of Nations.") About forty concordats were signed in the interwar period.[29]

These papal diplomats tried to persuade scholars and government officials that neutrality on religious matters along the American or

French (after 1905) model should not become normative. If an individual's salvation depended on good standing within the church, and Catholic leaders had no doubt that it did, a state should promote such standing. In majority Catholic societies, church officials claimed responsibility for religious education in state schools or state funding for independent Catholic schools and wielded significant influence over family law and censorship policies. State officials in these majority Catholic countries did not disturb existing synagogues or churches or monitor private religious conduct, but public religious witness—certainly proselytizing—by Protestants was discouraged and, at times, as in Spain and Italy, made subject to fines and imprisonment.

Even in the early 1900s, Spanish Jesuits had protested when American occupiers of the Philippines had written guarantees of religious freedom into the territory's new constitution. As they explained:

> But if by liberty of religions is understood the granting to all religions—for example the worship of Confucius, or of Mohammed—and to all the Protestant sects equal rights to open schools, erect churches, create parishes, have processions and public ceremonies, with the Catholic Church, we believe that it would not only not be advisable, but it would be a lamentable measure for any government which may rule the destinies of the Filipinos.[30]

A generation later, many Catholics were even more certain. Poland's first constitution in 1921 did not, technically, endorse Catholicism, but still declared that "the Catholic confession as the religion of the overwhelming majority of the people takes first place among all equal confessions."[31] During the drafting process for the new Irish constitution in the 1930s, Irish Jesuits urged Prime Minister Eamon de Valera to recognize the "special position" of Catholicism as in "other Catholic constitutions."[32] The final text identified Catholicism as the "faith of the great majority of the citizens," but de Valera, sensitive to the plight of Catholics in the Protestant North and Dublin's tiny Jewish community, declined to declare Catholicism the state church. Cardinal Pacelli acknowledged the difficulty but regretted the phrasing. He thought it would be preferable to formally endorse Catholicism and then acknowledge that the constitution "tolerates" other faiths.[33]

III

CURIAL OFFICIALS triumphantly promulgated the first modern code of canon law in 1917, a bulky Latin volume that listed regulations on a bewildering array of topics, including the crucial insistence in Canon 329 that all episcopal appointments be made by the pope. (Saying so did not make it so. Governments in countries such as Spain played a role in the selection of bishops into the 1960s.) The language in Canon 218 registered ultramontane triumph: it claimed papal authority for not only "faith and morals" but anything "affect[ing] the discipline and government of the Church spread throughout the whole world."[34]

Bishops founded national conferences in the United States and a few other countries in the 1920s, but Vatican officials limited their influence. Boston's archbishop, William O'Connell, trained in Rome, complained of episcopal colleagues in the United States taking a "plebiscite among the bishops" in order to "diminish the authority of the Roman congregations."[35] Other bishops—even those highly placed within the Vatican itself—despaired at the unwillingness of curial officials to adapt their working patterns to the expanding needs of a global church and complained that important slots invariably went to well-connected Italians.[36]

The same Roman focus on autonomy scuttled participation in interreligious or ecumenical initiatives. Presbyterians, Anglicans, and Methodists, especially, developed ties with each other and with Orthodox Christians in the early twentieth century. Some Catholics, led by Belgium's Cardinal Désiré Mercier, participated in some of these discussions, but Benedict XV and his aides disliked the fact that Cardinal Mercier cheerfully referred to Protestants as "brothers and sisters in Christ." Roman officials warned Mercier, who ignored them, against dialogue with "pseudo-bishops."[37]

Pius XI thought such ecumenical efforts reeked of "dogmatic liberalism and modernism." He prohibited Catholic participation in ecumenical meetings in Switzerland and Germany, and in 1928 he issued an encyclical on religious unity, *Mortalium Animos*, that seemed less about unity than subjugation. Discussion of Christian cooperation could only proceed after recognition of the "authority and supremacy of Peter and his legitimate successor."[38] Small groups of Protestants in Rome and across Italy, often led by Italians who had converted from Catholicism while working in the United States, occupied an inordinate amount of the pope's attention, and he despaired at the Italian government's unwillingness to enact repressive measures against these "heretics."[39] While denouncing anti-Semitism, Pius XI also shut down a Catholic organization named Amici d'Israel (friends of Israel) out of fear that interreligious discussions, even about use of the phrase "perfidious Jews" in the Good Friday liturgy, might dilute doctrine.[40]

On paper, church regulations prohibited Catholics from attending a funeral in a synagogue or Protestant church or even attending a secular university without permission from the local bishop. One English Catholic recalled his childhood in a tight-knit parish in London in the 1920s and early 1930s.

> I was brought up not to enter a Protestant building, let alone take an active part in what took place there. Even to be present at the funeral or wedding of a non-Catholic relation required ecclesiastical permission and due care not to give the impression of taking part in the recitation of Protestant prayers or in hymn singing.[41]

IV

THE DISTINCTIVENESS OF the church was also highlighted on the battlefields of World War I. Soldiers repeatedly wrote of their pride that Catholics were more regular than Protestants in attending battlefield church services. The Latin liturgy remained a common thread, with German Catholic soldiers on one side of the trenches in France and French and British Catholic soldiers on the other attending identical services. Marian shrines, such as Lourdes in France, Knock in Ireland, La Vang in Vietnam, and Altötting in Bavaria, drew record numbers of pilgrims. New Marian apparition sites attracted new pilgrims, most famously at Fatima in Portugal beginning in 1917, but also at Ezkioga in the Spanish Basque country and Beauraing in Belgium.

If conventional portraits of post–World War I European and North American elites stress disillusionment and alienation, Catholic intellectuals, perhaps even ordinary Catholics, thought history moved in their direction. As one Hungarian Jesuit explained, "Protestants . . . sense very well, however much they may adhere to their confession, that Catholicism is the strongest fortress of the Christian faith and morality, the strongest bastion in the fight against liberal thought and destruction."[42]

The milieu was stronger than ever. The Netherlands contained not only Catholic schools, parishes, and universities in abundance, but also Catholic associations of laundry owners, tobacconists, barbers, and watchmakers.[43] When the Boy Scouts were introduced to the Netherlands as a potentially unifying youth movement, Catholic leaders created their own troops (as did Protestants) to avoid any taint of secularism.[44]

A French priest and dean of the faculty at the Institut Catholique de Paris equated the Allied victory in the war with a new opportunity for neo-Thomism and the defeat of "German philosophy."[45] Neo-Thomism

1932 Eucharistic Congress, Dublin. *(#2473 courtesy of Fr. Browne SJ collection)*

remained the underpinning for intellectual work within the Catholic world, and journals and institutes in that tradition continued to proliferate. (Many of the scholarly articles were still published in Latin.) This shared intellectual universe did not prevent rival Thomisms, but it did facilitate a genuinely international Catholic scholarly community. By 1939, alumni from the Gregorian University in Rome, a center of neo-Thomism, worked in twenty-eight nations.[46]

Eucharistic congresses, gatherings of Catholics from around the world for several days of Masses, processions, and exhortations, reached an extraordinary scale. Crowds of between five hundred thousand and over one million people attended the closing liturgies in Chicago (1926), Sydney (1928), Dublin (1932), Buenos Aires (1934), Manila (1936), and Budapest (1937). In Chicago, 150,000 people swarmed the train station to greet a special train of bright red coaches, dubbed the "Cardinals' Special," carrying several cardinals. In Buenos Aires, one priest recalled the scene:

> We had calculated badly. We did not believe many
> men would come. . . . As it turned out, it was impos-
> sible. Nobody could move a step in any direction. The
> nuns made hosts the whole afternoon, and continued
> the whole night. In the Cathedral, Mass was said con-
> tinually without interruptions, until past dawn. The
> priests brought the chalices on the Avenida de Mayo
> underground train. I heard confessions the whole night
> through, on the steps of the Loria station.[47]

A single Catholic parish in the town of Timaru, on New Zealand's South Island, counted only 2,350 registered souls but almost two dozen active organizations, from prayer groups to choirs to a cricket club. Rates of religious intermarriage in New Zealand were higher than in Catholic Europe or South America—only half of Catholics married other Catholics—but the subculture served a matchmaking role. Edicts against dancing, once strictly enforced, were set aside in an effort to promote social opportunities. A tennis club was said to claim a "record of Catholic marriages of which any matrimonial agency would be envious."[48]

1934 Parish Mission in Ireland.
(#3.62.6 courtesy of Fr. Browne SJ collection)

The primary mechanism for exerting influence on public life became Catholic Action, or, as proponents defined it, "the participation of the laity in the apostolate of the hierarchy." Begun by Pius X, the concept became the centerpiece of the pontificate of Pius XI, who dedicated a 1926 encyclical to the idea of "the Christian restoration of society in a Catholic sense."[49] Priests founded organizations for youth, women, university students, and farmers. Catholic Action was most successful in northern Europe, especially the Low Countries and France, but also vital in Canada, Italy, Mexico, Chile, and Brazil. Significant Catholic Action groups emerged in Ceylon (Sri Lanka), Uganda, and the Belgian Congo.

Military imagery suffused the movement—Belgians saw themselves as "a phalanx of the church of Christ"—with copious references to "knights" or "militia."[50] Huge gatherings in Rome of youth groups, women, or workers became routine, culminating in audiences with Pius XI.

The precise goals of Catholic Action remained hazy, and local circumstances dictated particular programs. Some of the most innovative work occurred in Catholic-affiliated unions. These unions enrolled only one-seventh as many workers as Europe's secular trade unions, but even in those secular unions Catholics became a key constituency. In Belgium, a young priest named Joseph Cardijn developed an influential methodology—See, Judge, Act—that allowed workers and young people to discuss their own solutions to the problems they encountered instead of simply listening to parents or chaplains. Cardijn explicitly saw himself competing with socialists for the allegiance of workers, and his work inspired other trade union activists across Europe.[51]

The ambitions of the JOC—after the French language abbreviation for Young Christian Workers—were immense. The slogan at one French national meeting was "Before we can convert Christians in the workshops, we must make the workshop Christian."[52] In front of eighty thousand Young Christian Workers in Paris in 1937, as the high point of a three-day festival of choral performances, meetings, and speeches, young workers carried a forty-foot-tall cross as a choir sang "Who builds the City?" and the crowd answered, "It is He."[53]

Running parallel to Catholic Action organization efforts were a new group of Catholic journals, including *Hochland* in Germany, *Criterio* in Argentina, *A Ordem* in Brazil, and *Commonweal* in the United States, typically founded by laypeople. No particular program united them beyond an uneasiness with secular liberalism and a desire, in the words of *Criterio*'s editors, to "prepare the Catholic conscience."[54]

V

WRITING FROM BERLIN in 1919, a city that in the span of a year witnessed the end of World War I, the collapse of the German Empire, a communist uprising, and the adoption of the democratic Weimar constitution, the influential German Jesuit Heinrich Pesch made a blunt assertion. "Capitalism has played itself out," he told his readers. "It is irretrievably lost. . . . We agree with Marxian socialism that the future no longer belongs to the economic license of individualistic capitalism."[55]

Catholics in the interwar era still understood political economy as indispensable for their social vision. Authority and justice remained its key words, not democracy or civil liberties. But in the 1920s, as opposed to the 1890s, Pesch's recipe of organized vocational groups, state intervention, and a limited free market seemed an ever more plausible "third way."

The same postwar moment offered the same possibilities elsewhere. In the United States, the Washington priest John Ryan drafted a plan for postwar reconstruction issued under the name of the American bishops, where they endorsed old-age and unemployment insurance, labor participation in management, a minimum wage, and a form of national health care. Workers and managers, the bishops recommended, should learn "the folly of excessive selfishness and senseless individualism." Higher taxes had the salutary effect of forcing a "small class of privileged capitalists . . . to return a part of their unearned gains to society."[56] A commentator for the liberal journal *The Nation* speculated that, as in Germany, secular reformers and Catholics might establish a new "kinship."[57]

An agricultural version of Catholic corporatism emerged, beginning in Belgium and spreading to Germany, Italy, and Mexico. In Calabria, Catholics began rural banks in order to "gradually acquire the consciousness of that solidarity which is their state."[58] Bavarian Catholics brought the idea of rural cooperatives and lending societies to South Africa.[59] In the United States, Catholic agricultural cooperatives sprouted in the rural Midwest.[60]

The most influential agricultural experiments occurred in Nova Scotia, where priest-professors from St. Francis Xavier University worked with farmers to set up marketing and production cooperatives, local stores, and insurance plans.[61] Thousands of visitors from around the Catholic world journeyed to Nova Scotia to learn the techniques of the Nova Scotia, or Antigonish, system of cooperatives. They adapted them for use in Jamaica, Guatemala, the Dominican Republic, and Peru as a mechanism for lessening the dependence of farmers on a particular harvest. (In the 1950s they expanded with great success to South Korea and what became Bangladesh.)[62]

The release of Pius XI's encyclical *Quadragesimo Anno* in May 1931 further energized Catholic corporatists. Drafted by two German Jesuits, Oswald von Nell-Breuning and Gustav Gundlach, its title marked forty years since Leo XIII's *Rerum Novarum*. Nell-Breuning and Gundlach were part of an activist circle meeting at Königswinter, on the Rhine, and eager to integrate theology and the social sciences. Both men published widely on a German economy marked by hyperinflation during the 1920s and then, after the 1929 stock market crash, high unemployment. They stressed the "completely unhealthy" reliance on the free market to solve the inequities generated by a capitalist economy.[63]

Published at the height of a global depression, *Quadragesimo Anno* was more radical than *Rerum Novarum*. Where *Rerum Novarum* stressed the rights of property owners, *Quadragesimo Anno* emphasized the "social character of ownership," and some neo-Thomists went further and dismissed conventional defenses of private property as "bourgeois." Where Leo XIII recommended workers' associations, Pius XI insisted that workers and employers jointly direct particular industries. The fact that the publication of *Quadragesimo Anno* coincided with the collapse of the Credit-Anstalt bank in Vienna and a subsequent run on banks across central Europe gave its recommendations even more punch.[64]

This papal notion of a more harmonious and less competitive economy always had a utopian flavor. When he first read a draft of *Quadragesimo Anno*, the Father General of the Jesuits asked Nell-Breuning, "How long do you think it will take to achieve this?" Nell-Breuning sheepishly replied, "It will never be achieved."[65] Still, the desire for experimentation strengthened as the economic crisis deepened. In Poland, Catholic activists supported the creation of strong workers' councils, aid to small businesses, and checks on a consumer economy based on the "artificial creation of unwholesome needs."[66] Vietnamese Catholics who had studied in Paris worked with French missionaries to bring Catholic Action ideas back to Southeast Asia. They sponsored numerous conferences and meetings on such topics as "Christian Social Doctrine and the Question of Work."[67]

Even in the United States, before the 1932 election, Democratic presidential candidate Franklin Roosevelt sent a giddy tremor through Catholic circles by quoting *Quadragesimo Anno* on the campaign trail. The encyclical, Roosevelt explained, was "just as radical as I am" and "one of the greatest documents of modern times."[68] The cornerstone program of Roosevelt's first term, the National Recovery Administration, with its attempt to set wages and prices, confirmed the Catholic view that planning, not economic growth, was the way forward. One writer viewed Roosevelt as moving toward "the Solidarism advocated by Father [Heinrich] Pesch . . . over forty years ago."[69]

VI

THE ZENTRUM PARLIAMENTARY REPRESENTATIVE, Helene Weber, one of the few women elected to the committee to draft Germany's democratic constitution in 1919, knew the task ahead would be challenging. Born in 1881, Weber began her professional career as a history instructor at an elite high school for women, where she was later remembered for her rigorous standards and the large briefcase of maps and graded essays she deposited on her desk before querying students on the day's lesson. She managed to attend university while teaching and eventually became the head of the *Katholischen Frauenbunde*, or Catholic Women's League.[70]

Weber merged an interest in economic reforms along the lines of *Rerum Novarum* (1891) with an equally distinctive vision of the family. For Weber, as for many socially minded Catholics, the widespread Catholic demand for a living wage for male workers doubled as a defense of traditional familial arrangements, since it was imperative, as Weber explained, that after having a child "a woman's job has to take the backseat and the family has to become the new center of her life."[71] Fathers exhausted from overwork and mothers forced to labor outside the home could not devote proper attention to raising their children. The Irish Constitution of 1937 insisted that private property be "regulated by the principles of social justice," but also regretted that some women felt economic pressure to take on paid labor "to the neglect of their duties inside the home."[72]

Laywomen such as Weber enrolled hundreds of thousands of members in Catholic women's organizations across Europe and North and South America. Instead of a false equality, in the words of one French activist, these women believed that the family was the "essential context for the woman question."[73] The Catholic women's movement in Italy only hesitantly took the name *movimento femminile cristiano* because of negative connotations around the term "feminist," which had come into use in the nineteenth century and gained ground in the twentieth.[74]

For women forced by circumstance to accept low-wage jobs, protective legislation limiting hours worked in a day seemed imperative, since, as one Chilean Catholic woman explained, "weakness is the origin of civil and social rights."[75]

Education for women was important, and nuns such as the Madames of the Sacred Heart and the Sisters of Notre Dame de Namur, based in northern Europe but with establishments all over the world, founded colleges or high schools for women. Thirty different congregations of women religious in Philadelphia ran three colleges, seventeen private academies, over two hundred elementary schools, eight hospitals, thirteen orphan asylums, eleven day nurseries, one settlement house, seven old-age homes, three homes for the handicapped, eight boarding houses for women, five homes for "unfortunate" women, and three visiting nurse associations.[76] In the Global South, the autonomy offered to women in religious orders meant a break with prevailing patriarchal customs. The decision of Bernadette Garatsa in Rhodesia to join a convent infuriated her father, leading to a lawsuit and Garatsa's eventual triumph in British colonial courts, affirming the right of an adult African woman to make life choices independent of paternal desires.[77]

Helene Weber focused on laywomen as leaders in the newly emerging profession of social work, where she encouraged Catholics to adopt modern methods. Her work paralleled that of Jane Addams in the United States, and Weber visited Addams in Chicago to exchange ideas. She and her Catholic peers nonetheless still viewed even social work through the lens of protecting the nuclear family. When drafting the Weimar constitution and through her service as an elected Center Party representative in the Reichstag, Weber fought against divorce law reform, which she and other Catholics viewed as less a tool to liberate women from oppressive marriages and more a vehicle to enable dissolute men. In Brazil, similarly, Catholic women led a petition drive against divorce well before they received the vote.[78] In Italy, Catholic women collected 3.5 million signatures in opposition to the reform of divorce laws.[79]

Around the world, male Catholic leaders (and some women) were initially equivocal on the topic of women's suffrage. Pius X allegedly told a German Catholic woman that he "approved of a cultured woman, one who knew Latin, even a woman doctor, but not a female voter."[80] Some German Catholic women insisted as late as 1918 that what they desired "is not the right to vote, but rather the possibility to become true housewives and mothers."[81]

Weber persuaded her colleagues in the Center Party to shift direction and support women's suffrage in the 1919 constitution, ignoring insinuations that she was an overly modern "Berliner." (She confided to a friend that some party members considered her "most unpleasant" for her advocacy of women's suffrage.)[82] Eventually, male Zentrum party leaders came around, partly as a matter of principle and partly as a competitive strategy. Catholics knew that many secular male liberals in France, Mexico, and elsewhere opposed women's suffrage precisely because they feared voting rights for women would enhance the power of Catholic parties. In France, liberals and socialists worried about a "government of priests" and a "Catholic mentality" shared by potential women voters. Women won the right to vote in France only in 1946.[83]

And in fact, Catholic women did support Catholic political parties and causes more consistently than Catholic men. In Germany, Catholic women were the most loyal Zentrum voters in the 1920s. Uruguayan women stressed that "the Communist woman, the Socialist woman" would exercise the ballot, and so Catholic women must "with the same firmness." Ecuador, the first country in Latin America to enfranchise women in 1929, also had the highest percentage of Catholics in its governing structure.[84]

A few Catholic activists debated whether they should emphasize elevating men's wages (even basing wages on the number of children in a family) or raise women's wages to equal men's. Most thought the answer obvious: focus on male heads of households and families. In France, Catholics rallied around the idea of allowances—*allocations familiales*— for married women raising children.[85] One woman laborer in Argentina, a leader in a Christian union, explained:

> I spend eight hours every day of the week in a factory. Nevertheless I tell you: *women should not have to work. . . .* God did not create her to supplement her husband's meager salary, but to be a companion, a girlfriend, a wife and

a mother. That's why we women are in the JOC. Because the JOC understands our vocation and our destiny, and will always struggle, unto death, to restore to women their lost Christian dignity.[86]

By the 1930s, though, some married Catholic women expressed a desire to work outside the home because of the meaning they derived from such work. Left-leaning French Catholics disparaged ideas of the "eternal feminine" and demanded equal pay for equal work. An Austrian woman urged clergy and politicians to recognize that "a woman's value is not determined merely by the calling to marriage and motherhood, but rather to other professions as well."[87]

VII

THE WEAKENING OF Victorian-era reticence on sexual and cultural matters marked the interwar period on both sides of the Atlantic. Writers and artists challenged obscenity laws, and public health officials advocated for the regulation of prostitution. Newly confident Catholics immersed themselves in these debates over censorship and sexuality, what Helene Weber termed protecting "public morality."[88] Irish bishops lamented the prevalence of the "dance hall, the bad book, the indecent paper, the motion picture and the immodest fashion in female dress."[89] Roman officials joined bishops and lay Catholic intellectuals (male and female) in Lithuania, the United States, France, and Ireland in regretting fashion trends that raised hemlines above the knee or encouraged the use of lipstick.[90]

Monitoring the production of books and newspapers was challenging given the decentralized publishing industry, although Weber and other Catholics bemoaned the "rising tide of filthy and dirty magazines."[91] Film, the era's most popular cultural form, offered more possibilities. In the Catholic view, movies promoted immorality if they depicted premarital (or extramarital) sex, divorce, or contempt for religous institutions. This assessment was not unique to Catholics, but only Catholics had the organizational capacity to do something about it. The International Union of Catholic Women's Leagues and priests involved with

Catholic Action programs worked to foster "good" cinema, and some of its members, as in Holland, sat on national boards of film censorship.[92]

Belgium became the home of the International Catholic Organization of Cinema, which encouraged Catholics not only to evaluate but to produce their own films. A Belgian Dominican priest saw the heightened influence of the media as requiring "nothing less than a total spiritual mobilization."[93] But the size of the American film industry meant that more could be accomplished in Los Angeles than in Brussels. Catholic bishops authorized the formation of the Legion of Decency in 1934 and encouraged millions of Catholics to take the Decency Pledge against attending objectionable movies. (Philadelphia's Cardinal Dougherty briefly forbade local Catholics from attending *any* films.)

Catholic pressure on the box office—or threats of such pressure—pushed studio executives to the bargaining table. An American Jesuit, Daniel Lord, devised guidelines for review and censorship of Hollywood films. Fr. Lord's use of natural law terminology—"the law which is written in the hearts of all mankind"—suggested his theological training. So, too, did his refusal to approve cinematic treatments of abortion, venereal disease, homosexuality, and birth control.[94] Parallel organizations emerged in Ireland, Italy, Mexico, Argentina, and Germany, essentially wherever Catholics possessed sufficient cultural influence to insert themselves into the censorship process. In Mexico, Catholic-dominated boards monitored new films, often to combat Hollywood stereotypes of salacious Latin American women or decadent Latin American men.[95] As late as the 1950s, Italian Catholic Action groups owned and ran over four thousand movie theaters, showing only Church-approved films.[96]

Censorship questions were controversial, but the most divisive topic—central to the entire twentieth-century history of Catholicism—was contraception. Most religious leaders in most religious traditions in the late nineteenth and early twentieth centuries thought contraception immoral. A distinctive Catholic campaign against contraception emerged only haltingly, scaling the hurdles of public reticence about sexual matters and widespread confusion among even physicians about the biological facts of a woman's reproductive cycle. As contraceptive practices and devices became more widespread, Catholic leaders overcame their hesitation. Sexual intercourse, Catholic philosophers explained, like freedom itself, had particular ends. And the primary end of intercourse remained procreation. Attempts to interfere with this end through contraception violated the natural law.

This interlocking set of assumptions fueled Catholic activism, but so, too, did the practice of confession. Protestant and Jewish leaders might oppose contraception, but such discussions, always intermittent, had an ethereal air. For Catholics, by contrast, contraception posed acute problems, since many Catholic adults attended confession monthly, or even weekly, and since all Catholics were formally required to attend confession after having committed serious sins.

Public awareness of Catholic opposition to contraception became widespread after 1921, when New York police broke up a public meeting of the American Birth Control Conference. Allegations that the police acted at the behest of New York's Cardinal Patrick Hayes remained unproven, although plausible. Hayes took the occasion to issue a pastoral letter, read out loud at each Sunday Mass in Manhattan, concluding that "Children troop down from Heaven because God wills it. . . . Woe to those who degrade, pervert, or do violence to the law of nature as fixed by the eternal decree of God Himself!"

Quick to define the contest as Catholics versus the enlightened, New York's Margaret Sanger, the world's most prominent advocate of contraception, immediately informed readers of the *Birth Control Review* that "you can no longer remain neutral. You must make a declaration of independence, of self-reliance, or submit to the dictatorship of the Roman Catholic hierarchy."

Into the 1930s, few public officials risked Catholic wrath by supporting or sponsoring legislation on birth control. In Britain and New Zealand, Catholic opposition intimidated the efforts of Labour Party activists to loosen restrictions on access to birth control. In Germany, Catholics in the Center Party such as Helene Weber agreed with many economic policies of the Social Democrats, but disagreed with plans to increase access to birth control. When American Catholics complained to President Franklin Roosevelt about federal workers promoting the use of birth control in an impoverished, predominantly Catholic Puerto Rico, Roosevelt immediately replied that his administration would refrain from "teaching Birth Control."[97] With

Vatican encouragement, Catholic diplomats from a number of countries strategized to prevent the League of Nations from promoting contraception.[98]

Frank discussion of birth control troubled Roman theologians. As early as 1925, cardinals assembled in Rome discussed a report from the apostolic delegate to the United States who worried that the "plague" of birth control was infecting American Catholics. Cardinal Eugenio Pacelli expressed the same fears about German Catholics.[99]

The first shift occurred among Anglicans, whose bishops in 1930 voted to permit married couples to use contraceptives for "a morally sound reason." In response, two Jesuits based in Rome—one Belgian and one German—drafted the first formal papal statement on contraception, the encyclical *Casti Connubii*, which consolidated Catholic teaching in the strongest terms. Procreation remained the final and most important end of sexual intercourse. No reason, "however grave," justified use of contraceptives, an act "intrinsically against nature." Released within four months of each other, each written in a prophetic, uncompromising tone, *Casti Connubii* and *Quadragesimo Anno* stretched Catholic teaching to its severest limits. Each document, the one on marriage and the other on the economy, called for wages to match family needs. In Washington, John Ryan, predictably, highlighted the passage in *Casti Connubii* that urged government officials to "do their utmost to relieve the needs of the poor."[100]

Casti Connubii was publicly greeted by Catholics around the world with great enthusiasm, but denouncing contraception at the height of a global depression did not suggest an overreliance on focus groups.[101] During the 1930s, anxious Catholic couples either abstained from sex or used contraceptives at higher rates. One knowledgeable priest in the United States privately admitted that "practically every priest who is close to the people admits that contraception is the hardest problem of the confessional today."[102]

Limits to the liberal faith in individual autonomy also became evident. In the early twentieth century, progressive reformers around the world became convinced that governments needed to pass laws requiring the sterilization of "imbeciles" and criminals. Sanger herself regretted that "anybody in this vast country is at perfect liberty to become a father or a mother"—including a "mental defective," a "pauper," and those bereft of "common decency."[103] Her British counterpart, Marie Stopes, explicitly worried about too many Catholic children, or, as she delicately put it, "soiled, diseased, desperate, and misbegotten reproductions."[104]

Catholics occasionally used eugenic language themselves. In New Zealand, Auckland's bishop worried that "the prolific Oriental" would reproduce in great numbers while Catholic women of European descent refused to bear the children God desired.[105] The most prominent German Catholic eugenicist, Fr. Hermann Muckermann, explained his "first concern" as preserving "the untouched, hereditary, elemental nature of the German people."[106]

Still, most Catholic intellectuals—even in Germany—could not reconcile forced sterilization and eugenics with *Casti Connubii*. Nazi officials fired Fr. Muckermann from his directorship at the Kaiser Wilhelm Institute for Anthropology because of his scruples about ambitious National Socialist programs of racial hygiene. Milan's Fr. Agostino Gemelli found himself repeatedly forced to explain to Italian eugenicists why he could not endorse the "moral error" of sterilization.[107] The most distinguished Catholic anthropologist in the United States eventually withdrew from contact with the nation's leading eugenic organizations because of their obsession with so-called Nordic races.[108]

In Britain, Poland, France, Quebec, and Latin America, Catholics, and usually only Catholics, challenged reformers wielding the authority of science in order to limit the reproductive capacities of the "unfit." No institution did more. The archbishop of New Orleans scorned the notion of a "millenium of supermen and superwomen as perfect specimens of the human animal, bred and reared according to the latest eugenic rules." Instead of forced sterilizations, he suggested, the state might guarantee that the poor were "properly housed and protected against the profiteer."[109]

VIII

THE CATHOLIC IDEA of a rightly ordered society extended beyond economics and the family to politics. After World War I, two patterns became evident. In Anglophone countries, Catholics eagerly participated in local and national politics and self-consciously acknowledged a democratic legacy stretching back to Ireland's Daniel O'Connell. One child of Irish Catholic migrants, Al Smith, ran for president as the first Catholic nominee of a major political party in the United States in 1928. Another child of Irish Catholic migrants, James Scullin, was elected prime minister of Australia in 1929.

In Italy and Germany, too, Catholic democrats became more visible. In 1919, Benedict XV welcomed the formation of the first Catholic Italian political party, the Partito Populare Italiano, or PPI, led by a charismatic Sicilian priest, Fr. Luigi Sturzo. Sturzo's passion for Catholic involvement in political life had already extended to serving in his native town's city government and founding its most important local newspaper. The PPI was an immediate electoral success, claiming 20 percent of the national vote in the first postwar elections and sending one hundred representatives to parliament. A few German Catholics, notably the convert Erik Peterson, in an essay dedicated to Sturzo, hoped that Catholics could underwrite "a harmonious welfare democracy with special regard for the weak classes."[110]

An equally important pattern, though, was for Catholic intellectuals and politicians to express doubts about democracy's future, especially as assassinations, chaotic parliamentary debates, and rotating chief executives destabilized democratic governments. Of the twenty-eight European parliamentary democracies in 1920, thirteen had become authoritarian governments by 1938. Democracies weakened or collapsed in South America's largest countries, including Brazil and Argentina.

Catholics stood at the center of this maelstrom. Democracy was the dog that rarely barked in Catholic social thought, and papal commentary evaded the term. Voluminous commentaries on workers' rights and just wages contrasted with terse examinations of politics. Catholics might found political parties and run for office, but Catholic theory lagged Catholic practice. In Europe, a surprising number of priests became presidents, prime ministers, and leading parliamentary figures, including Ignaz von Seipel in Austria, Willem Nolens in Holland, Josef Tiso in Slovakia, Ottokár Procházka in Hungary, and Ludwig Kaas in Germany. Despite their electoral successes, these men often displayed a contempt for parliamentary wrangling. This antidemocratic sensibility stemmed in part from the tendency of democratic governments to abolish or harass Catholic schools or expropriate Catholic property; in part it derived from neo-Thomism, with its emphasis on order and authority.

Democracy received little support in Rome. Pius XI, in his first encyclical, offered a condescending appraisal of "modern democratic states," which were "most exposed to the danger of being overthrown by one faction or another."[111] Vatican officials kept Fr. Sturzo's PPI at arm's length and eventually decided it was better to negotiate directly with Benito Mussolini after he seized power in 1922. Fearful of assassination by Mussolini's agents, Sturzo fled to London and then the United States.

One of the Nazi movement's opponents in Munich in the 1920s was Cardinal Michael Faulhaber, but Faulhaber viewed democratic politics with almost equal disdain. Dismayed by the absence of any recognition of God in the Weimar constitution, Faulhaber advocated for monarchy over republican institutions in a famous 1922 debate with Konrad Adenauer, later the first chancellor of West Germany but then a young Catholic mayor of Cologne and a defender of the Weimar government. Both men left the podium "with bright red faces."[112]

From his nuncio's office in Munich, Cardinal Eugenio Pacelli watched the growth of the Nazi Party with foreboding, especially since the movement at its origins counted many Catholic members eager to demonstrate their patriotic bonafides. Hitler's own anti-Catholic rhetoric soon soured many of these Catholics, notably his attacks in *Mein Kampf* on "ultramontanism" and the futility of an international church attempting to represent the "feelings of the German people."[113] Still, Pacelli privately speculated that nationalism might be the "most dangerous heresy of our time."[114]

The most important nationalist and authoritarian voice within the Catholic milieu was France's Charles Maurras, an unbeliever but also a royalist, an anti-Semite, and a nationalist dismayed by France's evolution toward secular democracy. The movement Maurras founded, Action Française, began during the turmoil of the Dreyfus affair in the 1890s, but his blend of nationalism and authoritarianism gained an international audience in the 1920s. One French Catholic recalled, with some hyperbole, the extent of Maurras's influence:

> [The Action Française exerted] an almost complete dicta-
> torship over Catholic intellectual circles. Whoever came
> out as a democrat in those circles was doomed to be an
> object of an ironical and scornful pity; he was looked
> down upon as a person behind the times, a survivor of
> another age.[115]

Outside of France, Catholics in French Canada, Italy, Spain, and South America shared with Maurras a disdain for "Anglo-Saxon" values and the unrestrained capitalism they associated with the United States.[116] An important Brazilian Catholic intellectual recalled Maurras's appeal this way: "We found that the religious movement of this era should parallel the political movement, against liberal democracy."[117]

Startled by Maurras and like-minded figures, Pius XI tried to redirect Catholics away from a toxic mixture of political authoritarianism and nationalism. He placed Maurras's writings on the Index of Forbidden Books and then in 1926 condemned the Action Française. He made a French cardinal unwilling to disavow Maurras resign his position, the first resignation of a cardinal in the modern era.

In the moment these papal hesitations about nationalism had only modest effect. Maurras's allies publicly pledged obedience to the pope while privately assuring each other that history would vindicate them. The class notes of a student at a Roman seminary directed by supporters of Maurras reveal a professor describing France as possessing "two souls." One soul was Catholic and opposed to the French Revolution. The other was a blend of "Masonry, Judaism and Protestantism."[118] "Despite the Pope, the Cardinal, the Nuncio and the rest," another Maurras supporter noted, "everybody here is in excellent form. This will pass. The Action Française is like the Church itself. Persecutions do it good."[119]

Still, a few Catholics began to register their concern. The era's most important scholar of nationalism, Columbia University's Carlton Hayes, a Catholic convert, explicitly attacked Maurras, Mussolini, and Hitler.[120] French Jesuit Henri de Lubac, destined to become one of the most influential theologians at the Second Vatican Council, tried to distinguish in his first published essay between an honorable patriotism and a destructive nationalism. He worried that Catholicism might become "an instrument of service to nationalist passions."[121]

IX

IN 1924 PLUTARCO CALLES, a determined anticlerical, was elected president of Mexico. The Mexican Constitution of 1917 had already formally banned religious instruction in all primary schools, prohibited monastic orders, banned public religious processions, and required priests to obtain government licenses while prohibiting them from voting or wearing clerical garb in public. But these laws were loosely enforced and a new group of Catholic organizations emerged to defend church interests.

Calles's election upset this equilibrium. Calles and his aides vowed to implement the provisions of the 1917 constitution and to make schools entirely secular, with the vocal support of American liberals such as the philosopher John Dewey. Dewey bluntly explained that "the Church can hardly escape paying the penalty for the continued ignorance and lack of initiative which it has tolerated if not cultivated."[122]

In response, prodded by Catholic Action organizations, Mexico's bishops declared a suspension of all Masses on August 1, 1926. Almost immediately, a civil war exploded between government forces and Catholic dissidents centered in the states of Michoacán, Guanajuato, and Jalisco. Perhaps fifty thousand Catholics took up arms against the government, calling themselves Cristeros after the idea promoted by Pius XI of a Christ the King standing above politics.

The welcome given to Calles's anticlerical initiatives differed from town to town. In one Michoacán village, educators and military officials described Catholic clergy as "deeply fanatical" and rallied villagers to force the local bishop into exile. In another Michoacán village, only federal troops could restore order after protesting crowds shouted "¡Viva Cristo Rey!" ("Long live Christ the King.")[123]

Twenty-five hundred Mexican bishops, priests, nuns, and lay leaders fled to the United States, making San Antonio, Texas, the hub of the resistance. (The Mexican Episcopal Committee met there for the duration of the war.) The Calles government deported other Catholics and used secret agents to monitor their activities. Both exiles and deportees encouraged anti-government sentiment and rallied Catholics around the world to the cause of religious liberty in Mexico. The Knights of Columbus, a US-based Catholic fraternal organization with many Mexican branches, organized meetings and raised funds for the Cristeros. The rebels seemed, in the words of a government informer, to have "plenty of sympathizers who are helping out with money and ammunition."[124]

The saga of one Mexican Jesuit, Miguel Pro, attracted much attention. Pro had studied in Mexico, Nicaragua, France, and Belgium. Upon his return to Mexico, he became active in the resistance to the Calles government by celebrating clandestine Masses and personally escorting groups of nuns across the Mexican-American border into Texas under cover of darkness.[125] After an acquaintance plotted the assassination of Calles, Pro and his brother were arrested and convicted without a trial, although it seems unlikely they knew anything of the conspiracy. A photo of Pro before his execution, kneeling, with a crucifix around his neck and a rosary in his hand, and uttering the words "¡Viva Cristo Rey!" became a talisman of Catholic resistance to a secular state. Believers exchanged it as a postcard. A French Canadian Jesuit who had met the young Pro in Europe wrote a biography that was immediately translated into multiple languages.[126]

Postcard of Mexican Jesuit Miguel Pro before his execution in 1927. *(Courtesy of Rare Books and Special Collections, Hesburgh Library, University of Notre Dame)*

Events in Mexico seemed to augur a new, more aggressive secularist agenda. When Poland's ambassador to the Vatican met with Pius XI, they discussed the Cristero Rebellion. The pope "asserted that when it comes to the Catholic countries, such as Poland, France, Spain, and South America, activities from Masonry on the one hand and communists on the other might lead to a total collapse of authority."[127]

Vatican officials commended Mexican Catholics for their resistance to the "impious laws" and a "persecuting government." In private memos they compared events in Mexico with events during the French Revolution.[128] But they, too, desired to end the war. After three years and ninety thousand deaths, Catholic leaders from the United States helped bring the Cristeros and the Calles government to the bargaining table. Leaders from both sides negotiated a cease-fire in 1929.

X

VINCENT LEBBE AND MA XIAOBANG continued to struggle for an authentically Chinese Catholicism. Lebbe counted as a friend the influential Belgian Jesuit and Louvain professor, Pierre Charles, who taught generations of future missionaries that their role was to plant Indigenous churches, not simply import an ultramontane European Catholicism. Charles invited Lebbe to speak at Louvain on such topics as "indigenous clergy in China" and "China and the foreigner."[129]

Sympathy for the view that Catholics must become integrated into host societies became more and more evident in Rome. The Vatican's Holy Office reversed course in 1936 and allowed Catholics to bow before the Yasukuni Shrine outside of Tokyo, a Shinto site dedicated to honoring Japanese war dead. Such gestures had once been forbidden—two students at Jesuit-run Sophia University had infuriated Japan's fascist leaders by refusing to bow in 1932—but now became defined as registering "patriotism and loyalty," not religious worship.[130] The Propaganda Fide revoked the 1704 papal condemnation of the Jesuit Chinese rites, a tacit admission that contemporary missionaries must acculturate to their surroundings in much the same way as the first Catholic missionaries to Asia. Missionaries who had once disparaged Confucius now described him as a sage.[131]

The Japanese invasion of Manchuria in 1931 energized Ma Xiaobang, and he addressed the national assembly on the necessity of a "moral rearmament."[132] In 1938, on his one hundredth birthday, Nationalist Party officials battling the Japanese took time to honor a feeble Ma with a celebration of his life and work, although he had been taken to Vietnam to escape Japanese bombing campaigns. He died unaware he had left his homeland.

Lebbe also threw himself into the struggle against the Japanese. His defense of the China he now called home—he became a citizen in 1933—included service in Chiang Kai-shek's Nationalist army (with the honorary rank of colonel), organizing a Catholic regiment for this "most just of wars," and volunteering his Little Brothers as stretcher bearers.[133] Chinese Catholics viewed Lebbe as a hero—in contrast to Italian Catholic missionaries willing to collaborate with the Japanese invaders—and lined up to confess their sins to him. Lebbe's close friend, Bishop Yu Bin, urged Chinese Catholics to "take up arms, defend their country and if necessary die for her, with honor."[134]

Chinese communists arrested Lebbe when the alliance between Mao Zedong's Communists and Chiang Kai-shek's Nationalists broke down in the late 1930s. They imprisoned him for eighty days. Desperately ill upon his release, Lebbe was flown to the Nationalist wartime capital of Chongqing and welcomed as a hero. He died in June 1940. In one of his last letters, he vowed to continue demonstrating, "even if I am alone in the world, Christian indignation against the demon of imperialism."[135]

EIGHT

Crisis

The Politics of the 1930s

I

IN THE SPRING OF 1933, Münster resident Edith Stein, a philosopher and convert to Catholicism from Judaism, wrote to Pope Pius XI. She gave the letter to the Benedictine abbot who served as her spiritual director, and he arranged for intermediaries to place the letter on the pope's desk. She referred to herself, significantly, not only as a "daughter of the Catholic Church" but also "as a daughter of the Hebrew people." In the weeks since Adolf Hitler and the National Socialist Party had taken control of the German government, she explained, the new government "had exhibited a total disregard of justice and humanity." Its leaders had long "preached hatred of the Jews." Why had the pope said nothing? "Not only the Jews," she explained, "but also thousands of faithful Catholics in Germany, and, I believe, the entire world, have been waiting and hoping

Edith Stein *(Katholiek Documentatie Centrum, Nijmegen, Photo: AFBK-2A9135)*

that the Church of Christ would make itself heard in condemning this abuse of the name of Jesus Christ. Is this idolatry of race and of the power of the state, with which the masses are bombarded daily over the radio, not open heresy?" She predicted that silence when crimes were committed against Jews would only encourage attacks on Catholicism, "carried out more quietly and in a less brutal way than that against the Jews."[1]

Born on Yom Kippur, as her mother liked to point out, into a devout Jewish family in Breslau, Germany (now Wrocław, Poland), in 1891, Stein was a brilliant student. While attending the university in Breslau she fell into the circle of young scholars interested in the work of the philosopher Edmund Husserl. She transferred from Breslau to the university in Göttingen to be near Husserl, whom she and other students called "the Master."

Husserl founded phenomenology, as much a method as a theory. Phenomenologists urged people to closely describe their individual experience, coming to grips with the things and emotions that structure day-to-day existence. Many Catholic neo-Thomists found Husserl's work appealing, especially those clustered around Belgium's Cardinal Mercier and working at the Catholic University of Louvain. They blended phenomenology with psychological experiments to gain a deeper understanding of such topics as memory and perception and spread Husserl's ideas around the world through their scholarly networks. Both Husserl and these Catholic admirers presumed the existence of an identifiable physical and moral order. One Belgian understood Husserl as proving from a different angle neo-Thomist claims about "objective truth."[2]

During World War I, Stein volunteered as a nurse on a typhoid ward and became an ardent German patriot. "I believe I can assert objectively," she wrote to a colleague in 1917, "that since Sparta and Rome there has never been as strong a consciousness of being a state as there is in Prussia and the new German Reich. That is why I consider it out of the question that we will now be defeated." On a break, she visited her family in Breslau. She could not bear the mundane chitchat and decided, in the moment, that "my individual life has ceased, and all that I am belongs to the state."[3]

The horrific last year of the war and its turbulent aftermath shattered this certainty. "Good and evil, knowledge and ignorance," she now concluded, "are mixed on all sides."[4] She grew interested in the limits of national loyalties and found herself drawn to religious questions. Because she was a woman, Stein could not pursue the second dissertation (or habilitation) that would qualify her for a university professorship, a policy Husserl chose not to challenge. Because she was Jewish, academic employment opportunities were limited. When apprised of an open teaching position in Hamburg, she declined to apply, since "there are already two Jewish philosophers there." More would not be welcome given the "present level of rampant anti-Semitism."[5]

Husserl himself was a nonobservant Jew who eventually converted to a nondogmatic form of Protestantism. His circle of students included men and women with a diverse set of religious commitments, most famously Martin Heidegger, a onetime Catholic seminarian, but also Max Scheler, one of Germany's most important philosophers and self-identified for a time as Catholic. Heidegger eventually developed a disdain for the Catholicism of his youth, and some Catholics began to regard Scheler's philosophical approach as insufficiently neo-Thomist. (Scheler's divorce and subsequent remarriage to one of his students also scandalized onetime admirers.) Stein knew Heidegger, and when she encountered him by chance at Husserl's home, she took a walk with him and another student to discuss "the philosophy of religion."[6]

Other Husserl students, including the Austrian Dietrich von Hildebrand, found in phenomenology inspiration for their conversion to Catholicism. Stein was a member of this second group, and she later wrote that phenomenology guided her into the "majestic temple of scholastic [or neo-Thomist] thought."[7] When she informed her mother of her conversion to Catholicism, it was the first time Stein had seen her cry. (Even a decade later Stein knew that her mother remained convinced that "everyone ought to live and die in the faith in which they were born.")[8] During the 1920s, Stein taught German literature and history at a teacher's college for women. She asked her local bishop for his permission to read authors listed on the Index of Forbidden Books: Bergson, Hume, Kant, Locke, and Spinoza. All were works she "formerly used in the study of modern philosophy."[9]

Despite a grueling teaching schedule, Stein completed major translation projects on Aquinas (from Latin into German) and John Henry Newman (from English into German). In 1929, Stein published a comparison of Aquinas and Husserl, with Aquinas winning the argument. (That same year, another brilliant young German Jewish philosopher, Hannah Arendt, also a onetime Husserl student, published her dissertation on St. Augustine.) Stein worked closely with the German-Polish Jesuit Erich Przywara and explained their shared goal as "a confrontation between traditional Catholic and modern philosophy."[10] Przywara put it this way: making sure Aquinas stands "eye to eye with Husserl, Scheler and Heidegger."[11]

II

ERICH PRZYWARA HAD once forecast a " 'Catholic renewal' . . . a positive view of 'Catholic' as a creative factor in the life of the spirit and culture."[12] But by the early 1930s, Przywara and other Catholics took a more defensive stance. The old enemies, after all, remained. Catholics continued to fulminate against socialists (who returned the favor) and Freemasons (likewise). One influential Polish priest urged Catholics to unite against a comprehensive list of foes: "international Masonry, international socialism, and international sects and heresies [as they] gather all their forces against Christ and His Church."[13]

Two groups—communists and Jews—took on new importance. Catholics had long denounced an atheistic communism, if often only in the abstract. The Russian Revolution of 1917 created an actual communist state, but Bolshevik policy toward Catholicism was at first less aggressive than anticipated—only 7 percent of Catholic churches had been closed in 1928. Yet while Vatican officials repeatedly attempted in vain to negotiate a concordat protecting Catholic institutions, the Soviets began to pressure Christian organizations.[14] A French priest based in Moscow uttered grave warnings about the future of the country's two million Catholics. "There is no apostolate," he explained to his superiors, "no religious instruction of the young, nobody to replace the priests who have died or fled, and no bishop. We are witnessing the death, slow but sure, of Latin Catholicism in Russia."[15]

A more open Soviet persecution of Christian churches of all types began in 1929, predicated on Joseph Stalin's suspicion that groups independent of the state might resist his agricultural collectivization program. Priests were imprisoned and parishes closed. Protests from Vatican diplomats and European supporters were unavailing, since as the commissar for foreign affairs calmly explained, "the Soviet government has an anti-religious orientation."[16] Soon, the price for serving on a parish council could be a decade in a Siberian gulag.[17] By 1938, the 1,217 Catholic parishes extant within the Soviet Union in 1917 had been reduced to exactly one, in Moscow, led by an American priest, Léopold Braun, who ministered to diplomats and a handful of local parishioners willing to brave monitoring by the secret police. At night, as Braun reported to his superiors, trucks deposited those arrested during the Great Terror of 1937 at the Lubyanka prison just a few yards from the parish.[18]

Earlier than their secular peers, Catholic intellectuals shrewdly recognized in Soviet communism a competing cosmology, or, in the words of Erich Przywara, a "religious spirit phenomenon."[19] They worried

Anton Walter family, 1932. Walter was sentenced in 1933 to a decade-long prison term in the Soviet Union for the crime of serving on a parish council. *(Courtesy of Rare Books and Special Collections, Hesburgh Library, University of Notre Dame)*

that these anti-religious sentiments might spread from Moscow across Europe. Revolutionaries in 1848 had hoped to topple decrepit monarchies and install governments committed to civil liberties and (male) suffrage. Revolutionaries in 1919 hoped to install atheist, communist governments. Germany's bishops organized 1,737 parish and diocesan meetings against radicalism and communism in the single year of 1931. On the first Sunday of Lent in 1932, every German pastor gave a sermon on "Bolshevism."[20] As one German priest speculated, the Soviet strategy was to "drive Germany to the side of Bolshevism" and create a "victorious united Soviet Germany and Soviet Russia." The Church could still lead an anti-communist movement, "but it will not be possible much longer." Austrian Catholics committed themselves to opposing "Bolshevism's battle against religion and Christian culture both inside and outside Russia."[21] Vietnamese Catholics, aware of communism's appeal to some contemporaries, worried about the "spirit of Bolshevism that is in the air."[22]

Catholic leaders in countries with barely perceptible communist movements were no less watchful. Brazilian bishops and priests portrayed communism as a "moral plague" and communists as "modern barbarians armed with sickle and hammer."[23] Ireland's bishops accused the Irish Republican Army of trying to "impose upon the Catholic soil of Ireland the same materialistic regime, with its fanatical hatred of God, as now dominates Russia and threatens to dominate Spain."[24]

Pius XI confided to a priest based in China that "the great danger is Bolshevism for China, India, Europe, throughout. The Bolsheviks are marvelous propagandists."[25] When Vincent Lebbe lived in Paris, he saw himself as competing for the allegiance of Chinese students with the future communist premier Zhou Enlai, also living in Paris and for a time a correspondent for Lebbe's newspaper. Ma Xiangbo worried about the allure of communism—defined as the "compulsory sharing of property and women"—to intellectuals.[26]

The Vatican convened conferences and organized museum exhibits in the mid-1930s on communism, the world's only "truly global organization" besides Catholicism, and founded a new Secretariat on Atheism.[27] Vatican officials, and subsequently French bishops, worried about Catholic trade unionists willing to consider alliances with communist counterparts, the so-called *main tendue,* or extended hand, since communism "despite certain occasional camouflages remains the worst danger."[28] More commonly, Catholic trade unionists needed no Roman encouragement to see themselves as in the vanguard of opposition to communist influence. Catholic members of the San Francisco long-shoreman's union successfully mobilized to defeat communist candidates in elections for shop leadership positions.[29]

Some of the same Catholics thought that Jews subverted national unity, too. A modern anti-Semitism emerged within Catholic circles in the nineteenth century, building on traditional religious tropes but translating them into a new idiom. The most virulent forms of this anti-Semitism were frankly conspiratorial, and its advocates across Europe and North America promoted the idea of the Jews as bent on "world domination."[30] But less conspiratorial Catholics also voiced anti-Semitic sentiments. In Hungary, Bishop Ottokár Prohászka translated *Rerum Novarum* into Hungarian and daringly entitled an early work *Modern Catholic,* a text that drew unfavorable scrutiny from Pius X's anti-modernist censors. During the brutal final months of World War I, with Hungary's armies enduring horrendous losses, this self-professed "modern" Catholic expressed his fears about a "militant phalanx" of Jews subverting the country's war effort. He falsely accused the country's Jews of not enlisting in the army in numbers proportionate to their presence in the population.[31] After the war, as a leading member of parliament, Bishop Prohászka advocated a quota for Jewish students at universities. Such laws, he claimed, represented a necessary cultivation of a "national Christian tendency."[32] For the same reason, some Polish Catholics fought for the same quotas on Jewish students in Polish universities.[33]

The idea of a link between Judaism and communism, what contemporaries termed a Judeo-Bolshevik conspiracy, became widespread. The notion was hardly limited to Catholics but nonetheless nestled within the Catholic milieu. In 1919, two future popes, Eugenio Pacelli (Pius XII) as a nuncio in Munich and Achille Ratti (Pius XI) as a nuncio in Warsaw, witnessed struggles with local communists firsthand. Pacelli stayed in Munich in 1919 during the city's short-lived Bavarian Soviet Republic, and by his own possibly self-aggrandizing account, revolutionaries with guns drawn threatened to shoot him on the steps of the nuncio's residence.[34] During the anxious days of Warsaw's siege during the Soviet-Polish War, Ratti also remained in the city.[35] Neither man distinguished revolution from communism or from the Jewish people. Pacelli feared a "grim Russian-Jewish-Revolutionary tyranny."[36] Ratti described Bolshevism as "essentially Jewish, anti-Catholic [and] anti-religious."[37]

Not all Catholic leaders were anti-Semitic, and in New York City and other places, Catholics and Jews occasionally developed alliances. When the head of the world's Jesuits, Włodzimierz Ledóchowski, proposed firing the Jewish dean of Fordham University's pharmacy school, simply because it seemed inappropriate for a dean at a Catholic university to be Jewish, the university's Jesuit community thwarted the effort.[38]

As the grip of the global depression tightened, however, Catholic anti-Semitism became more visible. By the 1930s, Fr. Charles Coughlin had become the most famous Catholic priest in the United States. Based in suburban Royal Oak, outside of Detroit, Michigan, Coughlin's weekly radio program drew an audience in the tens of millions. An early champion of Franklin Roosevelt's New Deal—"Christ's New Deal"—Coughlin began criticizing Roosevelt as insufficiently radical in the mid-1930s, urging him to nationalize the banking industry and inflate the currency. For a short time, he seemed to be Roosevelt's primary political rival.[39]

Always opposed to communism—he installed an anti-communist club for students in his parish grade school—Coughlin started promoting anti-Semitism in the late 1930s. He drew from the writings of Fr. Denis Fahey, an Irish priest educated in Rome by French anti-modernist clergy.[40] Fahey, and then Coughlin, reprinted the *Protocols of the Elder of Zion*, the fabricated document alleging a Jewish plot aimed at world domination. Notoriously, Coughlin defended violence against Jews on Kristallnacht, the night in November 1938 when Nazis encouraged the destruction of synagogues and Jewish-owned stores. Other American Catholics, notably Fr. John Ryan, immediately took to the airwaves to rebut Coughlin, and most Catholic newspapers and many bishops declaimed against Nazi violence. Still, the activities of paramilitary Christian Front organizations inspired by Coughlin, located in heavily

Catholic areas of Boston and New York, echoed fascist mobs tormenting Jews in Italy and Germany. They organized boycotts of Jewish-
owned stores, assaulted Jewish pedestrians, and claimed, as in Europe,
to counter communist influence.[41]

Other Catholics thousands of miles away followed the same path.
The Argentine priest Gustavo Franceschi delivered that country's most
popular radio broadcasts in the 1930s. Unlike Coughlin, he rejected
conspiracy theories. But he still thought Jews were motivated by "the
spirit of wealth and the power of gold."[42]

Some Catholic theologians and scholars, especially in central Europe,
used scientific racism to justify anti-Semitism. Europe's leading Catholic anthropologist, Austrian Wilhelm Schmidt, considered Nazi ideas
about Aryan superiority absurd, but he found some versions of racial
theory irresistible. In a 1934 essay on "The Jewish Question," Schmidt
lamented the predominance of Jews in the medical profession and the
film industry.[43] Karl Adam, a German Catholic theologian influential
for his support of ecumenicism, professed admiration for Nazi efforts to
unite German Protestants and German Catholics in a "blood unity."[44]

Poland's Cardinal Augustus Hlond offered a tortured defense of economic boycotts directed against Jews in 1936:

> One may love one's own nation more but one may not
> hate anyone. Not even Jews. It is good to prefer your
> own kind when shopping, to avoid Jewish stores and
> Jewish stalls in the marketplace, but it is forbidden to
> demolish a Jewish store, damage their merchandise, break
> windows or throw things at their homes.[45]

Hlond also offered another line of analysis. "It is a fact," he concluded, "that the Jews are fighting with the Catholic Church, that they
are embedded in free-thinking, that they constitute the avant-garde of
godlessness, the Bolshevik movement and revolutionary activities."[46]

Remarkably, then, Jews seemed to some Catholics implicated in
both capitalist and communist modernities. The German Jesuit Gustav
Gundlach rejected laws targeting Jews and reminded Catholics that Jews
remained a "chosen people within the divine and Christian economy

of salvation." But he also warned of the "truly harmful influence of the Jewish segment of the population in the areas of economy, politics, theater, cinema, the press, science and art." He thought it worrisome that Jews managed to "operate within the camp of world plutocracy" as well as "international Bolshevism."[47]

III

THE TWO MOST controversial Vatican concordats of the era—the 1929 Lateran Accords with Mussolini and the 1933 Reichskonkordat with Hitler—used diplomatic means to protect Catholic institutions. The Lateran Accords finally ended the long standoff with the Italian state that began with the country's unification in 1870 and granted the Holy See sovereignty in Vatican City. Mussolini also guaranteed Catholic instruction in state schools, ended legal divorce, and promised independence for Catholic Action organizations. Pius XI congratulated Mussolini for not sharing "the concerns of the liberal school."[48]

This positive appraisal of Mussolini was shared by a surprising number of non-Catholic intellectuals and politicians. But enthusiasm for Mussolini was especially notable among Catholics, including bishops and priests who had trained in Rome. In the United States, the bishop of rural Sioux Falls, South Dakota, who had spent eighteen years in Rome at the North American College seminary before his episcopal assignment, finagled an invitation to meet Il Duce in 1932. He "likened [Mussolini's] attitude to that of George Washington." The rare Italian priest in the diaspora community who publicly criticized Mussolini, such as Detroit's Giuseppe Ciarrocchi, a supporter of the now disbanded Partito Populare Italiano, endured efforts to silence him by Italian Fascist diplomats because he refused, in Ciarrocchi's words, to condone the "worship of Mussolini." No less an authority than Vatican secretary of state Eugenio Pacelli intervened to halt Ciarrocchi's embarrassing (to the Vatican) "anti-Fascist campaign."[49]

Within Italy, the agreement forged between the Vatican and the Italian state almost collapsed at its outset. In 1929 the pope had insisted, explicitly quoting the majority opinion in the US Supreme Court decision in *Pierce v. Society of Sisters* (1925), which prohibited the state of Oregon from banning Catholic schools, that parents, not the state, had the primary right (and duty) to educate their children.[50] In 1931, Pius XI protested with more vehemence Mussolini's decision to abolish Catholic youth groups and, in the pope's words, foster "Statolatry," or the "pagan worship of the State."[51] Still, until the late 1930s, Vatican and state intermediaries managed to smooth over differences between Pius XI and Mussolini occasioned by censorship of Catholic publications and restrictions on Catholic organizations.[52]

The Reichskonkordat negotiated between the Vatican and the new National Socialist government was signed in the summer of 1933. Until that moment, most German Catholic bishops had denied that Catholics in good standing could join the Nazi Party. German Catholic voters were the single voting bloc within Germany most resistant to Hitler's persuasive powers, and the most Catholic regions of Germany were the least likely to support the National Socialists.[53]

Hitler's electoral victory in 1933 presented new threats but also an opportunity. Always wary, Pius XI nonetheless credited Hitler in these early days with being "the first and only man of state who speaks against

Reichskonkordat signing, 1933, Vatican secretary of state Cardinal Eugenio Pacelli, the future Pope Pius XII, at center. *(KNA-Bild, #77146)*

the bolshevists. Until now, it [has] only been the Pope."[54] In Cardinal Pacelli's phrasing, by negotiating the Reichskonkordat with the National Socialists, Catholics dodged a "Kulturkampf much worse than in Bismarck's times."[55] A pleased Hitler told an aide that no one would have thought "that the Church would be ready to commit the bishops to this state." Cardinal Faulhaber of Munich, long critical of the National Socialists and once willing to forbid Catholics from joining the Nazi Party because of the Nazi belief in Aryan superiority, congratulated Hitler in a handwritten note. The letter conveyed Faulhaber's distaste for democratic politics. "What the old parliament and parties did not accomplish in sixty years," he admiringly told the new Reich Chancellor, "your statesmanlike foresight has achieved in six months."[56]

IV

THIS CLUSTER OF IDEAS—a fierce anti-communism, an underlying drumbeat of anti-Semitism, and skepticism about democratic politics—existed across the Catholic world in the mid-1930s. In majority Catholic states such as Brazil, Portugal, and Austria, the result was a distinct Catholic authoritarian vision, built on the corpse of a discredited liberalism but attempting to distinguish itself from Italian fascism and German Nazism. After a coup overthrew the Brazilian Republic in 1930, Rio de Janeiro's powerful bishop, Sebastião Leme, helped negotiate the resignation of Brazil's president and welcomed the new president, Getúlio Vargas. Leme mobilized Catholic supporters in two massive rallies in Rio de Janeiro, telling the cheering throngs that "either the state . . . will recognize the God of the people or the people will not recognize the state."[57]

Vargas, an agnostic who named his son Luther, nonetheless chose to work with Leme, even as his government substituted authoritarian rule for electoral politics. A year later, Leme presided at the dedication of a massive statue dedicated to Christ the Redeemer, paid for in part with state funds, overlooking Rio de Janeiro's magnificent harbor. Attending the ceremony were Vargas and every member of his cabinet, along with forty-five bishops. The constitution of 1934 did not officially recognize Catholicism, but it allowed the Vargas government to support Catho-

Christ the Redeemer statue dedication, Rio de Janeiro, 1931. *(Getty Images/Keystone France)*

lic schools and trade unions and to provide state subsidies for Catholic hospitals, seminaries, and colleges for the first time since the founding of the republic in 1889. State education officials even funded a Portuguese translation of Thomas Aquinas's *Summa Theologica*.[58] (At the exact same moment Dominican priests completed the first translation of the *Summa Theologica* into Czech.)[59]

A Brazilian Jesuit described his country as immune to "individualist excesses and socialist exaggerations." A modern Brazilian state would stress communal interests more than capitalist "oppression of the weak and the poor."[60] A political party with many Catholic supporters, the Ação Integralista Brasileira, described its platform as directed "against the false mystique of democracy and against the false mystique of communism."[61]

In Portugal, Antonio Salazar, a onetime Catholic youth leader and seminarian, became the country's dictator in 1932. As a young man, Salazar had endorsed *Rerum Novarum* and the idea of a more ordered economy. A stint in parliament, with its unstable coalitions, dismayed him. As he explained, "We are drawing near to the moment in political and social evolution in which a political party based on the individual, the citizen or the elector will no longer have sufficient reason for existence."[62]

In Austria, the newly elected chancellor, Engelbert Dollfuss, promised in 1933 to build a "Catholic German state" inspired by *Quadragesimo Anno*, and he dismissed as anachronistic "the era of liberal and capitalistic systems."[63] Dollfuss, like Salazar, eliminated not only rival political parties but also independent trade unions. Both Austria and Portugal banned the sale of birth control devices, and both disallowed forced sterilization, with Portuguese Catholics especially insistent on prohibiting sterilization as a "flagrant injustice." Both states thought family allowances were a way to promote large families and to allow mothers to remain in the home.[64]

Dollfuss and Salazar distinguished their movements from Nazism. Portuguese Catholic newspapers repeatedly criticized Nazi attempts to dismantle Catholic organizations in Germany, and Dollfuss was assassinated by Nazi thugs in 1934 in a failed plot to overthrow the government. Dollfuss and his successor, Kurt Schuschnigg, protected (and funded) Catholic scholars who disparaged Nazi views on race and physicians who refused to implement Nazi sterilization programs.[65]

Salazar's influence in the Catholic world extended not only to Portuguese-speaking Brazil but also to surprising places such as Britain, where writer G. K. Chesterton and other Catholic luminaries lauded the Portuguese experiment.[66] In France, especially, many Catholics saw this type of authoritarian politics as alluring, especially when they contemplated their own turbulent democracy. Jesuits in the Philippines pondered whether the elimination of political parties and a regime modeled on either Austria or Portugal might prove a worthy goal.[67]

When the British political theorist Michael Oakeshott surveyed the range of political options in Europe in the 1930s, he identified "representative democracy," "communism," "fascism," and "National Socialism." Referencing Portugal, Poland, Ireland, and Austria, he also listed "Catholicism."[68]

V

A CASCADING SERIES OF events in the late 1930s shattered this nationalist and authoritarian Catholic vision. The most important, and violent, occurred in Spain. Spain's left-wing movements had inherited a tradition of hostility and violence directed against Catholic leaders and institutions, and Spanish Catholics, in turn, had long insisted on the unity of nation and faith. This polarization made Spain's culture wars more enduring than those of Germany and France, which had been eased by the shared trauma of World War I.[69] The collapse of Spain's authoritarian government and the advent of the Second Republic in 1931 began an era of heightened tension. Spain's Catholic leadership saw the republic as born "in the shadow of unbelief and modern rationalism." Naturally, it would be "hostile to Religion."[70]

In these uncertain first days of the Spanish Republic, a Vatican scarred by its experience of anticlericalism in Mexico in the 1920s counseled caution. Bishops and laypeople alike knew that one-third of Spanish Catholics, primarily located in the north, actively practiced their faith, while another third, primarily in the south, were actively hostile.

To the dismay of most Catholics, however, the draft version of the new Spanish Constitution gave no special protection or financial aid to the Church, and it recommended the expulsion of all religious orders and the seizure of their property. One of the most reactionary Spanish bishops, Pedro Segura y Sáenz of Toledo, judged the constitution with its separation of church and state entirely unacceptable, a claim he supported with a torrent of references to Pius IX's Syllabus of Errors. He traced the constitution's lineage from the French Revolution to "democracies hostile to the Church." Republican leaders forced Segura into exile.[71]

The eventual Spanish Constitution banned only the Jesuits, not all religious orders, although it formally prohibited all men's and women's religious orders from teaching in publicly funded schools. Follow-up legislation removed all crucifixes from classrooms, secularized cemeteries, and legalized divorce. Revolutionaries began directing acts of violence against the church—including the assassination of thirty-four priests and the burning of fifty churches.

Francisco Franco led a group of Spanish military officers and their troops in a violent rebellion against the democratically elected republican government in 1936. The reaction of Catholic leaders was initially hesitant. Many in Franco's inner circle possessed anticlerical tendencies, and neither Franco nor his aides had provided church officials with advance notice of the insurrection. An early policy statement by a Franco lieutenant—"We believe that the Church ought to be separated from the State for the good of both institutions"—was not reassuring. Still, the cultural fault lines etched so deeply in Spanish history evolved into military divides. One cardinal who worried about Franco's eagerness to dominate the church still supported the rebellion because its failure would lead to "the installation of a Communist regime."[72]

Pius XI resisted the entreaties of his secretary of state, Eugenio Pacelli, to formally endorse Franco's nationalist Catholicism.[73] But wartime savagery on both sides squeezed out room for compromise. Loyalists (or Republicans) denounced Catholic tolerance of Nationalist war crimes, even tolerance of the execution of Basque priests sympathetic to the republic.[74] Catholics supporting the rebellion pointed to an unprecedented level of violence by Loyalists directed against the church. In a burst of iconoclasm, Loyalist militants "executed" (toppled) statues of Jesus and the Sacred Heart across Spain and then used dynamite to finish the job. They melted down church bells and burned altar cloths and vestments. Liturgies in Loyalist regions effectively ended. Thousands of church buildings were destroyed, and thirteen bishops, over two hundred nuns, and several thousand priests were killed, most in the first six months of the war. These assassinations and this destruction constituted the most comprehensive attack on Catholicism since the French Revolution, an event that many Spanish Catholics now saw as the "stepmother" to the Loyalist government in Spain.[75] Within Spain, bishops and Catholic intellectuals sacralized the conflict, defining it, in the words of one activist, as "a crusade against Communism, to save religion, the nation, and the family."[76]

With the Soviet Union sending material to the Loyalist armies and Hitler and Mussolini aiding Franco's Nationalist army, the civil war also became a global conflict. Liberals on both sides of the Atlantic rallied to support a democratic government threatened by a fascist rebellion, but Catholics around the world understood this mobilization as condoning anticlerical slaughter. When the Loyalists surrendered in the spring of 1939, the newly elected Pius XII sent a telegram to Franco congratulating him on this "long-desired Catholic victory in Spain." In return, the generalissimo expressed gratitude to the Holy Father for his prayers in the battle against "enemies of Religion, the Fatherland and Christian civilization."[77]

VI

THE SPANISH CIVIL WAR catapulted French philosopher Jacques Maritain into a newfound fame, and he soon became the world's most influential Catholic intellectual. His story was an unlikely one. After a personal crisis that included contemplation of suicide, Maritain converted to Catholicism, along with his wife, Raïssa, in 1906. He devoted himself to neo-Thomist analyses of aesthetics and culture, lecturing at Catholic universities and contributing to philosophical journals. His *Three Reformers* identified, in rote fashion, Luther, Descartes, and Rousseau as the men responsible for the modern world and "all the problems which torment it."[78]

Democratic politics seemed suspect. "The more I think about it," he wrote to a friend in 1914, "the more I am persuaded that we must have a political doctrine and that this doctrine can only be anti-revolutionary, anti-republican, anti-constitutional, and therefore monarchist."[79] In 1922, Maritain dismissed the work of the American philosopher William James as a "philosophy of Democracy" that "pictures the world as an immense swarm, with no established order or hierarchy, the wills of all members being equal in importance."[80]

For Maritain, the turning point came in 1926 with Pius XI's condemnation of Charles Maurras and the Action Française.[81] Maritain wholeheartedly accepted the pope's decision, and in a major break with onetime allies, ended his cooperation with the movement. As democracies crumbled across Europe and Latin America, Maritain began to write less about aesthetics and more about politics. He published an essay arguing that Thomas Aquinas had favored democracy as a form of government, implicitly challenging his onetime mentor, the Dominican priest Reginald Garrigou-LaGrange, the world's most prominent neo-Thomist and a top papal adviser. Garrigou-LaGrange admired the Action Française and thought only "arrivistes" and "incompetents" would run for office in a democracy.[82] In 1934, after the Nazis came to power in Germany and a right-wing demonstration in Paris ended with fifteen dead, Maritain drafted an anti-fascist manifesto, "For the Common Good."[83] In 1936, he published his masterpiece, *Integral*

Humanism, in Spanish and French and then in multiple translations, a text that became one of the key documents of twentieth-century political thought.

It was an unusual treatise. *Integral Humanism* contained sharp criticism of "imperious" atheism within the Soviet Union. But Maritain criticized with equal vigor "individualist liberalism." Like a surprising number of Catholic reformers, Maritain dove into the recently published manuscripts of the young Karl Marx and pondered the problem of worker alienation.[84] Another Catholic personalist and Maritain ally, Emmanuel Mounier, founded a journal, *Esprit,* preaching the need for a Catholicism able to circumvent dominant ideologies. "We reject the evil of East [communism] and West [capitalism] alike," he wrote in the journal's inaugural issue.[85]

For Maritain, the flourishing of the human "person" required respect for the person's embeddedness in communities such as the family, professions, and churches. No social theory should begin or end with an isolated individual quavering before a powerful state. "Person" was a term of art, and its varied meanings, filtered through translations of Maritain's meandering French prose, frustrated him. A decade later he complained that "there are at least a dozen personalist doctrines, which at times have nothing more in common than the word 'person.'"[86]

But in the 1930s Maritain was clear. "Persons" possessed an inherent "dignity"—another Catholic key word. A free market capitalism shorn of buffering institutions would not protect persons. Neither would communists obsessed with class conflict or National Socialists obsessed with race. Catholics described the primary danger faced by the world as "totalitarianism," a term popularized by two Maritain supporters, the German journalist and scholar Waldemar Gurian and the exiled leader of the Partito Populare Italiano, Fr. Luigi Sturzo. Debates about what constituted "totalitarianism" occurred around the Catholic world in the 1930s and 1940s.[87]

As a corollary, only a "pagan theology," in the words of the German theologian Erik Peterson, another Maritain admirer, could endorse what so many Catholics had long considered a worthy goal: a unity of church and state. Catholics should not equate theology with politics and should instead welcome pluralism. (Maritain's use of "pluralism" placed the term into widespread circulation.)[88] Democratic governments with universal suffrage followed from this distinction between religious and political authority, and Maritain drew on Aristotle to stress the vocation of the democratic politician, as opposed to a denigration of politics as "Machiavellian."[89]

Maritain promoted his version of personalism through ceaseless writing and traveling. Following a trip to Germany, he confided to Waldemar Gurian his dismay that some German Catholics had been won over by "the mystique of the Reich."[90] He made the first of many visits to North America in 1933, where he established contact with intellectuals and reformers in the United States and Canada. In Quebec, especially, his disciples challenged the patriotic chauvinism they associated with French Canadian Catholicism.[91] In 1934, Maritain gave a set of lectures on *Integral Humanism* in Santander, Spain, to little effect in a country hurtling toward a civil war.[92] He traveled to Poznań, Poland, where he gave seminars and addressed virtually all of Poland's Catholic elite at the International Thomistic Congress. Here, too, he cautioned against the "corporatist"—but not democratic—state favored by so many Catholics and became an inspiration for leaders of Poland's nascent Christian Democratic Movement.[93]

In Italy—where some Catholic intellectuals supported Mussolini into the late 1930s—Maritain's ideas thrilled a cadre of young activists disenchanted with Il Duce. These activists would later become leaders of the postwar Christian Democratic Party, including the future Italian prime ministers Alcide De Gasperi, Giulio Andreotti, and Aldo Moro. Giovanni Battista Montini, a Brescia native whose father had been active in the Partito Populare Italiano, admired Maritain and wrote an introduction for the Italian translation of *Integral Humanism*. Montini became one of the closest aides of Pius XII and in 1963 he would be elected Pope Paul VI.[94]

The outbreak of the Spanish Civil War gave Maritain a new international platform. Repeatedly, he explained to Catholics, even French cardinals, why Franco's rebellion should not be considered a "holy war."[95] In North America, Maritain and former German chancellor Heinrich Brüning inspired editors at *Commonweal* to draft a statement urging American Catholics not to believe that Franco will "inaugurate a beneficent and progressive social order." Even this mild criticism of Franco led to blistering attacks from other Catholic publications and a sharp decline in subscriptions.[96]

By then, Maritain had sailed for South America. In Rio de Janeiro, his lectures on *Integral Humanism* attracted the country's leading intellectuals. The director of the country's most influential Catholic center, a onetime enthusiast for the Action Française, identified himself as an "open Catholic, democratic and reformist" after listening to Maritain.[97]

In Buenos Aires, the reception was chillier. A few notables, including scientists who began a reading group dedicated to *Integral Humanism*, cheered on Maritain's efforts.[98] Still, important figures in the Argentine church, such as Fr. Gustavo Franceschi, questioned the wisdom of Maritain's "strong polemic." Franceschi agreed with Maritain that Catholics must reject Nazism and communism as "totalitarianisms . . . opposed to Catholic doctrine." But he thought Maritain too quick to dismiss

Jacques Maritain, right, just after arriving in Rio de Janeiro, 1936.

Portugal's Salazar and Spain's Franco. Franceschi's reports of his own visit to wartime Spain (where he brought supplies, including liturgical vestments, to embattled Spanish Catholic clergy) stressed persecution. "No Catholic in South America," he told Maritain in an open letter, "ignores that if the reds triumph in Spain, our continent will find itself in a very great danger." Argentine Catholics to the right of Franceschi flatly termed Maritain a communist.[99]

Maritain also reached out to like-minded Catholics in England. In London, the People and Freedom Group translated and reprinted essays by Maritain and his allies. Its executive secretary told Maritain that "your cause is our cause."[100] Even among Maritain's students, though, the sequence of opposition to individualism, emphasis on the human person, and support for democracy did not always unfold in predictable ways. One of his pupils, Yoshimitsu Yoshihiko, was one of the few Catholics among Japan's intellectual elite. He absorbed Maritain's criticism of the "isolated and abstract individual" but transposed it into an attack on a corrupt Western modernity and a justification for a "new East Asian spiritual civilization."[101]

VII

INTEGRAL HUMANISM also contained an attack on "racist totalitarianism" as exhibited by Mussolini and Hitler.[102] As Maritain knew, racism ran deep within the European and North American Catholic milieu. Poland's most distinguished young Thomistic philosopher, an admirer of Maritain, had not hesitated in 1930 to recommend that Poles "defend our special Polish culture from a deluge by the bankrupt Jewish culture, particularly in education, art and social mores."[103]

Married to Raïssa, a Jew, and with many Jewish friends, Maritain sought to untie this anti-Semitic knot. His evolution away from the anti-Judaism in Catholic circles was halting, and as late as 1937, he ruminated on divine "penalty" or "punishment" of Jews. But he also courageously denounced anti-Semitic laws. Others inspired by Maritain, often Catholic converts from Judaism based in Vienna, where they could still publish freely on the topic of next-door Nazi racism, thought it "absurd . . . to make today's Jews responsible for the crucifixation of Christ 2,000 years ago."[104]

This campaign against anti-Semitism overlapped with an equally fledgling campaign against colonialism and against racism directed toward people of Asian or African descent. Maritain admired the work of Mahatma Gandhi in India and supported Vincent Lebbe's effort to build an Indigenous church in China. Maritain told Lebbe that Christianity must be "truly Chinese in China, as it is French in France or Italian in Italy." No Catholic should consider "imposing the universal primacy of Greco-Latin culture." When a shipment of Maritain's books arrived in China, Lebbe offered Maritain his gratitude for the philosopher's "admirable work."[105]

On his first visit to North America, Maritain reached out to the American Jesuit John LaFarge. Beginning with a parish assignment among Black Catholics in southern Maryland, LaFarge had spent much of his career attempting to diminish Euro-American Catholic racism. LaFarge published English translations of Maritain's attacks on an "intrinsically inhuman" German racism and urged the French philosopher to view campaigns against anti-Semitism as part of a larger effort to "teach the Catholic world the principles of justice toward people of other races." (He also prepped Maritain on how to respond if Black Catholics pressed him on the question of whether "the Catholic Church justified slavery.") Maritain, in turn, described LaFarge's 1937 *Interracial Justice*, the first Catholic book to define racism as a violation of the "human dignity of the person," as a text of "first importance" and circulated it among European colleagues.[106]

Pierre Charles, the Belgian Jesuit who from his teaching post in Louvain taught thousands of future missionaries, became the most significant European Catholic critic of racism. (Charles knew and admired both Vincent Lebbe and Maritain.) He authored the first Catholic dissection of the fraudulent *Protocols of the Elders of Zion*, alleging a Jewish conspiracy to dominate the world, and continually insisted on humanity's common origins and the "substantial equality of different races."[107]

Crucially, and for the first time, Catholics from European colonies entered this conversation. They found their voice (and each other) not in West Africa or Vietnam or India but in European capitals such as Paris,

London, and Rome, where a growing number of students from the colonies arrived in the 1930s and where they formulated new ideas about
colonialism and race. African Catholic students, especially, having won
the opportunity to study in France through competitive examinations
in Catholic secondary schools, shared inexpensive Parisian apartments
or dormitories and discussed how to advance their native countries.

The most influential young African Catholic was Léopold Senghor.
Senghor grew up in rural Senegal, where he was educated in missionary schools and converted from Islam to Catholicism before winning a
scholarship to study in Paris. He excelled as a student, qualifying to teach
at an elite French lycée, or high school, and then at a French university.
He also fell in with a group of African Catholic students and writers,
including Paulette Nardal and Louis Thomas Achille, two cousins from
Martinique. Nardal began an important pan-African literary journal
and Achille, after his Paris sojourn, taught French at Howard University
in Washington, DC. All of these students admired the writers of the
Harlem Renaissance, and Senghor himself helped found the Negritude
movement, emphasizing Black African culture and its independence
from Western models. He became one of the first African-born writers to establish a major reputation in the West.[108] Senghor also read
both Maritain and Emmanuel Mounier, and he even wrote an admiring
tribute to the Reform Catholic hero of the French Revolution, Abbé
Grégoire.[109]

Both anti-fascist European Catholics and African Catholics studying in Paris were jolted into action by Benito Mussolini's decision to
send the Italian army into Ethiopia in 1935. Since the early twentieth
century, links between Italian Catholic missionaries and government
officials in North Africa had eased once formidable tensions between
state and church. In Libya, in the 1920s, missionaries provided up-to-
date maps for Italian soldiers.[110] In Ethiopia, missionaries and Catholic
antislavery activists founded "freedom villages" as "oases of Christianity" free from any taint of slavery.[111]

The invasion of Ethiopia, complete with atrocities that included the
wiping out of whole villages with poison gas, led to sanctions from
the League of Nations. Many Italian Catholics nonetheless endorsed
this military venture. Milan's Cardinal Schuster hailed the invasion

as opening Ethiopia to "Catholic faith and Roman civilization," and a delighted Mussolini broadcast the cardinal's speech on state radio. Another Italian bishop identified the country's critics as motivated by "Russian bolshevism, communism, international masonry [and] English Protestantism."[112]

Small groups of Catholics across Europe promoted a different view. Some French Catholics—including Maritain—denounced the "sophistry" of racism and mocked anyone who after the Italian invasion could with a straight face extol the "benefits of Western colonialism."[113] (The editors of *Civiltà Cattolica* wanly responded by recommending "prudence.")[114] Fr. Luigi Sturzo, now exiled to London, criticized an obviously "unjust war" from his vantage point as "a Catholic and as an Italian."[115]

Pius XI had expressed dismay at the prospect of the Italian invasion of Ethiopia before it occurred, but after the event he retreated into a studied neutrality. He pondered a direct appeal to Mussolini, acknowledging Italy's imperial ambitions but denying the justice of the particular conflict with Ethiopia. He quietly registered his disagreement with Cardinal Schuster's endorsement of the invasion.[116]

The pope knew that the invasion had had a disillusioning effect on African Catholics. Paulette Nardal and other African Catholic students based in Paris arranged lectures to Catholic groups across northern Europe on the importance of supporting Ethiopian independence. In Africa itself, European missionaries pleaded with the pope not to support Mussolini. The missionaries knew that African nationalists were castigating Catholics and their church for condoning the invasion, with rumors in places such as the Gold Coast (Ghana) of weekly church collections being secretly sent to Mussolini via the Vatican. The mood in the Gold Coast, worried one local Catholic, was now "charged with anti–Catholicism."[117]

VIII

JACQUES MARITAIN'S FEVERISH ACTIVITY made him the spokesman for anti-fascist Catholicism at a moment when Catholics around the world, beginning in Rome, were beginning to reconsider entanglements with fascist governments. After an extended drafting period, Pius

XI issued two encyclicals on the world situation in 1937. The first, *Mit Brennender Sorge* (With Burning Concern), was smuggled into Germany by church officials, secretly distributed, and then read out loud from pulpits on Palm Sunday. Fundamentally, the letter protested Nazi violations of the 1933 Reichskonkordat. The sections on race—attacking the "myth of race and blood" and defending the origins of the New Testament in the Hebrew Bible—became the most cited and were the most direct challenge to Nazi ideology, although the document did not contain a condemnation of anti-Semitism.[118]

The second encyclical, *Divini Redemptoris*, appeared three days later. It defined "bolshevistic and atheistic communism" as a "Satanic scourge" wherever it appeared—in the Soviet Union, Mexico, or Spain. While *Mit Brennender Sorge* pleaded for the protection of Church institutions— a conventional Catholic demand—*Divini Redemptoris* assailed communism for its effect not only on institutions but also on the human person. No ideology should be permitted to deny "human personality of all of its dignity."[119]

Mit Brennender Sorge infuriated Hitler and Joseph Goebbels and led to an intensified assault on independent Catholic institutions. After launching an expanded defamation campaign against the clergy—in one of the largest mass rallies of the era, Goebbels sneered at the "animalistic sexual degeneracy" that he believed to be "widespread" among priests— pressure on Catholic institutions increased. "We will have to bend the Churches to our will and make them serve us," Hitler told Goebbels. "The vow of celibacy must be eradicated. Church assets must be confiscated, and no one should be allowed to study theology before the age of twenty-four. With that we will rob them of their next generation. The monastic orders will have to be dissolved."[120] Goebbels's Propaganda Ministry, for a brief time, identified the battle against Catholicism as the government's "most important domestic confrontation."[121]

In 1936, Catholics in the town of Oldenburg successfully reversed the Nazi decision to remove all crucifixes from Catholic schools, with priests ringing church bells in protest, farmers erecting crucifixes in their fields, and women wearing small crucifixes as jewelry. In 1938, when the decree was reinstated, they could do little. When some parents attempted to organize a strike in protest, the Gestapo sent them to a concentration camp. The local government then closed all Catholic schools.[122]

The British ambassador to the Vatican noticed a shift. Until 1935, he reported, "The Vatican's consuming obsession was the fear of communism." Now, "the German persecution seemed to have displaced the Communist menace as the Vatican's major and immediate cause of preoccupation."[123]

In Italy, the promulgation of Nazi-inspired racial laws in 1938, including laws prohibiting marriage between Catholics and baptized Jewish converts, seemed yet another warning signal. Pius XI became more confrontational in his unscripted remarks and issued a plea for Catholic universities to discredit specious doctrines of a biological "race." He told a group of French trade unionists that limits must be placed on the state.[124] He told a group of Belgians that all Catholics were "spiritually" Semites. Racist legislation made him "ashamed to be an Italian."[125]

John LaFarge toured Europe that same year. When Pius XI learned LaFarge was nearby, he summoned him to the Vatican for a secret meeting and charged him with drafting an encyclical on race. "Say what you would say," Pius XI told LaFarge, "if you were Pope." He knew of LaFarge through reading the Jesuit's just published *Interracial Justice*. LaFarge spent a summer in Paris working with a German Jesuit, Gustav Gundlach, and a French Jesuit on the assignment.

LaFarge had studied in Innsbruck as a seminarian and had contacts across the continent. His letters to a friend in the United States—with coded references to evade German and Italian censors—registered a dawning realization that an entire Catholic civilization was at risk. LaFarge favored the Nationalists in the Spanish Civil War and hoped that Franco would accept Portugal's Salazar as a model and build a "Catholic cooperative state." But he worried, too, about the "subjugation of the Church" in Spain. (And one Spanish cardinal would soon be writing the pope to complain about "ostentatious Catholic ceremonies" endorsed by his peers that venerated the Franco regime.) In Rome, before meeting the pope, LaFarge was dismayed to find anti-Semitic materials translated from the German in the city's bookstores.[126]

While visiting a seminary classmate, now a pastor at the most prominent parish in Koblenz in the heart of the Catholic Rhineland, LaFarge was stunned by widespread misinformation. "We understand," parishioners told him, "that in Paris the streets are running with blood; there is a terrible revolution and people are being murdered by the Jews and Bolsheviks." When LaFarge denied this, one dismayed parishioner responded by denouncing "the stuff [the Nazis] have been handing out to us here." In late-night discussions at the rectory, local priests sardonically confided that while they remained "free to hold our beautiful pilgrimage and Corpus Christi processions," the Nazi government used this freedom to demonstrate "how much Hitler loved the Church." Honest criticism of the government, on the other hand, might lead to imprisonment in Dachau. LaFarge reflected:

> Here had flourished the center of a great organized campaign of intensive Catholic living, of charitable works, of religious instruction, of apostolic works for all classes, of social reform, of liturgical realization. Here the banner of Christ the King had been unfurled before vast multitudes in public squares. Here the clouds of godless Marxism had been rolled away, while Germany's great Catholic traditions were preserved or revived.

Would this Catholic world survive Nazism? "When things are definitely past," LaFarge worried, "they seem like dreams."[127]

LaFarge's collaborator, Gustav Gundlach, was more scathing. "We have to see clearly," he told LaFarge, "that this business of race could become no less a danger to the world than red communism." The new pope, Pius XII, elected in early 1939, declined to release the encyclical drafted by LaFarge and Gundlach. A dismayed Gundlach urged LaFarge to read a new biography of Charles Montalembert and see how "this great patriot and Catholic" had offered a positive vision at a moment when "so many prelates were resigning themselves to the system."[128]

In a subsequent letter, Gundlach regretted that "as a result of our own anti-communism, it was already secretly hoped that we could present ourselves as allies and companions, in one way or another, of the Authoritarians and Totalitarians." Catholics in South America might face a desperate choice between "communism and national totalitarian-

214 THE MILIEU AND ITS DISCONTENTS, 1870–1962

ism."[129] Alerted that the Gestapo might arrest him, Gundlach left Germany for Rome, where he would sit out the war. He complained that "modern anti-democratic Catholics" had proven too willing to conciliate dictatorial leaders. "Over and over again the historian will ask the question," he sadly concluded, "How could all this have happened without a protest as loud and clear as befitted the gigantic dimensions of events?"[130]

IX

PIUS XI AND Secretary of State Eugenio Pacelli discussed Edith Stein's plea for a denunciation of the Nazis in a private meeting in the spring of 1933, as evidenced in Pacelli's handwritten notes. Then negotiating the Reichskonkordat between Hitler and the Vatican, they sent only a form letter of acknowledgment.[131]

Only months before, like virtually every European Catholic intellectual in the interwar era, Stein had made her way to the home of Jacques and Raïssa Maritain, just outside of Paris, where the couple organized a long-running salon. Discussions began in the early afternoon, included tea, and occasionally went late into the evening. Stein spent a "wonderful day" there. Jacques Maritain then sent her an inscribed copy of one of his philosophical works. In reply, Stein regretted that her teaching duties at the Catholic Pedagogical Institute in Münster prevented her from devoting herself to "principally philosophical questions."[132]

Soon after Hitler took power, Stein lost her teaching position. Jews were no longer allowed to serve on college or university faculties. Martin Heidegger personally dismissed Husserl, his and Stein's teacher, from the university at Freiburg because of Husserl's Jewish ancestry. Stein decided to write her autobiography, focusing on her Jewish childhood and using the blank sides of a typescript of an essay on Aquinas. "I am not permitted to give any lectures this semester," she told a friend, "because of my Jewish descent."[133]

Stein formally entered a women's religious order, the Discalced Carmelites, at the age of forty-two, a few months after her letter to Pius XI. She took the religious name of Sister Teresa Benedicta of the Cross. The violence of Kristallnacht in November 1938, including the destruction of synagogues in nearby Cologne, impressed upon her the dangers she faced. She moved just across the German border to a Carmelite convent in Echt, Holland, founded during the Kulturkampf as a haven when Bismarck expelled nuns and priests from Germany in the 1870s. Stein's sister, Rosa, also a Catholic convert, made it to Holland as well. But German armies conquered and occupied the country in the spring of 1940. Stein began a desperate effort to find a new home. She arranged for a place in a Carmelite convent in Fribourg, Switzerland, but Swiss government officials rejected her request for asylum in order to avoid a "dangerous precedent."[134]

When the Dutch Catholic bishops courageously protested the Nazi treatment of the Jews on July 26, 1942, the German high command retaliated. A week later, two SS officers appeared in Stein's convent and required her to leave in only ten minutes. As a Catholic convert and nun she might be protected. As a Jew her presence was intolerable. Other nuns hurriedly helped her pack. All Jews who had converted to Catholicism were grouped together in a transit camp, and one detainee witnessed Stein comforting separated families. Rosa was also arrested. On August 5, Stein wrote to ask sisters still living in the convent to save her last scholarly manuscript. On August 6, she requested "woolen stockings [and] two blankets" and, for Rosa, a toothbrush, cross, and rosary. That night, about one thousand Jews were deported, jammed into freight cars despite the summer heat. On August 7, the train stopped in Schifferstadt, in eastern Germany, and a station master spoke briefly with Stein. She told him she was "traveling East." On August 9, 1942, she was murdered in the gas chambers at Auschwitz.[135]

NINE

Ressourcement

Opening the Milieu

I

Mary Magdalene dumping out her bottle of perfume, St. John resting his head on Jesus's chest, all the way to little Zacchaeus climbing up a tree—individuals who follow the impulses of their hearts. These are acts full of freshness. With such appetizing subjects, how is it we end up, Sunday after Sunday, with a mash so boring one can only take it in as punishment?

Doesn't it seem to you that we have a serious spiritual matter here as well, as there is in sacred art? For me, it's an analogous issue: it's that of the religious aesthetic, which we should display in all its breadth.[1]

Dominique de Menil conveyed her exasperation in this 1951 letter to her Dominican priest friend and mentor, Fr. Marie-Alain Couturier. In the first years after World War II, using the wealth amassed through the oil services company founded in France by her father and now run in Houston, Texas, by her husband, Jean, she began acquiring paintings and sculptures that would make her and her husband two of the twentieth century's greatest patrons.

She had few predecessors. The Catholic art produced during the ultra-montane revival—mass-produced statuary from the workshops on the streets of the Saint-Sulpice neighborhood in Paris, stained glass from Germany, paintings copied from Italian originals—had no place in the burgeoning world of galleries, journals, and museums. Antoni Gaudí, in Barcelona, might design an eccentric masterpiece such as the Basilica de La Sagrada Familia. But a fraught relationship existed between Catholicism and the modernism understood as the most innovative feature of the early-twentieth-century arts. T. S. Eliot and Ezra Pound expressed interest in Dante and Catholic imagery, but more artists disdained what they understood as an oppressive institution. The hectoring Jesuit in James Joyce's *A Portrait of the Artist as a Young Man* reflected this view. "Hating the Church fervently," Joyce privately vowed to "open war on it by what I write, and say and do."[2]

This hostility between Catholicism and the avante-garde diminished in the 1940s and 1950s. A group of painters, sculptors, novelists, and musicians did dismiss some of the piety associated with the ultramontane revival. The American writer Flannery O'Connor visited the healing waters at Lourdes, but less out of devotion than a sense of irony. She described the true "miracle" of Lourdes as the absence of epidemics. But the same artists—certainly O'Connor—found in Catholicism a vehicle for grappling with suffering, sin,

Dominique de Menil and architect Philip Johnson, River Oaks Theatre, Houston, November 1949. *(Courtesy of Menil Archives, The Menil Collection, Houston. Photo: The Houston Post)*

and God's presence (or absence).[3] The English writer J. R. R. Tolkien created a "fundamentally religious and Catholic" imaginary universe in his popular fantasy novels *The Hobbit* and *The Lord of the Rings*, with evocations of the trenches where he had served during World War I.[4] The French painter Georges Rouault invoked God's mercy through haunting portraits of prostitutes and beggars.[5] French filmmakers such as Robert Bresson and Italian filmmakers such as Roberto Rossellini, notably in his 1945 classic *Rome: Open City*, melded Catholic and left-wing political imagery. (The film included a priest, working with a communist, martyred in the anti-fascist resistance.) New York's Cardinal Francis Spellman would lobby to ban a later Rossellini film, *The Miracle*, which Spellman judged as sacrilegious. But even as Spellman lost his legal battle at the US Supreme Court, critics heralded a Catholic artistic renaissance.[6]

Dominique de Menil played an important role in this reengagement of Catholicism with the arts. Born Dominique Schlumberger in 1908 to an illustrious French Protestant family, she was raised in austere luxury in Paris and at the country estate of her maternal grandfather, one of France's most distinguished scholars and politicians. Her father, Conrad Schlumberger, a physics professor turned oil entrepreneur, eventually became one of the wealthiest men in France.

Jean de Menil came from an aristocratic French Catholic family. Two of Jean's older brothers died in combat during World War I, and another became a Dominican priest. The family lived in straitened circumstances— in contrast to the Schlumbergers—but Jean graduated from the prestigious Sciences Po and began a banking career. He drifted, like many young Catholic intellectuals, into the orbit of Charles Maurras in the 1920s and joined the nationalist Action Française. Pius XI's condemnation of the Action Française in 1926 jolted Jean, and along with a friend he fired off an eleven-page resignation letter. "We are Romans," the two men explained, who cannot commit the "original sin" of disobeying the pope.

Dominique and Jean met three years later at a ball in Versailles. They fell in love immediately, and their religious differences seemed no obstacle. As Dominique explained to Jean just weeks later, "It is absurd to think that the difference of religion between us could be a source of dissension. That would be an ecclesiastic, sectarian way of seeing things."

Conrad Schlumberger disagreed. An unbeliever himself, he had discouraged Dominique as a child from saying bedtime prayers. "God doesn't exist," he told her. "We can't speak with him. It is more honest not to pray." But the prospect of his brilliant Sorbonne-educated daughter, a possible successor in his firm, marrying a devout Catholic aroused latent confessional instincts. Grandmother Schlumberger chose this moment to send to Dominique a not so innocently titled volume, *The Genius of Protestantism*. Dominique laughed it off. "Clearly there is panic," she told Jean, "up and down the line."

Soon she was serious, even frantic. Her father had made it clear, as Dominique put it to Jean, "that I cannot bring children into the world in order to make them Catholic." She regretted that "your church" was so "intransigent" on the topic of raising children in the faith. Eventually, Jean and Conrad Schlumberger came to an agreement, in writing, with Dominique monitoring negotiations, to celebrate two wedding ceremonies and raise the children in both traditions. It helped that Jean seemed to Conrad not "at all to be a doctrinaire."[7]

Dominique had long veered between "great attraction for Catholicism" and distaste for the "stupidities" and "nonsense" spouted by Catholics. The couple's first stop on their honeymoon, though, was to visit with Jean's brother Patrice, the Dominican priest, at the Saulchoir Abbey in Belgium. (They then hopped on a train to Barcelona and flew to a Moroccan resort.)

Dominique converted to Catholicism in 1932, a year after her marriage, and never glanced back. Over a memorable week in January 1936, she and Jean attended a set of lectures by the Dominican priest Yves Congar in the giant Basilica of the Sacre Coeur in Montmartre. Perhaps remembering her family's uneasiness with her husband's Catholicism, Dominique resonated with Congar's message that Catholics should view Protestants as "separated brethren" (not heretics) and as already possessing "in greater or lesser degree what we desire to see fulfilled in them."[8] She composed an erudite article regretting that neo-Thomism had channeled Catholics away from an exploration of the beliefs Protestant and Catholics shared.[9] The book Congar eventually published out of his lectures, *Divided Christendom*, became one of the most important theological texts of the twentieth century. "I had the privilege to hear him," she recalled of the lectures, "and it marked me for life."[10]

The day after the final Congar lecture, Dominique and Jean attended an event they had organized, one of the first "dialogue" Masses held in Paris. These dialogue Masses emerged from the work of Belgian and German liturgists and became popular with youth groups and at university settings in the 1940s and 1950s. Dialogue meant engaging the congregation, not simply the altar boys or the choir, in the scripted Latin responses. The hope was to create a more communal feeling, less a sense that the Mass was hundreds of individuals engaged in acts of uncoordinated private prayer.

Like Congar, Dominique and Jean participated in the salon of Jacques and Raïssa Maritain at their home outside Paris. (Two of Dominique's cousins converted under the influence of the Maritains.) Jacques Maritain's writing on art exerted a gravitational pull in the Catholic cultural sphere, just as his writing on democracy shaped how Catholics viewed politics. He joined Leo XIII in understanding Thomism as an alternative to philosophies derived from the Enlightenment, but Maritain pivoted between Aquinas in the twelfth century to the avante-garde in the twentieth. Catholic art need not take as its subjects Lourdes or pious nuns. Art made by the believer, even in abstract forms, could signify religious meaning just as the eucharist signified more than a piece of bread and the sacrament of confirmation more than a dab of oil.[11]

Maritain's cosmopolitan sensibility made this neo-Thomist modernism real. His life and work influenced the composers Igor Stravinsky and Olivier Messiaen, the sculptor Eric Gill, and the painters Marc Chagall, Georges Rouault, and Gino Severini.[12] His friendships with gay artists—even as he cautiously discouraged homosexual activity—suggested a willingness to circumvent conventions. He may himself have been gay. Eight years into their marriage, Maritain and Raïssa took a private and highly unusual joint vow of chastity.[13]

Major writers, including Gabriela Mistral (Chile), David Jones (England), Jean Cocteau and Julien Green (France), Flannery O'Connor (United States), Czesław Miłosz (Poland), and Shūsaku Endō (Japan), attested to Maritain's influence. O'Connor, from a tiny town in Georgia, wryly termed herself a "hillbilly Thomist."[14] Dominique and Jean fell under Maritain's spell, too, and Dominique later funded the preservation of Maritain's vast archive. "He was the example," she recalled, "the saintliness of Maritain."

Dominique met her second interlocutor, Fr. Marie-Alain Couturier, at Maritain's salon. Dominique found Couturier mesmerizing and
began financially supporting his newly founded journal, *L'Art Sacré*.
"For him, the mediocrity of today's religious art is more than a defi-
ciency, it is a sin," she told Jean. "I am not far from thinking he is
right."[15]

Fr. Couturier spent the war years exiled in North America lecturing on art history to students at a Catholic women's college, serving as
a chaplain to Free French pilots in training, and haunting New York
galleries. At the same time, Couturier deepened his friendship with the
Menils and advised them on their first purchases, notably a painting by
Paul Cezanne ($300) in 1945 and major works by Henri Matisse, Pablo
Picasso, Alexander Calder, and Georges Rouault. (Matisse became one
of Couturier's closest friends.) He encouraged the Menils in their decision to hire the avatar of the International Style, architect Philip Johnson, to design Houston's first modernist home, even as he joked about
the Menils living in Texas, so far from "civilization."[16] When completed, Couturier placed a photo of the Menil home on the cover of
L'Art Sacré along with an essay by Dominique. She described a tour of
France she took with Couturier in the summer of 1952, visiting several
projects he had orchestrated, including a chapel designed by the world's
leading modernist architect, Le Corbusier. Maritain's views on modern
art were not identical to Couturier's: he found Matisse's work "enchant-
ing" but disliked Le Corbusier's glass towers. Still, the two men both
"detest[ed] the Neo-Gothic" because of what they considered its false
homage to the Middle Ages. Dominique also thrilled to the marriage
of Catholicism and modern forms.[17] "What does it matter if it isn't perfect?" she wrote. "The child is born: he will grow!"[18]

The highpoint of Dominique's tour of France in 1952 was Henri
Matisse's recently completed chapel in a convent in Vence, on the
French Riviera. Matisse and Couturier corresponded at length about
even small details in the design. When completed, Matisse judged it
his masterpiece, and so did Dominique. "So many churches today are
oppressive by their conventional style," she explained, "or injurious by
their aggressive forms; this chapel feels like a new proclamation."[19]

The disdain felt by Dominique de Menil and Couturier for popu-

Father Marie-Alain Couturier (far left) at the consecration of
La Chapelle du Rosaire, Vence, France, 1951. The chapel was
designed by Henri Matisse. *(Henri Cartier-Bresson, Courtesy of Menil Archives, The
Menil Collection, Houston)*

lar Catholic taste—from cookie-cutter neo-Gothic churches to mass-produced statues of the saints—anticipated controversy about the top-down reforms of the Second Vatican Council. (Neither reformers such as Menil and Couturier nor the bishops whose aesthetic sense they derided did much consulting of the faithful.) Couturier thought the art of Saint-Sulpice a "corruption of all that is purest in the Gospel."[20] He described the pious bric-a-brac hawked by shopkeepers at Lourdes as the "shame of the French church."[21]

As Dominique de Menil knew, controversy had engulfed Couturier even as they crisscrossed France.[22] The Vatican's Holy Office had decided to weigh in on the topic of sacred art. Archbishop Celso Costantini, himself a former sculptor, drafted the report. Costantini had promoted Indigenous Christian art as a missionary in China, but drew the line at abstract art created by atheist artists. He rejected the modernist conviction that Christian art must be modified to the "needs and conditions of modern times." He would later receive a private commendation from

Pius XII for his efforts to prevent "deformed" and "deplorable" art from desecrating the "house of God."[23]

Couturier responded in a front-page interview in the Parisian daily *Le Figaro*, conceding that "truly sacred art" might be impossible in a materialistic society but still holding out hope for "works of high 'religious' inspiration."[24] Privately, he became discouraged. He appreciated that some French bishops had defended his work, but he knew that others agreed with the Holy Office. "More and more I see the church as a mutilated tree," he wrote, "Successive crises have fashioned in Rome complexes of fear, defense mechanisms responding to serious problems with suspicions of hearsay and condemnation."[25]

II

THE REEXAMINATION OF so many dimensions of Catholic life by a loosely allied group of artists and scholars between the 1930s and 1960s is often called a "ressourcement." Theologian Yves Congar defined the term as literally meaning "return to the sources," but it also meant a wider evaluation of the ultramontanism these men and women had inherited.[26] The movement began in northern Europe, extended around the world, encountered resistance from Vatican officials in the era of Pius XII, and helped determine the outcome of the Second Vatican Council.

Reformers reconsidered a dazzling array of topics, including the liturgy, anti-Semitism and racism, marriage and sexuality, democratic politics, missions and decolonization, religious freedom, human rights, and the idea of conscience. They never formed a school—and divisions among them would become more evident during the turbulent 1960s and 1970s—but theological, political, and aesthetic visions often aligned. Those urging new forms of church architecture and art, such as Dominique de Menil, favored democratic governments and expressed dismay at papal reluctance to criticize fascist leaders. In 1939, Dominique de Menil criticized Vatican blindness as Spain's Francisco Franco moved "more and more toward tyranny."[27] More than most contemporaries, reformers demonstrated interest in the Global South during the era of decolonization and insisted, in Dominique's words, that the "church is not national." The Menils were among the first Western collectors of African art, and a Kongo crucifix hung in the main bedroom of their home.[28]

Even technical debates on the relationship of nature to grace in Thomistic theology reliably indicated which French Catholics supported the collaborationist Vichy government and which French Catholics supported the resistance.[29] While living in Bucharest in 1940, Jean de Menil worked undercover for French security forces and sabotaged oil transports headed for Germany.

Escaping France ahead of the Nazi armies, Maritain spent 1940 to 1944 in exile in the United States. At first, Maritain and his allies, many exiled like himself, despaired as they observed Spanish bishops blessing Franco and authoritarian priest-politicians, such as Joseph Tiso in Slovakia, allying themselves with the Nazis. Especially discouraging was the situation in France. After the German military victory, many French Catholics rushed to support Marshal Philippe Pétain's Vichy government with its slogan of "work, family, fatherland." The most influential personalist after Maritain, Emmanuel Mounier, admired the Catholic, at times personalist, rhetoric of Vichy leaders in 1940 and 1941. To Mounier, Maritain's "all or nothing" focus on democracy seemed untenable. Far better to recognize that "we are obliged now to find a place for freedom in authoritarian regimes."[30] After all, the Vichy constitution recognized the "liberty and dignity of the human person" as a "supreme value."[31]

"Catholic democracy," a discouraged Yves Simon told Maritain, "is condemned to produce only trash." Now teaching with Simon at the University of Notre Dame, another exile and Maritain friend, Waldemar Gurian, sardonically commented that "if St. Thomas lived today he would be for Franco, for Tiso, for Pétain."[32] When Simon learned that Fr. Reginald Garrigou-LaGrange, once a mentor to Jacques and Raïssa Maritain, supported the Vichy government, he exploded. "How disgusting this Garrigou!" he told Maritain. "Were I not so respectful of the sacerdotal character, I would, I think, write him that he is the one I will hold responsible if harm befalls one of my Jewish friends."[33]

Maritain persevered. In 1941 he defended democracy as a system of government superior to any alternative. "It is necessary to show," he told

Yves Simon, "that Thomism is what is strongest against false democracy. . . . St. Thomas was a democrat, in this sense . . . the Gospel works in history in a democratic direction."[34] In contrast to the reflexive anti-Americanism of personalists such as Mounier, Maritain expressed admiration for the authors of the Declaration of Independence and the United States Constitution. He pondered writing a new version of the Federalist Papers, applicable to France and "the entire world."[35]

In 1942 Maritain coordinated the drafting of a manifesto, "In the Face of the World's Crisis," signed by forty-three European Catholic scholars "sojourning in America" and published in Europe, Latin America, and the United States. The manifesto argued that democracy was the "issue at stake in the struggle" and insisted that a corporatist state "no longer sufficed."[36]

Pius XII himself may have drawn on Maritain's writings. In his 1944 Christmas address, after several caveats, the pope announced that "the democratic form of government" now appeared "to many as a postulate of nature imposed by reason itself." One of Maritain's close friends, a Swiss theologian, archly noted "numerous coincidences" between the papal address and Maritain's prose.[37]

Maritain also began a correspondence with Free French leader Charles de Gaulle, who later arranged for some of Maritain's writings to be dropped from Allied bombers into occupied France. "The error of those Catholics who follow Pétain in France or Franco in Spain," Maritain told de Gaulle, was an inability to distinguish between the "rights of the human person" and an "old paternalist conception." De Gaulle agreed with Maritain that France had suffered a "moral collapse," but he also insisted that he was "not worried for the future of democracy. Its enemies are only ciphers. I don't fear for the future of religion. The bishops have behaved badly but there are good curés, simple priests who are saving us."[38]

De Gaulle prevented the cardinal archbishop of Paris, perceived as sympathetic to Vichy, from celebrating a victory Mass at Notre Dame following the city's 1944 liberation. He named Maritain ambassador to the Vatican and insisted that he use his new post to force the resignation of bishops loyal to Vichy. Maritain castigated his former mentor, Garrigou-LaGrange. "When you took the side of Marshal Pétain," he told him, "you compromised Thomism through your political positions that were odious to those who were struggling for the liberation of our country."[39]

III

JACQUES MARITAIN'S PROGRAM intersected with efforts by a remarkable group of European and North American theologians. If Maritain reconsidered how Catholics approached art and politics, these scholars scoured ancient texts to recover a richer sense of Catholic engagement with the world. Leaders in this effort included the French Jesuits Henri de Lubac and Jean Daniélou, the French Dominican priests Yves Congar and Marie-Dominique Chenu, the German Jesuit Karl Rahner, and the American Jesuit John Courtney Murray. Each of these men was born between 1895 and 1904 and entered a religious order as a young man. Just reaching the height of their intellectual powers, they were disturbed by what the political crisis of the 1930s and then World War II revealed about their church, many of whose members (and leaders) seemed to understand religion as either a pious afterthought to daily life or a reliable bulwark to any social order. Unbelief seemed to them a consequence of this inward focus on institutions, fostered by the refutations of "modernity" that constituted much of the standard Catholic curriculum.

French Jesuits and French Dominicans, especially, sponsored what became called the *nouvelle théologie*.[40] Their first task was to reassess Thomas Aquinas, obscured, in the eyes of the reformers, by distorted textbook summaries. Chenu, living in the same Saulchoir abbey as Jean de Menil's brother, Patrice, urged Catholics to locate Aquinas in the "intellectual revolution of the thirteenth century," not simply to regurgitate formulas marred by "anti-protestant polemic." Theologians should discard a "state of siege."[41] (Chenu's recovery of the context in which Aquinas worked in the twelfth century also led to a new appreciation of Islamic thinkers, and he encouraged the founding of a Dominican center of Islamic studies in Cairo.)[42]

The second task was to plumb the patristic texts of early Christianity, well before Aquinas, in order to find models of church different from those of the ultramontane era. The same scholars began two publication series, one whose first volume was Yves Congar's *Christians Divided*, so important for Dominique de Menil. Congar prefaced this work with the hope that the "concept of the Church . . . recover the broad, rich, vital meaning it once had." De Lubac focused on the question of the relationship between nature and grace, which in his hands evolved into a plea for Catholics to engage the world beyond church walls.[43]

The experience of the war itself confirmed the intuition of these theologians about the inadequacy of church structures. In France, many of the leading figures in the *nouvelle théologie* participated in the resistance. Congar spent five years in a German prisoner of war camp. De Lubac helped edit *Témoignage Chrétien* (*Christian Witness*), a clandestine Catholic publication.[44] He worried that the complacency of so many Catholics about the political crisis revealed a "faith completely withdrawn into a private sphere."[45]

This desire for new ecclesiastical forms crossed the Rhine. Isolated groups of German Catholics resisted the Nazis, including the German Jesuit Alfred Delp, the group around Claus von Stauffenberg, the aristocratic leader of the July 20, 1944, assassination attempt on Hitler, and the Protestant and Catholic students in the White Rose group in Munich. Delp and the other members of the Kreisau Circle, a resistance group, drew on a Catholic vocabulary when they insisted that Germans must respect "the inviolable dignity of the human person."[46]

Most of those even tangentially involved in resistance against Hitler were discovered and executed. And their willingness to resist was exceptional. The average German Catholic clergyman and layperson accepted the idea, as one seminarian serving on the Eastern Front put it, of World War II as a necessary struggle between "the civilization of the Christian world" and "the Judeo-Bolshevik will to destruction."[47]

With rare exceptions, such as Münster's Clemens von Galen, who in a blistering trio of sermons denounced Nazi euthanasia programs designed to murder "unproductive" elderly and mentally ill citizens, German bishops did not challenge the regime. Even von Galen favorably quoted Adolf Hitler and his attacks on the "Judeo-Bolshevik rulers in Moscow."[48] Franz Jägerstätter, a Bavarian Catholic farmer executed for his refusal to swear an oath of loyalty to Hitler, noted how sad it made him "when we hear again and again from Catholics that this war, which Germany is leading, is perhaps not unjust because it will eradicate Bolshevism."[49]

This inchoate sense that Catholics and the church had failed did not negate the work of the Catholics scattered across Europe—including bishops, priests, nuns, and laypeople—who defied the Nazis and risked their lives to protect Jewish neighbors. But it prompted questions. Before his execution, in notes smuggled out of prison, Jesuit Alfred Delp worried about Catholicism at a "dead end." He wondered if the focus on preserving institutions had obscured a more pressing need for "personal regeneration and revitalization."[50]

The same fears haunt a set of sermons given in Munich just after the war by another German Jesuit, Karl Rahner. He first asked his listeners to recall the terror of nights spent in shelters during Allied bombing raids "waiting for a senseless death." He encouraged them to contemplate their own "rubbled over" condition. Belief should not be limited to what occurs within church walls on Sundays. "God must be sought and found *in* the world," he explained, "and every day must become God's day. . . . The everyday itself must be prayed."[51]

Strands of the *nouvelle théologie* filtered across the Atlantic. An American Catholic soldier who stayed in Paris after the war to assess this theological ferment, founded a theological journal, *CrossCurrents*, after his return to the United States, printing the first issues in his garage. These issues included translations of important essays by de Lubac, Congar, and Rahner.[52]

Vatican uneasiness with the *nouvelle théologie* was not entirely predictable. In 1943, Pius XII encouraged Catholic biblical scholars to avoid fundamentalist or literal readings of Scripture, dismantling barriers erected during the modernist crisis. In 1947, he encouraged a more participatory liturgy, even if he did reach all the way back to the 1786 Synod of Pistoia—an "illegal Synod"—as a caution against too much experimentation.[53]

The claims made by the proponents of the *nouvelle théologie* seemed less negotiable. At the height of the war, Holy Office officials found time to place Marie-Dominique Chenu's programmatic statement on the *nouvelle théologie* on the Index of Forbidden Books. They recoiled against Chenu's placing of Thomas Aquinas in historical context and described the conventional reading of Aquinas as "absolute and immutable."[54] After the war, as reformers became bolder, an apprehensive Pius XII ratcheted up the Vatican response. Having protected the church during the war, in his self-perception, Pius XII now fended off threats from within.

Following a series of challenges and denunciations, including one hyperbolic essay by Garrigou-Lagrange entitled "The *Nouvelle Théologie*, Where Is It Going?" Pius XII released the encyclical *Humani Generis* in 1950, which directly criticized proponents of the *nouvelle théologie* for substituting a "history of dogma" for permanently valid truths.[55] "It was quite necessary," Pius XII told an Italian cardinal, "everything was being lost!"[56] In the wake of *Humani Generis*, de Lubac was forbidden to teach in his own seminary, and librarians in the seminary pulled his books from the shelves.[57]

The most interesting pastoral experiment of the era—the worker-priest movement—came directly out of the *nouvelle théologie*. Chenu and Congar had written on the need for Catholics to develop more connections with an alienated working class, and Chenu offered one of the first postsecondary courses on Marx at Saulchoir. (A socially minded Chilean priest wrote an introduction to one of the first Spanish-language texts on Marx.)[58] A group of Dominican priests took this message to heart and began working with dockworkers in Marseilles. These clergy soon attracted followers from other religious orders and diocesan clergy. Many of these men moved to apartments near industrial sites, where they dressed in ordinary working men's clothes and took factory jobs. "The Church today," one priest in the movement wrote, "has lost the affection and the attention of the common people."[59]

No more than a few hundred priests and seminarians from France, Belgium, and the Netherlands participated in worker-priest experiments, but they attracted enormous attention. The young American Jesuit Daniel Berrigan studied in France in the early 1950s. "He has been in the factories for some eight years," a mesmerized Berrigan reported after meeting one priest dressed in work clothes, "so [he] can speak with authority." He thought the experiment a "marvelous and sacrificial and admirable departure."[60] A young Polish priest and future pope, Karol

Wojtyła, on summer break while studying in Rome, admired the "living testimony" of worker-priests laboring with Polish miners in Belgium.[61] Another future pope, Archbishop Montini of Milan, visited a worker-priest community incognito.[62]

Yet many Vatican officials and French bishops were not pleased. The disregard of divisions between priests and laity and the left-leaning politics saturating the movement seemed proof of an experiment gone awry. Orders came to close down "French innovations." Chenu was sent away from Paris and stripped of his teaching position.[63]

IV

JACQUES MARITAIN'S IDEAS underwrote one of the key achievements of twentieth-century political history: Christian Democratic parties. After almost a century of doubting the efficacy of democracy, at least in much of Europe and Latin America, Catholics became its guarantors. For all or part of the period between 1945 and 1980, Christian Democratic parties held power in Italy, Germany, Switzerland, Belgium, the Netherlands, Austria, Brazil, Chile, Venezuela, Ecuador, El Salvador, Guatemala, and Costa Rica. Even parties not formally identified as Christian Democratic—such as the Mouvement Républicain Populaire in France, the Democratic Party in Uganda, the Indische Katholieke Paritij in Indonesia or the Fianna Fáil in Ireland—adopted personalist language as they pushed for family allowances, supported trade unions, and encouraged small businesses. Maritain's influence would even be distantly felt in countries without Catholic political parties. In Canada, a young Pierre Trudeau, a future prime minister, found Maritain's ideas compelling.[64] In the United States, Sargent Shriver, John Kennedy's brother-in-law and the first director of the Peace Corps, read Maritain with care, as did future Minnesota senator Eugene McCarthy. (So did Joseph R. Biden, Sr., the father of a future US president.)[65]

Not only Catholics belonged to Christian Democratic parties, and they were never controlled by the institutional church. Maritain himself never deigned to participate in a political party. But the lineage is direct. In Italy, Catholics fighting in the resistance to Mussolini read Maritain in off moments, amazingly, and after the war worked to replace "economic liberalism" with a personalist democracy.[66] In West Germany, Catholics formed the Christian Democratic Union (and an even more Catholic counterpart, the Bavarian Christian Social Union). Both parties welcomed Protestants, but Catholics were numerically and ideologically the primary sponsors. The Cologne Guiding Principles adopted by the Christian Democratic Union are an undiluted sample of Maritain's personalism: "The spiritual dignity of the individual person will be recognized. The individual will be valued as a self-accountable person, not as a mere member of the community."[67]

The same European Christian Democrats also underwrote an unprecedented commitment to international organizations. They promoted the notion of an *Abendland*, or Christian West, where governments rested on top of an interlocking base of families, neighborhoods, churches, and regional groups. Christian Democracy must be distinguished from a discredited Prussian nationalism. Here, too, Maritain was a pioneer, and he argued in 1951 for a form of world government to match the "material unification" provided by a global economy.[68] Catholic scholars took the lead in positing an "Atlantic world."[69] Maritain wondered if the Atlantic Ocean had "taken the role of the Mediterranean" during the Roman Empire.[70]

This belief in a shared Christian past laid the groundwork for the European Economic Community (and eventually the European Union). So Catholic were the initial foundations of the European Economic Community that Swedish and British ministers expressed hesitation about aiding in the "consolidation" of a Catholic bloc.[71] The founders included Konrad Adenauer of West Germany, Alcide De Gasperi of Italy, and Robert Schuman of France, all postwar chancellors or prime ministers, all from minority regions within their homelands, all native German speakers, all committed Catholics. De Gasperi and Adenauer first met in 1921 at a gathering of German and Italian Catholic politicians. Mussolini's security forces imprisoned De Gasperi in the 1920s, and upon his release, he retreated into a job at the Vatican library. Adenauer was forced by the Nazis to resign as mayor of Cologne because he would not raise a Nazi flag over city hall. In 1944, he and his wife were detained by the Gestapo.[72]

Konrad Adenauer, chancellor of West Germany (center), Alcide De Gasperi, former prime minister of Italy (left), Robert Schuman, former prime minister of France (right), in 1957. All Catholics, all founders of the European Union. *(Getty Images/Keystone France #104406926)*

The evolution toward Christian Democracy, European cooperation, and an alliance with the United States was not inevitable. A Catholic socialism also emerged from the war, in part because socialists, communists, and Catholics had frequently worked together in local resistance movements. For these Catholics, modern capitalism was not just individualist, but morally unacceptable. In Poland, the priest-editor of the leading Catholic daily ventured in 1946 to make an "uncontroversial" claim: "No thinking person in Poland seriously wants to return to economic liberalism, with its anarchy of production and consumption, its cartels and trusts."[73] Other prominent Catholics such as the medievalist Étienne Gilson engaged in a fierce polemic with leading French intellectuals over the wisdom of military alliances with the United States. (Gilson thought NATO a needless provocation.) In New York City, pacifist Dorothy Day, developing her own brand of Catholic personalism in the Catholic Worker Movement, denounced capitalism even as she became the country's leading antinuclear activist.[74]

This more leftist Catholic politics never became a serious political force. The most Catholic regions of countries such as France proved to be the most resistant to the electoral appeal of the Communist Party.[75] In the long run (of two decades), Christian Democratic parties in Western Europe triumphed because of the economic growth and political stability they made possible. In West Germany, especially, labor unions, Christian Democratic politicians, and industrialists built a robust social welfare state infused with a Catholic sensibility. The leading such figure, Konrad Adenauer, served as West German chancellor from 1949 to 1963 and was the most significant European politician of his era. He won reelection in 1957 on a platform of *Keine Experimente,* or No Experiments.[76]

More leftist versions of Catholic politics also could not overcome an ever more passionate Catholic anti-communism. When Charles de Gaulle first met with Pius XII in 1944, he was startled by the pontiff's repeated circling back to the topic of communist influence.[77] Even on the day of Germany's surrender in May 1945, a Vatican cardinal confided to his diary that "there is a dark shadow still cast over the bloody skies of Europe: the threat of yet another Antichrist—atheist Communism."[78] Our Lady of Fatima, named after the apparition of Mary to three children in a Portuguese village in 1917, became one of the most popular Catholic devotions around the world after 1945, largely because one visionary claimed to have received from Mary a secret message against communism. Dozens of unofficial Marian apparitions in Europe and North America during the late 1940s and 1950s carried a similar anti-communist message. West German Catholics awarded Adenauer a prize for his promotion of "spiritual weapons" against communism.[79]

A crucial moment was the Italian election of 1948. Roughly one-third of Italians held some affiliation with the Communist Party, and the party's prestige because of its leadership in the resistance to the Nazis had never been higher. Just after the war, local communist cells invited left-leaning priests to address them on the topic of "The Social Revolution of Jesus Christ," even as bishops tried to forbid such priests from preaching "whether inside a church or in open air."[80]

That a communist party might triumph at the polls in the heart of Western Europe, and in the capital of global Catholicism, seemed unacceptable to New York's Cardinal Spellman, who urged Italian Catholics in the diaspora to encourage their compatriots to reject communism, and Pius XII, who informed Italians two weeks before the election that their ballots would be cast "either with or against Christ." The voters chose Christ, or the Christian Democrats, despite the gap between papal anti-communism and Italian villages where communist and Catholic neighbors often coexisted without rancor. In 1949, still fearful of communist inroads in France and Italy, Pius XII issued a decree excommunicating any Catholic willing to "defend or propagate" communism.[81] Unless you live in Rome, the Irish ambassador to the Vatican informed his government, you cannot understand how concerned Vatican officials are with "the menace of Communism" and the persecution of the Church behind the Iron Curtain.[82]

This persecution was not imagined. Catholic anti-communism during the 1950s included many excesses—notably the lurid campaigns to root out alleged communists from the federal government launched by Senator Joseph McCarthy in the United States—but the situation for Catholics in Eastern Europe, even as Christian Democratic parties took root in Western Europe, was sobering. Communists largely controlled Catholic organizations in much of the region—through imprisonment, infiltration by the secret police, creation of front organizations, and blackmail.[83]

The Italian Communist Party head Palmiro Togliatti evaded the topic of independent Catholic organizations in communist governments or so-called people's democracies. He euphemistically explained that "where the Communist Parties are in power" the government should not permit "conflicts on religious grounds."[84] Joseph Stalin could afford more candor. As he told the Politburo:

> It is necessary that we isolate the Catholic hierarchy and
> drive a wedge between the Vatican and the believers. . . .
> Our measures will divide lower-level priests from the
> hierarchy. Governments should order priests to take the
> citizen's oath, communist parties should force priests to

spread the ideas of Marx, Engels, and Lenin through religious classes and sermons, and whenever they have direct
contacts with their believers.[85]

In Albania, communist leaders virtually eradicated Catholicism,
murdering seven bishops and 115 of the country's 160 priests.[86] In
Czechoslovakia, monasteries were closed (and turned into prisons),
priests sent to labor camps, Catholic newspapers shuttered, and alternative "patriotic" Catholic organizations established.[87] In 1945, Hungarian Catholics began a journal named *Christianity and Democracy* and
explicitly invoked Maritain. Communist officials shut it down as an
"instrument of reaction."[88] When Hungary's Cardinal Mindszenty protested as communists closed all Catholic schools in 1948, he was jailed
and convicted in a show trial. His imprisonment—and that of the Czech
archbishop Josef Beran and the Yugloslav cardinal Alojzije Stepinac—
drew international attention.

Only in Poland was the story different. After the annihilation of
Poland's Jews and the expulsion of German (largely Protestant) residents
in 1945, Poland had become an overwhelmingly Catholic nation. The
experience of Nazi and then Soviet occupation had deepened the bonds
between priests and people, and Soviet observers professed themselves
"amazed" by the "strength and influence of the Catholic Church both
in educating children and in scholarship."[89]

Even in Poland, though, navigating between communist state officials and the Vatican proved challenging. Pius XII, long enamoured of
German culture, alienated Polish Catholics by not formally recognizing
Polish control over lands annexed from Germany after the war. Warsaw's Cardinal Stefan Wyszyński, seeking an accommodation with the
regime, struck an agreement in 1950 guaranteeing religious education in
most state schools and church autonomy in exchange for priests refrain-
ing from criticizing or opposing the government. Top aides to Pius
XII thought the agreement "simply disastrous," and the government's
decision in 1952 to close some seminaries and church organizations partially vindicated their skepticism. Wyszyński himself was placed under
house arrest along with other bishops, priests, and lay activists. In 1953,
the most important Polish Catholic journal, *Tygodnik Powszechny*, ceased

publication because its editors refused to print an admiring obituary for Stalin.[90]

Events in China followed a parallel pattern. The 1949 Constitution of the People's Republic of China defined freedom of religion as a right, but how the Communist Party would treat "foreign" religions—including the country's three million Catholics—remained uncertain. A few Chinese Catholics, including the Jesuit Aloysius Jin Luxian, who had studied in Paris and like so many Catholics had been impressed by the worker-priest movement, hoped for a Chinese version of socialism compatible with religious freedom. (In this Jin Luxian resembled those Poles who aspired to build a Catholic socialism within Poland.) As late as 1951, Zhou Enlai, the first premier of the People's Republic, met with Catholic representatives and acknowledged their need to adhere to the pope "in all spiritual matters."[91]

But already the Communist Party had developed a strategy for dividing the church. The success of Catholic youth groups, especially in Shanghai, and continued close ties between Chinese Catholics and international (and anti-communist) devotional groups such as the Irish-based Legion of Mary, disturbed party leaders, and soon the official line hardened. Chinese Catholics faced pressure to recant their beliefs and join a newly established "patriotic" Catholic church with communist-approved bishops. One party document outlined a plan to "destroy the [Roman] Catholic Church. This is the objective we aim to reach and for which we struggle."[92]

V

As CHRISTIAN DEMOCRATS TOOK center stage in Western Europe, and as communist leaders thwarted Christian Democrats in Eastern Europe, the first continent-wide meeting of Christian Democrats in South America occurred in Montevideo, Uruguay. The assembled delegates sent Jacques Maritain a telegram thanking him for providing the "ideal solution to our great political and economic difficulties."[93]

Family resemblances between Latin American and European Christian Democrats were obvious. The origins of Christian Democracy in Chile lay in a 1933 meeting between Maritain and Eduardo Frei, a young Catholic student and future Chilean president. Frei had traveled to Rome to attend an international Catholic Action youth meeting, where he also met Rafael Caldera, the future Venezuelan president. He took a side trip to Paris to sit in on a seminar with Maritain. In 1938, Frei and his Chilean colleagues founded a political party whose symbol became a red vertical arrow slashing through two slanted bars, signifying a resistance to both capitalist and socialist orthodoxies. He invoked the "dignity of the human person."[94]

Opposition to Maritain's ideas proved more persistent in South America and on the Iberian Peninsula because in those locations authoritarian politics had not been as discredited as in France, West Germany, and Italy. One of Maritain's most vociferous opponents was the Argentine priest Julio Meinvielle. Meinvielle referenced Joseph de Maistre and Pius IX in an effort to demonstrate that Maritain neglected the "anti-Christian" dimensions of the French Revolution and repeated the errors of Félicité Lamennais, the nineteenth-century ultramontane democrat attacked by Pope Gregory XVI. He despaired of "Jewish-Masonic-communist" influence within Maritain's Catholic orbit.[95]

Meinvielle naturally welcomed the emergence of Juan Perón as Argentina's strongman leader. More socially minded Catholics opposed the advent of Perón's regime in 1946, as did, initially, the country's bishops. But Perón deftly co-opted many Catholic positions, such as the family wage. By the early 1950s, though, this religious-political alliance foundered on Perón's desire to absorb independent Catholic trade unions and youth organizations into a state-run corporatism. "I do not understand," Perón told the Argentine bishops in 1954, "why they are being organized, these groups of Catholic labourers, Catholic lawyers, Catholic doctors and Catholic farmers. We are Catholics too!"[96]

Successful examples of Christian Democratic parties in Europe—Christian *and* democratic—made Perón and his wife Eva's authoritarian instincts less tolerable to Catholic activists. A desperate anticlerical campaign launched by Perón included banning priests from teaching in schools, expelling Catholics from the civil service, and closing Catholic schools by removing their tax exemptions. The government even forbade religious decorations at Christmas. Finally, military leaders—with Church support—overthrew Perón in 1955.[97]

VI

THE SAME PERSONALISM that underlay new Catholic understandings of art and politics also shaped new understandings of marriage and sexuality. Pius XI had identified procreation as the primary end of sexual intercourse in his 1930 encyclical *Casti Connubii* and denounced birth control and eugenics. He had hoped to end discussion of these topics, but beginning in central Europe, new doubts about church teaching emerged. Initial questions came from the Austrian Dietrich von Hildebrand, who trained as a philosopher with Edmund Husserl and became a close friend of Maritain. Procreation might be a primary end of marriage, von Hildebrand conceded, but the meaning of sexual intercourse within marriage also lay in forging a couple's "complete, unique community." Such bonds, sanctified in the marriage sacrament, were as important as bearing children. Nazi laws prohibiting marriages between Jews and Christians violated "the most intimate sphere of life."[98]

A German theologian, Herbert Doms, ventured the claim that procreation and the expression of marital love should be given equal weight. First trained as a biologist, Doms pointed out the inadequacies of nineteenth-century descriptions of human reproduction. Neither Doms nor von Hildebrand advocated for a change in Catholic teaching on contraception. But arguing that the purpose of marriage included both procreation and love and stressing the importance of an egalitarian marital bond opened new areas of reflection. If procreation was not the primary purpose of marriage, did each act of sexual intercourse need to be open to procreation? Doms wondered if the church might eventually welcome family limitation, since the "relative importance of the purposes of marriage is capable of some variation in the course of history."[99]

Vatican officials entered the debate, prohibiting new printings of Doms's work and stunting his career. In 1944, the Holy Office, in the words of one satisfied American Catholic ally, "definitely and conclusively" declared that the "primary end of marriage is the procreation and rearing of children."[100] Privately, Maritain regretted the Holy Office diktat. He termed it "another of those tragic examples where the church defends a truth by blockading it with ways of thinking that simple human experience has left way behind."[101]

After World War II, Catholics, even more than Protestants and Jews, married at younger ages and had more children as a baby boom swept across Western Europe and North America. As late as 1960, Catholic college-educated women, the group most likely to be aware of formal church teaching, chose "five" when surveyed on their ideal number of children. Families with six, eight, and ten children were routine.[102]

The photos of these smiling families at baptisms and first communions concealed strains. Especially challenging was the situation faced by the woman married at, say, twenty-one and bearing a fifth child at age thirty. Could she endure four or five more pregnancies? Would her husband's income sustain their family? Could they afford Catholic school tuition? Surveys of Catholic couples showed that from one-third to one-half of couples in West Germany and the United States used contraceptives by the 1950s. Even reform-minded priests and lay Catholics urged these couples to avoid "selfishness" by welcoming children and offering prophetic witness to the primacy of human life in a materialistic age.[103]

Prophetic witness is by definition not a mass movement. The starkness of the Catholic attack on contraception seemed draconian when measured against the circumstances that might lead couples to use contraceptives. Partial relief for Catholic couples became available with the so-called rhythm method, or, as Catholic moralists preferred, "periodic continence." By charting a woman's menstrual cycle, Catholic couples could schedule intercourse during infertile periods and not violate the ban on "artificial" contraception. In its modern form, the method dated only from the early 1930s, when reliable biological information on women's menstrual cycles became available.

To strict moralists in Europe and North America, this new, more reliable rhythm method at first seemed dubious.[104] The Apostolic Delegate in Washington, DC, acting on instructions from the Vatican, secretly warned bishops in 1936 that the rhythm method was an "extreme remedy" suitable only as a last resort. A Belgian theologian memorably described couples using the rhythm method as hedonists who "listen to the deafening noise of jazz on the radio to muffle the voices of their own conscience."[105]

Pius XII eased doubts about the rhythm method with an unequivocal endorsement when speaking to Italian midwives in 1951.[106] Lay couples interested in limiting family size, one American theologian explained to his peers, were not "selfish, materialistic people distrustful of divine providence." Still, the need for daily rectal temperature readings (for women), along with the uncertainty of those readings and subsequent anxieties about possible conception, limited its appeal.

Catholics continued to oppose public distribution of contraceptives. In 1948, in heavily Catholic Massachusetts, where Protestants had passed laws against contraception in the nineteenth century, Catholics led a successful campaign against an easing of legal restrictions. Supporters of reform argued that the "religious beliefs of some should not be forced upon all. This is an elementary matter of civil liberties in a democracy." Fifty-two percent of the state's voters disagreed, or, in the words of the Catholic publicity campaign against the measure, chose to believe that birth control was "still against God's law."[107]

Similarly, American Catholics serving in Japan after World War II challenged the promotion of birth control (along with legalization of abortion and forced sterilization for prisoners and the mentally ill). Working with Japanese Catholic allies, they orchestrated criticism from prominent Vatican officials, who expressed dismay that a "victor nation" such as the United States would permit the Japanese to "contradict the immutable natural law." Under Catholic pressure, the leader of the American occupation forces, General Douglas MacArthur, prohibited birth control advocate Margaret Sanger from visiting Japan for a series of lectures.[108]

At the same time, though, some Catholic theologians and doctors moved in a different direction. Belgium became the most important Catholic research hub on family life, with scholars stressing the importance of sexual pleasure (especially for women) and the bonding effects of sexual intercourse for married couples. Marital counselors at Catholic centers frankly discussed these issues and urged women to resist abusive relationships. In the Netherlands, theologians and sociologists detailed the potentially unhealthy consequences for young couples of either abstinence or children in quick succession.[109]

As this personalist understandng of marriage became more widespread, Catholics began to approach sex and marriage in ways unlike their parents. A best-selling book on marriage in West Germany, by a Catholic author, insisted that erotic attraction and sexual pleasure were "essential to marriage. They are at its center, not a side realm."[110] A Canadian priest and counselor explained that couples using approved methods such as rhythm should plan their families together. "The church," he felt compelled to explain, "has never advocated giving birth to the most children in the quickest possible time."[111]

Postwar interest in population control presented another challenge. Interest in the population question exploded in the 1950s as demographers pondered declining rates of infant mortality, longer life spans, and an unprecedented baby boom. Experiments in contraceptive distribution and, at times, forced sterilization followed population control funding in India, Puerto Rico, and other sites in the Global South. From the beginning, population control advocates, working through the Rockefeller Foundation, the World Health Organization, and government agencies understood Catholic teaching on contraception as a primary obstacle. One population control leader accused Catholics of stopping "human progress" in the name of "entrenched dogma."[112]

During the Great Depression some Catholics had pointed to declining birth rates as an argument against contraceptives, but the utility of that argument diminished during the postwar baby boom. Instead of flooding poor countries with contraceptives, some Catholics now argued, wealthy countries should share their resources. Milan Archbishop Giovanni Montini suggested that only such redistribution would be consistent with the "dignity of conjugal relations."[113]

VII

ONE WRITER TERMED the International Eucharistic Congress in Rio de Janeiro in 1955 "the greatest spectacle of faith ever seen in Brazil." It also signaled church-state reconciliation. In contrast to the late nineteenth century, when a republican government refused to countenance dealings with the church and even dropped the Christmas holiday from the official state calendar, Catholic agencies received government funds to support social welfare programs, orphanages, and Catholic schools. Nuns ran over half of the nation's hospitals. The Eucharistic Congress itself received a subsidy. One bishop later recalled working on the planning with Getúlio Vargas, Brazil's president:

> I remember when Vargas . . . insisted on sending a personal representative . . . to ensure that all the state apparatus was made available to us in preparation for the International Eucharistic Congress of 1954–55. Every door was opened to us, every facility was made available. That was how we were able to get a huge esplanade built across the bay right in the heart of Rio—the project was already under way, and we got it speeded up.

At once pilgrimage and tourist destination—Pan American Airlines signed on as a sponsor—the week-long sequence of Masses, processions, festivals, and lectures displayed the religiosity of a country frequently caricatured as an endless carnival. At one Mass, one million people received communion, including, organizers noted, well over three hundred thousand men. President Dwight D. Eisenhower and Pope Pius XII sent greetings. Bishops and state officials dedicated the new campus of the Pontifícia Universidade Católica de Rio de Janeiro, supported with state funds.[114] Knowledgeable analysts noted that many more Brazilian intellectuals and leaders identified themselves as practicing Catholics than in the early twentieth century.[115]

The ceremonies modeled themselves on the Olympics, with a Brazilian gold medal winner in the triple jump carrying a eucharistic torch from the statue of Christ the Redeemer perched far above the city down to the plaza constructed for the Eucharistic Congress. The lighting of the torch opened the congress and invoked those Catholics trapped in figurative darkness in Eastern Europe and China.

Twenty cardinals and three hundred bishops from around the world attended the congress, with many episcopal dignitaries staying on hotel boats docked in the harbor. The messages enunciated by speakers—criticizing "modern errors," respecting workers, denouncing communism, honoring the priesthood and the family—struck conventional notes.

In retrospect, hints of changes were evident. Brazilian elites were more Catholic than ever before, but church leaders grumbled about the slowly dropping percentage of Catholics in the general population, as Protestants, sometimes American missionaries, founded new congregations and Afro-Brazilian religions such as Umbanda gained adherents. One Belgian priest-sociologist reported that "in Rio there are already more than six hundred spiritist temples officially registered. In São Paulo, there are one hundred and eighty. . . . The Bishops are very worried about this situation because it affects mostly Catholics."[116]

Also indicating new directions at the Eucharistic Congress was the outdoor altar, capped by a towering mast to evoke a ship entering the harbor. "Let us not forget," explained the priest who commissioned modernist architect Lúcio Costa to design the altar, that "Brazil, and notably Rio, is the leading country in modern architecture."[117] Costa, along with his protégé, Oscar Niemeyer, moved directly from the Eucharistic Congress to planning for Brasília, the new national capital; his blueprint laid out the city in the shape of a cross. Niemeyer had already designed a controversial modernist church in the city of Belo Horizonte. In Brasília he would design a spectacular cathedral, a concrete tower, much of it underground, supported by sixteen swooping white pillars.

Costa and Niemeyer had trained with Le Corbusier, the French modernist hired by Fr. Couturier and admired by Dominique de Menil. She and Jean (now Anglicized to John) spent the 1950s in Houston, with frequent visits to New York, where John served on a board at the Museum of Modern Art and where they owned a townhouse, and to Paris, where they kept a family apartment.

When Dominique learned that a nearby parish in Houston anticipated building a new church, she arranged for Philip Johnson to be hired as its architect. Johnson drew up plans, but when news reached Texas of the dispute between the Holy Office, Couturier, and *L'Art Sacré* in France, he correctly predicted that "we are sure to have our troubles." The nervous bishop rejected Johnson's design.[118]

Dominique nonetheless persuaded the Basilian priests running the

University of St. Thomas to hire Johnson, and he designed a new section of their campus as a series of rigorously modernist buildings. She and John also commissioned their own chapel, originally planned for the St. Thomas campus but later located on a site owned by the Menils next to the museum they founded. It imagined Catholicism as part of an interreligious space painted by the abstract expressionist Mark Rothko. That Rothko was Jewish did not matter. What did matter was Rothko's somber canvases of pure color, which Dominique knew would create "an extraordinary mystical environment."[119]

TEN

Decolonization

A Catholic Global South

I

BEFORE WORLD WAR II, if they discussed economic growth at all, Catholic intellectuals warned against the ways in which growth might disrupt social hierarchies. Growth meant small businesses bought out by corporations, family farms swallowed by large landowners, or a desire for unnecessary luxuries (including mothers working outside the home when such income was unnecessary). Redistribution, not growth, seemed the most equitable solution to the global depression. *Quadragesimo Anno* (1931) promoted just wages for workers, not greater equality between rich and poor nations.

The onset of the Cold War raised a different alarm; policymakers became convinced that poverty fostered communism. The alternative was economic development, and Catholic institutions played a significant role, along with colonial governments and international aid agencies, in facilitating development programs. Bishops in the tiny West African country of Guinea, for example, received over seventy million francs from the French government in the single year of 1954 to build schools. Officials dedicated many of these schools to women's education, and these newly educated young women were encouraged to marry and form monogamous—not polygamous—Christian households.[1] The British government funded schools staffed by Irish and Canadian mis-

Barbara Ward, 1945. *(Getty Images)*

sionaries in Nigeria, and an estimated thirty thousand Catholic
teachers worked for the Nigerian bishops by the 1960s.[2] In
Ghana, women religious serving as missionary nurses helped
establish the country's modern
medical system.[3]

Two Catholics played a
significant role in the more
theoretical development conversation. The first was Barbara Ward. Born in 1914, Ward
graduated from Oxford as the
only woman in her year with
a first-class honors degree. She
started writing freelance articles
on foreign affairs and criticized
the many English Catholics who took Franco's side in the Spanish Civil
War. "If I were a trained nurse," she told her mother, "I should go to
Madrid to show that all papists aren't in league with Franco, Mussolini
and Goering."[4] By 1940 she was both a full-time writer for the British
newsweekly *The Economist*, one of the first women to hold such a role,
and secretary of Sword of the Spirit, a British group determined to demonstrate that Catholics should support Jacques Maritain and democracy as
opposed to Portugal's Catholic dictator, Antonio Salazar.[5]

Ward's reputation as a foreign affairs correspondent was such that the
British government sent her to Washington, DC, during World War
II. In that capacity she met with Eleanor Roosevelt and top Roosevelt
administration officials and attempted to persuade them that the "clerical fascist capitalism" on display in Europe and Latin America during the
1930s would have little postwar appeal.[6] She married a United Nations
diplomat from Australia, Robert Jackson, who spent his career working
on hydroelectric development projects. Ward accompanied Jackson to
postings in Australia, India, and the Gold Coast (Ghana). She became
friends with Jawaharlal Nehru, the first prime minister of an indepen-

dent India, and Kwame Nkrumah, the first prime minister of an independent Ghana. She published several books on development over the course of the 1950s, written with lightning speed even as she composed pieces for *The Economist* and lectured on both sides of the Atlantic. Willing to accept French colonialism (in Vietnam) and British colonialism (in Malaysia) if she perceived local nationalists as overly sympathetic to communism, she still reminded her readers that foreign aid was the least expensive way to combat the Soviets. Catholics must recognize "moral obligations which stretch beyond our own frontiers."[7] An "exclusive loyalty" to the nation-state was "especially repugnant."[8]

Ward's best-known study, *The Rich Nations and the Poor Nations*, appeared in 1962. Now a fixture on the New York–Washington–London policy circuit, collecting honorary degrees and awards, Ward became an adviser to the World Bank. The book garnered her a dinner invitation with President John F. Kennedy, who jotted in a notebook his conviction, taken from a conversation with Ward, that the Soviets feared only "a religion that transcends frontiers and can challenge the purpose and performance of the nation state."[9]

The second Catholic voice was that of Louis-Joseph Lebret. A pilot during World War I in the French air force who had been awarded the Legion of Honor, Lebret entered the Dominican order in 1923 eager to do missionary work. He began in Brittany, where he competed with communists for the allegiance of dockworkers, and observed with dismay the threat posed to local fishermen by multinational companies claiming the most productive waters.[10] He read Karl Marx intensely. In 1942, he founded a think tank focused on development issues—*Économie et Humanisme* (Economy and Humanism)—dedicated to understanding a world in "rapid evolution" with a growing gap between developed and "under-developed" nations.[11]

Lebret shared with American development experts a vigorous anticommunism. He shared with Latin American economists a focus on dependency and exploitation. His contribution was to move away from a single-minded focus on economic growth toward a wider view acknowledging "the human need for transcendence." Development meant not just "having more" but "being more." In the 1950s he hopscotched from Lebanon to South Vietnam to Uruguay to Rome, but his influence was greatest in West Africa and Brazil. He regretted that the United States so often acted as a "neo-imperialist" power and had become "hated" in much of the Global South.[12]

II

WARD AND LEBRET UNDERSTOOD that decolonization meant that Catholics must abandon the equation of the church with the West. Filipino independence from the United States in 1946, Indian independence from Britain in 1948, Indonesian independence from the Dutch in 1949, Vietnamese independence from France in 1954, and independence for thirty-three countries in Africa between 1954 and 1965, including Ghana, the Congo, Senegal, Nigeria, Uganda, and Kenya, did not move to a single tempo. But everywhere decolonization revealed new political constellations. Graham Greene, the English Catholic novelist, probed the tensions of the Cold War and decolonization from Nairobi to Havana to Saigon. When doing research, he repeatedly sought out Catholic informants, many of whom became thinly veiled characters in his fiction and who stressed how blurry the ideological lines between East and West became the further one traveled from Moscow or Washington. "One rather feels," he observed in 1959 after several weeks in the Congo observing Congolese Catholics along with missionary Belgian priests and nuns, "the end of European Africa is coming quickly."[13]

Along with other French Catholic intellectuals, Fr. Lebret coined the term *tiers monde*, or "third world," to identify nations not included in either the Soviet or American blocs. Figures from the ressourcement—many of whom knew Lebret—also chimed in. Theologian Jean Daniélou stressed that Christians must recognize the world's various civilizations—Indian, Chinese, African—and not dwell on Christianity's Greco-Roman origins.[14] Philosopher Étienne Gilson warned Catholics not to pine for an unrecoverable Middle Ages. "Christendom has passed," he insisted, "but Christianity remains."[15]

Nineteenth-century ultramontane missionaries had been global in their orientation, too, traveling to all corners of the world with their devotional objects, architectural plans, and Latin textbooks. What changed after World War II was that Indigenous people fully joined the conversation. Vatican officials had long encouraged the appointment of Indigenous clergy and bishops, often over objections from French, Portuguese, and Belgian colonial officials. Pius XI had appointed the first six native bishops in China (1926), the first native bishop in Japan (1927), and four native-born bishops in Vietnam and Ceylon (1933). Pius XII appointed twelve native-born bishops from all around the world, including the first native bishop from sub-Saharan Africa. Ordinary parish bulletins in Paris recognized the pope's goal in these appointments as an "affirmation of the universality of the Church and a condemnation of all racism."[16]

During World War II, the sheer difficulty of communication with Rome from East Asia, South Asia, and Africa expedited the appointment of native bishops and clergy to important posts. In India, the internment of Italian and German missionaries by the British made it crucial, in the words of one missionary, to push toward a "native priesthood."[17] "Do we seriously think," asked one Belgian missionary expert in 1944, "that Europe ravaged by wars, divided by hatreds, that Europe, where faith is declining in more than one country, is capable of indefinitely increasing its missionary effort?"[18]

Léopold Senghor served in the French National Assembly as an elected representative from Senegal after the war and like many other African Catholics understood political autonomy for his native country as inseparable from native leadership within the church. He knew that the old imperial order could not endure and clashed with European missionaries who complained about an African "lack of civilization."

Léopold Senghor, 1953, founder of the Negritude movement and first president of Senegal. *(Felix Man/Picture Post/Hulton Archive/Getty Images)*

"[The] missionaries who were the most liberal Europeans [in Africa] before the war," he explained, "fail to comprehend the evolution the war has wrought in minds and fact."[19] Senghor initially favored a confederation of French-speaking West African states still formally linked to France—a plan resembling Maritain's hope for a federal, non-nationalist Europe—but as that vision became less plausible he advocated independence. In 1960 he was elected Senegal's first president, and he immediately hired Fr. Lebret to develop the country's economic plan.[20]

At the same time, Senghor became fascinated with the writings of the French Jesuit and paleontologist Pierre Teilhard de Chardin. Teilhard knew from excavations in Zambia and South Africa that human civilization had originated in Africa, not Europe. In his writings, which circulated in samizdat fashion among French Catholics because Vatican officials doubted their orthodoxy, Teilhard pondered the theological implications of what he called a planetary consciousness.[21] Senghor served on the committee that arranged for the publication of Teilhard's work after the Jesuit's death in 1955. He invoked Teilhard when discussing his own version of a "universal civilization."[22]

One of Senghor's friends, Alioune Diop, another Senegalese convert to Catholicism, became a close friend of Emmanuel Mounier. In an open letter to Diop, published in the first issue of *Présence Africaine*, a journal Diop founded that would boast contributions from the leading intellectuals of the African diaspora, including W. E. B. DuBois and Aimé Césaire, Mounier encouraged his African readers to develop a distinct voice within both Catholicism and the larger society. Similarly, African seminarians and priests who met in Rome while taking theological degrees also began to publish essays urging European Catholics to accept Negritude and decolonization.[23] "In the Congo," one priest insisted, "[the Church] should be Congolese, in the construction of the church and in the making of sacred objects, one should carefully consider the lines, the colors and all the elements of Congolese art."[24]

By the 1950s, the formal question of racial equality no longer seemed controversial. Yves Congar described "the idea of race" as meaningless for Catholic theology, and John Courtney Murray thought the sinfulness of racial segregation "entirely clear." (He had been uncertain a decade earlier.)[25] Catholic colleges and schools in border states such as Missouri integrated their student bodies in advance of public institutions. The Vatican newspaper, *L'Osservatore Romano*, ran a front-page congratulatory article when a New Orleans archbishop excommunicated a handful of white Catholics for refusing to take communion from the hand of an African American priest. Similarly, it applauded Catholic opposition to apartheid in South Africa, with its "systematic contempt of the human person."[26]

The gap between principles and practice remained daunting, and here the traditional Catholic respect for community mores could serve as a pretext for discrimination. White bishops and clergy in South Africa only cautiously challenged the country's ban on interracial marriage and spent much time conciliating the often fiercely anti-Catholic architects of the apartheid regime. Steps taken to integrate what had already become a majority Black church were hesitant. One group of white Catholic laity in South Africa formally protested the Vatican decision to appoint the country's first Black African bishop in 1954, describing themselves as "vehemently against having a non-European bishop as bishop of Europeans." Resistance to integration of parishes and schools in the American South, and even in northern American cities where there were few legal barriers, could be violent.[27]

Dismantling colonial structures proved even more challenging. The majority of African bishops remained missionaries of European descent. Some of these men still held that Christianity and European civilization could not be distinguished. The most influential prelate of this type, Marcel Lefebvre, spent sixteen years in Gabon before his eventual appointment as apostolic delegate for Africa and archbishop of Dakar. Lefebvre thought it obvious that European Catholic culture shielded Africans from communism and an Islam that both depended on "fanaticism, collectivism and the enslavement of the weak."[28] The leading Belgian bishop in the Congo resented any government funds going to Protestant or secular schools because "Catholicism represents a stable factor."[29] Irish missionaries in Benin City, Nigeria, fended off complaints made by lay parishioners about British colonialism (in the state) and Irish colonialism (in the church).[30]

Other European and North American bishops, missionaries, and intellectuals viewed their work differently. One Belgian priest working in the Congo, fluent in Swahili and other African languages, composed a groundbreaking work entitled *Bantu Philosophy*, and Léopold Senghor and Alioune Diop arranged for its publication.[31] An American Jesuit anthropologist trained in Vienna began his work in the Philippines with a sense of the natives as exotic and the idea that he would write about them in *National Geographic* magazine. A decade later, he organized Catholic missionaries from across North America to challenge "ethnocentrism."[32]

A fascinating debate on whether Catholics had a "duty to decolonize" erupted in Paris in 1956 with more liberal clergy, influenced by African Catholic students, taking the affirmative and also, for the first time, urging Catholics to examine their history of complicity with slavery.[33] In 1956, a group of African Catholic students based in Paris authored a remarkable manifesto that reached the front page of *Le Monde*:

> We, the Catholic students of Black Africa in France, reaffirm our desire to stay simultaneously entirely Christian and entirely African; we cannot, in any circumstances or under any pressure, choose between these two loyal-

African Catholic students in France, 1950s. *(Courtesy of the Archives of the Congrégation du Saint-Esprit)*

> ties. . . . We affirm our attachment to the natural right
> of African peoples to self-determination [and] we ask
> French Catholics to make the necessary effort to under-
> stand the demands of this double loyalty to the church
> and to Africa.

Archbishop Lefebvre found such arguments a "serious problem." Along with his allies he stressed the benefit to Africans of colonial administration by "peoples more privileged than they."[34] During the papacy of Pius XII, this view received a hearing, and Lefebvre helped draft the first ever encyclical on the subject of Africa, *Fidei Donum.* Its primary aim was to plead for more missionaries, and in this it was successful, as the United States, Canada, Ireland, and other countries began sending more missionaries, including lay volunteers, to the continent. Even by the standards of 1957, however, the document's paternalism was striking. The pope applauded Africans "reaching out toward the highest civilization of our times." Belgian diplomats breathed a sigh of relief; they informed government officials in Brussels that the pope's real concern was not colonialism but the "grand battle of influence between the Soviet world and the Free World."[35]

A muted response came from African Catholic students, two hundred of whom had gathered in Rome on the weekend of the encyclical's release. "Should not the church take a solemn position against colonialism?" Joseph Ki-Zerbo, from Upper Volta, asked. The students met with the secretary of the Propaganda Fide, but an ailing Pius XII declined to join them.[36]

III

PARALLEL DYNAMICS OF Catholic decolonization became evident in Southeast Asia. In the Philippines, Horacio de la Costa had graduated from an elite Jesuit high school in Manila in the 1930s. Interned during the Japanese occupation of the Philippines during World War II, he obtained a doctorate in history from Harvard after the war. He soon became the first Filipino leader of the Jesuits, and his scholarly passion, even when writing on events in the sixteenth century, became the origins of a Filipino nationalist consciousness. As early as 1952, he insisted that Catholicism no longer be viewed as a Western import but instead as belonging "fully as much to Asia as to Europe."[37]

In Indonesia after 1945, Dutch Catholic church officials and political leaders scrambled to sustain the country as a colony by warning of "chaos" should a nascent independence movement succeed. Some of these Dutch Catholics and their Indonesian allies aligned themselves with the majority Muslim population to create "greater spiritual resilience against communism." But support for an independent republic also became apparent. The first native Indonesian bishop, Albertus Soegijapranata, played a crucial role. An aristocrat (and Jesuit) from Java, Soegijapranata had at first resisted calls to form a republic. But he became the region's most important Catholic figure during the Japanese occupation (when Dutch Catholics were imprisoned or placed under house arrest), and he developed contacts with republican leaders, some of whom were Catholic. He spoke of his "supernatural optimism" about an independent Indonesia. Other Indonesian Catholics protested the Dutch presence by placing pro-independence articles in liberal American and Dutch Catholic publications. Eventually, Soegijapranata cajoled many Dutch Catholic leaders into accepting the new republic and arranged for official recognition from the Vatican.[38]

Just as some missionaries worried about African Catholics becoming communists, so, too, did missionaries worry about Vietnamese Catholics becoming "communist sympathizers." Vietnamese Catholic students, like their African Catholic contemporaries, also studied in Paris in the 1930s, and again, like their African Catholic contemporaries, expressed doubts about conventional justifications for colonial rule. They began to ask, "What is the right of colonization?"[39]

After the war and the Japanese occupation, Bishop Ngô Đình Thục organized the Vietnamese bishops to support Vietnamese independence.[40] In this more nationalist setting, French missionary bishops and clergy came under attack as "undesirables and troublemakers, if not enemies of the nation." Vietnamese clergy barred some French priests from saying Mass. French priests, in turn, hid statues of French saints to prevent their destruction by Vietnamese Catholics. Outside of Paris, newly

President Ngô Đình
Diệm of South
Vietnam, 1957.
Bishop Ngô Đình
Thục, his brother, is
in the background
in clerical clothing.
(Keystone/Getty Images)

mobilized Vietnamese Catholic students congregated at a retreat center and sang patriotic songs.[41]

What eventually divided Vietnamese Catholics from Vietnamese communists was not a desire for independence, which they shared, but a recognition that communists in Vietnam might be as committed to persecution of Catholics as communists in Eastern Europe and China. What began as an anti-colonial struggle against the French became a front in the Cold War. The Vietnamese leader, and future president of North Vietnam, Ho Chi Minh, cheerfully attended the ordination of a Catholic bishop in 1945, but his subordinates began closing Catholic schools in areas under their control in the late 1940s.[42] A pastoral letter issued by fifteen Vietnamese bishops in 1951 declared agreement with Pius XII "that there exists the most complete opposition between the Catholic Church and Communism . . . it is absolutely impossible to be at the same time a Catholic and a Communist."[43]

After the French defeat in 1954 and the division of Vietnam into a communist North and a nominally democratic South, Ngô Đình Diệm of South Vietnam became the first Catholic head of state in Vietnamese history. He was the brother of Bishop Ngô Đình Thục, and he had been exposed to French personalism while studying in Paris. (He also met Vincent Lebbe there.)[44] Diệm's authoritarian governing style belied his democratic rhetoric, but along with other Vietnamese Catholic personalists he desired to dismantle the "distorted impression of freedom" promoted by both Marxism and a lightly regulated capitalism.[45]

Since Catholics lived primarily in the North, where they faced communist persecution, several hundred thousand fled to the South in the mid-1950s in one of the first postwar refugee crises. Bishop Thục and President Diệm mobilized aid for these refugees from contacts in Catholic circles in the United States, and an American Catholic medical missionary, Tom Dooley, gave the refugee crisis worldwide publicity in a series of hugely popular and anti-communist accounts, one entitled *Deliver Us From Evil*. On visits to the United States, President Diệm was praised by American bishops as a "God-fearing, anti-communist and courageous statesman."[46]

IV

CATHOLICS IN LATIN AMERICA had long oscillated between dismay with secular elites and alliances with authoritarian (and at least nominally Catholic) political leaders. In Guatemala, for example, the country's fiercely anti-communist archbishop, Mariano Rossell y Arellano, connived with the CIA and Catholics with links to Franco's Spain to overthrow a democratically elected, left-leaning leader in 1954. That the democratic government had firmly separated church from state appalled the archbishop, and he and his allies saw state control of education as "pure totalitarianism." He mobilized Catholic women, in particular, under the banner of a Francoist slogan, "God, Fatherland, Liberty."[47]

What emerged across Latin America in the 1950s, however, even in Guatemala, was also a sense that Catholics bore some responsibility for alleviating economic disparities. They could no longer run schools only for the children of wealthy Catholics or ignore the consolidation of land holdings to the benefit of a few families. Even as he supported the Guatemalan coup, Archbishop Rossell conceded that the current "distribution of the land and its riches is neither Christian nor equitable." He blamed "laissez-faire" and "free competition."[48]

A wave of missionaries augmented these reform impulses. Beginning in the 1940s, thousands of Catholic clergy and nuns arrived in Latin

America from Ireland, the United States, Canada, and Western Europe. (Some arrived after their expulsion from communist China.) These foreign-born clergy and nuns presumed that as Catholics they spoke the "spiritual language of Latin America."[49] But the travails of American missionaries to Peru are suggestive. Assigned to remote Aymara- and Quechua-speaking regions, they struggled to connect with illiterate villagers whose language they could not understand and whose Catholic identity revolved around festivals and local devotions, not sacraments and Catholic institutions. The tone of reports back to the United States could be condescending. "The people crowded around the altar," wrote one priest who had been sent to the Puno region, "with the decorum of children at a side-show, nothing like the order which usually attends Mass in the States."

At the same time, the missionaries often found themselves awed by the piety they encountered. Or as another American priest explained:

> I know they don't go to Mass or frequent the sacraments,
> that the Fiesta is for most a social event during which
> there is much drunkenness and other excesses. All this I
> know. But when I see them straining under the weight of
> the statue, when I see them crowding around our Blessed
> Mother, when I see them kneeling on the streets, when
> I see groups, many of whom are no more than children,
> dancing about the statue during the entire procession,
> then it seems to me that these poor uneducated Indians
> have a love, a faith in many ways deeper and more beau-
> tiful than that of which we sometimes feel so proud.[50]

Over time, missionary priests and nuns shifted their focus from building successful parishes or schools on the North American model to building social programs. In Peru, missionaries constituted a majority of clergy by 1960, and Peruvian church and government officials placed them in charge of entire regions. They trained catechists, but also built medical clinics and distributed aid provided by the US or West German governments.[51]

The most promising example of this reform emphasis within Catholicism was in Chile. Christian Democrat Eduardo Frei and his allies accused more traditional Chilean Catholics in the late 1940s of indulging in a "sterile and harmful anti-communism" and neglecting the cries of those who "suffer dreadful poverty." (A local bishop responded by terming Frei and his student allies "enemies of Christ.")[52] Frei welcomed the reform efforts of Alberto Hurtado, a Chilean Jesuit trained in social action in Europe, who founded homes for poor children, encouraged labor unions, and pushed Chile's Catholic elite to recognize economic disparities. In 1953, socially minded Catholics, supported for the first time by some bishops, mediated a widely publicized strike in Chile's rural Central Valley, helping negotiate an agreement favorable to agricultural workers.[53]

Even as missionaries and development experts descended upon Latin America, a small group of Latin American priests crossed the Atlantic in the opposite direction. They took degrees at Catholic universities, usually at Louvain in Belgium or the Institut Catholique in Paris, where they absorbed the ideas of the *nouvelle théologie*. The most influential of these men, Gustavo Gutiérrez, a Peruvian priest, studied in Louvain and Lyon, where he became fascinated by the worker-priest experiments. He met privately with Henri de Lubac, still prohibited from taking a faculty position, and adopted de Lubac's position that theology could not be separated from politics.

Sharing the belief that theology should inform politics did not mean that de Lubac and Gutiérrez shared a common program. De Lubac remained anti-communist, and he had long worried that "progressive Christians" might trap themselves into supporting the "totalitarians of the communist party."[54] Gutiérrez had no interest in Soviet atheism but believed that Marxist analysis shed light on Latin American inequality. Upon returning from France, Gutiérrez worked in the slums of Lima, and this experience solidified his conviction that conventional political and economic structures could not ameliorate the plight of the poor. He developed ties with Catholic students and activists in Brazil, who seemed more open to "Christian socialism" and less determined to "defend private property" than Christian Democrats influenced by

Jacques Maritain. In 1960, a group of Brazilian Catholic college students described capitalism as a "monstrous structure" and "against the dignity of the human person."[55]

If the Cold War accelerated Catholic development work in Africa, the Cuban revolution had the effect of a seismic boom in Latin America. In 1959, despite his Jesuit education, Fidel Castro installed a communist regime ninety miles from the United States. The initial Cuban Catholic response to the revolution was measured, even hopeful, since Castro's initial program of agrarian reform mapped onto ongoing Catholic efforts. By 1961, the decision of Cuban revolutionaries to expropriate private property and their increasingly anti-religious policies had changed this appraisal, and the vibrant Cuban Catholic exile community in Miami became a center of anti-communist activity.

Now more than ever, economic development in Latin America seemed a priority, and John F. Kennedy began his presidential administration with a massive infusion of funds into South America. Many of these Latin American development programs built upon existing Catholic ties. Kennedy administration official Sargent Shriver and Notre Dame's president, Theodore Hesburgh, arranged to send some of the first Peace Corps volunteers to projects initiated by Chilean Catholics. Attorney General Robert Kennedy visited Peru and annoyed the country's president by meeting with American missionaries and learning about rural Catholic cooperatives.[56] European Catholic development agencies—led by West Germans—also began funding programs identified by Catholic missionaries and Christian Democrats in Chile, Venezuela, and Brazil. This West German financial support was significant enough to eventually persuade the Brazilian bishops that they needed to elect a German-speaking bishop as the leader of their episcopal conference.[57]

The Vatican continued to fret about a Catholic Latin America vulnerable to communists, Protestant missionaries, and secularization. One top curial official pleaded with leaders of American and Canadian dioceses and religious orders to tithe 10 percent of their priests and nuns to Latin America, given the "well-known lack of clergy, and indeed of all apostolic workers."[58] Few met this goal, but another several thousand American, Canadian, and European Catholic nuns and priests moved to Latin America between 1960 and 1970, along with smaller numbers of lay volunteers. President Kennedy explicitly noted his hope that the world's bishops would continue to discuss development issues.[59]

V

THE EXPERIENCE OF World War II and then the Cold War allowed some Catholics and Protestants to dismantle walls erected during the culture wars of the nineteenth century. In North America, Jesuit John Courtney Murray led the way. Gifted with an icy intelligence and at ease in the circles of the Protestant establishment—he taught at Yale for a year and enjoyed the occasional round of golf with his close friend *Time* magazine publisher Henry Luce—Murray desired Catholics in the United States to take on greater responsibility as guardians of Western civilization.

Upon returning from four years of study in Rome in 1937, convinced that Catholics, Protestants, and Jews should work together to combat fascism, Murray began studying the problem of interreligious cooperation. Up until this point, Catholics everywhere had been forbidden from joint ventures with Protestants and Jews out of fear that such cooperation might imply equal validity for all religions. Catholics bold enough to participate in American groups such as the National Conference of Christians and Jews, including Columbia University professor Carlton Hayes, faced persistent sniping. Hayes told Murray of his wish that Catholic bishops would "frankly accept the *fact* of cultural pluralism among us."[60] Murray referenced Jacques Maritain and asserted that Catholics needed to take greater account of the "fundamental and primordial ethical value of the law of brotherly love."[61]

Across the Atlantic, at the same moment, theologians and scholars promoted new forms of ecumenical cooperation. Yves Congar, whose early work on this topic so inspired Dominique de Menil, brought together small groups of Catholics and Protestants in French- and German-speaking Europe in the late 1940s.

These ecumenical dialogues, like the worker-priest experiment and other initiatives connected to the *nouvelle théologie*, fell victim to Vatican retrenchment. In 1948, much to the embarrassment of Congar, Pius XII warned Catholics against even attending ecumenical gatherings. Over the next decade only scattered groups of Catholics engaged in such work. The most influential was the German Jesuit and top Vatican aide Augustin Bea, who encouraged a range of below-the-radar dialogues between Catholics and Jews. Bea surprised himself, as he admitted to a friend, by agreeing to shift away from his expertise in ancient texts—he was a Hebrew Bible scholar—to this new arena. Opportunity for dialogue awakened a "desire in my heart."[62]

Most Catholics, certainly most German Catholics, continued to understand themselves and their church as victims of the Nazis. Difficult as it is to imagine now, the topic of the Holocaust was barely discussed in the first decade after World War II. Pius XII told the German bishops that Nazism had been a "satanic ghost" and that they had emerged from the war "strengthened and purified." Belgium's Catholic political parties protested compensation paid to the country's few surviving Jews.[63]

Jacques Maritain was again a dissenting voice. Horrified by the Holocaust and instances of postwar anti–Semitism, including a pogrom at Kielce in Poland in 1946, Maritain privately pleaded with Pius XII, via his friend Archbishop Montini, to denounce anti–Semitism and eliminate the prayer for "perfidious Jews" from the Good Friday liturgy. Six million European Jews had been "liquidated," Maritain noted, and for this Catholics bore some responsibility. The pope should "tell the truth to the world and shed light on this tragedy."[64]

He did not receive a response. Reflection on these questions began not in Rome but at the grass roots in West Germany and Switzerland. Among the leaders was Gertrud Luckner, an Anglo-German convert from Quakerism to Catholicism, who had settled in Germany and helped rescue hundreds of Jews during the most desperate days of the war. After 1945 she facilitated Jewish-Catholic encounters through small conferences and a journal she edited, *Freiburger Rundbrief*. For her wartime heroism—and her postwar promotion of interreligious exchange—Luckner became the first German citizen officially invited to visit the newly founded State of Israel in 1951. She and her collaborators worked to discredit notions of Jews as Christ killers and with Fr. Bea's encouragement established ties with Jewish groups scattered across Western Europe.[65]

VI

ECUMENICAL OR INTERRELIGIOUS cooperation, with its underlying respect for the convictions of diverse believers, naturally fed into discussions of two other issues highlighted by the Cold War: human rights and the importance of conscience. Neo-Thomists in the early twentieth century had expressed little interest in human rights, since such claims depended on an individualism they rejected. In a book whose title, *The Rights of Man and Natural Law,* startled Catholics weaned on horror stories about the French Revolution, Jacques Maritain redirected the conversation. Yes, Maritain conceded, the French Declaration of the Rights of Man had lodged human rights within a "false rationalist perspective." (Thomas Jefferson's prose in the Declaration of Independence came closer to "the originally Christian character of human rights.") But the true origins of human rights lay "in the conception of man and of natural law established by centuries of Christian philosophy."[66]

Some Catholic scholars found Maritain's uniting of Thomas Aquinas, the natural law, and human rights unpersuasive. "What [Maritain] wants apparently," complained one scholar privately, "is a St. Thomas who, being completely divorced from his life in the thirteenth century, is free to live as a philosopher in the twentieth century and after."[67] But Maritain persevered, and the onset of the Cold War made the need to explain why the West promoted human rights and why the communist bloc did not only more acute. He played a leading role on the 1947 committee of philosophers charged with drafting the influential UNESCO Report on Human Rights. Maritain admitted that the drafters could not agree on "one and the same conception of the world," but he applauded the development of a "single body of beliefs for action."[68]

Postwar constitutions written by Christian Democrats struck similar notes. In Italy, Christian Democrats drafted a constitution that would, in the words of one advocate, "transcend the principles of 1789."[69] Article 3 was pitch-perfect Maritain: "It is the Republic's duty to remove obstacles of an economic or social order physically constricting the freedom and equality of citizens and thus impeding the full development of the human person." In West Germany, too, the *Grundgesetz*, or basic law, of 1949 can be understood in personalist terms. The first clause of article 1 asserted that "Human Dignity is inviolable," and the second clause endorsed "inviolable and inalienable human rights."[70]

Little of this was controversial. But navigating one particular human rights issue—freedom of religion—proved challenging. Debate about the role of Catholicism in democratic societies surged after World War II. The most vigorous discussion was in the United States, where the country's foremost philosopher, John Dewey, referred to Catholicism as a "reactionary world organization." Similarly, the journalist Paul Blanshard's best-selling book, *American Freedom and Catholic Power*, pleaded with liberals to form a "resistance movement" to counter the "antidemocratic social policies of the hierarchy."[71]

Could Catholics be trusted to support democratic governments? They voted in elections and ran for office. But Catholic support for fascism in the 1930s seemed to demonstrate an antipathy to the culture underpinning democracy. Blanshard highlighted Vatican treaties with Mussolini and Hitler and Catholic opposition to birth control. He mocked nuns and warned against the growing number of Catholic schools. He joined like-minded critics in pointing to Latin America, where Brazil's Catholics had long threatened to prohibit American Protestant missionaries from entering the country and where violent clashes between small groups of Protestants and the Catholic majority occurred beneath the public radar. The Argentinian bishops in 1945 had asserted that the "constitutional right of Protestants and dissidents to be respected in the exercise of their worship does not allow them the right to proselyte among Catholics."[72]

Prominent West German Protestants echoed Blanshard's complaints, with one announcing that "the present West German government was conceived in the Vatican and born in Washington. The continuance of the West German state means the death of continental Protestantism."[73] The same debate occurred in Australia and even Malawi, where Blanshard's arguments were used to challenge the formation of a Catholic political party.[74]

Both John Courtney Murray and Jacques Maritain dismissed Blanshard's criticisms. Murray thought that liberals such as Blanshard and his many allies tended to exalt democracy beyond a system of government into an all-encompassing theological claim. Maritain knew that standard church-state teaching was "odious" to non-Catholics, but he also thought that Americans were susceptible to a dangerous "total liberalism."[75]

Murray and Maritain nonetheless realized that Blanshard's hostile, even offensive, questions required better answers than Catholics had yet provided. In a series of dazzling, crisp essays, Murray argued against the standard Catholic view that the state should endorse the one, true church. While it was understandable that Pope Leo XIII had emphasized the desirability of a formal unity between church and state during the liberal nationalist persecutions of the 1870s and 1880s, a state-sponsored religion should no longer serve as a Catholic ideal. Nineteenth-century struggles should not determine twentieth-century Catholic responses.[76]

European Catholic intellectuals moved on parallel paths. A West German Jesuit, who like Murray had begun his scholarly career by encouraging cooperation between Catholics and Protestants, now promoted "full religious freedom as in the USA."[77] A French Jesuit wrote on the "modern papacy and freedom of conscience."[78] Maritain cited Murray in a series of lectures given at the University of Chicago. A young Theodore Hesburgh, just about to be named president of the University of Notre Dame, read the lectures and wrote Maritain with delight. "I was amazed," he told Maritain, "to see how closely your conclusions agree with those of Father Murray." He thought it certain that "this chapter of yours will answer the doubts of many thinking Americans who have long been perplexed by this subject."[79] Murray, in turn, read Maritain with care. He described Latin American criticism of Maritain as "vicious" and like Maritain had warm discussions with Archbishop Montini in Milan. Murray found the future Paul VI "personally sympathetic with my 'orientations' and rather wanted his hand to be strengthened."[80]

Schools proved the most controversial testing ground. Just as in the 1870s, expanding networks of Catholic schools in the 1940s seemed to many liberals incompatible with the need to prepare citizens for democratic self-government. French liberals bemoaned children educated in a "spiritual ghetto," and American Supreme Court justices privately regretted that the Court in 1925 had defended the right of Catholics to manage their own schools.[81]

By contrast, Catholics, even liberal Catholics, identified parents choosing Catholic schools for their children as a basic human right, preceding the right of the state to educate its citizens. A West German cardinal thought an absence of public funding for religious schools risked making democracy "nothing more than a shell." (A "strike" by forty thousand West German Catholic schoolchildren—organized by the bishops—reinforced the point.)[82] In the United States, the issue of public support for Catholic schools animated two of the era's most controversial Supreme Court decisions, as justices wary of Catholicism invoked Thomas Jefferson's offhand phrasing of a "wall of separation" to distinguish church from state.

The outcomes of this education debate varied. Funding for Catholic schools continued as before the war in the Netherlands and Canada. Funding continued in Belgium, but controversies over education extended to the Belgian Congo. (There Catholics founded the country's first university and threatened a student strike if funding was withdrawn, even as they attempted to rebut claims that they favored "theocratic" education.)[83] No government support of Catholic schools was allowed in the United States, although the Catholic school system continued to expand, peaking in 1965 with 12.5 million students in grade schools and high schools, entirely funded by parishes and parents and resting on the barely compensated labor of women religious, priests, and brothers. (By contrast, the federal government allowed veterans provided tuition funds as part of the GI Bill to spend those monies at Catholic colleges and universities, leading to a significant expansion of that system.) In France, government ministries denied funding for Catholic schools in the 1940s, but Charles de Gaulle instituted it in modified form at the beginning of the Fifth Republic in 1958.

John Courtney Murray, like so many reform-minded scholars, became an object of Vatican scrutiny. The leader of the Holy Office, Cardinal Alfredo Ottaviani, had Murray's essays on religious freedom in his sights when he gave a well-publicized speech endorsing not only the nineteenth-century view of church and state unity, but a recently signed treaty between the Vatican and Franco's Spain. (The treaty reaffirmed Catholicism's status as the country's official religion.) Many Catholic officials—even top papal aides—found Ottaviani's speech appalling. The mortified Irish ambassador to the Vatican privately lamented the "grave neglect by Rome of the mass of Catholic opinion in the West."[84]

But Ottaviani was head of the Holy Office and the Irish ambassador was not. Murray's two leading opponents in the United States, Fr. Joseph Fenton and Fr. Francis Connell, faculty members at Catholic University in Washington, DC, knew Ottaviani and welcomed their patron's blast. Fenton's suspicion of doctrinal development was such that he accused even the nineteenth-century English convert John Henry Newman of demonstrating the "unerring instinct of a minimizer." Connell barraged Ottaviani with complaints about Murray. In response, Murray privately complained to Connell that "it is particularly painful when suspicions of unorthodoxy are raised privately, by word of mouth in high places."[85]

By 1955, this Roman hostility toward Murray, even if Pius XII himself took a more measured view, was such that his Jesuit superiors silenced him. A Jesuit based in Rome advised Murray to avoid "that controverted question under present circumstances." Murray replied that this seems a "delicate way of saying 'You're through.'" A friend watched a depressed Murray comb his bookshelves in his room at the Maryland seminary where he taught: books on church-state issues went back to the library, since he could no longer write on the subject. Only books on other topics could remain.[86]

VII

BY THE LATE 1950S, Pius XII and his closest aides were seen as so sympathetic to American goals in the Cold War that some Italian observers wryly described them as Il Pentagone after the Virginia headquarters of the American military.[87] This support for the American military was not uniform across the Catholic world. One prominent American Jesuit, John Ford, had criticized Allied saturation bombing in 1944 for targeting innocent victims. Other philosophers and theologians had opposed the dropping of the atomic bomb in 1945. As late as 1957, the Oxford philosopher Elizabeth Anscombe delivered a stern indictment of President Truman's decision to drop the atomic bombs on Hiroshima and Nagasaki. She disagreed with the decision of her employer to award Truman an honorary degree. She thought "for men to choose to kill the innocent as a means to their end is always murder."[88]

But the dropping of the atomic bomb came to be understood as a special case, and Anscombe stood outside the mainstream of Catholic thought. The topic of conscientious objection to war remained almost taboo. In France, only the Algerian War of the 1950s (and a military draft) provoked interest in the subject, especially when some Catholic soldiers refused to torture Algerian prisoners. As late as 1960, though, the cardinal archbishop of Paris shunted off interest in conscientious objection by stating that "it is for the Church to teach the truth, not for the faithful to make the truth according to their inclination."[89] Chicago's cardinal archbishop similarly advised the United States Justice Department not to be concerned about Catholic conscientious objectors. "It seems to me," he explained, that if "civil authorities" declared war, "we do not allow personal opinion to override it." A German Jesuit testified before the West German parliament that antinuclear Catholic activists were incapable of "deciding such a complex question through their conscience."[90]

Flickers of change became perceptible through the *nouvelle théologie*. Theologians, philosophers, and historians interested in reform— such as France's Henri de Lubac, Yves Congar, Étienne Gilson, and Marie-Dominique Chenu; Germany's Erich Przywara and Edith Stein; Canada's Bernard Lonergan; and Italy's Don Giuseppe de Luca—read or even translated John Henry Newman in the decades before 1960. Two dimensions of Newman's work seemed newly relevant: his idea of doctrinal development and his discussion of the importance of the individual conscience.

One of the young scholars trying to grasp Newman's idea of conscience in light of twelve years of National Socialism was Joseph Ratzinger, the future Benedict XVI. A Bavarian, Ratzinger had been drafted into the German antiaircraft corps as a teenager in 1943. He escaped when he deserted and walked back to his hometown village during the war's last weeks. A generation younger than the theologians associated with the *nouvelle théologie*, Ratzinger shared their frustration with a static neo-Thomism. Encountering the writings of the most controversial nouvelle theologian, Henri de Lubac, was a "key reading event." Ratzinger participated in a two-year reading group on Newman immediately upon entering the seminary in 1946, and he welcomed the idea that following church teaching "does not rest on a cancellation of conscience."[91] Bernhard Häring had served as a chaplain in the *Wehrmacht* and witnessed the horrors of the Eastern Front. He invoked individual conscience (and Newman) in his monumental *The Law of Christ* (1954), the most influential postwar text on moral theology, and insisted that "Christian life may not be viewed solely from the point of formal enactment of law."[92]

The term "conscience" also lay beneath the first critical assessments of German Catholic complicity with Nazism. The protagonists were an American and a West German. The American, Gordon Zahn, was one of the few American Catholic conscientious objectors during World War II, inspired by the example of New York's Dorothy Day. After the war, he fell into the orbit of Eugene McCarthy, a Catholic Minnesota congressman, who gave him a staff job in Washington, DC while he worked at night on his doctorate. He managed to obtain a teaching position at Loyola University in Chicago and a fellowship to spend a year in West Germany. There he made contact with the small but vocal West German Catholic peace movement as he began researching the biography of Franz Jägerstätter, the Bavarian Catholic executed for his refusal to serve in the *Wehrmacht*. One of Zahn's friends, the Kentucky monk Thomas Merton, told Zahn that Jägerstätter was a "moving symbol of a lonely isolated Christian who was faithful to his conscience."[93] Rome's Augustin Bea, having just been named a Cardinal, and then promoting promoting ecumenical and interreligious dialogue with Protestants and Jews, proved uninterested in dialogue with Zahn. He asked Jesuit editors in the United States to sideline Zahn because he treated questions about German Catholic war guilt "simplistically."[94]

Zahn's work intersected with the efforts of a young West German Catholic lawyer, Ernst Böckenförde, and Munich's cardinal, Julius Döpner, would later place both men on a list of "nonconformist" activists. Böckenförde had protested in 1957 when a fellow Catholic, Chancellor Konrad Adenauer, endorsed the placement of American nuclear weapons on West German soil. Most West German Catholic intellectuals, notably the social theorist Gustav Gundlach, supported Adenauer. Gundlach insisted that "even the destruction of an entire people" in a just war was morally legitimate.[95] John Courtney Murray, so controversial on church-state questions, noted the West German debate and called the arguments of Catholic pacifists "alarming." Communism remained the "gravest possible menace to the moral and civilizational values that form the basis of the 'West." He cited an ambitious young American strategist, Henry Kissinger, in support of the need to consider, not condemn, the idea of a limited or tactical nuclear exchange.[96]

Böckenförde also became annoyed when his Münster bishop informed parishioners that it was a sin to vote for the Social Democratic Party as opposed to the Christian Democratic Union, then at the height of its power under Adenauer. In *Hochland*, a leading Catholic journal edited by his uncle, Böckenförde complained that Catholics had not yet adapted to the ethos of modern democracies and must resist an "inner affinity of the Church for authoritarian regimes."[97]

Böckenförde then grew bolder. He dissected an archive of Catholic texts from 1933 and 1934 where he found numerous German Catholics urging reconciliation between Catholicism and the new National Socialist regime. Böckenförde pointed especially to those German Catholics who transferred their desire for a more organic community to the Nazi movement. He quoted one prominent Benedictine abbot (and liturgical reformer) who had in 1933 welcomed the "Führer, [who] out of the loneliness of service and sacrifice, borne by an unswerving faith in the German Volk, has brought [the State] to a joyful affirmation of itself."[98]

Böckenförde was critical of Zentrum leaders willing to bargain with the National Socialists and Vatican officials, including the future Pope Pius XII, who had negotiated the 1933 Reichskonkordat. Böckenförde attributed these fateful decisions to a "deeply rooted anti-liberalism that had been characteristic of Catholic thinking since the nineteenth century." (Here Böckenförde noted the 1832 papal condemnation of Lamennais.) An obsession with neo-Thomism had blinded Catholics to the importance of democratic practice, as had knee-jerk rejections of the "ideas of 1789." "Can one seriously say," Böckenförde asked in the essay's provocative last line, "that the positions and political principles that led to the errors of 1933 have been overcome in the German Catholicism of today?"[99] The article provoked dozens of commentaries and in Böckenförde's wry phrasing "a medium sized earthquake." Zahn wrote Böckenforde of his admiration for the article, which in Zahn's view had implications for "Catholics in all lands." A few months later, Zahn published a book criticizing German Catholic passivity during the Nazi era.[100]

By then the term "conscience" had taken on a life of its own. Louis-Joseph Lebret asked Catholics to examine their "collective conscience" and work toward eliminating "racial ideas" and the gap between rich and poor nations.[101] The founder of Amnesty International, a British Catholic, dedicated the organization to assisting "prisoners of conscience." Soon married couples contemplating the use of contraceptives, opponents of racial segregation, and defenders of religious freedom would identify a person's conscience as making an inviolable, even sacred, claim.

VIII

THE TRIUMPH OF Catholic reformers was never assured. Yves Congar, John Courtney Murray, Henri de Lubac, Marie-Dominique Chenu, and other ressourcement figures remained silenced or in exile into the late 1950s. Jacques Maritain, himself, barely escaped censure for his views on church and state in a document drafted, but not released, by Vatican officials. Credible rumors of Latin American bishops pressing for a condemnation of Maritain circulated in Rome as late as 1960.[102] The importance of the Global South to Catholicism's future was clear, but the process of disentangling the church from imperialism had barely begun. Official church teaching on the desirability of a unity of church and state remained unchanged. Textbooks used in Catholic schools described the Jewish people as the murderers of Christ, doomed to wander the world and "cursed by God."[103]

To predict in 1958 that Catholics would witness more changes in their church in the next fifteen years than at any time since the French

Revolution would have seemed preposterous. Only the election of a new pope that year, Venetian cardinal Angelo Roncalli, or John XXIII, altered horizons. Roncalli had been raised in a peasant family near Bergamo, with cows grazing outside his front door. If Catholicism "is to be held vitally," Roncalli wrote in his journal as a seminarian, "we celebrate it with an energy that is wholly youthful."[104] Later, as a seminary professor, he taught the scholarly work of a friend and colleague, a historian of the church later excommunicated as a modernist. After his election as pope, he strolled over to the Holy Office, opened the dusty file on himself, and found a notation, "suspected of modernism."[105]

While serving as Apostolic Delegate to Turkey and Greece, Roncalli saved the lives of several thousand Jews by facilitating their transit from Nazi-occupied Europe. An American working in Istanbul sketched his personality. "Roncalli is a fascinator," he wrote in his diary, "Charming, vocal, amusing, political, friendly—he wins everyone."[106] As nuncio to France beginning in 1945, Roncalli helped Jacques Maritain replace several bishops deemed overly sympathetic to the wartime Vichy government. He encouraged diplomats laboring on a draft of the 1948 United Nations Universal Declaration of Human Rights.[107]

Still, Roncalli was also a seventy-eight-year-old churchman whose piety was entirely traditional. He had (privately) dismissed the Matisse chapel so beloved by Abbé Couturier and Dominique de Menil as a "perversion" of "liturgical and artistic taste."[108] A visitor to Roncalli's study in Paris observed him reading a new and controversial text, Yves Congar's *True and False Reform within the Church*. (Vatican officials prohibited its reprinting.) The visitor asked for an assessment. "A reform of the Church," Roncalli wondered in reply, "is such a thing really possible?"[109]

PART III

Vatican II and Its Aftermath

1962–2021

ELEVEN

Vatican II

A Church Transformed

I

PIUS XII HAD long pushed himself beyond exhaustion, and in 1950 and 1954 he had come close to death. He spent his days preparing detailed talks for an endless string of audiences, from astronomers to gynecologists. He pushed out of his inner circle aides with ties to the Catholic ressourcement, including Archbishop Montini, whom he removed from Rome by appointing him as archbishop of Milan. After suffering two strokes in three days, Pius XII died in October 1958. One of his physicians was an ophthalmologist whose salient professional credential was a brother working in the Vatican. He botched the embalming of the body and sold photos of the corpse. Allegedly, the pope's last words were "Pray, pray, pray that this unhappy situation for the Church may end."[1]

Pius XII had considered the church he led to be under siege. He perceived threats from Protestants (in Latin America), Muslims (in Africa), and communists (everywhere). Other threats existed within the church, although these challenges seemed more manageable. He had checked the ressourcement reformers of the 1930s and 1940s at almost every turn; their names and their ideas remained unknown to most of the world's five hundred million Catholics. These Catholics worshipped in an institution whose practices and structures, though reconstructed after the French Revolution, were routinely described as timeless. The liturgy remained in Latin, and Sacred Hearts, novenas, and rosaries constituted a common devotional language. Catholic schools, hospitals, universities, and associations multiplied and flourished.

Catholics still constituted a strong majority of the population in many European countries and in Central and South America. The Catholic population had increased steadily in both Western Europe and North America because of the postwar baby boom, and over half of the world's Catholics lived on those two continents. In both regions the primary problem seemed to be constructing an infrastructure to catch up with this growing population, now more likely to be located in fast-developing suburban areas. In the area around Cologne, 1,250 churches were constructed in the 1950s and 1960s, in part because so many churches had been destroyed during the war but in part because of migration into the suburbs. Outside of cities such as New York and Chicago, the pace of suburban growth—and church and school construction—was equally rapid. In Bologna, the city's cardinal dedicated eleven new church construction sites—placing a cross in the fields where a suburban church would be constructed—in one frantic day.[2] None of this growth matched what was occurring in Africa, where the Catholic population soared because of successful evangelization campaigns and high birth rates.

Warning signs were more subtle. Religious practice was declining, perhaps collapsing, among some sectors of the European and Latin American working class and was sporadic in regions of the world where the presence of the institutional church remained faint. Important intellectuals had lost interest in neo-Thomism, the intellectual underpinning of the milieu. The distinguished medievalist Étienne Gilson complained about neo-Thomism's outdated methods, "its lack of historical sense, the ignorance of or the snobbish inability to understand the latest research, the need to create heretics to cut up."[3] A few seminarians in the United States joked about "ghetto Thomism."[4] Some undergraduates at Jesuit-run Boston College ritually tossed their textbooks into a bonfire and a nearby reservoir to register discontent with the eight required courses in neo-Thomist philosophy.[5]

Catholic women on both sides of the Atlantic were becoming restless with prescribed roles. Women religious in the United States and Canada, especially, began to seek more extended training and educational opportunities, including the first advanced theology degrees for women. In West Germany, leaders of the country's largest Catholic women's organization, themselves lawyers, politely argued for marriage as an equal partnership, more professional opportunities for single and married women (with a caveat that mothers should focus first on children), and a more pragmatic acceptance of divorce.[6]

Another unexpected challenge was prosperity. The economic boom in Western Europe and North America after World War II pulled millions of Catholics, as much or more than any other group, into the middle class. Income levels for Catholics in both West Germany and the United States reached or exceeded national averages for the first time in the early 1960s.[7] One Jesuit sociologist wondered if "group solidarity" might wither. "It is not so much that religion and moral law are denied or rejected," he wrote, "[but that] they are simply judged not pertinent as guiding norms of practical action."[8]

II

ON JANUARY 25, 1959, three months after his election, "trembling a little with emotion," John XXIII stunned the world by announcing an ecumenical council. It would become one of the most important events of the twentieth century.

The hazy goal mentioned in John XXIII's announcement—the "enlightenment, education and joy of the entire Christian people"—provided little guidance.[9] After his announcement, the pope asked curial officials to poll bishops, nuncios, theologians, and heads of male religious orders, asking what topics they thought should be discussed "with complete freedom and honesty."[10] The extent to which authority had been centralized in the papacy since the First Vatican Council can be gauged by the unimaginative replies. Some respondents filled out the form with a bare couple of sentences. Of 3,000 topics tabulated, 250 mentioned the laity.[11] One church historian predicted to Giovanni Montini in Milan (who had just been named a cardinal) that the "elderly vultures" in the Curia would control the council's outcome.[12]

The pope established ten commissions organized by topic and a central coordinating committee. The Theological Commission, chaired by the head of the Holy Office, Cardinal Alfredo Ottaviani, was the most important. A native of the Trastevere neighborhood, a short walk from the Vatican, Ottaviani's episcopal motto—*semper idem*, or "always the same"—conveyed his sense of the council's purpose: to reiterate church teaching. In the 1930s, as a canon lawyer, he had published a bold article documenting the ways Stalin, Hitler, and Mussolini had infringed upon the rights of the church. That protective sense endured. "Not all that is new," he told one reporter, "is true and good merely because it is new."[13] During the 1950s he had opposed ecumenical ventures and supported traditional church teaching on the unity of church and state.[14] In 1961 he published a collection of essays entitled, in French, *Le Rempart* (The Rampart). Ressourcement theologian Henri de Lubac thought it should have been entitled "The Maginot Line."[15]

The men chosen to draft the schemata (or draft texts) were not a diverse group. All were priests. Most lived in Rome, where meetings were held, and many had spent their entire careers at Roman universities or in Vatican offices. They inhabited, de Lubac thought, "a small academic system, ultra-intellectualist without being intellectual."[16] The footnotes in the drafts referenced the decrees of the First Vatican Council and recent papal statements. Upon reading these drafts, Yves Congar, another French ressourcement theologian, concluded that "Ultramontanism really does exist."[17]

John XXIII barely involved himself in these preparations. Still, he indicated his desire for something other than familiar formulas. He appointed a number of reform-minded bishops to the commissions along with, remarkably, some of the theologians associated with the *nouvelle théologie*. Retrieved from theological exile, Henri de Lubac found himself on the Theological Commission exchanging cordial, if surreal, greetings with Italian and Spanish theologians who had denounced him to the Holy Office a decade before. To de Lubac's amusement, each commission member took an oath of secrecy, kneeling in front of Ottaviani, who sat in a throne-like chair with two lit candles on each side and a copy of the Bible. But de Lubac seemed unlikely to have much influence. After bumping into de Lubac and two other reform-minded theologians on a Roman side street, Yves Congar noted that they seemed "despondent and embittered." In their assessment, "No notice has been taken, or is being taken, of their opinions. Those based in Rome take care of everything among themselves."[18]

Innovation came from unexpected places. Agreeing to a proposal made by Cardinal Bea, John XXIII established a Secretariat for Promoting Christian Unity in 1960 and asked Bea to serve as chair. Bea asked Yves Congar to join him on the commission. Congar accepted the invitation, although he worried that the "Council was coming twenty years too soon." Yet he hoped that "the very announcement of a Council with an ecumenical goal could speed up certain processes."[19] One of Ottaviani's allies confided to his diary his surprise at Congar's new prominence. "It is hard to believe," he wrote, "that the Pope would put people like de Lubac and Congar on the [commissions]."[20]

Some speeding up occurred before the council began. John XXIII eliminated the phrase "perfidious Jews" from the Good Friday liturgy. He met with Jules Isaac, an eighty-seven-year-old Jewish historian from France, whose wife, daughter, and son-in-law had been murdered at Auschwitz. Following the meeting, the pope added the relationship with the Jewish people to Bea's portfolio. Bea drafted as consultants the handful of Catholics who had published on the topic in the 1940s and 1950s, and he solicited opinions from prominent rabbis and Jewish organizations, especially in the United States. The most significant Catholic voice in this conversation was Fr. Johannes (John) Oesterreicher, a convert from Judaism who had edited an anti-Nazi newspaper in Vienna before fleeing to the United States. His parents, too, had been murdered in concentration camps.

Two German theologians, Jesuit Karl Rahner and Fr. Joseph Ratzinger, served as theological advisers, Rahner to Cardinal Franz König from Vienna and Ratzinger to Cardinal Joseph Frings from Cologne. That fall, Ratzinger prepared an address for Frings to give in Genoa contrasting the era of the First Vatican Council with preparation for the Second Vatican Council. Then, liberalism in politics, economics, and theology seemed the most important concern. Now, the challenge was globalization. Ratzinger described how radio and television brought the world into once isolated homes while trains and passenger airplanes allowed much greater contact between diverse peoples. More than anything else, then, the church "must become in a fuller sense than here-tofore a world Church."

To Ratzinger, Europe's plunge into the abyss of two world wars had discredited any notion of Western superiority. Catholics must "recognize the relativity of all human cultural forms" and cultivate "a modesty which sets no human and historical heritage as absolute." Local liturgical practices should be encouraged and local episcopal authority strengthened. Archaic practices such as the Index of Forbidden Books should be jettisoned precisely because they mimicked "totalitarian" restrictions on the quest for truth.[21]

John XXIII obtained a copy of Frings's speech and summoned him to Rome. Frings joked with an aide that the meeting with the pope would be the last time he wore his cardinal's robes. Instead, the pope encouraged him. In the summer of 1962, when the preparatory commissions submitted their first texts, Frings and other bishops registered complaints. They judged most of the texts "completely unsuitable" and "so inadequate" and "excessively juridical and scholastic."[22]

In a radio address given one month before the council, John XXIII called for Christians to live in such a way so as to attract others less by doctrine than "by good example."[23] A week before the opening of the council, he visited Assisi, home of St. Francis. Large crowds greeted him at every train station. At Assisi, John XXIII said that the council must emphasize "the church of the poor."[24]

By now, saturation media coverage of the council had begun. Roughly ten thousand bishops, theologians, aides, and reporters descended on Rome. The 2,500 Council Fathers or voters (bishops, abbots, or heads of male religious orders), came from seventy-nine countries, a reminder of the church's global reach, with 38 percent from Europe, 31 percent from North and South America, 20 percent from Asia and Oceania, and 10 percent from Africa. Communist governments prevented the attendance of many bishops from behind the Iron Curtain, and for that reason a large crowd greeted the Polish bishops when they arrived at Rome's Termini train station. Most bishops from outside of Europe flew to Rome, but the Australians took a two-week voyage by sea, studying the preparatory texts on the way. Most bishops stayed in religious houses, but the 120 Americans confirmed stereotypes of excess by renting rooms in three hotels, including the Grand Hotel on the Via Veneto, a film star haunt in the era of *La Dolce Vita*. Bishops from wealthy churches, such as from the United States and West Germany, paid their own way and in addition helped the Vatican subsidize travel costs for almost all of the bishops from the Global South. At the end of each day's sessions, one observer noted, the African bishops piled onto a bus while each West German bishop hopped into an individual Mercedes.[25]

Most curial officials thought the council would quickly approve the preparatory texts. Perhaps the deliberations could conclude by Christmas. One Italian cardinal did worry about unreliable French and German bishops who had "never completely freed themselves from Protesant pressure. . . . They are fine people, but they do not realize that they are the heirs to a mistake-ridden history." He thought bishops from Catholic countries such as the Italians, the Mexicans, and members of the curia must stay alert to "false turns."[26]

III

THE OPENING OF THE council on October 11, 1962, went according to plan, although John XXIII's admonition to ignore "prophets of doom" set an unexpected tone. The fireworks began two days later. Elections were scheduled for commissions to consider the prepared texts, but a French cardinal proposed delaying the vote so that bishops could get to know one another. This proposal passed overwhelmingly, signaling that many bishops intended to resist the curia's dictation of the council's pace. The next week the council also approved a message to the world from the bishops. It had been drafted in part by the Dominican priest Marie-Dominique Chenu, a ressourcement theologian serving as an informal adviser to a bishop from Madagascar. Chenu complained that the editors of his text "drowned it in holy water." But a new tone came through. "Our concern," it read, is "first of all on those who are especially lowly, poor and weak." The message invoked "the dignity of the human person, whatever contributes to a genuine community of peoples."[27]

Opening Day of the Second Vatican Council, St. Peter's Basilica in
Rome, October 11, 1962. *(Getty Images)*

Grouped by region or language, bishops began meeting independently. The Latin American bishops had formed an episcopal conference in 1955 and this group reconvened in Rome. The Italian bishops,
long understood to answer only as individuals to the pope, began to
meet as a group. A Pan-African episcopal conference coalesced. Theologians associated with the ressourcement ran seminars and gave lectures
on biblical scholarship, the liturgy, and the nature of the church. The
Indonesian bishops, for example, a mix of Indonesian natives and Dutch
missionaries, arranged for theological advisers from the Netherlands to
organize a series of lectures and readings.[28]

Even as these unexpected dialogues began, discussion of the first
text, on the liturgy, proceeded in St. Peter's. The liturgical commission
in the run-up to the Second Vatican Council had been the only one of
the ten commissions stocked with ressourcement theologians. Joseph
Ratzinger's bleak assessment of the preparatory texts did not extend to
the liturgical schema. He applauded it for modeling John XXIII's plea
for a "renewal of Christian life."[29]

The liturgical reform movement had begun in France, Germany, and
Belgium in the late nineteenth century and had evolved into a vehicle
for increasing the participation of Catholics in the Mass. German Benedictine priests brought the movement to the United States and Brazil

in the 1930s, and in both countries it became linked to Catholic Action programs. (Conservative Brazilian Catholics, though, worried that new liturgical practices would further the "religious deterioration, moral and cultural, of the modern world."[30]) Even in Franco's Spain, by the 1950s, some Jesuits complained about the Mass as being more of a "spiritual marketplace than an assembly of brothers." Too many "saints on our altars" distracted from the building of a "community of the faithful."[31]

Catholics in the Global South generally favored liturgical reforms. Vatican officials authorized bilingual missals in South Asia and East Africa in the 1950s so that Catholics could follow the Mass in their native languages as they listened to the approved Latin text.[32] Dutch priests in Indonesia worked to make Catholic rituals such as baptism or confirmation resemble Indigenous feasts of initiation.[33] One student from Upper Volta studying in Paris, Joseph Ki-Zerbo, complained that the absence of "prayers, songs, and ritual gestures performed in unison" made French Catholicism seem "sterile."[34]

The key issue at the council was whether the Mass should continue to be celebrated in Latin or be translated into vernacular languages. Opponents of the change emphasized Latin's unifying effect and, impolitely, given Protestant observers in St. Peter's, associated linguistic diversity with Protestantism. Ottaviani opposed any change. The Los Angeles cardinal, James McIntyre, whose rudimentary Latin amused some bishops, thought "active participation [in the Mass] was frequently a distraction."[35]

Those bishops favoring reform urged not only vernacular languages but Indigenous art and a simpler rite. They included many bishops from the Global South attuned to "inculturation"—a term coined by a Belgian missionary in 1962.[36] African bishops requested that the schema drop the word "Western" before the word "liturgy," since the church was not, and never had been, limited to the West. A Japanese bishop worried that emphasizing the splendor of liturgical vessels such as the chalice worked against an Asian emphasis on simplicity.[37]

When the introduction and first chapter came up for a vote, it received overwhelming approval, with 1,992 Council Fathers out of 2,118 voting *placet*, or "approve." (The entirety of the text on the liturgy, after amendments, would be approved a year later.) This outcome revealed a massive, unexpected constituency for reform. Yves Congar, standing in St. Peter's when the vote was announced, recognized that "something irreversible has happened and been affirmed in the Church."[38] The final document called for the cultivation of "the art of our own days, coming from every race and region."[39] When Dominique de Menil read this passage, she felt confirmed in her belief that religious art and architecture, including her soon to be commissioned Rothko chapel in Houston, must reflect "the mood created by Vatican II: the Church renouncing triumphalism."[40]

By then conflicts had erupted over the other texts. To the reformers these texts contained the condemnations John XXIII had cautioned against. The text on sources of revelation, for example, implied that the Catholic tradition stood independent of scripture, a reversion in the eyes of reformers to an outdated and polemical anti-Protestantism. Karl Rahner and Joseph Ratzinger composed an influential critique of the schema on revelation that circulated among the bishops. Rahner put it this way: "The infallible magisterium of the Church is not lord over the revealed word of God that is contained in the scriptures, but rather is at its service."[41]

Ottaviani was aghast. "They talk of 'modern man,'" he complained in the first meeting of the Theological Commission to discuss the text on sources of revelation, "he does not exist! They want to be 'pastoral.' But the first pastoral duty is teaching. Afterwards let the parish priests do the adapting. They talk of 'ecumenism.' There is a great danger of minimalism." That same day the episcopal conferences of Germany, Japan, India and Ceylon, the Philippines, Africa, and Latin America registered their opposition to the prepared text on revelation, siding against Ottaviani and curial officials. The American bishops, too, defied senior leaders such as Cardinal Spellman of New York and Cardinal MacIntyre of Los Angeles and voted to scrap the text. By contrast, the Italian bishops, with important exceptions, such as Montini from Milan, endorsed the prepared texts. They blamed Rahner, Ratzinger, and their allies for these divisions and vowed "not to leave the Council and the Church in the hands of the Germans."[42]

In the final vote, 62 percent of the Council Fathers rejected the draft-text, and John XXIII on his own initiative pulled it from deliberation. By now, the Roman theologians and Cardinal Ottaviani understood that the dominant currents of the council pulled away from their intended direction. When Ottaviani bumped into Yves Congar in St. Peter's Square, he angrily accused him of aiding Rahner and Ratzinger.[43]

The draft-text on the church seemed to the reformers equally troubling. By its definition, the church was only the Roman Catholic Church, not Protestants, Orthodox Christians, and other "separated communities." It reiterated the standard Catholic teaching on church and state, recommending state endorsement of Catholicism. The image used to describe the church was the Mystical Body, drawing from Pius XII's 1943 encyclical, but in a strictly hierarchical fashion with laypeople under the direction of clergy, clergy subordinate to bishops, and bishops subordinate to the pope. Rahner thought the text "could have been formulated even in the 1800s."[44]

Worried about the huge mass of texts still not discussed, two cardinals offered a new plan for proceeding. Belgium's Cardinal Leo Jozef Suenens proposed that the future work of the council should be divided into two basic areas: texts on the church in its inner life and texts on its relationship to the world. The next day Cardinal Montini from Milan agreed. He had not signed the initial letters of concern issued by some bishops about the preparatory texts, but now he publicly expressed his unhappiness. In doing so he made clear that the man who many tabbed as John XXIII's successor sided with reform.

When the first session ended in early December, most bishops left Rome exhilarated. How long it would take to rewrite the remaining documents remained uncertain. Listening to dozens of speeches a day in a Latin they did not all speak, and in accents hard to decipher for those who did, was exhausting. But the sense that something had changed was palpable. Imperial within their own dioceses, but socialized to defer to Rome on theological matters, the bishops now understood themselves as a collective. The First Vatican Council had been dominated by the pope. The Second Vatican Council would be run, for the most part, by the bishops. "The episcopate has discovered itself," Congar wrote in his diary. "It has become aware of itself."[45]

One American bishop wrote to a friend just as the first session concluded: "We in the U.S. knew something of Latin America but now we have learned first-hand of the problems of Japanese Catholics, Indonesians, Africans, and Polynesians: the prelates from all over the globe who have spoken have helped us all to distinguish better what is essential to the Church and what is non-essential."[46]

IV

BETWEEN THE end of the first session in December 1962 and the beginning of the second session in October 1963, the world rushed in. Questions about development, contraception, anti-Semitism, and the Cold War all became more pressing outside Rome and then within debates at the council. These topics did not yet cause significant ruptures among Catholics—those would come after the council—but they did push the bishops to consider the fate not only of the church they led but of the world they inhabited.

John XXIII placed development on the conciliar agenda. He had long expressed interest in Louis-Joseph Lebret's work, and in 1961 Lebret helped draft his first major encyclical, *Mater et Magistra*. In that document, the pope welcomed the "attainment of political independence by the peoples of Asia and Africa." He warned against the "unbridled luxury, of the privileged few [which] stands in violent, offensive contrast to the utter poverty of the vast majority." Wealthy nations must not forget the "spiritual values" present in the less developed world—here Lebret's influence seems obvious—and do more than promote scientific or technical achievements.[47] When Santiago's new archbishop, inspired by the encyclical, told John XXIII that he would sell off church lands and support agrarian reform, John XXIII responded with a wink. "Do it," the pope said. "I will back you up."[48]

John XXIII had already welcomed Alioune Diop and other African Catholics to Rome and listened to their pleas to respect African "personhood" and not assume that only the "Western experience" contained "universal truths."[49] He met with Senegal's Léopold Senghor and stressed that "your country and Africa as a whole was particularly on Our mind." At a major conference in Abidjan, Ivory Coast, Senghor lauded *Mater et Magistra*. A genuine "unity of the Church" must be found beyond the narrow constraints of "western culture."[50] "Confronted with the undeveloped countries," John XXIII asserted in his radio address a month before the council, in a line that he specifically added with his own pen, "the Church presents itself as it is and wishes to be, as the Church of all, and particularly as the Church of the poor."[51] During the first session of the council, bishops committed to a "church of the poor" met under the aegis of Cardinal Gerlier from Lyons. One of the participants in the group, Bologna's Cardinal Lercaro, much admired by Léopold Senghor, urged the Council Fathers to make the "church of the poor" the "sole theme of Vatican II in its entirety."[52]

A second issue starting to shape the council was contraception. Beginning in 1961, the availability of easy-to-use and reliable oral contraceptives marked the dawn of a sexual revolution. John Rock, a Boston Catholic obstetrician and one of the developers of the birth control pill, published a widely reviewed book, *The Time Has Come*, which argued that taking the pill did not differ in a moral sense from the papally endorsed rhythm method. Both were "artificial." Rock appeared on national television and toured the United States to promote his view, much to the frustration of some theologians, who wished the Boston archdiocese could somehow squelch his commentary.[53]

The conversation about birth control was especially vigorous in the Netherlands, where some of the first oral contraceptives were manufactured, and Belgium, where leading theologians, not simply physicians such as Rock, argued that married Catholic couples could avail themselves of the birth control pill. A Dutch bishop, Rinus Bekkers, appeared on the country's lone television network in March 1963 and to an astonished national audience explained that a married couple alone should decide whether to use contraceptives, "a decision in which no-one may intervene." Bekkers sent a letter to every priest in his diocese of Den Bosch stating that no (married) Catholic should be excluded from the sacraments if he or she used contraceptives in good conscience. (Bekkers's statements were translated and circulated to members of the Christian Family Movement in the United States.) [54]

Here, too, John XXIII had responded. One of the Roman drafts had reiterated *Casti Connubii*, the 1930 encyclical forbidding contraception. The "natural, objective, specific, principal, primary, single and indivisible end" of sex within marriage remained procreation.[55] Overpopulation as a sociological fact, a Roman expert explained, did not alter "theological truth."[56] John XXIII authorized his ally, Cardinal Suenens of Belgium, to organize a secret committee—given the Vatican rumor mill not secret for long—to assess the issue.

A third topic, anti-Semitism and the relationship with the Jewish people, received a new impetus from an unlikely source: a hit play. *Der Stellvertreter,* or *The Deputy,* by the West German playwright Rolf Hochhuth, drew large audiences in major cities in Europe and North America in the spring of 1963. Its message—that Pius XII placed church concerns above the lives of Europe's Jews during World War II—became part of the reassessment of complicity in the Holocaust provoked by the Israeli trial of Adolf Eichmann.

As a drama, *The Deputy* suffered from wooden dialogue, but as a polemic it was a huge success. Pius XII's onetime aide, Cardinal Montini, recoiled at Hochhuth's script and authored a statement in Pius XII's defense. Public declarations in support of Europe's Jews during the war, Montini explained, "would have been not only futile but harmful."[57]

The Vatican under Pius XII had refused to recognize the new state of Israel and had even enlisted American Catholics in a futile effort to prevent American recognition in 1948.[58] Catholic bishops from Middle Eastern countries feared any declaration on the Jewish people might imperil Christian populations in Arabic countries such as Egypt, Iraq, and Syria. At the end of the first session, Cardinal Bea persuaded John XXIII to reconsider and place the topic on the conciliar agenda. Bea stressed that the "appalling crimes of National Socialism against six million Jews" required a "purification of spirit and conscience."[59]

Bea became the person most identified with transformations in the relationships of Catholics with Protestants and Jews. He traveled to Harvard University after the first session to address what became the largest ever gathering of Protestant and Catholic theologians. On the same trip, he met with New York City rabbi Abraham Heschel. Heschel had visited Bea in Rome and had taken the lead in discussions between American Jewish groups and the Secretariat for Promoting Christian Unity. In Boston and in New York City, they huddled together to discuss these topics as "old friends." Privately, Bea warned Heschel and other Jewish interloctutors of potential roadblocks, including anti-Semitism among Catholics and concerns expressed by Middle Eastern

Catholics and Arab governments. Publicly, Bea stressed the "integrity and permanent preciousness of Judaism and the Jewish people."[60]

By this time, John XXIII had begun to question the Cold War postures of both the United States and the Soviet Union. Two years into his papacy, in a gesture that would have seemed impossible in the era of Pius XII (or Joseph Stalin), John XXIII appealed to both countries to "face squarely the tremendous responsibilities they bear before the tribunal of history." Another peasant son, Soviet president Nikita Khrushchev, welcomed the "common sense" of John XXIII. Khrushchev then asked, maliciously, whether John Kennedy and Konrad Adenauer would lessen Cold War tensions and obey "the Pope of Rome?"[61]

Communist repression did not cease. Hungarian bishops who responded to the Vatican's invitation to send in topics for consideration by the council had their recommendations confiscated by the Hungarian state security agency. The Hungarian government eventually allowed some bishops to attend the council, escorted by secret police agents, because attendance might "enhance the international prestige of the socialist countries." (During the council, government-allied bishops transmitted internal council documents, which were then scoured by government security officials.) The Czechoslovakian government allowed four bishops to attend the opening session of the council, but insisted that they be escorted by clergy known to have ties with the secret police.[62]

In Poland, the situation was different. More than anywhere else in Eastern Europe, Polish Catholics had sustained their own institutions, established contacts with Catholics on the other side of the Iron Curtain, and protected church agencies from manipulation by state security agencies. Yet having been cut off from new theological currents since 1939, most of the Polish bishops had only a hazy awareness of topics raised by the *nouvelle théologie*. Defensively, they declared that "we firmly reject the accusation that we are somehow 'backward.' We in no way wish for a return to the bygone (and not always good) social forms in the middle ages."[63]

John XXIII disconcerted Kennedy administration officials with a suggestion that the United States and the Soviet Union jointly declare a "peace race" (as opposed to an arms race.)[64] His inclination toward dialogue was only reinforced by events during the first week of the council, when the American government announced that the Soviets had placed nuclear missiles in Cuba. During the next thirteen days, as the council held its first working sessions and as the world teetered on the verge of a nuclear exchange, John XXIII encouraged both sides to negotiate and through intermediaries played a modest role in defusing the conflict.

After the first session, John XXIII became bolder. He now encouraged outreach to even the most recalcitrant communist governments. He sent Cardinal König of Vienna to meet with Cardinal Mindszenty of Budapest, now in his seventh year of confinement in the American embassy following eight years in a Hungarian prison. Another papal envoy began negotiations to end the harassment of Cardinal Beran in Prague. These scattered initiatives marked the beginning of what came to be called *Ostpolitik*, or a Vatican policy of negotiations with communist governments to improve the situation of Catholics. This strategy was controversial, even scandalous, to Catholics accustomed to the anti-communist rhetoric of Pius XII. Some judged it naive. But it reflected John XXIII's refusal to be bound by the strictures of the Cold War.

John XXIII also instructed a Roman theologian to draft an encyclical, *Pacem in Terris* (Peace on Earth), released the day after Cardinal König visited Cardinal Mindszenty. Something of a grab bag, the encyclical defended human rights, attacked racial discrimination, and distinguished between errors (such as Marxism) and people who mistakenly believed them. It was addressed, significantly, not only to Catholics but to all men and women of goodwill. It repeatedly used the phrase "dignity of the human person," a phrase that had become central to Catholic opposition to totalitarianism in the 1930s and 1940s. The most important sentences were the following:

> Justice, right reason, and the recognition of man's dignity
> cry out insistently for a cessation to the arms race. The
> stock-piles of armaments which have been built up in
> various countries must be reduced all round and simulta-
> neously by the parties concerned. Nuclear weapons must
> be banned.[65]

President John Kennedy, typically reluctant to identify himself as a Catholic in public settings, chose one week later to praise the "penetrating analysis" of the encyclical in an address at Boston College. "As a Catholic," he said, "I am proud of it and as an American I learned from it." That fall he signed the first nuclear test ban treaty with the Soviet Union.[66]

V

JOHN XXIII's DEATH in June 1963 evoked heartfelt tributes from around the globe, a testimony to the widespread desire for a more pastoral approach to the world's problems. The former Cardinal Montini, now Paul VI, opened the second session of the council in October 1963. Paul VI's precise demeanor contrasted with John XXIII's ebullience, as did his long speeches, composed in elegant Latin, when compared with John XXIII's penchant for offhand remarks. More aware of ressourcement currents than any other bishop—he had welcomed the liturgical movement, become a close friend of Jacques Maritain, visited worker-priests, personally encouraged John Courtney Murray, Yves Congar, and Henri de Lubac, promoted Louis-Joseph Lebret's development work, and traveled to Latin America and Africa—Paul VI seemed an ideal successor to John XXIII. After all, the second session marked a second beginning. As Joseph Ratzinger put it, "the preparatory work was unsatisfactory, and the Council rejected the extant texts. But the question at this point was . . . What now?"[67]

The first document considered in the second session was the revised text on the church. Instead of referring to lay Catholics as "subjects" and to the church as "militant," it now used the phrases "people of God" and "pilgrim church." Instead of the "role" of the laity, it identified a "universal call to holiness" by virtue of baptism. Some conservatives viewed this call to holiness as dangerously close to a Protestant "priesthood of all believers," but in the final version of this document, now called *Lumen Gentium* and approved in 1964, the "people of God" came before any discussion of the priesthood or hierarchy.

The council also approved the first three chapters of a text on ecumenism that in its generosity of spirit would have been inconceivable even two years earlier. The last two chapters, on the Jews and on religious liberty, proved more troublesome. Paul VI worried that a text on the Jews might convey endorsement of Rolf Hochhuth's castigation of Pius XII for wartime silence. More reactionary bishops thought the text skirted the need for Jews to convert to Catholicism and should acknowledge that the ancestors of contemporary Jews had killed Christ. The text on religious liberty worried Latin American bishops, frustrated by the increasing number of evangelical Protestant missionaries from the United States moving to Brazil, Argentina, and other countries in the region.

John Courtney Murray, ordered to stop working on the issue less than a decade earlier, became a consultant on the religious liberty chapter. Murray denied an accusation made by some bishops that identifying religious liberty as a fundamental component of human dignity led to "indifferentism." Instead, promoting religious freedom reassured non-Catholics worried that the church would take away their liberties. Eventually, the bishops decided to postpone decisions on both the text on the Jews and the text on religious liberty. The text on the Jews would be folded into a new document on Catholicism's relationship with non-Christian religions. The text on religious liberty would become a separate declaration.

Controversy swirled around these two documents—often discussed simultaneously—because each highlighted doctrinal development. For reformers, a key intellectual resource became the work of John Henry Newman, whose interest in the development of doctrine seemed refreshingly unlike the ahistorical neo-Thomism dominant in seminaries and universities. Newman's ideas on development, published to acclaim in 1845, had fallen into obscurity by the 1920s, only to be recovered in subsequent decades by ressourcement theologians. Murray told an after-dinner audience during the second session that "Newman's idea of the evolution of dogma might well become one of the key ideas in Vatican Council II."[68]

Paul VI pushed the idea of ecumenical dialogue forward after the second session by making an unexpected and dramatic visit to Jerusalem. Surrounded by enormous crowds, he visited sites associated with the ministry of Jesus. He met with Athenagoras, the Orthodox patriarch based in Istanbul, in the first in-person encounter of a pope with an Orthodox patriarch since 1438.

After the second session ended, work on the texts on the Jews and religious liberty began anew. As a German, Bea defended the idea that no group merited collective guilt, since German Catholics after 1945 had rejected the idea of collective guilt for Nazi crimes. John Oesterreicher convinced Bea and other once-cautious theologians that by a "special promise the Jews constitute a special people, not because of their own merits, but because of the faithfulness of God." How could Catholics claim the Jews had rejected Jesus when Jesus's first followers had been Jewish?[69]

Meanwhile, Murray composed and circulated his first article on religious freedom in over a decade. Translated into Dutch, French, German, Portuguese, and Spanish, the article declared itself an exercise in ressourcement. It began by noting that not only Catholics in the United States but also Catholics in majority Islamic, Hindu, and Buddhist countries, as well as Catholics living behind the Iron Curtain, desired clarity on the matter of religious freedom. Murray stressed the topic's importance in a context of "limited government"—here he registered the last twenty-five years of reform-minded Catholics attacking totalitarianism—as opposed to an older notion of a state's obligation to promote true religion. And he called for religious freedom to be understood as an inescapable part of human dignity.[70]

The debate on religious liberty during the third session was fierce, with a sharpness in tone new for the council, even as the parade of speakers to the thirty-seven microphones scattered within the magnificent central nave of St. Peter's maintained a formal decorum. Opponents derided the very idea of religious liberty; in their view only one religion, Catholicism, was true. The church's teaching on the topic must be distinguished from the 1948 United Nations Declaration of Human Rights. The concordats signed with Spain (1953) and the Dominican Republic (1954), which confirmed an official role for Catholicism in majority Catholic countries, must be honored.

Marcel Lefebvre, onetime archbishop from Dakar and longtime defender of French colonialism in Africa, turned apocalyptic. If approved, he said, the declaration on religious freedom would do "great harm . . . to the respect the Catholic Church enjoys among all human beings." The Spanish bishops, too, registered their opposition. One Spanish bishop wondered why the "liberalism, so often condemned by the church, is now solemnly approved by Vatican Council II."

Using notes provided by Murray, support for the declaration came first from the Americans. Long accused of secretly plotting to diminish the liberties of fellow citizens, the bishops from the United States now thought it vital to "show that the Catholic Church promotes religious liberty rather than tries to repress it." Bishops from Eastern Europe argued with equal vigor that men and women "writhing under atheistic and Marxist regimes" needed the support that a declaration on religious liberty would provide. African bishops worried that newly independent secular states in Africa might restrict Catholic activities without the guarantee of religious liberty for all.[71]

As the discussion on religious liberty concluded, the debate began on the text outlining the church's relationship with non-Christian religions, eventually entitled *Nostra Aetate*. The new document included an uncontroversial paragraph on Muslims and short references to Hindus and Buddhists. The centerpiece was eight paragraphs on the relationship of people of the "new covenant" (Christians) with men and women of "Abraham's stock" (Jews). Bea opened the first presentation acknowledging that the topic had "aroused the greatest public interest." He knew that bishops from the Middle East wanted to drop the topic altogether and that the king of Jordan and other Arab leaders had urged Paul VI not to permit the discussion.

Bea insisted that the declaration on the Jews had nothing to do with the state of Israel or "political questions." Like Murray, Bea performed an act of ressourcement, moving beyond medieval (and even patristic) condemnations of the Jews as guilty of the death of Christ to an analysis of Paul's letter to the Romans and a conception of the Jews as possessing an ongoing covenant with God. He knew, too, that Abraham Heschel "had told the pope that any inclusion of the theme of conversion would produce exceedingly negative reactions in the Jewish communities, and would nullify the many good things that the document contained."[72]

Most bishops supported the text, but as in the debate over religious liberty, some bishops thought the text on the Jews meant revolution more than development. A few bishops made comments that reflected the persistence of anti-Semitism in Catholic circles. Why, asked the cardinal from Palermo, do we need a special statement on the Jews? Given Jewish support for the Freemasons, "the Jews should be forcefully exhorted to respond with love to the sincere love with which we treat them." By contrast and significantly, the West German bishops supported the new text. Boston's Cardinal Cushing, whose brother-in-law was Jewish, flatly said, in Latin marked by a Boston accent, that "we ought to confess humbly before the world that Christians have too often not acted as true Christian followers of Christ in their relations with their Jewish brothers."[73]

The council also began its consideration of Schema XIII, on the church's relationship to the modern world. This introductory discussion lasted a full twenty days. One bishop from Guinea thought the document overly Western:

> The schema has been conceived for Europe and perhaps
> for America, but not sufficiently for the Third World. . . .
> I find no mention in it of the difficulties of the peoples of
> Africa: underdevelopment, colonialism, discrimination
> according to race or color.[74]

This exhortation seemed timely given not only decolonization in Africa and Asia but awareness of the American civil rights movement. Already that fall, Paul VI had met with Martin Luther King Jr. King said the pope asked him "to tell the American Negroes that he is committed to the cause of civil rights in the United States." The meeting occurred despite frantic attempts by FBI director J. Edgar Hoover to scotch the meeting by claiming that King was a communist, using New York's Cardinal Spellman as an intermediary.[75] A group of American bishops requested that the council emphasize "the equality of everyone in the Church with no distinction on account of race." The Americans received support from a South African archbishop who argued that all people of color were "insulted by the racial sins of American, South

African and Rhodesian whites, because they are so deeply conscious of their identification with those who feel the lash of the white man's scorn in the United States or Southern Africa."[76]

The next major topic of discussion generated by Schema XIII was contraception. Despite reminders from the council moderators that John XXIII had established a special papal commission to discuss the topic, some bishops could not resist the microphone. Cardinal Suenens urged recognition of the "communion of spouses" within marriage as a goal equal in importance to procreation. He concluded with a rhetorical flourish, asking the bishops to "embrace science" on the topic and "avoid a new Galileo affair."[77] Waves of applause echoed in St. Peter's. Cardinal Ottaviani retorted that he, Ottaviani, was the eleventh of twelve children, born of parents who "never doubted Providence."[78] A furious Paul VI forced Suenens to publicly acknowledge that a decision on whether contraception was licit rested with the pope, not the council.

The end of this initial discussion of Schema XIII coincided with a pair of unprecedented papal interventions. Yves Congar had long worried that Paul VI might seek to conciliate members of the minority who invoked the "spectre of Pistoia" (the famous 1786 synod) and who worried about the diminishment of papal authority.[79] Paul VI now attached an explanatory note to the third chapter of the Dogmatic Constitution on the Church, *Lumen Gentium*, without discussion or vote. The note explained why the focus on episcopal authority in no way limited the authority of the pope. His phrasing, drawn from objections made by bishops in the minority, was that the pope "may exercise his power at any time, as he sees fit, by reason of the demands of his office."[80]

Lumen Gentium was still approved by an overwhelming majority. The majority also approved the Decree on Ecumenism, now termed *Unitatis Redintegratio*. The two documents were linked. *Lumen Gentium* suggested that while the true church "subsists" in Catholicism, elements of truth exist in other religions as well. *Unitatis Redintegratio* began with the statement that "the restoration of unity among Christians is one of the principal concerns of the Second Vatican Council." No mention was made of the longstanding claim that Orthodox or Protestant Christians should "return" to Catholicism.[81]

Paul VI's second intervention, announced through intermediaries, was to postpone the vote on the Declaration on Religious Liberty to the fourth and final session. Many bishops worried that delay meant burial and made pleas for a reconsideration on the council floor, to the dismay of Paul VI, watching on closed-circuit television. One Belgian bishop privately told Paul VI that he feared that the "declaration on religious freedom will be the object of sabotage maneuvers" developed by "certain influential members of the minority."[82] The American bishops lined up in the side aisles of St. Peter's to draft and sign a petition of protest (composed on a typewriter snuck out of a nearby curial office). It began with the phrasing, "Respectfully but insistently, even more insistently, very insistently, we request. . . ."[83]

Given the pope's unexpected intervention on *Lumen Gentium* and the postponement of the vote on the Declaration on Religious Liberty, the third session concluded on an uncertain note. Some referred to the week of the two interventions as the *settimana nera*, or "black week." The reforming majority of the Council Fathers remained in control, but Paul VI's interventions, made under pressure from members of the minority, signaled new strains.

A small group of bishops opposed to the direction of the council had now formed a lobby, the *Coetus Internationalis Patrum*, or International Group of Fathers. Their leaders were Geraldo de Proença Sigaud from Brazil and Marcel Lefebvre from France. Lefebvre's support for French colonialism and Sigaud's ties to the Tradition, Family, and Property movement in Brazil, a leading source of right-wing sentiment across Latin America, suggested how theological and political conservatism overlapped. These bishops pleaded for a condemnation of communism and a rejection of any development of church teaching on religious liberty or the Jews. They accused ressourcement theologians such as Congar and Chenu of steering the council in a "Marxist direction."[84] Sigaud chastised the Council Fathers for ignoring the need to "defend religious liberty against the threats of communism and Islam."[85]

Certainly the passage of *Lumen Gentium* marked a major accomplishment, even if the allocation of governance tasks among the pope, the bishops, and the curia remained uncertain. The "pilgrim" church had entered a new era of self-understanding. Joseph Ratzinger stressed this point:

> The spiritual awakening, which the bishops accomplished
> in full view of the Church, or, rather, accomplished as
> the Church, was the great and irrevocable event of the
> Council. It was more important in many respects than
> the texts it passed.[86]

Paul VI also cultivated a new sense of church when he took his second trip during the council, this time to India. On this journey he stressed that his goal was to make visible a more open church and a church of the poor. Already he had renounced the use of the jeweled papal tiara.[87]

The bishops had agreed that on the first Sunday of Advent, November 29, 1964, Catholics around the world would begin to implement the sacred constitution on the liturgy. The comprehensiveness of the changes—and their abruptness—was remarkable. Ornate altars were removed from the back wall of thousands of churches and simple altars installed closer to the congregation. Communion rails separating the priest from the congregation were dismantled. Statues of saints thought to clutter the altar disappeared. The priest faced the congregation instead of standing with his back to them. The prayers he uttered in Japanese, Portuguese, and Swahili now required the congregation to respond, and the congregation was encouraged, haltingly, to sing hymns instead of listening to a choir or organist. In time, communicants would receive the eucharistic host in the hand instead of on the tongue and while standing instead of kneeling.

Musical changes were equally significant. Much of the Gregorian chant and medieval music cultivated since the nineteenth-century ultramontane revival was discarded. Vernacular forms of music—paralleling the shift to vernacular languages—came to the fore. This often meant folk music with guitars in much of Western Europe and North America. (By 1976, a third of the parishes in one English diocese used English language folk hymns, often newly composed.) Janet Mead, a Sister of Mercy from Adelaide, Australia, had an international hit with her folk music version of the Our Father. In Latin America, folk music at Mass became pervasive as well, but with mariachis in Mexico or Andean music in Argentina.[88]

The reaction to the changes, the most sweeping since the development of the Roman rite in 1570, was mixed. Even some bishops committed to reform, such as Santiago's archbishop, worried that the devaluation of traditional devotions might appeal only to "neo-colonial elites."[89] In Cuernavaca, Mexico, home to a reform-minded bishop, some Catholics mourned the removal of beloved saints' statues and portraits from the altar and their subsequent storage in the church basement.[90] In countries where Latin texts and music consolidated religious identity for a Catholic minority, the change to the vernacular could be painful. The English novelist Evelyn Waugh complained to London's cardinal archbishop that "every attendance at Mass leaves me without comfort or edification."[91]

Most Catholics, especially young people, welcomed the changes, and survey data and first-person accounts confirm this enthusiasm. Even London's cardinal archbishop, a skeptic, responded to Waugh that "the *vast* majority (my priests tell me) enjoys the English in the Mass: even many who were opposed before."[92] The top-down process for the reforms mattered less than the sense that ordinary Catholics participated more in the Mass instead of observing it.

The most enthusiastic reception was in Africa and other parts of the Global South, where the Latin language and Western musical forms had long seemed less a unifying language than an imposition. Well into the twentieth century in mission territories such as colonial British West Africa, Igbo Catholics referred to the Latin Mass as the "*uka Fada*" or "priest's Mass" because the priest seemed the sole actor.[93] Now worship was more communal. One of the Catholic founders of the Negritude movement in Paris in the 1930s, Paulette Nardal, dedicated herself to composing choral hymns in Creole to be used by parishioners in her native Martinique. The archbishop of Abidjan asked Catholics to rejoice in the fact that "God asks us to sing his praises, to honor him and pray to him in harmony with our African soul."[94]

VI

JOHN XXIII CONVENED the council in part to reassess the church's relationship with the world, but consensus on just what that relationship should be proved elusive. Since the early nineteenth century, the dominant strategy had been to build institutions and shield Catholics from a potentially hostile modernity. The mutating Schema XIII (on the Church in the Modern World) proposed something different: for Catholics and the church to take on the world's problems as their own. Theologians defending the schema, notably its principal author, Marie-Dominique Chenu, saw it as a natural culmination of decades of work to move Catholics beyond church walls. We must begin, Chenu asserted, "by observing the human condition in order then to move on to Christ." We do not need, in a document aimed at the whole world, to deduce a "Christian anthropology" but instead to "discern the 'signs of the times' in the concrete reality of history."[95]

Another group of ressourcement theologians, including Henri de Lubac and Joseph Ratzinger, thought that the draft's plea for engagement with the world underestimated the world's corruption. Optimism about technology and the "scientific spirit" was naive. "The Christian message," Ratzinger explained, "cannot have as its purpose the glorification of the technological—technology does not need that—but the provision of critical norms by which to judge it." He added that the church must first recognize that "the definitive answers to the pressing questions of the human race are found in Christ."[96]

The discussions were vigorous. At one meeting, a German bishop gesticulated with such force that his episcopal ring flew off his finger. The two sides eventually reconciled, with the final document, now named *Gaudium et Spes*, or Joy and Hope, fundamentally reflecting Chenu's vision. The opening line urged Catholics to immerse themselves in the world's "joys and hopes, griefs and anxieties." Like the Declaration on Religious Freedom, it stressed the importance of the individual conscience in ways almost unthinkable to anyone accustomed to the focus on clerical authority in the ultramontane era.[97]

As the fourth session began in late September 1965, exhaustion threatened to derail the council. Wrangling the weary bishops became more difficult, and attendance more erratic. Council Fathers took a grueling 256 votes on eleven documents in ten weeks. Halfway through the debate on *Gaudium et Spes*, the attention of the council moved west. Paul VI had embarked on a third international trip during the council, this time to New York City to address the United Nations and celebrate Mass at Yankee Stadium.

Again the media coverage was spectacular, with satellites beaming Paul VI's speech around the world. One theme of his address was the importance of development programs addressing global poverty, and behind the scenes, the British journalist and foreign policy expert Barbara Ward helped lay the groundwork for development to become a central preoccupation of the post-conciliar church. A widely circulated memo Ward prepared as part of the discussion around *Gaudium et Spes* argued that the "Christian conscience of the West" must recognize the current imbalance between wealth and population. The ecumenical progress made at the council, she thought, made this an issue for all Christians and "has raised such hopes and expectations" that "disillusion" would set in without a vigorous response.[98]

Paul VI placed equal emphasis on peace. The passage "*Jamais plus la guerre! Jamais plus la guerre!*" in Paul VI's French, or "War never again," became the headline. He flew back to Rome and was driven directly from the airport to St. Peter's, where as he strode up the main aisle, the assembled bishops rose and greeted him with applause.

Paul VI's plea for an end to war highlighted another topic in *Gaudium et Spes*, whether the council would endorse the just war tradition or take a more pacifist stance. American and British bishops urged the council to recognize the possibility of a just war, even one conducted with nuclear weapons. Alternatively, one bishop invoked Franz Jägerstätter—the Bavarian peasant who had refused on the basis of conscience to serve in the Wehrmacht during World War II and was executed—as a model of Gospel living. *Gaudium et Spes* eventually straddled the line between pacifism and the just war tradition. But the notion of "conscience" and "witness" on matters of war, peace, and human rights was becoming central to Catholic self-understanding.[99]

No place more vividly displayed the intersection of decolonization and the Cold War than Vietnam. President Lyndon Johnson decided to massively increase the number of American troops to Vietnam in early 1965, and this decision may have sparked Paul VI's antiwar address to the United Nations. Left-leaning Italian Catholics, especially, took the lead in European opposition to the American involvement in Vietnam, with Giorgio La Pira, Florence's mayor and a friend of Paul VI, making a well-publicized (and futile) visit to Hanoi, the capital of communist

North Vietnam. A radical priest encouraged Italian Catholics to declare their conscientious objection to service in the Italian military.[100] In the United States, shockingly, a young Catholic Worker volunteer splashed gasoline over his body and immolated himself in front of the United Nations building in New York City. Two American priests (and brothers), Daniel and Phillip Berrigan, signed a "statement of conscience" in opposition to the war, much to the dismay of New York's Cardinal Spellman.[101]

The most controversial section of *Gaudium et Spes* was on marriage and, implicitly, birth control. The treatment was personalist. Procreation was only one purpose of marital sex, no more important than cultivating love between the spouses. Church teaching on contraception was conveyed as open to development.

Defenders of *Casti Connubii*, the 1930 encyclical forbidding use of contraception, leapt into action. The American Jesuit John Ford, working through Cardinal Ottaviani and other Vatican contacts, urged Paul VI to resist any change in church teaching. Ford knew that even two years earlier most US bishops had not favored a change in church teaching, but he also knew that opinions were rapidly shifting. His notes detailing his meetings with the pope suggest the drama of the moment. Called suddenly to the Vatican on the morning of November 22 ("luckily I was at home"), Ford spoke with Paul VI for an hour about the proposed text. "They say *Casti Connubii* is obsolete," Ford complained. The pope replied, "It is not obsolete. *Casti Connubii è tuttora valido*" (is still valid). Ford also emphasized to the pope that "human nature can't change."

The next day, Ottaviani announced his receipt of a letter from Paul VI, drafted by Ford and another papal adviser, requesting that *Gaudium et Spes* reassert the authority of *Casti Connubii*. The American cardinal chairing the commission charged with composing the text, Detroit's John Dearden, marked the folder containing his copy of the letter "of great historical importance."[102]

How to integrate the papal letter with the working draft caused further discussion, and moderates such as Dearden successfully persuaded the committee to retain the notion that marriage had two ends (or goals): procreation and spousal love. The final version of *Gaudium et Spes* referred to *Casti Connubii* in one famous footnote but did not render a verdict on contraception. (Dearden later revealed that he had privately gone over every line with Paul VI.) Better, the bishops decided, to await the verdict of the papal commission on the subject.[103]

VII

FINALLY, THE COUNCIL ENDED. The bishops approved the three documents announcing a new relationship between church and world— *Gaudium et Spes* (On the Church in the Modern World), *Dignitatis Humanae* (Declaration on Religious Freedom), and *Nostra Aetate* (Declaration on the Relation of the Church to Non-Christian Religions)—by majorities well above the two-thirds threshold. Against the odds, Paul VI had steered the council to a harmonious conclusion. As he put it, a church that "in the present century was absent and cut off" had reengaged with the modern world.[104] In rural Australia, an editorial writer explained more matter of factly that "there is no longer the urge to build walls around pious Catholics; to regard the Church as a fortress inside which the good should keep themselves unspotted from the world."[105]

The phase of Catholic history beginning with the ultramontane revival of the early nineteenth century had concluded. Working under the glare of the world's media, the bishops and their theologians had managed to compose, debate, and approve four constitutions (on the liturgy, the church, divine revelation, and the church's relationship with the modern world), three declarations (including on religious freedom and the church's relationship with other religions), and nine decrees. (The constitutions and the declarations were understood to be the council's core texts; the nine decrees were less consequential.) The respectful tone adopted by the council toward the world, the absence of condemnation, remained consistent throughout the texts, and this rhetorical posture proved almost as important as the documents themselves.[106]

What the bishops had not done—a crucial omission—was assess the structures of the church they had inherited. The liturgy might be in the vernacular, and the laity and the clergy had together become members of the people of God, but the pope and the bishops saw their authority, if anything, enhanced. The uneven but genuine evolution toward transparency and shared governance marking most institutions in the developed world in the 1970s and 1980s, from universities to government agencies to corporations, had no Catholic analogue. The centralization of church authority, the determination to avoid "scandal" or revelations of misdeeds, and the desire to shield church procedures from a meddling state endured. Paul VI unilaterally created a synod of bishops in the last conciliar session, but its role in conjunction with the curia remained uncertain. That Paul VI withdrew the topics of birth control and priestly celibacy from conciliar deliberations hinted at a coming storm over gender, sex, and authority.

Still, for the first time, the bishops had acted as a global church with Brazilian, Polish, and Filipino bishops jostling for time at the microphones and meeting each other at the coffee bars. In the nineteenth century, Karl Rahner explained, the church "exported a European religion as a commodity it did not really want to change." The outcome of the Second Vatican Council was different. "The victory of the vernacular in the church liturgy," he argued, "signals unmistakably the coming-to-be of a world Church whose individual churches exist with a certain independence in their respective cultural spheres, inculturated, and no longer a European export."[107] The Japanese novelist Shusaku Endō published his most influential work, *Silence*, just after the completion of the council. Its main characters wrestle with the necessity of adapting Catholicism to local contexts, even while preserving the core of the faith.

Endō had studied with a student of Jacques Maritain. On the last day of the council, Paul VI paid tribute to Maritain, his old friend. Maritain had recently retired to a French monastery but had followed news reports of the council's work. He had consulted with Paul VI on the Declaration on Religious Freedom and the paragraphs on the relationship with the Jewish people in *Nostra Aetate*. He welcomed the endorsement of democracy in *Gaudium et Spes*, vindication for a man who in the desperate days of the 1930s articulated the Catholic argument for democracy when it seemed likely to perish.[108]

This sense of triumph soon vanished. Paul VI had optimistically announced near the end of the council, "Discussion finishes; comprehension begins."[109] Catholics knew, or thought they knew, how to resist a dangerous modern world. Now how to engage it? Answering this question proved more challenging than anticipated. Three years after the council, Maritain surprised his onetime colleagues in the ressourcement by publishing a sour reflection on the post-conciliar church. He described its intellectuals as abjectly "kneeling before the world."[110]

What seemed an orderly set of changes to bishops meeting in Rome became a pell-mell dash on the ground, at least in Western Europe and North and South America. Aspects of church life once taken for granted were now in flux, beginning with the reformed liturgy but extending to new architectural forms, the culling of traditional devotions, and a rethinking of parish and school missions. Priests and nuns entered into unprecedented soul-searching about their ministry. The flight from a depleted neo-Thomist synthesis was blindingly fast.[111]

A young British anthropologist, Mary Douglas, offered a shrewd assessment. She admired the accomplishments of the council. But she wondered if the pace of the changes had outrun the capacity of Catholics to accommodate them. Douglas had attended a London boarding school run by the Sisters of the Sacred Heart. She respected the educational standards of the nuns but even more their sense of abnegation and the clear roles in the school for everyone from the headmistress to first-year students. As a doctoral student at Oxford, she began her examination of ritual and hierarchy among the Lele people in what was then the Belgian Congo, studying how Catholicism did or did not become integrated into local practices. Her *Purity and Danger*, published in 1966 when she was thirty-four, became one of the most influential texts in the history of her discipline.[112]

She then turned her anthropological gaze on the post-conciliar church. Reformers in the heady days after the council congratulated themselves on liberating Catholics from "formal, ritualistic conformity." Douglas was less sure. She worried about the "collapse of symbolic form." She bristled at bishops and theologians implementing the conciliar texts with little consideration for the devotional culture they swept away. A seemingly minor decision such as abandoning the requirement that Catholics not eat meat on any Friday was for Douglas an attack on "sacramental forms of worship." Many Catholics—including Douglas's "Bog Irish" ancestors—had taken such demands with great seriousness.

Now these rules no longer applied. Equating religion with ethics—why not eat meat on Fridays and give money to the poor?—made religion less compelling. If Catholics become "unritualistic," she predicted, they "will eventually lose their capacity for responding to condensed symbols such as the Blessed Sacrament." They might cease being Catholic.[113]

TWELVE

Liberation

Freedom and Human Rights in the 1970s

I

BORN IN 1909 to a family of modest means and with twelve siblings—only four of whom survived to adulthood—Hélder Pessoa Câmara enrolled in the local seminary at age fourteen. Because of his youth, his ordination to the priesthood in 1931 required a special dispensation from the Vatican. He became active in intellectual circles and in the Ação Integralista Brasileira, Brazil's rightist political party, even wearing the green shirts favored by party members beneath his clerical uniform.[1] Portugal's António Salazar and his putatively Catholic state was their ideal.

Câmara's abilities drew him into the inner circle of Rio de Janeiro's cardinal, Sebastião Leme. Partially under the influence of Jacques Maritain, who had visited Brazil in 1936, Câmara edged away from the right-wing politics of his youth. He soothed tensions between Catholics and the country's beleaguered Protestant minority, whose members praised Câmara's "noble Christian spirit."[2] He exchanged ideas about economic development with Louis-Joseph Lebret. He traveled to Rome in 1950 and met with Giovanni Montini, who encouraged him to organize the Brazilian bishops into a national conference even as Câmara himself was named an auxiliary bishop of Rio de Janeiro. Working with a like-

Archbishop Dom
Hélder Câmara, Paris,
1968. *(Getty Images)*

minded Chilean colleague, he orchestrated the first meeting of bishops
from all of Latin America in 1955, an organization named CELAM for
its Spanish acronym. The meeting occurred during the International
Eucharistic Congress, which Câmara had also organized in conjunction
with the Brazilian government.

By now the epitome of the wheeling and dealing bishop, the dimin-
utive Câmara, just over five feet tall, moved with ease from baptisms
and weddings for Rio de Janeiro's elite to meetings in Rome and con-
sultations in government ministries. He worked (and prayed) from
before dawn until midnight, gathering with friends at favored restau-
rants for diversion. But his interests had begun to shift. One of the
French cardinals attending the International Eucharistic Congress in
Rio de Janeiro in 1955, Pierre-Marie Gerlier, asked Câmara if the opulence on display—including a bejeweled monstrance for the eucharistic host and military honor guards in dress uniform—was appropriate.
The two men toured Rio de Janeiro's slums, or favelas, packed with
migrants from rural areas. Câmara later recalled another question posed
by Gerlier:

Brother Dom Hélder, why don't you use this organizing talent that the Lord has given you in the service of
the poor? You must know that although Rio de Janeiro is
one of the most beautiful cities in the world it is also one
of the most hideous, because all these favelas in such a
beautiful setting are an insult to the Lord.[3]

The question struck him like a lightning bolt. The success of the
Eucharistic Congress resulted in that rarest of public goods, a surplus,
and Câmara decided to use the funds to build a housing complex in one
of the favelas. He coordinated a statement from the country's bishops
that urged Brazilians to not "overlook the cry of the masses, who, vic-
timized by the specter of hunger, are reaching the depths of desperation."[4] When Montini, now cardinal archbishop of Milan, visited Brazil
in 1960, Câmara escorted him on a tour of the same favelas.[5]

At the Second Vatican Council, Câmara served on one of the preparatory commissions, and his leadership of the Brazilian bishops' conference,
the third largest after the United States and Italy, gave him an influential
platform. When Yves Congar lectured to the Brazilian bishops during the
first session, he described Câmara as "not only very open but full of ideas,
imagination and enthusiasm. He has what is missing in Rome—vision."[6]

Câmara composed letters twice a week—293 in total—to a circle
of friends in Rio de Janeiro, detailing events in Rome. He identified
with the council's reformers, especially those bishops such as Gerlier
who formed the "church of the poor" group. He encouraged artists and
statesmen (such as Léopold Senghor) who promoted a "black Christ."
He championed dialogue with "atheists and particularly Marxists."[7] He
privately asked John XXIII: "Isn't it true, Holy Father, that communism
is not the worst enemy?" John XXIII agreed.[8]

Between the second and third sessions, Paul VI appointed Câmara
as archbishop of Olinda-Recife. Recife had long been a center of both
Catholic and communist activism in Brazil's impoverished Northeast.[9]
Upon his arrival, Câmara moved out of the episcopal mansion into a
small, neighboring building. He declined to wear the archbishop's purple
sash. He hitchhiked into the city center instead of using his official car.

Three weeks after Câmara's appointment, Brazilian generals over-threw the elected president. Those bishops who welcomed the coup tended to be supportive of Brazil's Tradition, Family, and Property movement, which had just coordinated a series of huge anti-commu-nist rallies, led by an American priest, Patrick Peyton (whose work was funded in part by the CIA), and a Brazilian nun, Sr. Ana de Lourdes. Leaders urged the praying of the rosary and invoked Mary to help Bra-zil avoid the fate and suffering of "Cuba, Poland, Hungary and other enslaved nations."[10]

Another group of bishops, led by Câmara, regretted the coup and resented what they identified as a right-wing American and Brazilian obsession with communism. In Câmara's first address in his new dio-cese, he insisted that "Christ is called Zé, António, Severino." He urged Brazilians not to "denounce as communists those who merely hunger and thirst for social justice and Brazil's development."[11]

During the third session of the council, Câmara became one of the bishops drafted to analyze the "signs of the times" for the commission composing *Gaudium et Spes*. During the fourth session, he led a group of forty-two bishops who traveled outside Rome to a church associated with the catacombs during the early Christian era. The assembled bish-ops all vowed to live "in the ordinary manner of our people."[12]

Upon returning to Recife, Câmara set up credit unions, required seminarians to live with poor families, and arranged for lay theolo-gians (including women) to be trained by the archdiocese. His critical statements about the military government drew unwelcome attention. Police searched Câmara's office and tapped his phone. Downplaying fears about communism, he orchestrated a statement by bishops of the northeast region, seized by the police before it could be distributed, insisting that "there is neither development nor Christianity" when "the people are not given first consideration."[13] By the late 1960s, Brazilian church officials led the opposition to the military regime. The govern-ment imprisoned eighteen priests and fifty-seven pastoral workers in 1968.[14] In 1969, one of Câmara's priest-aides was tortured and mur-dered, presumably by government forces.

Dressed in simple clerical clothes, wearing a black beret, and eager to do interviews, sometimes between connecting flights, Câmara became a celebrity. Invitations arrived at such a rate, and the situation within Brazil was so repressive, that Câmara spent months at a time giving lectures around the world. His ability to criticize individual violent acts while denouncing structural violence proved appealing, and he described himself, in a book title, as *Violent for Peace*. At the annual meeting of the Katholikentag in West Germany, Munich's Cardinal Döpfner asked in mock exasperation if the German church had "no other problem" than those identified by the charismatic Câmara.[15]

Critics within and outside the church accused Câmara of practicing a Catholic version of radical chic. The criticism reflected the rapidity of change within Brazil, where the pastor on the plantation and chaplain in the military had for most of the twentieth century symbolized the church's role as an integrative, not oppositional, institution. In the 1950s, Rio de Janeiro's archbishop traveled the country by courtesy of a military jet and officially served as vicar of the air force.[16]

A generation later, furious Brazilian government officials called Câmara "Fidel Castro in a cassock."[17] He became one of the foremost voices of the global human rights movement, an unimaginable role for a Brazilian Catholic bishop in the 1950s. When Dominique de Menil created an annual award in honor of the twenty-fifth anniversary of the United Nations Declaration of Human Rights in 1973, she invited Câmara to Houston and the pair became friends. Câmara spoke at the Rothko Chapel, inveighed against torture, and urged "development yes, but not at an inhuman price."[18]

II

DOM HÉLDER CÂMARA'S CAREER—from right-wing politics in the 1930s to the Second Vatican Council to champion of human rights—captures an important twentieth-century arc. But if the global Catholic story beginning in the early nineteenth century and up to the Second Vatican Council can be summarized as ultramontane triumph and then, in the 1950s, erosion, the narrative of the tumultuous decade after the council is more fragmented.

One new emphasis was development. During the debate over *Gaudium et Spes*, a cluster of experts and bishops had come together under the auspices of the Working Group on the Poor to discuss development issues. Paul VI chartered a new Vatican commission after the council, *Iustitia et Pax*, or Justice and Peace, which became the model for dozens of other similar commissions at the national and diocesan level around the world. Câmara founded one of the first of these diocesan commissions in Recife. Barbara Ward mobilized contacts ranging from U Thant, United Nations secretary-general, to Robert Kennedy to England's Cardinal Heenan in support of this effort, and major international Catholic charities began to place the word "development" in their charters, even though such an emphasis "did not exist," in the words of one French expert, only two decades before.[19]

Paul VI also began work just after the council on a social encyclical. The center of Catholic gravity on questions of political economy had steadily moved left since the early twentieth century, beginning with Pius XI's grave doubts about capitalism as expressed in *Quadragesimo Anno* at the height of the global depression. When a young American Catholic, William F. Buckley, a founder of the American conservative movement, complained in 1952 that Yale University faculty promoted socialism, major Catholic intellectuals dismissed him. Fr. John LaFarge complained that Buckley was mistaken in "asserting the absolute rights of Free Enterprise."[20] In West Germany, Fr. Oswald von Nell-Breuning scorned the idea of a "pure economy of competition."[21]

The tension between free market–oriented reformers and advocates of Catholic social thought also became visible in Chile. In the 1950s, at the Universidad Católica in Santiago, administrators accepted a proposal to form an independent economics institute (and eventually school) funded by the American government and private foundations and staffed by faculty and recent PhDs from the University of Chicago, the economics department in the world most committed to a free market approach. Bishop Manuel Larrain, on the board of the university, protested permitting "a brand of conservative economics where social justice considerations do not exist."[22] Some of the Chicago economists, in turn, worried about religious restrictions on their work.

Among those assisting Paul VI in the drafting process for his social encyclical were Barbara Ward and a dying Fr. Louis-Joseph Lebret, both crucial to Catholic development work in the postwar era. Released in early 1967, *Populorum Progressio* struck new notes. Development "cannot be restricted to economic growth alone," Paul VI explained. "To be authentic, it must be well rounded; it must foster the development of each man and of the whole man." He stressed the importance of "integral human development" and described "a type of capitalism" in bleak terms:

> These concepts present profit as the chief spur to economic progress, free competition as the guiding norm of economics, and private ownership of the means of production as an absolute right, having no limits nor concomitant social obligations.[23]

Paul VI would soon link development to the environmental movement and the need to battle the "permanent menace" of pollution.[24] The *Wall Street Journal* dismissed such claims as "warmed over Marxism." Jibes of this sort could be ignored, but the pope's stern assessment of capitalism during a period of robust economic growth suggested the importance Catholics now placed on the gap between rich and poor.[25] Alioune Diop, the Senegalese Catholic who had become an interlocutor between the Vatican and sub-Saharan Catholic Africa, repeated the phrasing of his friend, Fr. Lebret, that integral human development meant not just "having more" but "being more."[26] European Christian Democrats, eager to sustain their influence in the Global South in the postcolonial era, studied the encyclical with care.[27]

Populorum Progressio had its most consequential impact in Latin America. Dom Hélder Câmara congratulated Paul VI on a "courageous encyclical," and bishops from the Dominican Republic and other countries immediately began to encourage "authentic human development" and urge limits on private property rights.[28]

In Chile, rebellious students invoked the encyclical as they challenged the presence of free market economists at the Universidad Católica in Santiago. After occupying several campus buildings, although not the economics school, then located in a bucolic suburb, students examined the place of economics in the curriculum. One Chilean priest complained that "even courses which are as proper for an economics school such as Economic Development or as proper for a Catholic university as socio-economic Doctrine of the Church tend to be qualified as instruments of 'ideological indoctrination.' "[29]

The second meeting of CELAM, the organization of Latin American bishops, occurred at Medellín, Colombia, in 1968. Paul VI opened the meeting as part of the first papal visit to South America and received a thunderous welcome. Just a month before Medellín, Gustavo Gutiérrez had addressed a group of priests in his native Peru. The title of the talk was "Theology and Development," but at the last moment Gutiérrez scratched out the term "Development" and substituted "Liberation."[30]

The new term stuck. What many Latin American Catholic intellectuals and activists took from the Second Vatican Council, and even more from their lived experience in a region so marked by inequality, was the need for liberation from an oppressive economic system. The assembled bishops and theologians at Medellín rejected violence—a fact neglected by liberation theology's opponents—but they also committed themselves to the "authentic liberation" of the poor. Commissions on peace and

Gustavo Gutiérrez, one of the founders of liberation theology, 1979. *(Katholiek Documentatie Centrum, Nijmegen/photo: AFBK-2A3459)*

justice should be developed in every diocese, in part to foster "concientización," borrowing a term from the Brazilian educator Paulo Freire, who had moved to Chile in 1964 after the military coup in Brazil and whose "pedagogy of the oppressed" had wide influence among Catholics. "Concientización" meant that the church should attempt to help form socially aware Christian citizens. These Christians would then alleviate "the misery that besets large masses of human beings in all of our countries."[31]

Gutiérrez had welcomed *Populorum Progressio*, later remembering it as "a trumpet call."[32] He published his masterpiece, *Teología de la Liberación*, in 1971. Along with theologians from Brazil, Uruguay, and Central America, he departed from the vision of Jacques Maritain. He rejected the pluralist "separation of planes" between politics and religion, each granted a certain autonomy, that Maritain promoted in the 1930s and 1940s as a corrective to the long-standing Catholic preference for church-state unity. By contrast, Gutiérrez emphasized the need to liberate humans from both unjust economic structures and sin. Latin America, he bluntly concluded, "cannot develop within the capitalistic system."[33]

Liberation theology's reception was electric. If the church in Latin America had long been compromised by alliances with anti-communist dictators—as late as 1967 a Guatemalan archbishop personally sprinkled holy water on fifty-four Ford Broncos sent by the American government for use by security forces—no place now seemed more obviously the Catholic "future" as one immodest Brazilian theologian put it.[34] Scholars and church leaders organized eleven major conferences on liberation theology during 1970–1971 in Latin America.[35] A bevy of European and North American priests, nuns, and scholars had migrated to the region in the early 1960s, and their work and connections also made ideas of development and liberation in Latin America more visible.[36]

The emphasis of liberation theologians and their allies on direct work with the poor melded with the existing ecclesial base communities, where small groups read the scriptures together and developed plans for social action. Thousands of such communities had been organized in Brazil in the early 1960s, across South and Central America over the next decade, and then in other areas of the Global South, including the Philippines and India. This combination of theory (liberation theology) and organizational strategy (ecclesial base communities) allowed more Catholics than ever before to work with the poor. In the Indian state of Kerala, Catholic activists led the successful effort to rein in commercial fisheries and protect the livelihood and culture of the region's one million fishing families. In many areas of the subcontinent, they became among the leading defenders of Dalits, or untouchables, as well as Adivasi, or tribal peoples.[37]

Ecclesial base communities simultaneously fostered catechetical work among Quechua- and Aymara-speaking people in Peru and Bolivia, Xoco people in the Amazon, and Mayans in Mexico. Sometimes priests and nuns ventured out into remote areas with little fear of competition. In other locales, the work of Protestant missionaries, quick to translate the Bible into Indigenous languages and form local congregations, pressured Catholic bishops to consider new methods. Bishop Samuel Ruiz, in the Chiapas region of Mexico, began his career in the early 1960s wary of communist influence and hoping to "civilize" Mayans. Within a decade, collaborating with foreign missionaries from Europe and North America, Ruiz changed course and founded dozens of agricultural cooperatives. "If the Church does not turn Tzeltal here," one group of activists challenged Ruiz, "we don't understand how it can be Catholic at all." Gustavo Gutiérrez founded a center in Lima named after Bartolomé de las Casas, the sixteenth-century Spanish defender of Indigenous people.[38]

More surprising was the impact of liberation theology in North America and Western Europe. In Canada, for example, the circuit of missionaries to Peru, Bolivia, and Brazil and then back to Montreal and Toronto prepared the way for a visit by Gutiérrez.[39] Contact with liberation theologians inspired the formation of base communities in Spain and led to a "prophetic denunciation" of a church as "capitalist and linked to power."[40] "*Dios está en el base*," wrote Spain's most prominent theologian, José María González Ruiz, or "God is at the roots." The church needed a "theology of revolution" just as much as a "revolution in theology." Or as González Ruiz explained in 1967: "Capitalism must be considered from a Christian moral perspective as intrinsically perverse."[41]

Left-leaning West German Catholics seized on the writings of liberation theologians with particular enthusiasm. Here was a theology with a mistrust for how capitalism ordered the world. Here was a focus on poverty and how Jesus's example should shatter middle-class complacency. Johann Baptist Metz, a student of Karl Rahner, trained many Latin American students in Münster even as he, himself, was profoundly influenced by Gutiérrez and other liberation theologians. Another German theologian and bishop, Karl Lehmann, recognized the power of the term "liberation" as opposed to Western notions of "freedom."[42]

Bishops from South America and North America held their first joint meetings in the late 1960s, with Latin American experts urging the assembled bishops to remember that an inculturated church could not derive its identity solely from an "Aristotelian-Thomistic-Mediterranean culture." The bishops read and discussed Gustavo Gutiérrez, pondering "the theological meaning of 'liberation' in general." Just what liberation meant remained hazy. Or as Chile's Cardinal Raúl Silva Henriquez admitted to his North American colleagues, "In all these meetings there occur [a] series of criticisms against capitalism, but . . . no one ever offers a new, functional, valid system to replace it."[43]

III

COULD THAT new, functional, valid system be socialism? Simultaneous with the end of the council, Karl Rahner, Yves Congar, and other major figures participated in multiple Catholic-Marxist exchanges. Paul VI's grim characterization of capitalism in *Populorum Progressio* buoyed these discussions, even if the pope cautioned against blurring socialist and Christian categories.

This new openness toward socialism drew attention away from Christian Democratic parties. During the Second Vatican Council, the Christian Democratic movement seemed at high tide. German Christian Democrats had held a parliamentary majority without interruption since 1949. Italian Christian Democrats had an equally successful record, as did Christian Democratic parties in Belgium and the Netherlands. In Chile, Jacques Maritain's protégé, Eduardo Frei, had just been elected president. More than any other figure in South America, Frei promoted explicitly Christian and democratic politics—some Chilean Catholics called it "social action in power, without clericalism"—and his 1964 campaign depended on support from Catholic officials (and a Central Intelligence Agency eager to counter communist influence). Another Maritain disciple and Christian Democrat, Rafael Caldera, would soon be elected president of Venezuela.[44]

Even so, Maritain's influence was waning. In 1966, one philosopher wondered whether a Maritain center recently founded at the University of Notre Dame had missed its moment. "In the flurry of writing that accompanied and succeeded Vatican II," he noted, "there was little reference to Maritain, an astonishing thing considering his intellectual preeminence in the Church a couple of decades back."[45] British Catholic leftists challenged what they viewed as Maritain's reluctance to link theology and revolution.[46] Catholic student groups in northern Italy had once named themselves after Maritain and Emmanuel Mounier, but in the late 1960s they chose the names Camillo Torres (the ex-priest killed in 1966 as a revolutionary in Colombia), Fidel Castro, and Che Guevara.[47] So, too, in Brazil and Mexico, where Catholic students in the left-leaning Juventud Universitaria Católica or the Corporación de Estudiantes Mexicanos shifted from reading Maritain and Louis-Joseph Lebret to reading secular radicals.[48]

In West Germany, the Christian Democrats formed a coalition government with the Social Democrats in 1966; Italian Christian Democrats lost ground to the Italian Communist Party. Christian Democratic politicians, with their bargaining and compromises, now seemed to students and labor activists to stand in the way of more ambitious social goals. Even Aldo Moro, Italy's most prominent Christian Democratic politician, had begun to worry that a vibrant Catholic party had become "the party of the state."[49] Allied to often inchoate demands made by student activists was a new informality in style marking the gap between rebellious youth and establishment figures. If students favored long hair and jeans, Moro, as a matter of decorum, wore a tie and dark suit to the beach—at least whenever photographers might be present.

Old antagonisms dissolved. In 1966, the Italian Communist Party encouraged its members to join forces with "progressive Catholics." In Bologna, the city's cardinal, Giacomo Lercaro, who in the 1950s had scoffed at the idea that "Catholic life can coexist with atheist Marxism," was honored by the city's communist government.[50] This drift away from Christian Democratic parties was also noticeable in Chile. Cardinal Silva of Santiago remained hesitant about reducing Catholicism to "a socioeconomic and political system," but he recognized in Catholic support for socialist Salvador Allende the desire for a "pluralistic and democratic socialism."[51] Some radical Catholics explicitly favored Allende in the 1970 presidential election, even if most Catholics remained committed Christian Democrats. An aggravated President Richard Nixon complained to top aides that one of the biggest changes in Latin America had "been the deterioration of the attitude of the Catholic Church." Nixon described himself as "pro-Catholic," and he had long collaborated with American Catholics in anti-communist efforts. Now he wondered if the church in Latin America could "play an effective role on a serious question."[52]

IV

COLLEGE ENROLLMENTS SOARED in the 1960s in the United States, and to a lesser degree in Europe and Latin America, and the percentage of Catholic young people enrolled in college may have increased at an even faster rate. When these students participated in the student revolts that so marked the period, they frequently combined criticism of political and university leaders with attacks on religious paternalism. When students closed down Louvain (Leuven) in Belgium in 1966, the presenting incident was tension over whether the university would become bilingual for French-speaking and Flemish-speaking students. But at center stage was a conflict between the bishops dominating the board of trustees and a former seminarian leading the students. As one student put it, "Almost everyone present in [Louvain/Leuven] at that time came from Catholic high schools and had experienced at least eighteen years of Catholic upbringing. There were people present who, at this particular moment, [wanted to] settle their accounts with that past."[53]

At Milan's Università Cattolica del Sacro Cuore, or Sacred Heart University, enrolled students had to be baptized Catholics, and the university automatically expelled student couples living together outside of marriage. (To deter such relationships, the university housed women students with watchful Catholic families.) In 1967, a protest against an increase in student fees metastasized into meetings about the future of the university and the church. Protesters referenced Karl Marx but also Karl Rahner. Observers noted that women students involved in the protests wore pants instead of skirts.[54]

Student protests in the United States and Western Europe soon coalesced around a shared opposition to the American military effort in Vietnam. Vatican diplomats were not far behind. Instead of the concordat strategy of Pius XI and Pius XII, Paul VI directed papal foreign policy away from traditional realpolitik. As early as 1965, days after the conclusion of the Second Vatican Council, he urged the Johnson administration to search for a peaceful settlement, appealing for a Christmas truce and later offering to mediate peace talks.[55] These efforts clashed with the stance of New York's Cardinal Spellman, who visited American and South Vietnamese troops in Southeast Asia nine times and defined the conflict in Vietnam as "a war for civilization." Even in 1966 Spellman expressed the hope that "we shall soon have the victory for which all of us in Vietnam and all over the world are hoping and praying, for less than victory is incomprehensible."[56]

Left-leaning Catholic students and activists, especially in France and Italy, immediately declared a challenge: "Who speaks in the name of the Church? Cardinal Spellman for war or the Pope for peace?"[57] Australian Catholics formed a new group, Catholics for Peace, and lambasted Sydney's cardinal for supporting Spellman. A nun in New Zealand recalled how most (although not all) of her colleagues became opposed to New Zealand's involvement in the conflict. Some later marched against the war in full habit.[58] When President Johnson decided to attend Spellman's funeral in 1967 in New York City, antiwar protesters immediately gathered outside St. Patrick's Cathedral. More hawkish on the war in 1965 than the average citizen, Catholics in the United States would become significantly more opposed to the war than the average citizen by 1970.[59]

Bologna's Cardinal Lercaro—an ally of Paul VI as one of the four moderators at the Second Vatican Council, where he advocated for a pacifist (as opposed to just war) position—denounced the United States from the pulpit on New Year's Day in 1968 for not suspending the bombing of North Vietnam. Or as he put it, "The Church cannot be neutral in the face of evil, but must be prophetic."[60]

The headlines generated by Lercaro's homily prompted Paul VI to ask for his resignation. Other Catholics also acted. Senators Eugene McCarthy and Robert F. Kennedy declared their candidacies for US president because of their opposition to President Johnson's escalation of American involvement in Vietnam. The Berrigan brothers, Daniel and Philip, became leaders in what members called the Catholic resistance. Daniel Berrigan had remained close to worker-priests in France after first meeting them in the early 1950s and compared the American military effort in Vietnam to the ill-fated French effort in Algeria.

At a Selective Service office in suburban Baltimore, Maryland, members of the resistance broke in, seized draft files, and burned them in the parking lot. Before their trial, some of these activists implored Dom Hèlder Câmara to assist them. Instead of reporting for his prison sentence, Daniel Berrigan became a fugitive, occasionally delivering quick antiwar speeches to delighted audiences. FBI agents, also often Catholic, finally arrested Berrigan after he had evaded them for four months. They nabbed Philip Berrigan, also a fugitive, as he hid in the rectory of a New York City parish.[61]

V

THE MOST DARING DIALOGUES occurred across the Iron Curtain. Reforms announced in Czechoslovakia in the spring of 1968 seemed to herald a new day as the Alexander Dubček government released hundreds of imprisoned priests and lay Catholics as part of its rejection of Stalinism. In turn, twenty-two thousand Catholics signed a petition asking Dubček to honor freedom of religion in practice, not just theory, and abandon surveillance and blackmail.[62] Newly freed Catholic political prisoners asked "informed and honorable Marxists" to disavow past repression and invoked Vatican II in calling for a dialogue between an "open Christianity and an open Marxism."[63]

Leonid Brezhnev's decision to send Soviet tanks into Prague in August 1968 eliminated such hopes. Combined with parallel events in Poland, including a purge of Jewish intellectuals, enthusiasm for Christian-Marxist dialogue diminished. By the early 1970s, as in Western Europe and parts of Latin America, many left-leaning Catholics in Eastern Europe dismissed politics as a dead end.

They did so for different reasons. In Western Europe and Latin America, formal politics seemed less vital than new forms of collective action. The most famous European experimental religious community, Isolotto, founded in a poor suburb of Florence in the 1950s, evolved into a space where the priest faced the people during Mass (even before the council), laypeople offered homilies, and small group Bible reading replaced traditional forms of Catholic Action. Isolotto's several thousand parishioners engaged in a years-long confrontation with a new, more conservative bishop in the late 1960s. (Upon presenting the new bishop to Catholics in Florence's famous duomo, or cathedral, the retiring, more liberal bishop introduced him with the following words: "I present to you the new bishop who has been sent to me from Rome without me having asked for him.") One priest from a working-class family in Spain recalled how his mother, proud that her son had become a priest, sobbed when she first visited the ramshackle house in a poor suburb of Madrid where he had moved with other young clergy. He didn't own a car. No one called him "Don Pedro."[64]

Eastern European Catholics shared this eagerness to build a new church, but they worried that Catholics in Western Europe and North America had become consumed by struggles against ecclesiastical authority figures. They hungered for the civil liberties and political parties that some Catholics in the West dismissed as bourgeois conventions. "I fulfilled my oppositional desires," recalled one Hungarian Catholic activist, "not by living against something, not by denying something, but in a positive struggle for values."[65]

Many Eastern European Catholics were skeptical of the Vatican policy of *Ostpolitik*, which allowed Paul VI to at once criticize government-sponsored atheism in the Eastern bloc but also insist that the church would not cut itself "off from the adherents of these systems."[66] The top Vatican diplomat, Agostino Casaroli, visited Poland three times in the first two years after the council, circumventing Poland's hardline Cardinal Wyszyński. He also reached out to every other country in the Eastern Bloc and Cuba. In Cuba, a Vatican official declared that "I consider the Church to be aware of the change of political system in this country; it is an incontrovertible fact which is now irreversible. As a result the Church should adapt to these changes, as it has shown in Europe."[67] In Yugoslavia, Vatican diplomats angered some Catholics by beginning negotiations with the communist leadership without involving local bishops. These bishops accurately predicted that agreements to protect religious freedom would be worthless.[68] In 1972, the Vatican permitted the naming of four Czechoslovakian bishops whom both sides knew to be collaborators with the secret police, members of a government-sponsored group entitled, without irony, *Pacem in Terris*. The plan was that the remaining episcopal slots would go to priests independent of the regime—but the Czech government did not permit those appointments. Catholic intellectual life continued, furtively; some of the most distinguished priests, such as Tomáš Halík, secretly ordained in 1978, kept day jobs. (Halík did not even confide in his mother.)[69]

Only in Poland did the church remain an imposing presence in civil society. Polish Catholics celebrated a millennium of Christianity in 1966, with recitations of a vow pledging the Polish nation to Mary in every parish and ceremonies across the country. After communist authorities "arrested" the icon of the Black Madonna of Jasna Gora as it was transported from Lublin to Warsaw, Cardinal Wyszyński continued the procession with an empty frame—attracting even larger crowds. Anxious state officials eventually returned the icon, and the Madonna again took pride of place.[70]

No *Ostpolitik* penetrated Chinese borders. None could. In the 1950s, almost all of the foreign missionaries running schools and orphanages had been imprisoned, forced to leave China, or killed. Chinese Catholics were divided between those affiliated with state-approved patriotic Catholic churches and Roman Catholic churches, although the lines were blurry in particular locales. The Catholics most likely to remain affiliated with Roman-approved parishes lived in isolated, often majority Catholic villages. Even many of these Catholics renounced their faith during the savage persecution of the Cultural Revolution in the late 1960s. In Shanxi Province, state officials mounted a museum exhibition explaining why Catholicism threatened the state. Red Guards ordered Catholics from local villages to attend the exhibit and then forced them to kneel for hours outside the museum, poking them with sticks and making them eat dirt.[71]

VI

THE WORLD'S MOST DISTINGUISHED neo-Thomist philosopher, Alasdair MacIntyre, considered belief in human rights "one with belief in witches and in unicorns."[72] Liberation theologians, approaching the question from another angle, arrived at the same conclusion. They desired social transformation, not a delusory focus on individual freedoms, which could mutate into a defense of free market economics. One Uruguayan Jesuit saw human rights as an "ideological trap set for the most deprived countries on earth."[73]

These views rested comfortably within an enduring Catholic skepticism about human rights, originating in a neo-Thomist tradition that valued community over the individual. After Jacques Maritain's defense of human rights in the 1940s, few Catholics explored the topic as the pressures of the Cold War and decolonization shifted attention away from the rights of individuals to the formation of nation-states.

Still, spurred by the texts of Vatican II, Catholics were consistently among the leading figures in the burst of human rights activism that marked the 1970s, especially in Eastern Europe and Latin America. Already in 1968 the Polish bishops, in a gesture that would have seemed out of character a generation earlier, celebrated the twentieth anniversary of the United Nations Declaration of Human Rights, although they thought "human dignity"—a term that first garnered wide used during the battle against communism and fascism in the 1930s—a better starting point than "individual rights."[74]

Dissidents in Czechoslovakia took on a new prominence with the 1975 Helsinki Accords. These accords formally acknowledged Soviet control over Eastern Europe. But in part because of Vatican diplomats, the same accords required Eastern European governments to weave commitments to "the inherent dignity of the human person" into their constitutions. (This language may have been the crowning achievement of *Ostpolitik*.)[75]

Almost immediately after the signing of the treaty, Protestant, Catholic, and secular dissidents in Czechoslovakia—taking advantage of a practical ecumenicism forged while in prison or in jointly run organizations—composed and signed a statement, Charter 77, demanding that the state respect civil liberties. The playwright Václav Havel was the leading figure and an unbeliever, but during his imprisonment, he spent long hours pondering Christian texts with two priest-cellmates committed to the movement.[76] Jan Patočka, a no-longer-practicing Catholic trained in the phenomenology so important to Catholic intellectual life in the mid-twentieth century, and inspired by Yves Congar, Karl Rahner, and other figures of the ressourcement, became another guiding presence. Patočka died from a heart attack following interrogation by the police, which generated enormous sympathy.[77] Meanwhile, Czech bishops linked to the government accused the Charter 77 signatories of not recognizing "the good our socialist society does for the happiness of the people."[78]

In the 1950s, Polish editor Tadeusz Mazowiecki had hoped to develop a Catholic communism. He had been present in Rome for much of Vatican II and had long favored Marxist-Catholic dialogue. By 1970, he was disillusioned. He now urged Polish Catholics to focus on the "most basic human matters," and he even invoked the failure of German and Polish Catholics to protest attacks on the Jews in the 1930s as proof that "national traditions" could become "rotten."[79]

Long focused on protecting their institutions from Stalinist predators, Polish Catholic intellectuals such as Mazowiecki pivoted toward the world. There they met Adam Michnik, a leading secular activist and former communist who, after the government crackdown of 1968, had set himself the task of bridging the longstanding gulf between university and reform circles and Polish Catholicism. "The Church now stands stubbornly on the side of the persecuted and the oppressed," Michnik explained to skeptical colleagues. Indeed, "the enemy of the Left is not the Church but totalitarianism."[80] "We were no longer Marxist dissidents," he recalled, "but members of the anti-totalitarian opposition."[81]

A parallel process occurred in Latin America. The military coup in Chile in 1973, culminating with President Salvador Allende's suicide and an authoritarian regime led by General Augusto Pinochet, marked a turning point. In the 1950s, Catholic leaders would not have challenged a dictator's authority. Now Chilean bishops organized an ecumenical human rights campaign to document torture and murder by Chilean security forces. Named the Vicariate of Solidarity—again solidarity as the key term—this team of lawyers, educators, and social workers investigated human rights violations and assisted victims. In a defiant gesture, Santiago's Cardinal Silva placed the offices of the Vicariate in Santiago's central square, next to the cathedral. Its efforts drew international attention and inspired imitators across the region. In Paraguay, Catholics led efforts to defend Indigenous land rights. In Brazil, the Commission of Justice and Peace in São Paulo monitored the actions of the military government.[82]

In 1977, a new United States president, Jimmy Carter, claimed human rights as central to American foreign policy in a commencement address at Notre Dame. The university's president, Fr. Theodore Hesburgh, had recently founded a center on civil and human rights, and Carter met with its affiliated faculty along with Cardinal Paolo Evaristo Arns of São Paulo, also receiving an honorary degree and one of the leaders of Brazil's human rights movement. When Carter later visited Brazil, he made a point of seeking out Cardinal Arns. In Santiago, where General Pinochet still ruled with an iron hand, Cardinal Silva boldly declared 1978 a "year of human rights" with the motto "every man has the right to be a person."[83]

In the 1950s, intellectuals around the world questioned the capacity of Catholics to sustain democracies. By the 1980s, intellectuals applauded Catholicism's role in fostering them.[84] A church once entirely committed to the defense of the West in the Cold War now possessed a significant pacifist wing. A church once suspicious of interfaith and ecumenical dialogue now explored contested issues with Orthodox Christians, Anglicans, Jews, and Muslims. A church once skeptical of freedom of religion and other human rights had become their champion.

THIRTEEN

Exodus

Sex, Gender, and Turmoil

I

THE 1960S MARKED the moment when Christian churches (Protestant and Catholic) ceded much of the formal and informal control they had long exercised over culture. As late as 1952, students and faculty members at universities such as Notre Dame had to request permission to read texts by authors on the Index of Forbidden Books, including philosophers such as John Locke and Thomas Hobbes. (The books were kept in a locked cage in the basement of the library.)[1] Vatican officials could still consider forbidding Catholics from reading a "disturbed, confused and audacious" novel, *The Power and the Glory*, written by Graham Greene about an alcoholic priest persecuted by state officials in Mexico. Archbishop Giovanni Montini used his influence to sideline the condemnation—although Greene received a cautionary letter.

A decade later adventurous readers could safely ignore both church and state. When Greene met Montini, now Paul VI, in 1965, the pope smiled and told him to "pay no attention" to the dispute. The next year, Paul VI officially shut down the Index of Forbidden Books.[2]

Mass audiences now patronized European and then American films that included nudity and treated once taboo topics. The Legion of Decency, the once feared international Catholic group, changed its name to the more anodyne National Catholic Office for Motion Pictures. Its members could no longer intimidate film producers with a rating of "condemn" when diocesan papers might give the same film a glowing review.

More positively, the push toward engagement with the world so evident at Vatican II extended to culture. On October 5, 1964, over eight hundred Council Fathers attended a special screening of Pier Paolo Pasolini's *The Gospel According to St. Matthew*. Directed in the unadorned Italian neorealist style, the film used amateurs, not trained actors, in the leading roles and depicted Jesus's life with a scriptural fidelity and simplicity that echoed the conciliar call for a less triumphal church. The score included a selection from a Congolese liturgy. Pasolini, gay and politically radical, dedicated the film to the late John XXIII, whose openness had inspired him.

II

CHANGING IDEAS ABOUT gender and sexual morality were much more destabilizing. John XXIII had welcomed improvements in the status of women in one paragraph of *Pacem in Terris*, but with the exception of a handful of comments by bishops, women as a discrete topic barely registered at the Second Vatican Council. Excluded from the coffee bars set up in St. Peter's, the women auditors at the council convened at a separate coffee bar sardonically named Bar Nun.

Between 1965 and 1975 the climate changed. The demands of the women's movement—wage equality, entrance into male-dominated professions, and bodily autonomy—rippled across Western societies in one of the most important transformations of the twentieth century. Catholic women's organizations began holding conferences on such themes as "Women's Freedom in the Modern World." During the conciliar discussions on development, one of the world's leading experts, Barbara Ward, had been prevented from speaking because Paul VI thought it ill-advised for a woman to address the bishops. She arranged for a male colleague to read her remarks. Another woman initially scheduled to speak, Pilar Bellosillo, the Spanish head of the World Union of Catholic Women's Organizations, also agreed to step aside.[3]

Ward privately compared the plight of women in a "patriarchal society" with the "subjugation of the colonial nations." Slavery had once been thought acceptable; ignoring "50 percent of the human race" still was. She zeroed in on the birth control commission. She found it absurd "to discuss birth control without an examination in depth of the full vocation of women." She wondered about the "chances of women, too, making a breakthrough to full humanity."[4]

As Ward knew, many bishops no longer accepted the traditional teaching on contraception. South African Archbishop Denis Hurley had arrived at the council opposed to any use of contraceptives. But his involvement in the drafting of *Gaudium et Spes* and extended conversations with a friend, a Catholic mother of eight, changed his mind. He sent a letter—a "nuclear bomb"—to Cardinal Ottaviani explaining his support for married couples using contraceptives.[5] In Massachusetts, where Catholics had successfully blocked efforts to increase access to contraceptives for married couples in 1942 and 1948, a civil liberties expert commented in 1962 on "an increasing number of statements by liberal, educated Catholics expressing the view that we must 'live and let live' and that no religious group, even if it is the majority group, should impose its views on others." Here, John Courtney Murray played a behind-the-scenes role. Then laboring over the Declaration of Religious Liberty at the Second Vatican Council, Murray composed the 1965 statement that reoriented the Catholic policy position in Massachusetts, insisting that it is not "the function of civil law to prescribe everything that is morally right and to forbid everything that is morally wrong." Given that contraceptive devices had "received official sanction by many religious groups within the community," Catholics should not oppose their legalization.[6]

The birth control commission held its final meetings in 1966. New members appointed by Paul VI included three couples, one each from Canada, France, and the United States. The American couple, Patricia and Patrick Crowley from suburban Chicago, were longtime leaders of a Catholic Action group, the Christian Family Movement. Patricia Crowley mobilized the couples on the commission to poll other couples. The response was overwhelming. Both men and women, but especially women, wrote searing letters—shared with commission members— describing their struggles with the ban on contraception. The letters detailed broken marriages, anxiety about pregnancy, and exhaustion from large families. They revealed anger directed toward those priests (a rapidly diminishing number) who still advocated the rhythm method while not themselves having to delay sexual intercourse with a spouse.[7]

Another new voice on the commission was John Noonan, a law professor at Notre Dame. Noonan's *Contraception*, published in 1965, received enormous, flattering attention and was immediately translated into multiple languages. (He was personally encouraged by Belgium's Cardinal Suenens.) After detailing the emancipation of women, the acknowledgment by many theologians that procreation need not serve as the single, primary goal of sexual intercourse, and the support for change now expressed by married couples, priests, and bishops, Noonan concluded that "it is a perennial mistake to confuse repetition of old formulas with the living law of the church. The church, on its pilgrim's path, has grown in grace and wisdom."[8]

Theologians weighed in. Bernhard Häring, the German moral theologian who helped draft the section on marriage in *Gaudium et Spes*, had once opposed contraception but now thought the entire subject looked "altogether different with the passage of time."[9] In a talk given just before his death, John Courtney Murray regretted that on contraception the church had "reached for too much certainty too soon, it went too far. Certainty was reached in the absence of any adequate understanding of marriage."[10]

Ultimately, all of the lay members, nine of the twelve bishops, and fifteen of the nineteen theologians on the commission voted for a change in church teaching. Disgruntled conservatives drafted an unofficial minority report that challenged the majority recommendation. Both the majority report favoring a change in church teaching and the unofficial minority report were leaked simultaneously to *Le Monde*, the London *Tablet*, and the *National Catholic Reporter*. This publicity heightened expectations for change, and Catholic commentators from Brazil to the United States to West Germany openly discussed the need for a new perspective on human sexuality not limited to what one Brazilian priest called "essentialist" approaches.[11]

Paul VI hesitated. He commissioned reports from theologians and surveyed bishops. His friend and ally at the council, Belgium's Cardinal

Suenens, arranged for twenty-seven European bishops to sign a document urging change. Suenens, himself, pleaded with Paul VI to modify past church teaching in light of "new facts." Modification did not mean a "rupture in doctrinal continuity."[12] Another ally, Cardinal Döpfner of Munich, notified Paul VI that the German bishops had voted in favor of change, thirty-four to five. One poll of Catholics in West Germany found that well over 80 percent of respondents felt that contraception should either "be allowed" or, more ominously, "was not a matter for the Church."[13]

Released on July 29, 1968, *Humanae Vitae* began with a reaffirmation of *Gaudium et Spes* on the dual purposes of sex within marriage: procreation and the unity of the couple. The pope had eliminated a reference to the traditional judgment of contraception as a mortal sin. He encouraged priests meeting with couples to approach the topic with compassion.

And yet Paul VI declared "artificial" contraception "intrinsically wrong." This claim—conveyed in headlines as "Pope bans pill"—made *Humanae Vitae* the single most controversial document in the modern history of Catholicism. Everywhere Catholics in large majorities rejected the encyclical. One meticulous US survey of "devout" Catholic women in 1971 found not a single Catholic woman younger than thirty-five (out of seventy-three interviewed) opposed to using contraceptives. Spain's Pilar Bellosillo and her colleagues in the World Union of Catholic Women's Organizations regretted that the encyclical viewed women solely in their role as mothers, without acknowledging "other concerns."[14]

The deeper blow was to the church's authority. Some passages in *Humanae Vitae* now seem prescient about the ways in which changing mores might repackage sexual exploitation, not end it. Like contemporary feminists, for example, Paul VI cautioned against men manipulating women as "mere instrument[s] for the satisfaction of [their] own desire[s]." Brazilian bishops worried about a "society completely turned toward profit, exploitation of women and materialism."[15]

Given the unpopularity of a ban on contraception for married couples, these warnings were not—could not—be heard. Cardinal Ottaviani and other conservatives had urged Paul VI to condemn contraception less out of conviction in the natural law arguments made for the teaching than from a sense that an alteration would weaken the church's teaching authority. Upholding the teaching did far more damage. "It could be," theologian Marie-Dominique Chenu speculated in a letter to the French bishops, "that Rome has lost, in a stroke, the authority that it took sixteen centuries to build."[16]

In Europe and North America, most theologians rejected the document's reasoning as inconsistent with new understandings of conscience and marriage in *Gaudium et Spes*. National groups of bishops issued statements on the encyclical—again unprecedented—and many statements, such as from West Germany, allowed couples to dissent "from a non-infallible church teaching in their private theory or practice."[17]

In a few areas of the world, Paul VI received strong episcopal support. "A child," the Polish bishops explained, "is not the private concern of the parent but a value about which the entire society must be concerned."[18] In Latin America, the Paul VI of *Populorum Progressio* mattered more than the Paul VI of *Humanae Vitae*. He received an enthusiastic welcome at Medellín in 1968, just one month after the release of *Humanae Vitae*. Dom Hélder Câmara had sent Paul VI a telegram pledging his adherence to *Humanae Vitae*. He admired Paul VI's dedication to economic development in the Global South and did not hide his distaste for European and American experts convinced that "the poor should limit the number of children they have."[19]

At a stormy 1968 meeting of Pax Romana, an international Catholic organization, these divisions burst into view. The Mexican American labor leader César Chávez, then at the height of his fame for organizing farmworkers in California, joined with Polish delegates to defend *Humanae Vitae*. As one delegate explained: "all the Third World delegations were strongly in favor of *Humanae Vitae* because they considered birth control and family planning as a weapon of American imperialism directed at them."[20]

The same dynamics evident in the birth control controversy—if in a less explosive key—became evident in discussions of divorce. In some European and Latin American countries, divorce had long been almost unobtainable, despite de facto marital separations. The most publicized debate occurred in Italy. Socialist legislators pushed through a liberalization of Italian divorce laws in 1970. Aggrieved Christian Democrats arranged for a referendum on the matter—Paul VI was more circumspect, sensing the unpopularity of the old restrictions—and were humiliated by a resounding defeat, with 60 percent of Italians rejecting "indissoluble marriage."[21] At the same time and for the same reasons, a liberal Catholic, Prime Minister Pierre Trudeau, maneuvered a Canadian law legalizing no-fault divorce through Parliament over the objections of Catholic bishops. He stressed the need to replace a language of "sin" or "theology" (words not in the legal code but used to discredit his opponents) with a secular vocabulary.[22]

Efforts to change divorce laws in majority Catholic countries such as the Philippines, Ireland, and Chile were unsuccessful. Filipino bishops fought off efforts to loosen divorce laws in the 1970s, and an Irish opinion poll of 1971 showed only 22 percent of adults in favor of removing the ban on divorce from the country's constitution. (Ireland's Cardinal William Conway stressed the ban as sustaining the "fabric of family life.")[23] Irish voters rejected a loosening of divorce laws as late as 1985. Chilean legislators—urged on by the country's bishops—rejected reform as late as 2004.[24] Still, the overall evolution had become clear. Voters and legislators were increasingly willing to take apart a Catholic moral code on censorship, contraception, and divorce, inserted into public law in much of the world in the early twentieth century and now seen as an unjust imposition of religious mores onto more secular societies.

III

THE PRIESTHOOD, oddly enough, had been a secondary topic at the Second Vatican Council when compared with the extended discussion of episcopal authority and the laity. The ontological difference "in essence" between ordained and lay Catholics was reiterated in *Lumen Gentium*. But the day-to-day role of priests among lay Catholics now called to holiness by virtue of their baptism received little explication.[25]

Celibacy was the hot-button issue. Catholics in the late 1960s resumed a conversation about celibacy begun in the decades after the French Revolution and sidelined by the ultramontane revival. Before the last session of the Second Vatican Council, a Brazilian bishop floated the idea of ordaining married men as diocesan priests due to the perennial lack of clergy across Latin America. In Brazil, the average parish nominally contained over seventeen thousand people, and 40 percent of the country's priests came from outside the country, with Italy contributing fourteen hundred men and West Germany and Holland together contributing over nine hundred.[26]

Paul VI withdrew the topic of celibacy from consideration at the Second Vatican Council, but his decision delayed a debate, rather than preventing one. The bishops had approved married male deacons over the objections of some bishops who thought such a practice threatened the celibate ideal. Ecumenical initiatives with Orthodox churches, even enhanced contact with Eastern rite Catholic churches, highlighted the presence of married male clergy in other traditions.

Celibacy itself did not cause an unprecedented exodus of men from the priesthood in the decade after the council. Uncertainty about clerical roles and hesitation about lifetime commitments probably played a bigger role. Regardless, the result was shocking. When men left the priesthood in the mid-twentieth century, as a handful did, their departure was treated as something between a scandal for the church and a source of grave shame for the individual. By 1970, departures could no longer be ignored. Over fifty thousand men left the priesthood between 1964 and 1986. Two-thirds of the priests who left were under the age of fifty-five.[27] A seminary rector in South Africa, where fifteen of sixty-one students left in a single year, wrote to his superiors of "a serious questioning attitude both as regards seminary life and as regards the priesthood itself."[28]

In the United States, a full 10 percent of clergy left the priesthood in the decade after the Second Vatican Council. In Spain, three thousand priests left in just over a decade, and the number of men in religious orders fell by a quarter. In Brazil, already burdened by a low priest-to-parishioner ratio, some 10 percent of the parishes by 1970 had no priests at all, and in some dioceses, such as the archdiocese of São Paulo, the number of men ordained in a given year was significantly lower than the number of men who departed.[29] In other locations, such as Poland and much of sub-Saharan Africa, the number of priests increased in the first generation after the council. But even when the retention crisis eased, as it did by the 1980s, clerical recruitment in most parts of the world never replicated the levels of the mid-twentieth century.[30]

In 1970, Brazilian bishops voted to ordain married men. They thought married clergy necessary to serve Amazonian regions where congregations went months without sight of a priest and because of this absence could not celebrate the eucharist.[31] At a 1971 episcopal synod, bishops from not just Brazil but also Canada, Holland, and Belgium supported ending mandatory celibacy. At least a thousand Dutch priests—out of eight thousand—endorsed a recommendation to make celibacy optional.[32]

The hierarchies of Zambia, Cameroon, and South Africa petitioned Rome to allow married men to serve as priests, in part because the growing number of African Catholics outpaced the more slowly growing number of African priests and in part, they claimed, because celibacy was less comprehensible in a context where kinship and family were so central to identity. (Some African bishops opposed any change of the rule on celibacy out of fear that married clergy would always be second class in Roman eyes.) Reports circulated of significant numbers of African priests, especially in rural areas, living with common-law families.

Paul VI rebuffed these requests. He first defended celibacy in a 1967 encyclical as a "brilliant jewel" and a countersign against "modern opinion."[33] The pope's arguments were "clear and abstract," one Chilean bishop replied, but neglected assessing the "signs of the times" as suggested by *Gaudium et Spes*.[34]

Paul VI also rejected arguments for women's ordination. He gestured, certainly, toward greater influence for women within the church. Perhaps to his regret, he granted an audience to Betty Friedan, author of *The Feminine Mystique*, who could not resist a jibe at a Vatican where "the only skirts . . . are those worn by the priests."[35] More substantively, he established a special study commission on women, asked the newly formed International Theological Commission whether women could, like men, be ordained as deacons, and requested the Pontifical Biblical Commission to assess whether women could be ordained as priests.

The answer to the last question was "possibly," according to the Pontifical Biblical Commission in 1975—the commission could find no scriptural warrant for not ordaining women. According to a statement by the Congregation for the Doctrine of the Faith the following year, however, the answer was "no."

These answers did not halt discussion. Women appointed to the papal study commission complained that the "inductive method used by *Gaudium et Spes* was not used."[36] They were correct. Arguments against women's ordination to the priesthood or the diaconate, or even women as homilists in ordinary parish settings, drew on the techniques of ressourcement but stacked the deck in favor of continuity. Here, too, scholars dove into the history of the early church, discerning whether Jesus's teaching to the disciples (who included women) differed from his teaching to the apostles (who included only men) and whether the liturgies of early Christian communities included any equivalent to women clergy.

Theologians and even bishops wondered why doctrinal development made sense in the area of religious liberty, but not in the type of person considered eligible for ordained ministry. It might be true, as theologian Karl Rahner noted, that since the early church only men had been ordained. It might also be true that this tradition should "be understood as a 'human' tradition like other traditions in the Church which were once unquestioned, had existed for a long time and nevertheless became obsolete as a result of sociological and cultural change."[37]

In the 1950s, as a top aide to Pius XII and then as archbishop of Milan, Giovanni Montini had been the establishment figure most supportive of ressourcement. In the 1970s, though, Paul VI resisted reforms around sexuality and gender. He knew that the women's movement had as yet barely reached Eastern Europe, Latin America, or Africa. In Nicaragua, as late as 1969, the country's bishops published a pastoral letter forbidding women to attend Mass without their heads covered.[38] Even in the United States, while a few liberal bishops lobbied for a proposed Equal Rights Amendment to the Constitution, a Catholic, Phyllis Schlafly, mobilized thousands of working- and middle-class women in a successful campaign against the amendment. She warned it would allow husbands to abandon their wives with little penalty and devalue traditional women's roles.[39]

These debates over women's equality occurred at the same time as the collapse of a separate women's sphere within the church. For almost every men's Catholic organization in the ultramontane era there existed a women's counterpart. This parallel world of women's schools, altar societies, and auxiliaries began to crumble as women entered the paid labor force in growing numbers. The daughters of the women who had once staffed and supported these organizations, sometimes the women themselves, came to resent, or find unnecessary, a segregation that now could seem less about differentiation than about inferiority.

The most dramatic changes occurred among women religious. The bishops at the council required all religious orders—men and women—to reassess their charism. Hundreds of religious orders involving hundreds of thousands of members embarked on this quest. They met in general congregations, researched the spiritual directives and writings of their founders, and tore away encrusted practices such as required prayer times or onerous clothing restrictions.

Members of men's and women's religious orders often discovered in their founders a piety less formulaic than the spiritual practices consolidated during the ultramontane era. They drew from these documents and conciliar texts to make the training of seminarians or novices less structured. In their schools, universities, and hospitals, they vowed to serve not only middle-class Catholics but the poor. Missionary work continued, but with cautions against assumptions of Western superiority and attempts at inculturation. The largest men's religious order, the Jesuits, at a turbulent General Congregation in Rome in 1974–1975, pledged "solidarity with the poor."[40]

The reassessment among women religious in Western Europe and North America was especially sweeping because it coincided with the women's movement. Few women religious in the 1960s described themselves as feminists. But they balked at the disjunction between their regimented lives and the call to engage the world emanating from the Second Vatican Council. In the United States, a Pittsburgh nun noted that a policeman might stop traffic and allow her to cross the street on a red light, but her own superiors required her to ask permission before attending a high school basketball game. When she proposed joining Dr. Martin Luther King's 1965 march at Selma, as many nuns did, her superior responded by informing her that "we can do more by staying home and praying" and saying, "We don't go out late in the evening, sister."[41]

The experience of the Dutch women's religious community, the Sisters of Charity of Our Lady Mother of Mercy, is illustrative. Founded in 1832, the Sisters of Charity expanded to England, the United States, and the Dutch colonies of Indonesia and Suriname in the nineteenth century and to Rhodesia, Germany, Brazil, and the Philippines in the twentieth. They numbered 3,447 sisters in 1962, 84 percent born in the Netherlands. Wherever a convent was located, whatever its members were doing, daily rhythms of prayer, mealtimes, and prescribed reading were predictable. Novices from outside Holland traveled to the home country for initial training, and sisters everywhere ate on Dutch plates and used Dutch cutlery. Mother superiors automatically enrolled sisters in the Catholic People's Party in the Netherlands for the "good of Catholic affairs" and in opposition to the "threat of communism." "We learned to do everything in the same way," recalled one General Superior in 1964, "working, eating, praying, having recreation, indeed dressing and undressing."[42]

After the council, many members of the Sisters of Charity abandoned markers of distinctiveness: moving into apartments in groups of three or four (as opposed to large convents) and abandoning the religious habit. One nun vividly recalled her shock at an international meeting of the order when she realized that some of the reform-minded Dutch sisters had begun wearing earrings.

When Catholic schools and hospitals closed in North America and Europe, in part because of competition with secular equivalents, in part because Catholic assimilation made them seem less necessary, some sisters shifted out of traditional roles as teachers and nurses. More volunteered for missionary work (notably in Brazil) and for direct parish ministry (alongside priests). Their commitment to the social justice dimensions of the conciliar documents surpassed that of any other group in the church.

Then there were fewer of them. The number of entrants into women's religious orders began declining before the council, not after. But the decline accelerated after 1965. Women religious, like men in religious orders, assessed whether they were called to celibacy with the added question of whether they wanted to labor in an institution in which they always, even if indirectly, answered to men. After the council, many members of the Sisters of Charity left, and far fewer women entered, with the total number of women in the order tumbling from close to four thousand in the early 1960s to below two thousand by 1990. (In once devout redoubts such as Quebec, the number of new entrants to women's religious orders fell an almost unbelievable 98.5 percent.)[43]

This exodus meant that even as the women's movement swept through the developed world, as the number of women doctors, lawyers, corporate leaders, government officials, and university professors increased, the leadership cadre within Catholicism became more male. The rate of departures from women's religious orders eventually stabilized, as it did for priests, but in North America and Western Europe the number of entrants to women's religious orders never came close to recovering the peak numbers of the 1940s and early 1950s or even the significantly reduced numbers of the 1970s.

One practical consequence of diminishing numbers of women religious was massive financial pressure on Catholic elementary schools, which had long relied on their devoted and inexpensive labor. Another consequence was a decrease in the number of single-sex women's Catholic secondary schools and colleges, as their justification became less clear and as the declining number of nuns made them vulnerable to takeover by once single-sex male but now coeducational competitors. In the dizzying speed of a generation, leaders of many women's religious orders in North America and Western Europe contemplated either their own abolition or the recruitment of members from the Global South. The single flourishing province within the Sisters of Charity in 1990— with a sizable number of young members—was in Indonesia.

IV

A FINAL ISSUE, abortion, left a more enduring policy footprint. Just as contraception became legal and available almost everywhere, and just as divorce laws were loosened, an abortion rights movement emerged. Illegal in most of the world in 1960—except in Japan and most of the communist bloc—abortion became legal in most Western European and North American countries by 1980.

The process was contentious everywhere, but the most explosive debate occurred in the United States. Many Catholics involved in the civil rights and antiwar movements glided into antiabortion activism because they identified that cause, too, with a commitment to social justice. The Archdiocese of San Francisco Social Justice Commission declared in 1967 that its members had "consistently supported principles of social justice, and their concrete application, in such community concerns as race relations, elimination of poverty, collective bargaining for farm workers and similar issues concerning human dignity." "We believe it entirely consistent," they continued, ". . . to now urge your opposition to the Beilenson Bill [which] abridges the right to life of an unborn child and thereby works a grave injustice."[44]

Witness—to use the vocabulary of the day—in opposition to abortion law reform faced two obstacles. The first was obvious. Public opinion polls in the late 1960s revealed that Catholics were increasingly sympathetic to changes in abortion laws, although more opposed reform than either Protestants or Jews.[45] Catholic women were as conservative as Catholic men on the issue, and women played as important a role in the struggle to maintain laws restricting abortion as they did in the effort to abolish them. The typical antiabortion activist after 1973 was a married, lower-middle-class Catholic woman. A self-described Long Island Catholic housewife, Ellen McCormack, ran for the Democratic nomination

Pro-life rally in Washington, DC, 1979. *(Bettmann via Getty Images)*

for president of the United States in 1976 on a pro-life platform, scorned by feminist women leaders and male Democratic Party officials, but also capturing 3 to 5 percent of the vote in each primary she entered.[46]

Catholic credibility on the topic of abortion remained limited because of the absence of women in clerical roles. On one side, pro-choice women spoke of the terrors of unwanted pregnancy and the dangers of illegal abortions. On the other side, priests or (male) Catholic lawyers outlined in abstract terminology their opposition to the taking of innocent life. As one sympathetic colleague told law professor John Noonan, the "impasse over [abortion] will not be broken by talking (as Catholics have been prone to talk) only about the right to life. If nothing else, that has been a principle which has precluded the need to look at the evidence, or listen to the testimony of women who want abortions." Exploiting this weakness, pro-choice activists encouraged pro-choice Catholic women to step into the spotlight. The director of the National Organization to Repeal Abortion Laws recommended that a Massachusetts organizer find a "Catholic woman to organize other Catholics with the same conviction."

Catholic views on contraception were the second obstacle. Most Catholic intellectuals in the late 1960s believed that abortion and contraception were distinct issues: one could justify a change in teaching on contraception, on Catholic grounds, without favoring the legalization of abortion. But separating the two issues in the public mind was easier said than done. When the American Civil Liberties Union reversed itself and took a position in favor of abortion on demand in 1967, one Notre Dame law school professor (and active member) complained that the organization had abandoned the "first principle of secular ethics . . . that life is an absolute value." The same professor conceded that the "medieval attitude" of Catholic leaders on contraception diminished Catholic credibility, but he still found the resolution of "human problems by the destruction of life" appalling. The director of the ACLU replied that he and his colleagues now equated "anti-abortion positions with anti-birth control ones, and the defenders [of restrictions on abortion] with an effort to enact theological positions into law."[47]

Abortion rights advocates had as many losses as wins at the ballot box and in state legislatures but proved stunningly successful at the US Supreme

Court. The scope of the *Roe v. Wade* decision in 1973—overturning fifty state laws—generated an antiabortion campaign in the United States, led initially by Catholics, that became one of the most enduring social movements of the twentieth and twenty-first centuries. Some of the same debates occurred in France, West Germany, and Italy. Here, too, Catholic activists regretted that *Humanae Vitae* had complicated their ability to frame abortion as a human rights issue, instead of an example of religious special pleading. But more communal understandings of society in Western Europe meant that access to legal abortion came with more significant restrictions on abortion during the later stages of pregnancy and more generous maternity benefits for women carrying pregnancies to term.[48] In Italy, for example, the abortion issue virtually disappeared from public life after a public referendum in 1981, with defeats for two competing proposals to either make abortion illegal or to eliminate almost all restrictions on the procedure. In Portugal and Spain, the legislative process was more contentious but the outcomes were similar.[49]

V

WRITING FROM PARIS during the turbulent summer of 1968, Yves Congar thought it "unjust and even stupid to attribute to the council the difficulties that we are having today." Still, even Congar conceded that "everything is being called into question at the same time."[50] A discouraged Paul VI admitted a few weeks later that no one had predicted the "acute and complex internal revolution" occurring inside the church.[51]

The question is simple: Did the reforms of the Second Vatican Council cause the decline in Catholic practice or did they limit its effect?

The decline was real. Catholic attendance at weekly services had long been higher than Protestant attendance in every industrial country. In West Germany in 1965, over half of Catholics attended church services each week compared with less than 10 percent of Protestants.[52] Other sacramental indicators were equally robust. Virtually every baby born in Spain, for example, was baptized Catholic into the early 1980s, and over 90 percent of marriages included a Catholic ceremony.[53]

This high level of practice made the descent more wrenching. The pace was not uniform: the falloff was initially much less drastic in the

United States, West Germany, and Chile than in French-speaking Canada. But the pattern was clear. Mainline Protestant church attendance and affiliation declined, too, perhaps at an even faster rate, but Protestants had not just completed the largest ecumenical council in history designed to energize religious practice.

The negative reaction to *Humanae Vitae* played a role. The disjunction between church teaching that formally defined using birth control as a sin and an overwhelming majority of couples willing to use birth control acted as a significant deterrent to confession, a sacramental practice that collapsed almost instantaneously in the early 1970s.[54]

If the reflex reaction for Catholics during the ultramontane era had been to build their own institutions to protect the faithful from a hostile modernity, the reaction after the council was to encourage engagement. The theme for the 1968 Katholikentag, held in Essen, West Germany, and attended by overflowing crowds of delegates and observers, was *"Mitten in dieser Welt"* or "in the midst of the world."

How should the world be engaged? In Quebec, lay Catholics urged church officials to relinquish responsibilities for education and social welfare, not, at least initially, out of a desire to secularize the society but from a conviction that laypeople must bring Catholic ideals into state agencies.[55] In France, especially, but across much of Western Europe, Catholic trade unions diminished their confessional identity in order to enhance their influence.[56]

Tracking the path of conciliar reform in one country, the Netherlands, and then one parish outside of Denver, Colorado, is illuminating.

Prior to the council, Dutch Catholicism seemed an unequivocal ultramontane success story. Mass attendance was the highest in Western Europe and religious vocations numerous. Dutch Catholics numbered only 1 percent of the world's total but supplied 10 percent of the world's missionaries. Ninety percent of Catholic children—and there were many Catholic children, given one of the highest birth rates in Europe—attended Catholic schools. Fewer than 10 percent of Dutch Catholics married outside the faith. When a Dutch Catholic died, the deceased was automatically buried in a Catholic cemetery. One comedian explained Dutch Catholicism this way: "In our church formerly everything was forbidden, except what was allowed—and you had to do that."[57]

No bishops had been more committed to reform than the Dutch, and as a group they published a pastoral letter anticipating conciliar themes.[58] They challenged the preparatory texts and promoted ecumenical dialogue. Within Holland itself, saturation coverage of the council produced high levels of awareness of events in Rome. Divides between Catholics and Protestants had long been the central cleavage in Dutch society. But attitudes were shifting. When Princess Irene converted to Catholicism in 1963 and announced plans to marry a Spanish Catholic nobleman, polls suggested that most Dutch citizens thought she should remain in the line of succession to the historically Protestant throne. (She eventually withdrew.)[59]

Catholic practice in the first years after the council changed almost instantly. Liturgical experiments were widespread—including Masses using Beatles songs. Priests and nuns trained in university-sponsored theological centers, as opposed to stand-alone seminaries or novitiates. Catholic trade unions merged with Protestant counterparts. Catholic boy scouts merged with Protestant and secular troops.[60] When Tomáš Halík managed to leave communist Czechoslovakia for the first time in the spring of 1967, he did so on a student exchange with Holland's Catholic Tilburg University. Upon his arrival, he was startled to learn that Dutch students considered texts by Jacques Maritain and Emmanuel Mounier, obtained by Halík with difficulty in communist Prague, "thirty years out of date." On the evening of Halík's arrival, the students in Tilburg had organized a seminar entitled "God Is Dead and Has Left His Mausoleum: The Church." An astonished Halík realized that the students were also coordinating a protest directed against the local bishop, who had disapproved of the recent civil marriage of the university's priest-chaplain.[61]

The Dutch bishops issued a catechism that replaced the existing catechism aimed at children. (The subtitle of the English translation, revealingly, was "Catholic Faith for Adults.") It became an unlikely best seller. "We too," the text began, "as Christians, are men with enquiring minds." Church teaching on contraception was judged open to "development," and other religions were assessed sympathetically.[62]

Even as they authorized the catechism, Dutch bishops organized a massive National Pastoral Council involving laypeople, priests, nuns, and bishops to discuss Catholicism's future. Bishops spoke at such gatherings "as individuals and as a college" but not as figures demanding obedience. The optimism of synod participants, the sense that they were building something unprecedented, was palpable, even delirious. "I feel in writing you like Moses before the burning bush," wrote one Dutch bishop, "as I stand before a moment of history, an event that history before us has never before seen and of which we do not know how it will turn out."

The Roman response was more restrained. Paul VI, and then, more reluctantly, the Dutch bishops, ordered investigations of the catechism. Later editions were printed with appendices stressing original sin and hierarchical authority. The pope expressed his disappointment at the unwillingness of Dutch Catholics, even Dutch bishops, to defend celibacy as a "principal law of our Latin Church."[63]

Dutch Catholicism in 1978 was more oriented toward social justice, more collegial in its governance, and more ecumenical in its outreach than the Dutch Catholicism of 1958. It was also less stable. The reaction to *Humanae Vitae* was explosive. Most bishops made it clear that they thought contraception permissible, as did the overwhelming majority of Dutch Catholic women.[64] The priesthood entered a state of permanent crisis. Eleven men resigned from the priesthood in 1960; 243 in 1970. Mass attendance declined 20 percent in a ten-year period.[65] Most Catholics still baptized their children, and most couples married within the church, but these numbers, too, soon began a precipitous slide. One in three baptized Dutch Catholic children born in the 1960s would abandon the church entirely. Within another generation, sociologists would identify the Netherlands, one of the most religious places in the industrial world in the 1950s, as one of the most secular.[66]

VI

HALF A WORLD AWAY from the Netherlands, at St. Jude's Parish in a booming suburb outside of Denver, Colorado, an energetic young pastor began the construction of an open-plan church in the architectural spirit of the Second Vatican Council. Parishioners had gathered for years in the gym of Alameda Public High School—jokingly dubbed Our Lady of Alameda—so the new building was welcome. On the first Sunday, parishioners entering the new church gasped in amazement. Instead of the customary ornate decorations, the building was constructed out of simple materials so as to focus attention on the celebration of the Mass. A stark altar faced the congregation. The stained glass windows had abstract designs. No altar rail separated priests from people.[67]

These suburban Coloradans delighted in their new church. They recalled amusement, not just anguish, among both priests and laypeople upon learning of *Humanae Vitae*, since it seemed counter to what they considered good sense. They liked dialogue homilies, where their pastor engaged parishioners in an informal conversation. They took communion in the hand, as at a meal, instead of kneeling and on the tongue. They celebrated intimate Masses on weeknights in parishioners' homes. A folk guitar choir led the congregation in singing.

Despite a daunting 1,100 children registered in the parish, the pastor and the parish council (itself a conciliar innovation) agreed not to build a school. No nuns seemed willing or able to staff it. The emphasis instead was on small faith-sharing groups, which were popular, and after-school or Sunday catechesis for children, which was hit or miss.

A commitment to social justice and a global church became evident, and the parish sent 5 percent of its income to various good causes, including a sister parish in Uganda. The parish sponsored Vietnamese Catholic refugee families as they fled to the United States after the end of the Vietnam War. When nuns from a local college protested the presence of nuclear weapons at a facility outside of Denver, some parishioners supported their efforts.

The end result, as in Holland, was a more communal parish responsive to a Second Vatican Council welcomed by both priests and laypeople. But stability was elusive. The charismatic founding pastor at St. Jude's, exhausted from the strains of parish management and struggling to control an alcohol problem, resigned from the priesthood. He later married. Even the modernist architecture that once seemed so refreshing became viewed by some parishioners as uninspired. In a later refurbishment, a large crucifix and statues of Mary and Joseph were placed near the altar, facing out toward the congregation.

VII

BY THE LATE 1970S, the reaction against post-conciliar turmoil had become obvious. One bishop, France's Marcel Lefebvre, a founder of the conservative Coetus Internationalis Patrum group at the council, rejected the Vatican II documents on the liturgy, religious liberty, and relationships with non-Christians. In a telling comparison, he termed the council a "French revolution." He formed a breakaway church in 1975 and named it after the anti-modernist pope, Pius X. Lefebvre would eventually be excommunicated for ordaining his own bishops along with dozens of priests.[68]

The most painful disputes occurred within the church. Many leading conciliar figures—Cardinal Suenens, Cardinal Lercaro, Marie-Dominique Chenu, Yves Congar—thought controversy after the council reflected a failure of nerve, not an overly ambitious pace of change. Other conciliar veterans were more skeptical. They continued to endorse the council they had done so much to shape, but they became wary of reforms proposed in its name. They agreed with Henri de Lubac, who worried that "today we are witnesses to an endeavor that wants to dissolve the Church into the world."[69]

Joseph Ratzinger became their leader. Ratzinger had doubted the logic of *Humanae Vitae* and expressed openness toward remarriage within the church for divorced Catholics. Now he saw reform as a false path. Rebellious students disrupted his Tübingen classroom during the 1968 protest movements; the experience dismayed him. He described the church as "thoroughly shaky and deeply divided." "The sacramental principle is no longer self-evident," he grimly announced. Some Catholics mistakenly believed that "the only reliable thing is democratic control."[70] After cautiously endorsing *Gaudium et Spes* in 1965, he now bemoaned its "tragic one-sidedness."[71]

Paul VI did not engage in these polemics. But he spent the final years of his life distressed by ecclesial turmoil. He never issued another encyclical following the traumatic reception of *Humanae Vitae*. He regretted that Catholicism contained so many "baptized people who for the most

Two of the most influential theologians of the twentieth century: Karl
Rahner, S.J. (left), and Joseph Ratzinger, in 1971. *(KNA Bild, #100216)*

part have not formally renounced their Baptism but who are entirely
indifferent to it and not living in accordance with it."[72]

The creases in Paul VI's face revealed the strains of the office. Just
after his eightieth birthday, he learned of the kidnapping of his friend,
Aldo Moro, five-time prime minister and current president of the Christian Democratic Party, by the Red Brigades terrorist group. Paul VI had
first met Moro while serving as a chaplain for a Catholic youth group
in the 1930s, and the two men had worked together for political and
religious reform. Just as Moro attempted to loosen a sclerotic Christian
Democratic Party bureaucracy, Paul VI attempted to reform the curia.

In the days after the kidnapping, Paul VI scoured press reports and
watched news broadcasts. He knew that Moro—an advocate of collaboration between Christian Democrats and communists—had enemies. One Italian cardinal confided to a friend (on a phone tapped by
the police) that Moro "had gotten what he deserved."[73] Moro wrote
directly to the pope. He asked Paul VI for assistance in the name of a

shared "Christian humanism." Paul VI stayed up past midnight drafting a response, which his office released in photocopy form, giving
reporters a glimpse of the pope's own handwriting. He pleaded with
"the men of the Brigades" to release a "good and upright man" who
"shares with you the common dignity of a brother in humanity." He
covertly gathered funds to support a ransom effort but he also hesitated
to challenge government leaders unwilling to negotiate with the Red
Brigades. Moro thought this unwillingness a rejection of Catholicism's
"long humanitarian tradition."[74] "Everything is useless," he complained
in a final note, "when you do not wish to open the door." He added,
unfairly, "The Pope did little."[75]

The Red Brigade kidnappers executed Moro on the fifty-fifth day of
his captivity. They stuffed his body in the trunk of a car and parked it
on a Roman street before alerting the media. Breaking Vatican protocol
to celebrate a layperson's funeral, Paul VI arrived three days later at the
enormous cathedral of St. John Lateran surrounded by police with
machine guns drawn. He knew that members of Moro's immediate
family would not attend the liturgy, so infuriated were they with Christian Democratic officials, whom they judged to have betrayed their husband and father. The distraught pope dwelt in his homily on the "unjust

Funeral Mass of Aldo Moro, Rome, 1978. *(Getty photos)*

outrage" committed against Moro, who had done so much for the Italian people. He wondered about the "silence of God."[76]

Paul VI continued to meditate on his friend's imprisonment and death in the following months. He jotted down a reference to Luke 21:19 on the ability to "know how to suffer."[77] Dom Hélder Câmara met with Paul VI in Rome that summer. The pope described himself, using a Portuguese term, as "*saudade*," or gripped by melancholy. He urged Câmara to continue preaching "justice and love."[78]

By this time, the Brazilian church—leading the resistance to the military junta, with thousands of parishes and schools and roughly fifty thousand ecclesial base communities—was the world's most radical. Activists stressed "starting from the poor and their historic project."[79] But would these ideas and these institutions endure? The baroque prose favored by many liberation theologians and the disdain some expressed for popular piety did not endear them to all Catholics. "What's the use of venerating pretty images of Christ," Câmara once asked an audience for whom this veneration had long been encouraged, "if we fail to see in him those who need to be rescued from their poverty?"[80] Millions of onetime Catholics became members of Protestant Pentecostal churches led by ministers preaching a gospel of free markets and social mobility.[81]

Paul VI died three months after burying Aldo Moro. When the world's cardinals assembled to choose his successor, they selected an amiable Italian. He took the name John Paul in honor of his two immediate predecessors. He died a month later.

When the cardinals gathered again, for the second time in six weeks, the mood was somber. After two Italian cardinals deadlocked in the opening ballots, the electors turned to the young (only fifty-eight), charismatic, polyglot cardinal archbishop of Kraków, Karol Wojtyła. He became the first pope born outside of Italy since the sixteenth century and the longest-serving occupant of the office since Pius IX.

Immediately after his election, John Paul II began to crisscross the globe at a relentless pace. He made 109 trips outside of Italy as pope, speaking to more people than any person in human history, utterly comfortable on every stage. His first visit to Brazil in 1980 included a four-hour lecture to a mute assembly of Brazil's bishops, often lauded for their focus on social justice. Cardinal Arns in São Paolo had only the year before supported striking metalworkers and a young union activist and future president, Luis Inácio Lula Da Silva, as part of his resistance to Brazil's military regime. Now John Paul II instructed the bishops to avoid "partisan struggles or . . . strife among groups and systems." He urged them not to diminish their spiritual charism for "political commitments."[82]

When he landed in Recife, John Paul II greeted Dom Hélder Câmara with evident delight, referring to him as the "brother of the poor, my brother." His homily at a Mass held in one of Recife's favelas, attended by one million people, pleaded for a just distribution of land and for preservation of Brazil's natural environment. But the man he appointed as Câmara's successor in 1985 would shutter Câmara's vaunted Justice and Peace Commission. Upon the site a developer erected a shopping mall.[83]

FOURTEEN

Charisma

John Paul II and the End of the Cold War

I

HIS LIFE POSSESSED A cinematic grandeur. Born in 1920 in a village twenty miles southwest of Kraków, Karol Wojtyła witnessed some of the most harrowing moments of Poland's harrowing twentieth century. Karol was a bright, athletic student, admired across the town's religious divides. He played on the Jewish side in soccer games between the town's Catholic and Jewish boys. His older sister died before Wojtyła's birth; his mother when Wojtyła was nine. An older brother died when Wojtyła was twelve. Beginning his university studies in Kraków in 1938, Wojtyła put most of his energy into college theatrical productions. After the German invasion of Poland in 1939, he and his father fled east until they realized that Stalin had arranged with Hitler for Soviet armies to occupy the eastern half of the country. They returned to Kraków, where the Germans closed Wojtyła's university. His father died, leaving him bereft of any family. He spent the first years of World War II laboring in a quarry, rubbing petroleum jelly on his face to protect himself against bitterly cold winds on the thirty-minute walk to work. In off hours, he attended a clandestine seminary, once evading a dragnet while hiding in a basement closet as Gestapo officers searched the upper floors. After the war, sent to Rome to study by his archbishop, he wrote a hurried dissertation on the sixteenth-century Spanish mystic John of the Cross.

Returning to Poland, he translated into Polish a major text of the German phenomenologist Max Scheler, influential for Jacques Maritain and many other Catholic intellectuals. He criticized Scheler for veering toward relativism and avoiding the "normative ought." But he admired Scheler's focus on concrete human experience and blended it with the neo-Thomism he had absorbed in Rome and Kraków.[1] As a parish priest and university professor, he was an immediate success. He often took the night train from Kraków to Lublin, arriving in time to teach classes at the Catholic University. He counseled college students and young professionals not only after class, but also on hiking trips and retreats, saying Mass outdoors in violation of government protocols.

Appointed a bishop at the age of thirty-eight, he played a significant role at the Second Vatican Council through participation in the debates over the draft texts for the Declaration on Religious Freedom and *Gaudium et Spes*. His charisma was compelling. As Yves Congar recorded, Wojtyła "made a very great impression. His personality is imposing. A power radiates from it, an attraction, a certain prophetic force that is very calm, but incontestable."[2] Henri de Lubac thought Wojtyła possessed "a profound Christian sense, without being at all rigid."[3]

Wearing sunglasses and his episcopal robes, Wojtyła could evoke a clerical James Bond. After the council, despite visa hassles with wary Polish state officials, he deepened his ties to church figures across the world through trips to the United States (twice), Canada, the Philippines, and Australia. These visits confirmed his assessment of a "false irenicism, humanism and even secularism" infecting Western European and North American Catholic intellectuals.[4] At the invitation of Paul VI, he offered a Lenten retreat for the pope and the curia. With Paul VI taking copious notes, he analyzed "dechristianization." It occurred "by force" in Eastern Europe; by osmosis in the West.[5]

Wojtyła made his version of personalism especially visible through two post-conciliar issues. The first was contraception. Like personalists everywhere, he saw marriage as about more than procreation, as a "genuine union of persons." But while many personalists moved from this definition of marriage to support for married couples using contraception, Wojtyła did not. Working with Wanda Półtawska, a physician who had survived four years in the Ravensbrück concentration camp, Wojtyła came to see contraception as itself a violation of the human person. His 1960 *Love and Responsibility* defined sexual intercourse as possessing "full value" only "when it contains the conscious acceptance of the possibility of parenthood."[6]

Placed on the expanded papal birth control commission by Paul VI, Wojtyła did not play an active role, but he did cast one of the few votes against an alteration to church teaching and personally conveyed his views to Paul VI in the run-up to *Humanae Vitae*. After the encyclical's release, he welcomed its conclusions but wished it had been made "more easily accessible to the modern world."[7] In the early 1970s, he established dozens of family counseling and marriage preparation centers in the Kraków archdiocese, hoping to create a "Polish model of pastoral care for families." (He also pressured Polish writers who endorsed contraceptives to alter their views.)[8]

The second area of Wojtyła's personalist influence was human rights. If in the 1950s Wojtyła shared conventional Catholic anxieties about the alienation produced by capitalism, in the late 1960s he stressed threats to the human person. As he confided to Henri de Lubac, "the evil of our times consists in the first place of a kind of degradation indeed in a pulverization of the fundamental uniqueness of each human person."[9]

Wojtyła's *The Acting Person*, published in Polish in 1969, is a dense, almost impenetrable text. (Kraków priests joked that it would be assigned in purgatory.) But its focus on solidarity and the common good as existing beyond particular communities fed into claims for human rights.[10] Adam Michnik, the secular Polish intellectual most dedicated to establishing common ground with the church, recalled Wojtyła as someone "who used our language and talked clearly about human rights . . . we knew we could count on his sympathy."[11] After government officials prohibited a student group in Kraków from organizing a lecture on "Orwell's 1984 and Poland Today," Wojtyła arranged for the lecture to be hosted in a local parish.[12]

II

JOHN PAUL II'S ENERGY, before the onset of the Parkinson's disease that marred his final years, makes it tempting to substitute his biography for a history of the church in the late twentieth century. Along with his closest aide, Joseph Ratzinger, who became his prefect for the Congregation of the Doctrine of the Faith in 1981 and his successor in 2005 as Benedict XVI, John Paul II set the terms of discussion within the church—and occasionally within the wider world—for more than a generation. Together, the two men would work for thirty-five years to reconstitute Catholic life in a world where, in Ratzinger's view, "the classical supports of a Christian society have been destroyed."[13]

John Paul II immediately reassessed how Catholics should navigate the challenges of the Cold War. Six months after his election, John Paul II returned to his native Poland. From the moment he arrived, with church bells pealing across the country as his plane touched down, his presence conveyed a more confrontational message than that carried by the cautious Vatican (and West German) policy of *Ostpolitik*. Speaking in Warsaw's Victory Square, he noted that the underground Polish army had launched a doomed uprising in 1944 against the *Wehrmacht* from that very spot, while Soviet armies on the other side of the Vistula River refused to assist them. "In how many places in Europe and the world has [the Polish soldier] cried with his death," he emphasized, "that there can be no just Europe without the independence of Poland marked on its map!"[14] The crowds packing every event—25 percent of the Polish population attended a papal Mass in person—drove the point home. Newspapers and television cameras covered nothing else. This "most fantastic pilgrimage in the history of contemporary Europe," in the words of Adam Michnik, became a tutorial on nonviolent resistance to the communist state.[15]

John Paul II did not instigate the formation of an independent trade union, Solidarity, a year later. But the "awakened consciences" of Polish workers, in the words of a contemporary analyst, stemmed in part from the exhilarating papal visit. The term "solidarity" had diverse roots,

Pope John Paul II in Kraków, Poland, 1979. *(Bettman via Getty Images)*

but its resonance within Catholic circles and in John Paul II's writing was deep.[16]

Within a year, the Solidarity movement enrolled a stunning ten million workers. At shipyards in the port city of Gdańsk, the epicenter of the movement, workers attended daily Mass around an altar inside Gate #2. On the gate they pinned a large color photograph of John Paul II. One of the workers, Lech Wałęsa, soon Solidarity's leader, began a practice of speaking about the goals of workers after the conclusion of the Mass. Polish bishops sent out communiques invoking *Gaudium et Spes* and the "right of workers to free association in unions which genuinely represent them."[17] John Paul II published an encyclical outlining the need for "solidarity" in light of the "exploitation of the workers."[18] In turn, the first official Solidarity statement of goals invoked the encyclical.[19]

The Polish government crushed this initial phase of the movement with the declaration of martial law and the imprisonment of many Solidarity leaders in December 1981. Still, the circulation of dissident materials and clandestine meetings between various opposition groups did not cease. American trade unions and Christian Democratic governments in Western Europe secretly provided financial aid. So, too, did the new American president, Ronald Reagan. Reagan's rhetoric was not subtle—he termed the Soviet Union the "evil empire"—but he shared with John Paul II a not-so-utopian conviction that the current geopolitical order would not endure.

At the same time, the stagflation (high unemployment and high inflation) tormenting the developed world in the 1970s, and the even more devastating economic crisis sweeping through the communist bloc, prompted new questions. Catholics more enamoured of free markets than the authors of papal encyclicals seized the opportunity to reassert the importance of economic growth and entrepreneurship. Some of the first Catholics to do so emerged from the unlikely setting of Franco's Spain, where a group of priests and laypeople fused conservatism on moral and sexual matters with economic liberalism. The primary carriers of this ideology were members of Opus Dei, a religious movement founded in the early 1930s. The first generation of Opus Dei priests and lay affiliates did not challenge Franco's restrictions on civil liberties, but they dedicated themselves to a modernization of the Spanish economy, emphasizing ties with the European community and quietly countering Franco's instinct to isolate Spain from global markets.[20] They founded Spain's leading business school, the University of Navarra, in Pamplona in 1958 and established affiliated campuses across Latin America.[21]

Given his repeated warnings against consumerism, John Paul II fit no one's definition of a libertarian. Still, he challenged not just Soviet control of Poland, but the entire communist project, with its restrictions on freedom of religion, most of all, but also its restrictions on free markets. Unsurprisingly, John Paul II warmed to the traditional piety and market-friendly ethos of Opus Dei, and in 1982 he made Opus Dei a personal prelature reporting to the Vatican and not to local bishops. He fast-tracked the canonization of the movement's founder.

Similar ideas about the relationship between markets and human flourishing resonated in the United States. Here the protagonists were not Opus Dei technocrats but the onetime radical journalist Michael Novak, the writer and (later) papal biographer George Weigel, the Lutheran pastor and, after his conversion, Catholic priest Richard John Neuhaus, and the former secretary of the treasury William Simon. These men translated John Paul II's economic vision into a variant on Reagan-era Republican Party orthodoxy. Novak's 1982 *The Spirit of*

Democratic Capitalism, dedicated to John Paul II, argued that capitalism properly understood protected human dignity far better than socialism or ill-formed notions of "class struggle." When the American bishops authored a pastoral letter urging government officials to substantially enhance services for the poor and reduce income inequality, positions that placed them to the left of the Democratic Party, Novak coordinated a statement lambasting the bishops for ignoring the virtues of "free economic institutions . . . free economic activism, property rights, markets, incentives and invention."[22] Neuhaus learned with delight that John Paul II and the papal household subscribed to his newly founded journal *First Things*.[23]

The same alliances shaped a brief skirmish over the nuclear arms race. Even as Catholic views on the economy shifted to the left in the 1970s, so too did church leaders around the world become more pacifist, more skeptical of nuclear deterrence than would have seemed possible during Pius XII's papacy. Lay Catholic groups inspired by the council, most notably the Sant'Egidio group based in Rome, helped negotiate an end to conflicts in places as diverse as Mozambique and the Balkans. Bishops began to speak out. In 1983 alone, in reaction to the Reagan administration boost in defense spending and the NATO decision to place intermediate nuclear missiles in Western Europe, a dozen bishops' conferences from Japan to Belgium to Hungary released statements decrying the arms race.[24]

West German and American bishops issued the most sophisticated documents. In both countries, the process of drafting the letters, including numerous public discussions, signaled a new episcopal confidence on the public stage. The West German bishops and leading Catholic intellectuals engaged the leader of the West German Social Democratic Party in a dialogue on "peacemaking."[25] Eminences such as George Kennan, a leading architect of American Cold War strategy in the 1940s, called the American bishops' letter the "most profound and searching inquiry" of warfare in the nuclear age.[26]

The same Catholics attracted to President Reagan's free market views challenged these efforts to edge away from nuclear deterrence, with Michael Novak accusing the bishops of not "defending the innocent, by having no deterrent at all."[27] The secretaries of defense and state in the Reagan administration, as well as the head of the National Security Council, registered their opposition. Reagan himself wrote John Paul II emphasizing his own determination to eliminate nuclear weapons, but he thought the first step required a nuclear buildup, not a freeze in arms production. When Reagan first met John Paul II, he showed him spy satellite photos of Soviet nuclear missile placements in Poland.

John Paul II summoned the leader of the United States bishops' conference to Rome and urged him not to encourage unilateral disarmament or pacifism given Soviet militarization. He would soon appoint a former military chaplain, John O'Connor, as archbishop of New York. Privately convinced that the bishops underestimated Soviet recalcitrance, Reagan remained publicly upbeat. When queried at a press conference after the publication of the final draft of the bishops' letter, Reagan insisted that the bishops and the administration "were doing the same thing."[28]

III

John Paul II made a second papal visit to Poland in 1983. Five hundred thousand people attended one event, one million the next, with crowds chanting the pope's name. Solidarity remained banned, but John Paul II slipped the phrase "fundamental solidarity between human beings" into a homily, and the crowd roared with laughter and applause. "The first visit broke through a barrier of fear," one intellectual speculated, "perhaps this one can break through the barrier of hopelessness."[29] In Hungary, communist secret agents had infiltrated almost every Catholic group. In East Germany, the Stasi (Ministry for State Security) secretly tape-recorded parishioners in the confessional. But in Poland, independent Catholic activists and organizations remained major political actors.[30]

A young Warsaw priest, Jerzy Popiełuszko, joined the crowds welcoming the pope. Sent by Cardinal Wyszyński to minister to workers in a steel mill, Popiełuszko's sermons, broadcast over Radio Free Europe, attracted large audiences. His stress on "human dignity" invoked the Second Vatican Council just as his pleas to "live in truth" referenced Czech dissident Václav Havel.[31] Popiełuszko's kidnapping, the search for his kidnappers, the discovery of his battered body tossed into a reservoir, and the arrest of unrepentant officials from the Interior Ministry mesmerized the nation. One of the largest crowds since the imposition of martial law gathered outside the church for Popiełuszko's funeral, with Solidarity activists such as Lech Wałęsa offering eulogies.

The alliance between church leaders and leading intellectuals strengthened. A Gdańsk shipyard pastor offered a homily in tribute to Adam Michnik, imprisoned for much of the decade, "for being loyal to the cause of human solidarity in Poland."[32] When John Paul II visited Poland for a third time as pope, in 1987, he again made a point of using the word "solidarity" and defined it "as an essential part of the consistent message of the Church's social teaching."[33]

The collapse of communist rule in Poland and Eastern Europe rested more on Mikhail Gorbachev's unwillingness to send tanks to Warsaw, Prague, and East Berlin than efforts by Polish activists or John Paul II. Still, the Catholic role was significant. As the Polish economy crumbled in the late 1980s, desperate communist leaders permitted the first free elections since the 1920s, and the political party formed out of Solidarity registered stunning triumphs. (The party did best in regions where Mass attendance was the highest.)[34] In September 1989, Tadeusz Mazowiecki, friendly with John Paul II since the 1950s, a close observer of the Second Vatican Council, and a founder of Solidarity, became the first noncommunist prime minister of an independent Poland since before World War II. Two months later the Berlin Wall fell. Leaders of both the Soviet Union (before its dissolution) and the United States agreed to destroy part of their nuclear arsenal in treaties far more ambitious than any imagined during the debate on the arms race less than a decade before.

John Paul II assessed the post–Cold War world in 1991 with *Centesimus Annus*, an encyclical marking the one-hundredth anniversary of *Rerum Novarum*. The pope consulted with numerous economists, including Jeffrey Sachs, the American leading Poland's transition from a communist command economy to a market system. Sachs compared Poland and Spain—two rural Catholic countries on Europe's periphery with populations and economies of roughly similar size in 1950, but with Spain's per capita income four times that of communist Poland by 1989.[35]

More admiring of capitalism than his predecessors, John Paul II praised the free market as "the most efficient instrument for utilizing resources and effectively responding to needs."[36] In the United States, Richard John Neuhaus broke the press embargo on the encyclical and published a fawning assessment in the *Wall Street Journal* beneath the headline "The Pope Affirms the 'New Capitalism.' "[37]

The headline was misleading. Even as he acknowledged the importance of markets, John Paul II added that "there are many human needs which find no place on the market." He lamented a "destructive competitiveness" imposed on workers and a "superficial" consumerism. He hoped that the world would not fall prey to an "unbridled affirmation of self-interest."[38] When he visited Poland again that same year, he scolded more than he celebrated. He urged compatriots not to be "trapped by all of these forces of desire which slumber in you as a source of sin."[39]

IV

IF IN POLAND and much of Eastern Europe the struggle against communism culminated in independence and triumph, events in South Korea and the Philippines were equally thrilling. The contexts were different. South Korean Catholics numbered perhaps 10 percent of the population, although they were overrepresented in elite sectors because of a long-standing Catholic focus on education. In the Philippines, as in Poland, Catholics were an overwhelming majority. Eighty percent of the population claimed to attend Mass once a month, and Catholicism had long ago fused with national identity.[40] The most revealing comparison was with the Catholic experience in Latin America. Authoritarian dictators in both South Korea and the Philippines, like those in Argentina and Brazil, had long counted on Catholic support for strongman rule. Both in Latin America and East Asia an American economic and military presence remained palpable. In both regions, too, dictators used the threat of communist agitation to justify limits on civil liberties.

In South Korea and the Philippines, the texts of the Second Vatican Council, along with inspiration provided by liberation theologians, inspired new social movements. In South Korea, security police arrested Bishop Daniel Chi Hak-Soun in 1974 for aiding student demonstrators against the authoritarian government. The event—and Bishop Chi Hak-Soun's insistence in a "Declaration of Conscience" that his criticism of the regime stemmed from his Catholicism—mobilized the country's previously quiescent Catholic community.

Seoul's Cardinal Stephen Kim, appointed by Paul VI in 1968, became the titular leader of a resistance movement that included both Protestants and Catholics. Kim had grown up in a poor family, entered the seminary, and spent several years in Münster, Germany, obtaining a sociology degree and ministering to migrant Korean miners and nurses and their families. He expressed passionate support for the Second Vatican Council and saw it as his mission to cultivate the public engagement championed in *Gaudium et Spes*. He regretted that the church in South Korea had for so long been focused on "its own good while neglecting other affairs in the world." Myeongdong Cathedral, in Seoul, became a sanctuary for protesters in the 1980s, and activists circulated works by Gustavo Gutiérrez. In the culminating protest against the regime in 1987, just before its collapse, thousands of citizens and students camped inside and outside the cathedral. Kim informed government leaders that police attempting to arrest protesters would have to "trample on me first, priests secondly, and then sisters."[41]

In the Philippines, President Ferdinand Marcos declared martial law in 1972, stressing the link between stability, social justice, and the "conquest of mass poverty." At the time, many Catholics supported Marcos and welcomed the "restoration of peace and order."[42] As in Latin America, though, human rights advocacy and liberation theology generated a new dynamic. *Populorum Progressio* was widely read, and the country's bishops resolved "more than ever [to] be a Church of the poor."[43] Gustavo Gutiérrez's writings had a major influence among men and women in religious orders and as in Latin America, North American and European missionaries played a significant role. Base communities formed on the Latin American model, and some Catholics nurtured collaborations with the local Communist Party. Military officials targeted Filipino Catholic activists and foreign missionaries during the era of martial law and conducted raids on church establishments. In response, one Filipino nun, Sr. Mariani Dimaranan, became the leader of a national task force to monitor torture and human rights violations and a major contributor to the work of Amnesty International.

The 1983 murder by security forces of Senator Benigno Aquino, the leader of the opposition to Marcos, eventually propelled Catholic leaders, notably Cardinal Jaime Sin, to turn to electoral politics. (The Manila archdiocese controlled the one radio station able to evade government censorship.) Sin openly supported the presidential candidacy of Corazon Aquino, the devout wife of the murdered opposition leader. President Marcos's attempt to steal the 1986 election prompted Sin to mobilize crowds of up to two million people in a "people power" revolution that eventually overthrew the government, with pro-democracy Catholics at the center of the resistance. "If we did nothing," the bishops wrote, "we would be party to our own destruction as a people."[44]

V

MORE AMBIGUOUS late Cold War dramas played out in South and Central America. Authoritarian leaders, typically generals, ruled most of the region in the 1970s and 1980s. Once upon a time these dictators and juntas could count on church officials as reliable allies. No longer. Across Latin America, Catholic activists took leading roles in opposition movements, often putting themselves at risk. Security forces murdered eight hundred priests, nuns, and lay Catholic activists across Latin America over the course of the 1970s. (More Catholics died resisting authoritarian governments in Latin America during the 1970s than resisting communism in Eastern Europe in the 1980s.) When members of the Argentinian military interrogated Catholic activists in Argentina, they accused John XXIII and Paul VI of "ruining" the church and detected "communism" in the documents drafted at Medellín.[45]

How would John Paul II assess these tensions? When Karol Wojtyła met with Latin American bishops at a 1974 synod in Rome, he expressed hesitation. He acknowledged the injustice of the region's prevailing inequality. Poland was also poor. But Wojtyła thought the focus needed to be on the "spiritual freedom of man, the freedom of the human soul, the freedom of conscience, the freedom of religion." Or as he put it in a homily recorded by the Polish secret police:

> We understand well that the act of human emancipa-
> tion is multifaceted. It involves not only emancipating
> man from material misery, from the unjust social, politi-
> cal, and economic structures that cause such misery, but
> it also involves the emancipation of man in the spiritual
> sense, from all forms of limitation, from all forms of spir-
> itual slavery. It also involves matters like the freedom of
> conscience and freedom of religion.[46]

Just two months into his papacy, John Paul II journeyed to Puebla, Mexico, to attend the first meeting of the Latin American bishops since the 1968 meeting in Medellín. A buoyant crowd of one million peo- ple greeted him when he landed in Mexico City, a celebration once unimaginable in a country where Catholic guerrillas and the Mexican army had clashed in a civil war as recently as the 1920s and where the Vatican still could not obtain diplomatic standing. (The pope traveled on an ordinary tourist visa.) John Paul II donned a sombrero for pho- tographers and waved to the crowds pouring onto the street during his ten-mile ride from the airport to the metropolitan cathedral. He made a pilgrimage to the Basilica of Our Lady of Guadalupe, where the devout believed the Virgin Mary had appeared to Juan Diego in 1531, a place reminiscent, as John Paul II stressed in his remarks, of equally venerable Marian shrines in Poland.

In Puebla, John Paul II did not criticize liberation theology. But he criticized efforts to diminish Christ's divinity and depictions of "Jesus as politically committed, as one who fought against Roman oppres- sion and the authorities, and also as one involved in the class struggle."[47] The Puebla meeting produced an unwieldy final document of no less than 1,310 paragraphs. Nonetheless, it coined a potent new phrase—"a preferential option for the poor"—that became shorthand not just for liberation theology but the more general orientation of the church in the region.

The challenge of applying this "preferential option" to concrete situations had already come into focus in Central America. In Nicaragua, Catholic bishops and leaders had long been associated with the Somoza family dynasty. But the documents of the Second Vatican Council and Medellín pointed in new directions, as did activism among students, supported by Jesuits working at the Universidad Centroamericana, in San Salvador.[48] American priests and nuns with experience in the region encouraged the US Congress to hold hearings on human rights in Central America, as both American and Nicaraguan clergy documented torture by security forces.[49]

After Somoza fell in 1979, the Sandinista government posed new challenges. Catholics such as the liberation theologian and ecclesial base community leader Fr. Ernesto Cardenal took cabinet-level positions in the newly formed Sandinista government. Regions with the densest concentration of ecclesial base communities were the most supportive of the new regime.[50] Sandinista leaders congratulated themselves for making Christians an "integral part of our revolutionary history to a degree unprecedented in any other revolutionary movement in Latin America and possibly the world."[51]

Other Catholics, including Managua's archbishop, Miguel Obando y Bravo, had been opposed to the Somoza regime—Obando once accepted a Mercedes as a gift from President Somoza and immediately sold it and gave the funds to the poor—but now expressed reservations about the Sandinistas. Sandinista tolerance of restrictions on markets, free speech, and religion, combined with pious invocations of Fidel Castro's Cuba, set off alarm bells. Obando said Mass for leaders of the rebel Contra insurgency in Miami even as the United States government funded the insurgents and coordinated an economic boycott.

John Paul II, too, voiced his displeasure. On landing at the Managua airport in 1983, the pope wagged an angry finger at Fr. Cardenal as the priest knelt on the tarmac for a blessing.[52] Annoyed by chants of "power to the people" during a liturgy attended by five hundred thousand people in Managua's main plaza, sweating profusely in 100-degree heat, the pope called out "silenzio" and denounced "godless communism" to little effect. In the United States, on national television, Ronald Reagan attacked Nicaraguans who "insulted and mocked the Pope."[53]

Preventing another Nicaragua in El Salvador became the goal in Washington, Rome, and San Salvador. Early patterns had been similar. Belgian missionaries from Louvain became affiliated with Catholic student groups in El Salvador in the mid-1960s. They encouraged students to move beyond traditional conceptions of private property and toward a stronger sense of the "common good and the right to land and life." Reading groups and journals proliferated.[54]

One El Salvadoran Jesuit, Rutilio Grande, drew international attention in the 1970s for his work with students. "In our country," he insisted, "there exists a false democracy, a democracy in name only." In one homily, he derided critics from the *Wall Street Journal* and "international high finance circles" who knew nothing of poverty. Instead, he invoked Paul VI on development and "the Martyrdom of the Church in various countries of Latin America."[55]

Grande's own martyrdom occurred a month later. Right-wing security squads assassinated him, and among those asked to identify his body was San Salvador's new archbishop, Óscar Romero. Romero's training at the Colegio Pio Latino Americano in Rome and his work as a seminary rector had hardly prepared him for the cauldron of El Salvadoran politics. At Grande's funeral, he hesitantly warned against "any liberation that does not move beyond this world's ideologies, interests and realities."[56] But Grande's death radicalized Romero, and within the year he was speaking on the political situation to overflowing crowds at the city's cathedral. On the anniversary of Grande's death, he lauded the dead Jesuit's vision of "authentic liberation" and his ability to help people "see in their poverty and suffering the source of salvation, liberation, and redemption."[57]

Celebrated by reporters, human rights activists, and socially minded Catholics, Romero used his fame to leverage support for political reforms. He shuttled between leftist revolutionaries, Christian Democratic politicians, and military leaders. He attended funerals for murdered trade unionists and teachers and explained to a dubious papal nuncio why his presence was "faithful to the spirit of Vatican II, translated for Latin America by Medellín and Puebla."[58]

In Rome, Romero met with John Paul II, but left the meeting dis-

Archbishop Óscar Romero. *(Image ID: PRETHK, Alamy)*

couraged by the pope's references to complaints within El Salvador about Romero's activism. By this time, although Romero did not know it, Carter administration officials were asking John Paul II to ensure that Romero played a "responsible and constructive role."[59] By contrast, he felt supported by West German Catholics who funded his initiatives through their development agencies. He received an honorary degree from the Catholic university at Louvain, where he explained that "persecution [of the Church] has been occasioned by the defense of the poor."[60]

On February 17, 1980, Romero pleaded with the United States to stop sending military aid to El Salvador and "truly defend human rights."[61] Before another huge crowd, in an address broadcast via radio across Latin America, Romero referenced the Second Vatican Council, the meeting of the Latin American bishops at Medellín, and Amnesty International as he made an impassioned plea to stop state-sponsored violence. "The church," he concluded, "preaches your liberation just as we have studied it in the Holy Bible today." The congregation interrupted the homily with applause five times.[62]

Four American church-
women murdered in
El Salvador in 1980.
Clockwise from top
left: Sr. Dorothy Kazel,
Sr. Maura Clark, Jean
Donovan, Sr. Ita Ford.
(Courtesy of Maryknoll Archives)

A week later, on March 24, 1980, while saying Mass, Romero was shot dead by members
of the security forces he had denounced. Later
that same year, members of the same security forces raped and killed three missionary
American nuns and a laywoman. Jean Donovan, the laywoman, a twenty-seven-year-old
from Cleveland, had trained as an accountant
before searching for more meaningful work.
She had lived in El Salvador for just over a
year. She saw Archbishop Romero as a "great
guy. He is the leader of Liberation Theology in
practice. . . . He really is the voice of the people." She found "Christ a lot more in a group
of lay people joined in prayer, genuinely caring for one another, than in John Paul II and
giant masses in Washington or wherever." One of her last letters was
to Senator Edward Kennedy, pleading with him to "stop the actions of
our government."[63]

United States Ambassador Robert White, also a Catholic, had dined
with the four American churchwomen on the night before their deaths.
He supervised the exhumation of their bodies and became a thorn in
the side of the new Reagan administration by emphasizing the need
to apprehend the murderers. John Paul II also mourned the deaths of
Romero and the American churchwomen, but if in Poland John Paul
II encouraged defiance of a dictatorial government, in Central America
he worried about a destabilizing radicalism. Reagan administration officials commenting on the murders of the four churchwomen were callous. Jeanne Kirkpatrick, soon to be appointed American ambassador to
the United Nations, insisted that the "nuns were not just nuns . . . they
were political activists."

Over the next decade, divisions among Catholics deepened as the
civil war continued, with a devastating death toll for a small nation.
American secretary of state Alexander Haig, himself Catholic with a
brother who was a Jesuit, thought "liberal Catholics" in El Salvador and

the United States did little more than echo Soviet and Cuban talking points. Senate Republicans held hearings on the connection between "theologies of liberation" and "violent Marxist revolution."[64] Meanwhile, more liberal Catholics in the United States and Europe, including former Ambassador White and a young Democratic senator from Delaware, Joseph Biden, insisted that American aid to El Salvador be tied to the arrest and conviction of the men who had killed the four missionaries. The keynote speaker at the 1984 Democratic Convention, New York's Catholic governor Mario Cuomo, denounced Republicans for giving "money to Latin American governments that murder nuns, and then lie about it."[65]

That same year, El Salvadorans elected as president a Christian Democrat, José Napoleón Duarte, who arranged for the conviction of five national guardsmen for the killing of the churchwomen. El Salvadoran security forces, in another spasm of violence, murdered six Jesuits, including one of the region's leading liberation theologians, Ignacio Ellacuría, as well as their housekeeper and her daughter in 1989, a week after the fall of the Berlin Wall. The murders prompted more protests organized by Catholics in Latin America, Western Europe, and the United States.

The context, though, was now different. As head of the Congregation for the Doctrine of the Faith, Joseph Ratzinger had already begun to discipline liberation theologians he deemed heterodox. He published a statement criticizing Gustavo Gutiérrez for his "uncritical acceptance of the Marxist conception of history."[66]

More broadly, capitalism as a method of organizing the economy now seemed inevitable, even just. With the fall of the Berlin Wall, Eastern Europeans rushed to abandon Soviet-style planning. The expansion of global markets had already brought tens of millions of once impoverished residents of South Korea, Hong Kong, Taiwan, and Singapore into the middle class. The most prosperous Latin American countries, such as Chile, were those most integrated into international trading patterns. These capitalist triumphs posed a conceptual challenge to Brazilian bishops working with ecclesial base communities, who continued to invoke "socialism" as "God's Kingdom on Earth."[67] Gutiérrez and other liberation theologians jettisoned a "Marxist version" of class struggle for a more anthropological, less overtly political examination of how the religious experience of the poor could instruct Catholics.[68]

Absent the Cold War, Latin America moved from the center of international diplomacy to its margins. Catholics in the US Congress, led by Speaker of the House Tip O'Neill, whose aunt was a Maryknoll nun, limited the ability of officials in the Reagan and George H. W. Bush administrations to fund the Contra army attempting to overthrow the Sandinista government. In 1990, the Sandinistas were defeated in free elections. In 1992, El Salvador's government signed a peace accord with guerrilla forces. The world's most important leftist political party, Brazil's Workers' Party, still depended on socially minded Catholics for its electoral popularity, but its successes seemed anomalous in an increasingly capitalist age.[69]

John Paul II proclaimed an era's end. His focus turned away from Latin America and toward the rebuilding of Catholic institutions in the liberated Baltic countries, Eastern Europe, and Ukraine. He regretted that "the sincere desire to be on the side of the oppressed and not to be cut off from the course of history" had led some Catholics to seek "an impossible compromise between Marxism and Christianity."[70] Joseph Ratzinger thought it time to close the liberation theology chapter. The collapse of communism, he wrote, "turned out to be a kind of twilight of the Gods for that theology."[71]

VI

CATHOLICISM in sub-Saharan Africa moved on a different trajectory. The buoyancy of the 1960s in newly independent African nations matched the optimism of the Second Vatican Council. No longer would the church "appear as a religion in service to the political and cultural imperialism of the West," a Cameroonian priest explained.[72]

Many of the African countries gaining independence had Catholics as their first presidents, including Léopold Senghor in Senegal and Julius Nyerere in Tanzania. The "faithful socialism" Senghor attempted to develop in Senegal, as well as Nyerere's version of socialism in Tanzania, had both Catholic and African roots. Nyerere agreed to speak at the motherhouse of the Maryknoll nuns in Ossining, New York, because he had worked with Maryknoll nuns in Tanzania. He referenced *Populorum Progressio* and urged Catholics "to recognize the need for social revolution and to play a leading role in it."[73] Paul VI and Nigeria's bishops mobilized these African Catholic presidents and a vast Catholic relief apparatus to alleviate the humanitarian crisis caused by Biafra's secession from Nigeria in 1967 and the subsequent civil war.[74]

Catholic toleration of apartheid regimes ended. The anti-apartheid movement in South Africa was led by secular and Protestant Black activists, but a few Catholics, such as Durban archbishop Denis Hurley, determinedly supported this vanguard. Catholics played a more significant role in Rhodesia (Zimbabwe), where Bishop Donal Lamont and a handful of Catholics became some of the most important internal critics of their government. Dominican nuns admitted "colored" students to their "white" schools in acts of civil disobedience. Lamont accused a white Catholic minister for the government of practicing "moral terrorism" on the African majority.[75]

One dimension of African Catholicism in the post-conciliar era was the development of African-led institutions. In Rhodesia (Zimbabwe) in the late 1960s and 1970s, African seminarians repeatedly went on strike, convinced that their English Jesuit professors treated them with a racist condescension. The seminarians alleged that their instructors judged them barely capable of being "simple parish priests"; they demanded that African priests join the teaching staff.[76] Faculty from Louvain, in Belgium, founded a faculty of theology at Lovanium University, in the Congo. Its members produced some of the first twentieth-century theological texts composed by Africans.[77]

About one-fifth of the 311 African bishops at the Second Vatican Council were native Africans, and fourth-fifths were European or American missionaries. The appointment of native African bishops proceeded quickly, though, and they were a majority by the mid-1970s. Priests and bishops from Latin America had long held the most important posts in that region, but now natives from Africa and South and East Asia took on key leadership roles both in their native countries and, increasingly, in Rome.[78]

Generally, post-conciliar Catholic leaders in Africa became more attached to global Catholic structures, not less. Developments in Uganda are revealing. The Great Lakes region of Uganda, Rwanda, Tanzania, and Burundi became the African Catholic heartland in the twentieth century, with Catholics either a majority or close to a majority in each country. In Uganda, atypically, native Ugandans, not foreign missionaries, held the most important church offices as early as 1950. The first African-born bishop, Joseph Kiwanuka, had trained in Rome as a canon lawyer and written a dissertation (in Latin) on Christian marriage, a daring topic for a student from a region where polygamy remained widespread. The schools Kiwanuka built, the devotions he encouraged, and the Latin he drilled into his seminarians—some were said to speak it more fluently than English—made his diocese of Masaka resemble a similarly structured diocese in, say, Austria.[79] Ugandan parishes remained poor—into the 1970s not a single parish in one diocese owned a working phone—and the model of evangelization through catechists and the building of parishes and schools remained traditional. An innovation was that many catechists now possessed a bicycle and were able to pedal from village to village.[80]

At the Second Vatican Council, Kiwanuka spoke eloquently of the need for Indigenous music to be integrated into the liturgy. He organized a ceremony in St. Peter's Square where Paul VI canonized twenty Ugandan martyrs killed in 1884, and beatified in 1920, with the voices of an African choir harmonizing over the beat of African drums. (Forty thousand Ugandans attended a parallel canonization Mass in Kampala.) In the first papal journey to Africa, Paul VI visited Uganda for three days in 1969, paying tribute to the same Ugandan martyrs and meeting with the region's bishops and Catholic politicians. He claimed "no other desire than to foster what you already are: Africans and Catholics."[81]

Given this optimism, the descent of so many African states—Uganda, certainly, but Nigeria, Ghana, and many others as well—into authoritarian rule or civil war proved all the more disheartening. Postcolonial democracy in Africa, it turned out, would not be the stable party system familiar to North Americans and Western Europeans (at least since 1945), but a kaleidoscope of shifting coalitions. The head of the Democratic (and deeply Catholic) Party in Uganda, Benedicto Kiwanuka worked closely with Archbishop Kiwanuka (no relation). Just as Archbishop Kiwanuka developed ties to the broader Catholic world by studying in Rome, Benedicto Kiwanuka studied law in London and came to see himself and his party as embarked on a project paralleling the Christian Democratic Union in West Germany or the Catholic People's Party in the Netherlands. He was elected the country's first prime minister in 1962, but could not prevent his successor from suspending Parliament and plunging Uganda into strongman rule in 1966. He urged a continuation of democracy. "A country's Constitution," Kiwanuka wrote, should not be "thrown away by a single person as easily as throwing a dirty handkerchief in a bedroom basket."[82]

Idi Amin's regime, beginning in 1971, sent Uganda into further disarray. Benedicto Kiwanuka had at first accepted Amin's leadership and even taken an appointment as chief justice. (The two men and their families shared one Christmas dinner.) Catholics were never a particular target of Amin's wrath, but independent sources of power were, and Amin soon embarked on a campaign against foreign influence in Uganda that extended to Catholics as pawns of a global church. He expelled fifty-five priests from the country and arranged for Benedicto Kiwanuka to be kidnapped as he left morning Mass. On Amin's orders, Kiwanuka was then savagely tortured and executed. Amin later

Two Catholic politicians: Benedicto Kiwanuka, chief minister of Uganda, and John F. Kennedy, president of the United States, 1961. *(Abbie Rowe. White House Photographs. John F. Kennedy Presidential Library and Museum, Boston)*

ordered the assassination of the priest-editor of the country's leading Catholic newspaper, in part because of his investigation into Benedicto Kiwanuka's death.[83]

VII

EXPERTS IN THE 1960S had predicted that Christianity, Protestant and Catholic, would fade in importance after so many African countries achieved independence. Missionary schools might have educated African elites, but after independence, state institutions would take on that role. Guinea's first president, Sékou Touré, refused to permit Catholic schools and even imprisoned his childhood friend, Guinea's archbishop, for several years to signal complete independence from European institutions.[84]

But Guinea was an exception. The Catholic growth rate in Africa was higher than in any other region and higher than the growth rate of the African population. John Paul II made thirteen separate trips to the continent, visiting almost every country. His evident joy when traveling in Africa stemmed from the buoyancy with which he was received and perhaps from the resemblance to the Poland of his youth, with its large families and packed seminaries and convents. Among the saints John Paul II canonized was Sr. Josephine Bakhita, once enslaved in the Sudan, then an Italian nun, and now a symbol of Catholic support for human rights and resistance to human trafficking. (Catholic-sponsored Radio Bakhita became South Sudan's leading radio station in the early twenty-first century.)[85] One Nigerian seminary enrolled more students than any other seminary in the world, and the pattern of sending African priests to Western Europe and North America for parish assignments (and funds for their home dioceses) became widespread.[86]

In country after country, Catholic schools played a significant role in the educational enterprise, and Catholic hospitals supplied much medical care. Their relative independence, in an era of failed African states, commended them. In Zambia, to take a typical example, Catholics provided up to 60 percent of the country's medical care in rural areas. They ran 15 percent of the country's schools, ranging from grade schools to a Catholic university. The reputations of the schools made them attractive to students and parents, and their graduates proved more likely than peers to take places at universities and assume leadership roles.

Many African Catholic dioceses, parishes, and institutions remained dependent on European and North American funding through development agencies such as Catholic Relief Services (United States), Adveniat (Germany), Trōcaire (Ireland), Cordaid (Holland), and the 165 Catholic aid groups that constituted the Caritas Internationalis network. The same uneasiness about corruption or inadequate supervision within state institutions that led parents to enroll children in Catholic schools or visit Catholic medical clinics also encouraged international aid agencies to channel funds through Catholic networks. Dioceses and parishes started to administer microfinance, water sanitation, and conflict resolution projects. Jesuit Refugee Services, for example, founded in 1980, spent over half of its budget in Africa in a typical year, and over half of these funds came from governments and UN agencies.

Here the risk became that development projects, however integral to the Catholic mission, might swamp the capacity of church leaders to perform more conventional religious tasks.[87] Sustaining a Catholic identity in their institutions was also challenging. Fee-paying parents (and at times governments) might resent theology classes or mandatory liturgies or courses whose emphasis on social justice (after the Second Vatican Council) cast an unwelcome light on local political arrangements. The willingness to admit non–Catholic students after the Second Vatican Council gestured toward ecumenicism (and financial stability) but also made institutional identity less coherent. In 1969, religious brothers and women religious made up one-third of the staff in Zambian Catholic schools; in 2004, just 3 percent. At some well-regarded Catholic schools in central Africa but also in India and other locations in the Global South, Catholics were only one-third or less of the pupils.[88]

Unlike in Europe and North America, secularization touched only the most urbanized parts of the African continent, but religious competition among Catholics, Protestants, and Muslims existed everywhere. A Pentecostal, or charismatic, renewal movement, including speaking in tongues and direct encounters with the Holy Spirit, emerged in the United States in the early twentieth century and spread across the world, eventually touching hundreds of millions of people. The roots of this

Pentecostalism lay within an often anti-Catholic wing of Protestantism, but after the Second Vatican Council, unexpectedly, a charismatic or Pentecostal movement became embedded within the Catholic church. The detachment of Pentecostal leaders from ordinary diocesan structures and the destabilizing emphasis on a personal encounter with the Holy Spirit created anxieties among bishops similar to those felt by their predecessors at Lourdes and elsewhere in the nineteenth century when Mary appeared to ordinary believers and attracted unruly crowds of the devout. Belgium's Cardinal Suenens attended Catholic Pentecostal meetings incognito for five days in the United States before conveying his endorsement of the movement to Paul VI.[89]

Never more than a small presence in North America and Western Europe, Catholic Pentecostalism became influential in Africa, Brazil, and India. In a typical pattern, a priest and nun from South Bend, Indiana, after working with middle-class Catholics in the United States, brought Pentecostal practices to western Uganda in the Fort Portal region in the early 1980s. Merging the healing practices and devotions of nineteenth-century ultramontanism and twentieth-century Pentecostalism proved surprisingly easy: both traditions saw the world as locked in a struggle between God and Satan.[90]

At times, Catholics absorbed witchcraft practices (in Uganda and Cameroon) and sorcery (in Zaire). Here the challenge of inculturation became evident. If church officials repudiated such practices and the healing ceremonies that accompanied them, they lost adherents. If they included them, they stretched orthodoxy beyond recognizable limits. The Ghanaian bishops produced manuals on the charismatic movement, acknowledging that healing and exorcisms marked Christ's ministry, but demanding "wise pastoral guidance and discernment of spirits."[91]

In Zambia, Emmanuel Milingo, educated by White Father missionaries and appointed archbishop of Lusaka in 1969, began to practice faith healings and exorcisms for large crowds. In 1982, Paul VI forced Milingo to resign his position as archbishop and move to Rome. There he married and formed a breakaway church.[92] Less provocatively, a Cameroonian priest and theologian, Meinrad Hebga, a Jesuit with a doctorate from the Sorbonne and a pioneer in calling for an African-led church in the 1950s, established a healing ministry. He, too, had first encountered Pentecostal Catholicism in the United States. Meeting with groups of followers in Cameroon, Hebga anointed men and women claiming damage from witchcraft or diabolical possession, as well as initiating dialogues with supplicants about their day-to-day challenges. Until his death in 2008, Hebga served as the spiritual guide for two hundred groups of Cameroonian Catholic charismatics. He traveled to London and Paris to meet with offshoot groups founded by Cameroonian migrants.[93]

VIII

AS IN POLAND, South Korea, the Philippines, and much of Latin America, democracy in sub-Saharan Africa deepened its Catholic roots. During the 1970s, except in the apartheid nations of Rhodesia and South Africa, where they became more outspoken in opposition to white minority rule, African Catholic leaders had tended to focus on preserving the Catholic institutions they led.

The end of the Cold War allowed more maneuvering room. Reluctance on the part of the United States and other Western nations to prop up anti-communist dictators after 1989 encouraged a second wave of democratization that proved more enduring than the post-independence democratic movements of the 1960s. In Francophone Africa, Catholic visibility was striking. Benin's archbishop presided over the national conference convened to draft a constitution. He governed the country until the first free election. In Gabon and Togo, bishops played similar roles, as they did in Zaire and the Congo.[94]

Bishops and lay Catholic leaders were only slightly less influential in the former British colonies. In Malawi, Catholics numbered less than 20 percent of the population, but the bishops' pastoral letter entitled *The Truth Will Set You Free* became the single most important public criticism of Malawi's one-party state. The letter began with a reference to the preferential option for the poor and regret that "many people still live in circumstances which are hardly compatible with their dignity as sons and daughters of God." John Paul II had visited Malawi in 1989 and encouraged both democracy and respect for human rights. When in 1992 it was announced that a popular majority had voted for a multiparty government, a jubilant crowd marched, significantly, to the local bishop's house.[95]

A gruesome exception to this pattern of Catholics building more stable democracies occurred in Rwanda. The 1994 genocide there—with eight hundred thousand people slaughtered in one hundred days—had multiple causes. Still, Catholic acceptance or even encouragement of ethnic divides between the Hutu and Tutsi peoples, dating back to the era of Belgian colonization, was among the most potent. In the 1950s, French and Belgian White Father missionaries helped persuade the colonial government to place primarily Hutu Catholics—roughly 80 percent of the population—into leadership positions. A bloody 1959 revolt ended the monarchy and forced thousands of Tutsi into exile in neighboring Uganda and Burundi.

Rwanda's first president after gaining independence from Belgium in 1962, Grégoire Kayibanda, a Hutu, had edited a Catholic newspaper and run a Catholic cooperative.[96] But he did little to thwart episodic Hutu killings of Tutsi students. Church leaders formally condemned the violence, but pleading with readers to love one's neighbor, "even if he is an enemy," seemed more accepting of conflict than eager to end it. One Italian missionary described the scene at his parish as a "spectacle of blood, fighting, pillaging and fires above all." He asked, "How can I celebrate Mass in a community divided by hate? How can I give the sacraments to a community in which the majority has been complicit in these events, led by politicians with a diabolical plan to eliminate the Tutsi?"[97]

Like so much of sub-Saharan Africa, Rwanda had a promising democratic dawn after 1989, when Catholic leaders, especially the editors of the national Catholic newspaper, attempted to guide the country toward a multiparty democracy. The country's bishops released a letter decrying ethnic division and inequality. But after the presidents of Rwanda and Burundi died in a mysterious plane crash in 1994, simmering conflicts metastasized into a war of extremist Hutu against Tutsi (and even moderate Hutu). The massacres provoked acts of desperate heroism, including Hutu priests and nuns sacrificing their lives while defending Tutsi parishioners. One Hutu nun, Sr. Felicitas Niyitegeka, ferried Tutsi across the border into Zaire and was captured upon her return. Because her brother was a colonel in the army, she was offered a chance to save her life, but she refused to abandon her colleagues and the Tutsi they protected. She was subsequently murdered and thrown naked into a common grave. Rwanda's bishops condemned the violence in abstract terms, without mentioning terrorism directed against the Tutsi. A few priests and nuns participated in the genocide, even killing trembling coreligionists seeking sanctuary within church buildings.[98]

Here inculturation meant an incapacity to reach across ethnic divides. A papal envoy, French cardinal Roger Etchegaray, crisscrossed the country during the genocide, attempting to reconcile warring parties. He regretted that the "blood of tribalism proved deeper than the waters of baptism."[99] John Paul II did not fly to Rwanda and try to broker an end to the slaughter as some commentators urged. (Neither did the secretary general of the United Nations, the president of France, or the president of the United States.) When confronted with evidence of priests and nuns participating in the genocide, the pope denounced such actions, but in a defensive way. "The Church in itself," he insisted, "cannot be held responsible for the misdeeds of its members who have acted against evangelical law."[100]

This distinction—between a pure church and its sinful members—was entirely traditional. It would soon come under scrutiny because it deflected questions about how institutions formed individuals, who in turn manipulated institutions. This relationship between institutions and individuals lay at the core of another problem long shrouded in secrecy: clergy sex abuse. Reckoning with that horror was just beginning.

FIFTEEN

Sexual Abuse (and Its Cover-Up)

I

THE AUSTRALIAN CITY of Ballarat, a gold rush boom town in the nineteenth century and a tourist destination in the twenty-first, is a ninety-minute drive west from Melbourne. The first itinerant priests said Mass in a tent adjacent to the mining fields.[1] Irish migrants built the city's neo-Gothic cathedral, inevitably named St. Patrick's. Ballarat's first bishop, the Irish-born Michael O'Connor, wrote to Dublin's Car-

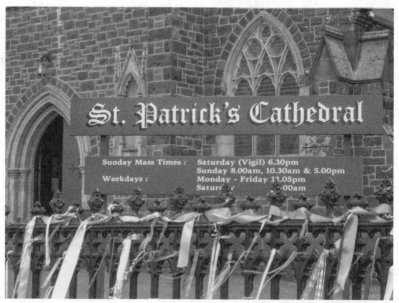

Ribbons placed on the fence outside of St. Patrick's Cathedral in Ballarat, Australia, to protest clerical sexual abuse. *(REUTERS/Jonathan Barrett—Image ID: 2CKBY53 via Alamy)*

dinal Paul Cullen in 1875, promising that he was "keeping up a per-
petual agitation on the Education question," and over time Ballarat's
Catholics constructed a daunting number of schools, orphanages, and
associations in the manner of the ultramontane revival.[2]

Some of these parishes and schools became crime scenes. The documentation available to trace the Catholic sexual abuse crisis in Ballarat
is unusual, the result of an investigation conducted by the Australian
Royal Commission on Institutional Responses to Child Sex Abuse.[3]
What the documentation reveals is not unusual. It encapsulates why the
sexual abuse crisis is the most traumatic episode in Catholicism's modern history.

The number of lives destroyed and families shattered by the abuse
crisis is unknowable, but some numbers are obtainable: in Australia,
4,444 people made sexual abuse claims against Catholic institutions,
with episodes overwhelmingly located in the period between 1950 and
1989. Most of the perpetrators were priests or brothers, and half of all
incidents involving priests and brothers occurred on church and school
grounds. Over 70 percent of abuse survivors were boys. Survivors made
credible claims of sexual abuse against 5 to 7 percent of priests and
brothers working in Australia during this period.

Clerical sexual abuse touched hundreds of families in Ballarat, a city
of just over one hundred thousand people. One survivor endured the
suicides of two brothers and a cousin; all four boys were victims of
abuse.[4] Two Ballarat Catholic institutions, St. Alipius school and St.
Patrick's high school were the sites for a large number of the claims, and
the Christian Brothers who ran both institutions received the highest
number of claims of any religious order.

The Royal Commission report begins with a Christian Brother, Gerald
Fitzpatrick, who began his career in 1950 working with "delinquent"—
also vulnerable—boys as their probation officer and at an orphanage. He
kissed and fondled boys while holding them on his lap, and encouraged
the boys to join him for nude swimming sessions at school picnics. After
parental complaints and hazy warnings from clerical supervisors to stay
away from young people, Brother Fitzpatrick was transferred from school
to school. As late as 1978, near the end of his career, observers saw him
visit the "junior dormitory and play with the boys."

Another Christian Brother, Stephen Farrell, taught for two years in Ballarat and in that time abused several young boys, including one boy on multiple occasions and in multiple sites on the parish and church grounds. He then abused that boy's brother. When a parent complained to the pastor about Farrell's behavior, she was told, "Don't go to the police," and the pastor moved Farrell out of the parish with no word to parishioners.

Another Christian Brother, Peter Toomey, was accused of touching boys inappropriately at a Christian Brothers school, but no investigation was ever made. He taught sex education classes, remarkably, and was said to have been "speaking freely of sex and asked too personal questions of boys." He worked in other parishes and schools and committed further acts of abuse. Much later, he was sentenced to a prison term.

Another Christian Brother, Edward Dowlan, was accused of putting his hands down a student's pants in 1973. The student who made the complaint was made to apologize in front of the entire school for spreading rumors. Nothing happened when another student told the principal of the school that Dowlan was "hurting me." A year later Dowlan is alleged to have raped a boy in the middle of the night. His parents immediately withdrew their son from the school, but Dowlan continued teaching at the boarding school and at other Catholic institutions for eight years after Christian Brothers provincials and leaders knew of accusations against him. He was removed only after police began an investigation. Dowlan was eventually convicted of sexual offenses against twenty boys and sentenced to multiple prison terms.

Monsignor John Day, a prominent diocesan priest, abused both boys and girls in the early 1970s. Five witnesses testified, courageously, to this fact, and the police also found evidence that Msgr. Day rented hotel rooms with young people. The police officer first assigned to the case was Msgr. Day's "best friend" and reluctant to investigate the claims. Two disgusted detectives took it upon themselves to inform the bishop that Day's conduct was "general knowledge among the Catholic and non-Catholic community in this area." In response, another priest in the parish warned an investigating officer to "drop the inquiry into Monsignor Day or you'll be out of a job." Monsignor Day resigned his position as rumors swirled through the parish, but no public statement was made beyond a cryptic announcement that the monsignor suffered from "ill health." Day demanded to be reassigned to another parish on the opposite end of the diocese from Ballarat, since no charges had been filed, and the bishop and diocesan board of consultors agreed to do so. He served in that parish until his death.

Fr. Gerard Ridsdale became the most notorious abuser. Following studies in Italy and England, Fr. Ridsdale returned to Ballarat in 1961, where he spent twenty-nine years as a priest in sixteen different assignments. He served for some time as an assistant to another abuser, Msgr. Day. He admitted committing sexual abuse to his bishop in 1975, was sent for desultory therapy sessions in Melbourne, then was reassigned. He later took a teenage boy (whose parents had separated) into the rectory to live with him. He abused him repeatedly, even daily. The boy's mother contacted the bishop, asking, "How can you let a child live in a presbytery with a priest?" She was ignored. After Ridsdale's removal from parish work, seventy-eight people claimed to have been sexually abused by him. He later confessed to acts of abuse while working in seven different parishes.

Most sexual abuse occurs in families, and much sexual abuse has occurred in secular organizations. The Australian Royal Commission depicts this in nauseating detail. But Catholic institutions and Catholic religious professionals received a high number of claims. Scholars have only begun to study sexual abuse, and assessments are necessarily tentative. Still, the spiritual manipulation conducted by perpetrators, combined with the spiritual desolation felt by survivors, may be a distinctive Catholic contribution to the crisis.[5] The idealization of priests and the priesthood meant perpetrators often had free reign. They could manipulate mothers eager to find male role models for their sons, or abuse young women seeking counseling. They could expect deference from parishioners and law enforcement officials. Survivors often reported that their own parents refused to believe initial accusations against beloved clergy.

The findings in Ballarat mimic what dozens of investigations (with more ongoing) have found in the United States, Chile, Germany, and elsewhere. Protecting priests and the church's reputation, instead of acknowledging the pain and suffering of survivors, was usually paramount. Whether liberal or conservative, whether supportive of Vatican II (as in Ballarat) or dubious, bishops fobbed off complaints by transferring abusive priests to new parishes and schools, where they might abuse again. Sexual abuse survivors and their supporters now cover the wrought iron fence outside St. Patrick's Cathedral in Ballarat with ribbons—to the applause of some parishioners and the consternation of others—in order to stress the centrality of Catholicism to one of the most painful wounds in the city's history.[6]

The ways in which global Catholic networks facilitated the crisis are becoming clear. Abusive priests were often sent to ineffective treatment programs in Australia, North America, and Rome. The then conventional wisdom that sexual abusers could be treated and sent back into active ministry was not unique to Catholicism. But it held unusual appeal for bishops because clergy could not be easily removed from the priesthood and because they remained in such high demand. Some Ballarat clergy did stints at an especially dubious treatment program in New Mexico, in the United States. The center—with branches eventually located in seven countries—began with a focus on priests struggling with alcoholism or other forms of substance abuse. Its founder did not think that men capable of sexually abusing minors should be rehabilitated for parish ministry and thought "such unfortunate priests should be given the alternative of a retired life within the protection of monastery walls or complete laicization." His cautions were ignored. In the 1970s, priests who had committed sexual abuse and who were undergoing treatment at the center took on weekend parish assignments, where they sometimes scouted out new victims.[7]

The hundreds of thousands of cases uncovered in the last twenty years—in Ballarat and around the world—will almost certainly not be replicated. The deference to clergy and trust between priests and parishioners that set the stage for abuse have greatly diminished. Significant safeguards are also often in place. In Australia, only a handful of Catholic abuse cases date from the twenty-first century. The 2018 grand jury report on sexual abuse within eight dioceses in Pennsylvania, in the United States, combined evidence of horror with evidence of progress. The chilling details of abuse included a network of priests passing abuse victims from one to another in a chain of sexual exploitation. What they also revealed is that the clerical sexual abuse crisis in Pennsylvania—if measured by the volume of cases—may have ended, with the overwhelming majority of incidents dating from thirty and forty years earlier. Yet if the abuse crisis is measured by its effects on survivors, many of whom first acknowledge and begin to process their abuse decades after it occurred, the ending will not be in our lifetime.[8]

What about Catholicism enabled predators? All answers remain contested. The most ambitious young priest in the diocese of Ballarat in the 1970s was Fr. George Pell, an alumnus of St. Patrick's College, who had completed his studies in Rome and Oxford before returning to his hometown. In quick succession, John Paul II appointed Pell as an auxiliary bishop, archbishop of Melbourne, archbishop of Sydney, and then cardinal, a position that included service on the influential Congregation of Bishops, charged with making recommendations to the pope for episcopal appointments around the world. A gruff former Australian Rules football player, Pell fit the John Paul II mold. His views were consistent: against the "normalization" of homosexuality, condom distribution, and any consideration of women priests.[9] These positions alienated him from many Australian Catholics, but even more from an increasingly secular Australian society.

Pell's first response to the abuse cases in Ballarat in the 1970s was dismissive. He admitted hearing "gossip" about multiple cases, including the "great scandal" caused by Msgr. Day, which had reached the Melbourne newspapers. He shared a rectory at one point with Ridsdale, although he denied knowing anything about Ridsdale's abuse. He later acknowledged a common blindness: if a priest denied committing abuse, he, like many other Catholics, instinctively believed the priest and not the survivor.

As the crisis deepened while he served as archbishop of Melbourne, Pell did establish one of the first programs to respond to victims. (Survivors and their attorneys claimed that the program's unstated goal was to avoid large financial settlements, as evidenced by aggressive tactics used by archdiocesan attorneys.) In 2015, Pell's decision to testify in front of the Australian Royal Commission about events in Ballarat by video from Rome, where he was then the first cardinal prefect for the Secretariat for the Economy, rather than in person before the Australian Royal Commission, generated headlines. When Pell, himself, was accused in 2017 of committing sexual abuse two decades previously, he was immediately convicted in the court of public opinion, so damaged was the reputation of Catholicism and so pugnacious were Pell's views on sexual ethics. One trial ended in a mistrial. A second jury convicted him. He spent thirteen months in jail until the conviction was unanimously dismissed as implausible by a seven-judge appeals panel.

Pell's experience with sexual abuse as it played out in Ballarat and Melbourne, and then his imprisonment for crimes that by a fair reading of the evidence he did not commit, prompted few reassessments. Press coverage tilted toward the sensational, focusing on Pell's guilt or innocence while ignoring the structures that permitted abuse. Pell, in turn, has taken to nostalgic reflections on the Catholicism of his youth. Then, Catholics believed in hell and eternal punishment. Now, "every Western society has seen an exodus of Church members and diminished practice." Indeed, the "prophets of gloom and doom" dismissed by John XXIII on the opening day of the Second Vatican Council "have been vindicated, unfortunately and unexpectedly, by a series of brutal reversals across the board."[10]

II

THE EXPERIENCE OF the Second Vatican Council and its turbulent aftermath instilled in many Catholics an openness toward change. Within the church, these changes included modernist architectural designs, the liturgy in the vernacular, revised missions for Catholic organizations, and new roles for laypeople, priests, and nuns.

Outside church walls, changes included new interest in human rights, democracy, and ecumenical and interreligious dialogue. John Paul II welcomed the church's public role. No pope in the modern era spoke more firmly in support of human rights, and John Paul II's first address to the United Nations included a meditation on the "dignity of the human being."[11] No pope condemned anti-Semitism with more vigor. John Paul II made the first papal visit to a synagogue soon after his election. He canonized the convert philosopher Edith Stein, or Sr.

Teresa Benedicta of the Cross, murdered at Auschwitz in 1942 not far from the pope's childhood home because of her Jewish ancestry. His pilgrimage to Israel in the millennial year of 2000 included stops at Yad Vashem, the Holocaust memorial, and at the Wailing Wall in Jerusalem, and he publicly voiced regrets for Christian anti-Semitism. In Morocco, after negotiating religious freedom for Catholic institutions in that overwhelmingly Muslim country, he made a touching plea to eighty thousand Muslim teenagers in a soccer stadium in Casablanca to find in God the "source of all joy."[12]

Within the church, John Paul II and Joseph Ratzinger understood their task as one of stiffening spines. "After the phase of 'indiscriminate openness'," Ratzinger told an interviewer shortly after moving to Rome "it is time that the Christian reacquire the consciousness of belonging to a minority." The church and its members must discard an overly "euphoric post-conciliar solidarity."[13]

The documents of the Second Vatican Council emphasized the authority of bishops, but the ceaseless activity of John Paul II conveyed a different message. In just over twenty years, he authored a best-selling book, fourteen encyclicals, and hundreds, even thousands, of lectures and homilies. He arranged for the drafting and publication of the first Roman-approved catechism since the sixteenth century.

This torrent of prose came naturally to a former university professor. It also reflected John Paul II's conviction that papal charisma could circumvent unsympathetic elites and reach ordinary believers. He founded World Youth Day in Rome in 1986, moved it to Buenos Aires in 1987, and then held it every three years in locations including Santiago de Compostela in Spain, Denver in the United States, and Manila in the Philippines. Each time, the event drew hundreds of thousands of young people for several days of Masses, concerts, and service activities. John Paul II's critics underestimated the event's appeal, which recognized that religious identity, especially among young people, was more than ever a conscious decision instead of a familial expectation. But at a moment when many of the world's parishes were losing members and when vocations to the priesthood and religious life were diminishing, such events could seem more spectacle than strategy. No spikes in Catholic practice resulted. The ultramontane revival of the nineteenth century, which reached from villages to the Vatican, not just the other way around, produced a more enduring set of spiritual forms.[14]

John Paul II and Joseph Ratzinger also limited the role of regional or national episcopal conferences. As head of the Congregation of the Doctrine of the Faith, Ratzinger required the leaders of bishops' conferences from Western Europe and the United States to meet with him in Rome to discuss a common approach to nuclear proliferation. John Paul II later issued an apostolic letter limiting the authority of such conferences and requiring that their documents undergo "review by the Holy See."[15]

Synods of bishops, established as a governance mechanism by Paul VI at the end of the Second Vatican Council, made little impact. John Paul II was observed reciting the rosary—or dozing or discreetly reading a book—during synod working sessions he nominally supervised. He allowed little genuine debate. Synod documents were largely prepared in advance by curial officials and approved in rote fashion.[16] A bishop, complained one Brazilian cardinal after attending a synod, is not "the local branch manager of the International Spiritual Bank Inc."[17]

Church administration at the local level followed much the same pattern. Bishops, priests, nuns, and laypeople launched national or diocesan synods in West Germany, the United States, and other places in the years after the council, but these typically foundered on widespread uneasiness with decentralized decision-making. Even parish councils— never mandated—struggled to assert themselves against the occasional recalcitrant pastor or to attract the commitment of parishioners accustomed to top-down governance.

Having admonished the liberation theologians, Joseph Ratzinger pursued other theological foes. Implementing liturgical reforms was a top priority for Asian Catholics after the Second Vatican Council, as they tried to rebut the commonly held view (among Catholics and non-Catholics) that Catholicism remained rooted in European culture. On the Indonesian island of Flores, for example, Dutch missionaries began to use locally made vestments and integrated Indigenous music and art into worship services. Masses celebrated in the fields were coordinated with the agricultural seasons, and seeds and tools were blessed during the liturgy.[18]

Such syncretism raised hackles in Rome, and Ratzinger began disciplinary proceedings against theologians based in South Asia, including a Belgian priest, Jacques Dupuis, who had spent thirty-six years teaching and writing in India, and a Sri Lankan theologian, Tissa Balasuriya. He judged Dupuis, especially, as overly eager to see the work of God and salvation in sacred Hindu texts. Ratzinger's own 2000 instruction, *Dominus Iesus*, stressed the centrality of Christ for any person's salvation. This might seem boilerplate coming from the prefect of the Congregation for the Doctrine of the Faith, but its tone rested uneasily next to *Nostra Aetate*, the more irenic document on non-Christian religions at the Second Vatican Council. Ratzinger lamented a "religious relativism which leads to the belief that 'one religion is as good as another.' "[19] "Yes, it is true there will be no authentic evangelization without announcing Jesus Christ Savior of the whole human race," responded a wary Cardinal Julius Darmaatmadja of Jakarta, "but for Asia, there will be no complete evangelisation unless there is dialogue with other religions and cultures."[20]

The biggest geopolitical challenge was in China. Both John Paul II and Benedict XVI favored some form of engagement with the People's Republic of China and its nine million Catholics, nominally members of either patriotic (government-approved) or underground churches, but in reality often attending both. By 2018, Vatican diplomats had negotiated a treaty with the People's Republic and even some voice for the state in episcopal appointments. Chinese Catholics and outside observers differed in their assessment of this strategy. Some of the leading pro-democracy activists in Hong Kong, notably Martin Lee, were Catholic. Along with Hong Kong's Cardinal Joseph Zen, they expressed fears that Vatican officials would be manipulated by Chinese communists. The roles of the 1930s were reversed. Then, Secretary of State Eugenio Pacelli favored concordats to protect Catholic institutions while liberals urged a principled stand against fascism. Now, Cardinal Zen and his admirers judged agreements with authoritarian rulers in China a betrayal of religious freedom while Vatican officials favored diplomatic overtures.

John Paul II's minimal interest in administering the curia contrasted with Paul VI, for whom the ins and outs of the papal bureaucracy were second nature. John Paul II did involve himself in episcopal appointments, choosing men based on his personal assessments of their character and their sympathy with his program. Some of his first appointments—Joseph Bernardin in Chicago, Carlo Maria Martini in Milan—were moderates, but over time his determination to appoint men sharing his countercultural sensibility became clear. Often they were plucked from relative obscurity, with specific checks on whether they supported *Humanae Vitae* (required), women's ordination (unacceptable), or married male clergy (unacceptable). In Chicago, Bernardin devoted his final years to the Catholic Common Ground Initiative aimed at uniting an increasingly polarized American church, only to have cardinals in the John Paul II mold scotch the effort. The most vocal, Cardinal Bernard Law in Boston, solemnly warned that "dialogue as a way to mediate between truth and dissent is mutual deception."[21] Bernardin's successor in Chicago, Francis George, described liberal Catholicism as an "exhausted project" and later made a melodramatic forecast: he would die in his bed, as he did, but his immediate successor would die "in prison and his successor will die a martyr in the public square."[22]

An even more abrupt shift in direction occurred in Latin America. Across the region John Paul II appointed bishops more committed to strict versions of orthodoxy. His choice as Lima's archbishop proved so threatening to liberation theologians that Gustavo Gutiérrez chose to become a priest in the Dominican order (as opposed to remaining a member of Lima's diocesan clergy) in order to gain greater distance from episcopal authority.[23]

III

JOHN PAUL II and Joseph Ratzinger accepted the expansion of capitalism after the fall of the Berlin Wall, although Ratzinger frequently noted that "democratic socialism was and is close to Catholic social doctrine."[24] They proved less malleable on matters of gender and sexuality. After 1989, the distinguishing characteristic of Catholic engagement on these topics became enlistment in a culture war. In part these clashes were inevitable: an institution with a sharply etched vision of family, gender, and sexuality could not avoid conflict in an environment (at least in the North Atlantic) where customs changed with astonishing speed. In part the clashes stemmed from John Paul II's rhetorical style. Instead of the long tradition of Catholic casuistry, or reasoning about how to balance individual cases with abstract principles, John Paul II favored absolutes. He saw Western societies as decayed and reasserted the importance of "universal moral norms" and prohibitions on acts deemed "intrinsically evil."[25]

The most rapidly shifting norm was gender equality. On John Paul II's first visit to the United States in 1979, Sr. Theresa Kane, speaking at a papal Mass in Washington DC's Basilica of the Immaculate Conception, urged the pope to recognize that women religious had fully "entered into the renewal efforts in an obedient response to the call of Vatican II." She asked him, in a reference to women's ordination, to "include women in all the ministries of the church."[26]

John Paul II greeted Kane graciously when she walked over to his chair and requested a blessing. But over the next two decades he would encounter advocates of women's ordination wherever he traveled in North America and Western Europe. After all, the rapidly growing number of women in professional roles was one of the defining markers of the age. This expansion of women's roles was less visible in John Paul II's Poland and less visible still in the Global South. Still, the Anglican Church ordained women beginning in the 1970s—one of the reasons Paul VI had first spoken against the idea—as did other Protestant denominations and some branches of Judaism. Continued Vatican resistance to ordination deepened the alienation of the first generation of female Catholic theologians, whose indictments of the church as a patriarchal institution became ever more comprehensive.[27]

John Paul II repeatedly insisted that women deserved legal and social equality with men but could not be ordained to the priesthood. This insistence took the form not only of an apostolic letter on the "dignity of women" but of a series of meditations on what became termed his theology of the body. He stressed sexual differentiation, not similarity, buttressed by a particular, even peculiar, interpretation of Genesis. Women possessed a "feminine genius."[28]

These papal meditations challenged the emerging academic conceit that all gender differences were social constructions. But the continued refusal to ordain women, and the limits to authority within the church for those not ordained, obscured any message of equality between the sexes. When the Vatican under John Paul II issued a ruling prohibiting girls from serving even as altar servers, parishioners erupted, with one mother in the United States pleading with her bishop to recognize that while her own faith could not be "altered by the decisions of men," younger women had become "further alienated." (The edict was revoked.)[29] Even as women took on the bulk of pastoral jobs in parishes and diocesan offices, Vatican officials tightened the connection between ordination and formal authority.[30] In the United States, fresh off widely celebrated pastoral letters on the nuclear arms race and the economy, the nation's bishops abandoned a letter on women, so difficult was it to draft something acceptable both to moderate bishops and to Joseph Ratzinger's Congregation for the Doctrine of the Faith.

In 1994, John Paul II issued an awkwardly worded statement declaring women's ordination impossible, even claiming that this teaching might be infallible. He demanded an end to theological discussion. Further theological discussion ensued. The British Catholic anthropologist, Mary Douglas, described papal statements against women's ordination as a "heavy bludgeon." Unlike most theologians, men or women, she did not favor women's ordination, because she thought ordination distracted from more fundamental questions of gender and power. But limiting ordination to men, she stressed, only became tenable if the Vatican recognized that since "women are the other half of humanity, they should not be left out of the church's official structure. There should be a commission for women, entrusted with specific areas of responsibility; anything that is proposed in those areas should be passed first by the Women's Commission on Doctrine."[31]

No commission was chartered. Instead, for Catholics in the developed world, church teachings on sex and gender became ever more out of sync with contemporary sensibilities. Given the depth of its Catholic culture, Ireland is a revealing case study. Until 1966, students studying in the library at University College Dublin stood at 12 p.m. and 6 p.m. for a recitation of the Angelus, a Catholic prayer. Into the 1970s, a mind-boggling 91 percent of Catholics claimed weekly Mass attendance, and church authority remained omnipresent, not only in parishes but in schools, legislative offices, and social service agencies. Paul

VI told a visitor in 1977 that "Ireland was a Catholic country—perhaps the only one left. It should stay that way. Laws should not be changed in a way that would make it less Catholic."[32]

Through the 1960s, government agencies and even quasi-independent firms such as Aer Lingus required women to leave full-time positions once they married, at least in part influenced by church teaching on the importance of women's roles as mothers and the need to provide jobs for male heads of households. (Such "marriage bars" had been abandoned in other countries a generation earlier.)[33] Contraceptives remained illegal until 1979, although doctors often prescribed birth control pills—conspiring with women patients—under the euphemism of "cycle regulation."[34] Even after *Humanae Vitae* in 1968, and what one observer called a "genuine and widespread crisis of conscience" among married couples, Irish priests rarely discussed birth control in public forums. "Doctrine must be emphasized," explained the longtime conservative Dublin archbishop John McQuaid, "before compassion."[35]

When John Paul II visited Ireland in 1979, he received a rapturous reception. A third of the country's population attended a single papal Mass in Dublin. One out of ten boys born in Ireland the next year was named John Paul. Alert to the impact of *Roe v. Wade* in the United States, Irish Catholic leaders persuaded voters to place a ban on abortion into the nation's constitution in 1983.

As the credibility of the Catholic sexual ethic waned, however, public opinion shifted. Negative appraisals of church teaching on contraception and women's ordination appeared in women's magazines. A popular bishop, Galway's Eamonn Casey, a Vatican II–style liberal who had attended Óscar Romero's funeral in San Salvador and headed Trōcaire, the highly regarded international development agency founded by the Irish church, generated months of headlines in 1992. His secret lover, Annie Murphy, revealed that Casey had fathered a son with her and used church monies to arrange for the son's care. The odyssey of a fourteen-year-old girl impregnated by the father of one of her friends and not permitted to travel to Britain for an abortion elicited from the Irish courts a ruling: abortions could be permitted in instances where a mother's mental health was at risk. This case, too, sparked a passionate discussion.

The first revelations from homes or workhouses for single women in Ireland occurred at the same moment. These institutions were founded in the late nineteenth or early twentieth century, funded in large part by the state and typically administered by women's religious orders. The stigma of single motherhood was such that pregnant women were often abandoned by families and local communities and saw these institutions as their only recourse. Upon entering, expectant mothers would sign a form pledging "to make my child available for adoption to any person [the mother superior] considers fit and proper." Children were often offered for adoption to couples who understood in return that they should make a donation to the convent or home. Some mothers stayed on as ill-paid laborers. Living conditions were grim. One bishop, as late as the 1950s, recommended "high boundary walls" for these residences.[36] Onetime residents of the homes began discussing their experiences in well-publicized interviews in the early 1990s, and government officials, after many delays, launched investigations. Writing in the wake of these events, one analyst attributed growing public skepticism in Ireland about church teaching to a "fundamental shift in attitudes and behavior relating to the equality of the sexes."[37]

IV

THE ISSUE OF ABORTION sparked an enduring Catholic mobilization, although regional variations were significant. John Paul II's stress on the issue was extraordinary. In a 1995 encyclical, he defined the struggle over abortion as the central battle in an all-encompassing struggle between a "culture of death" and a "culture of life." At two separate United Nations conferences on population and development, in Cairo in 1994 and in Beijing in 1997, the Vatican used its diplomatic leverage to fight against defining access to abortion as a human right. Just before the Cairo conference, John Paul II sent a letter to all papal nuncios decrying "certain fringes" of activists in wealthy countries eager to impose "contraceptive imperialism."[38]

These gestures rallied many delegates from Latin America and the Middle East. After all, the original justification for many contraceptive programs, which often include access to abortion services, seemed less pressing as birth rates plummeted across the developed world. That population control advocates had hesitated to criticize India's program of forced sterilization for women with three children in the late 1960s or even China's one child policy of the 1980s, where state officials pressured women pregnant with a second child to undergo abortions, compromised their status as spokespersons for women's empowerment.

The same population control advocates and women's groups struck a nerve, though, by pointing out that what Vatican officials or bishops described as Catholic teaching most Catholics rejected. An overwhelming majority of Catholic women (and men) supported contraceptive use by married couples, and a smaller but still substantial number supported legal abortion. Mariana Aylwin, a Chilean Christian Democrat, thought Vatican officials incapable of listening to diverse views. "Are we going to look at pluralistic society as a threat or an opportunity?" she asked. "At Beijing," she asserted, "Muslims and Catholics seemed to share a pessimistic vision of the changes in the modern world, which was sometimes expressed in stances that were defensive and dismissive of what happened there."[39]

John Paul II did not budge. In Poland, he encouraged bishops to (successfully) fight a law that allowed abortions in the first weeks of a pregnancy, even though the procedure required the approval of two doctors.[40] In Germany, after reunification in 1990, jurist Ernst-Wolfgang Böckenförde helped author a constitutional court ruling that declared abortion illegal, but not criminal if a woman seeking an abortion agreed to a counseling sesssion. German Catholics ran 15 percent of the counseling facilities in the country and saw in them an opportunity to offer support to women contemplating an abortion. John Paul II and Cardinal Ratzinger equated support with complicity. They required German Catholics to close counseling centers so the global church could "speak unanimously and with one voice."[41]

John Paul II especially admired the work of Mother Teresa, then the world's most prominent Catholic woman. Born and raised in Albania and then trained in Ireland, Mother Teresa founded the Missionaries of Charity in Calcutta in 1948, dedicated to serving the world's most desperately poor. Her work attracted patrons as diverse as Ronald Reagan, Indira Gandhi, Desmond Tutu, and Britain's Princess Diana.

Her commitment to the homeless and the dying commended her to John Paul II, but so, too, did her disinterest in women's ordination and her orthodox views on sexual ethics. In her 1979 Nobel Peace Prize acceptance speech, she advocated natural family planning (or the rhythm method of birth control) and described abortion as the "greatest destroyer of peace today."[42]

In the United States, the abortion issue's integration into partisan divisions—one party, the Democrats, increasingly pro-choice and one party, the Republicans, increasingly pro-life—prevented the compromises typical in Western Europe. In 1984, the Democratic Party platform described reproductive freedom as a "fundamental human right." In 1992, Pennsylvania Governor Robert Casey, a Catholic and the leading pro-life Democrat, was prohibited from speaking at the Democratic National Convention. By the early 2000s, in turn, some John Paul II–style bishops began encouraging priests to withhold communion from pro-choice Catholic Democratic politicians, and several did so during the 2004 presidential campaign of Massachusetts senator John Kerry. When the University of Notre Dame invited the newly elected pro-choice president, Barack Obama, to speak at commencement and receive an honorary degree in 2009, dozens of bishops registered their disapproval—Chicago's cardinal archbishop, Francis George, called it an "extreme embarrassment"—even as the vast majority of students and faculty greeted the president with standing ovations.[43]

The overall trend toward legalization of abortion was clear. Contrary to the expectations of pro-choice advocates, young people in many countries became slightly more pro-life over time, not less, with prenatal technology making the case that fetal life deserved greater protection. Still, modest shifts in public opinion rarely translated into decisive pro-life legislative or electoral victories, with even pro-life voters unwilling to punish women procuring abortions or doctors performing them. In majority Catholic Croatia, abortion restrictions after 1989 were minimal, as church leaders became entangled with party politics and discredited in their attempt to enforce moral norms. In Poland, Solidarity activists such as Lech Wałęsa favored the criminalization of abortion, while more left-leaning colleagues supported fewer restrictions. Polish bishops, then at the height of their moral authority, resisted a plebiscite on the issue in part because they judged the right to life a matter of "basic human rights . . . and not the result of the assent of any societal group." (By contrast, they dropped their opposition to contraceptive distribution, since "such a ban simply could not be enforced. For that reason alone it is not worth pursuing.") Eventually, strict limits on legal abortion passed the Polish parliament, but controversy over the issue endured.[44] In Ireland, in 2018, a generation after placing a ban on abortion in the country's constitution, voters legalized the procedure in the first months of pregnancy, with younger and urban voters supporting the measure by overwhelming margins.

Public opinion in Latin America was divided, and many doctors and nurses in the region refused to perform abortions when legally permitted to do so. In Brazil, as late as 2004, the Workers' Party dropped support for abortion legalization in its platform in order to assuage a core constituency of left-leaning, pro-life Catholics. But in 2012 the Brazilian Supreme Court ruled abortion legal in the first three months of a pregnancy.[45] Argentine legislators legalized abortion in 2020, and the Supreme Courts of Mexico and Colombia decriminalized the procedure.[46]

V

MORE DRAMATIC SHIFTS in both public and Catholic opinion resulted from changing perceptions of homosexuality. Nothing had prepared Catholics for the emergence of a gay rights movement. To the extent that gays and lesbians were discussed, as was true beyond Catholic circles, experts diagnosed their orientation as one part medical problem and one part moral failing. A British study group chartered by the cardinal archbishop of London in the 1950s did recommend decriminalizing homosexual activity. Theologians such as the German Bernhard Häring, later famous for his rejection of the official teaching on birth control, agreed that private sexual conduct did not require "penal sanctions." But he also encouraged Catholics to "energetically oppose" the "claim that the vice is something natural."[47]

Homosexuality was not mentioned in any of the documents or public discussions at the Second Vatican Council. Catholic groups advocating for homosexuals emerged with the stirrings of gay rights activism in the United States, Britain, the Netherlands, and West Germany in the late 1960s. In the United States these groups took the name Dignity—invoking the Second Vatican Council—and dedicated themselves to "work for the development of the church's sexual theology and for the acceptance of gays as full and equal members of the one Christ." The first empathetic theological treatments of homosexuality appeared in English and French. By 1977, the leading professional society for Catholic theologians in the United States felt emboldened to argue that "a homosexual engaging in homosexual acts in good conscience has the same rights of conscience and the same rights to the sacraments as a married couple practising birth control in good conscience."[48]

The early response from bishops was measured. Bewildered is perhaps the better term. They reaffirmed that homosexuals remained welcomed as Catholics but condemned homosexual acts. West German bishops agreed with their government that homosexual acts did not merit legal punishment. Still, bishops in cities with large gay populations found themselves maneuvering between anticlerical and secular gay activists, newly mobilized gay parishioners, and Catholics willing to denounce any conciliatory gestures to a receptive Vatican.[49]

The fact that a significant percentage of priests were gay—and that some might, for the first time, identify as such—made the issue more volatile. Vatican officials unsuccessfully pressured the Jesuits to prevent the publication of a reform-minded text on Catholicism and homosexuality by John McNeill, one of their American members. A World War II veteran who joined the Jesuits in the late 1940s, McNeill had long known of (and struggled with) his homosexuality and had begun writing on the topic as a problem in sexual ethics after the Second Vatican Council. (He also had begun living secretly with a male partner.)[50]

As McNeill knew firsthand through a busy speaking schedule, many urban dioceses in Western countries now included seminarians or priests who had acknowledged to friends that they were gay or in a few instances had become active in support of gay rights. A remarkable 1979 private letter from Boston's Cardinal Humberto Medeiros to the cardinal prefect of the Congregation for the Doctrine of the Faith hinted at this new situation. Medeiros noted the presence of "widespread" and "open" gay communities in large American cities, with gay men asserting that sexual orientation "is of no consequence to anyone except themselves." He expressed concern about "the problem of homosexuality" in Catholic seminaries "which reflect our local American culture" and asserted that he had weeded out many homosexuals from the local seminary. He assured the Vatican that he would continue to "turn back the number of homosexuals who, for many reasons, are being drawn towards the sacred priesthood."[51]

As in other areas of sexual ethics, John Paul II and Cardinal Ratzinger dug in. Ratzinger authored an instruction in 1986 that, while deploring violence directed against gays and lesbians, identified a homosexual orientation (using neo-Thomist vocabulary) as "a more or less strong tendency ordered toward an intrinsic moral evil." Defined this way, "the inclination itself must be seen as an objective disorder."[52] The reaction within the gay community to Ratzinger's "Halloween" letter (released on October 31) fused anger and despair. John McNeill, breaking a silence imposed on him by his superiors, publicly announced his rejection of the Ratzinger letter. The Jesuits dismissed him and he left the priesthood.

Support for gay and lesbian rights in Western nations was also propelled by the AIDS pandemic. By 1986, about twenty-five thousand people in the United States and a roughly equivalent number in Western Europe had died of AIDS, with the majority of deaths occurring among gay men. (These numbers were only the beginning: by 2002, over five hundred thousand deaths from AIDS had been recorded in the United States.) In the United States, protests led by gay advocacy groups centered on government agencies charged with approving new treatment programs and unsympathetic officials in the Reagan administration. But these protests extended to the church, in part because of Cardinal Ratzinger's 1986 instruction and in part because of Catholic opposition to the distribution of condoms as a public health measure. In New York City, Cardinal John O'Connor's opposition to laws protecting homosexuals from discrimination in employment or housing had already pitted the hierarchy against gay activists. The AIDS crisis provoked an explosion. Hundreds of demonstrators affiliated with ACT-UP, the most radical activist group, poured into New York City's St. Patrick's Cathedral waving condoms during one Sunday Mass in 1989, desecrating communion wafers and chaining themselves to pews. Parallel protests occurred in Los Angeles, with a squabble between the archdiocese and the local public television station over the showing of a film sympathetic to the ACT-UP protests.[53] Protests in other cities—notably in Buenos Aires and West Berlin—were less provocative but equally pointed.[54] In the Philippines, public health officials decried Cardinal Jaime Sin's description of condoms as "intrinsically evil."[55]

Beneath these headlines the story was more complicated. In Brazil, public health and church officials framed AIDS as a societal problem instead of a homosexual disease, and some Brazilian Catholic leaders won plaudits for their work on AIDS education efforts.[56] In the United States, because so many women religious ran hospitals, nuns encountered the AIDS crisis firsthand. When patients at St. Vincent's Hospital, run by the Sisters of Charity and located in the heavily gay neighborhood of Greenwich Village in New York City, complained of isolation and mistreatment, ACT-UP activists invaded the hallways and tied condoms to crucifixes in the building. Listening sessions led by the nuns in charge of the hospital, focused on the experience of gay patients, led to procedural changes, and over time the hospital became a leading center of AIDS treatment.[57]

In the less industrialized world, where most people diagnosed with AIDS were heterosexual and where case numbers in areas such as sub-Saharan Africa shot up to terrifying levels, the question of condom distribution again became controversial. In regions marked by failing states, independent Catholic agencies, with their deep local ties, attracted major funders. The US government pumped over one billion dollars a year into AIDS care programs organized by Catholic Relief Services for southern Africa, and Catholic hospitals and clinics led the effort against AIDS in regions as disparate as South Sudan and Papua New Guinea. In India, Catholics, who numbered less than 2 percent of the population, were the second largest provider of health care for AIDS victims, after only the government itself.[58]

Even when visiting Africa, John Paul II insisted that wearing condoms to prevent AIDS was morally illicit. Benedict XVI was equivocal. Both men accurately emphasized that condoms alone could not solve a public health crisis with complex epidemiological and behavioral roots.

But condoms could save lives. Reporters discovered that employees of Catholic aid agencies, especially women religious, ignored papal pronouncements and found ways to distribute condoms when they judged such distribution necessary. When queried by a Dutch virologist on her willingness to educate villagers on condom use, one nun replied that "Rome is very far away from Namibia."[59]

As the debate over gay and lesbian rights traversed a winding path from employment law to service in the military to civil unions to gay marriage, Vatican and often episcopal opposition was a constant. Instead of discussing how a Catholic university might welcome gay and lesbian students, for example, Lima's archbishop ordered the Pontifical Catholic University of Peru to distribute pamphlets describing homosexuality as a curable illness.[60] In 2003, as debates over civil unions and same-sex marriage animated political life on both sides of the Atlantic, Joseph Ratzinger insisted that Catholics could not condone civil unions for gay and lesbian partners because to do so would inhibit "the proper development of human society, especially if their impact on society were to increase."[61] His instruction tied the hands of more moderate bishops, notably Jorge Bergoglio, archbishop of Buenos Aires and the future Pope Francis, who welcomed efforts to legally recognize same-sex relationships and give partners health and visitation rights, while deflecting proposals to legalize gay marriage.[62]

During these two decades of debate, Catholics made some of the most important arguments on both sides. Andrew Sullivan, a British journalist working in the United States, wrote perhaps the most influential treatise advocating both gay marriage and the admission of gays into the military. Spurred by the AIDS death toll and the denial of visiting rights in some hospitals to gay partners, Sullivan paid special attention to Cardinal Ratzinger's 1986 statement. He agreed with Ratzinger that homosexual persons were "made in the image and likeness of God," but then wondered how their inclination to same-sex activity could be described as intrinsically disordered. He dismissed the idea, defended by Ratzinger, that married gay couples would weaken the heterosexual family.[63]

By contrast, Oxford and Notre Dame professor John Finnis and Princeton professor Robert George argued that healthy societies, in

Finnis's words, should not equate heterosexual and homosexual cou-
plings as a "valid, humanly acceptable choice and form of life."[64] George,
especially, became a sought-after interlocutor for conservatives in both
the United States and Latin America.[65]

Over time, these conservative voices became minority voices. As
public opinion shifted in favor of legal divorce, access to contraception,
legal abortion (with restrictions), and gay rights, leading Catholic politicians in Europe, Latin America, and the United States became more
open about their disagreement with how John Paul II, Benedict XVI,
and many bishops translated church teaching into policy recommendations. Some of this disagreement was principled; some of it expedient.
All of it created a gap between bishops and Catholic politicians greater
than any that had existed before the 1980s. In Chile, over a thirteen-
year period, fierce debates occurred on divorce (ultimately allowed
with some restrictions in order to protect children), civil unions for
gays and lesbians (passed in 2004), and abortion (made legal to save the
life of the mother, if the pregnancy was caused by rape, or if the fetus
was not viable). In each instance, Catholic bishops and the papal nuncio decried changes in the law and insisted that Christian Democrats
who supported the measures only "called themselves Catholics." In each
instance, Christian Democrats in the legislature, virtually all Catholics,
moved ahead. One of the country's leading Christian Democrats later
regretted how clumsy episcopal interventions, from phone calls to legislators to pastoral letters, obscured the message of *Gaudium et Spes*, which
had encouraged lay Catholic professionals to carve out a new role in the
public sphere.[66]

Billionaire philanthropist Melinda French Gates, head of the world's
largest foundation devoted to public health, repeatedly stressed her commitment to her Catholicism. Her memoir referenced the pacifist Dorothy Day, Dutch theologian Henri Nouwen, and Mother Teresa. But
Gates also emphasized the importance of contraceptives for women's
development and described ordaining only men as "male dominance."
When criticized on the front page of the Vatican newspaper *L'Osservatore
Romano* for her advocacy of contraception, she was inundated with messages, including from priests and nuns working in the development field,
expressing their support.[67] Kenyan bishops opposed to Gates Foundation

programs repeated familiar arguments about cultural imperialism and described contraceptives as "dehumanizing" and "an insult to the dignity and integrity of the human person." But knowledgeable observers judged the credibility of the same bishops, who had unsuccessfully opposed a popular new constitution because it allowed for abortion in limited circumstances, as at a new low.[68]

VI

THE CLERICAL SEXUAL ABUSE crisis unfolded in starts and stops. Public awareness of sexual abuse in families and institutions crystallized in North America and Western Europe in the 1980s and 1990s, overcoming an earlier naivete about "liberation" and "consent" that discounted the devastating effects of sexual coercion on children and vulnerable adults. Because the authority of bishops in their dioceses and priests in their parishes on personnel matters remained close to absolute, sexual abuse within Catholic settings only episodically popped into public view. One priest from Northern Ireland, guilty of abusing dozens of young people, fled south to the Republic of Ireland (where the fumbling of an extradition request helped cause the collapse of the government). Cases also came to light of the same priest committing abuse in the United States. Investigative reporters in rural Louisiana highlighted sexual abuse cases involving a different priest in the mid-1980s. Victims started to come forward, and dioceses (and their insurance companies) began authorizing settlement payments. These turned out to be a harbinger of what would become billions of dollars in payments to victims and their lawyers.

Inquiries also began in the 1990s into other Catholic institutions. Some of the most startling revelations came in the investigations of boarding schools for Indigenous students in the United States, Canada, and Australia, typically funded by the state but frequently administered by Catholic religious orders. Often required to leave their families, living far from home, Indigenous young people were especially vulnerable to physical or sexual abuse by religious authority figures. Most of these schools were founded in the early twentieth century and closed by the 1970s, but little grappling with their impact had occurred. Findings of mass graves of young people in Canada next to two former residential schools in 2020 and 2021 produced a tidal wave of headlines and suggested a callous disregard for Indigenous life. Demands for formal apologies coincided with calls for reparation and redress.

Protestants had run similar boarding schools and orphanages. But Catholics committed to institutional autonomy and with a dedicated labor pool of priests, nuns, and brothers had run more of them for longer periods of time. State officials, for their part, despite after-the-fact posturing, had welcomed the budgetary relief provided by religious organizations. (Many priests and nuns laboring for state or local governments received only minimal wages.)

None of these revelations prepared the world's Catholics for the explosion of January 2002, when *Boston Globe* reporters detailed how priests in Boston accused of sexual abuse had been reassigned to other parishes. The *Globe* devoted over two hundred stories, many on the front page, to the crisis in its first four months, and for their efforts its editors and reporters received a Pulitzer Prize. A film based on these events received the Academy Award for Best Picture.

An ailing eighty-two-year-old John Paul II convened the American cardinals and Vatican officials in Rome four months after the first *Boston Globe* stories, but the meeting became a public relations fiasco of conflicting statements. The country's bishops partially recovered their balance at the national meeting in Dallas in June, where under the leadership of the future cardinal archbishop of Washington, DC, Wilton Gregory, they adopted a "one-strike" policy prohibiting any priest guilty of sexual abuse from serving in active ministry.

Following revelations of sexual abuse in the Anglophone world, public authorities in Belgium, the Netherlands, and Germany uncovered numerous incidents of clerical sexual abuse, including at a prestigious Berlin Jesuit high school and a Bavarian choir school. Beginning in the late nineteenth century, Catholics had fought to make their institutions autonomous from the state; these efforts now ground to a halt. Because internal church processes were so discredited, some governments started monitoring parish appointments, and state authorities (as in Australia) challenged the privacy of the confessional. In the United States, class action lawsuits became the most successful strategy for winning financial recompense for survivors. Lawyers for victims followed the template established by litigation against tobacco companies, who had known of the health damage caused by cigarettes in the same way that many bishops had known about sexually abusive priests. Thousands of victims sued for damages in this fashion, pushing numerous dioceses into bankruptcy. Legislators dropped statute of limitation restrictions given mounting public fury against the church, opening the door to yet another wave of difficult-to-adjudicate and long-ago claims of abuse.[69]

In England, incidents of abuse at two leading Catholic boarding schools, Ampleforth and Downside, and recalcitrance toward reforms by the Benedictine monks in charge—one headmaster-monk allegedly burned several wheelbarrows of documents—prompted a government minister, not a bishop or a religious superior or a school board, to pause admissions for a year.[70] In Chile, the most notorious case involved Fr. Fernando Karadima, a charismatic Santiago priest accused of abuse as early as 1984. When new accusations surfaced in the wake of the Boston revelations, Santiago's archbishop, judging them beyond the statute of limitations, ignored them. Only in 2010, after multiple victims came forward amid a national outcry, did a government investigation lead to the dismissal of Karadima from active ministry. By 2020, the Inter-American Commission on Human Rights had pledged to hold accountable those Catholic bishops accused of ignoring abuse cases.

As the focus shifted from abuse cases to cover-up, attention turned toward Rome. Canons limiting public exposure of priests accused of crimes, even concordats that explicitly prohibited priests and bishops from being tried in civil courts, came under scrutiny. So did a body of canon law that treated sexual abuse primarily as departure from clerical chastity, not a violation of children and vulnerable adults.

The initial Vatican response proved disastrous. Given his experience in communist Poland, where state security officials frequently manufactured accusations of sexual misconduct to discredit clergy, John Paul II was incapable of conducting an institutional audit. His first statements on sexual abuse, in the early 1990s, urged punishment for guilty priests but also cautioned against a media that "feeds on sensationalism."[71] Even after 2002, Vatican officials disliked what they perceived as a draconian "one-strike" rule drafted by bishops in the United States and defined the American policy as an exception to standard protections of clerical rights. John Paul II's secretary of state Cardinal Angelo Sodano repeatedly downplayed the crisis. As papal nuncio to Chile, he had declined to investigate Fr. Karadima. He tried to persuade Irish president Mary McAleese to thwart investigations of the church. As late as 2010, when he was no longer secretary of state, Sodano dismissed rumors and accusations of sexual abuse as "idle gossip."

The term "gossip" concealed a more disturbing reality. The global nature of the ultramontane revival and the parallel church structures built up in almost every country made national variations on sexual abuse less striking than similarities. Bishops and heads of male religious orders all felt pressure to ordain sufficient numbers of men for the priesthood. They also found it difficult to remove clerical offenders from the priesthood because the process depended on a Vatican bureaucracy eager to remind bishops and clergy that ordination meant a lifelong commitment. The most grotesque cases attracted the most press scrutiny—a handful of priest predators in each country committed a significant percentage of sexual crimes—but the systems enabling abuse drew more attention as the crisis dragged on. With significant exceptions, in parish after parish, in school after school, in diocese after diocese, in religious order after religious order, clerical leaders accustomed to thinking of theirs as a distinct caste ignored or concealed the crimes of priests. They failed to see the victims standing in front of them.

Everywhere, the majority of cases involved priests and teenage boys or priests and vulnerable adults such as seminarians. Everywhere, the absence of women from positions of authority enabled abuse patterns similar to those observed in other once all-male fraternities, such as police officers, military units, the Boy Scouts, and athletic teams.

Cover-ups—and actual acts of abuse—compromised bishops and cardinals around the world with diverse ideological views. But the scandals surrounding men appointed by John Paul II were especially notable. Bernard Law, cardinal archbishop of Boston, resigned following the revelations of cover-ups (although John Paul II gave him a sinecure appointment in Rome). Hans Hermann Groër, cardinal archbishop of Vienna, appointed only after John Paul II circumvented the normal appointment process, resigned after credible accusations of sexual abuse. Keith O'Brien, cardinal archbishop of Edinburgh, described gay marriage as "moral degradation" but then resigned after confessing to making sexual advances on a number of seminarians and clergy. Henry Gulbinowicz, cardinal archbishop of Wrocław, was forbidden from any public ministry because of credible claims of abuse.

Other abusers flourished in religious movements that emerged outside of normal diocesan structures, especially in the more experimental atmosphere of the 1960s and 1970s. The most appalling case was that of Fr. Marcial Maciel Degollado and the Legionaries of Christ.[72] Born in 1920, Maciel was raised in a Mexican family active in the Cristero rebellion, the guerrilla war against a government committed to the secularization of Mexican society. As a newly ordained priest, he founded a men's religious order, eventually named the Legionaries of Christ, and located its seminary in the ideologically congenial climate of Franco's Spain in the 1950s. Accusations of drug use and sexual abuse dogged Maciel and the Legionaries from the beginning, but he emerged unscathed from a Vatican investigation, spared, it seems, only because of Pius XII's death. When John Paul II visited Mexico in 1979, Maciel stood by his side. The Legionaries of Christ experienced exponential growth in the 1970s and 1980s. By 2003, the order ran a network of eleven colleges or universities and 150 high schools, as well as an affiliated movement for laypeople with fifty thousand members. Legionary of Christ clergy—row upon row of clean-shaven young men professing traditional views on sex and gender—became proof points for John Paul II's new evangelization. (John Paul II once ordained sixty Legionaries in a single liturgy.) They displayed their militancy by successfully promoting the canonizations of Mexican Cristero martyrs. Specific sums are unknown, but Maciel was a prodigious fundraiser for papal initiatives, with rumors of suitcases of cash accompanying him on trips to Rome.

American journalists broke the first stories of sexual abuse by Maciel and other Legionaries. His supporters in the United States, Mexico, and Rome leapt to his defense. Fr. Richard John Neuhaus declared Maciel's innocence a "moral certainty." When survivors conveyed accusations of abuse to Rome, Cardinal Joseph Ratzinger and the Congregation for the Doctrine of the Faith began, and then halted, presumably under pressure from John Paul II's aides, an investigation. Only after John Paul II's death and his own election as pope could Benedict XVI restart the investigation. Without releasing the details, he stripped Maciel of his position in 2006 and required him to lead a life of penance and prayer.

The details turned out to be salient. By the time of his death in exile in the United States in 2008, Maciel stood credibly accused of multiple sexual assaults on young men and boys, some of whom became Legionary priests and then committed acts of abuse themselves. He fathered six children with four different women and may have abused two of his own children.

This second phase of the sexual abuse crisis—focused on cover-ups as much as abuse incidents—culminated in 2018. Washington, DC's emeritus cardinal archbishop, Theodore McCarrick, was stripped of his status as cardinal and then removed from the priesthood. Complaints about McCarrick inappropriately touching seminarians, and eventually, credible accusations of sexual abuse of at least one minor decades before, wound their way from New Jersey and New York to Rome. Just-installed procedures for oversight of bishops, and not only priests, worked in this instance, although only belatedly. Rumors of McCarrick's abuse of seminarians had circulated for over twenty years among the region's clergy.

In the fall of 2020, Vatican officials released an unprecedented, admirably detailed report detailing McCarrick's ascent in the hierarchy from his appointment as bishop in 1977 to his last decade as cardinal archbishop emeritus of Washington, when he acted as a globe-trotting ambassador for humanitarian causes.[73] McCarrick's audacity was breathtaking. He had helped author the "one-strike" American policy in 2002 knowing his own complicity. He told John Paul II in a personal letter that he had "never had sexual relations with any person, male or female, young or old, cleric or lay, nor have I ever abused another person or treated them with disrespect."[74]

McCarrick was on the moderate wing of the US hierarchy but he was a longtime friend of John Paul II, whom he had met on the future pope's first visit to the United States in 1976. Like Maciel, he was a charismatic, effective fundraiser on behalf of the papacy, and while the report discounted any link between McCarrick's benefactions and the honors bestowed upon him, that particular question remains open. New York's Cardinal John O'Connor recommended against McCarrick's promotion, in a hedging letter, but other American bishops, when queried by Vatican officials, implausibly denied knowing anything disqualifying. John Paul II's longtime secretary, Bishop Stanisław Dziwisz, did not act on the negative testimony about McCarrick that did reach Rome. By the time of the McCarrick report, Dziwisz stood accused of the cover-up of abuse cases following his appointment as cardinal archbishop of Kraków, although he has denied the claims. Even in Poland, where a John Paul II Street or Plaza marks many cities and where the country's leading Catholic university carries his name, complaints about the handling of sexual abuse cases reached a crescendo. Two documentary films on clerical sexual abuse drew huge audiences and included interviews with survivors and claims of cover-up. Activists toppled a statue of a priest-chaplain to Solidarity who had been credibly accused of abuse. Some academics urged the media not to tar John Paul II with the brush of sexual abuse, arguing that a trusting pope had been fooled by manipulative clergy. Others demanded a Truth and Reconciliation commission. One distraught Polish priest told reporters that "we must establish what was happening in the papal court, especially among John Paul II's closest entourage."[75]

John Paul II's canonization, a process begun by Benedict XVI just six weeks after the pope's death, now seemed premature. Scholars, church officials, and survivors began to assess the damage done by twenty years of revelations about sexual abuse, not just to John Paul II's reputation but to the church he once so confidently led.

Pope Francis in Manila in 2015. *(Alamy)*

Pope Francis and Beyond

I

LET'S END WHERE we began.

France, the country where the ultramontane revival had such a profound impact in the wake of the revolution, and which sent more missionaries around the world than any other place, is now a missionary destination. Fewer than 10 percent of French Catholics attend Mass weekly, and hundreds of churches are falling into disrepair. The number of Catholic weddings is down 60 percent in twenty-five years. The sexual abuse crisis followed a now familiar pattern, with a 2021 report finding that over four thousand clergy or other Catholic personnel had committed acts of abuse over seven decades.[1]

Declining practice marks Catholicism not only in France but in all of Europe, as it does, in varying degrees, in Latin America, North America, and parts of East Asia. This Catholic pattern is not unique, and declines in Protestant church membership are sometimes more severe. (In France, the most vibrant religious community is Islam.) Conversions to Catholicism are also noteworthy, including four million adults in the United States alone since the 1980s. But the dominant pattern is disaffiliation. In once-Catholic countries such as Spain and Ireland, nonpracticing Catholics rarely convert to other faiths, but their inherited identity seems unlikely to transfer across generations. In Boston, one of the world's most Catholic urban areas sixty years ago, lapsed Catholics outnumber practicing Catholics. Forty-four percent of cradle Catholics in Britain and 34 percent of cradle Catholics in the United States no longer identify as such.

In Latin America, the decline has become more evident in countries battered by the sexual abuse crisis, such as Chile, even as it may have tapered off in Brazil, the nation with the world's largest number of Catholics. Two-thirds of Brazilians identify as Catholic, although one-fifth of baptized Catholics describe themselves as not affiliated with any church. Even in some African countries, including South Africa and Kenya, Catholics display high rates of drift. In Germany, low birth rates explain some of the decline in the Catholic population, but tax data reveal a steady stream of German Catholics formally renouncing church membership. Weekly Mass attendance for Catholics declined from 50 percent in 1950 to 27 percent in 1985 to 15 percent in 2002.[2]

Understanding the decline is challenging. Certainly, the sexual abuse crisis has resulted in an ongoing credibility crisis for church leaders. So, too, has the alienation of many women and perceptions of Catholicism as unwelcoming to gays and lesbians. In the United States, the association of religion with political conservatism during the last two decades has been off-putting to young people who are often more liberal on social issues.[3] At the same time, more liberal churches and synagogues have not flourished during this period either. Religious leaders from many backgrounds are struggling to find spiritual forms appealing to a mass audience in a fragmented age.

Migration is one form of renewal. In the nineteenth century, some thirty million Irish, German, Italian, Spanish, and Polish Catholics left Europe, primarily for North and South America. During much of the twentieth century, two world wars and legal barriers limited migration. But over the past fifty years, Catholic migrants showed some of the same propensity for institution building as their predecessors. In London, Tamil migrants from India pack novenas at a shrine to St. Anthony, originally built for the city's Italians and Irish. Polish Catholics now constitute a majority of the growing Catholic community in Norway. Filipinos are among the most significant Catholic populations in Sydney, Hong Kong, Rome, Los Angeles, and the Middle East. Vietnamese Catholics are disproportionately influential—with numerous vocations to the priesthood and religious life—in France and the United States. Catholics from Latin America and the Caribbean—Mexico above all, but also Cuba, the Dominican Republic, Guatemala, and El Salvador—come to the United States in large numbers. These Catholics and their descendants are now more likely to be practicing than the descendants of nineteenth-century European Catholic migrants. Devotion to Our Lady of Guadalupe extends far beyond Mexico City.[4]

Neither decline nor migration should overshadow a more important shift: the center of gravity within the Catholic world has moved south. In 1900, over two-thirds of the world's Catholics lived in Europe. Now less than one-third do. The largest number of Catholics reside in Latin America, and the fastest-growing Catholic population is in Africa. High birth rates and high rates of adult conversion mean that African influence within the global church will continue to grow. Already, the roughly 230 million African Catholics represent one-sixth of all Catholics worldwide. Soon, the ten countries with the largest Catholic populations will include not only Brazil, Mexico, and the Philippines but also Nigeria. More Catholics will live in the Democratic Republic of the Congo than in Spain.[5]

If fault lines in the nineteenth century were between Protestant and Catholic or between secular and Catholic, fault lines in the twenty-first century—in the Philippines, Sri Lanka, Sudan, Malaysia, and Nigeria—are more likely to be between Muslim and Catholic.[6] Indonesia has the largest Muslim population of any country in the world, but the nation also includes a significant Catholic minority, and the country's post-1960 history has been marked by a mix of violent clashes between Christians and Muslims, with culpability on both sides, and significant rates of intermarriage and extensive dialogue. Both Muslims and Christians at various points in the country's recent history desired acknowledgment of God in the country's constitution, and both puzzled over the role of religion in publicly funded education.[7]

Turmoil in the Middle East over the last generation has diminished the region's religious diversity, as Catholics and other Christians have fled ancestral homelands in Iraq, Iran, Egypt, and Syria.[8] Some of this turmoil resulted from the American invasions of Afghanistan and Iraq, initiated over the fierce objections of Vatican diplomats and John Paul II, who anticipated the inability of the United States to impose democratic governments. Some of it rests on Muslim persecution of Christians. Two men linked to the Islamic State murdered an eighty-five-year-old French priest saying Mass in 2016 in a working-class parish in Normandy. Islamic radicals orchestrated Easter Sunday bombings in Colombo, Sri Lanka, in

2019, partially destroying two Catholic churches and killing three hundred worshippers. The event mobilized members of Sri Lanka's Catholic diaspora in such far-flung locales as Toronto to urge renewed commitment to the country's long history of religious pluralism.[9]

That Catholics built so many institutions during the ultramontane era means that their influence often outweighs their numbers. The total number of pupils enrolled in Catholic nursery, primary, and secondary schools in 2016 was a staggering 62.5 million, up from 43.4 million in 1995. Growth is primarily in the Global South.[10] Hindu nationalist attacks on the small Catholic minority in India—small in India still means twenty million people—have recently created a new climate of fear.[11] But many of India's most prestigious secondary schools are Catholic—in the region around the city of Ranchi, in northeast India, the number of students enrolled in Jesuit high schools grew from just over two thousand in 1970 to almost eighteen thousand in 2010—and citizens of all faiths vie to enroll their children in them.[12] Twenty-five percent of Australian children receive their education in Catholic schools, funded primarily by the state since the early 1970s, even as day-to-day practice of the faith by Australian Catholics has declined.

In countries or regions where governmental presence is minimal—or corrupt—Catholic institutions remain crucial. Haiti is predominantly Catholic, and church officials are as influential as government leaders after an earthquake or hurricane. Catholics make up only 8 percent of the population in Chad, one of the world's most impoverished countries in a predominantly Muslim region. But Chad contains sixty-four Catholic schools, nine Catholic hospitals, and 102 parishes.[13]

Even French Catholicism showed the occasional vital sign. Some recent presidential candidates have stressed their Catholicism—violating a taboo—and citizens who rarely attend Mass but identify as Catholic remain a significant percentage of the population. In a country where many organizations, including political parties, the military, and trade unions, enroll fewer people than in the immediate postwar era, and where sociologists fret about the absence of common bonds, Catholicism is a potential binding agent. Self-consciously Catholic arguments about the nature of the family and, now, climate change shape cultural life well beyond vibrant communities of the devout. France's secular president,

Emmanuel Macron, startled some of his secular admirers by reaching out to Catholic audiences, referencing nouvelle theologian Henri de Lubac in one 2018 address where he asserted that "the link between Catholicism and the French nation is indestructible."[14] When a fire ripped through the Cathedral of Notre Dame in Paris, a medieval structure rebuilt in the nineteenth century along with much of French Catholicism, the event dominated global news coverage. Standing outside the cathedral, as firefighters dashed into the structure, Macron pledged to immediately rebuild.

II

THE UNLIKELY PERSON identifying a path forward is Jorge Bergoglio, or Pope Francis. Bergoglio was born in 1936 to parents whose families had migrated to Argentina from different towns near Turin. Before entering the Jesuits, he trained as a chemist. As a Jesuit superior, he joined his seminarians in required manual labor, including cleaning out the pigsty on the farm next to the seminary. He insisted that seminarians familiarize themselves with the challenges faced by poor families, becoming "pastors of large flocks, not strokers of a few preferred sheep." He welcomed liberation theology's focus on the poor, but dismissed the "absurd pretension [of some theologians] to become the 'voice' of the people, imagining perhaps that they don't have one."[15]

During the military dictatorship in Argentina in the 1970s and 1980s, small groups of "third world" clergy, nuns, and laypeople clashed with the security forces of an increasingly repressive regime. Bergoglio found himself pinned between these activists (including some Jesuits) and other Catholics willing to collaborate with the government. Tensions were such that his superiors removed him from Buenos Aires, sending him to Germany to begin a dissertation and then assigning him to the more rural setting of Córdoba in Argentina.[16]

John Paul II appointed Bergoglio first as an auxiliary bishop and then cardinal archbishop of Buenos Aires. Benedict XVI's unexpected resignation in 2013, a giant step away from a monarchical understanding of the papacy, allowed Bergoglio's election. When he greeted the crowd in St. Peter's Square, Francis did so as the first Jesuit pope and the first pope from Latin America. He joked that the cardinals had elected someone from the "end of the earth."

His predecessors as pope were a theologian and a philosopher, but Bergoglio never completed his doctorate. He did study spirituality. Long a scholarly backwater, the topic underwent a renaissance before the Second Vatican Council, led by nouvelle theologians, who in this area as in so many others used classic Christian texts to pose new questions. The term "discernment" became an interpretive key. Instead of what Bergoglio termed a "decadent or largely bankrupt Thomism," with prepackaged answers to familiar questions, discernment meant ascertaining God's will for a particular person—or a global church—at a particular moment. Discernment took time, required midcourse corrections, and necessitated "looking at the signs, listening to the things that happen, the feeling of the people, especially the poor."[17]

Soon after his election, Francis began to edge the church away from the front lines of culture wars over sexuality and gender. His own opposition to abortion and same-sex marriage was traditional, and he recognized that Catholics in the Global South, as a rule, were more conservative, not less, on these issues. He rattled liberals by referencing the active role of the devil. But his tone was different. He famously answered "Who am I to judge?" when asked about gay Catholics. He expressed support for same-sex civil unions. He mentioned abortion only occasionally.

Discernment applied to his own decisions. Francis's first assessments of the ongoing sex abuse crisis were defensive. He prematurely dismissed as "slander," for example, evidence that Chilean bishops had neglected victims while protecting their own reputations and priests guilty of abuse. Then he changed his mind. After sending a special papal investigator, who drafted a twenty-six-hundred-page report validating many claims made by survivors, Francis required all of the Chilean bishops to meet with him in Rome and submit their resignations (a number of which he accepted). He conducted long, searching conversations with survivors of abuse, notably Juan Carlos Cruz, an openly gay man and graduate of an elite Chilean Catholic high school. Francis appointed Cruz to a Vatican commission on sexual abuse in 2021.[18]

These conversations created momentum for Francis to develop mechanisms for oversight of bishops, not only priests. He commissioned the thorough report on the laicized Cardinal McCarrick, promoted by John Paul II and treated with kid gloves by Benedict XVI. The next challenge will be to implement reforms in parts of the world such as sub-Saharan Africa and South Asia, where claims of clerical sexual abuse are multiplying, including abuse of nuns by priests, but without the media scrutiny, legal mechanisms, or reformed church structures to provide voice for survivors.

Francis repeatedly picked up threads left dangling at the death of Paul VI and urged Catholics to recommit themselves to the texts of the Second Vatican Council. Like Paul VI, he limited the ability of priests to say the pre–Vatican II rite of the Latin Mass (after Benedict XVI expanded its availability) because many liturgical traditionalists had promoted the rite as part of a more general opposition to the council.

Also like Paul VI, Francis focused much of his energy on social questions. He stressed integral human development and the gap between rich and poor, but wove into this vision an emphasis on the natural environment, or, as he called it, "our common home." He became the world's leading voice on climate change through his major encyclical, *Laudato Si'*, which connected "the cry of the earth and the cry of the poor."[19] It began in the inductive manner of *Gaudium et Spes* with an analysis of relevant science, and Francis timed its release to encourage those conducting climate change talks in Paris. As he told an interviewer, "The green and the social go hand in hand. The fate of creation is tied to the fate of all humanity."[20]

Francis's rejection of "neoliberalism"—a term he used before it became fashionable—as causing the "human family to fall apart" aligned him with reform currents.[21] Already in *Gaudium et Spes* the world's bishops had written of a "human interdependence" that "grows more tightly drawn and spreads by degrees over the whole world."[22]

Other Catholics made the point about cultivating solidarity in different ways. The German jurist Ernst-Wolfgang Böckenförde wondered whether the focus on procedures and rights within contemporary liberalism could sustain the resources necessary for its survival. In the medieval period, religion had been "the strongest bonding force for the political order and the life of the state." After the French Revolution, distinctions between church and state meant people needed to find a "new togetherness."[23] The Canadian philosopher Charles Taylor spent part of the 1950s and early 1960s absorbed in the texts of the *nouvelle théologie*, arguing against a "dualism between Church and world." He later claimed that while modern notions of human rights and dignity required the collapse of medieval Christendom, the sustenance of such notions rested on religious sources of meaning.[24]

One form of solidarity comes from withdrawal. If the Second Vatican Council marked a moment of Catholic engagement with the world, the subsequent sixty years also witnessed a push among many Catholics for a more clear-cut identity. The Scottish-born Marxist-turned-Catholic philosopher Alasdair MacIntyre ended his most influential study calling for "new forms of community within which moral life could be sustained, so that both morality and civility might survive the coming ages of barbarism and darkness."[25] Benedict XVI agreed. Ever since the 1950s, as he reflected on the German Catholic experience under National Socialism, Joseph Ratzinger had harbored doubts about the ability of church structures to respond to the challenges posed by secular societies. He wondered if the bureaucracy of organizations such as Caritas, the West German Catholic social welfare agency, which employed 283,000 people in the 1970s, could sustain any missionary vibrancy.[26] He later warned Catholics not to be bound by institutions, an almost heretical thought for anyone raised in the ultramontane milieu. He borrowed the phrase "creative minorities" to describe small groups of Catholics who could convince others to join them by "their joy."[27]

This focus on Catholicism as a minority religion became especially visible in the United States. Although Catholics numbered only 20 percent of the population, they now constituted a majority on the US Supreme Court. Five Catholics were appointed to the court by Republican presidents—Clarence Thomas, John Roberts, Samuel Alito, Brett Kavanaugh, and Amy Coney Barrett—and a sixth justice appointed by a Republican president, Neil Gorsuch, was raised as a Catholic and studied with the prominent Catholic legal scholar, John Finnis. Their jurisprudence stressed the autonomy of religious institutions in an increasingly secular milieu. By 2020, they spoke and wrote less about the morality of contraception or gay marriage—lost causes in terms of public opinion—than did their predecessors. But they did emphasize free markets and free speech. These libertarian impulses would have surprised their nineteenth-century ultramontane ancestors, who thought such ideas rested on a misguided individualism. They also seemed poised to overrule the 1973 Supreme Court decision on abortion, *Roe v. Wade*, ending one chapter in the long American struggle over the issue and beginning a new phase of legislative debates.

At the same time, populist Catholic attacks on international organizations marked an abrupt reversal from the ethos cultivated by Jacques Maritain in the 1940s and Paul VI and John Paul II in the 1970s and 1980s. Maritain and his disciples had promoted democracy, the United Nations, and what would become the European Union. Giorgio La Pira, later mayor of Florence, insisted that a Catholic view "is resolutely opposed to every nationalist, racial or class-based conception of the political order."[28] Now Stephen Bannon, Donald Trump's 2016 campaign manager, and a few intellectuals offer tributes to nationalists such as Hungarian president Victor Orbán.

President Donald Trump's contempt for democratic procedures resonated in these same circles and blended with an increasingly open opposition to Pope Francis. A Republican Catholic congressman from Arizona boycotted Pope Francis's address to Congress because of the pope's emphasis on climate change, and championed false allegations of voting fraud in the 2020 presidential election. One of Pope Francis's antagonists, Archbishop Carlo Maria Viganò, the onetime Vatican nuncio to the United States, released a series of conspiratorial letters and videos supporting President Trump that linked a "deep state" with a "deep church." Viganò called on Francis to resign in 2018 and then raved about the threats posed by vaccination programs during the COVID-19 pandemic, "globalism," and a "New World Order." Other so-called traditionalists teetered on rejection of the Second Vatican Council itself.[29]

Provoking these open Catholic attacks on a pope, unprecedented in the modern era, have been modest ecclesiastical reforms. Doubts about the centralization of authority in the papacy—raised at the Second Vatican Council but submerged during the papacies of John Paul II and Benedict XVI—resurfaced after Francis's election, and he organized a cabinet of cardinals from every continent to work alongside the curia. More daringly, he revived the idea of synodal governance. The most controversial moments of Francis's papacy have involved synods in which he convened bishops, clergy, nuns, and laypeople to discuss family, youth, and the Amazon region. Planned for 2023 is a synod on the future of the church. A synod is not a legislative assembly. Its participants are not elected and do not pass laws. But Francis's willingness to follow synodal recommendations to allow divorced and remarried Catholics to receive communion sparked an intense reaction, as did his consideration of married male clergy in the Amazon and his encouragement of a distinctive Amazonian liturgical rite along the lines of the Zairian rite approved in the aftermath of the Second Vatican Council. (During the John Paul II and Benedict XVI era, proposed rites for India and the Philippines were rejected.)

Whether Francis's more synodal church will tackle internal questions such as the role of women and how bishops are selected is unclear. National synods in Australia and Germany—prompted in part by fallout from the sexual abuse crisis—are underway. German bishops and laypeople, in particular, are revisiting officially closed questions about married male clergy and blessings for gay couples.

Francis's desire for a more outward-facing, less "self-referential" church does possess an allure. On the day of his inauguration, Joseph Biden placed a photo of himself with Francis on his desk in the White House. A bitterly divided American episcopate simultaneously debated whether to withhold communion from pro-choice politicians such as Biden, but after meeting with Francis at the Vatican, a delighted Biden reported that the pope had told him to keep taking communion.

All Catholics dwell in local parishes and communities, not an abstraction called global Catholicism. But the causes Francis has emphasized— the environment and the plight of refugees—emphasize collaboration beyond the nation-state. He urges Catholics in Latin America to think of themselves as sharing a regional identity. He repeatedly recalls the founding of the European Union by Catholics who had endured World War II, the twentieth century's most damaging breakdown in collective governance.[30] Nigeria's Cardinal John Onaiyekan echoes Francis in seeing "the hand of God in the process of globalization." He stresses that "the genie is out of the bottle. We are all together and we shall remain together."[31]

An oddity of the moment is that two of the world's most admired Anglophone writers are also Nigerian Catholics. Chimamanda Ngozi

Adichie's ancestors converted to Catholicism in the 1920s under the tutelage of Irish Catholic missionaries. As a child, her family attended Mass every Sunday at the Catholic chapel at the University of Nigeria in Nsukka, and she recalls singing in Igbo and English, as well as "gold pendants at women's throats, their headscarves flared out like the wings of giant butterflies; men's caftans crisply starched; children in frilly socks and uncomfortable clothes." Her adult relationship to Catholicism is fraught, but enduring, since "to be raised Roman Catholic is to be inducted into a culture that clings, that slides between your soul's crevices and stays." Characters in her fiction visit a Lourdes shrine and claim to see the Virgin Mary. A priest travels to work in Germany because of that country's clergy shortage. The villain of one novel is an abusive Catholic father; a hero is an aunt whose Catholicism is more humane. Adichie declares herself "proud" of Pope Francis because he "seems to value the person as much as the institution."[32]

Uwem Akpan trained as a Jesuit priest, and his short stories reveal the world through the eyes of children. One scrambles to survive in a Kenyan slum and hopes to celebrate a modest Christmas. Another makes a dangerous journey through Catholic and Muslim regions of Nigeria. A third clutches the family crucifix while evading warring mobs in Rwanda. Akpan's focus on the vulnerable people of a continent in turmoil rests on his reading of *Gaudium et Spes* and especially its first line, frequently referenced by Francis: "The joys and hopes, the grief and anguish of the people of our time, especially of those who are poor or afflicted, are the joys and hopes, the grief and anguish of the followers of Christ as well."[33]

In the nineteenth century, European Catholics brought the devotional objects, textbooks, and architectural drawings of the ultramontane revival to every corner of the globe. In 1961, a young Joseph Ratzinger predicted that "we cannot yet imagine the riches to come when the charisms of Asia and Africa make their contributions to the whole church."[34] That same year, Karl Rahner observed that "today everybody is the next-door neighbour and spiritual neighbour of everyone else in the world."[35]

What will the next sixty years bring? An enduring legacy of the Second Vatican Council has been to catapult Catholics and their institutions onto a more global stage. What happens in Lisbon or London must now be understood in the context of what happens in Lagos.

Gauging what requires central control and what requires decentralized experimentation is not easy. Still, many of the arguments now animating Catholics may dissipate, less because of tidy resolutions and more because the world, and the church, will have moved on. "We are not living," Francis tells us, "in an era of change but a change of era."[36]

The ultramontane milieu constructed in the wake of the French Revolution is sliding into history, beyond living memory. A Catholic baptized today is as distant from the Second Vatican Council as Joseph Ratzinger and Karl Rahner were in 1961 from the nineteenth century. Let's hope that these young Catholics will be better positioned, in the words of Francis, to be "citizens of our respective nations and of the entire world, builders of a new social bond."[37]

Acknowledgments

Writing the history of modern Catholicism has its perils, but the community of scholars interested in the topic is a welcoming one. Members of the Colloquium on Religion and History in the History Department at Notre Dame dissected chapter drafts. Scott Appleby, Colin Barr, Paul Baumann, Ted Cachey, Pete Cajka, Kathleen Cummings, Darren Dochuk, Felipe Fernández-Armesto, Brad Gregory, Paul Kollman, CSC, Tom Kselman, Mark Noll, Robert Norton, Linda Przybyszewski, Stephen Schloesser, SJ, Sarah Shortall, Tom Tweed, and Ignacio Walker offered cogent advice. So, too, did the students in History 43979, Modern Religious History. Fr. Robert Sullivan read the manuscript, twice, with dispatch and wisdom. The almost one hundred participants from a dozen countries taking part in a 2018 conference on global Catholicism sponsored by the Cushwa Center for the Study of American Catholicism improved this book with their scholarship and suggested new paths for an emerging field.

In-person and Zoom audiences at St. Michael's College at the University of Toronto, Edinburgh University, Cambridge University, the Catholic University of Lublin, the Pontificia Universidad Católica in Santiago, Princeton University, and the University of Virginia allowed me to think out loud. Jennifer Ratner-Rosenhagen and Kevin Schultz, convenors of the Midwest Intellectual History Conference, did the same.

Help on photos and documents came from Elizabeth Foster, Charles Keith, David Morgan, Fr. Paulinus Odozor, Kim Christiaens and Luc Vints from KADOC in Leuven, Frank Kleinehagenbrock and Christoph Kösters from the Kommission für Zeitgeschichte in Bonn, Hans Krabbendam from the Katholiek Documentatie Centrum in Nijmegen, and Claude Lorentz from the Bibliothèque Nationale Universitaire in Strasbourg. Ibb Mayr provided translations from German; Ana Lopez Almanzar from Spanish. Two gifted department chairs—Jon Coleman and Elisabeth Köll—facilitated my return to full-time teaching and research. I am honored to receive research funds through the faculty position endowed in the name of Francis A. McAnaney, a New York lawyer and Notre Dame graduate from the class of 1929.

I had never written a book while teaching a course on the same topic. Turns out it's fun. I am grateful to the talented students in three iterations of History 30350, Global Catholicism. Maria Sermersheim and Francine Shaft excelled as students in the first version of the course and then even more as research assistants during that first COVID-19 year. Their intelligence and hard work improved the final product; their buoyant spirits lifted my own. Bryan Fok did similarly good work checking sources on the final manuscript.

Teaching assistants Susanna De Stradis, Lauren Hamblen, Melissa Coles, Julie Mullican, Edith LaGarde, and Samuel Roberts brought the course to life. One assignment drew on material culture items in Notre Dame's Hesburgh Library, a couple of which snuck into this volume as photographs. I'm delighted to acknowledge colleagues—including Rachel Bohlmann, Aedín Clements, Hye-jin Juhn, Erika Hosselkus, Natasha Lyandres, and Jean McManus—who nurture those collections for students and researchers. During the pandemic I sometimes worked, masked, on the eleventh and twelfth floors of the library. Perusing the journals and books located there made me even more grateful to the archivists and librarians who over generations built and sustained that magnificent resource.

This is my second go-round with W. W. Norton; it's again an honor. Alane Salierno Mason brilliantly edited the manuscript with one eye on the big picture and another on the details. Geri Thoma and Dan Conaway served as agents and cheerleaders. Friends at *Commonweal*—

including its editor Dominic Preziosi, publisher Tom Baker, and fellow board chairs Mark Dalton and Barbara Rosiello—inspired me with their dedication to that enterprise.

I sent off this manuscript with Patrick and Leo beginning college and Margaret about to finish. Nora is now an accomplished journalist. I've written it before but it's still true so I'll write it again. Sharing this family adventure with Jean remains my greatest gift.

Notes

INTRODUCTION

1 A few examples with a global or transnational emphasis all published since 2010: *Local Church, Global Church: Catholic Activism in Latin America from Rerum Novarum to Vatican II*, eds. Stephen J. C. Andes and Julia G. Young (Washington 2016); Edward Baring, *Converts of the Real: Catholicism and the Making of Continental Philosophy* (Cambridge MA 2019); Colin Barr, *Ireland's Empire: The Roman Catholic Church in the English Speaking World, 1829–1914* (Cambridge 2020); *Weltreligion im Umbruch: Transnationale Perspektiven auf das Christentum in der Globalisierung*, eds. Olaf Blaschke and Francisco Javier Ramón Solans (Frankfurt 2019); James Chappel, *Catholic Modern: The Challenge of Totalitarianism and the Remaking of the Church* (Cambridge MA 2019); Luca Codignola, *Blurred Nationalities across the North Atlantic: Traders, Priests, and Their Kin Travelling between North America and the Italian Peninsula, 1763–1846* (Toronto 2020); John Connelly, *From Enemy to Brother: The Revolution in Catholic Teaching on the Jews, 1933–1965* (Cambridge MA 2012); Kathleen Cummings, *A Saint of Our Own: How the Quest for a Holy Hero Helped Catholics Become American* (Chapel Hill 2019); *Neo-Thomism in Action: Law and Society Reshaped by Neo-Scholastic Philosophy 1880–1960*, eds. Wim Decock, Bart Raymaekers, and Peter Heyrman, (Leuven 2022); Jonathan L. Earle and J. J. Carney, *Contesting Catholics: Benedicto Kiwanuka and the Birth of Postcolonial Uganda* (Rochester, NY, 2021); Elizabeth A. Foster, *African Catholic: Decolonization and the Transformation of the Church* (Cambridge MA 2019); *Religious Internationals in the Modern World: Globalization and Faith Communities since 1750*, eds. Abigail Green and Vincent Viaene (London 2012); Udi Greenberg, "Catholics, Protestants, and the Violent Birth of European Religious Pluralism," *American Historical Review* 124 (Apr. 2019), 511–538; Henrietta Harrison, *The Missionary's Curse: And Other Tales from a Chinese Catholic Village* (Berkeley 2013); *Katholizismus transnational: Beitrage zur Zeitgeschichte und Gegenwart in Westeuropa und den Vereinigten Staaten*, eds. Andreas Henkelmann, Christoph Kösters, Rosel Oehmen-Vieregge, and Mark Edward Ruff (Münster 2019); Patrick J. Houlihan, *Catholicism and the Great War: Religion and Everyday Life in Germany and Austria-Hungary, 1914–1922* (Cambridge 2015); Theresa Keeley, *Reagan's Gun-Toting Nuns: the Catholic Conflict over Cold War Human Rights Policy in Central America* (Ithaca 2021); Piotr H. Kosicki, *Catholics on the Barricades: Poland, France, and 'Revolution,' 1891–1956* (New Haven 2018); *Más Allá De Los NacionalCatolicismos: Redes Transnacionales de Los Catolicismos Hispánicos,* eds. José Ramón Rodríguez Lago and Natalia Núñez Bargueño (Madrid 2021); James McCartin, *Prayers of the Faithful: The Shifting Spiritual Life of American Catholics* (Cambridge MA 2010); Florian Michel, *La pensée catholique en Amérique du Nord: Réseaux intellectuels et échanges culturels entre l'Europe, le Canada et les États Unis (années 1920–1960)* (Paris 2010); Maria Mitchell, *The Origins of Christian Democracy: Politics and Confession in Modern Germany* (Ann Arbor 2012); Brenna Moore, *Kindred Spirits: Friendship and Resistance at the Edges of Modern Catholicism* (Chicago 2021); Samuel Moyn, *Christian Human Rights* (Philadelphia 2015); Sarah Shortall, *Soldiers of God in a Secular World: Catholic Theology and Twentieth-Century*

French Politics (Cambridge MA 2021); Brian Stanley, *Christianity in the Twentieth Century: A World History* (Princeton 2018); Robert A. Ventresca, *Soldier of Christ: The Life of Pius XII* (Cambridge MA 2013); Albert Monshan Wu, *From Christ to Confucius: German Missionaries, Chinese Christians, and the Globalization of Christianity, 1860–1950* (New Haven 2016); Ernest P. Young, *Ecclesiastical Colony: China's Catholic Church and the French Religious Protectorate* (New York 2013).

2   John T. McGreevy, *Parish Boundaries: The Catholic Encounter with Race in the Twentieth Century Urban North* (Chicago 1996); McGreevy, *Catholicism and American Freedom: A History* (New York 2003); McGreevy, *American Jesuits and the World: How an Embattled Religious Order Made Modern Catholicism Global* (Princeton 2016).

3   David A. Bell, "The Global Turn," *New Republic* (Oct. 7, 2013).

4   Brahmabandhab Upadhyay, "Are Miracles Possible?" in *The Writings of Brahmabandhab Upadhyay,* eds. Dr. Julius Lipner and Dr. George Gispért-Sauch, S.J. (Bangalore 1991), I: 45–47; Pierre-Marie Hoog, S.J., *L'Église Saint Ignace* (Paris, n.d.), 22; Jeremy Clarke, S.J., "Our Lady of China: Marian Devotion and Jesuits," *Studies in the Spirituality of Jesuits* 41 (2009): 14–15.

5   C. F. G. de Groot, *Brazilian Catholicism and the Ultramontane Reform, 1850–1930* (Amsterdam 1996), 60.

6   Charles Keith, *Catholic Vietnam: A Church from Empire to Nation* (Berkeley 2012), 150–151.

7   Canon 218 in *The 1917 or Pio-Benedictine Code of Canon Law,* ed. Edward N. Peters (San Francisco 2001), 93–94.

8   Shanshan Lan, "The Catholic Church's Role in the African Diaspora in Guangzhou, China," in *Catholicism in China, 1900–Present,* ed. Cindy Yik-yi Chu (New York 2014), 219-236.

9   Peter Seewald, *Benedict XVI: A Life,* trans. Dinah Livingstone (London 2020), 1: 338.

10   *Gaudet Mater Ecclesia* (1962), §§14, 26.

11   Joseph Ratzinger, "On the Schema On the Sources of Revelation: Address to the German Speaking Bishops October 10, 1962," copy in Jared Wicks, "Six Texts by Joseph Ratzinger as Peritus before and during Vatican Council II," *Gregorianum* 89 (2008): 283.

12   Joseph A. Komonchak, "Benedict XVI and the Interpretation of the Council," *Cristianesimo nella Storia* 28 (2007): 330.

13   Benedict XVI, Address to the Roman Curia, December 22, 2005, copy in *The Crisis of Authority in Catholic Modernity,* eds. Michael J. Lacey and Francis Oakley (New York 2011), 358–362.

14   Bernard J. F. Lonergan, "The Transition from a Classicist Worldview to Historical Mindedness," [1967] in Lonergan, *A Second Collection,* eds. William F. J. Ryan, S.J., and Bernard J. Tyrrell, S.J. (Philadelphia 1974), 1–11.

ONE: REVOLUTION

1   C. Sneyd Edgeworth, *Memoirs of the Abbé Edgeworth: Containing His Narrative of the Last Hours of Louis XVI* (London 1815), 78.

2   Henry Essex Edgeworth de Firmont to Usher Edgeworth, Sept. 1, 1796, *Letters from the Abbé Edgeworth to His Friends, Written between the Years 1777 and 1807; with Memoirs of His Life,* ed. Thomas R. England (London 1818), 96–97; Marquis de Beaucourt, "Le mot de l'abbé Edgeworth" in *Captivité et derniers moments de Louis XVI* (Paris 1892), 2: 353–369.

3   M. V. Woodgate, *The Abbé Edgeworth (1745–1807)* (New York 1946), 27.

4   Edgeworth to Moylan, Jan. 9, 1791, in *Letters from the Abbé Edgeworth,* 63.

5   Dominic Aidan Bellenger, *The French Exiled Clergy in the British Isles after 1789* (Bath 1986), 13.

6   Moylan to Burke, Dec. 20, 1793, in *Letters from the Abbé Edgeworth,* 182, 184.

7   Michael O'Brien, *Mrs. Adams in Winter: A Journey in the Last Days of Napoleon* (New York 2010), 98.

8   Edgeworth to Usher Edgeworth, Oct. 30, 1800, in *Letters from the Abbé Edgeworth,* 144.

9   Woodgate, *The Abbé Edgeworth,* viii.

10   Joseph de Maistre, *Considerations on France*, ed. Richard A. LeBrun (Cambridge [1797] 1994), 21.

11   Fr. Jan Roothaan to Fr. Leonardo Fava, Feb. 1, 1848, in Ioannis Phil. Roothaan, *Epistolae* (Rome 1940), 3: 173.

12   John Cooney, *John Charles McQuaid: Ruler of Catholic Ireland* (Dublin 1999), 70.

13   Christian Sorrel, "Le concile d'un évêque missionnaire: Mgr. Michel Bernard, archevêque de Brazzaville, à Vatican II," in *L'Afrique et la mission: Terrains anciens, questions nouvelles avec Claude Prudhomme*, eds. Oissila Saaïda and Laurick Zerbini (Paris 2015), 119.

14   Alyssa Goldstein Sepinwall, *The Abbé Grégoire and the French Revolution: The Making of Modern Universalism* (Berkeley 2005), 111.

15   Ronald Schechter, *Obstinate Hebrews; Representations of Jews in France, 1715–1815* (Berkeley 2003), 89–94.

16   Sepinwall, *The Abbé Grégoire and the French Revolution*, 172.

17   Thomas Paine, *Common Sense*, ed. Thomas Slaughter (Boston 2000), 82.

18   Sepinwall, *The Abbé Grégoire and the French Revolution*, 130–131.

19   Susan Dunn, *The Deaths of Louis XVI: Regicide and the French Political Imagination* (Princeton 1994), 17.

20   Dale K. Van Kley, the subject's leading scholar, coined the term. See Dale K. Van Kley, *Reform Catholicism and the International Suppression of the Jesuits in Enlightenment Europe* (New Haven 2018).

21   Ulrich L. Lehner, *The Catholic Enlightenment: The Forgotten History of a Global Movement* (New York 2016), 7.

22   Paula Findlen, "The Pope and the Englishwoman: Benedict XIV, Jane Squire, the Bologna Academy and the Problem of Longitude," in *Benedict XIV and the Enlightenment: Art, Science, and Spirituality*, eds. Rebecca Marie Messbarger, Christopher M. S. Johns, and Philip Gavitt (Toronto 2016), 45.

23   Margaret R. Ewalt, *Peripheral Wonders: Nature, Knowledge, and Enlightenment in Eighteenth-Century Orinoco* (Lewisburg, PA, 2008), 113; Charles E. Ronan, *Francisco Javier Clavigero, S.J., (1731–1787) Figure of the Mexican Enlightenment: His Life and Works* (Chicago 1977), 133.

24   Ulrich L. Lehner, *On the Road to Vatican II: German Catholic Enlightenment and Reform of the Church* (Minneapolis 2016), 53.

25   Lodovico Antonio Muratori, *The Science of Rational Devotion. From the Writings of the Learned and Celebrated Muratori* (Dublin 1789), 114.

26   Ernest Wangermann, "The Austrian Enlightenment" in *The Enlightenment in National Context*, eds. Roy Porter and Mikuláš Teich (Cambridge 1981), 131.

27   Richard Butterwick, "Catholicism and Enlightenment in Poland-Lithuania," in *A Companion to the Enlightenment in Catholic Europe*, eds. Ulrich L. Lehner and Michael O'Neill Printy (Leiden 2010), 321.

28   Benedict Maria von Werkmeister, "My Principles Regarding the Power of the Church" [1789], in *Early Modern Catholic Sources: The Catholic Enlightenment: A Global Anthology*, eds. Ulrich L. Lehner and Shaun Blanchard (Washington 2021), 175-176.

29   Simon Ditchfield, "Decentering the Catholic Reformation: Papacy and Peoples in the Early Modern World," *Archiv für Reformationsgeschichte* 101 (2010): 186–208.

30   David A. Brading, *The First America: The Spanish Monarchy, Creole Patriots, and the Liberal State 1492–1867* (Cambridge 1991), 508.

31   Sacred Congregation of the Propagation of the Faith to a Chinese missionary superior, Sept. 13, 1760, in *One Hundred Roman Documents Concerning the Chinese Rites Controversy (1645–1941)*, trans. Donald F. St. Sure, ed. Ray R. Noll (San Francisco 1992), 64.

32   Ernest P. Young, *Ecclesiastical Colony: China's Catholic Church and the French Religious Protectorate* (New York 2013), 14.

33   Brading, *The First America*, 503.

34   Jeffrey Burson, "Introduction: The Culture of Jesuit Erudition in the Age of Enlightenment," *Journal of Jesuit Studies* 6 (2019): 387–415.

35   T. C. W. Blanning, *Reform and Revolution in Mainz 1743–1803* (Cambridge 1974), 103.

36   Dale K. Van Kley, "Catholic Conciliar Reform," in *Religion and Politics in Enlightenment Europe*, eds. James E. Bradley and Dale K. Van Kley (Notre Dame 2001), 61.

37   Dale K. Van Kley, "Plots and Rumors of Plots: The Role of Conspiracy in the International Campaign against the Society of Jesus, 1758–1768," in *The Jesuit Suppression in Global Context: Causes, Events, and Consequences*, eds. Jeffrey D. Burson and Jonathan Wright (Cambridge 2015), 117–138.

38   Sabina Pavone, *The Wily Jesuits and the Monita Secreta*, trans. John P. Murphy, S.J. (St. Louis 2005), 85–98.

39   Emanuele Colombo and Niccolò Guasti, "The Expulsion and Suppression in Portugal and Spain: An Overview," in *The Jesuit Suppression in Global Context*, 1–39.

40   Joep van Gennip, "'Contulit hos virtus, expulit Invidia': The Suppression of the Jesuits of the Flemish-Belgian Province," in *The Survival of the Jesuits in the Low Countries, 1773–1850*, eds. Leo Kenis and Marc Lindeijer (Leuven 2019), 96.

41   Thomas M. McCoog, S.J., "'Lost in the Title': John Thorpe's Eyewitness Account of the Suppression," in *The Jesuit Suppression in Global Context*, 173.

42   Lehner, *On the Road to Vatican II*, 154.

43   Francis Oakley, *The Conciliarist Tradition: Constitutionalism in the Catholic Church 1300–1870* (New York 2003), 193; Daniele Menozzi, "Prospettive sinodali nel Settecento" in *Il Sinodo Di Pistoia Del 1786: atti del convegno internazionale per il secondo centenario Pistoia-Prato, 25–27 settembre 1986*, ed. Claudio Lamioni (Rome 1991), 23–31.

44   Richard Herr, *The Eighteenth-Century Revolution in Spain* (Princeton 1973), 400–407; Shaun Blanchard, *The Synod of Pistoia and Vatican II: Jansenism and the Struggle for Catholic Reform* (New York 2020), 214.

45   Pamela Voekel, *Alone before God: The Religious Origins of Modernity in Mexico* (Durham 2002), 51–52.

46   Mark Goldie, "Alexander Geddes at the Limits of the Catholic Enlightenment," *Historical Journal* 53 (Mar. 2010): 74.

47   Quentin Skinner, *The Foundations of Modern Political Thought* (Cambridge 1978), 2: 113–134; Dale Van Kley "Religion and the Age of 'Patriot' Reform," *Journal of Modern History* 80 (2008): 252–295.

48   Toleration Act of the Emperor Joseph II, Oct. 13, 1781, copy in *Church and State through the Centuries: A Collection of Historic Documents with Commentaries*, eds. Sidney Z. Ehler and John B. Morrall (Westminster, MD, 1954), 226.

49   Richard Butterwick, *The Polish Revolution and the Catholic Church, 1788–1792: A Political History* (Oxford 2012), 214; John McManners, *Church and Society in Eighteenth-Century France* (Oxford 1998), 2: 644–660.

50   Petition of the Catholics, 1762, in *The Catholic Church in Sri Lanka: The Dutch Period*, ed. V. Perniola, S.J. (Dehiwala 1985), 3: 199.

51   Gilles Chaussé, "French Canada from the Conquest to 1840" in *A Concise History of Christianity in Canada*, ed. Terrence Murphy (Toronto 1996), 59.

52   Aaron Willis, "The Standing of New Subjects: Grenada and the Protestant Constitution after the Treaty of Paris (1763)," *Journal of Imperial and Commonwealth History* 42 (2014): 1–21.

53   Alexander Hamilton, "A Full Vindication of the Measures of Congress" [1774] at founders.archives.gov.

54   Catherine O'Donnell, "British Atlantic Catholicism in the Age of Revolution and Reaction," in *Imagining the British Atlantic after the American Revolution*, eds. Michael Meranze and Saree Makdisi (Toronto 2015), 92–95.

55   John Carroll [pseudonym Pacificus] to John Fenno [1789], in *Early Modern Catholic Sources: The Catholic Enlightenment: A Global Anthology*, eds. Ulrich Lehner and Shaun Blanchard (Washington 2021), 277.

56   "Remarks on an Act for Regulating Elections," Jan. 29, 1787, in *The Papers of Alexander Hamilton*, eds. Harold C. Syrett and Jacob E. Cooke (New York 1962), 4: 30.

57   Katherine Carté, *Religion and the American Revolution: An Imperial History* (Chapel Hill 2021), 269.

58   Colin Haydon, *Anti-Catholicism in Eighteenth-Century England, c. 1714–80: A Political and Social Study* (Manchester 1993), 212–213.

59   George Washington, General Orders, Nov. 5, 1775, at founders.archives.gov; Carté, *Religion and the American Revolution*, 280.

60   Eamon Duffy, "Ecclesiastical Democracy Detected: I (1779–1787)," *Recusant History* 10 (1970): 199.

61   Lehner, *The Catholic Enlightenment*, 121.

62   Document No. 3 [1788] in Joaquim Heilodoro da Cunha Rivara, *Goa and the Revolt of 1787*, trans. Renato da Cunha Soares (New Delhi [1875] 1996), 133.

63   McManners, *Church and Society in Eighteenth-Century France*, 1: 29.

64   John Hardman, *Louis XVI* (New Haven 1993), 125.

65   Edgeworth to Moylan, Aug. 13, 1777, in *Letters from the Abbé Edgeworth*, 28.

66   McManners, *Church and Society in Eighteenth-Century France*, 2: 731.

67   Bernard Plongeron, *Conscience religieuse en Révolution* (Paris 1969), 201.

68   Timothy Tackett, *Religion, Revolution, and Regional Culture in Eighteenth-Century France: The Ecclesiastical Oath of 1791* (Princeton 1986), 69; Dale K. Van Kley, "The Abbé Grégoire and the Quest for a Catholic Republic," in *The Abbé Grégoire and His World*, ed. Jeremy Popkin and Richard Popkin (Dordrecht 2000), 85.

69   P. G. M. Dickson, "Joseph II's Reshaping of the Austrian Church," *Historical Journal* 36 (1993): 89–114.

70   Butterwick, "Catholicism and Enlightenment in Poland-Lithuania," 314, 344.

71   Ulrich Lehner, *Enlightened Monks: The German Benedictines, 1740–1803* (Oxford 2011), 74.

72   Emile Perreau Saussine, *Catholicism and Democracy: An Essay on the History of Political Thought*, trans. Richard Rex (Princeton 2012), 9–10.

73   John Carroll to Joseph Berington, July 10, 1784, *The John Carroll Papers*, ed. Thomas O'Brien Hanley, S.J. (Notre Dame 1976), 1: 147–149; Catherine O'Donnell, "John Carroll and the Origins of an American Catholic Church, 1783–1815," *William and Mary Quarterly* 68 (Jan. 2011): 115–117.

74   Michael D. Breidenbach, *Our Dear-Bought Liberty: Catholics and Religious Toleration in Early America* (Cambridge MA 2021), 169–230.

75   Edgeworth to Moylan, Nov. 6, 1790, in *Letters from the Abbé Edgeworth*, 56.

76   Gérard Pelletier, *Rome et la Révolution Française. La théologie et la politique du Saint-siège devant la Révolution française, 1789–1799* (Rome 2004), 137; Pius VI to French bishops in the National Assembly, March 10, 1791, in *The French Revolution Confronts Pius VI*, trans. Jeffrey J. Langan (South Bend 2020), 1: 39.

77   Pius VI to French bishops, 1: 39

78   Pierre Rosanvallon, *The Demands of Liberty: Civil Society in France since the Revolution*, trans. Arthur Goldhammer (Cambridge MA 2007), 19.

79   Amir Minksy, "The Men Who Stare at Cathedrals: Aesthetic Education, Moral Sentiment, and the German Critique of French Revolutionary Violence, 1793–1794," *Central European History* 53 (2020): 24; Timothy Tackett, *The Coming of the Terror in the French Revolution* (Cambridge MA 2015), 256–261, 315–316.

80   Sudhir Hazareesingh, *Black Spartacus: The Epic Life of Toussaint Louverture* (New York, 2020), 45; Laënnec Hurbon, "Le clergé catholique et l'insurrection de Saint-Domingue," in *L'Insurrection des esclaves de Saint-Domingue*, ed. Laënnec Hurbon (Paris 2000), 29–39.

81   Terry Rey, *The Priest and the Prophetess: Abbé Ouvière, Romaine Rivière, and the Revolutionary Atlantic World* (New York 2017), 117.

82   Hazareesingh, *Black Spartacus*, 275; *Mémoires De Grégoire, ancien évêque de Blois . . .* (Paris [1837] 1989), 84.

83   James Smyth, *Henry Joy McCracken* (Dublin 2020), 35.

84 Thomas Bartlett, *Ireland: A History* (Cambridge 2010), 208.
85 Dáire Keogh, *The French Disease: The Catholic Church and Irish Radicalism 1790–1800* (Dublin 1993), 140, 182–186.
86 S. Karly Kehoe, *Creating a Scottish Church: Catholicism, Gender and Ethnicity in Nineteenth-Century Scotland* (Manchester 2010), 35; Luca Codignola, "Roman Catholic Conservatism in a New North Atlantic World, 1760–1829," *William and Mary Quarterly* Third Series 64 (Oct. 2007): 736.
87 Van Kley, *Reform Catholicism*, 258–260.
88 Blanning, *Reform and Revolution*, 330.
89 Chadwick, *The Popes and European Revolution*, 476–480.
90 Herr, *The Eighteenth-Century Revolution*, 308.
91 Michael Broers, *The Politics of Religion in Napoleonic Italy: The War Against God, 1801–1814* (New York 2002), 28.
92 Vittorio Emanuele Giuntella, *La religione amica della democrazia: I cattolici democratici del triennio rivoluzionario (1796–1799)* (Rome 1990), 197.
93 Chadwick, *The Popes and European Revolution*, 451, 475.
94 Helena Rosenblatt, *The Lost History of Liberalism: From Ancient Rome to the Twenty First Century* (Princeton 2018), 55.
95 Sepinwall, *The Abbé Grégoire and the French Revolution*, 137, 145.
96 Gaspar Melchor de Jovellanos, "Report on the Agrarian Law," in *Report on the Agrarian Law (1795) and Other Writings*, eds. Gabriel Pacquette and Álvaro Caso Bello (London 2016), 84.
97 María Victoria López-Cordón Cortezo, "The Merits of the Good *Gobierno*: Culture and Politics in the Bourbon Court," in *The Spanish Enlightenment Revisited*, ed. Jesús Astigarraga (Oxford 2015), 29–30.
98 Darrin M. McMahon, *Enemies of the Enlightenment: The French Counter-Enlightenment and the Making of Modernity* (Oxford 2001), 59.
99 Sylvio Hermann De Franceschi, "L'Autorité Pontificale Face Au Legs De L'Antiromanisme Catholique et Régaliste Des Lumières," *Archivum Historiae Pontificiae* 38 (2000): 119–163.
100 Hervé Hasquin, *Population, Commerce et Religion au Siècle Des Lumières* (Brussels 2008), 228–229.
101 Edmund Burke, *Reflections on the Revolution in France*, ed. J. C. D. Clark (Stanford 2001), 323.
102 Bernard Plongeron, "L'Eglise et les Déclarations des droits de l'homme au XVIII siècle," *Nouvelle Revue Théologique* 101 (1979): 366.
103 Butterwick, *The Polish Revolution and the Catholic Church*, 279.
104 Kenneth Ballhatchet, *Caste, Class and Catholicism in India 1789–1914* (Richmond 1998), 85.
105 Shaun Blanchard, "The Ghost of Pistoia: Evocations of *Auctorem Fidei* in the Debate over Episcopal Collegiality at Vatican II," *Theological Studies* 79 (2018): 66.
106 Ricci to Grégoire, Oct. 29, 1798, in *Rivista Di Storia e Letteratura Religiosa* 52 (2016), 270.
107 *Discourse of His Eminence Cardinal Chiaramonti, Bishop of Imola, afterwards Pope Pius VII, Addressed to his Diocesans on Christmas Day, 1797*, reprinted in *United States Catholic Miscellany* (Sept. 1826): 6, 10.
108 C. A. Bayly, *The Birth of the Modern World 1780–1914* (Malden 2004), 108.
109 Klaus Epstein, *The Genesis of German Conservatism* (Princeton 1966), 607.
110 Sudhir Hazareesingh, *The Saint-Napoleon: Celebrations of Sovereignty in Nineteenth-Century France* (Cambridge 2004), 3–4.
111 Ricci to Henri Grégoire, Sept 20, 1806 in *Correspondance Scipione de' Ricci-Henri Grégoire (1796–1807)*, ed. Maurice Vaussard (Florence 1963), 140–145.
112 Ambrogio A. Caiani, *To Kidnap a Pope: Napoleon and Pius VII* (New Haven 2021), 4.
113 *The Memoirs of Chateaubriand*, trans. and ed. Robert Baldick (New York 1961), 291.

114 Henrietta Harrison, *The Missionary's Curse and Other Tales from a Chinese Catholic Village* (Berkeley 2013), 47.

115 Dominique Julia, "La Restauration de la Compagnie de Jésus," in *La Compagnie De Jésus Des Anciens Régimes Au Monde Contemporain (XVIII–XX Siècles)*, eds. Pierre-Antoine Fabre, Patrick Goujon, S.J., and Martín M. Morales, S.J. (Rome 2020), 67.

TWO: REVIVAL

  1 Mary C. Sullivan, R.S.M., *Catherine McAuley and the Tradition of Mercy* (Notre Dame 1995), 150.

  2 Door to Door Petition [1827] in *The Correspondence of Catherine McAuley, 1818–1841*, ed. Mary C. Sullivan, R.S.M. (Dublin 2004), 38.

  3 Daniel Murray to Cardinal Mauro Cappellari, Apr. 17, 1830, in *The Correspondence of Catherine McAuley*, 44.

  4 Act of Profession of Vows [1831] in *The Correspondence of Catherine McAuley*, 47.

  5 Sullivan, *Catherine McAuley*, 280.

  6 Jo Ann Kay McNamara, *Sisters in Arms: Catholic Nuns through Two Millennia* (Cambridge MA 1996), 555, 566.

  7 Ralph Gibson, *A Social History of French Catholicism 1789–1914* (New York 1989), 105–108; Claude Langlois, "Le catholicisme au féminin," *Archives des sciences sociales des religions* 29 (1984) 29–53.

  8 Helmut Walser Smith, *German Nationalism and Religious Conflict: Culture, Ideology, Politics, 1870–1914* (Princeton 1995), 94.

  9 Suellen Hoy and Margaret MacCurtain, *From Dublin to New Orleans: Nora and Alice's Journey to America, 1889* (Dublin 1994), 48.

 10 Charles Hergenroeder, C.SS.R., "Blessed Barbara Maix (1818–1873) and the Redemptorists of Vienna," *Spicilegium Historicum* 63 (2015): 137–156.

 11 Mary Ewens, "Removing the Veil: The Liberated American Nun," in *Women of Spirit: Female Leadership in the Jewish and Christian Traditions*, eds. Rosemary Radford Ruether and Eleanor McLaughlin (New York 1979), 259.

 12 S. Karly Kehoe, *Creating A Scottish Church: Catholicism, Gender and Ethnicity in Nineteenth-Century Scotland* (Manchester 2010), 119–120.

 13 Catherine McAuley, "On the Passion of Jesus Christ," [c. 1834] in *A Shining Lamp: The Oral Instructions of Catherine McAuley*, ed. Mary C. Sullivan, R.S.M. (Washington 2017), 103.

 14 Catherine McAuley, "Imitating Jesus Christ," [c. 1834] in *A Shining Lamp*, 66.

 15 Desmond Bowen, *The Protestant Crusade in Ireland, 1800–1870: A Study of Protestant-Catholic Relations between the Act of Union and Disestablishment* (Dublin 1978), 8.

 16 McAuley to Rev. John Rice, O.S.A., Dec. 8, 1833, in *The Correspondence of Catherine McAuley*, 55.

 17 McAuley to Sr. M. Frances Warde, May 11, 1839, in *The Correspondence of Catherine McAuley*, 194.

 18 Sr. Mary Vincent to Mother Mary Cecilia, Nov. 16, 1841, in Sullivan, *Catherine McAuley*, 244.

 19 Gerald Izenberg, *Impossible Individuality: Romanticism, Revolution, and the Origins of Modern Selfhood, 1787–1802* (Princeton 1992), 300–301.

 20 Vincent Viaene, *Belgium and the Holy See from Gregory XVI to Pius IX, 1831–1859: Catholic Revival, Society and Politics in 19th-Century Europe* (Leuven 2001), 42.

 21 Paul Gottfried, "Catholic Romanticism in Munich," (Yale University PhD 1968), 83.

 22 Friedrich von Schlegel, *The Philosophy of History in a Course of Lectures Delivered at Vienna*, trans. James Burton Robertson (London [1828] 1873), 455.

 23 Thomas Babington Macaulay, "Ranke's History of the Pope" [1840] in *Critical and Historical Essays*, ed. Hugh Trevor Roper (New York 1965), 277, 312–313.

 24 Viscount de Chateaubriand, *The Genius of Christianity* (Baltimore 1856), 474; Gibson, *A Social History of French Catholicism*, 167.

25 Brian Porter-Szücs, *Faith and Fatherland: Catholicism, Modernity, and Poland* (New York 2011), 19.

26 Ernest Sevrin, *Les Missions Religieuses en France sous la Restauration (1815–1830)* (Saint-Mandé 1948–1959), 1: 50.

27 Marc Lindeijer, S.J., Jo Luyten, and Kristien Suenens, "The Quick Downfall and Slow Rise of the Jesuit Order in the Low Countries," in *The Survival of the Jesuits in the Low Countries 1773–1850*, eds. Leo Kenis and Marc Lindeijer, S.J. (Leuven 2019), 29–30; Christopher Clark, "The New Catholicism and the European Culture Wars," in *Culture Wars: Secular-Catholic Conflict in Nineteenth-Century Europe*, eds. Christopher Clark and Wolfram Kaiser (Cambridge, UK, 2003), 17.

28 John T. McGreevy, *American Jesuits and the World: How an Embattled Religious Order Made Modern Catholicism Global* (Princeton 2016), 35.

29 Francis A. Sullivan, S.J., *Salvation outside the Church? Tracing the History of the Catholic Response* (Eugene 1992), 109.

30 Charles A. Bolton, *Church Reform in 18th Century Italy (The Synod of Pistoia, 1786)*, (The Hague 1969), 90.

31 Bolton, *Church Reform in 18th Century Italy*, 10–11; Eamon Duffy, *Saints and Sinners: A History of the Popes* (New Haven 2014), 249.

32 *Auctorem Fidei* (1794), proposition 62.

33 Joseph de Guibert, S.J., *The Jesuits: Their Spiritual Doctrine and Practice: A Historical Study*, trans. William J. Young, S.J. (Chicago [1953] 1964), 500.

34 Jon Vanden Heuvel, *A German Life in the Age of Revolution: Joseph Görres, 1776–1848* (Washington 2001), 339.

35 Wolfgang Schieder, "Church and Revolution: Aspects of the Social History of the Trier Pilgrimage of 1844," trans. Richard Deveson [1974], in *Conflict and Stability in Europe*, ed. Clive Emsley (London 1979), 65–95.

36 Parker to Dr. John Ronge, Boston, May 19, 1854, in John Weiss, *Life and Correspondence of Theodore Parker* (New York 1864), 1: 376.

37 Luca Codignola, *Blurred Nationalities across the North Atlantic: Traders, Priests, and Their Kin Travelling between North America and the Italian Peninsula 1763–1846* (Toronto 2019), 121.

38 Paul Cullen to Bishop Francis Kenrick, [Dec. 8] 1833, in Colin Barr, *Ireland's Pope: Paul Cullen, 1803–1878*, forthcoming, Cambridge University Press.

39 Klaus Schatz, *Papal Primacy from Its Origins to the Present*, trans. John A. Otto and Linda Maloney (Collegeville, MN, 1996), 148.

40 Michael Printy, "Protestantism and Progress in the Year XII: Charles Villers's *Essay on the Spirit and Influence of Luther's Reformation* (1804)," *Modern Intellectual History* 9 (2012): 306.

41 Frédéric Ozanam to Ernest Falconnet, Feb. 10, 1832, in *Frédéric Ozanam: A Life in Letters*, trans. and ed. Joseph L. Dirvin, C.M. (St. Louis 1986), 18.

42 Eric Yonke, "Cardinal Johannes von Geissel," in *Varieties of Ultramontanism*, ed. Jeffrey Von Arx (Washington 1998), 18.

43 McGreevy, *American Jesuits and the World*, 16.

44 C. Michael Shea, "Giovanni Perrone's Theological Curriculum and the First Vatican Council," *Revue d'Histoire Ecclésiastique* 110 (2015): 796.

45 John Henry Newman to Mrs. John Mozley, July 25, 1847, in *The Letters and Diaries of John Henry Newman* (Oxford 2016), 12: 104.

46 C. Michael Shea, *Newman's Early Roman Catholic Legacy 1845–1854* (Oxford 2017), 164–185.

47 Klaus Epstein, *The Genesis of German Conservatism* (Princeton 1966), 615.

48 Frances Lannon, *Privilege, Persecution, and Prophecy: The Catholic Church in Spain, 1875–1975* (New York 1987), 59.

49 Jose Luis Mora, "On Ecclesiastical Wealth" [1831], in *Nineteenth-Century Nation Building and the Latin American Intellectual Tradition: A Reader*, eds. Janet Burke and Ted Humphrey (Indianapolis 2007), 38.

50   "Madison's Detached Memoranda" [c. 1820], ed. Elizabeth Fleet, in *William and Mary Quarterly* 3 (Oct. 1946): 556–557.

51   Johann Adam Möhler, *The Spirit of Celibacy* (Chicago [1828] 2007), 75.

52   Gibson, *A Social History of French Catholicism*, 62.

53   Kenneth Ballhatchet, *Caste, Class and Catholicism in India 1789–1914* (Richmond 1998), 8–12.

54   Robert Darnton, *The Corpus of Clandestine Literature in France 1769–1789* (New York 1995), 202–204.

55   E. Clare Cage, *Unnatural Frenchman: The Politics of Priestly Celibacy and Marriage, 1720–1815* (Charlottesville 2015), 92–96, 98.

56   Cage, *Unnatural Frenchmen*, 139.

57   Annabelle Melville, *Louis William DuBourg: Bishop of Louisiana and the Floridas, Bishop of Montauban, and Archbishop of Besançon, 1766–1833* (Chicago 1986), I: 282.

58   Brian F. Connaughton, *Clerical Ideology in a Revolutionary Age: The Guadalajara Church and the Idea of the Mexican Nation, 1788–1853* trans. Mark Allen Healey (Calgary 2003), 150.

59   Jonathan Sperber, "Churches, the Faithful, and the Politics of Religion in the Revolution of 1848," in *Europe in 1848: Revolution and Reform*, trans. David Higgins, eds. Dieter Dowe, Heinz-Gerhard Haupt, Dieter Langewiesche, and Jonathan Sperber (New York 2000), 727.

60   Dagmar Herzog, *Intimacy and Exclusion: Religious Politics in Pre-Revolutionary Baden* (Princeton 1996), 24–35.

61   C. F. G. de Groot, *Brazilian Catholicism and the Ultramontane Reform*, 1850–1930 (Amsterdam 1996) 33, 40–41.

62   Kenneth P. Serbin, *Needs of the Heart: A Social and Cultural History of Brazil's Clergy and Seminaries* (Notre Dame 2006), 51.

63   Möhler, *The Spirit of Celibacy*, 87, 94.

64   Ballhatchet, *Caste, Class and Catholicism*, 102–103; Yvan Lamonde, *The Social History of Ideas in Quebec 1760–1896*, trans. Phyllis Scott and Howard Scott (Montreal 2013), 248.

65   Gibson, *A Social History of French Catholicism*, 57.

66   Luca Codignola, "The Catholic Clergy in the North Atlantic Area, 1763–1830: Patterns of Deviancy," *Almanack* 26 (2020): 1–34; Margaret Lavinia Anderson, "The Limits of Secularization: On the Problem of the Catholic Revival in Nineteenth-Century Germany," *Historical Journal* 38 (Sept. 1995): 652–54.

67   Jacob Ramsay, *Mandarins and Martyrs: The Church and the Nguyen Dynasty in Early Nineteenth-Century Vietnam* (Stanford 2008), 26.

68   Adrian Hastings, *The Church in Africa 1450–1950* (Oxford, 1994), 373.

69   R. G. Tiedemann, "Indigenous Agency, Religious Protectorates, and Chinese Interests: The Expansion of Christianity in Nineteenth Century China," in *Converting Colonialism: Visions and Realities in Mission History, 1706–1914*, ed. Dana L. Robert (Grand Rapids 2008), 207–213.

70   Jean-Marie Kreins and Josy Brisens, S.J., "Les jésuites luxembourgeois et l'expérience missionnaire dans le monde aux XIXe et XXe siècles," in *Le Face-à-Face des Dieux: Missionnaires luxembourgeois en Outre-Mer*, ed. Andre Neuberg (Bastogne 2007), 127–131.

71   *Annales de la Propagation de la Foi* (29), 1857. Circulation figures in Cage, *Unnatural Frenchmen*, 269.

72   Claude Prudhomme, *Stratégie missionnaire du Saint-Siège sous Léon XIII (1878–1903): centralisation romaine et défis culturels* (Rome 1994), 414–43.

73   Henrietta Harrison, "'A Penny for the Little Chinese': The French Holy Childhood Association in China, 1843–1951," *American Historical Review* 113 (Feb. 2008): 72–92; Hillary Kaell, "The Holy Childhood Association on Earth and in Heaven: Catholic Globalism in Nineteenth-Century America," *American Quarterly* 72 (2020): 827–851.

74   Ballhatchet, *Caste, Class and Catholicism*, 3.

75   Jan Roothaan, "On Desire for the Missions" [1831], in *Renovation Reading*, revised and enlarged edition (Woodstock, MD, 1931), 58.

76   Nicholas Point, S.J., to Fr. Fremiot, S.J., Mar. 1850 in *Lettres des nouvelles missions du Canada, 1843–1852*, ed. Lorenz Cadieux (Montreal 1973), 614–615.

77   Kevin M. Doak, "Catholicism, Modernity, and Japanese Culture," in *Xavier's Legacies: Catholicism in Modern Japanese Culture*, ed. Kevin M. Doak (Vancouver 2011), 9.

78   Ramsay, *Mandarins and Martyrs*, 27.

79   Susan Bayly, *Saints, Goddesses and Kings: Muslims and Christians in South Indian Society 1700–1900* (Cambridge 1989), 358–359.

80   Prudhomme, *Stratégie Missionnaire*, 397.

81   Ernest P. Young, *Ecclesiastical Colony: China's Catholic Church and the French Religious Protectorate* (New York 2013), 40; Susan Sleeper-Smith, "Women, Kin, and Catholicism: New Perspectives on the Fur Trade," *Ethnohistory* 47 (2000): 431–432.

82   Claude Savart, *Les Catholiques du France au XIXe siècle: Le témoignage du livre religieux* (Paris 1985); Kevin Molloy, "Religious Texts for the Catholic Migrant: International Print Networks and the Irish-Australian Book Trade," in *Religion and Greater Ireland: Christianity and Irish Global Networks 1750–1950*, eds. Colin Barr and Hilary M. Carey (Montreal 2015), 71–93.

83   McGreevy, *American Jesuits and the World*, 108; Saul Zalesch, "The Religious Art of Benziger Brothers," *American Art* 13 (Summer 1999): 58–79.

84   Cordula Grewe, *Painting the Sacred in the Age of Romanticism* (Burlington, VT, 2009), 7, 288.

85   Timothy Blanning, *The Romantic Revolution: A History* (New York 2010), 128–129.

86   Augustus Welby Northmore Pugin, *Contrasts* (Edinburgh [1836] 1898), 1.

87   Augustus Welby Northmore Pugin, *An Apology for the Revival of Christian Architecture in England* (Edinburgh [1843] 1895), 30–31.

88   Christopher M. S. Johns, *The Visual Culture of Catholic Enlightenment* (University Park, PA, 2015), esp. 1–31.

89   Kevin Starr, *Continental Achievement: Roman Catholics in the United States, Revolution and Early Republic* (San Francisco 2020), 271–272.

90   Friedrich von Schlegel, *The Aesthetic and Miscellaneous Works of Frederick von Schlegel*, trans. E. J. Millington (London 1849), 171–172.

91   Michael J. Lewis, *The Politics of the German Gothic Revival: August Reichensperger* (Cambridge MA 1993), 35–36.

92   McAuley to Sr. M. Josephine Warde, Dec. 24, 1839 in *The Correspondence of Catherine McAuley*, 227.

93   Malcolm Thurlby, "The Roman Catholic Churches of Joseph Connolly (1840–1904)," in *Gothic Revival Worldwide: A. W. N. Pugin's Global Influence*, eds. Timothy Brittain-Catlin, Jan De Maeyer, and Martin Bressani (Leuven 2016), 81.

94   Bayly, *Saints, Goddesses and Kings*, 437–438.

95   McGreevy, *American Jesuits and the World*, 146; Marie Baboyant, "Le Gesù, le baroque nouveau et le nouveau Montréal," *Société canadienne d'histoire de l'Église catholique* 53 (1986): 109–120.

96   Herzog, *Intimacy and Exclusion*, 24.

97   Katherine Bergeron, *Decadent Enchantments: The Revival of Gregorian Chant at Solesmes*, (Berkeley 1998), 20.

98   Cuthbert Johnson, O.S.B., *Prosper Guéranger (1805–1875): A Liturgical Theologian: An Introduction to His Liturgical Writings and Work* (Rome 1984), 264–265, 288.

99   Austin Gough, *Paris and Rome: The Gallican Church and the Ultramontane Campaign 1848–1853* (Oxford 1986), 168.

100 Dale Light, *Rome and the New Republic: Conflict and Community in Philadelphia Catholicism between the Revolution and the Civil War* (Notre Dame 1996), 270; Roberto Perin, "French-Speaking Canada from 1840," in *A Concise History of Christianity in Canada*, 200.

101 Garrett Sweeney, "The 'Wound in the Right Foot': Unhealed?" in *Bishops and Writers:*

Aspects of the Evolution of Modern English Catholicism, ed. Adrian Hastings (Wheathampstead, 1977), 218.

102 Luca Codignola, "Benjamin Franklin and the Holy See, 1783–4: The Myth of Non-Interference in Religious Affairs," *Journal of Early American History* 6 (2016): 220–228.

103 Edward Sinnott, S.J., to Peter Kenney, S.J., Aug. 27, 1837, and Edward Sinnot, S.J., to Clement Rice, Jan. 20, 1839, in *Collectanea Hibernica* 48 (2006) 137, 148.

104 Young, *Ecclesiastical Colony*, 29.

105 Julia Gaffield, "The Racialization of International Law after the Haitian Revolution," *American Historical Review* 125 (2020): 862.

106 Leslie Bethell, "A Note on the Church and Latin American Independence," in *The Cambridge History of Latin America*, ed. Leslie Bethell (Cambridge 1985), 3: 232; Austen Ivereigh, *Catholicism and Politics in Argentina, 1810–1960*, (New York 1995), 48.

107 Bernard Plongeron, "The Practice of Democracy in the Constitutional Church of France, 1790–1801," in *Election and Consensus in the Church*, eds. Giuseppe Alberigo and Anton Weiler (New York 1972), 121.

108 Ballhatchet, *Caste, Class and Catholicism*, 68.

109 Gilbert Chaussé, "French Canada from Conquest to 1840," in *A Concise History of Christianity in Canada*, eds. Terrence Murphy and Roberto Perin (Toronto 1996), 99; Yvan Lamonde, *The Social History of Ideas in Quebec*, 87–88.

110 Luís Maria Ignacio Maria de Peñalver y Cárdenas, "Religious Conditions in Louisiana," Nov. 1, 1795, in John Tracy Ellis, *Documents of American Catholic History* (Milwaukee 1956), 181–183.

111 Charles Edwards O'Neill, "'A Quarter Marked by Sundry Peculiarities': New Orleans, Lay Trustees and Pere Antoine," *Catholic Historical Review* 76 (1990): 240–241; Pope Leo XII to Bishop Rosati on the Cathedral Trustees, Aug. 16, 1828, in *Louisiana Historical Quarterly* 31 (1948): 964–966.

112 Frances Trollope, *Belgium and Western Germany in 1833* (Philadelphia 1834), 1: 67, 96.

113 Viaene, *Belgium and the Holy See*, 170.

114 Trollope, 1: 24.

115 Viaene, *Belgium and the Holy See,* 194.

116 Viaene, *Belgium and the Holy See*, 306–307.

117 Viaene, *Belgium and the Holy See*, 195.

118 David Hempton, *Methodism: Empire of the Spirit* (New Haven 2005), 151–77; Cemil Aydin, *The Idea of the Muslim World: A Global Intellectual History* (Cambridge MA 2017).

119 Viaene, *Belgium and the Holy See*, 203.

THREE: DEMOCRACY

1 Christopher Domínguez Michael, *Vida de Fray Servando* (Mexico City 2004), 672–678.

2 David A. Brading, *The First America: The Spanish Monarchy, Creole Patriots, and the Liberal State 1492–1867* (Cambridge 1991), 583–590.

3 Fray Servando Teresa De Mier, *The Memoirs of Fray Servando Teresa De Mier*, trans. Helen Lane, ed. Susana Rotker (New York 1998), 32–33.

4 Nancy Vogeley, *The Bookrunner: A History of Inter-American Relations—Print, Politics, and Commerce in the United States and Mexico, 1800–1830* (Philadelphia 2011), 56.

5 Kevin Whelan, "The Green Atlantic: Radical Reciprocities between Ireland and America in the Long Eighteenth Century," in *A New Imperial History: Culture, Identity and Modernity in Britain and the Empire 1660–1840*, ed. Kathleen Wilson (Cambridge 2004), 224–227; Brading, *The First America*, 590.

6 Richard A. Warren, "Displaced 'Pan-Americans' and the Transformation of the Catholic Church in Philadelphia, 1789–1850," *Pennsylvania Magazine of History and Biography* 128 (2004), 343–366.

7 Dale Light, *Rome and the New Republic: Conflict and Community in Philadelphia Catholicism between the Revolution and the Civil War* (Notre Dame 1996), 126–127.

8   Warren, "Displaced 'Pan-Americans,'" 354; Martin I. J. Griffin, "Life of Bishop Conwell of Philadelphia," *Records of the American Catholic Historical Society* 25 (1914): 167.

9   Light, *Rome and the New Republic*, 261–267; Luca Codignola, *Blurred Nationalities across the North Atlantic: Traders, Priests, and Their Kin Travelling between North America and the Italian Peninsula, 1763–1846* (Toronto 2019), 123–124, 131.

10 Michael P. Costeloe, *Church and State in Independent Mexico: A Study of the Patronage Debate 1821–1857* (London 1978), 59.

11 Michael, *Vida de Fray Servando*, 665–66.

12 Mier to Bernardino Cantú, Aug. 31, 1826, in *Fray Servando Teresa de Mier: Antología del Pensamiento Político Americano*, ed. Edmundo O'Gorman (Mexico City 1945), 41.

13 R. R. Palmer, *The Age of Democratic Revolutions: A Political History of Europe and America, 1760–1800* (Princeton [1959–64] 2014).

14 Linda Colley, *Britons: Forging the Nation 1707–1837* (New Haven 1992), 18.

15 Simón Bolivar, "Letter from Jamaica" [1815] in *El Libertador: Writings of Simón Bolivar*, trans. Fredrick H. Fornoff, ed. David Bushnell (Oxford 2003), 19.

16 John Lynch, *New Worlds: A Religious History of Latin America* (New Haven 2012), 115.

17 Maurizio Isabella, "Citizens or Faithful? Religion and the Liberal Revolutions of the 1820s in Southern Europe," *Modern Intellectual History* 12 (2015): 555–557; C. A. Bayly, *Recovering Liberties: Indian Thought in the Age of Liberalism and Empire* (Cambridge 2012), 42–46.

18 José M. Portillo Valdés, "De la Monarquía Católica a la Nación de los Católicos," *Historia y Política* 17 (2007): 17–35.

19 Richard Herr, "The Constitution of 1812 and the Spanish Road to Parliamentary Monarchy," in *Revolution and the Meaning of Freedom in the Nineteenth Century*, ed. Isser Woloch (Stanford 1996), 390.

20 Javier Fernández Sebastián, "Toleration and Freedom of Expression in the Hispanic World between Enlightenment and Liberalism," *Past and Present* 211 (May 2011): 175.

21 Brian Hamnett, *The Enlightenment in Iberia and Ibero-America* (Cardiff 2017), 245–249.

22 M. Dominique Georges Frédéric De Pradt, *The Colonies and the Present American Revolutions* (London 1817), 403.

23 Brading, *The First America*, 571.

24 Jeffrey Klaiber, "The Church and Latin American Independence," in *The Cambridge History of Religions in Latin America*, eds. Virginia Garrard-Burnett, Paul Freston, and Stephen C. Dove (Cambridge 2016), 231–50.

25 E. Bradford Burns, "The Role of Azeredo Coutinho in the Enlightenment of Brazil," *Hispanic American Historical Review* 44 (May 1964): 145–160.

26 John Adams to James Lloyd, Mar. 27, 1815, at founders.archives.gov; John Adams to Thomas Jefferson, May 26, 1817, at founders.archives.gov.

27 Caitlin Fitz, *Our Sister Republics: The United States in the Age of Revolution* (New York 2016), 66.

28 Thomas Jefferson to Luis di Onís, Apr. 28, 1814, at founders.archives.gov.

29 J. Lloyd Mecham, *Church and State in Latin America: A History of Politico-Ecclesiastical Relations*, rev. ed. (Chapel Hill 1966), 96.

30 Glauco Schettini, "Confessional Modernity: Nicola Spedalieri, the Catholic Church and the French Revolution, c. 1775–1800," *Modern Intellectual History* 16 (2019): 24.

31 Isabella, "Citizens or Faithful?," 563.

32 Robert Walsh, *Notices of Brazil in 1828 and 1829* (Boston 1831), 1: 367–371.

33 John Keane, *The Life and Death of Democracy* (London 2009), 439–440.

34 Scott Eastman, *Preaching Spanish Nationalism across the Hispanic Atlantic, 1759–1823* (Baton Rouge 2012), 142, 160.

35 Linda Colley, *The Gun, the Ship and the Pen: Warfare, Constitutions and the Making of the Modern World* (New York 2021), 191.

36 Gemma Marie Del Duca, "A Political Portrait: Félix Varela y Morales, 1788–1853" (University of New Mexico, PhD 1966), 165.

37 Gabriel Paquette, *Imperial Portugal in the Age of Atlantic Revolutions: The Luso-Brazilian World, c. 1770–1850* (Cambridge 2013), 136–137.

38 Hilda Sabato, *Republics of the New World: The Revolutionary Political Experiment in 19th Century Latin America* (Princeton 2018).

39 Michael, *Vida de Fray Servando,* 667.

40 Brading, *The First America,* 650.

41 Joseph de Maistre, "On the Nature of Sovereignty" [1794–1795], in *The Generative Principle of Political Constitutions: Studies on Sovereignty, Religion and Enlightenment,* trans. and ed. Jack Lively (New York 1965), 125.

42 Alan J. Reinerman, *Austria and the Papacy in the Age of Metternich* (Washington 1979), 1: 58.

43 Reinerman, *Austria and the Papacy in the Age of Metternich,* I: 53.

44 Yvan Lamonde, *The Social History of Ideas in Quebec, 1760–1896,* trans. Phyllis Scott and Howard Scott (Montreal 2013), 37, 75.

45 Lamonde, *The Social History of Ideas in Quebec,* 113.

46 John Carroll to Charles Plowden, Feb. 3, 1791, in *The John Carroll Papers,* I: 492; John Carroll to Joseph-Octave Plessis, July 28, 1800, in *The John Carroll Papers,* 2: 312.

47 John Carroll to Henri Grégoire, Sept. 9, 1809, in Jacques M. Gres-Gayer, "Four Letters from Henri Grégoire to John Carroll, 1809–1814," *Catholic Historical Review* 79 (Oct. 1993): 681–703.

48 Patrick M. Geoghegan, *King Dan: The Rise of Daniel O'Connell, 1775–1829* (Dublin 2008), 22–23.

49 Catholic Emancipation Act in Great Britain and Ireland (1829), copy in *Church and State through the Centuries,* trans. and eds. Sidney Z. Ehler and John B. Morrall (Westminster, MD, 1954), 256–270.

50 J. C. D. Clark, *The Language of Liberty 1660–1832: Political Discourse and Social Dynamics in the Anglo-American World* (Cambridge 1994), 289.

51 James E. Bradley and Dale K. Van Kley, "Introduction," in *Religion and Politics in Enlightenment Europe,* eds. James E. Bradley and Dale K. Van Kley (Notre Dame 2001), 4.

52 Lamennais to Marquis de Coriolis, Apr. 30, 1825, in *Lamennais: Correspondance Générale* (Paris 1971), 3: 51–52; Lamennais to Comte de Senfft-Pillatsch, Dec. 22, 1826, in *Lamennais: Correspondance Générale,* 3: 255–258.

53 Lamennais to Comte de Senfft-Pilasch, July 13, 1830, in *Lamennais: Correspondance Générale,* 4: 306–307.

54 "On the Separation of Church and State," *L'Avenir* (Oct. 18, 1830), reprinted in *Lamennais: A Believer's Revolutionary Politics,* eds. Richard A. Lebrun and Sylvain Milbach (Leiden 2018), 44.

55 Daniel O'Connell to Christopher Fitz-Simon, Sept. 11, 1830, in *The Correspondence of Daniel O'Connell,* ed. Maurice O'Connell (Dublin 1977), 4: 203–205.

56 "On the Future of Society," *L'Avenir* (June 28–29, 1831), reprinted in *Lamennais,* 92.

57 Daniel O'Connell to Christopher Fitz-Simon, Sept. 11, 1830, in *The Correspondence of Daniel O'Connell,* 4: 203.

58 "Act of Union" (Nov. 15, 1831), reprinted in *Lamennais: A Believer's Revolutionary Politics,* 115–116.

59 Henk de Smaele, "Catholic Republicanism Revisited," in *World Views and Worldly Wisdom,* eds. Jan De Maeyer and Vincent Viaene (Leuven 2016), 70.

60 Lacordaire to Prosper Lorain, July 2, 1830, in *Henri-Dominique Lacordaire, Correspondance,* eds. Guy Bedouelle and Christoph-Alois Martin (Paris 2001), 1: 283.

61 "Révolution de Pologne," *L'Avenir* (Dec. 17, 1830).

62 O'Connell to Mary, Mar. 19, 1820, in *The Correspondence of Daniel O'Connell,* 2: 246.

63 Germán Ramírez Aledón, "El clero español en el exilio londinense," in *Londres y el*

liberalismo hispánico, eds. Daniel Muñoz Sempere and Gregorio Alonso García (Madrid 2011), 55.

64   Norman Ravitch, "Liberalism, Catholicism and the Abbé Gregoire," *Church History* 36 (1967): 439.

65   Montalembert, "Saint-German l'Auxerrois," *L'Avenir* (July 12, 1831) in *L'Avenir 1830– 1831,* ed. Guido Verucci (Rome, 1967), 604 ; Jean-Francois Brière, "Abbe Gregoire and Haitian Independence," *Research in African Literatures* 35 (2004): 34.

66   "Farewell from M. de Lamennais" (Nov. 15, 1831), reprinted in *Lamennais,* 124.

67   John Iwicki, C.R., with James Wahl, C.R., *Resurrectionist Charism: A History of the Congregation of the Resurrection* (Rome 1986), 1: 21–23.

68   Reinerman, *Austria and the Papacy in the Age of Metternich,* 2: 251.

69   Reinerman, *Austria and the Papacy in the Age of Metternich,* 2: 135.

70   Angiolo Gambaro, *Sulle Orme Del Lamennais in Italia I: Lamennais A Torino* (Torino 1958).

71   Emmet Larkin, "Cardinal Paul Cullen," in *Varieties of Ultramontanism,* ed. Jeffrey P. Von Arx (Washington 1998), 66.

72   Votum of R.P. Ventura [1831], in *La Condamnation de Lamennais,* eds. M. J. Le Guillou and Louis Le Guillou (Paris 1982), 105–116, esp. 106, 112.

73   Votum of R.P. Rozaven [1831] in *La Condamnation de Lamennais,* 116–126.

74   *Mirari Vos* (1832), §14, 15.

75   Lamennais to Baron de Vitrolles, Nov. 15, 1832, in *Lamennais: Correspondance Générale,* 5: 217–218.

76   Lamennais to Abbé Gerbet, Jan. 28, 1832, in *Lamennais: Correspondance Générale,* 5: 80–81.

77   Louis de Robiano to Comtesse de Robiano, Sept. 27, 1832, in *Catholicisme et Politique Documents inédit (1832–1909),* ed. A. Simon (Wetteren 1955), 73.

78   Félicité de Lamennais, *Words of a Believer* (New York 1834), 99.

79   Lamonde, *The Social History of Ideas in Quebec,* 134.

80   Richard F. Costigan, *Rohrbacher and the Ecclesiology of Ultramontanism* (Rome 1980), 74–75.

81   Lamennais to Montalembert, Jan. 1, 1834, in *Lamennais: Correspondance Générale,* 6: 15.

82   Giuseppe Mazzini, "On the Superiority of Representative Government," [1832] in *A Cosmopolitanism of Nations: Giuseppe Mazzini's Writings on Democracy, Nation Building, and International Relations,* trans. Stefano Recchia, eds. Stefano Recchia and Nadia Urbinati (Princeton 2009), 43.

83   Mazzini to Lamennais, Oct. 12, 1834, in *Mazzini's Letters,* trans. Alice De Rosen Jervis (Westport [1930] 1979), 23.

84   Dale K. Van Kley, "From the Catholic Enlightenment to the Risorgimento: The Exchange between Nicola Spedalieri and Pietro Tamburini, 1791–1797," *Past and Present* 224 (2014): 154.

85   Mazzini to Lamennais, July 3, 1838, in *Rivista di Storia della Chiesa in Italia* 15 (1962): 317.

86   Lacordaire to Montalembert, Apr. 8, 1837, in *Lacordaire-Montalembert Correspondance 1830–1861,* Louis Le Guillou ed. (Paris 1989) 351.

87   Oliver P. Rafferty, S.J., " 'The People—The Real Governors of Today': The Irish Catholic Church and Democracy, c. 1825–1923," *Studies* 107 (2018): 349.

88   John Wolffe, *The Protestant Crusade in Great Britain 1829–1860* (Oxford 1991), 318–319.

89   Merle d'Aubigne to Jules Michelet, Oct. 23, 1843, in Jules Michelet, *Correspondance Générale,* ed. Louis Le Guillou (Paris 1995), 4: 186.

90   Kehoe, *Creating a Scottish Church,* 40.

91   George Cheever, *Wanderings of a Pilgrim in the Shadow of Mont Blanc* (New York 1846), 19.

92   Caroline Ford, "Private Lives and Public Order in Restoration France: The Seduction of Emily Loveday," *American Historical Review* 99 (1994): 21–43.

93   Peter Coffman, "Meanings of Gothic in Atlantic Canada, c. 1840–1890," in *Gothic*

Revival Worldwide: A. W. N. Pugin's Global Influence, eds. Timothy Brittain-Catlin, Jan De Maeyer and Martin Bressani (Leuven 2016), 66.

94   Rev. J. F. Nicholson to O'Connell, Mar. 4, 1839, in *The Correspondence of Daniel O'Connell*, ed. Maurice O'Connell (Dublin 1972), 6: 219.

95   Jon Vanden Heuvel, *A German Life in the Age of Revolution: Joseph Görres, 1776–1848* (Washington 2001), 335.

96   Francisco Bilbao, "Chilean Sociability" [1844], in *Nineteenth-Century Nation Building and the Latin American Intellectual Tradition*, eds. Janet Burke and Ted Humphrey (Indianapolis 2007), 109.

97   John T. McGreevy, *American Jesuits and the World: How an Embattled Religious Order Made Modern Catholicism Global* (Princeton 2016), 10–11.

98   James E. Sanders, *The Vanguard of the Atlantic World: Creating Modernity, Nation, and Democracy in Nineteenth-Century Latin America* (Durham 2014), 138; Geoffrey Cubitt, *The Jesuit Myth: Conspiracy Theory and Politics in Nineteenth-Century France* (Oxford 1993), 137.

99   Jorge Enrique Salcedo Martínez, S.J., *Las vicisitudes de los jesuitas en Colombia: Hacia una historia de la Compañía de Jesús, 1844–1861* (Bogotá 2014), 166.

100 O'Connell to Rev. W. A. O'Meara O.F.M., Sept. 9, 1841, in *The Correspondence of Daniel O'Connell*, 7: 114–115.

101 O'Connell to William Higgins, Apr. 10, 1841, in *The Correspondence of Daniel O'Connell*, 7: 35–36.

102 Rafferty, "'The People—The Real Governors of Today,'" 350.

103 John Morley, *The Life of William Ewart Gladstone* (New York 1921), 3:62.

104 Donal A. Kerr, *Peel, Priests and Politics: Sir Robert Peel's Administration and the Roman Catholic Church in Ireland, 1841–1846* (Oxford 1982), 272.

105 Paul Cullen to Francis Kenrick, Sept. 17, 1847, cited in Colin Barr, *Ireland's Pope: Paul Cullen, 1803–1878*, forthcoming Cambridge University Press.

106 Vincent Viaene, *Belgium and the Holy See*, 462.

107 Charles Montalembert, *Oeuvres de M. le comte de Montalembert* (Paris 1860), 2: 457–459.

108 Gioacchino Ventura Da Raulica, *The Funeral Orations Preached on the Death of the Liberator* (Dublin 1847), 40.

FOUR: TRIUMPH

1   Lucien Jaume, *L'individu effacé ou le paradoxe du libéralisme français* (Paris 1997), 193–237.

2   Alexis de Tocqueville, *Democracy in America*, trans. Arthur Goldhammer (New York 2004), 332.

3   Entry of July 20, 1835, in *Alexis de Tocqueville's Journey in Ireland July–August 1835*, trans. and ed. Emmet Larkin (Washington 1990), 46–47.

4   Austin Gough, *Paris and Rome: The Gallican Church and the Ultramontane Campaign, 1848–1853* (Oxford 1986), 62.

5   André Jardin, *Tocqueville: A Biography*, trans. Lydia Davis and Robert Hemenway (New York 1988), 384.

6   John Connelly, *From Peoples into Nations: A History of Eastern Europe* (Princeton 2020), 159.

7   Alexis de Tocqueville, *Recollections: The French Revolution of 1848*, trans. George Lawrence, eds. J. Mayer and A. Kerr (New Brunswick 1997), 103.

8   Albert Paul Schimberg, *The Great Friend: Frederic Ozanam* (Milwaukee 1946), 215.

9   Klaus Schatz, *Geschichte der deutschen Jesuiten* (Münster 2014), 1: 131–132.

10   Christopher Clark, "Why Should We Think about the Revolutions of 1848 Now?" *London Review of Books* 41 (Mar. 7, 2019), 12–16.

11   Tocqueville to Francisque de Corcelle, July 22, 1854, in *The Tocqueville Reader: A Life in Letters and Politics*, eds. Olivier Zunz and Alan S. Kahan (Oxford 2002), 271.

12   Dale K. Van Kley, "From the Catholic Enlightenment to the Risorgimento: The

Exchange Between Nicola Spedalieri and Pietro Tamburini, 1791–1797," *Past and Present* 224 (2014): 154.

13   John T. McGreevy, *American Jesuits and the World: How An Embattled Religious Order Made Modern Catholicism Global* (Princeton 2016), 11.

14   Giacomo Martina, S.J., *Pio IX (1846–1850)* (Rome 1974), 541.

15   David I. Kertzer, *The Pope Who Would be King: The Exile of Pius IX and the Emergence of Modern Europe* (New York 2018), 153.

16   Eugenio F. Biagini, "Mazzini and Anticlericalism: The English Exile," in *Giuseppe Mazzini and the Globalisation of Democratic Nationalism* (Oxford 2008), 165.

17   Margaret Fuller to Mary Roach, May 23, 1847, in *"My Heart Is a Large Kingdom": Selected Letters of Margaret Fuller*, ed. Robert N. Hudspeth (Ithaca 2001), 245; Dispatch of Jan. 6, 1850, in *These Sad but Glorious Days: Dispatches from Europe 1846–1850*, eds. Larry J. Reynolds and Susan Belasco Smith (New Haven 1992), 321.

18   Martina, *Pio IX (1846–1850)*, 298.

19   Tocqueville to Francisque de Corcelle, July 30, 1849, in Tocqueville, *Oeuvres Complètes*, ed. J. P. Mayer (Paris 1983), 15/1: 340–341.

20   Tocqueville to Francisque De Corcelle, May 13, 1852, in Tocqueville, *Oeuvres Complètes*, 15/2: 55.

21   Tocqueville to Henry Reeve, Oct. 7, 1856 in Tocqueville, *Oeuvres Complètes*, 6: 199.

22   Gough, *Paris and Rome*, 79.

23   Yves M. Congar, "L'Ecclésiologie De La révolution Française Au Concile Du Vatican, Sous Le Signe De L'affirmation De L'Autorité," in *L'Ecclésiologie au XIXe Siècle* (Paris 1961), 103; Andrzej Walicki, *Philosophy and Romantic Nationalism: The Case of Poland* (Oxford 1982), 229–236; Sol Serrano, *¿Qué Hacer con Dios en la República? Política y secularización en Chile (1845–1885)* (Santiago 2008), 84.

24   Charles Mercier, *La Société de Saint-Vincent de Paul: Une mémoire des origines en mouvement 1833–1914* (Paris 2006), 49.

25   McGreevy, *American Jesuits and the World*, 113.

26   Douglass Sullivan-González, *Piety, Power and Politics: Religion and Nation Formation in Guatemala 1821–1871* (Pittsburgh 1998), 73.

27   Julia A. Clancy-Smith, *Mediterraneans: North Africa and Europe in an Age of Migration, c. 1800–1900* (Berkeley 2011), 274–275; Sr. Mary Carol Schroeder, O.S.F., *The Catholic Church in the Diocese of Vincennes 1847–1877* (Washington 1946), 97.

28   Abigail Green, "Nationalism and the 'Jewish International': Religious Internationalism in Europe and the Middle East c. 1840–c. 1880," *Comparative Studies in Society and History* 50 (2008): 550.

29   *Quanta Cura* (1864), appendix §80.

30   Brian Porter-Szücs, *Faith and Fatherland: Catholicism, Modernity, and Poland* (New York 2011), 96.

31   Colin Barr, "Paul Cullen, Italy and the Irish Catholic Imagination 1826–1870," in *Nation/Nazione: Irish Nationalism and the Italian Risorgimento*, eds. Colin Barr, Michele Finelli, and Anne O'Connor (Dublin 2014), 147.

32   John Molony, *The Roman Mould of the Australian Catholic Church* (Melbourne 1969), 78.

33   Raymond McCluskey, "Scots Pilgrimages to Rome (1877–1903): Educational Fieldwork for Victorians and Edwardians?" *Innes Review* 57 (2006): 182–205.

34   Thomas W. Spalding, *Martin John Spalding: American Churchman* (Washington 1973), 229.

35   Lord John Russell to Bishop Dr. Maltby of Durham, Nov. 4, 1850, copy in E. R. Norman, *Anti-Catholicism in Victorian England* (New York 1968), 159–160.

36   Frans Groot, "Papists and Beggars: National Festivals and Nation Building in the Netherlands during the Nineteenth Century," in *Nation and Religion: Perspectives on Europe and Asia*, eds. Peter van der Veer and Hartmut Lehmann (Princeton 1999), 172.

37   Christopher Clark, "The New Catholicism and the European Culture Wars," in *Culture*

Wars: Secular–Catholic Conflict in Nineteenth-Century Europe, eds. Christopher Clark and Wolfram Kaiser (Cambridge 2003), 35.

38 Gough, *Paris and Rome*, 131.
39 Ruth Harris, *Lourdes: Body and Spirit in the Secular Age* (London 1999), 124.
40 Louis Veuillot to Théodore Foisset, Oct. 12, 1850, in Veuillot, *Oeuvres Complètes*, ed. Pierre Gibert (Paris 1983), 15: 251.
41 Gough, *Paris and Rome*, 211.
42 Colin Barr, *Ireland's Empire: The Roman Catholic Church in the English-Speaking World, 1829–1914* (Cambridge 2020), 312.
43 Serrano, ¿*Qué hacer con Dios en la República?*, 192.
44 Fr. Daniele Comboni to Bishop Luigi di Canossa, Feb. 1, 1868, in *The Writings of St. Daniel Comboni: Correspondence and Reports (1850–1881) of the Founder of the Comboni Missionaries*, trans. Catharine P. Marcelin-Rice and Louis Marcelin-Rice, ed. Fr. John M. Troy (London 2005), 474.
45 I. Ciampi, S.J., *Prospectus for St. Austin's Society for the Diffusion of Useful and Religious Knowledge* (Bombay 1866), v.
46 Colin Barr, "Giuseppe Mazzini and Irish Nationalism," in *Giuseppe Mazzini and the Globalisation of Democratic Nationalism*, 126, 134.
47 Donoso Cortes, "Discourse on Dictatorship" [1849], in Cortes, *Readings in Political Theory*, trans. Vincent McNamara and Michael Schwartz, ed. R. A. Herrera (Naples, FL, 2007), 64.
48 Lamonde, *The Social History of Ideas in Quebec*, 265.
49 Ralph Waldo Emerson to Thomas Carlyle, Sept. 26, 1864, in *The Correspondence of Thomas Carlyle and Ralph Waldo Emerson, 1834–1872* (Boston, 1883), 2: 286.
50 John Stuart Mill, *Collected Works of John Stuart Mill*, eds. John M. Robson and Jack Stillinger (Toronto 1981), 1: 45.
51 Rev. J. Balmes, *Protestantism and Catholicity Compared in Their Effects on the Civilization of Europe* (Baltimore [1842]1851), 27, 419.
52 Orestes Brownson to Jeremiah Cummings, Oct. 30, 1849, I–3–i, Brownson papers, University of Notre Dame Archives; Félix Frias, "Paris y Roma," in Frias, *Escritos y Discursos*, ed. C. Casavalle (Buenos Aires 1884), 1: 340.
53 Josep M. Fradera, *Jaume Balmes: Els fonaments racionals d'una política catòlica* (Barcelona 1996), 167–213; Wilhelm Emmanuel von Ketteler, "The Christian Concept of the Private Property Right" [1848], in *The Social Teachings of Wilhelm Emmanuel von Ketteler Bishop of Mainz 1811–1877*, trans. Rupert J. Ederer (Washington 1981), 10–11.
54 Jonathan Sperber, *Popular Catholicism in Nineteenth-Century Germany* (Princeton 1984), 89.
55 Wilhelm Emmanuel von Ketteler, "Freedom, Authority and the Church" [1862], in *The Social Teachings of Wilhelm Emmanuel von Ketteler*, 117.
56 William Edward Hogan, *The Development of Bishop Wilhelm Emmanuel von Ketteler's Interpretation of the Social Problem* (Washington 1946), 115–143; Emiel Lamberts, *The Struggle with Leviathan: Social Responses to the Omnipotence of the State, 1815–1965* (Leuven [2011] 2016), 258–260.
57 Karl Marx to Friedrich Engels, Sept. 25, 1869, in Karl Marx and Friedrich Engels, *Selected Correspondence 1846–1895* (Westport, CT, 1975), 263.
58 Fr. Félix Varela, "Abolition!" [c. 1822] in *The Cuba Reader: History, Culture, Politics*, eds. Aviva Chomsky, Barry Carr, and Pamela María Smorkaloff (Durham 2003), 96.
59 Albert Garcia Balañà, "Antislavery Before Abolitionism: Networks and Motives in Early Liberal Barcelona, 1833–1844," in *Slavery and Antislavery in Spain's Atlantic Empire*, eds. Josep M. Fradera and Christopher Schmidt-Nowara (New York 2013), 240.
60 Kenneth P. Serbin, *Needs of the Heart: A Social and Cultural History of Brazil's Clergy and Seminaries* (Notre Dame 2006), 46–49.

61 Montalembert to Lacordaire, Sept. 20, 1839, in *Lacordaire-Montalembert Correspondance, 1830–1861*, ed. Louis Le Guillou (Paris 1989), 449.

62 Daniel O'Connell, "Daniel O'Connell and the Committee of the Irish Repeal Association of Cincinnati" [1843], in *Union Pamphlets of the Civil War, 1861–1865*, ed. Frank Freidel (Cambridge MA, 1967), 2: 811.

63 Thomas Paul Thigpen, "Aristocracy of the Heart: Catholic Lay Leadership in Savannah 1820–1870" (Emory University, PhD, 1995), 591.

64 Sarah A. Curtis, "Anne-Marie Javouhey and the Colony at Mana, French Guiana, 1827–1848," in *Views from the Margins: Creating Identities in Modern France*, eds. Kevin J. Callahan and Sarah A. Curtis (Lincoln 2008), 37.

65 Francis Patrick Kenrick, *The Acts of the Apostles, the Epistles of St. Paul, the Catholic Epistles, and the Apocalypse* (New York 1851), 497.

66 John T. McGreevy, "Catholicism and Abolition: A Historical (and Theological) Problem," in *Figures in the Carpet: Finding the Human Person in the American Past*, ed. Wilfred M. McClay (Grand Rapids 2007), 415.

67 "Fr. James Ryder, S.J., Criticizes Abolitionism" [1835] and "A Jesuit Priest Witnesses Anguish at Newtown" [1838], in *Facing Georgetown's History: A Reader on Slavery, Memory and Reconciliation,* eds. Adam Rothman and Elsa Barraza Mendoza (Washington 2021), 127, 136–137; John T. McGreevy, "Catholicism and Abolition," 415.

68 McGreevy, "Catholicism and Abolition," 415.

69 Luigi Taparelli to Veuillot, Feb. 23, 1849, in *Carteggi del P. Luigi Taparelli D'Azeglio della Compagnia di Gesù*, ed. Pietro Pirri (Torino 1932), 262–263.

70 Lamonde, *The Social History of Ideas in Quebec*, 287.

71 Luigi d'Azeglio Taparelli, *Saggio teoretico di dritto naturale appoggiato sul fatto* (Rome [1849] 1949), 478. On regional identity, Christopher Clark, "From 1848 to Christian Democracy," in *Religion and the Political Imagination*, eds. Ira Katznelson and Gareth Stedman Jones (Cambridge 2010), 211–12.

72 Giacomo Martina, S.J., "Motivi e radici dell'opposizione piemontese alla compagnia di Gesù," in *La Compagnia di Gesù nella Provincia di Torino: dagli anni di Emanuele Filiberto a quello di Carlo Alberto*, eds. Bruno Signorelli and Pietro Uscello (Turin 1998), 421–422.

73 Mauricio Tenorio-Trillo, *Latin America: The Allure and Power of an Idea* (Chicago 2017), 51–52.

74 Francisco Javier Ramón Solans, "The Creation of a Latin American Catholic Church: Vatican Authority and Political Imagination, 1854–1899," *Journal of Ecclesiastical History* 71 (2020): 316–336.

75 Thomas C. Bruneau, *The Political Transformation of the Brazilian Catholic Church* (Cambridge 1974), 23; Ivereigh, *Catholicism and Politics in Argentina*, 47.

76 Derek Williams, "Negotiating the State: National Utopias and Local Politics in Andean Ecuador, 1845–1875" (SUNY Stony Brook, PhD 2001), 142; John Lynch, *New Worlds: A Religious History of Latin America* (New Haven 2012), 208–211.

77 Kerby A. Miller, *Emigrants and Exiles: Ireland and the Irish Exodus to North America* (New York 1985), 297, 569; Kevin Robert Ostoyich, "The Transatlantic Soul: German Catholic Emigration during the Nineteenth Century" (Harvard University, PhD 2006), 159–160.

78 Kevin Kenny, "Irish Emigrations in a Comparative Perspective," in *The Cambridge Social History of Modern Ireland*, eds. Eugenio F. Biagini and Mary E. Daly (Cambridge 2017), 405–422.

79 *Annual Report All Hallows College* (Dublin 1848), 2.

80 Molony, *The Roman Mould of the Australian Catholic Church*, 24, 28.

81 Beverly Zimmerman, *The Making of a Diocese: Maitland, Its Bishop, Priests and People 1866–1909* (Melbourne 2000), 196.

82 Oliver P. Rafferty, S.J., "The Catholic Church, Ireland and the British Empire, 1800–1921," *Historical Research* 84 (May 2011): 295.

83   S. K. Kehoe, "Catholic Collaborators: Britain and the Catholic Church in Trinidad, c. 1820–1840," *Slavery and Abolition* 40 (2019): 136.
84   Bernard Aspinwall, "Scots and Irish clergy Ministering to Immigrants, 1830–1878," *Innes Review* 47 (1996): 51.
85   McGreevy, *Catholicism and American Freedom*, 30.
86   Terence J. Fay, *A History of Canadian Catholics: Gallicanism, Romanism and Canadianism* (Montreal 2002), 181.
87   McGreevy, *American Jesuits and the World*, 101, 72.
88   Mark Peterson, *The City-State of Boston: The Rise and Fall of an Atlantic Power, 1630–1865* (Princeton 2019), 575.
89   Comte de Montalembert, *On the Subject of National Education in France; Delivered in the Chamber of Peers April 16, 1844*, trans. Professor Walter (Philadelphia 1844).
90   Jardin, *Tocqueville*, 364.
91   R. P. Jonquet, *Mgr. Bonjean Oblat de Marie Immaculée Premier Archevêque de Colombo* (Nîmes 1910), 1: 125.
92   McGreevy, *Catholicism and American Freedom*, 7–12, 41.
93   Angelo Secchi S.J. to his mother, Oct. 19, 1848, copy in *Bulletin of the American Association of Jesuit Scientists* 17 (1940): 128–132.
94   McGreevy, *Catholicism and American Freedom*, 13.
95   Donald M. MacRaild, "Transnationalizing 'Anti-Popery': Militant Protestant Preachers in the Nineteenth-Century Anglo World," *Journal of Religious History* 39 (2015): 224–243.
96   Alessandro Gavazzi, *Father Gavazzi's Lectures in New York*, ed. and trans. Madame Julie de Marguerites (New York 1853), 276.
97   McGreevy, *Catholicism and American Freedom*, 24.
98   Abraham Lincoln to Joshua Speed, Aug. 24, 1855, in *Collected Works of Abraham Lincoln*, ed. Roy P. Basler (New Brunswick 1953), 2: 321–323.
99   Edwin Williamson, *The Penguin History of Latin America* (New York [1992] 2009), 242.
100   Constitution of Mexico (1857), article V.
101   McGreevy, *Catholicism and American Freedom*, 59, 87–88.
102   Pablo Mijangos Y González, *The Lawyer of the Church: Bishop Clemente de Jesús Munguía and the Clerical Response to the Mexican Liberal Reforma* (Lincoln 2015), 79–82; David A. Brading, "Ultramontane Intransigence and the Mexican Reform: Clemente de Jesús Munguía," in *The Politics of Religion in an Age of Revival: Studies in Nineteenth-Century Europe and Latin America*, ed. Austen Ivereigh (London 2000), 122, 132–133.
103   John W. O'Malley, *Vatican I: The Council and the Making of the Ultramontane Church* (Cambridge MA, 2018), 114.
104   Richard F. Costigan, S.J., *The Consensus of the Church and Papal Infallibility* (Washington 2015), 173.
105   Jonquet, *Mgr. Bonjean Oblat de Marie Immaculée*, 195.
106   Colin Barr, " 'Imperium in Imperio': Irish Episcopal Imperialism in the Nineteenth Century," *English Historical Review* 123 (2008): 611.
107   Lord Acton to Richard Simpson, Nov. 2, 1862, in *The Correspondence of Lord Acton and Richard Simpson*, eds. Jozef Louis Altholz and Damian McElrath (Cambridge 1971), 3: 45.
108   Thomas Albert Howard, *The Pope and the Professor: Pius IX, Ignaz von Döllinger, and the Quandary of the Modern Age* (New York 2017), 110; John P. Boyle, "The Ordinary Magisterium: Towards a History of the Concept, I," *Heythrop Journal* 20 (1979): 380–398.
109   Owen Chadwick, *A History of the Popes 1830–1914* (Oxford 1998), 318.
110   James J. Hennesey, *The First Council of the Vatican: The American Experience* (New York 1963), 147.
111   Schatz, *Papal Primacy*, 149.

112   "Ripugnanza del Concetto di Cattolico liberale," *Civiltà Cattolica* Series VII 8 (1869): 18.

113   McGreevy, *Catholicism and American Freedom*, 47.

114   Montalembert, *L'église libre dans l'état libre discours prononcés a l'Assemblée Générale des Catholiques à Malines* (Brussels 1863), 21, 150–151.

115   Adolphe Deschamp to Comtesse M. De Robiano, Dec. 17, 1869, in *Catholicisme et Politique Documents inédits (1832–1909)*, ed. A. Simon (Wetteren 1955), 103.

116   Montalembert to Deschamps, Oct. 2, 1869, in *Correspondance Entre Charles Montalembert et Adolphe Deschamps 1838–1870*, ed. Roger Aubert (Brussels 1993), 205–206.

117   Montalembert to M. Lallemand, Feb. 28, 1870, in *Charles de Montalembert Journal Intime Inédit Tome VIII: 1865–1870*, eds. Louis Le Guillou and Nicole Roger-Taillade (Paris 2009), 792–796.

118   O'Malley, *Vatican I*, 165; Carol E. Harrison, *Romantic Catholics: France's Postrevolutionary Generation in Search of a Modern Faith* (Ithaca 2014), 273.

119   O'Malley, *Vatican I*, 213.

120   O'Malley, *Vatican I*, 196–97.

121   Gladstone to Joseph Bickersteth, Dec. 9, 1874, in *The Correspondence of Henry Edward Manning and William Ewart Gladstone*, ed. Peter C. Erb (Oxford 2013), 3: 399–400; W. E. Gladstone, *The Vatican Decrees in Their Bearing on Civil Allegiance: A Political Expostulation* (New York 1875), 24.

122   Kenneth Parker, "Saint John Henry Newman, Development of Doctrine and Sensus Fidelium: His Enduring Legacy in Roman Catholic Theological Discourse," *Journal of Moral Theology* 10 (2021): 69.

123   John Henry Newman to Lady Simeon, Nov. 18, 1870, in *The Letters and Diaries of John Henry Newman*, eds. Charles Stephen Dessain and Thomas Gornall, S.J. (Oxford 1974), 25: 231.

124   Thomas Albert Howard, *The Pope and the Professor*, 153.

125   David I. Kertzer, *Prisoner of the Vatican: The Pope's Secret Plot to Capture Rome from the New Italian State* (Boston 2004), 107.

126   McGreevy, *Catholicism and American Freedom*, 106–107.

FIVE: MILIEU

 1   Rebecca Ayako Bennette, *Fighting for the Soul of Germany: The Catholic Struggle for Inclusion after Unification* (Cambridge MA, 2012), 33; Franz Theodor Helmken, *The Cathedral of Cologne*, trans. J. W. Watkins (Cologne 1884), 32.

 2   Margaret Lavinia Anderson, *Windthorst: A Biography* (New York 1981), 159.

 3   Wilhelm Emmanuel von Ketteler, "Liberalism, Socialism and Christianity" [1871], in *The Social Teachings of Wilhelm Emmanuel von Ketteler Bishop of Mainz (1811–1877)*, trans. Rupert J. Ederer (Washington 1981), 501–507.

 4   Albert Monshan Wu, *From Christ to Confucius: German Missionaries, Chinese Christians, and the Globalization of Christianity, 1860–1950* (New Haven 2016), 36.

 5   Heidi Bossard-Borner, "Village Quarrels and National Controversies: Switzerland," *Culture Wars: Secular–Catholic Conflict in Nineteenth-Century Europe*, eds. Christopher Clark and Wolfram Kaiser (New York 2003), 266.

 6   Paola Chenillo Alazraki, "Liberalismo a prueba: La expulsión de 'extranjeros perniciosos' en México durante la República Restaurada (1867–1876)," *Revista de Indias* 72 (2012): 377–408.

 7   Austen Ivereigh, *Catholicism and Politics in Argentina: 1810–1960* (New York 1995), 53.

 8   Prince Bismarck [1877] and Notes on Professor Atwater's Lectures on Civil Government [1878], *The Papers of Woodrow Wilson*, ed. Arthur S. Link (Princeton 1966), 1: 313, 427.

 9   Owen Chadwick, *A History of the Popes 1830–1914* (Oxford 1998), 235–236.

10   Émile de Laveleye, *Protestantism and Catholicism, in Their Bearing upon the Liberty and Prosperity of Nations: A Study of Social Economy* (London 1875), 11, 59, 52.

11   Richard L. Kagan, "Prescott's Paradigm: American Historical Scholarship and the Decline of Spain," in *Imagined Histories: American Historians Interpret the Past*, eds. Anthony Molho and Gordon Wood (Princeton 1998), 324–348.

12   Thomas Nipperdey, "Max Weber, Protestantism, and the Context of the Debate around 1900," in *Weber's Protestant Ethic: Origins, Evidence, Contexts*, eds. Hartmut Lehmann and Guenther Roth (Cambridge 1993), 77–78.

13   James McMillan, "'Priest Hits Girl': On the Front Line in the 'War of the Two Frances,'" in *Culture Wars*, 79.

14   Ivereigh, *Catholicism and Politics in Argentina*, 54.

15   John T. McGreevy, *Catholicism and American Freedom: A History* (New York 2003), 91–99.

16   C. F. G. de Groot, *Brazilian Catholicism and the Ultramontane Reform, 1850–1930* (Amsterdam 1996), 44.

17   Ulrike Harmat, "'Till Death Do You Part': Catholicism, Marriage and Culture War in Austria-Hungary," in *Marriage, Law and Modernity: Global Histories*, ed. Julia Moses (London 2018), 112; Max Herbert Voegler, "Religion, Liberalism and the Social Question in the Habsburg Hinterland: The Catholic Church in Upper Austria, 1850–1914" (Columbia University, PhD 2006), 160–161.

18   Dain Edward Borges, *The Family in Bahia, Brazil: 1870–1945* (Stanford 1992), 130.

19   Protesta por la erección de una estatua a Giordano Bruno [1889], *Documentos Colectivos Del Episcopado Español 1870–1914*, ed. Jesús Iribarren (Madrid 1974), 74–75.

20   Matteo Sanfilippo, "Genesi, nascita e inizio delle Delegazioni apostoliche negli Stati Uniti e in Canada," *Archivum Historiae Pontificiae* 52 (2018): 31–56.

21   Eamon Duffy, *John Henry Newman: A Very Brief History* (London 2018), 22.

22   Owen Chadwick, *Catholicism and History: The Opening of the Vatican Archives* (Cambridge 1978), esp. 72–143; Valentina Merla, *Papi che leggono Dante: la ricezione dantesca nel magistero pontificio da Leone XIII a Benedetto XVI* (Bari 2018), 11–30.

23   Leo W. Shields, "The History and Meaning of the Term Social Justice" (University of Notre Dame, PhD 1941), 26.

24   *Libertas* (1888), §11.

25   *Aeterni Patris* (1879), §26.

26   Thomas A. Hartley, *Thomistic Revival and the Modernist Era* (Toronto 1971), 34–35.

27   Edward Baring, *Converts to the Real: Catholicism and the Making of Continental Philosophy* (Cambridge MA 2019), 27.

28   Colin Barr, "The Failure of Newman's Catholic University of Ireland," *Archivium Hibernicum* 55 (2001): 136.

29   Anderson, *Windthorst*, 535.

30   Frances Lannon, *Privilege, Persecution, and Prophecy; The Catholic Church in Spain, 1875–1975* (Oxford 1987), 69.

31   Harold Laski, *Studies in the Problem of Sovereignty* (New Haven 1917), 219.

32   Pius IX to Archbishop Ledóchowski, June 25, 1874, copy in *Il 'Kulturkampf' in Italia e nei paesi di lingua tedesca*, eds. Rudolf Lill and Francesco Traniello (Bologna 1992), 269.

33   James E. Bjork, *Neither Pole Nor German: Catholicism and National Indifference in a Central European Borderland* (Ann Arbor 2008), 25–27.

34   S. Karly Kehoe, *Creating a Scottish Church: Catholicism, Gender and Ethnicity in Nineteenth-Century Scotland* (Manchester 2010), 158–159.

35   John T. McGreevy, *Parish Boundaries: The Catholic Encounter with Race in the Twentieth-Century Urban North* (Chicago 1996), 7–28.

36   Colin Barr and Daithí Ó Corráin, "Catholic Ireland, 1740–2016," *The Cambridge Social History of Modern Ireland*, eds. Eugenio F. Biagini and Mary E. Daly (Cambridge 2017), 73–74.

37   Patricia Londoño-Vega, *Religion, Culture and Society in Colombia: Medellin and Antioquia, 1850–1930* (Oxford 2002), 178.

38   John Louis Ciani, "Across a Wide Ocean: Salvatore Maria Brandi, S.J., and the *Civiltà*

Cattolica from Americanism to Modernism, 1891–1914" (University of Virginia, PhD 1992), 63.

39 Charles Loring Brace, *The Dangerous Classes of New York, and Twenty Years' Work among Them* (New York [1872] 1880), 154.

40 Edward Ross Dickinson, *The Politics of German Child Welfare from the Empire to the Federal Republic* (Cambridge MA, 1996), 94–97.

41 Colin Barr, *Ireland's Empire: The Roman Catholic Church in the English-Speaking World 1829–1914* (Cambridge 2020), 364.

42 Patrick J. Houlihan, *Catholicism and the Great War: Religion and Everyday Life in Germany and Austria-Hungary, 1914–1922* (Cambridge 2015), 22.

43 Jan De Volder, *Cardinal Mercier in the First World War: Belgium, Germany and the Catholic Church* (Leuven 2018), 13; Ivereigh, *Catholicism and Politics in Argentina*, 60.

44 Sven Sterken and Eva Weyns, "Introduction: Faith and Its Territories," in *Territories of Faith: Religion, Urban Planning and Demographic Change in Post-War Europe*, eds. Sven Sterken and Eva Weyns (Leuven 2022), 14; Porter-Szücs, *Faith and Fatherland*, 82.

45 John Lynch, *New Worlds: A Religious History of Latin America* (New Haven 2012), 232.

46 Lannon, *Privilege, Persecution, and Prophecy*, 8–18.

47 Hugh McLeod, *Piety and Poverty: Working-Class Religion in Berlin, London and New York, 1870–1914* (New York 1996), 208–209.

48 Walter Nugent, *Crossings: The Great Transatlantic Migrations, 1870–1914* (Bloomington 1992), 14.

49 James Sanders, *The Education of an Urban Minority: Catholics in Chicago, 1833–1965* (New York 1977), 70.

50 Leslie Woodcock Tentler, "Who Is the Church? Conflict in a Polish Immigrant Parish in Late Nineteenth-Century Detroit," *Comparative Studies in Society and History* 25 (1983): 241–276; Brian McCook, *The Borders of Integration: Polish Migrants in Germany and the United States, 1870–1924* (Athens 2011), 105–106.

51 Circular Letter Promoting a National Parish at San Francisco, 1871, in *¡Presente!: U.S. Latino Catholics from Colonial Origins to the Present*, eds. Timothy Matovina and Gerald E. Poyo (Maryknoll, NY, 2000), 101.

52 Donna Gabaccia, *Italy's Many Diasporas* (Seattle 2000), 4, 58–59.

53 Robert Anthony Orsi, *The Madonna of 115th Street: Faith and Community in Italian Harlem, 1880–1950* (New Haven 1985), 55.

54 Miranda Lida, "La Europeización Del Catolicismo Argentino Y Sus Transformaciones Desde 1880 Hasta La Década De 1960," in *Más Allá De Los Nacionalcatolicismos: Redes Transnacionales de Los Catolicismos Hispánicos*, eds. José Ramón Rodríguez Lago and Natalia Núñez Bargueño (Madrid 2021), 153–176; Kenneth P. Serbin, *Needs of the Heart: A Social and Cultural History of Brazil's Clergy and Seminaries* (Notre Dame 2006), 75–76.

55 Rolando Iberico Ruiz, "La Roma del Perú: resurgimiento católico, espacio público y política en Arequipa (1860–1925)," (Pontificia Universidad Católica Del Peru, MA 2017), 33.

56 Londoño-Vega, 167–172.

57 Lynch, *New Worlds*, 233.

58 Ralph Della Cava, *Miracle at Joaseiro* (New York 1970), 48.

59 Lisa M. Edwards, *Roman Virtues: The Education of Latin American Clergy in Rome, 1858–1962* (New York 2011), 17, 15, 65.

60 Richard A. Sundt, "From Late Gothic to Gothic Revival in Latin America," in *Gothic Revival Worldwide: A. W. N. Pugin's Global Influence*, eds. Timothy Brittain-Catlin, Jan De Maeyer, and Martin Bressani (Leuven 2016), 121–129.

61 Charles A. Hale, *The Transformation of Liberalism in Late Nineteenth-Century Mexico* (Princeton 1989), 154.

62 Joop Vernooij, C.Ss.R., "The Seven Redemptorist Bishops of Suriname," *Spicilegium Historicum* 60 (2012): 247.

63 Leslie Woodcock Tentler, *Seasons of Grace: A History of the Catholic Archdiocese of Detroit* (Detroit 1990), 3.

64 Peter Paul Cahensly to Cardinal Simeoni, June 10, 1884, in *For the Love of Immigrants: Migration Writings and Letters of Bishop John Baptist Scalabrini (1839–1905)* (New York 2000), 176.

65 Petition of the Italian Colonists of Benevento, State of Espirito Santo, Brazil to Bishop of Cremona, Mar. 5, 1887, in *For the Love of Immigrants*, 165.

66 Kathleen Sprows Cummings, *A Saint of Our Own: How the Quest for a Holy Hero Helped Catholics Become American* (Chapel Hill 2019), 100–101; Leslie Woodcock Tentler, *American Catholics: A History* (New Haven 2020), 142.

67 McGreevy, *Catholicism and American Freedom*, 121.

68 [Matteo Liberatore], "L'Unità italiana e l'intervento straniero," *Civiltà Cattolica* Series VIII 2 (1871): 145–146.

69 Rosa Bruno-Jofré, *The Missionary Oblate Sisters: Vision and Mission* (Montreal 2005), 27.

70 Laura Crago, "Nationalism, Religion, Citizenship, and Work in the Development of the Polish Working Class and the Polish Trade Union Movement, 1815–1929: A Comparative Study of Russian Poland's Textile Workers and Upper Silesian Miners and Metalworkers" (Yale, PhD 1993), 83.

71 Paul Misner, *Social Catholicism in Europe: From the Onset of Industrialization to the First World War* (New York 1991), 204; Edward G. Bagshawe, *Mercy and Justice to the Poor: The True Political Economy* (London 1885), 7.

72 *Rerum Novarum* (1891), §§3, 19–20, 46, 45.

73 Heinrich Pesch, *Lehrbuch Der Nationalökonomie*, trans. Rupert Ederer (Lewiston, ME [1923] 2002), 1: 1, 32; 2: 1, v.

74 Serbin, *Needs of the Heart*, 67.

75 Alan Knight, *The Mexican Revolution* (Lincoln [1986] 1990), 1: 40.

76 John A. Ryan, "A Great Catholic Work on Political Economy," *Fortnightly Review* 17 (May 1910): 289.

77 John A. Ryan, *A Living Wage: Its Ethical and Economic Aspects* (New York 1912), vii.

78 Jorge Adame Goddard, *El Pensamiento Político y Social de los Católicos Mexicanos (1867–1914)* (Mexico City 2004), 221–223; Paul Smyth, "Reclaiming Community? From Welfare Society to Welfare State in Australian Catholic Social Thought," *Australian Journal of Politics and History* 49 (2003): 17–30.

79 McGreevy, *Catholicism and American Freedom*, 143.

80 José David Lebovitch Dahl, "The Roman Catholic Church in the Formation of Modern Anti-Semitism: *La Civiltà Cattolica*, 1850–1879," *Modern Judaism* 23 (2003): 180–197.

81 Porter-Szücs, *Faith and Fatherland*, 21–23.

82 Balázs Trencsényi, Maciej Janowski, Monika Baar, Maria Falina, and Michal Kopecek, *A History of Modern Political Thought in East Central Europe: Volume I: Negotiating Modernity in the "Long Nineteenth Century"* (Oxford 2016), 552–553.

83 John W. Boyer, *Political Radicalism in Late Imperial Vienna* (Chicago 1981), 212.

84 Ruth Harris, *Dreyfus: Politics, Emotion, and the Scandal of the Century* (New York 2010), 183.

85 Daniel Unowsky, "Local Violence, Regional Politics, and State Crisis: The 1898 Anti-Jewish Riots in Hapsburg Galicia," in *Sites of European Anti-Semitism in the Age of Mass Politics 1880–1918*, eds. Robert Nemes and Daniel Unowsky (Hanover 2014), 15, 33.

86 P. M. Jones, *Politics and Rural Society: The Southern Massif Central c. 1750–1880* (Cambridge 1985), 235.

87 Malcolm Deas, "The Role of the Church, the Army and the Police in Colombian Elections," in *Elections Before Democracy: The History of Elections in Europe and Latin America*, ed. Eduardo Posada Carbó (London 1996), 167.

88 Emiel Lamberts, "Catholic Congresses as Amplifiers of International Public Opinion,"

450 NOTES TO PAGES 130–136

in *The Papacy and the New World Order: Vatican Diplomacy, Catholic Opinion and International Politics at the Time of Leo XIII 1878–1903*, ed. Vincent Viaene (Leuven 2005), 213–225.

89 Jonathan Sperber, *The Kaiser's Voters: Electors and Elections in Imperial Germany* (Cambridge 1997), 281.

90 Grant Grams, "Der Volksverein Deutsch-Kanadischer Katholiken: The Rise and Fall of a German-Catholic Cultural and Immigration Society, 1909–1952," *Catholic Historical Review* 99 (2013): 482.

91 Timothy R. Scully, *Rethinking the Center: Party Politics in Nineteenth and Twentieth Century Chile* (Stanford 1992), 51–52.

92 Knight, *The Mexican Revolution*, 1: 400–404.

93 Tom Buchanan, "Britain," in *Political Catholicism in Europe, 1918–1965*, eds. Tom Buchanan and Martin Conway (Oxford 1996), 264.

94 Vincent Viaene, "Catholic Mobilisation and Papal Diplomacy during the Pontificate of Pius IX (1846–1878)," in *The Black International: The Holy See and Militant Catholicism in Europe*, ed. Emiel Lambert (Leuven 2002), 168–174.

95 Roger Haight, S.J., "Bremond's Newman," in *Newman and the Modernists*, ed. Mary Jo Weaver (Lanham, MD, 1985), 119–137; *The Reception of Pragmatism in France and the Rise of Roman Catholic Modernism 1890–1914*, ed. David G. Schultenover, S.J. (Washington 2009).

96 George Tyrrell, *Medievalism* (Allen, TX [1908] 1994), 42, 84; George Tyrrell to Maria Longworth Storer, Apr. 5, 1900, in *Letters from a "Modernist": The Letters of George Tyrrell to Wilfrid Ward 1893–1908* (London 1981), 166.

97 Friedrich Von Hügel to Maude Petre, July 3, 1906, in *The Letters of Baron Friedrich von Hügel and Maude D. Petre*, ed. James, J. Kelly (Leuven 2003), 46.

98 Gabriel Daly, O.S.A., *Transcendence and Immanence: A Study in Catholic Modernism and Integralism* (Oxford 1980), 234; Claus Arnold, "Antimodernismo e magistero romano: la redazione della *Pascendi*," *Rivista di storia del cristianesimo* 5 (2008): 3–64.

99 Copy of Anti-Modernist Oath in Fergus Kerr, *Twentieth-Century Catholic Theologians: From Neoscholasiticsm to Nuptial Mysticism* (Oxford 2007), 223.

100 A. R. Vidler, *Variety of Catholic Modernists* (Cambridge 1970), 104.

101 Klaus Schatz, S.J., "Jesuit Journals and the First World War: On Nationalism and Dialogue," *Civiltà Cattolica* (Oct. 4, 2018), online edition.

102 Mark McGowan, *The Imperial Irish: Canada's Irish Catholics Fight the Great War, 1914–1918* (Montreal 2017); Barr, *Ireland's Empire*, 460–461.

103 John T. McGreevy, *American Jesuits and the World: How an Embattled Religious Order Made Modern Catholicism Global* (Princeton 2016), 174.

104 Houlihan, *Catholicism and the Great War*, 53.

105 Désiré Mercier, *The Voice of Belgium: Being the War Utterances of Cardinal Mercier* (London 1917), 18, 20.

106 John Deak, "Ignaz Seipel (1876–1932): Founding Father of the Austrian Republic," *Contemporary Austrian Studies* 21 (2012): 41.

107 Lynch, *New Worlds*, 237.

108 McGreevy, *Catholicism and American Freedom*, 100.

SIX: EMPIRE

1 Robbie Aitken, "Selling the Mission: The German Catholic Elite and the Educational Migration of African Youngsters in Europe," *German History* 33 (2015): 30.

2 *Moniteur de Rome,* July 7, 1887, copy in Claude Prudhomme, *Stratégie missionnaire du Saint-Siège sous Léon XIII (1878–1903)* (Rome 1994), 600.

3 Mgr. Henri Vieter, *Chronique de la fondation de l'Eglise catholique au Cameroun 1890–1903*, trans. J. B. Schmitt (Cameroon [1903] 2013), 281.

4 Heinrich Berger, *Mission und Kolonialpolitik: Die Katholische Mission in Kamerun Während der Deutschen Kolonialzeit* (Freiburg 1978), 174–175.

5   Vieter, *Chronique de la fondation de l'Eglise catholique au Cameroun*, 137.

6   Prudhomme, *Stratégie Missionnaire*, 211.

7   Charles Keith, *Catholic Vietnam: A Church from Empire to Nation* (Berkeley 2012), 29.

8   Albert Monshan Wu, *From Christ to Confucius: German Missionaries, Chinese Christians, and the Globalization of Christianity, 1860–1950* (New Haven 2016), 47.

9   Charles Duparquet to Superior General, Feb. 8, 1868, in *Le Père Duparquet: espoirs et échec de la mission en terre portugaise Lettres et Écrits*, ed. Gérard Vieira (Paris 2013) 2: 373–374.

10 Henrietta Harrison, *The Missionary's Curse and Other Tales from a Chinese Catholic Village* (Berkeley 2013), 104.

11 John Mary Waliggo, "The Bugandan Christian Revolution: The Catholic Church in Buddu, 1879–1896," in *Christianity and the African Imagination: Essays in Honour of Adrian Hastings*, eds. David Maxwell with Ingrid Lawrie (Leiden 2002), 87–89.

12 Julia A. Clancy-Smith, *Mediterraneans: North Africa and Europe in an Age of Migration, c. 1800–1900* (Berkeley 2011), 268; Prudhomme, *Stratégie Missionnaire*, 226.

13 Harrison, *The Missionary's Curse*, 106–108.

14 A. Planque to unknown, May 7, 1877, copy in *Rapports du Père Planque, de Mgr Lavigerie et de Mgr. Comboni sur l'Association Internationale Africaine*, ed. R. P. Marcel Storme (Brussels 1957), 12.

15 Emma Rothschild, *An Infinite History: The Story of a Family in France over Three Centuries* (Princeton 2021), 269.

16 Storme, *Rapports du Père Planque*, 39, 45.

17 Silvia Cristofori, "Costantino l'africano: Il progetto politico-religioso di Charles Lavigerie per l'Africa centrale (1878–1885)," *Cristianesimo nella Storia* 36 (2015): 591.

18 Daniele Comboni to Fr. Francesco Bricolo, Apr. 23, 1865, in *The Writings of St. Daniel Comboni: Correspondence and Reports (1850–1881) of the Founder of the Comboni Missionaries* (London 2005), 311.

19 Daniele Comboni to Cardinal Alessandro Barnabò, Feb. 25, 1865, in *The Writings of St. Daniel Comboni*, 296.

20 Adrian Hastings, *The Church in Africa: 1450–1950* (Oxford 1994), 451.

21 Quoted in Paul Kollman, "Christianity and Abolition in Africa," (2021), in *Oxford Encyclopedia of Africa* at https://doi.org/10.1093/acrefore/9780190277734.013.944.

22 Waliggo, "The Bugandan Christian Revolution," 92.

23 François Renault, *Cardinal Lavigerie: Churchman, Prophet, and Missionary*, trans. John O'Donohue (London, [1992]1994), 175.

24 Joseph W. Peterson, "Honor, Excrement, Ethnography: Colonial Knowledge between Missionary and Militaire in French Algeria," *Journal of Modern History* 93 (2021): 45–47.

25 Olivier Sibre, *Le Saint Siège et L'Extrême Orient (Chine, Corée, Japon): De Léon XIII À Pie XII (1880–1952)* (Rome 2012), 20.

26 Prudhomme, *Stratégie Missionnaire*, 215.

27 J. P. Daughton, *An Empire Divided: Religion, Republicanism, and the Making of French Colonialism, 1880–1914* (New York 2006), 124–125.

28 Philippe Delisle, "Bretons in Conquest of a Former Colony: French Catholic Missionaries in Haiti, 1860–1915," in *In God's Empire: French Missionaries and the Modern World*, eds. Owen White and J. P. Daughton (Oxford 2012), 70.

29 Patrick Cabanel, "Introduction," in *Le Grand Exil: Des Congrégations Religieuses Françaises 1901–1914*, eds. Patrick Cabanel and Jean-Dominique Durand (Paris 2005), 7–11.

30 Michael Sutton, *Nationalism, Positivism and Catholicism: The Politics of Charles Maurras and French Catholics 1890–1914* (Cambridge 1982), 97–98.

31 C. F. G. de Groot, *Brazilian Catholicism and the Ultramontane Reform, 1850–1930* (Amsterdam, 1996), 112.

32 Daughton, *An Empire Divided*, 157.

33 Elizabeth A. Foster, *Faith in Empire: Religion, Politics, and Colonial Rule in French Senegal, 1880–1940* (Stanford 2013), 1–2, 76–78.

34 Gambetta Speech in the Chamber of Deputies, May 4, 1877, in *Nineteenth-Century Europe: Liberalism and Its Critics*, eds. Jan Goldstein and John W. Boyer (Chicago 1988), 359.

35 Rothschild, *An Infinite History*, 291–292.

36 Daughton, *An Empire Divided*, 182, 197.

37 Vincent Viaene, "King Leopold's Imperialism and the Origins of the Belgian Colonial Party, 1860–1905," *Journal of Modern History* 80 (2008): 741–790.

38 John S. Lowry, *Big Swords, Jesuits, and Bondelswarts: Wilhelmine Imperialism, Overseas Resistance and German Political Catholicism, 1897–1906* (Leiden 2015), 138–139.

39 Joseph Schmidlin, *Die Katholischen Mission in den Deutschen Schutzgebieten* (Münster 1913).

40 Katherine D. Moran, *The Imperial Church: Catholic Founding Fathers and United States Empire* (Ithaca 2020), 23–135.

41 John T. McGreevy, *American Jesuits and the World: How an Embattled Religious Order Made Modern Catholicism Global* (Princeton 2016), 191.

42 Kenneth Ballhatchet, *Caste, Class and Catholicism in India 1789–1914* (Richmond 1998), 15.

43 Emmet Larkin, *The Roman Catholic Church and the Creation of the Modern Irish State, 1878–1886* (Philadelphia 1975), 176.

44 Karina Urbach, "On Her Majesty's Secret Service. Gladstone, Ireland and Pope Leo XIII, 1881–1885/86," in *Vatican Diplomacy, Catholic Opinion and International Politics at the Time of Leo XIII (1878–1903)*, ed. Vincent Viaene (Brussels 2005), 181–194.

45 Colin Barr, *Ireland's Empire: The Roman Catholic Church in the English-Speaking World, 1829–1914* (Cambridge 2020), 203.

46 Frederick Cooper, "The Problem of Slavery in African Studies," *Journal of African History* 20 (1979): 103–125.

47 Daniele Comboni, Annual Letter to the Cologne Association [1869], in *The Writings of St. Daniel Comboni*, 561.

48 Daniele Comboni to a Priest from Trent, June 24, 1873 in *The Writings of St. Daniel Comboni*, 997.

49 Paul V. Kollman, *The Evangelization of Slaves and Catholic Origins in Eastern Africa* (Maryknoll, N.Y., 2005), 126–128.

50 Amalia Ribi Forclaz, *Humanitarian Imperialism: The Politics of Anti-Slavery Activism, 1880–1940* (Oxford 2015), 20–24.

51 Carolina Nabuco, *Life of Joaquim Nabuco* (Stanford [1929] 1950), 162.

52 John T. Noonan, Jr., *A Church that Can and Cannot Change* (Notre Dame 2005), 112–113.

53 Daniele Comboni to the President of the Society of Cologne Report for the Year 1867, December 27, 1867 in *The Writings of Daniel Comboni*, 458–469.

54 Foster, *African Catholic*, 203; Forclaz, *Humanitarian Imperialism*, 17.

55 Roberto Italo Zanini, *Bakhita: From Slave to Saint*, trans. Andrew Matt (San Francisco 2013).

56 Kollman, *Evangelization of East Africa*, 128–138.

57 Zanini, *Bakhita*, 68, 88.

58 Daniele Comboni to Fr. Francesco Bricolo, Jan. 15, 1865 in *The Writings of St. Daniel Comboni*, 283.

59 McGreevy, "Catholicism and Abolition," 416.

60 Philippe Laburthe-Tolra, "La Mission catholique allemande du Cameroun (1890–1916) et la missiologie," in *Diffusion et acculturation du christianisme (XIXe–XXe.)*, ed. Jean Comby (Paris 2005), 228.

61 James B. Bennett, *Religion and the Rise of Jim Crow in New Orleans* (Princeton 2005), 162–192; Barr, *Ireland's Empire*, 200–201; Stephen J. Ochs, *Desegregating the Altar: The Josephites and the Struggle for Black Priests 1871–1960* (Baton Rouge 1990), 179, 302.

62 Dain Borges, "Catholic Vanguards in Brazil," in *Local Church, Global Church: Catholic Activism in Latin America from Rerum Novarum to Vatican II*, eds. Stephen J. C. Andes and

Julia G. Young (Washington 2015), 29; Sergio Rosas, "Los Dominicos Españoles Y La Restauración De La Orden De Predicadores En América Latina (1880–1938)," in *Más Allá De Los Nacionalcatolicismos: Redes Transnacionales de Los Catolicismos Hispánicos,* eds. José Ramón Rodríguez Lago and Natalia Núñez Bargueño (Madrid 2021) 330–335.

63 Thomas Jefferson Morgan, *Roman Catholics and Indian Education: An Address* (n.p. 1893), 2.

64 Margaret D. Jacobs, *White Mother to a Dark Race: Settler Colonialism, Maternalism, and the Removal of Indigenous Children in the American West and Australia, 1880–1941* (Lincoln 2009), 157.

65 Christine Choo, "The Role of the Catholic Missionaries at Beagle Bay in the Removal of Aboriginal Children from Their Families in the Kimberley Region from the 1890s," *Aboriginal History* 21 (1997): 14–29.

66 J. R. Miller, *Shingwauk's Vision: A History of Native Residential Schools* (Toronto 2000), 199–204.

67 Sylvia Caiuby Novaes, *The Play of Mirrors: The Representation of Self Mirrored in the Other,* trans. Izabel Murat Burbridge (Austin 1997), 79.

68 Emma Anderson, "Residential School Saint: The Life, Death, and Turbulent Afterlife of Rose Prince of the Carrier Nation," *Church History* 89 (2020): 598–599.

69 Kathleen Holscher, "A Right No Power Can Take Away: Religious Freedom and the Fight for Catholic Schools among the Osage," *Catholic Historical Review* 106 (2020): 1.

70 McGreevy, *American Jesuits and the World,* 183–184; R. Ollivier S.J. to Fr. E. Chambellan, May 27, 1877, FAM collection, box 56, Mission Nouvelle Orleans file, Archives of the French Province, Society of Jesus, Vanves, France.

71 McGreevy, *American Jesuits and the World,* 183–184.

72 McGreevy, *American Jesuits and the World,* 198; Pedro S. De Achútegui, S.J., and Miguel A. Bernad, S.J., *Religious Revolution in the Philippines: Life and Church of Gregorio Aglipay 1860–1960* (Manila 1960), 1: 27.

73 David Strong, S.J., *A Call to Mission. A History of the Jesuits in China 1842–1955* (Adelaide 2018), 1: 401; Harrison, *The Missionary's Curse,* 108–115; Anthony E. Clark, *Heaven in Conflict: Franciscans and the Boxer Uprising in Shanxi* (Seattle 2015).

74 Wu, *From Christ to Confucius,* 103, 1.

75 Léon Joly, *Le Christianisme et l'Extrême-Orient* (Paris 1907), 1: 403.

76 Ernest P. Young, *Ecclesiastical Colony: China's Catholic Church and the French Religious Protectorate* (New York 2013), 149–150.

77 Vincent Genin, "Arthur Vermeersch on Colonial and Conjugal Morality: A Presentist Approach to St. Thomas," in *Neo-Thomism in Action: Law and Society Reshaped by Neo-Scholastic Philosophy 1880–1960,* eds. Wim Decock, Bart Raymaekers, and Peter Heyrman, (Leuven 2022) 249.

78 Brahmabandhab Upadhyay, "Are We Hindus?" in *The Writings of Brahmabandhab Upadhyay,* eds. Julius Lipner and George Gispért-Sauch, S.J. (Bangalore 1991), I: 24–25.

79 Keith, *Catholic Vietnam,* 79, 1.

80 Harry R. Rudin, *Germans in the Cameroons 1884–1914: A Case Study in Modern Imperialism* (New Haven 1938), 373.

81 Engelbert Mveng, *Histoire Du Cameroun* (Paris 1963), 463–464.

82 Salvador Eyezo'o, "Polémique entre Mgr Alexandre Le Roy et le cardinal Willem van Rossum: Sur la relève des pallotins allemands au Cameroun. Entre intérêt politique national et catholicité de l'Eglise romaine (1919–1923)," in *L'Afrique et la mission: Terrains anciens, questions nouvelles avec Claude Prudhomme,* eds. Oissila Saaïdia and Laurick Zerbini (Paris 2015), 104.

83 Meredith Terretta and Benjamin N. Lawrance, "'Sons of the Soil': Cause Lawyers, the Togo-Cameroun Mandates, and the Origins of Decolonization," *American Historical Review* 12 (2019): 1709–1713.

84 Ochs, *Desegregating the Altar,* 284.

85 Aylward Shorter, *African Recruits and Missionary Conscripts: The White Fathers and the Great War (1914–1922)* (London 2007), 138.

86 Hermann Nekes, 'Vierzig Jahre im Dienste der Kamerunmission: Zum Tode des schwarzen Lehrers Andreas Mbange," *Stern der Heiden* 39 (1932): 317–23; Hermann Nekes, "Andreas Mbange und seine Gefährten," *Stern der Heiden* 40 (1933): 4–14.

87 Mveng, *Histoire Du Cameroun*, 461–466.

88 Shorter, *African Recruits and Missionary Conscripts*, 176–177.

89 Zanini, *Bakhita*, 109.

SEVEN: Nation

1 Li Tiangang, "Christianity and Cultural Conflict," trans. Ruth Hayhoe, in *Ma Xiangbo and the Mind of Modern China 1840–1939*, eds. Ruth Hayhoe and Lu Yongling (Armonk, NY, 1996), 107–111.

2 Tiangang, "Christianity and Cultural Conflict," 120.

3 Ma Xiangbo, "A Letter to the Pope Asking Him to Promote Education in China," [1912], in *Ma Xiangbo and the Mind of Modern China*, 219–222.

4 Vincent Lebbe to Dom Bède, May 1, 1900, in *Lettres du Père Lebbe*, eds. Paul Goffart and Albert Sohier (Tournai 1960), 30.

5 Vincent Lebbe to Dom Bède, July 13, 1901, in *Lettres du Père Lebbe*, 39.

6 Vincent Lebbe to Antoine Cotta, Mar. 10, 1908, in *Lettres du Père Lebbe*, 80.

7 Maurice Cheza, "Le chanoine Joly inspirateur du Père Lebbe? Un moment du Débat sur la rénovation des méthodes missionnaires," *Revue Théologique de Louvain* 14 (1983): 315.

8 Anthony E. Clark, *China Gothic: The Bishop of Beijing and His Cathedral* (Seattle 2019), 66.

9 Ernest P. Young, *Ecclesiastical Colony: China's Catholic Church and the French Religious Protectorate* (New York 2013), 160, 178–179.

10 Young, *Ecclesiastical Colony*, 188.

11 Young, *Ecclesiastical Colony*, 178.

12 Vincent Lebbe to Bishop Reynaud, Sept. 18, 1917, in *Lettres du Père Lebbe*, 143.

13 Antoine Cotta to Vincent Lebbe, Mar. 3, 1920, in *Recueil Des Archives Vincent Lebbe: Pour L'Église Chinoise III. L'Encyclique Maximum Illud*, ed. Claude Soetens (Louvain 1983), 26.

14 Claude Soetens, "Introduction," in *Recueil Des Archives Vincent Lebbe: Pour L'Église Chinoise III*, 19.

15 Vincent Lebbe quoted in 1925 talk, *Recueil Des Archives Vincent Lebbe: Un an d'activité du Père Lebbe: 1926*, ed. Claude Soetens (Louvain 1984), iii–v.

16 Young, *Ecclesiastical Colony,* 243; Arnulf Camps, "Celso Constantini, Apostolic Delegate in China, 1922–1933," in Camps, *Studies in Asian Mission History* (Leiden 2000), 171; Thomas Coomans," Indigenizing Catholic Architecture in China: From Western-Gothic to Sino-Christian Design 1900–1940," in *Catholicism in China, 1900–Present: The Development of the Chinese Church*, ed. Cindy Yik-yi Chu (New York 2014), 132–136.

17 Vincent Lebbe to Bishop Reynaud, Sept. 18, 1917, in *Lettres du Père Lebbe*, 154.

18 Paul P. Mariani, S.J., "The First Six Chinese Bishops of Modern Times: A Study in Church Indigenization," *Catholic Historical Review* 100 (2014): 486–513.

19 Vincent Lebbe to Antoine Cotta, Oct. 17, 1926, in *Recueil Des Archives Vincent Lebbe: Un an d'activité du Père Lebbe: 1926*, 229; Vincent Lebbe to Msgr. Braun, Oct. 31, 1926, in *Recueil Des Archives Vincent Lebbe: Un an d'activité du Père Lebbe: 1926*, 233.

20 Young, *Ecclesiastical Colony,* 243.

21 Helmut Walzer Smith, *Germany: A Nation in Its Time* (New York 2020), 299.

22 Patrick J. Houlihan, *Catholicism and the Great War: Religion and Everyday Life in Germany and Austria-Hungary, 1914–1922* (Cambridge 2015), 62.

23 Andrzej Walicki, "The Troubling Legacy of Roman Dmowski," *East European Politics and Societies* 14 (2000): 32.

24 Margaret Todaro Williams, "Pastors, Prophets and Politicians: A Study of the Brazilian Catholic Church, 1916–1945" (Columbia, PhD 1971), 427.

25 Thomas J. Morrisey, S.J., *From Easter Week to Flanders Field: The Diaries and Letters of John Delaney, S.J., 1916–1919* (Dublin 2015), 123.

26 Elizabeth A. Foster, *Faith in Empire: Religion, Politics, and Colonial Rule in French Senegal, 1880–1940* (Stanford 2013), 107.

27 Guiliana Chamedes, *A Twentieth-Century Crusade: The Vatican's Battle to Remake Christian Europe* (Cambridge 2019), 2.

28 Larry Wolff, *Woodrow Wilson and the Re-Imagining of Eastern Europe* (Stanford 2020), 98.

29 Chamedes, *A Twentieth-Century Crusade*, 34–68; *Ubi Arcano Dei Consilio* (1922), §45.

30 John T. McGreevy, *American Jesuits and the World: How an Embattled Religious Order Made Modern Catholicism Global* (Princeton 2016), 189.

31 Houlihan, *Catholicism and the Great War*, 64.

32 Séan Faughnan, "The Jesuits and the Drafting of the Irish Constitution of 1937," *Irish Historical Studies* 26 (1988): 8.

33 Dermot Keogh, *Ireland and the Vatican: The Politics and Diplomacy of Church-State Relations 1922–1960* (Cork 1995), 134–137.

34 Canon 329 and Canon 218 in *The 1917 or Pio-Benedictine Code of Canon Law*, ed. Edward N. Peters (San Francisco 2001), 132–133, 93–94.

35 Gerald Fogarty, "Cardinal William Henry O'Connell," in *Varieties of Ultramontanism*, ed. Jeffrey Von Arx (Washington 1998), 137.

36 Hans de Vlak, " 'Some Matters That Should Be Improved in the Government of the Church,' a Remarkable Proposal for the Reform of the Roman Curia, 1931," in *Suavis Laborum Memoria: Essays in Honour of Marcel Chappin, S.J., on His 70th Birthday*, eds. Paul Van Geest and Roberto Regoli (Vatican City 2013), 183–208.

37 J. Dessain, "Le progrès de l'oecumenisme: l'incident Mercier 1919–1922," *Revue Théologique de Louvain* 5 (1974): 469–476.

38 John Pollard, "The Unpublished Encyclicals of the Pontificate of Pope Pius XI: *De Ecclesia Christi*, 1931," *Cristianesimo nella storia* 38 (2017): 813–866.

39 Kevin Madigan, *The Popes against the Protestants: The Vatican and Evangelical Christianity in Fascist Italy* (New Haven 2021).

40 Hubert Wolf, *Pope and Devil: The Vatican's Archives and the Third Reich*, trans. Kenneth Kronenberg (Cambridge 2010), 81–126.

41 Clifford Longley, *The Worlock Archive* (London 2000), 28.

42 Paul A. Hanebrink, *In Defense of Christian Hungary: Religion, Nationalism, and Antisemitism, 1890–1944* (Ithaca 2006), 91.

43 John A. Coleman, *The Evolution of Dutch Catholicism, 1958–1974* (Berkeley 1978), 97.

44 Kristin Mennen and Marijn Molema, "The Role of Religion in the Dutch Scout Movement (1911–1973)," *Revue d'Histoire Ecclésiastique* 111 (2016): 642.

45 Philippe Chenaux, "The 1920s Francophone Thomistic Revival," in *Neo-Thomism in Action: Law and Society Reshaped by Neo-Scholastic Philosophy 1880–1960*, eds. Wim Decock, Bart Raymaekers, and Peter Heyrman (Leuven 2022), 42.

46 Edward Baring, "Ideas on the Move: Context in Transnational Intellectual History," *Journal of the History of Ideas* 77 (2016): 574–583.

47 Austen Ivereigh, *Catholicism and Politics in Argentina: 1810–1960* (New York 1995), 76–77.

48 Christopher Van Der Krogt, "Catholic Religious Identity and Social Integration in Interwar New Zealand," *Catholic Historical Review* 86 (2000): 47–65.

49 John Pollard, "Pius XI's Promotion of the Italian Model of Catholic Action in the World-Wide Church," *Journal of Ecclesiastical History* 63 (2012): 758–784.

50 Martin Conway, "Building the Christian City: Catholics and Politics in Interwar Francophone Belgium," *Past and Present* 128 (1990): 122–125.

51 *Between Cross and Class: Comparative Histories of Christian Labour in Europe 1840–2000*, eds. Lex Heerma van Voss, Patrick Pasture, and Jan De Maeyer (Bern 2005).

52 Gerd Ranier-Horn, *Western European Liberation Theology: The First Wave (1924–1959)* (New York 2008), 26.

53 Philip Nord, "Catholic Culture in Interwar France," *French Politics, Culture and Society* 21 (2003): 7.

54 Ivereigh, *Catholicism and Politics in Argentina*, 75.

55 Franz H. Mueller, "I Knew Heinrich Pesch," *Social Order* 1 (1951): 147–148.

56 Program of Social Reconstruction, February 12, 1919, in *Pastoral Letters of the United States Catholic Bishops* (Washington 1984), I: 255–271.

57 Raymond Swing, "The Catholic View of Reconstruction," *Nation* 108 (Mar. 29, 1919), 467–468.

58 Jonathan Steinberg, "The Poor in Christ: Peasants, Priests and Politics in the Cosenza General Strike, November 1920," in *History, Society and the Churches: Essays in Honour of Owen Chadwick*, eds. Derek Beales and Geoffrey Best (Cambridge 1985), 257–278.

59 Fr. Marcel Dischl, C.M.M., *Transkei for Christ: A History of the Catholic Church in the Transkeian Territories* (n.p. 1982), 173–179.

60 Christopher Hamlin and John T. McGreevy, "The Greening of America, Catholic Style, 1930–1950," *Environmental History* 11 (July 2006): 464–500.

61 Leo R. Ward, C.S.C., *United For Freedom: Co-operatives and Christian Democracy* (Milwaukee 1945).

62 Catherine LeGrand, "The Antigonish Movement of Canada and Latin America: Catholic Cooperatives, Christian Communities, and Transnational Development in the Great Depression and the Cold War," in *Local Church, Global Church: Catholic Activism in Latin America from Rerum Novarum to Vatican II*, eds. Stephen J. C. Andes and Julia Young (Washington 2016), 237–244; Richard Timm, *Father of the Credit Unions in Bangladesh: Life of Father Charles J. Young, CSC* (Dhaka 2010), 91.

63 Oswald von Nell-Breuning, S.J., "The Drafting of Quadragesimo Anno," in *Readings in Moral Theology No. 5: Official Catholic Social Teaching*, eds. Charles Curran and Richard A. McCormick (New York 1986), 60–68; Noah Benezra Strote, *Lions and Lambs: Conflict in Weimar and the Creation of Post-Nazi Germany* (New Haven 2017) 61–63.

64 James Chappel, "The Thomist Debate over Inequality and Property Rights in Depression Era Europe," in *So What's New about Scholasticism? How Neo-Thomism Helped Shape the Twentieth Century*, eds. Rajesh Heynickx and Stéphane Symons (Berlin 2019), 21–38.

65 Nell-Breuning, "The Drafting of Quadragesimo Anno," 64.

66 Leszek Kuk, "A Powerful Catholic Church, Unstable State and Authoritarian Political Regime: The Christian Democratic Party in Poland," in *Political Catholicism in Europe 1918–1945: Volume I*, eds. Wolfram Kaiser and Helmut Wohnout (New York 2004), 157.

67 Keith, *Catholic Vietnam*, 196–197.

68 *The Public Papers and Addresses of Franklin D. Roosevelt: Volume One: The Genesis of the New Deal 1928–1932*, ed. Samuel I. Rosenman (New York 1938), 778.

69 Joseph Thorning, S.J., "Principles and Practice of the NRA," *Catholic Mind* 32 (Oct. 8, 1934), 363.

70 Luise Jörissen, "Als Oberlehrerin in Köln," in *Ernte eines Lebens: Helene Weber (1881–1962)*, eds. Anne Mohr and Elizabeth Prégardier (Essen 1991), 13–15.

71 Antonia Schilling, "Helene Weber (1881–1962)—Ein Weimarer Zentrumspolitiker," in *Die Frauen und der politische Katholizismus: Akteurinnen, Themen, Strategien*, eds. Markus Raasch and Andreas Linsenmann (Paderborn 2018), 268–269.

72 *Irish Constitution* (1937), Articles 41 and 43.

73 Susan Pedersen, *Family, Dependence, and the Origins of the Welfare State: Britain and France, 1914–1945* (Cambridge MA 1993), 394.

74 Helene Dawes, "The Catholic Church and the Woman Question: Catholic Feminism in Italy in the Early 1900s," *Catholic Historical Review* 97 (2011): 499.

75 John A. Ryan, *A Living Wage: Its Ethical and Economic Aspects* (New York 1906), 133;

Ericka Kim Verba, *Catholic Feminism and the Social Question in Chile, 1910–1917: The Liga de Damas Chilenas* (Lewiston 2003), 129.

76 Kathleen Sprows Cummings, *New Women of the Old Faith: Gender and American Catholicism in the Progressive Era* (Chapel Hill 2009), 3.

77 Nicholas M. Creary, *Domesticating a Religious Import: The Jesuits and the Inculturation of the Catholic Church in Zimbabwe, 1879–1980* (New York 2011), 49.

78 C. F. G. de Groot, *Brazilian Catholicism and the Ultramontane Reform, 1850–1930* (Amsterdam 1996), 121–123.

79 Dawes, "The Catholic Church and the Women's Question," 509.

80 Dawes, "The Catholic Church and the Women's Question," 516.

81 Douglas J. Cremer, "The Limits of Maternalism: Gender Ideology and the South German Catholic Workingwomen's Associations, 1904–1918," *Catholic Historical Review* 87 (2001): 450.

82 Schilling, "Helene Weber," 277.

83 Steven C. Hause with Anne R. Kenney, *Women's Suffrage and Social Politics in the French Third Republic* (Princeton 1984), 238, 255.

84 Christine Ehrick, *The Shield of the Weak: Feminism and the State in Uruguay 1903–1933* (Albuquerque 2005), 175–176; Adam Przeworski, "Conquered or Granted?: A History of Suffrage Extensions," *British Journal of Political Science* 39 (2009): 315–319.

85 Nord, "Catholic Culture in Interwar France," 1–20.

86 Ivereigh, *Catholicism and Politics in Argentina*, 98.

87 Emmanuel Mounier, "Manifeste au Service Du Personnalisme" [1936], in Mounier, *Oeuvres (1931–1939)* (Paris 1961), 1: 560; Laura S. Gellott, *The Catholic Church and the Authoritarian Regime in Austria, 1933–1938* (New York 1987), 331.

88 Laurie Marhoefer, *Sex and the Weimar Republic: German Homosexual Emancipation and the Rise of the Nazis* (Toronto 2015), 108.

89 Kevin Rickett, "Protectionism and Catholic Film Policy in Twentieth Century Ireland," in *Moralizing Cinema: Film, Catholicism and Power*, eds. Daniel Biltereyst and Daniela Treveri Gennari (New York 2015), 192.

90 Indre Cuplinskas, "National and Rational Dress: Catholics Debate Female Fashion in Lithuania, 1920s–1930s," *Church History* 88 (2019): 696–719; Ines Weber, "Kann denn Mode Katholisch sein? Katholischer Mediendiskurs und die Medienkommission des KDFB," in *Katholiken und Moderne: Katholische Frauenbewegung zwischen Tradition und Emanzipation*, ed. Gisela Muschiol (Münster 2003), 143–162; Maryann Valiulis, "Neither Feminist nor Flapper," in *Chattel, Servant or Citizen: Women's Status in Church, State and Society*, eds. Mary O'Dowd and Sabine Wichert (Belfast 1995), 168–178; Sally Dwyer-McNulty, "Hems to Hairdos: Cultural Discourse and Philadelphia Catholic High Schools in the 1920s, a Case Study," *Journal of American Studies* 37 (2003): 179–200.

91 Schilling, "Helene Weber," 286.

92 Guido Convents, "Resisting the Lure of the Modern World: Catholics, International Politics and the Establishment of the International Catholic Office for Cinema (1918–1928)," in *Moralizing Cinema*, 19–32.

93 Daniel Biltereyst, " 'I Think Catholics Didn't Go to the Cinema': Catholic Film Exhibition Strategies and Cinema-Going Experiences in Belgium, 1930s–1960s," in *Moralizing Cinema*, 259.

94 McGreevy, *Catholicism and American Freedom*, 156–157.

95 Francisco Peredo Castro, "Catholicism and Mexican Cinema: A Secular State, A Deeply Conservative Society and a Powerful Hierarchy," in *Moralizing Cinema*, 72–73.

96 Paul Ginsborg, *A History of Contemporary Italy: Society and Politics 1943–1988* (London 2003), 169.

97 Atina Grossmann, *Reforming Sex: The German Movement for Birth Control and Abortion Reform, 1920–1950* (New York 1995), 50–51; Neil Riddell, "The Catholic Church

and the Labour Party," *Twentieth Century British History* 8 (1997): 179–182; McGreevy, *Catholicism and American Freedom*, 160.

98 Matthew Connelly, *Fatal Misconception: The Struggle to Control World Population* (Cambridge 2008), 73.

99 Lucia Pozzi, "The Problem of Birth Control in the United States under the Papacy of Pius XI," in *Pius XI and America*, eds. Charles R. Gallagher, David I. Kertzer, and Alberto Melloni (Berlin 2010), 209–232; Eugenio Pacelli report of Nov. 18, 1929, in *Die Lage der Kirche in Deutschland: Der Schlußbericht des Nuntius vom 18. November 1929* (Paderborn 2006), 125.

100 McGreevy, *Catholicism and American Freedom*, 163.

101 Guillaume Cuchet, "Quelques Données Concernant L'Encyclique *Casti Connubii*," in *Pie XI et La France*, ed. Jacques Prévotat (Rome 2010), 347–348.

102 McGreevy, *Catholicism and American Freedom*, 232.

103 McGreevy, *Catholicism and American Freedom*, 223.

104 Charlotte Wildman, "Irish-Catholic Women and Modernity in 1930s Liverpool," in *Women and Irish Diaspora Identities: Theories, Concepts and New Perspectives*, eds. D. A. J. MacPherson and Mary J. Hickman (Manchester 2014), 73.

105 Christopher Van Der Krogt, "Exercising the Utmost Vigilance: The Catholic Campaign against Contraception in New Zealand during the 1930s," *Journal of Religious History* 22 (1998): 325.

106 John Connelly, *From Enemy to Brother: The Revolution in Catholic Teaching on the Jews 1933–1965* (Cambridge MA 2012), 15.

107 Francesco Cassata, *Building the New Man: Eugenics, Racial Science and Genetics in Twentieth-Century Italy* (New York 2011), 145.

108 Sharon Leon, " 'Hopelessly Entangled in Nordic Presuppositions': Catholic Participation in the American Eugenics Society in the 1920s," *Journal of the History of Medicine and Allied Sciences* 59 (2004): 41–49.

109 McGreevy, *Catholicism and American Freedom*, 224–225.

110 Michael Hollerich, "Catholic Anti-Liberalism in Weimar: Political Theology and Its Critics," in *The Weimar Moment: Liberalism, Political Theology and Law*, eds. Rudy Koshar and Len Kaplan (Lexington 2012), 37.

111 *Ubi Arcano Dei Consilio* (1922), §12.

112 Wilhelm Ribhegge, "Joseph Mausbach (1860–1931) and His Role in the Public Life of the Empire and the Weimar Republic," trans. Ralph Keen, *The Catholic Historical Review* 84 (1998): 37.

113 Derek Hastings, "How 'Catholic' Was the Early Nazi Movement? Religion, Race, and Culture in Munich, 1919–1924," *Central European History* 36 (2003): 383–433; Brendan Simms, *Hitler: A Global Biography* (New York 2021), 102–103.

114 Ventresca, *Soldier of Christ*, 62.

115 Yves Simon, *The Road to Vichy, 1918–1938*, trans. James A. Corbett and George J. McMorrow (Lanham, MD, 1988), 42.

116 Maurice Demers, *Connected Struggles: Catholics, Nationalists and Transnational Relations between Mexico and Quebec, 1917–1945* (Montreal 2014), 79.

117 Olivier Compagnon, "Le Maurrassisme en Amérique Latine: Etude comparée de cas argentin et brésilien," in *Charles Maurras et L'Étranger L'Étranger et Charles Maurras*, eds. Olivier Dard and Michel Grunewald (Bern 2009), 289.

118 Philippe J. Roy, "La Préhistoire Du Coetus Internationalis Patrum: Une Formation Romaine, Antilibérale et Contre-révolutionnaire," in *La Théologie Catholique Entre Intransigeance et Renouveau*, eds. Gilles Routhier, Phillipe J. Roy, and Karim Schelkens (Louvain 2011), 333.

119 Eugen Joseph Weber, *Action Française* (Stanford 1962), 232.

120 Carlton J. H. Hayes, *The Historical Evolution of Modern Nationalism* (New York 1931), 212–231.

121 Henri de Lubac, "Patriotisme et Nationalisme" [1933], in de Lubac, *Résistance chrétienne au Nazisme*, eds. Renée Bédarida and Jacques Prévotat (Paris 2006), 14.

122 John Dewey, "Church and State in Mexico" (1926), in Dewey, *The Later Works, 1925–1953*, ed. Jo Ann Boydston (Carbondale 1984), 2: 197–198.

123 Matthew Butler, *Popular Piety and Political Identity in Mexico's Cristero Rebellion: Michoacán, 1927–1929* (Oxford 2004), 87.

124 Julia G. Young, "The Calles Government and Catholic Dissidents: Mexico's Transnational Projects of Repression, 1926–1929," *The Americas* 70 (2013): 75, 83–84.

125 Julia G. Young, "Cristero Diaspora: Mexican Immigrants, the U.S. Catholic Church, and Mexico's Cristero War, 1926–1929," *Catholic Historical Review* 98 (2012): 279.

126 Demers, *Connected Struggles*, 64–72.

127 Porter-Szücs, *Faith and Fatherland*, 337.

128 Stephen J. C. Andes, *The Vatican and Catholic Activism in Mexico and Chile: The Politics of Transnational Catholicism, 1920–1940* (New York 2014), 83–84.

129 An Vandenberghe, "Beyond Pierre Charles: The Emergence of Belgian Missiology Refined," in *Mission & Science: Missiology Revised/Missiologie Revisitée, 1850–1940*, eds. Carine Dujardin and Claude Prudhomme (Leuven 2015), 163.

130 Klaus Schatz, "The Yasukuni Shrine Affair: Paolo Marella and the Revision of the Prohibition of Eastern Rites," *Archivum Historiae Societas Iesu* 81 (2012): 459.

131 Wu, *From Christ to Confucius*, 161–189.

132 Olivier Sibre, *Le Saint-Siège et L'Extrême-Orient (Chine, Corée, Japon) De Léon XIII À Pie XII (1880–1952)*, (Rome, 2012), 579.

133 Vincent Lebbe to Dom Bède, Sept. 20, 1939, in *Lettres du Père Lebbe*, 306–307.

134 Sibre, *Le Saint-Siège et L'Extrême-Orient*, 625; Harrison, *The Missionary's Curse*, 143.

135 Lebbe to Dom Bede, Sept. 20, 1939, in *Lettres du Père Lebbe*, 307.

EIGHT: CRISIS

1 Edith Stein to Pius XI, Apr. 12, 1933, copy in Emma Fattorini, *Hitler, Mussolini, and the Vatican: Pope Pius XI and the Speech That Was Never Made*, trans. Carl Ipsen (Cambridge 2011), 202–203.

2 Edward Baring, *Converts to the Real: Catholicism and the Making of Continental Philosophy* (Cambridge 2019), 51.

3 Edith Stein to Roman Ingarden, Feb. 9, 1917, in *Letters to Roman Ingarden*, trans. Hugh Candler Hunt, ed. Maria Amata Neyer, O.C.C. (Washington 2014), 44.

4 Edith Stein to Erna Stein, July 6, 1918, in Edith Stein, *Self-Portrait in Letters: 1916–1942*, trans. Josephine Koeppel, O.C.D. (Washington 1993), 27.

5 Edith Stein to Roman Ingarden, Nov. 11, 1919, in *Letters to Roman Ingarden*, 164.

6 Edith Stein to Roman Ingarden, June 8, 1918, in *Letters to Roman Ingarden*, 108.

7 Baring, *Converts to the Real*, 75.

8 Edith Stein, *Life in a Jewish Family 1891–1916: An Autobiography,* trans. Josephine Koeppel, O.C.C. (Washington 1986), 17; Edith Stein to Gertrud von le Fort, Oct. 9, 1933, in *Self-Portrait in Letters*, 158–159.

9 Edith Stein to Dr. Ludwig Sebastian, Feb. 21,1926, in *Self-Portrait in Letters,* 49–50.

10 Baring, *Converts to the Real*, 75.

11 Hannah-Barbara Gerl-Falkovitz, "'His Whole Life Consisted of a Search for Religious Truth': Edith Stein in Conversation with John Henry Newman," trans. Jonathan Knutsen, in *Contemplating Edith Stein*, ed. Joyce Avrech Berkman (Notre Dame 2006), 161.

12 Thomas O'Meara, "Alois Dempf: Culture and Religion in the History of Thinking," *Gregorianum* 96 (2015): 288.

13 Brian Porter-Szücs, *Faith and Fatherland: Catholicism, Modernity, and Poland* (New York 2011), 282.

14   Todd H. Weir, "A European Culture War in the Twentieth Century? Anti-Catholicism and Anti-Bolshevism between Moscow, Berlin, and the Vatican 1922 to 1933," *Journal of Religious History* 39 (2015): 285; Philippe Chenaux, *L'Église catholique et le Communisme en Europe, 1917–1989: de Lénine à Jean-Paul II* (Paris 2009), 57–83.

15   G. M. Hamburg, "Father Léopold Braun: An Assumptionist Priest in Stalin's Moscow, 1934–1945," in Leopold L. S. Braun, AA, *In Lubianka's Shadow: The Memoirs of an American Priest in Stalin's Moscow, 1934–1945* (Notre Dame 2006), xxix.

16   Weir, "A European Culture War in the Twentieth Century?," 289.

17   See biographical note for Anton Walter in *Book of Remembrance: Biographies of Catholic Clergy and Laity Repressed in the Soviet Union (USSR) from 1918 to 1953*, eds. Father Bronisław Czaplicki and Irina Osipova, trans. Geraldine Kelley (Moscow 2000), available at https://biographies.library.nd.edu/about/translation.

18   Braun, *In Lubianka's Shadow*, xxviii–xxxv, 112.

19   Paul Silas Peterson, "Erich Przywara on Sieg-Katholizismus, Bolshevism, the Jews, Volk, Reich and the Analogia Entis in the 1920s and 1930s," *Journal of the History of Modern Theology* 19 (2012): 118.

20   Weir, "A European Culture War in the Twentieth-Century?," 296–297.

21   Guiliana Chamedes, *A Twentieth-Century Crusade: The Vatican's Battle to Remake Christian Europe* (Cambridge MA 2019), 123.

22   Keith, *Catholic Vietnam*, 113.

23   Scott Mainwaring, *The Catholic Church and Politics in Brazil, 1916–1985* (Stanford 1986), 133.

24   Keogh, *Ireland and the Vatican*, 83

25   Olivier Sibre, *Le Saint Siège et L'Extrême Orient (Chine, Corée, Japon): De Léon XIII À Pie XII (1880–1952)* (Rome 2012), 587.

26   Weizheng, "Statesman and Centenarian," in *Ma Xiangbo and the Mind of Modern China*, 70.

27   Chamedes, *A Twentieth-Century Crusade*, 147.

28   Oscar Arnaz, "Stillborn Alliance: Catholic Divisions in the Face of the Main Tendue," *Journal of Modern History* 51 (1979): D1016.

29   William Issel, *For Both Cross and Flag: Catholic Action, Anti-Catholicism and National Security Politics in World War II Era San Francisco* (Philadelphia 2010), 75.

30   Nina Valbousquet, "Tradition catholique et matrice de l'antisémitisme à l'époque contemporaine," *Revue D'Histoire Moderne & Contemporaine* 62 (2013): 75.

31   Paul Hanebrink, "Transnational Culture War: Christianity, Nation and the Judeo-Bolshevik Myth in Hungary, 1890–1920," *Journal of Modern History* 80 (2008): 55.

32   Bettina Reichmann, *Bischof Ottokar Prohaszka (1858-1927): Krieg, christliche Kultur und Antisemitismus in Ungarn* (Paderborn 2015), 211.

33   Piotr H. Kosicki, *Catholics on the Barricades: Poland, France and "Revolution," 1891–1956* (New Haven 2018), 36.

34   Robert A. Ventresca, *Soldier of Christ: The Life of Pius XII* (Cambridge MA 2013), 54.

35   Stanislaw Wilk, SBD, "Achille Ratti: Visiteur Apostolique et Premier Nonce Dans La Pologne Renaissante," in *La Papauté Contemporaine*, eds. Jean-Pierre Delville and Marco Jačov (Vatican City 2009), 345–357.

36   Wolf, *Pope and Devil*, 79.

37   Entry of Jan. 17, 1920, in *I Diari Di Achille Ratti*, 2: 207.

38   Thomas J. Shelley, *Fordham: A History of the Jesuit University of New York: 1841–2003* (New York 2016), 198–199.

39   Alan Brinkley, *Voices of Protest: Huey Long, Father Coughlin and the Great Depression* (New York 1982), 82–106, 133–138.

40   Sr. Mary Christine Athans, *The Coughlin-Fahey Connection: Father Charles E. Coughlin, Father Denis Fahey, C.S.Sp., and Religious Anti-Semitism in the United States, 1938–1954* (New York 1991).

41   Charles R. Gallagher, *The Nazis of Copley Square: The Forgotten Story of the Christian Front* (Cambridge MA 2021).

42   Graciela Ben-Dror, *The Catholic Church and the Jews: Argentina, 1933–1945* (Lincoln 2008), 46.

43   Suzanne Marchand, "Priests among the Pygmies: Wilhelm Schmidt and the Counter-Reformation in Austrian Ethnology," in *Worldly Provincialism: German Anthropology in the Age of Empire,* eds. H. Glenn Penny and Matti Bunzl (Ann Arbor 2003), 283–317.

44   Udi Greenberg, "Catholics, Protestants, and the Violent Birth of European Religious Pluralism," *American Historical Review* 124 (2019): 519–524; John Connelly, *From Enemy to Brother: The Revolution in Catholic Teaching on the Jews 1933–1965* (Cambridge MA 2012), 19.

45   Ronald Modras, "The Interwar Polish Catholic Press on the Jewish Question," *Annals* of the *American Academy of Social and Political Science* 548 (1996): 179.

46   Porter-Szücs, *Faith and Fatherland*, 311.

47   Gustav Gundlach, "Anti-Semitism" [1930], reprinted in Georges Passelecq and Bernhard Suchecky, *The Hidden Encyclical of Pius XI*, trans. Steven Rendall (New York 1997), 47–49.

48   David I. Kertzer, *The Pope and Mussolini: The Secret History of Pius XI and the Rise of Fascism in Europe* (New York 2014), 111.

49   Peter R. D'Agostino, *Rome in America: Transnational Catholic Ideology from the Risorgimento to Fascism* (Chapel Hill 2004), 270, 278.

50   David Upham, "Pope Pius XI's Extraordinary—But Undeserved—Praise of the American Supreme Court," *Rutgers Journal of Law and Religion,* 14 (2012) at https://lawandreligion.com/volume-14.

51   *Non Abbiamo Bisogno* (1931), §44.

52   Sergio Palagianio, "Le series Affari del fondo P. Pietro Tacchi Venturi SJ (1861–1956) nel Archivum Romanum Societatis Iesu (ARSI): lavori archivistici e primi rilevi," *Archivum Historiae Societas Iesu SI* 85 (2016): 97–185.

53   Maps of Catholic voting patterns in *Catholics and Third Reich: Controversies and Debates,* eds. Karl-Joseph Hummel and Michael Kissener (Paderborn [2010] 2018), 310–31.

54   Laura Pettinaroli, *La Politique Russe Du Saint-Siège (1905–1939)* (Rome 2015), 750.

55   Wolf, *Pope and Devil*, 177.

56   Ian Kershaw, *Hitler: 1889–1936 Hubris* (New York 1998), 488; Kardinal Michael Faulhaber to Adolf Hitler, July 24, 1933, copy in Hubert Gruber, *Katholische Kirche und Nationalsozialismus 1930–1945: Ein Bericht in Quellen* (Paderborn 2006), 111.

57   Ralph Della Cava, "Catholicism and Society in Twentieth-Century Brazil," *Latin American Research Review* 11 (1976): 13.

58   Kenneth Serbin, "State Subsidization of Catholic Institutions in Brazil, 1930–1964," Working Paper #181, Kellogg Institute of International Studies (Oct. 1992).

59   Jakub Štofaník, "Reception and Adaptation of Neo-Thomism in East-Central Europe, Between the Intellectual and Social Involvment of the Catholic Church," in *Neo-Thomism in Action: Law and Society Reshaped by Neo-Scholastic Philosophy 1880–1960,* eds. Wim Decock, Bart Raymaekers, and Peter Heyrman (Leuven 2022), 101.

60   Erika Helgen, *Religious Conflict in Brazil: Protestants, Catholics, and the Rise of Religious Pluralism in the Twentieth Century* (New Haven 2020), 34.

61   Margaret Todaro Williams, "Integralism and the Brazilian Catholic Church," *Hispanic American Historical Review* 54 (Aug. 1974): 438.

62   Tom Gallagher, "Portugal," in *Political Catholicism in Europe, 1918–1965,* eds. Tom Buchanan and Martin Conway (Oxford 1996), 133.

63   Laura S. Gellott, *The Catholic Church and the Authoritarian Regime in Austria, 1933–1938* (New York 1987), 7.

64   Richard Cleminson, *Catholicism, Race and Empire: Eugenics in Portugal, 1900–1950* (New York 2014), 76.

65 Connelly, *From Enemy to Brother*, 103–146; Monika Löscher, "Eugenics and Catholicism in Interwar Austria," in *Blood and Homeland: Eugenics and Racial Nationalism in Central and Southeast Europe, 1900–1940*, eds. Marius Turda and Paul Weindling (New York 2006), 310–312.

66 Tom Villis, *British Catholics and Fascism: Religious Identity and Political Extremism between the Wars* (New York 2013), 94, 190–191.

67 James Chappel, "Exploring the Catholic Turn to Rights," in *Christianity and Human Rights Reconsidered*, eds. Sarah Shortall and Daniel Steinmetz-Jenkins (Cambridge MA 2020), 73–77; McGreevy, *American Jesuits and the World*, 212.

68 Michael Oakeshott, *The Social and Political Doctrines of Contemporary Europe* (New York [1939] 1950), xx; Samuel Moyn, *Christian Human Rights* (Philadelphia 2015), 35–36.

69 Francisco Javier Ramón Solans, " 'El Catolicismo Tiene Masas': Nación, Política y Movilización en España, 1868–1931," *Historia Contemporánea* 51 (2015): 427–454.

70 Callahan, *The Catholic Church in Spain*, 276.

71 Pedro Segura, "Sobre el proyecto de Constitución y deberes de los católicos" [1931], in *Documentos colectivos del episcopado español*, ed. Jesús Ibarren (Madrid 1974), 146.

72 Callahan, *The Catholic Church in Spain*, 345.

73 Wolf, *Pope and Devil*, 133.

74 Julian Casanova, *A Short History of the the Spanish Civil War* (London 2013), 200.

75 Maria Thomas, "Disputando la esfera pública: violencia anticlerical conflictividad y el Sagrado Corazón de Jesús, abril de 1931–julio de 1936," *Cuadernos de Historia Contemporánea* 33 (2011): 49–69; Callahan, *The Catholic Church in Spain*, 298.

76 Callahan, *The Catholic Church in Spain*, 349.

77 Telegrams in Gonzalo Redondo, *Historia de la Iglesia en España 1939–1939* (Madrid 1993), 2: 607–608.

78 Jacques Maritain, *Three Reformers: Luther, Descartes, Rousseau* (New York 1929), 4.

79 James Chappel, *Catholic Modern: The Challenge of Totalitarianism and the Remaking of the Church* (Cambridge MA 2018), 36.

80 Jacques Maritain, "William James and His Impetuous Philosophy," *Living Age* 24 (1921): 392–396.

81 Eugen Weber, *Action Française: Royalism and Reaction in Twentieth-Century France* (Stanford 1962), 219–255.

82 Ruedi Imbach, "Démocratie ou monarchie?: La Discussion Sur Le Meilleur Régime Politique Chez Quelques Interprètes Français De Thomas D'Aquin (1893–1928)," in *Saint Thomas XXe siècle: Actes du colloque du Centenaire de la "Revue Thomiste" 1893–1992*, ed. Fr. Serge-Thomas Bonino, O.P. (Paris 1994), 344.

83 Jacques Maritain, "For the Common Good: The Christian's Responsibility for the Present Crisis" [1934], trans. Bernard Doering, in *Notes et Documents*, 20 (1980): 1–20.

84 Jacques Maritain, *Integral Humanism, Freedom in the Modern World, and a Letter on Independence*, trans. Otto Bird, Joseph Evans, and Richard O'Sullivan, K.C., ed. Otto Bird (Notre Dame [1936] 1996), 175, 252.

85 Tony Judt, *Past Imperfect: French Intellectuals 1944–1956* (New York [1992] 2011), 172.

86 Jacques Maritain, *The Person and the Common Good*, trans. John J. Fitzgerald (New York 1947), 13.

87 James Chappel, "The Catholic Origins of Totalitarianism Theory in Interwar Europe," *Modern Intellectual History* 8 (2011): 561–590; Michael Schäffer, "Luigi Sturzo as a Theorist of Totalitarianism," in *Totalitarianism and Political Religions*, ed. Hans Maier (London 2004), 22–31; Diego Mauro, "El Huevo De La Serpiente: Los Seguidores De Luigi Sturzo En Argentina Y El Debate Sobre El Totalitarismo (1927–1945)," in *Más Allá De Los NacionalCatolicismos: Redes Transnacionales de Los Catolicismos Hispánicos*, eds. José Ramón Rodríguez Lago and Natalia Núñez Bargueño (Madrid 2021), 203–228.

88 Erik Peterson, "Monotheism as a Political Problem: A Contribution to the History of Political Theology in the Roman Empire" [1936], in Peterson, *Theological Tractates*,

trans. and ed. Michael J. Hollerich (Stanford 2011), 104; H. S. Jones, "Catholic Intellectuals and the Invention of Pluralism in France," *Modern Intellectual History* 18 (2021): 497–519.

89   Jacques Maritain, "The End of Machiavellianism," *Review of Politics* 1 (1942): 1–33.

90   McGreevy, *Catholicism and American Freedom*, 199.

91   Jean-Philippe Warren, "Pax Romana: un des vecteurs de diffusion du maritainisme (1939–1952)," *Etudes d'histoire religieuse* (2013): 71–91.

92   Javier Tusell, "Jacques Maritain et Le Personnalisme En Espagne," in *Jacques Maritain En Europe: La réception de sa pensée*, ed. Bernard Hubert (Paris 1996), 181–188.

93   Kosicki, *Catholics on the Barricades* 43–50.

94   Rosario Forlenza and Bjorn Thomassen, *Italian Modernities: Competing Narratives of Nationhood* (New York 2016), 78–80.

95   Jacques Maritain to Cardinal Alfred Baudrillart, Sept. 28, 1939, in *Les Carnets Du Cardinal Baudrillart 11 Avril 1939–19 mai 1941*, ed. Paul Christophe (Paris 1998), 977–980.

96   McGreevy, *Catholicism and American Freedom*, 199–200.

97   Michael Löwy and Jesús García-Ruiz, "Les Sources Françaises du christianisme de la libération au Brésil," *Archives de sciences sociales des religions*, 42 (1997): 14–18.

98   Miguel De Asúa, "Argentine Catholic Democratic Scientists and Their Projects for a Research University (1932–1959)," *Catholic Historical Review* 106 (2020): 111.

99   Gustavo Francesci to Jacques Maritain, July 29, 1937, and Maritain to Franceschi, Aug. 8, 1937, in Franceschi file, Maritain papers, Bibliothèque Nationale Universitaire, Strasbourg [BNS]; Austen Ivereigh, *Catholicism and Politics in Argentina, 1810–1960* (New York 1995), 117–122.

100   Barbara Barclay Carter to Maritain, June 7, 1938, Barbara Barclay Carter file, Maritain papers, BNS; Wolfram Kaiser, *Christian Democracy and the Origins of European Union* (Cambridge 2007), 136–150.

101   Yoshimitsu Yoshihiko, "The Theological Grounds of Overcoming Modernity" [1942], in *Overcoming Modernity: Cultural Identity in Wartime Japan*, trans. and ed. Richard F. Calichman (New York 2008), 86, 90.

102   Maritain, *Integral Humanism,* 323–332.

103   Kosicki, *Catholics on the Barricades*, 45.

104   Connelly, *From Enemy to Brother,* 139–141.

105   Jacques Maritain to Marie-Alain Couturier, July 26, 1942, in Couturier collection, box 4, file 7, Menil Foundation Archives [MFA]; Jacques Maritain to Vincent Lebbe, [July–Aug. 1927], in Maritain, *Oeuvres complètes* (Fribourg 1984) 16: 411–414; Pierre Sauvage, "Jacques Maritain et La Belgique," in *Jacques Maritain En Europe* 141.

106   McGreevy, *Catholicism and American Freedom*, 210; John T. McGreevy, "Catholicism and Abolition: A Historical (and Theological) Problem" in *Figures in the Carpet: Finding the Human Person in the American Past*, ed. Wilfred M. McClay (Grand Rapids 2007), 424–426.

107   Connelly, *From Enemy to Brother*, 53–54.

108   Emily Musil Church, "In Search of the Seven Sisters: A Biography of the Nardal Sisters of Martinique," *Callaloo* 36 (2013): 379.

109   Alyssa Goldstein Sepinwall, *The Àbbé Gregoire and the French Revolution: The Making of Modern Universalism* (Berkeley 2005), 224.

110   Albert Sbacchi, "The Archives of the Consolata Mission and the Formation of the Italian Empire, 1913–1943," *History in Africa* 25 (1998): 319–340.

111   Forclaz, *Humanitarian Imperialism*, 122–126.

112   Peter C. Kent, "Between Rome and London: Pius XI, the Catholic Church and the Abyssinian Crisis of 1935–1936," *International History Review* 11 (1989): 265; David I. Kertzer, *The Pope and Mussolini*, 220–226, 458.

113   The manifesto appears as Appendix Two in Yves R. Simon, *The Ethiopian Campaign and French Political Thought*, ed. Anthony O. Simon (Notre Dame 2009), 93–105.

114   Lucia Ceci, *Il papa non deve parlare: Chiesa, fascismo e guerra d'Etiopia* (Rome 2010), 222.

115   Chamedes, *A Twentieth-Century Crusade*, 198.

116   Ceci, *Il papa non deve parlare*, 54–62.

117   Kent, "Between Rome and London"; S.K.B. Asante, "The Catholic Missions, British West African Nationalists, and the Italian Invasion of Ethiopia, 1935–36," *African Affairs* 73 (1974): 204–216.

118   *Mit Brennender Sorge* (1937), §17.

119   *Divini Redemptoris* (1937), §§3, 7, 10; Moyn, *Christian Human Rights*, 38–39.

120   Volker Ullrich, *Hitler: Ascent 1889–1939*, trans. Jefferson Chase (New York 2016), 652–653.

121   Brendan Simms, *Hitler: A Global Biography* (New York 2021), 289.

122   Jeremy Noakes, "The Oldenburg Crucifix Struggle of November, 1936: A Case Study of Opposition in the Third Reich," in *The Shaping of the Nazi State*, ed. Peter D. Stachura (London 1978), 210–233.

123   Report of 1937 in *Anglo-Vatican Relations, 1914–1939: Confidential Annual Reports of the British Ministers to the Holy See*, ed. Thomas Hachey (Boston 1972), 370–371.

124   Alberto Guasco, "Un termine e le sue declinazioni: Chiesa cattolica e totalitarismi tra bibliografia e ricerca," in *Pius XI: Keywords*, eds. Alberto Guasco and Raffaella Perin (Berlin 2010), 94–9.

125   Fattorini, *Hitler, Mussolini, and the Vatican*, 161–165; Kertzer, *The Pope and Mussolini*, 356.

126   Mary Vincent, "Expiation as Performative Rhetoric in National-Catholicism: The Politics of Gesture in Post-Civil War Spain," *Past and Present* 203 (2009): 238; Passelecq and Suchecky, *The Hidden Encyclical of Pius XI*, 29–40.

127   John LaFarge, *The Manner Is Ordinary* (New York 1954), 226, 234.

128   Gustav Gundlach, S.J., to John LaFarge, S.J., Mar. 15, 1939, reprinted in Passelecq and Suchecky, *The Hidden Encyclical of Pius XI*, 80.

129   Gustav Gundlach, S.J., to John LaFarge, S.J., May 10, 1939, reprinted in Passelecq and Suchecky, *The Hidden Encyclical of Pius XI*, 86.

130   Gustav Gundlach, S.J., unpublished manuscript [1940], copy in file 4, box 1, George Shuster papers, Archives of the University of Notre Dame.

131   Wolf, *Pope and Devil*, 185–189.

132   Edith Stein to Jacques Maritain, Nov. 6, 1932, in *Self-Portrait in Letters*, 124–125.

133   Edith Stein to Elly Dursy, May 7, 1933, in *Self-Portrait in Letters*, 140–141.

134   Philibert Secretan, *Edith Stein et La Suisse: Chronique d'un asile manqué* (Geneva 1997).

135   Edith Stein to Mother Ambrosia Antonia Engelmann, OCD, Aug. 5, 1942, in *Self-Portrait in Letters*, 352; Edith Stein to Mother Ambrosia Antonia Engelmann, OCD, Aug. 6, 1942, in *Self-Portrait in Letters*, 353.

NINE: RESSOURCEMENT

1   Dominique de Menil to Marie-Alain Couturier, Aug. 25, 1951, copy in Ryan Dohoney, *Saving Abstraction: Morton Feldman, the De Menils, and the Rothko Chapel* (New York 2019), 94.

2   James Joyce to Nora Barnacle, Aug. 29, 1904, copy in Richard Ellman, *James Joyce* (New York [1959] 1982), 169.

3   Flannery O'Connor to Elizabeth Bishop, June 1, 1958, in O'Connor, *The Habit of Being: Letters of Flannery O'Connor*, ed. Sally Fitzgerald (New York 1979), 286.

4   Nicholas Boyle, *Sacred and Secular Scriptures: A Catholic Approach to Literature* (Notre Dame 2005), 252.

5   Stephen Schloesser, "Notes on the *Miserere* Plates Exhibited in *Mystic Masque*," in *Semblance and Reality in Georges Rouault 1871–1958*, ed. Stephen Schloesser (Chestnut Hill MA 2008), 157–180.

6   Anthony B. Smith, "The Circulation of Presence: Rossellini, Fellini, and the Boundaries of Religious Film," *Annali di scienze religiose* 14 (2021), 67–99.

7   William Middleton, *Double Vision: The Unerring Eye of Art World Avatars Dominique and John de Menil* (New York 2018), 77, 113–114, 151, 155.

8   Yves Congar, *Divided Christendom: A Catholic Study of the Problem of Reunion* (London [1937] 1939), 247.

9   Dominique de Menil, "Pour l'unité du monde chrétien," *La Vie intellectuelle* (Feb. 15, 1936), 383–388.

10 Dominique de Menil, Address on the Opening of the Rothko Chapel, February 26, 1971, in De Menil, *The Rothko Chapel: Writings on Art and the Threshold of the Divine* (New Haven 2010), 17–19.

11 Stephen Schloesser, *Jazz Age Catholicism: Mystic Modernism in Postwar Paris, 1919–1933* (Toronto 2005), 148–155, 163–167.

12 *The Maritain Factor: Taking Religion into Interwar Modernism*, eds. Rajesh Heynickx and Jan De Maeyer (Leuven 2010); *Maritain et les artistes: Rouault, Cocteau, Chagall . . .* , ed. Claude Lorentz (Strasbourg 2016).

13 Schloesser, *Jazz Age Catholicism*, 72–73.

14 Flannery O'Connor to Robert Macaulay, May 18, 1955, in *The Habit of Being*, 81.

15 Middleton, *Double Vision*, 174, 185.

16 Couturier to Dominique and Jean de Menil, Jan. 1951, in Couturier collection, box 2, file 7, Menil Foundation Archives [MFA], Houston, Texas.

17 Maritain to Couturier July 8, 1948, in Couturier collection, box 4, file 7, MFA; Schloesser, *Jazz Age Catholicism*, 163.

18 Dominique de Menil, "Impressions américaines en France," *L'Art Sacre* 7–8 (1953): 2–31.

19 Middleton, *Double Vision*, 344.

20 M. A. Couturier, "Sacred Arts and Its Public" [1951], in Couturier, *Sacred Art*, trans. Granger Ryan, eds. Dominique de Menil and Pie Duployé (Austin 1983), 59.

21 Antoine Lion, "Art sacré et modernité en France: le rôle du P. Marie-Alain Couturier," *Revue de l'histoire des religions* 227 (2010): 121.

22 François Caussé, *La Revue "L'Art Sacré": Le débat en France sur l'art et la religion (1945–1954)* (Paris, 2010), 499–542.

23 G. B. Montini to Celso Constantini, Dec. 17, 1952, in *Il Ritratto Segreto del Cardinale Celso Constantini in 10.000 lettere dal 1892 al 1958*, ed. Bruno Fabio Pighin (Venice 2012), 509.

24 Aidan Nichols, O.P., "The Dominicans and the Journal 'L'Art sacre,'" *New Blackfriars* 88 (2007): 42.

25 Marie-Alain Couturier, notebook entry of 1951, in *La vérité blessée* (Paris 1984), 245.

26 Yves Congar, *True and False Reform in the Church*, trans. Paul Philibert (Collegeville [1950] 2011), 39–40.

27 Middleton, *Double Vision*, 201.

28 De Menil, "Pour l'unité du monde chrétien," 385; Kristina Van Dyke, "The Menil Collection Houston Texas," *African Arts* 40 (2007): 45.

29 Joseph A. Komonchak, "Theology and Culture at Mid-Century: The Example of Henri de Lubac," *Theological Studies* 51 (1990): 579–602.

30 J. W. Hellman, "Emmanuel Mounier: A Catholic Revolutionary at Vichy," *Journal of Contemporary History* 8 (1973): 10, 15.

31 Samuel Moyn, *Christian Human Rights* (Philadelphia 2015), 51.

32 Gurian quoted in Yves R. Simon to Jacques Maritain, July 16, 1941, in *Jacques Maritain-Yves Simon Correspondance (Les Années américaines 1941–1961)* (Tours 2008), 2: 64–66.

33 Yves R. Simon to Jacques Maritain, Sept. 3, 1941, in *Jacques Maritain-Yves Simon Correspondance*, 2:69–71.

34 Jacques Maritain, *Christianity and Democracy* (New York 1944), 58; Jacques Maritain to Yves R. Simon, June 15, 1941, in *Jacques Maritain-Yves Simon Correspondance*, 2: 60–62 .

35 Jacques Maritain to Yves Simon, Oct. 3, 1941, in *Jacques Maritain-Yves Simon Correspondance*, 2: 76.

36 "In the Face of the World's Crisis: A Manifesto by European Catholics Sojourning in America," *Commonweal*, 36 (1942): 414–421.

37 "Pope's Christmas Message, 1944," *Catholic Mind* 43 (Feb. 1945), 68; Charles Journet to Jacques Maritain, Apr. 5, 1945, in *Journet-Maritain Correspondance*, eds. Mgr. Pierre Magie and George Cottier, O.P. (Fribourg 1996), 3: 310.

38 Jacques Maritain to Charles de Gaulle, Nov. 21, 1941, and Charles De Gaulle to Jacques Maritain, July 1, 1942, in *Cahiers Jacques Maritain* 16–17 (Apr. 1988): 61.

39 Bernard Doering, *Jacques Maritain and the French Catholic Intellectuals* (Notre Dame 1983), 223.

40 The foundational study is now Sarah Shortall, *Soldiers of God in a Secular World: Catholic Theology and Twentieth-Century French Politics* (Cambridge MA 2021).

41 Marie-Dominique Chenu, *Une École de théologie: le Saulchoir* (Paris [1937] 1985), 122, 143.

42 Minlib Dallh, "From Le Saulchoir to *Nostra Aetate*," in *The Promise of Renewal: Dominicans and Vatican II*, ed. Michael Attridge et al. (Adelaide 2017), 259–276.

43 Gabriel Flynn, O.P., "Ressourcement, Ecumenicism and Pneumatology," in *Ressourcement: A Movement for Renewal in Twentieth-Century Catholic Theology*, eds. Gabriel Flynn and Paul D. Murray (Oxford 2012), 222; Komonchak, "Theology and Culture at Mid-Century," 579–602.

44 Henri de Lubac, *Christian Resistance to Anti-Semitism: Memories from 1940 to 1944*, trans. Elizabeth Englund, O.C.D. (San Francisco 1990), 49.

45 Henri de Lubac, "Explication Chrétienne de Notre Temps" [1941], in De Lubac, *Résistance chrétienne au nazisme* (Paris 2006), 130.

46 Basic Principles of the Reconstruction, Aug. 9, 1943, draft, Kreisau Circle, in *Behind Valkyrie: German Resistance to Hitler: Documents*, ed. Peter Hoffmann (Montreal 2011), 77.

47 Lauren N. Faulkner, "Against Bolshevism: Georg Werthmann and the Role of Ideology in the Catholic Military Chaplaincy, 1939–1945," *Contemporary European History* 19 (2010): 12.

48 Sermon of Bishop Clemens August Count von Galen, July 20, 1941, copy in Beth A. Griech-Polelle, *Bishop von Galen: German Catholicism and National Socialism* (New Haven 2002), 178; Beth A. Griech-Polelle, "Bishop von Galen and the Judeo-Bolshevik Conspiracy," *Kirchliche Zeitgeschichte* 15 (2002): 436.

49 Jägerstatter Notebook II (1942), in *Franz Jägerstätter: Letters and Writings from Prison* (Maryknoll, NY, 2009), 181.

50 Alfred Delp, S.J., "The Fate of the Churches" [1944], in *Prison Meditations of Alfred Delp* (New York 1963) 116–117.

51 Karl Rahner, "Opening Our Hearts" and "Prayer in the Everyday" [1946], in *The Need and the Blessing of Prayer*, trans. Bruce W. Gillette (Collegeville 1997), 7, 45.

52 Jerry Ryan, "Faithful Ferryman," in *Fireworks: Jerry Ryan in Commonweal*, ed. Patrick Jordan (New York 2020), 134–136.

53 *Mediator Dei* (1947), §64.

54 Fergus Kerr, *Twentieth-Century Catholic Theologians: From Neoscholasticism to Nuptial Mysticism* (Malden, MA, 2007), 19.

55 *Humani Generis* (1950), §15.

56 Joseph A. Komonchak, "Popes Pius XI and Pius XII and the Idea of an Ecumenical Council" (2011), 10, link at Background to Vatican II, jakomonchak.wordpress.com.

57 Henri de Lubac, S.J., *At the Service of the Church: Henri de Lubac Reflects on the Circumstances That Occasioned His Writings* (San Francisco 1992), 60–79.

58 Gerd-Ranier Horn, *Western European Liberation Theology: The First Wave (1924–1959)*, (New York 2008), 105–109; Rosa Bruno-Jofré, "The Catholic Church in Chile and the Social Question in the 1930s: The Political Pedagogical Discourse of Fernando Vives Del Solar, S.J.," *Catholic Historical Review* 99 (2013): 723.

59 M. R. [Jacques] Loew, O.P., *Mission to the Poorest*, trans. Pamela Carswell (New York 1950), 100.

60 Daniel Berrigan to Philip Berrigan, Jan. 6, 1954, in *The Berrigan Letters: Personal Correspondence between Daniel and Philip Berrigan*, eds. Daniel Cosacchi and Eric Martin (Maryknoll, NY, 2016), 11.
61 Jonathan Luxmoore and Jolanta Babiuch, *The Vatican and the Red Flag: The Struggle for the Soul of Eastern Europe* (London 1999), 47
62 Gerd-Ranier Horn, *The Spirit of Vatican II: Western European Progressive Catholicism in the Long Sixties* (New York 2015), 63.
63 Yves Congar, *Journal d'un theologian: 1946–1956* (Paris 2001), 232–272.
64 Pierre Elliott Trudeau, *Memoirs* (Toronto 1993), 40.
65 Scott Stossel, *Sarge: The Life and Times of Sargent Shriver* (New York, 2004), 628; Dominic Sandbrook, *Eugene McCarthy: The Rise and Fall of Postwar American Liberalism* (New York 2005), 154; David Brooks interview with President Joseph R. Biden, Jr., *New York Times*, May 21, 2021.
66 Bjorn Thomassen and Rosario Forlenza, "Christianity and Political Thought: Augusto Del Noce and the Ideology of Christian Democracy in Post-War Italy," *Journal of Political Ideologies* 21 (2016): 181–199.
67 Maria D. Mitchell, *The Origins of Christian Democracy: Politics and Confession in Modern Germany* (Ann Arbor 2012), 90–91.
68 Jacques Maritain, *Man and the State* (Chicago 1951), 194.
69 Bernard Bailyn, "The Idea of Atlantic History," *Itinerario* (1996): 22–25.
70 Maritain to Journet, July 5, 1951, *Journet-Maritain Correspondence*, 4: 121.
71 Tony Judt, *Postwar: A History of Europe Since 1945* (New York 2005), 158.
72 Kaiser, *Christian Democracy and the Origins of European Union*, 191–252.
73 Brian Porter-Szücs, *Faith and Fatherland: Catholicism, Modernity, and Poland* (New York 2011), 146.
74 Florian Michel, *Étienne Gilson: une biographie intellectuelle et politique* (Paris 2018), 187–204.
75 Hervé Le Bras and Emmanuel Todd, *L'Invention De La France: Atlas anthropologique et politique* (Paris 2012), 346–347.
76 Jeffrey R. Fear, *Organizing Control: August Thyssen and the Construction of German Corporate Management* (Cambridge MA 2005), 677–709.
77 Julian Jackson, *De Gaulle* (Cambridge MA 2019), 318–319.
78 Entry of May 7, 1945, in *The Secrets of a Vatican Cardinal: Celso Costantini Wartime Diaries, 1938–1947*, trans. Laurence B. Mussio, ed. Bruno Fabio Pighin (Montreal 2014), 418.
79 Colleen Doody, *Detroit's Cold War: The Origins of Postwar Conservatism* (Urbana 2013), 76–92; Monique Scherr, "Catholic Piety in the Early Cold War Years or: How the Virgin Mary Protected the West from Communism," in *Cold War Cultures: Perspectives on Eastern and Western Societies*, eds. Annette Vowinkel, Marcus M. Payk, and Thomas Lindenberger (New York 2012), 130.
80 Horn, *Western European Liberation Theology*, 162–163.
81 Decree of the Holy Office, July 1, 1949, reprinted in Yvon Tranvouez, *Catholiques et communistes: La crise du progressisme chrétien, 1950–1955* (Paris 2000), 42; Rosario Forlenza, "The Enemy Within: Catholic Anti-Communism in Cold War Italy," *Past and Present* 235 (2018): 207–242.
82 Dermot Keogh, *Ireland and the Vatican: The Politics and Diplomacy of Church-State Relations, 1922–1960* (Cork 1995), 313.
83 G. Simon, "The Catholic Church and the Communist State in the Soviet Union and Eastern Europe," in *Religion and Atheism in the USSR and Eastern Europe*, eds. B. Bociurkiw and J. W. Strong (London 1975), 208.
84 Minutes of the Third Conference, Session II, Comrade Togliatti's report, Nov. 17, 1949, in *The Cominform: Minutes of the Three Conferences 1947/1948/1949*, ed. Giuliano Procacci (Milan 1994), 797–799.
85 Anne Applebaum, *Iron Curtain: The Crushing of Eastern Europe 1944–1956* (New York 2012), 269.

86   Luxmoore and Babiach, *The Vatican and the Red Flag*, 38.
87   Sabrina Petra Ramet, "The Catholic Church in Czechoslovakia 1948–1991," *Studies in Comparative Communism* 24 (1991): 381–386.
88   Charles Andras, "Maritain en Hongrie," in *Jacques Maritain en Europe*, 256–259.
89   John Connelly, *Captive University: The Sovietization of East German, Czech, and Polish Higher Education 1945–1956* (Chapel Hill 2000), 74.
90   Kosicki, *Catholics on the Barricades*, 157–162; Robert Ventresca, *Soldier of Christ: The Life of Pope Pius XII* (Cambridge MA 2013), 251; Christina Manetti, "Catholic Responses to Poland's 'New Reality,' 1945–1953," *East European Politics and Societies* 26 (2012): 309.
91   *The Memoirs of Jin Luxian*, trans. William Hanbury Tenison (Hong Kong 2012), 1:101–103; Paul Philip Mariani, *Church Militant: Bishop Kung and Catholic Resistance in Communist Shanghai* (Cambridge MA 2011), 57.
92   Mariani, *Church Militant*, 5.
93   Déclaration à Montevideo, Apr. 18–23, 1947, in *La Démocratie Chrétienne Dans Le Monde: Résolutions et déclarations des organisations internationales démocrates chrétiennes de 1947 à 1973*, ed. Gino Crotti (Rome 1973), 159–163.
94   Eduardo Frei to Bishop Manuel Larraín, Sept. 9, 1942, copy in Carlos González Cruchaga, *Historia De Una Polémica: Monseñor Manuel Larraín Y Los Orígenes De La Democracia Cristiana En Chile* (Santiago 1997), 39; Paul E. Sigmund, "The Transformation of Christian Democratic Ideology: Transcending Left and Right, or Whatever Happened to the Third Way?," in *Christian Democracy in Latin America: Electoral Competition and Regime Conflicts*, eds. Scott Mainwaring and Timothy R. Scully (Stanford 2003), 67.
95   Florian Michel, *La pensée catholique en Amérique du nord: réseaux intellectuels et échanges culturels entre l'Europe, le Canada et les Etats-Unis (années 1920–1960)* (Paris 2010), 262–265; Javier Tusell, "Jacques Maritain en le personnalisme in Espagne," in *Jacques Maritain en Europe*, ed. Bernard Hubert (Paris 1996), 188–196.
96   Juan Domingo Perón, "A Denunciation of Certain Argentine Churchmen" [1954], in *The Conflict Between Church and State in Latin America*, ed. Frederick B. Pike (New York 1964), 184–185.
97   Austen Ivereigh, *Catholicism and Politics in Argentina: 1810–1960* (New York 1995), 143–202.
98   Chappel, *Catholic Modern*, 115–123.
99   Herbert Doms, *The Meaning of Marriage* (New York 1939), 197.
100   Fr. Francis J. Connell, C.SS.R., "The Catholic Doctrine on the Ends of Marriage," *Proceedings of the Catholic Theological Society of America* 1 (1946): 35.
101   Jacques Maritain to Charles Journet, Nov. 15, 1948, in *Journet-Maritain Correspondance* 3: 715.
102   Norman B. Ryder, Charles F. Westoff, and Raymond H. Potvin, *College Women and Fertility Values* (Princeton 1967), 42–44.
103   Benjamin Ziemann, *Encounters with Modernity: The Catholic Church in West Germany 1945–1975* (New York 2014), 119; McGreevy, *Catholicism and American Freedom*, 233.
104   Martine Sevegrand, "La méthode Ogino et la morale catholique: une controverse théologique autour de la limitation des naissances (1930–1951)," *Revue d'histoire de l'Eglise de France* 78 (1992): 77–99.
105   McGreevy, *Catholicism and American Freedom*, 233; W. Dupont, "Of Human Love: Catholics Campaigning for Sexual Aggiornamento in Postwar Belgium," in *The Schism of '68: Catholicism, Contraception and "Humanae Vitae" in Europe, 1945–1975*, ed. Alana Harris (London 2018), 52.
106   Lucia Pozzi, "I Gesuiti e i discorsi dei papi: L'allocuzione di Pio XII alle ostetriche del 1951," in *I Gesuiti e i papi*, eds. Michela Catto and Claudio Ferlan (Bologna 2016), 131–156.
107   McGreevy, *Catholicism and American Freedom*, 234, 230.

108 Aiko Takeuchi-Demirci, "Sexual Diplomacy: U.S. Catholics' Transnational Anti-Birth Control Activism in Postwar Japan," in *Devotions and Desires: Histories of Sexuality and Religion in the Twentieth-Century United States*, eds. Gillian Frank, Bethany Moreton, and Heather Rachelle White (Chapel Hill 2018), 113–131.

109 Chris Dols and Maarten van den Bos, "Humanae Vitae: Catholic Attitude to Birth Control in the Netherlands and Transnational Church Politics, 1945–1975," in *The Schism of '68*, 23–48; Anne-Sophie Crosetti, "The 'Converted Unbelievers': Catholics in Family Planning in French-Speaking Belgium (1947–73)," *Medical History* 64 (2020): 267–286.

110 Dagmar Herzog, "Desperately Seeking Normalcy: Sex and Marriage in the Wake of the War," in *Life after Death: Approaches to a Cultural and Social History of Europe during the 1940s and 1950s*, eds. Richard Bessel and Dirk Schumann (Cambridge 2003), 176–177.

111 Michael Gauvreau, *The Catholic Origins of Quebec's Quiet Revolution, 1931–1970* (Montreal 2005), 199.

112 McGreevy, *Catholicism and American Freedom*, 235–236.

113 Monsignor J. B. Montini to Cardinal Siri [1953], copy in Rev. Anthony Zimmerman, S.V.D., *"Overpopulation": A Study of Papal Teachings on the Problem, with Special Reference to Japan* (Washington 1957), 305.

114 Kenneth Serbin, "Church-State Reciprocity in Contemporary Brazil: The Convening of the International Eucharistic Congress of 1955 in Rio de Janeiro," *The Hispanic American Historical Review* 76 (1996), 721–751.

115 Alceu Amoroso Lima, "Brazil," in *The Church and the Nations*, ed. Adrian Hastings (London 1959), 204.

116 Francois Houtart to unknown, July 30, 1954, copy in Madeleine Adriance, *Opting for the Poor* (Kansas City 1986), 15–16.

117 Serbin, "Church-State Reciprocity in Contemporary Brazil," 721–751.

118 Catherine R. Osborne, *American Catholics and the Church of Tomorrow: Building Churches for the Future, 1925–1975* (Chicago 2018), 42.

119 David Snell, "Rothko's Chapel—The Painter's Final Testament," *Smithsonian* 2 (1971), 52.

TEN: DECOLONIZATION

1 Elizabeth A. Foster, *African Catholic: Decolonization and the Transformation of the Church* (Cambridge MA 2019), 3, 48–50.

2 Paul Gifford, *Christianity, Development and Modernity in Africa* (New York 2013), 86; Adrian Hastings, *The Church in Africa, 1450–1950* (Oxford 1994), 562.

3 Barbra Mann Wall, *Into Africa: A Transnational History of Catholic Medical Missions and Social Change* (New Brunswick 2015), 37.

4 Jean Gartlan, *Barbara Ward: Her Life and Letters* (London 2010), 5.

5 Joan Keating, "Discrediting the 'Catholic State': British Catholics and the Fall of France," *Catholicism in Britain and France since 1789*, eds. Frank Tallett and Nicholas Atkin (London 1996), 27–42.

6 Gartlan, *Barbara Ward*, 15.

7 Barbara Ward, *Faith and Freedom* (New York 1954), 261.

8 Barbara Ward, "Two Worlds," in *Christianity and Culture*, ed. Stanley Murphy, C.S.B. (Baltimore 1960), 32–38.

9 Arthur Schlesinger, Jr., *A Thousand Days: John F. Kennedy in the White House* (Boston 1965), 108.

10 Denis Pelletier, *Économie et Humanisme: De L'Utopie Communautaire au Combat Pour Le Tiers-Monde 1941–1966* (Paris 1996).

11 Lydia Garreau, *Louis-Joseph Lebret, Précurseur de Vatican II* (Paris 2011), 239.

12 Giuliana Chamedes, "The Catholic Origins of Economic Development After World War II," *French Politics, Culture and Society* 33 (2015): 56–73.

13 Graham Greene to Catherine Watson, Feb. 18, 1959, in *Graham Greene: A Life in Letters*, ed. Richard Greene (New York 2007), 242.

14   Jean Daniélou, "Les Orientations présentés de la pensée religieuse," *Etudes* 249 (1946): 20.

15   Florian Michel, *Étienne Gilson: une biographie intellectuelle et politique* (Paris 2018), 137–138.

16   Vesna Drapac, *War and Religion: Catholics in the Churches of Occupied Paris* (Washington 1998), 54.

17   Richard Gribble, *The Implementation of Vatican II in Eastern Africa: The Contribution of Bishop Vincent McCauley, C.S.C.* (Lewiston 2009), 15.

18   Joseph Masson, S.J., *Vers l'église indigène: catholicisme ou nationalisme?* (Brussels 1944), 22.

19   Foster, *African Catholic*, 22.

20   Jacques Maritain, *L'Europe et L'idée Fédérale* (Paris [1940s] 1993); Frederick Cooper, *Citizenship, Inequality and Difference: Historical Perspectives* (Princeton 2018), 116–117.

21   André Dupleix and Jules Carles, *Teilhard de Chardin* (Paris 1991), 65.

22   Léopold Sédar Senghor, *Pierre Teilhard de Chardin et la politique africaine* (Paris 1962), 13–65.

23   Meinrad Hebga, "Christianisme et Négritude," in *Des Prêtres Noirs S'Interrogent*, eds. A. Abble et al. (Paris 1956), 189–203.

24   Vincent Mulago, "Nécessité L'Adaptation Missionnaire Chez Les Bantu Du Congo," in *Des Prêtres Noirs S'Interrogent*, 21–26.

25   Yves Congar, O.P., *The Catholic Church and the Race Question* (Paris 1953), 40; McGreevy, *Catholicism and American Freedom*, 209–211.

26   R. Bentley Anderson, " 'To Save a Soul': Catholic Mission Schools, Apartheid, and the 1953 Bantu Education Act," *Journal of Religious History* 44 (2020): 164–165.

27   Stuart C. Bate, "The Church under Apartheid," in *The Catholic Church in Contemporary South Africa*, eds. Joy Brain and Philippe Denis (Pietermaritzburg 1999), 153; John T. McGreevy, *Parish Boundaries: The Catholic Encounter with Race in the Twentieth-Century Urban North* (Chicago 1996), 79–110.

28   Foster, *African Catholic*, 194.

29   Adrian Hastings, *A History of African Christianity 1950–1975* (Cambridge 1979), 64.

30   Uyilawa Usuanlele, "The 1951–52 Benin City Catholic Church Crisis: Irish Catholic Clergy versus African Nationalism," *Journal of Religion in Africa* 49 (2019), 181–216.

31   Piet Clement, "Tempels Revisited: The Conversation of a Missionary in the Belgian Congo, 1930s–1960," in *Religion, Colonization and Decolonization in Congo: 1885–1960*, eds. Vincent Viaene, Bram Cleys, and Jan De Maeyer (Leuven 2020), 241–260.

32   John T. McGreevy, *American Jesuits and the World: How an Embattled Religious Order Made Modern Catholicism Global* (Princeton 2016), 218.

33   John T. McGreevy, "Catholicism and Abolition: A Historical (and Theological) Problem" in *Figures in the Carpet: Finding the Human Person in the American Past*, ed. Wilfred M. McClay (Grand Rapids 2007), 424–426.

34   Foster, *African Catholic*, 115, 124–125.

35   *Fidei Donum* (1957) §§7, 13; Guy Vanthemsche, "Le Saint Siège et la fin du Congo Belge (1958–1960)," *Revue D'Histoire Ecclésiastique* 109 (2014): 206–207.

36   Foster, *African Catholic*, 146–147.

37   McGreevy, *American Jesuits and the World*, 220.

38   Gerry Van Klinken, *Minorities, Modernity and the Emerging Nation: Christians in Indonesia, a Biographical Approach* (Leiden 2003), 175–187.

39   Charles Keith, *Catholic Vietnam: A Church from Empire to Nation* (Berkeley 2012), 196–200.

40   An Appeal of the Vietnamese Bishops in Favor of the Independence of Their Country, Sept. 23, 1945, in *Voices of Decolonization: A Brief History with Documents*, ed. Todd Shepherd (Boston 2015), 52–53.

41   Charles Journet to Jacques Maritain [1948], in *Journet-Maritain Correspondance*, eds. Mgr. Pierre Magie and George Cottier, O.P. (Fribourg 1996), 3: 671–675.

42   Ronald H. Spector, "Phat Diem: Nationalism, Religion and Identity in the Franco-Viet Minh War," *Journal of Cold War Studies* 15 (2013): 34–46.

43   Keith, *Catholic Vietnam*, 237.

44   Scott McConnell, *Leftward Journey: The Education of Vietnamese Students in France, 1919–1939* (New Brunswick 1989), 91–92.

45   Phi Van Nguyen, "The Vietnamization of Personalism: The Role of Missionaries in the Spread of Personalism in Vietnam, 1939–1961," *French Colonial History* 17 (2017): 117.

46   James T. Fisher, *Dr. America: The Lives of Thomas A. Dooley, 1927–1961* (Amherst 1997), 231.

47   Kirsten Weld, "The Other Door: Spain and the Guatemalan Counter-Revolution, 1944–54," *Journal of Latin American Studies* 51 (2019): 307–331; Patricia Harms, "'God Doesn't Like the Revolution': The Archbishop, the Market Women, and the Economy of Gender in Guatemala, 194–1954," *Frontiers* 32 (2011): 111–139.

48   Archbishop Mariano Rossell y Arellano, "Enemies of Christ" [1954], in *The Guatemala Reader: History, Culture, Politics,* eds. Greg Grandin, Deborah T. Levenson, and Elizabeth Oglesby (Durham 2011), 226–227.

49   Susan Fitzpatrick-Behrens, *The Maryknoll Catholic Mission in Peru, 1943–1989: Transnational Faith and Transformation* (Notre Dame 2012), 39.

50   Fitzpatrick-Behrens, *The Maryknoll Catholic Mission in Peru*, 59, 62.

51   Fitzpatrick-Behrens, *The Maryknoll Catholic Mission in Peru*, 94–114.

52   Ignacio Walker, "The Future of Chilean Christian Democracy," in *Christian Democracy in Latin America: Electoral Competition and Regime Conflicts,* eds. Scott Mainwaring and Timothy R. Scully (Stanford 2003), 166.

53   Timothy R. Scully, *Rethinking the Center: Party Politics in Nineteenth and Twentieth Century Chile* (Stanford 1992), 131–132.

54   Henri de Lubac, *At the Service of the Church: Henri de Lubac Reflects on the Circumstances that Occasioned His Writings* (San Francisco 1992), 240–242.

55   Michael Löwy and Jesús García-Ruiz, "Le Sources françaises du Christianisme de la Libération au Brésil," *Archive de sciences sociales des Religion* 97 (1997): 21–22; Colin M. Snider, "Catholic Campuses, Secularizing Struggles: Student Activism and Catholic Universities in Brazil, 1950–1968," in *Local Church, Global Church: Catholic Activism in Latin America from Rerum Novarum To Vatican II,* eds. Stephen J. C. Andes and Julia G. Young (Washington 2016), 185–204.

56   Patrick Lacroix, *John F. Kennedy and the Politics of Faith* (Lawrence 2021), 67–70; Fitzpatrick-Behrens, *The Maryknoll Catholic Mission in Peru*, 128.

57   Thomas C. Bruneau, *The Political Transformation of the Brazilian Catholic Church* (Cambridge 1974), 124.

58   Address of Msgr. Agostino Casaroli, Aug. 17, 1961, copy in Gerald M. Costello, *Mission to Latin America: The Successes and Failures of a Twentieth Century Crusade* (Maryknoll, NY, 1979), 275.

59   "Kennedy Writes Pope on Council," *New York Times*, Oct. 6, 1962.

60   McGreevy, *Catholicism and American Freedom*, 204–205.

61   John Courtney Murray, S.J., "Current Theology: Christian Co-Operation," *Theological Studies* 3 (1942): 424.

62   Saretta Marotta, "L'Ecumenista Bea Alla Luce Del Suo Archivio privato (1951–1961)," in *Il Concilio Vaticano II E I Suoi Protagonisti Alla Luce Degli Archivi,* eds. Philippe Chenaux and Kiril Plamen Kartaloff (Rome 2017), 75.

63   Tony Judt, *Postwar: A History of Europe since 1945* (New York 2005), 805.

64   Maritain to Montini, July 12, 1946, and Maritain to Montini, Apr. 12,1948, in Philippe Chenaux, *Paul VI et Maritain: Les rapports du "Montinianisme" et du "Maritainism"* (Brescia 1994), 104–107.

65   John Connelly, *From Enemy to Brother: The Revolution in Catholic Teaching on the Jews 1933–1965* (Cambridge MA 2012), 191–196.

66   Jacques Maritain, *The Rights of Man and Natural Law* (New York [1943] 1949), 80–81.

67   McGreevy, *Catholicism and American Freedom*, 201.

68   Jacques Maritain, "Introduction," in *Human Rights: Comments and Interpretations* (London 1949), 10.

69   Bjorn Thomassen and Rosario Forlenza, "Catholic Modernity and the Italian Constitution," *History Workshop Journal* 81 (2016): 21.

70   Michael Rosen, *Dignity: Its History and Meaning* (Cambridge MA 2018), 90–100.

71   McGreevy, *Catholicism and American Freedom*, 166–167.

72   Erika Helgen, *Religious Conflict in Brazil: Protestants, Catholics and the Rise of Religious Pluralism* (New Haven 2020), 29–58, 122–162; David F. Amico, "Religious Liberty in Argentina during the First Perón Regime, 1943–1955," *Church History* (1977): 491–492.

73   Mitchell, *The Origins of Christian Democracy*, 187.

74   H. Mayer, *Catholics and the Free Society: An Australian Symposium* (Melbourne 1961); Ian Linden, *Global Catholicism: Diversity and Change since Vatican II* (New York 2009), 229.

75   Jacques Maritain to Charles Journet, May 1, 1950, in *Journet-Maritain Correspondance*, 4: 57.

76   John Courtney Murray, S.J., "Leo XIII and Pius XII: Government and the Order of Religion" [1955], in Murray, *Religious Liberty: Catholic Struggles with Pluralism*, ed. J. Leon Hooper, S.J. (Louisville, KY, 1993), 51.

77   Max Pribilla, S.J., "Dogmatic Intolerance and Civil Toleration," *The Month* 4 (1950): 254; Udi Greenberg, "Catholics, Protestants, and the Tortured Path to Religious Liberty," *Journal of the History of Ideas* 89 (2018): 469–472.

78   Joseph Lecler, S.J., "La papauté moderne et la liberté de conscience," *Études* 249 (1946): 289–309.

79   Theodore Hesburgh to Maritain, Apr. 27, 1951, in Hesburgh file, Maritain papers, BNS.

80   McGreevy, *Catholicism and American Freedom*, 192.

81   Marco Duranti, *The Conservative Human Rights Revolution: European Identity, Transnational Politics, and the Origins of the European Convention* (Oxford 2017), 311; McGreevy, *Catholicism and American Freedom*, 182.

82   Mark Edward Ruff, *The Battle for the Catholic Past in Germany, 1945–1980* (Cambridge 2017), 57–67.

83   Patrick M. Boyle, "School Wars: Church, State, and the Death of the Congo," *Journal of Modern African Studies* 33 (1995): 451–468.

84   Keogh, *Ireland and the Vatican*, 340.

85   Thomas J. Shelley, "Three Popes and a Cardinal: Pius XII, John XXIII, Paul VI and Francis J. Spellman," in *La Papauté Contemporaine XIXe–XXe Siècles*, eds. Jean-Pierre Delville and Marco Jačov (Vatican City 2009), 521; McGreevy, *Catholicism and American Freedom*, 207–208.

86   Susanna De Stradis, "Not Quite Silenced: Understanding the Censoring of John Courtney Murray," *Commonweal* (December 9, 2021); Donald E. Pelotte, *John Courtney Murray: Theologian in Conflict* (New York 1976), 53; Walter J. Burghardt, "A Half Century of *Theological Studies*: Retrospect and Prospect," *Theological Studies* 50 (Dec. 1989): 772.

87   Entry of Mar. 4, 1962, in Henri de Lubac, *Vatican Council Notebooks*, trans. Andrew Stefanelli and Anne Englund Nash (San Francisco 2015), 1: 101.

88   John C. Ford, S.J., "The Morality of Obliteration Bombing," *Theological Studies* 5 (1944): 261–309; G. E. M. Anscombe, *Mr. Truman's Degree* (Oxford 1958), 2.

89   Rachel M. Johnson-White, "A New Primacy of Conscience? Conscientious Objection, French Catholicism and the State During the Algerian War," *Journal of Contemporary History* 54 (2019): 130.

90   McGreevy, *Catholicism and American Freedom*, 256; Ruff, *The Battle for the Catholic Past in Germany*, 130.

91   Joseph Ratzinger, *Milestones: Memoirs 1927–1977*, trans. Erasmo Leiva-Mierikakis (San Francisco 1998), 98; Cardinal Joseph Ratzinger, "Newman Belongs to the Great Teach-

ers of the Church" [1990] in *Benedict XVI and Cardinal Newman*, ed. Peter Jennings (Oxford 2005), 33.

92   Bernard Häring, *The Law of Christ: Moral Theology for Priests and Laity* trans. Edwin G. Kaiser (Westminster MD, 1963), 1: 154, vii.

93   Peter Cajka, *Follow Your Conscience: The Catholic Church and the Spirit of the Sixties* (Chicago 2021), 149.

94   Ruff, *The Battle for the Catholic Past in Germany*, 99.

95   Ruff, *The Battle for the Catholic Past in Germany*, 152; Michael Hollerich, "Total War and Limited Government: The German Catholic Debate at the Dawn of the Nuclear Age," in *Theology and World Politics: Metaphysics, Genealogies, Political Theologies*, ed. Vassilios Paipais (Cham, Switzerland, 2020), 245.

96   John Courtney Murray, S.J., "Remarks on the Moral Problem of War," *Theological Studies* 20 (1959): 40, 58.

97   Ernst-Wolfgang Böckenförde, "The Ethos of Modern Democracy and the Catholic Church" [1957], in Böckenförde, *Religion, Law and Democracy: Selected Writings*, eds. Mirjam Künkler and Tine Stein (Oxford 2020), 75.

98   Ernst-Wolfgang Böckenförde, "German Catholicism in 1933: A Critical Examination" [1961], in Böckenförde, *Religion, Law and Democracy*, 93.

99   Böckenförde, "German Catholicism in 1933," [1961], 101, 104.

100   Biographical Interview with Ernst-Wolfgang Böckenförde [2011] in Böckenförde, *Law, Religion and Democracy*, 375; Gordon Zahn to Böckenförde, Feb. 18, 1962, in Bundesarchiv Koblenz, Nachlass Böckenförde, #575. I am grateful to Professor Mark Ruff for providing me with a copy of this letter.

101   L.J. Lebret and Theodore Suavet, *An Examination of Conscience for Modern Catholics*, trans. Bernard J. Gilligan (New York 1961), 143.

102   Henri de Lubac recalled hearing this rumor five years later. Entry of Sept. 23, 1965, in de Lubac, *Vatican Council Notebooks*, 2: 369.

103   Claire Huchet Bishop, *How Catholics Look at Jews: Inquiries into Italian, Spanish and French Teaching Materials* (New York 1974), 11–31.

104   Jared Wicks, S.J., *Investigating Vatican II: Its Theologians, Ecumenical Turn, and Biblical Commitment* (Washington 2018), 19.

105   Lawrence Elliott, *I Will Be Called John: A Biography of John XXIII* (New York 1973), 92.

106   Peter Hoffmann, "Roncalli in the Second World War: Peace Initiatives, the Greek Famine and the Persecution of the Jews," *Journal of Ecclesiastical History* 40 (1989): 90.

107   Mary Ann Glendon, *A World Made New: Eleanor Roosevelt and the Universal Declaration of Human Rights* (New York 2001), 132.

108   Étienne Fouilloux, "Le Nonce Roncalli et L'Eglise De France (1944–1953)," in *La Papauté Contemporaine*, 535.

109   Entry for Oct. 19, 1965, Yves Congar, *My Journal of the Council* (Collegeville, MN, 2012), 816; Yves Congar, O.P., "Preface to the Second Edition" [1967], in Yves Congar, *True and False Reform in the Church*, trans. Paul Philibert (Collegeville [1950] 2011), 2.

ELEVEN: VATICAN II

1   Robert A. Ventresca, *Soldier of Christ: the Life of Pope Pius XII* (Cambridge MA 2013), 295–303.

2   Stephen M. Koeth CSC, "The Suburban Church: Catholic Parishes and Politics in Metropolitan New York, 1945–1985," (Columbia University, PhD, 2019); Sven Sterken and Eva Weyns, "Introduction: Faith and Its Territories," in *Territories of Faith: Religion, Urban Planning and Demographic Change in Post-War Europe*, eds. Sven Sterken and Eva Weyns (Leuven 2022), 10, 23.

3   Henri de Lubac, "Foreword," in *Letters of Etienne Gilson to Henri de Lubac* (San Francisco 1996), 11.

4 Joseph M. Becker, S.J., *The Re-Formed Jesuits: A History of Changes in Jesuit Formation during the Decade 1965–1975* (San Francisco 1992), I: 290.

5 Patrick H. Byrne, "Meaning, Concreteness, and Subjectivity: American Phenomenology, Catholic Philosophy, and Lonergan from an Institutional Perspective," in *The Catholic Reception of Continental Philosophy in North America*, eds. Gregory P. Floyd and Stephanie Rumpza (Toronto 2020), 114–115.

6 Darra D. Mulderry, "Educating 'Sister Lucy': The Experiential Sources of the Movement to Improve Higher Education for Catholic Teaching Sisters, 1949–1964," *U.S. Catholic Historian* 33 (2015): 55–79; Regina Illemann, *Katholische Frauenbewegung In Deutschland 1945–1962: Politik, Geschlecht und Religiosität im Katholischen Deutschen Frauenbund* (Paderborn 2016), 135–145.

7 Andrew Greeley, *The American Catholic: A Social Portrait* (New York 1977), 43–47, 53–67; David P. Conradt, "Changing German Political Culture," in *The Civic Culture Revisited: An Analytic Study*, ed. Gabriel A. Almond and Sidney Verba (Boston 1980), 261–262.

8 John T. McGreevy, *Catholicism and American Freedom: A History* (New York 2003), 220.

9 *The Pope Speaks* 5 (1958–1959): 398–401.

10 Etienne Fouilloux, "The Antepreparatory Phase: The Slow Emergence from Inertia (January 1959–October 1962)," in *History of Vatican II*, eds. Giuseppe Alberigo and Joseph A. Komonchak (Maryknoll, NY, 1995–2006), 1: 94.

11 Foullioux, "The Antepreparatory Phase," 1: 143.

12 Guiseppe De Luca to Giovanni Montini, Aug. 6, 1959, in De Luca, *Carteggio 1930– 1962*, ed. P. Vian (Brescia 1992), 232.

13 Philippe Chenaux, "Pie XI et Le Communisme, (1930–1939): D'Après Les Archives Du Vatican," in *La Papauté Contemporaine, XIX–XX siècle*, eds. Jean-Pierre Delville and Marko Jačov (Vatican City 2009), 475–476; Xavier Rynne, *Vatican Council II* (New York 1968), 41.

14 Alfredo Ottaviani, *Duties of the Catholic State in Regard to Religion* (Kansas City 1953).

15 Entry of Sept. 12, 1961, in Henri de Lubac, *Vatican Council Notebooks*, trans. Andrew Stefanelli and Anne Englund Nash (San Francisco 2015), 1: 75.

16 Entry of Sept. 19–20,1961, in de Lubac, *Vatican Council Notebooks*, 1: 77.

17 Entry of Mar. 11, 1962, in Yves Congar *My Journal of the Council*, trans. Mary John Ronayne, OP, and Mary Cecily Boulding, OP (Collegeville 2012), 143.

18 Entry of Sept. 22, 1961, in Congar, *My Journal of the Council*, 54.

19 Entry of July 1960 in Congar, *My Journal of the Council*, 4.

20 Joseph P. Chinnici, *American Catholicism Transformed: From the Cold War through the Council* (New York 2021), 116.

21 Joseph Ratzinger, "The World and the Church: A Contrast between Vatican I and Vatican II" [1961], in Jared Wicks, "Six Texts by Prof. Joseph Ratzinger as Peritus before and during Vatican Council II," *Gregorianum* 89 (2008): 254–261.

22 Klaus Wittstadt, "On the Eve of the Second Vatican Council (July 1–October 10, 1962)," *History of Vatican II*, 1: 423–424.

23 John XXIII radio message of Sept. 11, 1962, *Council Daybook Vatican II. Session I, Oct. 11 to Dec. 8, 1962*, ed. F. Anderson (Washington 1964), 19–20.

24 Peter Hebblethwaite, *Pope John XXIII: Shepherd of the Modern World* (Garden City 1985), 425–426.

25 Ian Linden, *Global Catholicism: Diversity and Change since Vatican II* (New York 2009), 287.

26 Andrea Riccardi, "The Tumultuous Opening Days of the Council," in *History of Vatican II* 2: 2.

27 Message to Humanity, Oct. 20, 1962, in *The Documents of Vatican II*, ed. Walter Abbott (New York 1966), 6.

28 Jared Wicks, S.J., "Pieter Smulders and *Dei Verbum*: De Fontibus Revelationis during Vatican II's First Period, 1962," *Gregorianum* 82 (2001): 560–566.

29   Joseph Ratzinger, "Evaluation of the First Draft Texts for Vatican II" [Sept. 1962], in Wicks, "Six Texts by Joseph Ratzinger," 265.

30   Massimo Faggioli, "The Preconciliar Liturgical Movements in the United States and the Liturgical Reform of Vatican II," in *La Théologie Catholique Entre Intransigeance Et Renouveau: La Réception Des Mouvements Préconciliaires A Vatican II*, eds. Gilles Routhier, Philippe J. Roy-Lysencourt, and Karim Schelkens (Leuven 2011), 69–71; Rodrigo Caldeira, "Le Conservatisme Catholique au Brésil," in *La Théologie Catholique Entre Intransigeance Et Renouveau*, 314–351.

31   William Callahan, *The Catholic Church in Spain, 1875–1998* (Washington 2000), 95.

32   Mathijs Lamberigts, "The Liturgical Movement in Germany and the Low Countries," in *La Théologie Catholique Entre Intransigeance Et Renouveau*, 118–119.

33   Interview with Wilhelm Van Bekkum, S.V.D., in Vincent A. Yzermans, *A New Pentecost: Vatican Council II: Session 1* (Westminster, MD, 1963), 268–272.

34   Elizabeth A. Foster, *African Catholic: Decolonization and the Transformation of the Church* (Cambridge MA 2019), 141.

35   Mark Massa, S.J., *The American Catholic Revolution: How the Sixties Changed the Church Forever* (New York 2010), 91.

36   J. Masson, S.J., "L'Église ouverte sur le monde," *Nouvelle Revue Théologique* 84 (1962): 1032–1043.

37   Mathijs Lamberigts, "The Liturgy Debate," in *History of Vatican II*, 2: 117–149.

38   Massa, *The American Catholic Revolution*, ix.

39   *Sacrosanctum Concilium* (1963), §123.

40   William Middleton, *Double Vision: The Unerring Eye of Art World Avatars Dominique and John de Menil* (New York 2018), 185.

41   Giuseppe Ruggieri, "The First Doctrinal Clash" in *History of Vatican II*, 2: 238.

42   Ruggieri, "The First Doctrinal Clash," in *History of Vatican II*, 2: 246, 249.

43   Entry of Nov. 28, 1962, in Congar, *My Journal of the Council*, 268.

44   Brendan J. Cahill, *The Renewal of Revelation Theology (1960–1962): The Development and Responses to the Fourth Chapter of the Preparatory Schema De Deposito Fidei* (Rome 1999), 137.

45   Giuseppe Alberigo, "The Conciliar Experience 'Learning on Their Own,'" in *History of Vatican II*, 2: 575–576.

46   Chinnici, *American Catholicism Transformed*, 163.

47   *Mater et Magistra* (1961), §§49, 69, 176.

48   Sol Serrano and Luz María Dîaz de Valdés, "Catholic Mobilization and Chilean Revolutions, 1957–1989," in *Catholics in the Vatican II Era: Local Histories of a Global Event*, eds. Kathleen Sprows Cummings, Timothy Matovina, and Robert A. Orsi (New York 2018), 163.

49   Foster, *African Catholic*, 90.

50   Léopold Senghor, "Postface: Des prêtres noirs s'interrogent et suggèrent," in *Personnalité africaine et catholicisme* (Paris 1963) 283–293.

51   John XXIII radio message of Sept. 11, 1962, *Council Daybook Vatican II*, 19–20.

52   Denis Pelletier, "Une marginalité engagée: le groupe Jésus, L'Eglise et les Pauvres," in *Les Commissions Conciliaires De Vatican II*, eds. M. Lamberigts, C. Soetens, and J. Grootaers (Leuven 1996), 63–89.

53   McGreevy, *Catholicism and American Freedom*, 239.

54   Chris Dols and Maarten van den Bos, "Humanae Vitae: Catholic Attitudes to Birth Control in the Netherlands and Transnational Church Politics, 1945–1975" in *The Schism of '68: Catholicism, Contraception and Humanae Vitae in Europe, 1945–1975*, ed. Alana Harris (New York 2018), 33; Market Derks, "Debating the Council on the Air: Media, Personality, and the Transformation of the Dutch Church," in *Catholics in the Vatican II Era*, 211; Robert McClory, *Turning Point: The Inside Story of the Papal Birth Control Commission, and how Humanae Vitae Changed the Life of Patty Crowley and the Future of the Church* (New York 1995), 46.

55   Joseph A. Komonchak, "The Struggle for the Council during the Preparation of Vatican II (1960–1962)," in *History of Vatican II*, 1: 253.

56   Entry of Mar. 9, 1962, in de Lubac, *Vatican Council Notebooks*, 1: 112.

57   Paul VI, "Pius XII and the Jews," *The Tablet* (June 29, 1963), 714.

58   Adriano Ciani, "The Vatican, American Catholics and the Struggle for Palestine, 1917–1958: A Study of Postwar Roman Catholic Transnationalism" (University of Western Ontario, PhD 2011), 141–208.

59   John Connelly, *From Enemy to Brother: The Revolution in Catholic Teaching on the Jews, 1933–1965* (Cambridge MA 2012), 249.

60   Edward K. Kaplan, *Abraham Joshua Heschel: Mind, Heart, Soul* (Lincoln 2019), 253–292.

61   Gerald P. Fogarty, "Vatican II and the Cold War," in *Vatican II: Behind the Iron Curtain*, ed. Piotr H. Kosicki (Washington 2016*)*, 27.

62   András Fejérdy, *Pressed by a Double Loyalty: Hungarian Attendance at the Second Vatican Council, 1959–1965* (Budapest 2016), 59, 182–186; Árpád von Klimó, "Vatican II and Hungary," in *Vatican II: Behind the Iron Curtain*, 56; James Ramon Felak, "Vatican II and Czechoslovakia," in *Vatican II: Behind the Iron Curtain*, 103–104.

63   Brian Porter-Szücs, *Faith and Fatherland: Catholicism, Modernity, and Poland* (New York 2011), 112.

64   Andrew Preston, *Sword of the Spirit, Shield of Faith: Religion in American War and Diplomacy* (New York 2012), 513.

65   *Pacem in Terris* (1963), §112.

66   Address at Centennial Celebration of Boston College, Apr. 20, 1963, online archives of the John F. Kennedy presidential library, digital item JFKPOF-043-034.

67   Gérard Philips, "Deux tendances dans la théologie contemporaine: En marge du IIe Concile du Vatican," *Nouvelle Revue Théologique* 85 (1963): 225–238; Joseph Ratzinger, *Theological Highlights of Vatican II* (New York 1966), 148.

68   McGreevy, *Catholicism and American Freedom*, 237.

69   Connelly, *From Enemy to Brother*, 247.

70   John Courtney Murray, S.J., "The Problem of Religious Freedom," *Theological Studies* 25 (1964): 503–575.

71   Miccolli, "Two Sensitive Issues," in *History of Vatican II*, 4: 109, 111–115, 126.

72   John Connelly, "The Church and the Mission to the Jews," in *After Vatican II: Trajectories and Hermeneutics*, eds. James Heft and John O'Malley (Grand Rapids 2012), 108.

73   Miccolli, "Two Sensitive Issues," in *History of Vatican II*, 4: 157, 159.

74   Norman Tanner, "The Church in the World (Ecclesia Ad Extra)," in *History of Vatican II*, 4: 290.

75   Curt Gentry, *J. Edgar Hoover: The Man and the Secrets* (New York 1991), 570–571.

76   John T. McGreevy, *Parish Boundaries: The Catholic Encounter with Race in the Twentieth-Century Urban North* (Chicago 1996), 152.

77   Tanner, "The Church in the World," in *History of Vatican II*, 4: 310.

78   McClory, *Turning Point*, 61.

79   Congar, *My Journal of the Council*, 426

80   *Lumen Gentium* (1964) explanatory note, section 4.

81   *Lumen Gentium* (1964), §8; *Unitatis Redintegratio* (1964), §1.

82   Luis Antonio Tagle, "The 'Black Week' of Vatican II," in *History of Vatican II*, 4: 402.

83   John W. O'Malley, *What Happened at Vatican II* (Cambridge MA 2008), 241.

84   Entry of Feb. 8, 1965, in Congar, *My Journal of the Council*, 721.

85   Benjamin Cowan, "The 'Beauty of Inequality' and the Mythos of the Medieval: Brazil and the Forging of Global Catholic Traditionalism," *Luso-Brazilian Review* 56 (2019): 105–129.

86   Ratzinger, *Theological Highlights of Vatican II*, 132.

87   Paul VI, Homily of Dec. 4, 1964, Bombay, at http://www.vatican.va.

88   John Ainslie, "English Liturgical Music since the Council," in *English Catholic Worship: Liturgical Renewal in England since 1900*, eds. J. D. Crighton, H. E. Winstone, and

J. R. Ainslie (London 1979), 103; T. M. Scruggs, "(Re) Indigenization?: Post-Vatican II Ritual and 'Folk Masses' in Nicaragua," *The World of Music* 47 (2005): 99–101.

89   Evangelista Vilanova, "The Intersession (1963–1964)," *History of Vatican II*, 3: 478.

90   Jennifer Scheper Hughes, "Traditionalist Catholicism and Liturgical Renewal in the Diocese of Cuernavaca, Mexico," in *Catholics in the Vatican II Era*, 64–65.

91   Evelyn Waugh to Archbishop Heenan, Jan. 3, 1965, in *A Bitter Trial: Evelyn Waugh and John Carmel Cardinal Heenan on the Liturgical Changes*, ed. Dom Alcuin Reid (San Francisco 2011), 71.

92   Archbishop Heenan to Evelyn Waugh, Jan. 17, 1965, *A Bitter Trial*, 72.

93   Uchenna Aba, *The Reception of the Second Vatican Council's Liturgical Reforms in Nigeria (Nsukka Diocese)* (Zurich 2016), 89.

94   Robert P. Smith, Jr., "Black Like That: Paulette Nardal and the Negritude Salon," *CLA Journal* 45 (2001): 66; Vilanova, "The Intersession," 482.

95   Joseph A. Komonchak, "The Redaction and Reception of *Gaudium et Spes*: Tensions within the Majority at Vatican II," 7, at https://jakomonchak.files.wordpress.com.

96   Joseph Ratzinger, "Proposed Revision of the Church in the Modern World, October 17, 1965," in Wicks, "Six Texts by Prof. Joseph Ratzinger," 291–293.

97   Entry of Sept. 16, 1965, in Congar, *My Journal of the Council*, 779.

98   Jean Gartlan, *Barbara Ward: Her Life and Letters* (London 2010), 132.

99   Karl Rahner, "Theological Investigations on the Concept of 'Witness'" [1972], in Rahner, *Theological Investigations* XIII (New York 1975), 152–168.

100   James Edward Miller, "Ambivalent about America: Giorgio La Pira and the Catholic Left in Italy from NATO Ratification to the Vietnam War," in *The United States and the European Alliance Since 1945*, eds. Kathleen Burk and Melvyn Stokes (Oxford 1999), 127–150.

101   Komonchak, "The Redaction and Reception of *Gaudium et Spes*," 15.

102   McGreevy, *Catholicism and American Freedom*, 244; Leslie Woodcock Tentler, *Catholics and Contraception: An American History* (Ithaca 2004), 247–261.

103   Giovanni Turbanti, *Un Concilio Per Il Mondo Moderno: La redazione della costituzione pastorale 'Gaudium et Spes' del Vaticano II* (Bologna 1998), 744–749.

104   Peter Hünermann, "The Final Weeks of the Council," *History of Vatican II*, 5: 475.

105   Jill Blee, *From the Murray to the Sea: The History of Catholic Education in the Ballarat Diocese* (Ballarat 2004), 148.

106   O'Malley, *What Happened at Vatican II*, 43–52.

107   Karl Rahner, S.J., "Towards a Fundamental Theological Interpretation of Vatican II," *Theological Studies* 40 (1979): 716–727.

108   Philippe Chenaux, *Paul VI et Maritain: Les rapports du 'Montinianisme' et du 'Maritainisme'* (Brescia 1994), 83–85, 111–114.

109   Luis Antonio G. Tagle, *Episcopal Collegiality and Vatican II: The Influence of Paul VI* (Manila 2004), 304.

110   Jacques Maritain, *The Peasant of the Garonne: An Old Layman Questions Himself about the Present Time* (New York 1968), 53–63.

111   Bernard Lonergan, "The Scope of Renewal" [1973], in *Collected Works of Bernard Lonergan: Philosophical and Theological Papers 1965–1980*, eds. Robert C. Corken and Robert M. Doran (Toronto 2004), 282–286.

112   Mary Douglas, "The Lele of the Congo," in *The Church and the Nations: A Study of Minority Catholicism*, ed. Adrian Hastings (London 1959), 73–89.

113   Mary Douglas, "The Contempt of Ritual I," *New Blackfriars* 49 (1968): 475–482.

TWELVE: LIBERATION

1   Margaret Todaro Williams, "Integralism and the Brazilian Catholic Church," *Hispanic American Historical Review* 54 (1974): 444.

2   Erika Helgen, *Religious Conflict in Brazil: Protestants, Catholics, and the Rise of Religious Pluralism in the Early Twentieth Century* (New Haven 2020), 249–250.

3   Dom Hélder Câmara, *The Conversations of a Bishop* (New York 1979), 151–512.

4 Scott Mainwaring, *The Catholic Church and Politics in Brazil, 1916–1985* (Stanford 1986), 40.

5 Gianni La Bella, "Paolo VI e L'America Latina," *Revue d'Histoire Ecclésiastique* 113 (2018): 789.

6 Entry of Oct. 21, 1962, in Yves Congar, O.P., *My Journal of the Council*, trans. Mary John Ronayne, O.P., and Mary Cecil Boulding, O.P. (Collegeville, MN, 2012), 87.

7 Letter of Nov. 24–25, 1963, in Dom Hélder Câmara, *Lettres conciliaires 1962–1965*, trans. José de Broucker (Paris 2007), 1: 372–375; Letter of Oct. 26–27, 1965, in *Lettres conciliaires 1962–1965*, 2: 964–965.

8 Entry of 21 Oct. 1962 in Congar, *My Journal of the Council*, 109.

9 Richard Marin, *Dom Hélder Câmara, Les Puissants et Les Pauvres: Pour une histoire de l'Eglise des pauvres dans le Nordeste brésilien (1955–1985)* (Paris 1995), 77–103.

10 Richard Gribble, CSC, "Anti-communism, Patrick Peyton, CSC and the CIA," *Journal of Church and State* 45 (2003): 549–558; Robert M. Levine, *The History of Brazil* (New York 1999), 126.

11 Dom Hélder Introduces Himself to the People of Olinda and Recife [1964], in *Dom Hélder Câmara: Essential Writings*, ed. Francis McDonagh (New York 2009), 42–43.

12 Church of the Catacombs statement [1965], in Maria Clara Bingemer, *Latin American Theology: Roots and Branches* (Maryknoll, NY, 2016), 51–53.

13 Mainwaring, *The Catholic Church and Politics in Brazil*, 96–97.

14 Richard Marin, "Les Églises et le pouvoir dans le Brésil des militaires (1964–1985), *Vingtième Siècle* 105 (2010): 131.

15 Chris Dols and Benjamin Ziemann, "Progressive Participation and Transnational Activism in the Catholic Church after Vatican II: The Dutch and West German Examples," *Journal of Contemporary History* 50 (2015): 481.

16 Kenneth P. Serbin, *Secret Dialogues: Church-State Relations, Torture, and Social Justice in Authoritarian Brazil* (Pittsburgh 2000), 27.

17 Joseph A. Page, "The Little Priest Who Stands Up to Brazil's Generals," *New York Times Magazine*, May 23, 1971, 26.

18 Dom Hélder Câmara opening address, Dec. 8, 1973, Rothko Chapel files, box 3 file 6, MFA.

19 Barbara Ward to Joseph Gremillion Nov. 21, 1966, in folder 1, box 11, Joseph Gremillion papers, Archives of the University of Notre Dame; allocution of Msgr. Rhodain, president of Caritas International, Oct. 23, 1966, in Rome, Sec. Oct.–Nov. 1966 file, box 11, Joseph Gremillion.

20 John T. McGreevy, "Catholics, Catholicism and the Humanities since World War II," in *The Humanities and the Dynamics of Inclusion since World War II*, ed. David A. Hollinger (Baltimore 2006), 190–191.

21 Noah Benezra Strote, *Lions and Lambs: Conflict in Weimar and the Creation of Post-Nazi Germany* (New Haven 2017), 195.

22 Juan Gabriel Valdés, *Pinochet's Economists: The Chicago School of Economics in Chile* (Cambridge 1995), 25.

23 *Populorum Progressio* (1967), §14.

24 *Octogesima Adveniens* (1971), §21.

25 Ian Linden, *Global Catholicism: Diversity and Change Since Vatican II* (New York 2009), 107.

26 Fabien Kange-Ewane, "Alioune Diop à travers son commentaire de l'encyclique «Progressio Populorum» (Rome, 1968): Le développement solidaire de l'humanité," *Présence Africaine* 125 (1983): 310–325.

27 Jacopo Cellini, *Universalism and Liberation: Italian Catholic Culture and the Idea of International Community, 1963–1978* (Leuven 2017), 121.

28 La Bella, "Paolo VI e L'America Latina," 800; Dominican Bishops' Statement [1967], in *The Dominican Republic Reader: History, Culture, Politics*, eds. Eric Paul Roorda, Lauren Derby, and Raymundo González (Durham 2014), 398–402.

29 Valdés, *Pinochet's Economists*, 205–206.

30 Lucia Ceci, *La Teologia della Liberazione in America Latina: l'Opera di Gustavo Gutiérrez* (Milan 1999), 101–102.

31 "Human Promotion" [1968], in *The Church in the Present Day Transformation of Latin America in the Light of the Council* (Bogotá 1970), II: 57, 58, 65.

32 Gustavo Gutiérrez, "The Church and the Poor: A Latin American Perspective," in *The Reception of Vatican II*, eds. Giuseppe Alberigo, Jean-Pierre Joshua, and Joseph A. Komonchak (Washington 1987), 184.

33 Gustavo Gutiérrez, "Notes for a Theology of Liberation," *Theological Studies* 31 (1970): 243–261.

34 Kirsten Weld, "The Other Door: Spain and the Guatemalan Counter-Revolution, 1944–1954," *Journal of Latin American Studies* 51 (2019): 359; Leonardo Boff, *Jesus Christ Liberator* (Maryknoll, NY, 1978), 44.

35 Christian Smith, *The Emergence of Liberation Theology: Radical Religion and Social Movement Theory* (Chicago 1991), 178.

36 Olivier Chatelain, "Michel Quoist, François Houtart: Deux Itinéraires Entre Sociologie Religieuse et Désire d'Amérique Latine (Années 1950–1960)," *Revue d'Histoire Ecclésiastique* 112 (2017): 215–238; Caroline Sappia, "Un Institut des hautes etudes doctrinales pour l'Amérique latine a Louvain?" in *Mission et engagement politique après 1945: Afrique, Amérique latine, Europe*, eds. Caroline Sappia and Olivier Servais (Paris 2010), 51–70.

37 Robert Calderisi, *Earthly Mission: The Catholic Church and World Development* (New Haven 2013), 86–87.

38 Jan Hoffman French, "A Tale of Two Priests and Two Struggles: Liberation Theology from Dictatorship to Democracy in the Brazilian Northeast," *The Americas* 63 (2007): 409–443; Guillermo Trejo, "Religious Competition and Ethnic Mobilization in Latin America: Why the Catholic Church Promotes Indigenous Movements in Mexico," *American Political Science Review* 103 (2009): 323–342; Juan Manuel Lombera, "The Church of the Poor and Civil Society in Southern Mexico: Oaxaca, 1960s–2010s," *Journal of Contemporary History* 54 (2019): 646–647.

39 Fred Burill and Catherine C. LeGrand, "Progressive Catholicism at Home and Abroad," in *Within and Without the Nation: Canadian History as Transnational History*, eds. Karen Dubinsky, Adele Perry, and Henry Yu (Toronto 2015), 311–340.

40 William J. Callahan, *The Catholic Church in Spain, 1875–1998* (Washington 2000), 517, 632–633.

41 Gerd-Rainier Horn, *The Spirit of Vatican II: Western European Progressive Catholicism in the Long Sixties* (Oxford 2015), 55.

42 Dagmar Herzog, "The Death of God in West Germany: Between Secularization, Post Fascism, and the Rise of Liberation Theology," in *Die Gegenwart Gottes in der modernen Gesellschaft: Transzendenz und Religiöse Vergemeinschaftung in Deutschland*, eds. Michael Geyer and Lucian Hölscher (Göttingen 2006), 449.

43 Rev. Edgar Beltran Position Paper, Inter-American Bishops Meeting, Caracas, June 3–5, 1969, box 13, folder 16, Cardinal John Dearden papers, Archives of the University of Notre Dame; Memo from Bishop Joseph L. Bernardin, Jan. 19, 1970, box 13, folder 18, Cardinal John Dearden papers; Minutes of Inter-American Bishops Meeting, June 3–5, 1969, Caracas, box 13, folder 15, Dearden papers.

44 Entry of Sept. 1, 1964, in Henri de Lubac, *Vatican Council Notebooks*, trans. Andrew Stefanelli and Anne Englund Nash (San Francisco 2015), 102–103.

45 Memorandum from Ernan McMullen, June 1966, in Joseph Evans file, Maritain collection, BNS.

46 Jay P. Corrin, *Catholic Progressives in England after Vatican II* (Notre Dame 2013), 346–352.

47 Horn, *The Spirit of Vatican II*, 115–125.

48 Colin M. Snider, "Catholic Campuses, Secularizing Struggles: Student Activism and

Catholic Universities in Brazil, 1950–1968," in *Local Church, Global Church: Catholic Activism in Latin America from Rerum Novarum to Vatican II*, eds. Stephen J. C. Andes and Julia G. Young (Washington 2016, 205–206; Jaime M. Pensado, "A 'Third Way' in Christ: The Project of the Corporation of Mexican Students (CEM) in Cold War Mexico," in *Local Church, Global Church*, 165–84.

49   Roy Domenico, *The Devil and the Dolce Vita: Catholic Attempts to Save Italy's Soul, 1948–1974* (Washington 2021), 336.

50   David I. Kertzer, *Comrades and Christians: Religion and Political Struggle in Communist Italy* (Cambridge 1980), 109–110.

51   Sol Serrano and Luz María Díaz de Valdés, "Catholic Mobilization and Chilean Revolutions, 1957–1989," in *Catholics and the Vatican II Era: Local Histories of a Global Event*, eds. Kathleen Sprows Cummings, Timothy Matovina, and Robert A. Orsi (New York 2018), 170.

52   Conversation of March 5, 1971, *Foreign Relations of the United States 1969–1976*, Vol. E–10, Documents on American Republics, 1969–1972.

53   Horn, *The Spirit of Vatican II*, 181.

54   Horn, *The Spirit of Vatican II*, 196–200; Alberto Savorana, *The Life of Luigi Giussani*, trans. Mariangela C. Sullivan and Christopher Bacich (Montreal 2018), 399.

55   Telegram from the Embassy in Italy to the Department of State, December 29, 1965, in *Foreign Relations in the United States, 1964–1968*, Volume III, Vietnam, June–December 1965.

56   Thomas J. Shelley, "Slouching toward the Center: Cardinal Francis Spellman, Archbishop Paul J. Hallinan and American Catholicism in the 1960s," *U.S. Catholic Historian* 17 (1999): 41.

57   Sabine Rousseau, *La Colombe et le napalm: Des chrétiens français contre les guerres d'Indochine et du Vietnam 1945–1975* (Paris 2002), 170.

58   Alessandro Santagata, "Les catholiques italiens et La Guerre Du Vietnam (1965–1968)," *Revue d'Histoire Ecclésiastique* 110 (2015): 213–232; Pauline O'Regan, *A Changing Order* (Wellington 1986), 98–99.

59   Patricia McNeal, *Harder Than War: Catholic Peacemaking in Twentieth-Century America* (New Brunswick 1992), 167.

60   Giuseppe Battelli, "I vescovi e la dialettica pace-guerra. Giacomo Lercaro (1947–1968)," *Studi Storici* (2004): 367–414.

61   James Carroll, *An American Requiem: God, My Father, and the War That Came Between Us* (Boston 1996), 200.

62   Luxmoore and Babiuch, *The Vatican and the Red Flag*, 141.

63   James Ramon Felak, "Vatican II and Czechoslovakia," in *Vatican II: Behind the Iron Curtain*, ed. Piotr Kosicki (Washington 2016), 107–108.

64   Horn, *The Spirit of Vatican II*, 151–163.

65   *Europe's 1968: Voices of Revolt*, eds. Robert Gildea, James Mark, and Anette Warring (New York 2013), 218, 230 .

66   *Ecclesiam Suam* (1964), §102.

67   John M. Kirk, *Between God and the Party: Religion and Politics in Revolutionary Cuba* (Tampa 1989), 118–119.

68   Luxmoore and Babiuch, *The Vatican and the Red Flag*, 136.

69   Sabrina Petra Ramet, "The Catholic Church in Czechoslovakia, 1948–1991," *Studies in Comparative Communism* 24 (1991): 380; Tomáš Halík, *From the Underground Church to Freedom*, trans. Gerald Turner (Notre Dame 2019), 97.

70   Brian Stanley, *Christianity in the Twentieth Century: A World History* (Princeton 2018), 53.

71   Henrietta Harrison, *The Missionary's Curse and Other Tales from a Chinese Catholic Village* (Berkeley 2013), 164–165.

72   Alasdair C. Macintyre, *After Virtue: A Study in Moral Theory* (Notre Dame 1984), 69.

73   Juan Luis Segundo, "Human Rights, Evangelization, and Ideology," in Juan Luis Segundo, *Signs of the Times: Theological Reflections* (Maryknoll, NY, 1993), 66.

74 Brian Porter-Szücs, *Faith and Fatherland: Catholicism, Modernity, and Poland* (New York 2011), 149–150.

75 Marco Lavopa, "L'Ostpolitik vaticana di Mons. Agostino Casaroli et lo 'spirito di Helsinki' (1963–1975)," *Democrazia e Diritto* 1–2 (2013): 510–518; Giovanni Barberini, *Ostpolitik della Santa Sede: un dialogo lungo e faticoso* (Bologna 2007), 370–371.

76 Jonathan Luxmoore and Jolanta Babiuch, "In Search of Faith, Part 2: Charter 77 and the Return to Spiritual Values in the Czech Republic," *Religion, State and Society* 23 (1995): 295.

77 Michael Gubser, *The Far Reaches: Phenomenology, Ethics and Social Renewal in Central Europe* (Stanford 2014), 151–187.

78 John M. Kramer, "The Vatican's 'Ostpolitik,'" *Review of Politics* 42 (1980): 297.

79 Piotr H. Kosicki, "Vatican II and Poland," in *Vatican II: Behind the Iron Curtain*, 174–179; Tadeusz Mazowieki, "Les chrétiens et les droits d' l'homme," in *Nous, chrétiens de Pologne*, ed. Jean Offredo (Paris 1979), 159–167.

80 Adam Michnik, "What Is Dialogue?" in *The Church and the Left*, ed. David Ost (Chicago 1993), 182.

81 Adam Michnik, "Anti-Authoritarian Revolt: A Conversation with Daniel Cohn-Bendit," in *Letters from Freedom: Post-Cold War Realities and Perspectives*, ed. Irena Grudzińska Gross (Berkeley 1998), 50.

82 Rene Harder Horst, "The Catholic Church, Human Rights Advocacy, and Indigenous Resistance in Paraguay, 1969–1989," *Catholic Historical Review* 88 (2002): 723–744; Patrick William Kelly, *Sovereign Emergencies: Latin America and the Making of Global Human Rights Politics* (Cambridge 2018), 40–45.

83 Samuel Moyn, *The Last Utopia: Human Rights in History* (Cambridge MA 2010), 145.

84 Samuel P. Huntington, "Democracy's Third Wave," *Journal of Democracy* 2 (1991): 12–34.

THIRTEEN: Exodus

1 Christopher Scott Temple, "Fostering Elite Science at an American Catholic University: The Rise of a Research Culture at the University of Notre Dame, 1842–1967," (University of Notre Dame, PhD 2020), 479.

2 Peter Godman, "Graham Greene's Vatican Dossier," *Atlantic* 288 (2001): 84–88.

3 Jean Gartlan, *Barbara Ward: Her Life and Letters* (London 2010), 135; Ian Linden, *Global Catholicism: Diversity and Change Since Vatican II* (New York 2009), 293.

4 Barbara Ward to Msgr. Joseph Gremillion, Feb. 24, 1966, box 11, folder 6, Gremillion papers, Archives of the University of Notre Dame.

5 Philippe Denis, "Archbishop Hurley, the Principle of Overriding Right and the Post-Conciliar Debates on Contraception and Collegiality," *Revue D'Histoire Ecclésiastique* 113 (2018): 325.

6 John Courtney Murray, S.J., Memo to Cardinal Cushing on Contraception Legislation [1965], in *Bridging the Sacred and the Secular: Selected Writings of John Courtney Murray, S.J.*, ed. J. Leon Hooper, S.J. (Washington 1994), 82–84.

7 Leslie Woodcock Tentler, *Catholics and Contraception: An American History* (Ithaca 2004), 221–223.

8 Joseph P. Chinnici, *American Catholicism Transformed: From the Cold War Through the Council* (New York 2021), 271; John T. Noonan, Jr., *Contraception: A History of Its Treatment by the Catholic Theologians and Canonists* (Cambridge MA [1965] 1986), 532.

9 John T. McGreevy, *Catholicism and American Freedom: A History* (New York 2003), 240.

10 John Courtney Murray, S.J., "Appendix: Toledo Talk" [1967], in *Bridging the Sacred*, 335–336.

11 Benjamin A. Cowan, *Securing Sex: Morality and Repression in the Making of Cold War Brazil* (Chapel Hill 2016), 57.

12 Gilfredo Marengo, *La Nascita Di Un Enciclica: Humanae vitae alla luce degli Archivi Vaticani* (Rome 2018), 91.

13   Klaus Große Kracht, "'Elternrecht' und 'Ehenot': Familienbilder und Wertewandel im westdeutschen Katholizismus der 1950er und 1960er Jahre," in *Liebe und tu, was du willst? Die "Pillenzyklika" Humanae vitae von 1968 und ihre Folgen* (Paderborn 2021), 181; Declerck, "La réaction du cardinal Suenens et de l'épiscopat belge a l'encyclique *Humanae Vitae*," *Ephemerides Theologicae Lovanienses* 84 (2008): 9.

14   Leon F. Bouvier and S. L. N. Rao, *Socioreligious Factors in Fertility Decline* (Cambridge 1975), 165; Immaculada Blasko and Mónica Moreno Seco, "Españolas En El Catolicismo International: La UMOFC, De La 'Personalidad De La Mujer' A La Demanda De 'Derechos Inalienables,'" in *Más Allá De Los NacionalCatolicismos: Redes Transnacionales de Los Catolicismos Hispánicos*, eds. José Ramón Rodríguez Lago and Natalia Núñez Bargueño (Madrid 2021), 415

15   *Humanae Vitae* (1968), §17; Cowan, *Securing Sex*, 67.

16   Martine Sevegrand, *L'Affaire Humanae vitae: L'Eglise catholique et la contraception* (Paris 2008), 158.

17   K. Erner and M. Mesner, "Attempted Disobedience: *Humanae Vitae* in West Germany and Austria," in *The Schism of '68: Catholicism, Contraception and Humanae Vitae in Europe, 1945–1975*, ed. Alana Harris (London 2018), 125.

18   Brian A. Porter-Szücs, *Faith and Fatherland: Catholicism, Modernity, and Poland* (New York 2011), 357.

19   Dom Hélder Câmara, *The Gospel with Dom Hélder Câmara*, trans. Alan Neame (London 1986), 21.

20   Piotr H. Kosicki, "The Catholic 1968: Poland, Social Justice and the Cold War," *Slavic Review* 77 (2018): 656.

21   Mark Seymour, *Debating Divorce in Italy: Marriage and the Making of Modern Italians, 1860–1974* (New York 2006), 199.

22   Anna Grzymała-Busse, *Nations under God: How Churches Use Moral Authority to Influence Policy* (Princeton 2015), 310.

23   Mary E. Daly, *Sixties Ireland: Reshaping the Economy, State and Society, 1957–1973* (Cambridge 2016), 378.

24   William Lies, C.S.C., and Mary Fran T. Malone, "The Chilean Church: Declining Hegemony?" in *The Catholic Church and the Nation-State: Comparative Perspectives*, eds. Paul Christopher Manuel, Lawrence C. Reardon, and Clyde Wilcox (Washington 2006), 96.

25   *Lumen Gentium* (1964), §10.

26   Thomas C. Bruneau, *The Political Transformation of the Brazilian Catholic Church* (Cambridge 1974), 245–246.

27   Michael Gaine, "The State of the Priesthood," in *Modern Catholicism: Vatican II and After*, ed. Adrian Hastings (New York 1991), 246–248.

28   Philippe Denis, "Clergy Training," in *The Catholic Church in Contemporary South Africa*, eds. Joy Brain and Philippe Denis (Pietermaritzburg 1999), 137.

29   Anthony J. Blasi and Joseph F. Zimmermann, *Transitions from Vowed to Lay Ministry in American Catholicism* (Lewiston, ME, 2004), 6–7; Juan Antonio Cazorla-Sanchez, "A Different Path? National Catholicism, Laicization and Dechristianization in Spain, 1939–1975," in *The Sixties and Beyond: Dechristianization in North America and Western Europe, 1945–2000*, eds. Michael Gauvreau and Nancy Christie (Toronto 2013), 362–363; Bruneau, *The Political Transformation of the Brazilian Catholic Church*, 129.

30   Brian Conway, "Context of Trends in the Catholic Church's Male Workforce: Chile, Ireland and Poland Compared," *Social Science History* 40 (2016): 405–432.

31   Jose Oscar Beozzo, "Le Concile Vatican II (1962-1965): La Participation de la Conférence Épiscopale du Brésil-CNBB," *Cristianesimo nella Storia* 23 (2002): 192.

32   Horn, *The Spirit of Vatican II*, 87–88.

33 *Sacerdotalis Caelibatus* (1967), §1.

34 F. J. Laishley, "Celibacy," in *Modern Catholicism: Vatican II and After*, ed. Adrian Hastings (New York 1991), 237.

35 Betty Friedan, "A Visit with Pope Paul" [1974], in Friedan, *"It Changed My Life": Writings on the Women's Movement* (Cambridge MA 1998), 372.

36 Peter Hebblethwaite, *Paul VI: The First Modern Pope* (New York 1993), 641.

37 Karl Rahner, "Women and the Priesthood," trans. Edward Quinn, in Rahner, *Theological Investigations* XX (New York 1981), 45.

38 Philip J. Williams, *The Catholic Church and Politics in Nicaragua and Costa Rica* (Pittsburgh 1989), 27.

39 Donald T. Critchlow, *Phylllis Schlafly and Grassroots Conservatism: A Woman's Crusade* (Princeton 2005).

40 Thirty Second General Congregation, Decree Four in *Documents of the 31st and 32nd General Congregations of the Society of Jesus*, ed. John W. Padberg, S.J. (St. Louis 1977), 428.

41 John T. McGreevy, *Parish Boundaries: The Catholic Encounter with Race in the Twentieth-Century Urban North* (Chicago 1996), 219.

42 Carmen M. Mangion, "A New Internationalism: Endeavouring to 'Build from this Diversity, Unity', 1945–1990," *Journal of Contemporary History* 55 (2020): 579–601; Sr. Alix van de Molensoft, *It All Began with Three Beguines: History of Ten Thousand Sisters of Charity 1832–1964*, trans. Sr. Therese Mary Barnett (Preston 1992), 161, 182, 201.

43 Kevin J. Christiano, "The Trajectory of Catholicism in Twentieth Century Quebec: Institutional Religion and Elite Politics During an Era of Change," in *The Church Confronts Modernity: Catholicism since 1950 in the United States, Ireland and Quebec*, ed. Leslie Woodcock Tentler (Washington 2007), 28–29.

44 Daniel K. Williams, *Defenders of the Unborn: The Pro-Life Movement before Roe v. Wade* (New York 2016); McGreevy, *Catholicism and American Freedom*, 268–269.

45 Judith Blake, "Abortion and Public Opinion: The 1960–1970 Decade," *Science* 171 (Feb. 12, 1971), 544; Kristin Luker, *Abortion and the Politics of Motherhood* (Berkeley 2008), 194–197.

46 Stacie Taranto, *Kitchen Table Politics: Conservative Women and Family Values in New York* (Philadelphia 2017), 68–92, 129–161.

47 McGreevy, *Catholicism and American Freedom*, 260–261, 267–268.

48 Mary Ann Glendon, *Abortion and Divorce in Western Law: American Failures, European Challenges* (Cambridge MA 1987).

49 Merike Blofield, "Women's Choices in Comparative Perspective: Abortion Policies in Late-Developing Catholic Countries," *Comparative Politics* 40 (2008): 399–419.

50 Yves Congar, "Afterward, July 1968," in Congar, *True and False Reform in the Church*, trans. Paul Philibert (Collegeville, MN, [1968] 2011), 341.

51 Paul VI quoted in Alberto Savorana, *The Life of Luigi Giussani*, trans. Mariangela C. Sullivan and Christopher Bacich (Montreal 2018), 414.

52 Herzog, "The Death of God in West Germany," 432.

53 Callahan, *The Catholic Church in Spain*, 472.

54 Leslie Woodcock Tentler, "Souls and Bodies: The Birth Control Controversy and the Collapse of Confession," in *The Crisis of Authority in Catholic Modernity*, eds. Michael J. Lacey and Francis Oakley (New York 2011), 293–316.

55 Michael Gauvreau, *The Catholic Origins of Quebec's Quiet Revolution, 1931–1970* (Montreal 2005).

56 James Chappel, *Catholic Modern: The Challenge of Totalitarianism and the Remaking of the Church* (Cambridge MA 2018), 241–247.

57 John A. Coleman, *The Evolution of Dutch Catholicism, 1958–1974* (Berkeley 1978), 77, 144.

58   Yves Chiron, "Paul VI et le Peri-Concile," in *La Papauté Contemporaine, XIXe–XXe siècle*, ed. Jean-Pierre Delville and Marko Jačov (Vatican City 2009), 590.

59   Coleman, *The Evolution of Dutch Catholicism*, 131.

60   Matthew Fox, *The Pope's War: Why Ratzinger's Secret Crusade Has Imperiled the Church and How It Can be Saved* (New York 2010), xvii; Kristian Mennen and Marijn Molema, "The Role of Religion in the Dutch Boy Scout Movement (1911–1973)," *Review d'Histoire Ecclesiastique* 111 (2016): 630–657.

61   Thomáš Halík, *From the Underground Church to Freedom*, trans. Gerald Turner (Notre Dame 2019), 46–47.

62   Kevin Smyth, *A New Catechism: Catholic Faith for Adults* (New York 1973), 3, 402–403.

63   Coleman, *The Evolution of Dutch Catholicism*, 175, 154, 194.

64   Dols and van den Bos, "Humanae Vitae," 23–48.

65   Coleman, *The Evolution of Dutch Catholicism*, 209, 302.

66   Peter Van Rooden, "Secularization, Dechristianization and Rechristianization in the Netherlands," in *Säkularisierung, Dechristianisierung, Rechristianisierung im neuzeitlichen europa: Bilanz und Perspektiven der Forschung*, ed. Hartmut Lehmann (Göttingen 1997), 131–153.

67   All details on St. Jude's parish in this and subsequent paragraphs are from Colleen McDannell, *The Spirit of Vatican II: A History of Catholic Reform in America* (New York 2011), 151–206.

68   Archbishop Marcel Lefebvre, *Open Letter to Confused Catholics* (Kansas City 1986), 100–109.

69   Massimo Faggioli, *A Council for the Global Church: Receiving Vatican II in History* (Minneapolis 2015), 124.

70   Joseph Ratzinger, "Introductory Thoughts on the State of the Church," in Ratzinger and Hans Urs von Balthasar, *Two Say Why*, trans. John Griffiths (Chicago 1973), 67–75.

71   Selection from Joseph Ratzinger, "Der Christ und die Welt von heute" [1973], trans. David Kirchhoffer, in *The Ratzinger Reader: Mapping a Theological Journey*, eds. Lieven Boeve and Gerard Mannion (London 2010), 122.

72   *Evangelii Nuntiandi* (1975), §56.

73   Alberto Melloni, "Pochino: Un Esame Delle Fonti E Della Ricerca Su Paolo VI, La Chiese E I Cattolici Nella Vicenda Moro," in *La Papauté Contemporaine*, 610.

74   Aldo Moro to Eleanora Moro, Apr. 27–30, 1978, in Leonardo Sciascia, *The Moro Affair*, trans. Sacha Rabinovitch (New York 1987), 96.

75   Melloni, "Pochino," 633–634.

76   May 13 remarks at funeral, in *Paolo VI e La Tragedia Di Moro: 55 Giorni Di Ansie Tentative, Speranze E Assurda Crudeltà*, ed. Pasquale Macchi (Milan 1998), 51.

77   Ripensamento, May 17, 1978, in *Paolo VI e La Tragedia Di Moro*, 54.

78   Ivanir Antonio Rampon, *Paolo VI e Hélder Câmara: un'Amicizia Spirituale* (Padova 2016), 170.

79   Ann Mische, *Partisan Publics: Communication and Contention across Brazilian Youth Activist Networks* (Princeton 2008), 119; Andrew Dawson, "The Origins and Character of the Base Ecclesial Community: A Brazilian Perspective," in *A Cambridge Companion to Liberation Theology*, ed. Christopher C. Rowland (Cambridge 2007), 139–158.

80   Calderisi, *Earthly Mission*, 14.

81   Thomas C. Bruneau, "Obstacles to Change in the Church: Lessons from Four Brazilian Dioceses," *Journal of Interamerican Studies and World Affairs* 15 (1973): 395–414.

82   Address to Brazilian Bishops, July 10, 1980, in John Paul II, *Addresses and Homilies Given in Brazil* (Washington 1980), 2: 101.

83   Homily at Mass in Recife, July 7, 1980, in *Addresses and Homilies Given in Brazil*, 1: 93–105; Francis McDonagh, "Introduction," in *Dom Hélder Câmara: Essential Writings*, 34.

FOURTEEN: CHARISMA

1 Michael Gubser, *The Far Reaches: Phenomenology, Ethics, and Social Renewal in Central Europe* (Stanford 2014), 188–211.

2 Entry of Feb. 2, 1965, in Yves Congar, O.P., *My Journal of the Council*, trans. Mary John Ronayne, O.P., and Mary Cecil Boulding, O.P. (Collegeville, MN, 2012), 714.

3 Entry of Mar. 31, 1965, in Andrew Stefanelli and Henri de Lubac, *Vatican Council Notebooks*, trans. Anne Englund Nash (San Francisco 2015), 2: 321.

4 Peter Hebblethwaite, *Synod Extraordinary: The Inside Story of the Rome Synod November–December 1985* (New York 1986), 25.

5 "Gli Appunti Di Paolo Vi Durante Gli Esercizi Spirituali Dettati Dal Card. Wojtyła," ed. Angelo Maffeis, *Istituto Paolo VI Notiziario* 49 (2005): 66–75; Karol Wojtyła, *Sign of Contradiction* (New York 1979), 132–133.

6 Karol Wojtyła, *Love and Responsibility*, trans. Grzegorz Ignatik (Boston 2013), 213.

7 Agnieszka Kościańska, "Humanae Vitae, Birth Control and the Forgotten History of the Catholic Church in Poland," in *The Schism of '68: Catholicism, Contraception and Humanae Vitae in Europe, 1945–1975*, ed. Alana Harris (London 2018), 187–208; Gilfredo Marengo, *La Nascita Di Un Enciclica Humanae Vitae alla luce degli Archivi Vaticani* (Rome, 2018), 99–100.

8 Sylwia Kuźma-Markowska and Agata Ignaciuk, "Family Planning Advice in State-Socialist Poland, 1950s–1980s: Local and Transnational Exchanges," *Medical History* 64 (2020): 260, 265.

9 Karol Wojtyła to Henri de Lubac, Feb. 1968, in Henri de Lubac, *At the Service of the Church: Henry de Lubac Reflects on the Circumstances that Occasioned His Writings*, trans. Anne Elizabeth Englund (San Francisco 1993), 171–172.

10 Cardinal Karol Wojtyła, *The Acting Person*, trans. Andrzej Potocki (Dordrecht [1969] 1979), 284–285.

11 Jonathan Luxmoore and Jolanta Babiuch, *The Vatican and the Red Flag: The Struggle for the Soul of Eastern Europe* (New York 1999), 196.

12 Timothy Garton Ash, *The Polish Revolution: Solidarity*, 3rd ed. (New Haven 2002), 23.

13 Joseph Ratzinger, "Sources and Transmission of the Faith," trans. Thomas Langan, *Communio* 10 (1983): 18.

14 John Paul II, Victory Square Homily, June 2, 1979, at http://www.vatican.va.

15 Adam Michnik, "A Lesson in Dignity" [1979], in Michnik, *The Church and the Left*, ed. and trans. David Ost (Chicago 1993), 223–231.

16 Ash, *The Polish Revolution*, 80; Steinar Stjernø, *Solidarity in Europe: The History of an Idea* (Cambridge 2004), 62–75.

17 Ash, *The Polish Revolution*, 66, 322–323.

18 *Laborem Exercens* (1981), §8.

19 Ash, *The Polish Revolution*, 239.

20 José V. Casanova, "The Opus Dei Ethic, the Technocrats and the Modernization of Spain," *Social Science* 22 (1983): 27–50.

21 Bethany Moreton, "Our Lady of Mont Pelerin: The 'Navarra School' of Catholic Neoliberalism," *Capitalism* 2 (2021): 88–153.

22 Michael C. Novak, *The Spirit of Democratic Capitalism* (Lanham [1982] 1991), 248; Michael Novak and William E. Simon, "Liberty and Justice for All" [1986], https://www.crisismagazine.com/1986/special-report-liberty-and-justice-for-all.

23 Randy Boyagoda, *Richard John Neuhaus: A Life in the Public Square* (New York 2015), 303.

24 Mark Heirman, "Bishops' Conferences on War and Peace in 1983," *Cross Currents* 33 (Fall 1983): 275–288.

25 Mark Edward Ruff, "Ernst-Wolfgang Böckenförde and the Rapprochement of Catholicism and Socialism," *Oxford Journal of Law and Religion* 7 (2018): 13–14.

26   George F. Kennan, "The Bishops' Letter," *New York Times*, May 1, 1983, sec. 4, p. 21.

27   Michael C. Novak, *Moral Clarity in the Nuclear Age* (Nashville 1983), 58.

28   Jared McBrady, "The Challenge of Peace: Ronald Reagan, John Paul II, and the American Bishops," *Journal of Cold War Studies* 17 (2015): 129–152.

29   Timothy Garton Ash, *The Uses of Adversity: Essays on the Fate of Central Europe* (New York 1989), 47–60.

30   John Connelly, *From Peoples into Nations: A History of Eastern Europe* (Princeton 2020), 668–671.

31   Father Jerzy Popiełuszko, "I am Prepared for Anything" [1984], in Grażyna Sikorska, *Jerzy Popiełuszko: A Martyr for the Truth* (Grand Rapids 1985), xi; Sikorska, *Jerzy Popiełuszko*, 56.

32   Michnik, "Preface," in *The Church and the Left*, xvi.

33   George Weigel, *Witness to Hope: The Biography of Pope John Paul II* (New York 1999), 546.

34   Brian Stanley, *Christianity in the Twentieth Century: A World History* (Princeton 2018), 55.

35   Jeffrey Sachs, *Poland's Jump to the Market Economy* (Cambridge MA 1993), 25.

36   *Centesimus Annus* (1991), §34.

37   Boyagoda, *Richard John Neuhaus: A Life in the Public Square*, 296.

38   *Centesimus Annus* (1991), §§34, 41, 17.

39   Stephen Engelberg, "Pope Calls on Poland to Reject Western Europe's Secular Ways," *New York Times*, June 8, 1991.

40   Anna Grzymała-Busse and Dan Slater, "Making Godly Nations: Church-State Pathways in Poland and the Philippines," *Comparative Politics* 50 (2018), 545–564.

41   Denis Kim, S.I., "For You and for All: Stephen Cardinal Kim, Church and Civil Society in South Korea," *Gregorianum* 96 (2015): 351–354.

42   Robert L. Youngblood, *Marcos against the Church: Economic Development and Political Repression in the Philippines* (Ithaca 1990), 37, 173.

43   Report of the Philippine Hierarchy of the People of God in the Philippines on Their Deliberations at the Annual Bishops' Conference, in *Responses to the Signs of the Times: Selected Documents: Catholic Bishops' Conference of the Philippines*, ed. Abdon Ma C Jasol, C.S.S.R. (Quezon City 1991), 68.

44   Post Election Statement [1983] in *Responses to the Signs of the Times*, 268–271; Ian Linden, *Global Catholicism: Diversity and Change Since Vatican II* (New York 2009), 167–174.

45   Martín Obregón, *Entre La Cruz Y La Espada: La Iglesia católica durante los primeros años del "Proceso"* (Buenos Aires 2005), 86.

46   Brian Porter-Szücs, *Faith and Fatherland: Catholicism, Modernity, and Poland* (New York 2011), 151.

47   Address of John Paul II, Puebla, Mexico, Jan. 28, 1979, I.4, at http://www.vatican.va.

48   Philip J. Williams, *The Catholic Church and Politics in Nicaragua and Costa Rica* (Pittsburgh 1989), 24–25.

49   Theresa Keeley, *Reagan's Gun-Toting Nuns: The Catholic Conflict over Cold War Human Rights Policy in Central America* (Ithaca 2020), 49.

50   Tommie Sue Montgomery, "Cross and Rifle: Revolution and the Church in El Salvador and Nicaragua," *Journal of International Affairs* 36 (1982): 209–221.

51   Sandinista National Liberation Front (FSLN): Communique of the National Directorate of the FSLN concerning Religion (February 1981), in *Liberation Theology: A Documentary History*, ed. Alfred T. Hennelly, S.J. (Maryknoll 1990), 318–322.

52   Weigel, *Witness to Hope*, 454.

53   Keeley, *Reagan's Gun-Toting Nuns*, 38.

54   Joaquín M. Chávez, "Catholic Action, the Second Vatican Council, and the Emergence of the New Left in El Salvador (1950–1975)," *The Americas* 70 (2014): 475.

55   Rutilio Grande, S.J., "Homily at Apopa, February 13, 1977," in *Rutilio Grande, S.J.:*

Homilies and Writings, trans. and ed. Thomas M. Kelly (Collegeville, MN, 2015), 111–124.

56 Homily at Funeral Mass of Rutilio Grande, Mar. 14, 1977, in *A Prophetic Bishop Speaks to His People: The Complete Homilies of Archbishop Óscar Arnulfo Romero*, trans. Joseph Owens, S.J. (Miami 2015), 1: 61.

57 Homily of Mar. 5, 1978, in *A Prophetic Bishop Speaks to His People*, 2: 290–296.

58 Entry of Apr. 14, 1978 in *Archbishop Óscar Romero: A Shepherd's Diary*, trans. Irene B. Hodgson (Cincinnati 1993), 40; entry of Aug. 11, 1979 in *Archbishop Óscar Romero: A Shepherd's Diary*, 306.

59 Keeley, *Reagan's Gun-Toting Nuns*, 91.

60 Óscar Romero, "The Political Dimension of the Faith from the Perspective of the Option for the Poor," [Feb. 2, 1980], in Archbishop Óscar Romero, *Voice of the Voiceless: The Four Pastoral Letters and Other Statements*, trans. Michael J. Walsh (New York 1985), 182.

61 Óscar Romero, "Letter to President Carter" [Feb. 17, 1980], in Romero, *Voice of the Voiceless*, 189.

62 Óscar Romero, "The Church and Human Liberation," Mar. 23, 1980, in *Romero: Martyr for Liberation* (London 1984), 32.

63 Ana Carrigan, *Salvador Witness: The Life and Calling of Jean Donovan* (New York 2005), 109–110, 234.

64 Keeley, *Reagan's Gun-Toting Nuns*, 109, 114, 146–147.

65 Mario Cuomo, "Transcript of Keynote Address by Cuomo to the Convention," *New York Times*, July 17, 1984.

66 Congregation for the Doctrine of the Faith, "Ten Observations on the Theology of Gustavo Gutiérrez" [1983], in *Liberation Theology: A Documentary History*, 348–350.

67 Guillermo Trejo and Fernando Bizzarro Neto, "Religious Competition and the Rise of Leftist Parties: Why the Catholic Church Provided the Mass Base for the Workers' Party in Brazil" (paper in author's possession), 9.

68 Gustavo Gutiérrez, *The Truth Shall Make you Free: Confrontations*, trans. Matthew McConnell (Maryknoll 1990), 60–63.

69 Trejo and Neto, "Religious Competition and the Rise of Leftist Parties."

70 *Centesimus Annus* (1991), §26.

71 Linden, *Global Catholicism*, 152.

72 P. Meinrad Hebga, S.J., "Un Malaise Grave," in *Personnalité africaine et catholicisme* (Paris 1963), 11–12.

73 Julius K. Nyerere, "The Church and Society," in Julius K. Nyerere, *Freedom and Development: A Selection from Writings and Speeches, 1968–1973* (Dar Es Salaam, 1973), 225.

74 Gianni La Bella, "Paolo VI, la Diplomazia e L'Impegno Per La Pace," *Review d'Histoire Ecclesiatique* 110 (2015): 861–870; Gerard O'Connell, *God's Invisible Hand: The Life and Work of Francis Cardinal Arinze* (San Francisco 2006), 74–92.

75 Ian Linden, *The Catholic Church and the Struggle for Zimbabwe* (London 1980), 125–126.

76 Nicholas M. Creary, *Domesticating a Religious Import: the Jesuits and the Inculturation of the Catholic Church in Zimbabwe, 1879–1980* (New York 2011), 105.

77 Linden, *Global Catholicism*, 177–189.

78 Adrian Hastings, *A History of African Chrisitanity, 1950–1975* (Cambridge 1979), 171.

79 Adrian Hastings, *The Church in Africa: 1450–1950* (Oxford 1994), 572–573.

80 Ronald Kassimir, "The Social Power of Religious Organization: The Catholic Church in Uganda, 1955–1961" (University of Chicago, PhD 1996), 105.

81 Paul VI homily of July 31, 1969, in Kampala, at http://www.vatican.va.

82 Jonathan L. Earle and J. J. Carney, *Contesting Catholics: Benedicto Kiwanuka and the Birth of Postcolonial Uganda* (Rochester, NY, 2021), 24, 43–48.

83 Hastings, *A History of African Christianity, 1950–1975*, 194–195.

84 Elizabeth A. Foster, *African Catholic: Decolonization and the Transformation of the Church* (Cambridge MA 2019), 1–3.

85 Christopher Tounsel, "Two Sudans, Human Rights, and the Afterlives of St. Josephine Bakhita," in *Christianity and Human Rights Reconsidered*, eds. Sarah Shortall and Daniel Steinmetz-Jenkins (Cambridge 2020), 261–275.

86 Philip Jenkins, *The Next Christendom: the Coming of Global Christianity* (Oxford 2007), 67.

87 Paul Gifford, *Christianity, Development and Modernity in Africa* (Oxford 2016), 94–97.

88 Brendan Carmody, "Catholic Church and State Relations in Zambian Education: A Contemporary Analysis," in *International Handbook of Catholic Education: Challenges for School Systems in the 21st Century*, eds. Gerald R. Grace and Joseph O'Keefe (Dordrecht 2007), 543–562; Gifford, *Christianity, Development and Modernity in Africa*, 86–90.

89 Valentina Ciciliot, "The Origins of the Catholic Charismatic Renewal in the United States: Early Developments in Indiana and Michigan and the Reactions of the Ecclesiastical Authorities," *Studies in World Christianity* 25 (2019): 251.

90 Heike Behrend, *Resurrecting Cannibals: The Catholic Church, Witch Hunts and the Production of Pagans in Western Uganda* (New York 2011), 87–90.

91 Mary Douglas, "Sorcery Accusations Unleashed: The Lele Revisited 1987" [1999], in *Mary Douglas: A Very Personal Method: Anthropological Writings Drawn from Life*, ed. Richard Farndon (London 2013), 79–94; Gifford, *Christianity, Development and Modernity in Africa*, 119.

92 Gerrie ter Haar and Stephen Ellis, "Spirit Possession in Modern Zambia: An Analysis of Letters to Archbishop Milingo," *African Affairs* 87 (1988): 185–206.

93 Ludovic Lado, *Catholic Pentecostalism and the Paradoxes of Africanization: Processes of Localization in a Catholic Charismatic Movement in Cameroon* (Leiden 2009), 21–25.

94 Paul Gifford, "Introduction: Democratisation and the Churches," in *The Christian Churches and the Democratisation of Africa*, ed. Paul Gifford (Leiden 1995), 1.

95 Kenneth R. Ross, "Not Catalyst but Ferment: The Distinctive Contribution of the Churches to Political Reform in Malawi 1992–1993," in *The Christian Churches and the Democratisation of Africa*, 98–107.

96 Timothy Paul Longman, "Christianity and Democracy in Rwanda: Assessing Church Responses to Political Crisis in the 1990s," in *The Christian Churches and the Democratisation of Africa*, 188–204.

97 J. J, Carney, *Rwanda before the Genocide* (New York 2013), 190–191.

98 Alison Des Forges, *"Leave None to Tell the Story": Genocide in Rwanda* (New York 1999), 248; Timothy Paul Longman, *Christianity and Genocide in Rwanda* (Cambridge 2010), 161–302.

99 J. J. Carney, "Waters of Baptism, Blood of Tribalism?" *African Ecclesial Review* 50 (2008): 9–30.

100 "Pope Says Rwandan Church Cannot be Held Responsible" [1996], at https://apnews .com/article/df4373f61b539678fc0ae216c958f144.

FIFTEEN: SEXUAL ABUSE (AND ITS COVER-UP)

1 Weston Bate, *Lucky City: The First Generation at Ballarat, 1851–1901* (Carlton, 2003), 20, 39.

2 Colin Barr, *Ireland's Empire: The Roman Catholic Church in the English-Speaking World, 1829–1914* (Cambridge 2020), 362.

3 *Royal Commission on Institutional Responses to Child Sex Abuse* (Canberra 2017). The data and quotations in the following paragraphs are drawn from two sections of this massive, multivolume report: volume 16, book 1, part D, chapter 13 on Catholic institutions and volume 16, Case Study 28 on Catholic Church authorities in Ballarat.

4 Jacqueline Williams, "A Gold Rush City Coming to Grips with the Sins of Its Clergy," *New York Times*, Apr. 29, 2018, A4.

5 Robert A. Orsi, "What Is Catholic about the Clergy Sex Abuse Crisis?" in *The Anthro-*

pology of Catholicism: A Reader, eds. Kristin Norget, Valentina Napolitano, and Maya Mayblin (Oakland 2017), 282–292.

6   I am grateful to Colin Barr for this information.

7   Tom Roberts, "Bishops Were Warned of Abusive Priests," *National Catholic Reporter*, Mar. 30, 2009.

8   Peter Steinfels, "The PA Grand Jury Report: Not What It Seems," *Commonweal* 146 (Jan. 25, 2019): 13–26.

9   George Pell, "Law and Morality," from *Cardinal George Pell, God and Caesar: Selected Essays on Religion, Politics and Society*, ed. M. A. Casey (Washington 2007), 21.

10 George Cardinal Pell, "Last Things," *First Things* (Dec. 2020), at https://www .firstthings.com.

11 John Paul II, Address to the United Nations, Oct. 2, 1979, §13.

12 George Weigel, *Witness to Hope: The Biography of John Paul II* (New York 1999), 540, 499.

13 Joseph Cardinal Ratzinger with Vittorio Messori, *The Ratzinger Report: An Exclusive Interview on the State of the Church*, trans. Savator Attanasio and Graham Harrison (San Francisco 1985), 36–37.

14 Charles Mercier, *L'Eglise, les jeunes et la mondialisation: une histoire des JMJ* (Paris 2020).

15 Ladislas Orsy, *Receiving the Council: Theological and Canonical Insights and Debates* (Collegeville 2009), 16–34.

16 Richard John Neuhaus, *Appointment in Rome: The Church in America Awakening* (New York 1999), 2, 26.

17 Peter Hebblethwaite, *Synod Extraordinary: The Inside Story of the Rome Synod November–December 1985* (New York 1986), 37.

18 Bernardus Boli Ujan, "Toward Inculturation: Traditional Seasonal Rites in Indonesia," *Vatican Council II: Reforming Liturgy*, eds. Carmen Pilcher, David Orr, and Elizabeth Harrington (Adelaide 2013), 81–94.

19 Congregation for the Doctrine of the Faith, *Dominus Iesus* (2000), §22.

20 Ian Linden, *Global Catholicism: Diversity and Change since Vatican II* (New York 2009), 238.

21 Cardinal Joseph Bernardin, "Catholic Common Ground News Conference" [1996], in *Selected Works of Joseph Cardinal Bernardin*, ed. Alphonse P. Spilly (Collegeville 2000), 2: 311–312; Bernard Cardinal Law, 'Response to 'Called to be Catholic,'" *Origins* 26 (Aug. 29, 1996): 170.

22 Cardinal Francis George, "How Liberalism Fails the Church," *Commonweal* (June 17, 2004); https://www.ncregister.com/blog/cardinal-george-the-myth-and-reality-of -will-die-in-my-bed.

23 Maria Olivia Mönckeberg, *El Imperio del Opus Dei En Chile* (Santiago 2016), 217–31; John L. Allen, "The Word from Rome," *National Catholic Reporter* (July 16, 2004).

24 Joseph Ratzinger, "The Spiritual Roots of Europe: Yesterday, Today and Tomorrow," in Joseph Ratzinger and Marcello Pera, *Without Roots: The West, Relativism, Christianity, Islam*, trans. Michael F. Moore (New York 2006), 72.

25 *Veritatis Splendor* (1993), §95, §96.

26 Sr. M. Theresa Kane, R.S.M., Welcome to Pope John Paul II, Oct. 7, 1979, in Christine Schenk, CSJ, *To Speak the Truth in Love: A Biography of Theresa Kane, RSM* (Maryknoll 2019), 265–266.

27 Rosemary Radford Reuther, "The Emergence of Chrisian Feminist Theology," in *Cambridge Companion to Feminist Theology*, ed. S. Frank Parsons (Cambridge 2002), 8.

28 *Letter to Women* (1995), §10.

29 Leslie Woodcock Tentler, "How Exceptional? U.S. Catholics Since 1945," in *Secularization and Religious Innovation in the North Atlantic World*, eds. David Hempton and Hugh McLeod (Oxford 2017), 283.

30 Philip Murnion, *New Parish Ministers* (New York 1992).

31   Mary Douglas, "The Gender of the Beloved," *Heythrop Journal* 36 (1995): 393–408.
32   Mary E. Daly, *Sixties Ireland: Reshaping the Economy, State and Society, 1957–1973* (Cambridge 2016), 192, 194; Dermot Keogh, *Ireland and the Vatican: The Politics and Diplomacy of Church-State Relations 1922–1960* (Cork 1995), 363.
33   Irene Mosca and Robert E. Wright, "The Long Term Consequences of the Irish Marriage Bar," IZA Discussion papers, #12301 (2019).
34   Laura Kelly, "The Contraceptive Pill in Ireland c. 1964–79: Activism, Women and Patient-Doctor Relationships," *Medical History* 64 (2020): 195–218.
35   Daly, *Sixties Ireland*, 210; Peter Murray, "The Best News Ireland Ever Got? *Humanae Vitae's* Reception on the Pope's Green Island," in *The Schism of '68*, 282.
36   Martin Sixsmith, *The Lost Child of Philomena Lee: A Mother, Her Son and a Fifty Year Search* (London 2009), inside cover; Department of Children, Equality, Disability, Integration and Youth, Government of Ireland, *Final Report of the Commission of Investigation into the Mother and Baby Homes* (Dublin 2020); quotation in Clair Wills, "Architectures of Containment," *London Review of Books* 43 (May 20, 2021), 20.
37   A. Connelly, "Women and the Constitution of the Republic of Ireland," in *Contesting Politics: Women in Ireland, North and South*, eds. Y. Galligan, E. Ward, and R. Wilford (Boulder 1999), 23.
38   Matthew Connelly, *Fatal Misconception: The Struggle to Control World Population* (Cambridge MA 2008), 365.
39   Ignacio Walker, "The Future of Chilean Christian Democracy," in *Christian Democracy in Latin America: Electoral Competition and Regime Conflicts*, eds. Scott Mainwaring and Timothy R. Scully (Stanford 2003), 185.
40   Anna Gryzmła-Busse, *Nations under God: How Churches Use Moral Authority to Influence Policy* (Princeton 2015), 175–177.
41   Ernst-Wolfgang Böckenförde, "A Christian in the Position of Constitutional Judge" [1999], in Böckenförde, *Religion, Law and Democracy: Selected Writings*, eds. Mirjam Künkler and Tine Stein (Oxford 2020), 285–286; Alessandra Stanley, "Pope Lectures German Bishops on Abortion," *New York Times*, Nov. 21, 1999.
42   Mother Teresa, Nobel Prize Lecture (1979), in Kathryn Spink, *Mother Teresa: A Complete Authorized Biography* (New York 2011), 324.
43   Liam Ford, "Cardinal Assails Notre Dame for Inviting Obama," *Chicago Tribune*, Apr. 3, 2009, sec. I, 11.
44   Grzymała-Busse, *Nations under God*, 172, 175.
45   J. Burdick, *Legacies of Liberation: The Progressive Catholic Church in Brazil at the Start of a New Millenium* (Burlington 2004), 88.
46   Inez San Martín, "Light Blue Is the Pro-Life Color in Argentina," *Crux* (Nov. 30, 2020).
47   "Homosexuality, Prostitution and the Law: Evidence Presented to the Wolfenden Commission by the Roman Catholic Advisory Committee," *Dublin Review* 230 (1956): 57–58; Bernhard Häring, *The Law of Christ: Moral Theology for Priests and Laity*, trans. Edwin G. Kaiser, CPPS (Westminster MD 1966), 3: 306.
48   *Human Sexuality: New Directions in American Catholic Thought: A Study*, ed. Anthony Kosnik (New York 1977), 216.
49   Jeffrey M. Burns, "Sexuality after the Council: Gay Catholics, Married Clergy, Rights and Change in San Francisco, 1962–1987," in *Catholics and the Vatican II Era: Local Histories of a Global Event*, eds. Kathleen Sprows Cummings, Timothy Matovina, and Robert A. Orsi (New York 2018), 3–27.
50   John McNeill, *Both Feet Firmly Planted in Midair: My Spiritual Journey* (Westminster, KY, 1998).
51   Cardinal Humberto Medeiros to Cardinal Seper, Feb. 12, 1979, reprinted in Investigative Staff of the *Boston Globe*, *Betrayal: The Crisis in the Catholic Church* (Boston 2002), 235–242.

52   *Letter to the Bishops of the Catholic Church on the Pastoral Care of Homosexual Persons* (1986), §3.

53   Benita Roth, *The Life and Death of ACT-UP LA: Anti-AIDS Activism in Los Angeles from the 1980s to the 2000s* (Cambridge 2017), 65–67.

54   Calvin Sims, "With Spray Paint, Students Wage 'Safe Sex' War," *New York Times*, Jan. 19, 1995, A4; James W. Jones, "Discourses on and of AIDS in West Germany, 1986–1990," *Journal of the History of Sexuality* 2 (1992): 443.

55   Philip Shenon, "Deadly Turning Point," *New York Times*, Jan. 21, 1996, A1.

56   Eduardo J. Gomez, "The Politics of Brazil's Successful Response to HIV/AIDS: Civic Movements, Infiltration, and 'Strategic Internationalization,'" *Brown Journal of World Affairs* 17 (2011): 51–64.

57   Michael O'Loughlin, "Plague: Untold Stories of AIDS and the Catholic Church. The Catholic Hospital That Pioneered AIDS Care." *America Media*, podcast.

58   Angela Kelly, "The Body of Christ Has AIDS: The Catholic Church Responding Faithfully to HIV and AIDS in Papua New Guinea," *Journal of Religion and Health* 48 (2009): 16–28; Robert Calderisi, *Earthly Mission: The Catholic Church and World Development* (New Haven 2013), 202–203.

59   Catherine Pepinster, "No Time to Lose," *The Tablet* 275 (Feb. 13, 2021): 7.

60   Lucien Chauvin, "Lima Students Decry Homosexuality Tract," *Chronicle of Higher Education* (Oct. 4, 2002): 55.

61   *Considerations Regarding Proposals to Give Legal Recognition to Unions between Homosexual Persons* (2003), §8.

62   Austen Ivereigh, *The Great Reformer: Francis and the Making of a Radical Pope* (New York 2014), 312–316; Ivereigh, "Defending Marriage is Not Enough," *Commonweal* (Oct. 28, 2020).

63   Andrew Sullivan, *Virtually Normal: An Argument about Homosexuality* (New York 1995), 19–55.

64   Julieta Lemaitre, "By Reason Alone: Catholicism, Constitutions, and Sex in the Americas," *ICON* 10 (2012), 493–51; John Finnis, "Law, Morality and 'Sexual Orientation,'" *Notre Dame Law Review* 69 (1994): 1070.

65   David D. Kirkpatrick, "The Conservative Christian Big Thinker," *New York Times Magazine*, Oct. 20, 2009, 24.

66   Ignacio Walker, *Cristianos sin Cristiandad (reflexiones de un legislador católico)* (Valparaíso 2020), 32, 43.

67   Melinda Gates, *The Moment of Lift: How Empowering Women Changes the World* (New York 2019), 71–74, 197–99.

68   Paul Gifford, *Christianity, Development and Modernity in Africa* (New York 2016), 99, 102.

69   Timothy D. Lytton, *Holding Bishops Accountable: How Lawsuits Helped the Catholic Church Confront Clergy Sexual Abuse* (Cambridge MA 2008).

70   *The Independent Inquiry into Child Sexual Abuse—Case Study Ampleforth and Downside* (London 2018).

71   Joseph P. Chinnici, O.F.M., *When Values Collide: The Catholic Chuch, Sexual Abuse, and the Challenges of Leadership* (New York 2010), 161.

72   Jason Berry and Gerald Renner, *Vows of Silence: The Abuse of Power in the Papacy of John Paul II* (New York 2004), esp. 166–204.

73   *Report On The Holy See's Institutional Knowledge And Decision-Making Related to Former Cardinal Theodore Edgar McCarrick (1930 to 2017)*, (Vatican City 2020).

74   Theodore McCarrick to Stanisław Dziwisz, Aug. 6, 2020, copy in *Report On The Holy See's Institutional Knowledge And Decision-Making*, 170.

75   Jonathan Luxmoore, "Polish Church Apologizes for Abuse Scandal," *The Tablet* (Nov. 10, 2020); Slawomir Mandes, "Clerical Sexual Abuse in an Illiberal State; The Case of Poland," *Journal of Church and State* 62 (2020): 86–109.

CONCLUSION: POPE FRANCIS AND BEYOND

1   Norimitsu Onishi and Aurelien Breeden, "Sexual Abuse Revelations Accelerate Sense of a French Church in Retreat," *New York Times*, Oct. 8, 2021.

2   Stephen Bullivant, *Mass Exodus: Catholic Disaffiliation in Britain and America since World War II* (Oxford 2019), 9–12, 28, 38; Pew Research Center, "In Western European Countries with Church Taxes, Support for the Tradition Remains Strong" (Washington 2019); Mark Edward Ruff, "The Post-Catholic Milieu in the Federal Republic of Germany," in *Die Gegenwart Gottes in der modernen Gesellschaft: Transzendenz und religiöse Vergemeinschaftung in Deutschland*, eds. Michael Geyer and Lucian Hölscher (Göttingen 2006), 364.

3   Robert D. Putnam and David E. Campbell, *American Grace: How Religion Divides and Unites Us* (New York 2010), 129–132.

4   Alana Harris, "'They Just Dig St. Anthony, He's Right Up Their Street, Religious Wise': Transnational Flows and Inter-Religious Encounters in an East London Parish," in *Migration, Transnationalism and Catholicism: Global Perspectives*, eds. Dominic Pasura and Marta Bivand Erdal (London 2016), 95–120; "'When Poland Became the Main Country of Birth among Catholics in Norway': Polish Migrants' Everyday Narratives and Church Responses to Demographic Re-Constitution," in *Migration, Transnationalism and Catholicism*, 259–290; Selva J. Raj, "Public Display, Communal Devotion: Procession at a South Indian Catholic Festival," in *Vernacular Catholicism, Vernacular Saints*, ed. Reid B. Locklin (Albany 2017), 143–147; Valentina Napolitano, *Migrant Hearts and the Atlantic Return: Transnationalism and the Roman Catholic Church* (New York 2016), 19–37, 127–149.

5   Philip Jenkins, *The Next Christendom: The Coming of Global Christianity* (Oxford 2011), 67, 227.

6   Eliza Griswold, *The Tenth Parallel: Dispatches from the Fault Line Between Christianity and Islam* (New York 2010).

7   *A History of Christianity in Indonesia*, eds. Jan Sihar Aritonang and Karel Steenbrink (Leiden 2008), 137–228.

8   Kent R. Hill, "On the Brink of Extinction: Christians in Iraq and Syria," in *Under Caesar's Sword: How Christians Respond to Persecution*, eds. Daniel Philpott and Timothy Samuel Shah (Cambridge 2018), 30–69.

9   Randy Boyagoda, "The Tragic Familiarity of the Sri Lankan Bombings," *New York Times*, Apr. 21, 2019.

10 Quentin Wodon, "More Schools, Larger Schools, or Both? Patterns of Enrollment Growth in K12 Catholic Schools Globally," *Journal of Catholic Education* 22 (2019), 140.

11 Mathew N. Schmalz, "The Indian Church: Catholicism and Indian Nationhood," in *The Catholic Church and the Nation State: Comparative Perspectives*, eds. Paul Christopher Manuel, Lawrence C. Reardon, and Clyde Wilcox (Washington 2006), 221–222.

12 Aditi Athreya, Rinald D'Souza, and Idesbald Godderis,"The Postcolonial Expansion of a Mission Jesuit Education in Ranchi, India, after 1950," in *Missionary Education: Historical Approaches and Global Perspectives*, eds. Kim Christiaens, Idesbald Goddeeris, and Pieter Verstraete (Leuven 2021), 97–98.

13 Marie Abi Habib and Andre Paultre, "Haiti Quake Destroyed Many Churches, Shredding a Mainstay of Support," *New York Times*, Aug. 22, 2021; Bryan T. Froehle and Mary L. Gautier, *Global Catholicism: Portrait of a World Church* (Maryknoll 2003), 132.

14 Henri Mendras and Alastair Cole, *Social Change in Modern France: Towards a Cultural Anthropology of the Fifth Republic* (Cambridge 1991), esp. 51–72; Emmanuel Macron, "Discours du Président de la République de Emmanuel Macron au Collége des Bernardins," at https://www.collegedesbernardins.fr/content/discours-du-president-de-la -republique-emmanuel-macron-au-college-des-bernardins.

15   Austen Ivereigh *The Great Reformer: Francis and the Making of a Radical Pope* (New York 2014), 181, 184.

16   Martín Obregón, *Entre la Cruz y la Espada: La Iglesia Católica durante los Primeros Años del 'Processo'* (Buenos Aires 2005); Ivereigh, *The Great Reformer,* 196–197.

17   *A Big Heart Open to God: A Conversation with Pope Francis*, interview by Antonio Spadaro, S.J. (New York 2013), 63, 14; John W. O'Malley, S.J., and Timothy W. O'Brien, S.J., "The Twentieth-Century Construction of Ignatian Spirituality: A Sketch," *Studies in the Spirituality of Jesuits* 52 (2020): 33.

18   Juan Carlos Cruz, James Hamilton, and José Andrés Murillo, *Abuso y poder: Nuestra lucha contra la Iglesia Católica* (Santiago, 2020).

19   *Laudato Si'* (2015), §49.

20   Pope Francis, *Let Us Dream: The Path to a Better Future* (New York 2020), 32.

21   *Fratelli Tutti* (2020), §168; Massimo Borghese, *The Mind of Pope Francis: Jorge Bergoglio's Intellectual Journey*, trans. Barry Hudock (Collegeville 2018), 193.

22   *Gaudium et Spes* (1965), §26.

23   Ernst Wolfgang Böckenförde, "The Rise of the State as a Process of Secularization" [1967], in Böckenförde, *Religion, Law and Democracy: Selected Writings*, eds. Mirjam Künkler and Tine Stein (Oxford 2020), 166; Peter E. Gordon, "Between Christian Democracy and Critical Theory: Habermas, Böckenförde, and the Dialectics of Secularization in Postwar Germany," *Social Research* 80 (2013): 173–202.

24   Charles Taylor, "Clericalism," *Downside Review* 78 (Summer 1960): 178–179; *A Catholic Modernity: Charles Taylor's Marianist Award Lecture*, ed. James L. Heft (New York 1999), 13–38.

25   Alasdair MacIntyre, *After Virtue*, 2nd ed. (Notre Dame [1981] 1984), 263.

26   Benjamin Ziemann, *Encounters with Modernity: The Catholic Church in West Germany, 1945–1975*, trans. Andrew Evans (New York 2014), 13; Wilhelm Damberg, "Is There an American Exceptionalism? American and German Catholics in Comparison," in *Secularization and Religious Innovation in the North Atlantic World*, eds. David Hempton and Hugh McLeod (New York 2017), 263.

27   Joseph Ratzinger response to Marcello Pera in Ratzinger and Pera, *Without Roots: The West, Relativism, Christianity, Islam*, trans. Michael F. Moore (New York 2006), 120–121; MacIntrye, *After Virtue*, 262–263.

28   Carlo Invernizzi Accetti, *What Is Christian Democracy? Politics, Religion and Ideology*, (Cambridge 2019), 133.

29   Archbishop Carlo Maria Viganò to Donald Trump, June 6, 2020, and Viganò to Trump, Oct. 30, 2020, at https://www.lifesitenews.com/news/abp-vigano-warns-trump-about-great-reset-plot-to-subdue-humanity-destroy-freedom.

30   *Fratelli Tutti* (2020), §10.

31   John Cardinal Onaiyekan with Emmanuel Ojeifo, *Let the Truth Prevail: Nocturnal Conversations on the Church, the Nation, and the World Today* (Abuja 2021), 147.

32   Chimamanda Ngozi Adichie, *Purple Hibiscus* (Chapel Hill 2012); Chimamanda Ngozi Adichie, "Raised Catholic," *Atlantic* (Oct. 14, 2015).

33   Uwem Akpan, *Say You're One of Them* (New York 2007); Uwem Akpan interview with Cressida Leyshon (2015), Newyorker.com; *Gaudium et Spes* (1965), §1.

34   Joseph Ratzinger, "The World and the Church: A Contrast between Vatican I and Vatican II: Lecture Text for Cardinal Frings" [1961], copy in Jared Wicks, "Six Texts by Joseph Ratzinger as Peritus before and during Vatican Council II," *Gregorianum* 89 (2008): 260.

35   Karl Rahner, S.J., "Christianity and the Non-Christian Religions" [1961], trans. Karl-Heinz Kruger, in Rahner, *Theological Investigations V* (London 1966), 117.

36   Address of the Holy Father, Meeting with the Participants at the Fifth Convention of the Italian Church, Nov. 10, 2015, at https://www.vatican.va.

37   *Fratelli Tutti* (2020), §66.

Index

Page numbers in *italics* refer to illustrations.